FOR REFERENCE

Do Not Take From This Room

The Greenwood
Encyclopedia of Daily Life
in America

Recent Titles in
The Greenwood Press "Daily Life Through History" Series

The Civil War
Paul A. Cimbala

Civilians in Wartime Europe, 1618–1900
Linda S. Frey and Marsha L. Frey, editors

The Vietnam War
James E. Westheider

World War II
G. Kurt Piehler

Immigrant America, 1870–1920
June Granatir Alexander

Along the Mississippi
George S. Pabis

Immigrant America, 1820–1870
James M. Bergquist

Pre-Columbian Native America
Clarissa W. Confer

Post-Cold War
Stephen A. Bourque

The New Testament
James W. Ermatinger

The Hellenistic Age: From Alexander to Cleopatra
James Allan Evans

Imperial Russia
Greta Bucher

4 WARTIME, POSTWAR,
AND CONTEMPORARY
AMERICA, 1940–PRESENT

The Greenwood
Encyclopedia of Daily Life
in America

Jolyon P. Girard
VOLUME EDITOR

Randall M. Miller
GENERAL EDITOR

The Greenwood Press "Daily Life Through History" Series

GREENWOOD PRESS
Westport, Connecticut • London

Library of Congress Cataloging-in-Publication Data

The Greenwood encyclopedia of daily life in America / Randall M. Miller, general editor.
　　　　p. cm.—(The Greenwood Press daily life through history series, ISSN 1080–4749)
　　Includes bibliographical references and index.
　　ISBN 978–0–313–33699–7 (set)
　　ISBN 978–0–313–33703–1 (v. 1)
　　ISBN 978–0–313–33704–8 (v. 2)
　　ISBN 978–0–313–33705–5 (v. 3)
　　ISBN 978–0–313–33706–2 (v. 4)
　　1. United States—Civilization—Encyclopedias.　2. United States—Social life and customs—
Encyclopedias.　3. United States—Social conditions—Encyclopedias.　I. Miller, Randall M.
E169.1.G7553　　　2009
973.03—dc22　　　2007042828

British Library Cataloguing in Publication Data is available.

Library of Congress Catalog Card Number: 2007042828
ISBN: 978–0–313–33699–7 (set)
　　　　978–0–313–33703–1 (vol. 1)
　　　　978–0–313–33704–8 (vol. 2)
　　　　978–0–313–33705–5 (vol. 3)
　　　　978–0–313–33706–2 (vol. 4)
ISSN: 1080–4749

First published in 2009

Greenwood Press, 88 Post Road West, Westport, CT 06881
An imprint of Greenwood Publishing Group, Inc.
www.greenwood.com

Printed in the United States of America

The paper used in this book complies with the
Permanent Paper Standard issued by the National
Information Standards Organization (Z39.48–1984).

10　9　8　7　6　5　4　3　2　1

Every reasonable effort has been made to trace the owners of copyright materials in this book, but
in some instances this has proven impossible. The editors and publisher will be glad to receive
information leading to more complete acknowledgments in subsequent printings of the book and in
the meantime extend their apologies for any omissions.

The publisher has done its best to make sure the instructions and/or recipes in this book are correct.
However, users should apply judgment and experience when preparing recipes, especially parents and
teachers working with young people. The publisher accepts no responsibility for the outcome of any
recipe included in this volume.

For my wife, Marilyn, a special contributor who has played the substantial role in my daily life.

CONTENTS

Contents

TOUR GUIDE: A PREFACE FOR USERS

During the time of the American Revolution, the writer Hector St. Jean de Crevecouer asked the fundamental question that has dogged Americans thereafter: "What then is this new man, this American." Countless students of American history have searched every aspect of political, economic, social, and cultural history to discover "this American." In doing so, they have often focused on the great ideas that inspired a "free people" and defined public interest since the inception of the United States; the great events that marked American history; and the great changes wrought by democratic, industrial, communications, and other revolutions shaping American life, work, and identities. And they have been right to do so. But more recently other students of history have insisted that finding the real American requires looking at the details of everyday life. Therein, they argue, Americans practiced what mattered most to them and gave meaning to larger concepts of freedom and to the great events swirling about them. The ways Americans at home and at work ordered their daily life have become the subject of numerous community studies and biographies of the so-called common man or woman that were created by combing through all manner of personal accounts in diaries, letters, memoirs, business papers, birth and death records, census data, material culture, popular song, verse, artistic expression, and, indeed, virtually any source about or by common folk.

But making sense of so much individual study and providing a clear path through the history of Americans in their daily life has waited on a work that brings together the many and diverse ways Americans ordered their individual worlds at home and at work. *The Greenwood Encyclopedia of Daily Life in America* promises such a synthesis; it also promises to find "this American" in what Americans ate, who they courted and married, how they raised their children, what they did at work, where they traveled, how they played, and virtually every aspect of social life that Americans made for themselves. As such, it brings to life "this American" on his or her own terms. It also suggests that by discovering the ordinary it becomes possible to understand that extraordinary phenomenon of the American.

Features and Uses

The Greenwood Encyclopedia of Daily Life in America is a reference work and guide that provides up-to-date, authoritative, and readable entries on the many experiences and varieties of daily life of Americans from the dawn of the republic through the first years of the twenty-first century. In spanning the roughly 250 years from the mid-eighteenth century to the new millennium, the four volumes of *The Greenwood Encyclopedia of Daily Life in America* employ both a chronological and a topical, or thematic, approach. Doing so invites many uses for the volumes as reference guides; as touchstones for inquiries to a host of questions about the social, cultural, economic, and political history of Americans and the nation; and, taken together, as a broad view of daily life in the United States.

Users can read the articles separately or as a running narrative, depending on interest and need. The organization of the work collectively according to time period and within each volume according to time period, geography, daily activity, and group allows readers to explore a topic in depth, in comparative perspective, and over time. Also, because each section of each volume opens with a synthetic overview for purposes of historical context, the material in each section becomes more readily linked to larger patterns of American social, cultural, economic, and political developments. By structuring the volumes in this manner, it becomes possible to integrate and apply the encyclopedia within modern and flexible pedagogical frameworks in the classroom, in the library, and in home-schooling settings.

Cross-referencing within the articles and the cumulative subject index to the encyclopedia found at the back of each volume together expand the reach of individual topics across time and in different places. Thus, for example, the discussion of marital patterns and habits in the antebellum period of the nineteenth century, which includes mentions of courtship patterns, marriage rites, family formation, parenting, and even divorce, easily bridges to treatments of the same topics in other periods. Likewise, a reader wanting to compare foodways as they developed over time might move easily from representations of the early American "down-home" cooking of a largely agricultural society, through the increased portability and packaging of foods demanded by an urbanizing society during the nineteenth century, to the recent preference for such paradoxes in food choices as fresh foods, exotic foods, and fast food in the post-industrial United States.

Readers might go backward as well as forward, or even sideways, in following their interests, looking for the roots and then growth and development of habits and practices that defined and ordered the daily lives of Americans. In doing so, they might discover that each successive modern society has had its own search for the simpler life by trying to recover and reproduce parts of a supposedly more settled and serene past. They also will discover not only the changes wrought by ever more modern means of production, transportation, communication, and social and economic organization but also some striking continuities. Old ways often continue in new days. Americans have been a people on the go from the beginning of the nation and have become more so over time. As such, staying in touch with family and friends has ever been central to Americans' sense of place and purpose in organizing their lives. Whether carrying a daguerreotype image while heading west or to war in the nineteenth century, shooting photos with a Kodak camera from the late nineteenth century well into the twentieth century, or taking pictures with a video camera, a digital camera, or even with a cell-phone in the twenty-first century, Americans sought ways to keep visual images of the people, animals, possessions, and places that mattered to them. Letter writing also has become no less important a means of communication when the words move electronically via e-mail than when they were scratched out with a quill pen on paper. The encyclopedia provides a ready way to measure and map such social and cultural patterns and developments.

In its organization and with its reference supports, the encyclopedia encourages such topical excursions across time. Thus, the encyclopedia promises ways to an integrated analysis of daily life and of the core values, interests, and identities of Americans at any one time and over time.

Sidebars (found in volumes 3 and 4, and called Snapshots), chronologies, illustrations, and excerpts from documents further enrich each volume with specific examples of daily life from primary sources. They add not only "color" but also significant content by capturing the sense of a particular people or place in song, verse, speech, letters, and image and by giving voice to the people themselves. Readers thus engage Americans in their daily life directly.

The life and use of the encyclopedia extends beyond the physical volumes themselves. Because the encyclopedia derives much of its material from the vast resources of the Greenwood Publishing Group archive of works in ongoing series, such as the *Greenwood Press Daily Life Through History* Series and the *Daily Life in the United States* Series, to name the two most prominent, and on the many encyclopedias, reference works, and scholarly monographs making up its list, and on the many document-based works in its collection, the encyclopedia includes up-to-date and reliably vetted material. It also plugs into the *Greenwood Daily Life Online* database, which ensures a continuous expansion, enhancement, and refinement of content and easy searching capabilities. In that sense, *The Greenwood Encyclopedia of Daily Life in America*, like the American people, literally exists in a constant state of renewal to live beyond its original creation.

Organization and Coverage

The Greenwood Encyclopedia of Daily Life in America has a wide sweep in terms of time, topics, and themes related to the ordering of the daily lives of Americans. It also includes the many and diverse Americans, understanding that no one experience or people spoke or speaks for the variety of daily lives in the United States or explains even the unity of common experiences many different Americans have had and sought. That said, the encyclopedia is not a simple fact-by-fact description of every group or daily activity conducted in the United States. The encyclopedia is consciously selective in topics and coverage, with an eye always to relating the most significant and representative examples of the daily lives of different Americans.

The coverage of particular people and topics varies due to the availability of sources by and about them. Thus, for example, such peoples as the Iroquois, Cherokee, and Lakota Sioux get more explicit notice than, say, the Shoshone, simply because they left a fuller record of their lives and were observed and written about, or painted or photographed, in their daily lives more fully than were some other Native peoples. Then, too, the daily life of immigrant peoples receives extensive coverage throughout the volumes, but the extent and depth of coverage varies due to the size of the group and, more important, due to the available source material about any particular group. Thus, for example, when combined, the several major governmental and foundation studies of eastern and southern European immigrant groups in industrial America in the late nineteenth and early twentieth centuries, the rich tradition of publishing ethnic newspapers, the relating of personal lives in memoirs and oral histories, and a conscious effort to recover an immigrant past by the children and grandchildren of the first generation all explain the wider focus on such groups as representative types for their day. We simply know much about such people at work and at home. Such coverage of some people more fully than others does not mean any one experience counts more than others. It is, rather, mainly a matter of the critical mass of information at hand.

The encyclopedia includes all age groups in its coverage, but, again, the documentary record is richer for people coming of age through their adult lives into retirement than it is for the very young or the very old. Then, too, more is known about the daily lives of the upper classes than the lower classes, the privileged than the underprivileged, and the free than the unfree. The encyclopedia boasts significant inclusion of the many diverse American people, irrespective of wealth, circumstance, race or ethnicity, religion, or any other marker, and, indeed, it makes special effort to embrace the fullest range and diversity of experiences of daily life from birth to death.

The four volumes, each of which was edited by a prominent specialist or specialists in the field, are arranged by time periods as follows.

- Volume 1: The War of Independence and Antebellum Expansion and Reform, 1763–1861; edited by Theodore J. Zeman
- Volume 2: *The Civil War, Reconstruction, and Industrialization of America, 1861–1900*; edited by James M. Volo and Dorothy Denneen Volo
- Volume 3: *The Emergence of Modern America, World War I, and the Great Depression, 1900–1940*; edited by Francis J. Sicius
- Volume 4: *Wartime, Postwar, and Contemporary America, 1940–Present*; edited by Jolyon P. Girard

Each volume follows a similar format in that it organizes the material into seven principal topics, which are then generally divided into the following subtopics.

Those subtopics are sometimes arranged in a different order within the volumes due to emphasis, but they remain continuous throughout the encyclopedia.

1. *Domestic Life:* Covering such subtopics as Men, Women, Children, Pets, Marriage, and so on.
2. *Economic Life:* Covering such subtopics as Work, Trade, Class and Caste, Urban and Rural Experience, and so on.
3. *Intellectual Life:* Covering such subtopics as Science, Education, Literature, Communication, Health and Medicine, and so on.
4. *Material Life:* Covering such subtopics as Food, Drink, Housing, Clothing, Transportation, Technology, and so on.
5. *Political Life:* Covering such subtopics as Government, Law, Reform, War, and so on.
6. *Recreational Life:* Covering such subtopics as Sports, Music, Games, Entertainment, Holidays and Celebrations, and so on.
7. *Religious Life:* Covering such subtopics as Religion, Spirituality, Ritual, Rites of Passage, and so on.

Users are guided through this enormous amount of material not just by running heads on every page but also by *concept compasses* that appear in the margins at the start of main topical sections. These compasses are adapted from *concept mapping*, a technique borrowed from online research methods and used in The *Greenwood Encyclopedia of Daily Life*. The concept compasses will help orient readers in the particular volume they are using and allow them to draw connections among related topics across time periods. Following is an example of a concept compass:

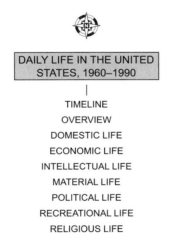

DAILY LIFE IN THE UNITED
STATES, 1960–1990
|
TIMELINE
OVERVIEW
DOMESTIC LIFE
ECONOMIC LIFE
INTELLECTUAL LIFE
MATERIAL LIFE
POLITICAL LIFE
RECREATIONAL LIFE
RELIGIOUS LIFE

The individual volumes also have several variations in their internal arrangements and coverage of topics that speak to the particular chronological period under review. Volume 1, for example, does not begin at a fixed date, as do the other volumes, and it covers a longer time period than any of the other volumes. Its primary focus is on the period from the American Revolution through the Civil War, but it also looks back in time in its descriptions of many elements of daily life that continued from the preindustrial colonial period through the first rumblings of the so-called market revolution of the early nineteenth century. It does so to provide not only an understanding of the continuities in many aspects of life—from the ways people raised crops and livestock, manufactured and sold goods, organized family life, worshipped, and practiced the rituals of birth, marriage, and death, to name several—but also to mark the changes wrought by the age of revolutions that came with new understandings of political, economic, social, cultural, and even parental authority following the American Revolution. In the subsequent volumes, there is some overlap in terms of beginnings and endings for the chronological periods because social history does not have neat markers as does American political history with its election cycles. Each of the final three volumes covers roughly a half-century of time, reflecting the growing complexity of life in the modern era.

The encyclopedia covers the whole of the United States. The geography of the United States has expanded mightily over time, but the importance of geographical identity within the United States has varied at different times and more recently has declined. The first three volumes recognize the salience of regional variations in defining daily life and break the material, in varying degrees, into regions within the United States (e.g., Northeast, South, Midwest, Pacific West). But the fourth volume, covering the last half of the twentieth century—by which time a national market, telecommunications, and popular culture had done much to break down regional identities and create a national culture—discounts the importance of region in many areas of daily life. To be sure, as Volume 4 reveals, regional identities still persisted, even pridefully so, in "the South" and "the West" especially, but throughout the United States the rhythms of life moved in strikingly similar ways in a nation increasingly knit together by interstate highways, television, and, more recently, by the Internet and by a mass consumption economy and culture. Class, race, and occupation, more than regional cultures, now count more in defining daily life and social ties. Religion, too, matters much in ordering individual lives and distinguishing groups from one another in the United States, easily the most "churched" nation in the industrial world. In some cases, particular subtopics disappear from successive volumes because Americans at different times gave up particular ways of working and living or because the representative ways of working and living changed, from those of an agricultural world to those of an industrial and urban one and then to a postindustrial suburban one, for example.

Throughout the encyclopedia the most basic ways people arranged their daily life make up the principal content of the volumes. But the coverage of any topic is not constant. Take time, for example. It is useful to note that historically over time, *time* literally has been speeding up for Americans. Americans who lived by Nature's times of season and sunrise and sunset occupied a different world than people who have made time a commodity to be metered out in nanoseconds for purposes of productivity and even pleasure. The multiplicity of clocks and watches made possible by the industrial revolution, the imposition of factory time in the workplace, the dividing of the nation into time zones demanded by the railroads, the breakdown of time ordered by the moving assembly line, the collapse of time realized by telecommunications and then the radio, and the more current compression of time by microchips in all manner of computers, cell phones, and gadgetry that seemingly now run daily life and work—all this change in understanding and managing time transformed not only the pace but also the direction of life. Each volume marks the changing of time, the ways people used their time, and the times. Thereby, the attention to matters of time becomes a topic of growing importance with each successive volume of the encyclopedia.

Finally, in terms of coverage and content, the encyclopedia combines a *macro* with the micro view of daily life. External factors such as wars, natural disasters (e.g., fires, floods, hurricanes and tornados, ice storms, and droughts), epidemic diseases, environmental transformation, economic and political change, and population movements profoundly affected how, where, and why people lived as they did and, indeed, even which people lived at all. The Revolutionary War and the Civil War, for example, uprooted countless people from their homes as armies tramped about, armies that also liberated enslaved people who then used the upheavals to run to freedom or to fight for it. Daily life for refugees, for the "freedpeople," for the losers of political power and economic advantage was altered to its core by war. Dealing with the loss of loved ones in the Civil War changed the ways many Americans approached the meaning and management of death—in embalming, in funerary practices, in memorializing the dead, in shifting family responsibilities in the wake of a parent's death. The total mobilization of World War II touched every American household, and the G.I. Bill that came with it opened up opportunities for education, home ownership, and medical benefits that helped make possible a middle-class life for many Americans. So, too, massive floods, such as the 1927 flooding of the Mississippi River basin, swept away people, possessions, and patterns of living across a wide swath. Government actions also influenced, even determined, people's daily life. The many New Deal programs that insured bank accounts; underwrote home mortgage loans; brought electricity to rural America; built dams for hydroelectric power and economic development; constructed roads, bridges, airports, and public buildings; encouraged the arts, music, and literature, and so much more left a physical, social, and cultural imprint that still matters in Americans' daily living. Thus, relating the *macrohistory* of larger historical events and developments to the ways such factors informed and influenced the *microhistory* of individual daily life is essential to understanding the dynamics and consequence of changes and continuities in the daily life of Americans. The panoramic perspective plots the landscape of social history, while the microscopic examination observes its many forms. All that said, the primary focus of this encyclopedia remains on what students of social and cultural history term "the infinite details" of Americans' social and material arrangements in their daily life. The title tells the tale.

The Greenwood Encyclopedia of Daily Life in America, in the end, still makes no claim to comprehensiveness in trying to bring in all Americans and all manner of life. No reference work dare do so. Recognizing such a limitation rather than retreating from it, this encyclopedia serves not only as an introduction to the varied and complex American peoples in their daily lives but also as an invitation to bring other peoples into view, which responsibility, one hopes, the students and teachers using this encyclopedia will assume.

A Note on the Conception and Creation of the Encyclopedia

The encyclopedia is the product of many hands. It is both a collective work and, in its separate volumes, also very much an individual one. The encyclopedia was developed collectively by editors at Greenwood Press, who originally sought to provide a companion encyclopedia to the very successful six-volume *Greenwood Encyclopedia of Daily Life*, which covered the world from prehistory to the end of the twentieth century. The editors at Greenwood also sought to capitalize on the many reference works and individual volumes Greenwood Press has published on various aspects of daily life in the United States. At Greenwood, Michael Herman conceived of the idea for such an encyclopedia and drafted the broad design for it. John Wagner then stepped in and in many essential ways translated idea into product. He helped recruit volume editors, managed relations with the editors by means of correspondence and providing sample materials and other forms of guidance, read the individual volumes for content and fit regarding the collective set, and managed the details of moving manuscripts to production.

Each author/editor assumed the primary, almost complete, responsibility for his or her individual volume. Early in the planning process, several author/editors gathered by correspondence and even in person to discuss the scope of the work, to mark off the time boundaries of the individual volumes, to agree on essential topics, and more. The general editor coordinated such discussions; guided the works in progress; read the individual volumes for content, coverage, and fit with the other volumes and overall purpose and design of the encyclopedia; and in other ways moved production along. It is important to note that each author/editor has assumed principal responsibility for the content of his or her volume, from selecting, arranging, and editing the articles, to getting permission to use materials, to providing the context for the articles, to fact-checking and proofreading the volume, to ensuring the highest quality in content and presentation. The general editor thus disclaims any responsibility for the specific content of or in any volume. The individual author/editor's name on the title page of each volume places the responsibility where it deservedly should rest, with the true creators. It also is important to note that in creating each volume, the author/editor did much more than compile, collate, and arrange materials derived from other sources. Each author/editor wrote the introductions to the respective volumes, the introductions to the subsections of each volume, the transitions within each article excerpting materials from other sources, the headnotes in each volume, and some of the text in each volume. Because of the uneven, or even nonexistent, source material on daily life for the two volumes treating the twentieth century, both Frank Sicius and Jolyon Girard wrote much original material. This was so much so in Girard's case that he became more author than editor of Volume 4.

In sum, then, the creation of this encyclopedia mirrors the American experience. It was, and is, an example of the nation's guiding principle of continuous creation as a people—e pluribus unum. It also is a recognition that people make history. We hope that by discovering the American people in their day-to-day lives and the life they have sought to create and live, readers will find that elusive "new man, this American" and themselves.

—Randall M. Miller

ACKNOWLEDGMENTS

As both an editor and author for the final volume in the *Daily Life in the United States* series, I would like to acknowledge the help of a number of people. Randall Miller and John Wagner provided valuable advice, assistance, and support throughout the project as series and project development editors, respectively.

The works of Eugenia Kaledin, *Daily Life in the United States, 1940–1959*, and Myron A. Marty, *Daily Life in the United States, 1960–1990*, provided the template for much of the organization and factual material for chapters 2 and 3.

Professor Darryl Mace, Cabrini College, contributed an important section on Intellectual Life, and Dr. Courtney Smith, a former undergraduate student of mine, wrote excellent reviews of sports in America for the volume. My senior class seminar students—Stephen Beierschmidt, Matthew Burge, Michael Bergamo, Dustin Carpenter, Gregory Cavacini, Jamie Curenden, Genevieve Cupaiuolo, Andrea Domacinovic, Brittany DeCicco, Marcy Fonseca, Charles Jaxel, Ryan Kelliher, Megan Keye, John Kolesnik, Christine MaGargee, Cari MaGoffin, Kevin Mairs, Megan McCourry, Deborah Maloney, Melina Moore, Matthew Paris, Angie Peso, Kevin Quinn, Tyler Sandford, Kristine Schmid, and Miriam Thompson—helped organize, edit, and review the entire volume.

Cabrini College provided a summer grant that enabled me to concentrate the necessary time on researching and writing the volume.

My son Geoffrey, an author in his own right and a devotee of popular culture in the United States, offered analysis and criticism throughout the project.

Finally, my wife Marilyn offered support, advice, and analysis. Since she provides the foundation of my daily life, and has for more than 40 years, this work is dedicated to her.

INTRODUCTION AND HISTORICAL OVERVIEW

Introduction

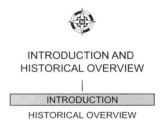

On December 7, 1941, Japanese military forces attacked the United States at Pearl Harbor in the Hawaiian Islands. The following day, President Franklin D. Roosevelt asked the Senate for a declaration of war, calling the December 7 attack a "date that will live in infamy." The American people entered World War II during the final month of 1941 after a decade-long national debate concerning the limits of U.S. involvement in the expanding world conflict.

During the 1930s, the American people had struggled with the domestic problems created by the Great Depression of 1929. Public views concerning U.S. involvement in world affairs remained broadly "isolationist" or "noninterventionist" as international tension and conflict developed during the decade. While President Roosevelt had encouraged the public to commit to aiding the enemies of Germany, Italy, and Japan (the Axis Powers), most Americans conceded only limited support for that position. As late as November 1941, public opinion polls backed the president's policy of "All Aid Short of War" (Cole 1968, 441). Those polls, however, failed to encourage direct American military involvement. The Pearl Harbor attack shattered that public position, and it changed the daily lives of Americans forever.

From the beginning of World War II to the first decade of the twenty-first century, the United States of America has witnessed remarkable and substantial changes in the daily **lives** of the men, women, and children who lived in the nation. In many aspects of life, both statistical and subtle, the United States has become a different society, and Americans have become different people. Many, if not most, of those alterations remain positive. Some are disturbing. This volume on daily life in America between 1940 and 2005 will examine the broad variety of factors, conditions, and issues that have influenced American life from the beginning of World War II to the present. This volume describes the lives of Americans at home, at work, and at play during more than a half-century of profound social, cultural, and economic transformation. Any effort as comprehensive as this volume and the set of which it is a part presents a daunting task, for a variety of reasons. Both the editor and the reader need to consider those reasons and understand them before engaging in the study.

CHRONOLOGY

Examining historical events in blocks of time (years, decades, centuries, etc.) remains an effective and traditional method for looking at human behavior. The years 1941 to 1945 defined the "war years" in America, even though American entry into World War II did not occur until the end of 1941. The period from 1945 to 1959 comprises the postwar decade for many historians, and that time period serves as a convenient way to examine how Americans responded to issues and pursued their daily lives following the war. Eugenia Kaledin subtitled her book *The United States, 1940–1959, Shifting Worlds*, to consider the era; so much changed, so quickly. Certainly, most Americans confronted a different daily life in 1945 than they did in 1959. Consider, as one example, the issue of African American civil rights. Black Americans in 1941 lived in a broadly different United States than they encountered by 1959. At the same time, however, some would argue that little had changed in the lives of African Americans, depending on who, where, and when. The famous *Brown v. Board of Education* Supreme Court decision in 1954 finally attacked segregated education, but discrimination and violence continued to challenge the evolving postwar civil rights movement.

Between 1960 and 1990, the same evolution of daily life occurred in a chronology difficult to define. Professor Myron Marty's book, *The United States, 1960–1990: Decades of Discord*, explored four key themes in his study of the generation and saw social and political discord as a central point. Yet, as much as Americans confronted clashes of conscience and policy, people in their daily lives often agreed on substantial issues that affected their communities and the nation. Clearly, daily attitudes about clothes, music, entertainment, and lifestyles altered dramatically between 1960 and 1990. People's lives do not alter so clearly from one year to the next, or even one decade to the next as chronological organization might indicate. Similar to a tidal change, the ebb and flow of American daily life often moved less clearly. This volume will, however, divide its timeframe as follows:

- 1940–1959—From World War II through the decade of the 1950s
- 1960–1990—Three decades of transition and diversity
- 1991–2005—The contemporary American scene

TOPICAL STUDIES

Looking at historical events and concerns topically poses a similar limitation. To discuss "daily life" in America from a topical perspective always provokes the rhetorical question, "whose daily life?" Sixteen million Americans entered the armed services during World War II, and there were similarities in their lives as part of that service. The service personnel who saw actual combat, however, had a vastly different daily life than those who had other assignments. Millions of African Americans looking for work migrated from the South into northern factories and businesses in the 1940s and 1950s. Were their daily lives similar to those of the black families that remained in the sharecropping system of the Cotton Belt states? Some 200,000 Mexicans came to the United States under the *bracero* legislation, to work in the agricultural regions of the American West. What impact did that move have on them and their families?

Protesters in the 1960s publicly voiced similar criticisms about American society in a torrent of discord that divided the country. Millions of Americans, however, took little or no interest in those protests and sought to live daily lives more reminiscent, in their view, of an earlier, less contentious era.

The volumes in this series are divided into both chronological and topical sections. They are designed to provide a sense of organization and clarity to the material covered in each volume. The reader, however, should always remember to examine with caution broad conclusions that either time or topic suggest in general terms. To organize the volume in topical format, the editors have examined the following subject areas:

- Domestic Life—Family life in America. The daily life of men, women, and children in a domestic environment.
- Economic Life—The commercial development of the nation and its impact on daily life.
- Intellectual Life—The role of ideas, thought, and conceptual views of American life from serious analysis to popular culture.
- Material Life—The influence of goods, products, and services on American daily life.
- Political Life—The ways political currents and issues have influenced the operation of society and the way that Americans have responded to their government and political issues.
- Recreational Life—A broad examination of how Americans spend their leisure time.
- Religious Life—The role of religion and spiritual themes in the daily lives of Americans.

REGIONALISM

In the preceding volumes of the series, the editors have given significant time to studying the daily life of Americans in regional terms. Distinct cultural and social conditions often developed and evolved in defined regional environments. Certainly, southern rural life in the nineteenth century differed broadly from American daily life in the emerging factories of the Northeast or the far West. That has not been the case, as much, in modern American life. To a significant degree, twentieth-century technology, demographics, commerce, and other factors have "homogenized" American daily life. Americans watch the same prime-time television shows, go to the same movies, eat at McDonald's, and shop at Wal-Mart. Regionalism, however, does play a continuing role in American life. Architecture in Arizona is different than in Massachusetts, as is a burrito served in San Antonio, Texas, compared to a lobster roll in Bar Harbor, Maine. At the same time, people in different parts of the country live in different demographic environments. Air conditioning and home heating systems notwithstanding, the rhythms of life move differently in the arid Southwest than in the humid Gulf Region or the wintry blasts of the Great Lakes. This volume will examine the explosion of suburban living in the United States following World War II. Still, millions of Americans live in urban centers and in the towns and small cities of rural America. Where people live is not just a matter of geographic location, it remains, as well, an issue of type—rural, urban, or suburban. The daily lives of Americans still reflect those aspects of regionalism even while the nation in the twenty-first century has become consistently more unified in culture and thought.

ANECDOTES AND STATISTICS

The use of statistical information and the addition of anecdotal examples tend to dominate the forms of presentation in studies of daily life. We need to know numbers, percentages, and the specific details that define how people lived. To talk about the evolution of a "car culture" following World War II, and to consider the impact that had on every aspect of American life makes little sense unless we know how many cars Americans bought yearly following the war and how many miles the average family drives each year. At the same time, the individual reflections of American men and women concerning their experiences protesting the war in Vietnam or worrying about a loved one fighting in Vietnam become an equally important aspect of understanding daily life in the country. Both methods of study seem equally fruitful. Whether one examines U.S. Census Bureau reports or Studs Terkel's oral histories, both demand a reader's attention. The issue to confront, however, hinges on how much weight to give to either or both statistics or anecdotes. Statistical data may be accurate in its detail, but it often omits the human element of historical conclusion. Statistics on car sales may tell a reader how many cars were sold in a given year, but may not indicate what people used the automobiles to do, or why the postwar "car culture" became such an emotional aspect of American life. Similarly, anecdotal quotes, conversations, or remarks give one a personal sense of daily life, but they can never explain broader views. In a sense, statistics show the reader "the forest, not the tree," and anecdotes show "the tree, not the forest." By using both, this volume promises a reasonable glimpse of both the forest and the trees of American's daily lives.

HISTORICAL OBSERVATION

Ultimately, location, economic condition, race, gender, culture, age, and other factors all play a significant role in how Americans saw and lived their daily lives. Those who study history must remain especially careful as they consider and present those variables. Different people do not naturally or necessarily agree on what is the "truth." Perspective and experience count much in determining how and what one sees of others and oneself. And people at certain times in history think about different things with different degrees of focus and intensity. An example of that relativity emerges in studies of the U.S. decision to use the atomic bomb to end World War II. At the time, in 1945, few Americans, including leaders of both political parties as well as the general public, disapproved of the decision to use the new, destructive weapon against Japan. In fact, most Americans applauded the action of President Truman in August 1945. Today, Americans view the issue from a perspective influenced by time and revision of thinking. In an August 2005 opinion poll "celebrating" the sixtieth anniversary of the end of World War II, 50 percent of the American public thought the use of the weapon inappropriate (*New York Times* 2005). Those who study history must carefully judge both points of view, and the historian who presents the material must also examine the issue with the same care.

FOR MORE INFORMATION

Bailey, Thomas A. *A Diplomatic History of the American People*. Englewood Cliffs, NJ: Prentice Hall, 1980.

Cole, Wayne S. *An Interpretive History of American Foreign Relations*. Homewood, IL: Dorsey Press, 1968.

New York Times (August 11, 2005). http://www.nytimes.com/gst.

Historical Overview

THE ROAD TO WAR, 1936–1940

Shortly after his election to a second term in 1936, Franklin Roosevelt gave a speech in Chicago condemning Germany, Italy, and Japan for their aggressive foreign policy and identifying them as threats to world peace and security. He called for a "quarantine" to check their dangerous behavior. The president sought to gain popular support for his view, but his "Quarantine Address" had little influence or impact with the American people. They had elected him to deal with the Depression, and most Americans showed little interest in the developing world crisis. Within four years, however, Roosevelt's insistence and the dramatic changes in world affairs had altered public views. By 1940, when Roosevelt ran for an unprecedented third

President and Mrs. Franklin D. Roosevelt, riding in Hyde Park, 1940. Library of Congress.

"I want you for the U.S. Army" recruitment poster, 1941. Library of Congress.

term as president, World War II had begun in Europe and Asia, and the United States had become a "Great Arsenal of Democracy," to quote the title of one of Roosevelt's fireside chats, aiding the enemies of Germany, Italy, and Japan. The war ended the Depression. Millions of Americans had gone back to work, and, in the process, they revitalized the nation's industry and their own lives. Still, a dramatic debate raged in the nation regarding the limits of U.S. involvement in World War II. The America First Committee and other "peace organizations" drew powerful public support arguing against direct U.S. involvement in the conflict. Senators, such as Gerald P. Nye of North Dakota, and popular national heroes, like Charles Lindbergh, warned of the dangers of conflict. Those isolationists or noninterventionists believed that Roosevelt would draw the nation into a war that would harm U.S. interests and produce the same flaws they believed had marked American involvement in World War I.

At the same time, other pressure groups like the Committee to Defend America by Aiding the Allies supported the president's policies and hoped to see the United States become more involved in the growing conflict. Nonetheless, Roosevelt won a third term by pledging to keep America out of the war through the use of aid programs and packages to those nations fighting against the Axis Powers. His leadership, and the worsening situation in Europe and Asia, had led most Americans to support "All Aid Short of War," but as late as November 1941, public opinion polls suggested that the people would go no further.

WORLD WAR II, 1941–1945

The Japanese attack at Pearl Harbor on December 7, 1941, ended the great debate in the United States. During the second week of December, the nation went to war. Both the federal government and the American people harnessed the full energy and resources of the nation to combat the Axis Powers of Germany, Japan, and Italy. From General Motors to Hollywood, from Washington, D.C., to Honolulu, Americans went to fight

"The Good War," to quote the title of Studs Terkel's 1984 book. Men, women, and children would experience major changes in their lives between 1941 and 1945 as a result of World War II. Many of those changes are discussed in the initial chapter of this volume.

A nation of 132 million people, with the most potent industrial capacity in history, geared for war in the winter of 1941–1942. During that conflict, 16 million Americans served in the armed forces (Millett and Maslowski 1994, 653). The factories worked overtime as the government budgeted billions of dollars to develop the supplies and weapons necessary to fight the war. Unemployment dropped to less than 1 percent. In noteworthy statistics dealing with ethnic minorities, more than 200,000 Mexicans immigrated legally to the United States to harvest crops.

Actress Marilyn Monroe poses for photographs after a performance during the Korean War, 1954. Chaiba.

African American employment in industry rose from 2.9 to 3.8 million workers. The female labor force rose by more than 50 percent and reached almost 20 million by 1945. Major demographic movement occurred within the United States as job opportunities developed and as servicemen and women moved from training bases to embarkation locations. The broad history of that effort and its influence on American daily life will form the first major section of this volume.

One can find astounding numbers in the money spent, the industrial and agricultural production developed, the rising wages, and the broad military operations across the face of the globe. The war, however, also involved the daily terror that combat produces. Half a million Americans were killed in World War II, thousands more wounded. Families at home agonized over those losses and feared the dreaded arrival of a letter from the government confirming the death or wounding of a loved one. Soldiers coming home brought their own memories of death and destruction as they reentered civilian society. The opening scene in the recent movie *Saving Private Ryan* (1998) vividly portrays that aspect of the conflict that many history textbooks neglect: Department of War typists sitting at rows of desks preparing letters to next of kin. A mother collapses in agony on her front porch as an officer arrives to tell her that her son has died. Doris Kearns Goodwin's *No Ordinary Time* (1999) also serves as an important study of American daily life during the war; in the movie, a visual moment of loss, in the book, a comprehensive study of the war years.

The "grand alliance" (using Winston Churchill's terminology) that the United States formed with the Soviet Union, Great Britain, and other nations defeated their Axis enemies in Europe by May 1945 and won in the Pacific with the surrender of Japan in August 1945. Americans breathed collective sighs of relief and joy having fought, in their view, the "Good War" against totalitarian regimes that threatened their security and the future of the world. Revisionist studies of history have questioned some of the flaws of that euphoria and have rightfully examined labor strikes, racial discrimination, black-market abuse of rationing, and other issues that indicate less-than-perfect public commitment and solidarity. Most Americans, however, celebrated in August 1945 and concluded that the war had been won as a result of collective effort and sacrifice.

POSTWAR AMERICA, 1945–1959

World War II had changed America's daily life. The Great Depression (1929–1941) provided a serious and severe blow to the nation's confidence in the free market system that had dominated the lives of Americans since the founding of the United States. The collapse of the economy, the millions of unemployed people, and the dramatic decline in American economic production had prompted the "New Deal," a broad series of government legislation that Franklin Roosevelt's government hoped would bring the country out of the Depression. Although a variety of federal programs worked to alleviate the symptoms the Great Depression created, millions of Americans remained unemployed into the late 1930s. The beginning of the war, and the upsurge of jobs and production demanded by a wartime economy and government spending to build the military arsenal that the United States would create in World War II ended unemployment and actually created a demand for labor. Sixteen million Americans would serve in the military during the war, and millions more would enter the factories to supply those forces. Agricultural production also grew significantly during World War II.

The federal government began to withhold taxes from employee paychecks during the war in order to develop a ready flow of cash, but those taxes did not prevent people from building a reservoir of postwar savings. Government rationing required many Americans to save money. The sale of War Bonds provided additional income that people could include in their savings. The Federal Deposit Insurance Corporation (FDIC), a New Deal program, ensured that the banks

Ford exhibit preview in New York City, 1948. Library of Congress.

would safeguard those savings. As a result, capital funds increased significantly during the war, and men and women would have more money to spend when it became feasible to do so. At the same time, the Depression and the war had re-created a demand market for goods and services that the Depression had limited or prevented in the 1930s. Effectively, by 1945, Americans had money to spend and things they hoped to purchase.

Additionally, the war itself had destroyed much of western Europe's economy and left American industry with few competitors. Some economists remained concerned that an end to World War II would push the country back into a depression. When wartime government contracts ceased, and when millions of servicemen and women returned to civilian life, they concluded, America would face a postwar economic decline. That failed to occur. Other economists pushed the view that a renewed consumer-driven economy with available capital and the industrial ability to shift from wartime to peacetime products would create a period of prosperity for the country. That did happen. In fact, American men and women found an open job market aggressively seeking employees and willing to provide not only wages but benefits (retirement and health), paid vacations, and other incentives to join the workforce. That postwar economic boom period meant many Americans could look forward to buying new homes, new cars, and new consumer conveniences that would have astonished them or their parents prior to 1941.

The benefits accorded a broad portion of the American public did not go to everyone. Although African Americans had found better pay and job opportunities in the factories and other professions during the war, they did not share proportionately in the progress that followed. They, and other Americans, continued to fight for civil rights, better jobs, fair housing, and equal educational opportunities. Other minority groups in the culture experienced similar oppression and exploitation and would also engage in efforts to redress their concerns. The impact of World War II, and the postwar era, would generate a renewed interest in and commitment to civil rights for those Americans. A people who had waged war against Nazism came to see the terrible "logic" of racism and discrimination in their own society. By the 1960s, a rights revolution swept the nation. The evolution of minority and women's struggles for self-realization and opportunity would become a hallmark of daily life in America between 1940 and 1990. It is an ongoing issue that continues to define America's commitment and character.

The postwar half-century saw an explosion of economic and social materialism. The consumer culture in America became an even more embedded aspect of daily life. Interpretations of that development have differed broadly among historians and observers of the society. Some economists believed that Americans had saved too much money during the 1920s, and they believed that it had caused the depression of 1929. In a "supply and demand" economy, unless one spent more money on goods and services, supply would exceed demand, production would decline, unemployment would rise, and a new postwar depression might ensue. It became imperative, therefore, to encourage enhanced, continual spending on goods and services in order to drive the new economy. Advocates of the new "consumerism" believed that Americans also wanted to throw off the prohibitions of spending that the Depression and the war had created. In simple terms, Americans had money and wanted to buy new things, and both they and the general economy would benefit from the indulgence of consumerism.

Critics have argued that the consumer culture has come to place too much emphasis on things as a measure of our society and culture. The mania to accumulate goods and services, they believe, weakened social cohesion and afflicted the daily lives of Americans with unhealthy eating, socializing, and hedonistic habits. Our culture, they have argued, became obsessed with possessions and self-indulgence found in what we own, not who we are. As an example, critics see the explosion of suburban home ownership and the growth in automobile purchases as threats to the community that existed in urban neighborhoods and public transportation. Americans rushed to buy single homes and park new cars in their driveways, but they then isolated themselves from day-to-day contact with their neighbors.

Whether positive, negative, or aspects of both, however, the mass consumption of goods, products, and services has been a dominant socioeconomic and cultural condition in American life since the end of World War II, and it remains inconceivable to examine the era without a clear look at the impact of that shift in behavior.

Intellectual Life

Many cultural historians identify the postwar era as an initial period (1945–1959) of conformity and social convention. To suggest, however, that people only lived in suburbs, watched television, and ate TV dinners is simplistic. A broad and significant variety of intellectual life took place during the era, and Americans were involved in that process. Americans not only watched Ed Sullivan's popular Sunday television variety show or listened to Elvis Presley records, they also supported symphony orchestras and read challenging new novels. Ernest Hemingway wrote his novella *The Old Man and the Sea* in 1951 and won the Nobel Prize for literature three years later. Jack Kerouac published *On the Road* in 1957, an iconic work for the "Beat Generation." Frank Lloyd Wright's Guggenheim Museum in New York City, completed in 1959, not only indicated an interest in architecture beyond "little pink houses" (a term from a song by John Mellencamp) in the suburbs, it was also built to house an outstanding art collection.

Material Life

The influence of mass consumption in the postwar free market economy raised materialism to a new significance in American daily life. One can certainly argue that people everywhere, and at all times, have sought material security in their lives— food, homes, and so on. That was certainly the case throughout American history, but, between 1941 and 1959, the interest in and commitment to mass consumption in America reached heights never seen in the past. The mass production of automobiles, durable goods (refrigerators, washing machines, etc.), housing and other items fueled the new consumer economy. Ten million homes were constructed during the 1950s. Americans had millions of new Bell Telephone System phones installed in their homes. By 1949, consumers purchased more than 250,000 television sets a month, compared to fewer than 17,000 three years earlier. Eight million cars rolled off the assembly lines in Detroit in 1950, 75 percent of the world's total production. Clearly, American consumers saw the accumulation of material goods as an essential aspect of their postwar daily lives (Tuttle and Perry 1970, 725–74).

Political Life

The two-party political system remained a viable aspect of American life during the period despite some signs of third-party activity in response to civil rights, fiscal policy, and the Cold War. The Democratic Party controlled the White House from 1940 to 1952 with Franklin Roosevelt leading a wartime government and Harry Truman (1949–1952) working to expand some of the ideas of the New Deal with his postwar Fair Deal programs and his development of a Cold War foreign policy to confront the Soviet Union. The Republican Party, however, regained control of the Congress following World War II, and Dwight Eisenhower, a moderate conservative war hero, won the presidency for the Republicans in 1952. The uncertainty and crisis of the Korean War (1950–1953) had shaken the complacency of the 1950s. So, too, had the internal problem caused by the influence of Senator Joseph McCarthy and others during the infamous "Red Scare" of the time. Those serious disturbances and the continued Cold War, including the threat of nuclear confrontation with the Soviet Union, however, seemed an acceptable aspect of America's new role as a world leader in defense of freedom. Perhaps the conservative nature of Eisenhower's administration, and that of the Congress, fit the mood of a people more interested in their own personal and professional lives than in the proactive, policy-driven governments that had operated during the Great Depression and World War II.

Recreational Life

With more money and more free time, most Americans experienced a renewed postwar interest in both spectator recreation and their own direct experiences. Movie attendance soared. Sports, at both the collegiate and professional levels, expanded in importance. Television slowly replaced radio as the in-home resource for relaxation and entertainment. Organized youth sports like Little League baseball served as social outlets for suburban families. Boy Scouts and Girls Scouts added to youth opportunities. That trend would continue throughout the remainder of the century.

Religious Life

From Alexis de Tocqueville's nineteenth-century observations in *Democracy in America* to contemporary social analysis, Americans have shown an abiding interest in religious affiliation and the relationship between organized religions and spiritual and moral behavior. Predominantly Christian in religious membership and cultural values, Americans seemed to become more interested in or involved with organized churches during and following the war. Postwar religious revivalism boomed

Natalie Wood displays new drive-in movie speakers. Library of Congress.

and traditional church membership increased significantly. The anecdotal inclusion of "under God" in the nation's Pledge of Allegiance and the inscription of "In God We Trust" on America's currency punctuated that focus. Forms of religious intolerance, such as anti-Catholicism, anti-Semitism, and a general distain for atheists and others outside of "mainstream" religious currents existed, but, again, significant numbers of Americans considered formal commitment to particular religious institutions a key aspect of their daily lives. And a nascent ecumenism appeared in the 1950s that promised a less turbulent and more accepting attitude in American society.

DECADES OF DISCORD, 1960–1990

American daily life did not alter abruptly with the election of President John F. Kennedy in 1960 and his inaugural promise of a "New Frontier." Yet, during the next 30 years, broad and significant changes in the national landscape did cause people in the country to look at themselves and their world in fundamentally different ways, often in a confrontational manner. Population changes alone had a significant impact on American life. The "Baby Boom" of the postwar era had produced millions of children who were entering adolescence or adulthood during the period. Those young people had not directly experienced either the economic and social privations of the Great Depression or the total commitment of the nation to a world war. The demographic shift to suburban life, the development of interstate highways, an immigrant influx, new technology such as telecommunications and computers, health benefits, an ever-expanding service economy and decline in the manufacturing sector, and the increasing complexity of America's international relations all brought changes in the daily lives of Americans.

A host of new critics arose to question "traditional" values, beliefs, and practices that many Americans had taken for granted during and following World War II. In every issue from foreign policy to the environment, from race relations to feminism, and from sexual behavior to popular culture, American attitudes shifted in the "decades of discord" that Myron Marty examined in his study of the era.

Domestic Life

While most Americans remained in single-family, traditional marriages, incidences of divorce, the decline in extended families, and a variety of other "aberrations" in domestic life occurred between 1960 and 1990. Statistics quantify the significance, but it remains important to analyze how and why those changes occurred. The significance and impact of children also changed during the period as their specific needs and interests enabled young people, from birth to adolescence, to demand a new focus and interest within the society. The evolution of a "teen culture," with all of its impact, from recreation to education, became a matter of absorbed attention. At the same time, life expectancy rose during the period. An expanded number of "senior citizens" with more retirement income than Social Security payments could provide, and longer life to enjoy the benefits of retirement, also created a new domestic force in the nation.

Economic Life

The American economy continued to grow during the 30-year period between 1960 and 1990, and the standard of living for most Americans appeared to improve. Occasional economic recessions, some serious, created concern, but the economy continued to expand. Growing energy needs made Americans increasingly dependent on foreign reserves. The rise of global competition challenged the postwar American economic dominance. Yet, the 30-year period between 1960 and 1990 witnessed a positive growth for the broad middle class. Still, Michael Harrington's *Other America* (1962) identified a population of families that the general prosperity of the postwar era had failed to reach. President Lyndon Johnson (1963–1969) recognized that condition and in proposing his "Great Society" programs declared a "War on Poverty" that would bring the full forces of the federal government to eradicate poverty and discrimination.

The issue of the extent and direction of public responsibility for addressing poverty and inequality in a free market economy remains a fundamental social argument to the present day. Can the richest, most powerful nation on earth tolerate any percentage of its population not having legitimate access to health, education, and economic opportunity? Or are there acceptable limitations on what the government can do in a free society to alleviate all social and economic ills? Between 1960 and 1990, that debate would provoke 30 years of discord. Ironically, the Vietnam War and changing domestic priorities in the 1960s through the 1970s undercut the Great Society programs and changed the direction of American economic life.

Intellectual Life

American colleges and universities, often bastions of conservative stability in the 1950s, experienced years of upheaval and intellectual debate, sometimes violent in approach. Higher education also saw a massive expansion in enrollments, an increase in resources, and more influence in an information-driven economy. A generation of professors and students challenged their elders regarding the direction and focus of American life. A range of artists, writers, musicians, and observers joined in the assault on traditional values and beliefs. As Rachel Carson's *Silent Spring* (1962) attacked the use of insecticides because of their effect on the environment, and Ralph Nader's *Unsafe at Any Speed* (1965) condemned General Motors for producing unsafe automobiles, a generation of social critics arose to question the safety of many products and technologies once thought to be boons to progress. Indeed, the paradox of modern life in America often focused on the benefits or flaws of advanced technology and science. How helpful or harmful were chemicals, for instance? The nation could study a new bibliography of criticism and provocative concern as books and articles questioned how the country operated and how Americans lived their daily lives.

Ohio National Guardsmen commence firing into student demonstrators at Kent State University, 1970. Library of Congress.

Hugh Hefner began to publish *Playboy* magazine in 1953. That monthly publication sought to popularize a sexual revolution previously studied seriously in works that Albert Kinsey had published in 1948 and 1953. In 1966, William Masters and Virginia Johnson published *Human Sexual Response*, providing scholarly substance to Hefner's commercial use of female nudity and male prurience that allowed him to become a wealthy entrepreneur. At every level of intellectual activity, Americans both questioned and defended the consequences of a national life that had surfaced following World War II.

Historians revised history to make it more inclusive of many voices and more contentious as they explored the roots of social problems. Novelists experimented with new narrative forms (Joseph Heller's *Catch-22*, 1961) or abandoned narrative altogether. Playwrights and artists challenged the canons of their crafts, sometimes eliminating color and dialogue. The period seemed a time of experimentation in lifestyles and ideas—and for many, of reassessment of old values in the face of bewildering intellectual and social ferment.

Material Life

Americans continued to pursue the consumer-driven materialism that surged anew following the war. Two cars became a family "necessity" in the middle-class commuting culture. Additional television sets went into "rec rooms" or bedrooms to accompany the novel color televisions in family living rooms. Technology rushed ahead with innovations made available to Americans products never considered previously outside of science fiction stories and movies. As an example, the space program produced Velcro as a necessity for zero-gravity use. Americans, in daily life, found other uses for the new product.

Political Life

President John Kennedy's election (1960) promised a "New Frontier" for Americans and the world. As a youthful, charismatic leader, Kennedy seemed to personify the hopes and aspirations of a postwar generation. His assassination on November 22, 1963, stunned the nation. His successor, Lyndon Johnson (1963–1969), developed the largest, most comprehensive federal program in history in his Great Society–War on Poverty initiative. The quintessential American political liberal, Johnson believed that racism, poverty, injustice, and all of the issues that had plagued the society, even as it prospered, could be attacked and eliminated. Certainly, the many programs that he and Congress developed helped. Yet, the Vietnam War, racial and civil unrest, and the assassinations of civil rights leader Martin Luther King Jr. and Senator Robert Kennedy convinced many Americans that President Johnson's domestic programs had failed to do their job.

Richard M. Nixon's election (1968) and his subsequent political history indicated a brief shift in political thinking in America, but the decade of protest and upheaval that confronted his administration continued unabated. The Watergate scandal that ended with Nixon's resignation (August 1974) further altered American attitudes about their government and the men and women who worked in Washington. The nation's bicentennial celebration in 1976 took place with a residue of cynicism and concern. While Presidents Gerald Ford (1974–1978) and

Nashville police officer, wielding a nightstick, holds an African American youth at bay during a civil rights march in Tennessee, 1964. Library of Congress.

Jimmy Carter (1979–1982) sought to find some transition in America's political attitudes, few real changes occurred until Ronald Reagan's presidential victory in 1980. The former movie actor and California governor brought a revived conservative philosophy to the White House that evoked a sympathetic and supportive response from many Americans. Weary with the cynicism and anti-American attitudes of far left critics of the country, Reagan's conservative base responded favorably to his upbeat, positive, pro-American positions. That political shift from traditional support for New Deal and Great Society federal liberalism to a broader conservative ideology remains one of the most significant changes in American politics since the end of World War II. It would drive the American political landscape to the present day.

Apollo 12 astronaut Alan Bean pauses during extravehicular activity on the moon, 1969. Chaiba.

Recreational Life

Since 1960, Americans have developed so many different ways to spend their recreation and leisure time and money that it seems silly to generalize. More time, more money, more options, more commercialism, and more access have all influenced the extensive opportunities for Americans to enjoy themselves. Examples are legion, from backyard barbecues to the National Football League's Super Bowls: television's profound and growing influence; sports betting and the growth of casinos; magazines and periodicals devoted to specific interests and recreational options; music, available in so many different varieties and new technologies, from stereo to tape decks to CDs; spectator sports that draw millions into stadiums and arenas and make multimillionaires out of athletes; recreational jogging, tennis, golf, bowling, and use of treadmills in a search of healthy exercise, weight loss, or personal enjoyment; society's expenditure of millions of dollars on pets. The new celebrities of American life are entertainers, whether athletes, musicians, or actors. Why and how that happened has roots in the nation's past, but the acceleration of that focus in American daily life occurred most rapidly between 1960 and 1990.

Religious Life

If Americans indicated a clear commitment to organized religious institutions following World War II, and opinion polls and scholarly observation seem to support that conclusion, the generation that lived between 1960 and 1990 offered broadly different commitments to church attendance and new forms of spirituality. A large percentage of the population continued to attend weekly church services, but polls and surveys alone do not always tell a clear story. Did Americans view their religious commitments differently? American Roman Catholics, for instance, began publicly to question key church traditions and policies, including church rules on birth control, homosexuality, and an all-male, unmarried priesthood. Issues of change or orthodoxy came under scrutiny and debate in Protestant and Jewish faiths as well. Vigorous evangelism, including increasing reliance on television and radio ministries and the draw of "felt" religious experiences, increased the numbers of people drawn to Pentecostal and fundamentalist churches. The "born again" Christian movement emerged as a key social and political force in the era. The alternate lifestyles that evolved from the youth movement of the 1960s created new options for spiritual growth outside of traditional religious belief. "New Age" concepts challenged weekly church attendance. Yet, in positive terms, mainline institutional churches and religions appeared to accept a new form of ecumenical acceptance of other faiths and religions, a clear effort to understand each other's differences.

If the period 1960–1990 exemplified "Decades of Discord," as Myron Marty has suggested, that conclusion does not necessarily mean that all discord was negative. Any new era of thought and behavior can always appear disruptive, and certainly these 30 years saw obvious elements of that confusion. Yet, the discord that had many Americans reexamining their past also yielded broad, contributive, and positive accomplishments that the encyclopedia will seek to examine.

THE MODERN ERA, 1991–2005

In 1992, Francis Fukuyama wrote *The End of History and the Last Man*. He seemed to suggest that the conclusion of the Cold War struggle between the United States and the Soviet Union had changed the evolution of history, both in America and throughout the world. The old international struggles between political and economic ideologies had ended, and free-market democracies, with America in the lead as a world "hyper-power," would face a new era. The book saw a positive, progressive conclusion to that theme. Yet, new issues emerged to demand the attention and concern of Americans as they led their daily lives, both international and domestic; terrorism and AIDS, globalization and genocide in Africa, energy demands, environmental concerns such as global warming, and a host of other problems required attention and affected American daily lives.

Nature itself seemed to reassert its claim to rule with a rash of violent weather, especially hurricanes, tornadoes, floods, and forest fires. If Americans had always faced those natural disasters, they appeared more disturbing in the modern era. The sense of powerlessness in the face of nature clashed with the contemporary view that science and technology gave Americans more control of their world. Who but a few specialists could have predicted the traumatic and destructive impact of Hurricane Katrina as it devastated the Gulf Coast and New Orleans in August 2005? At the same time, however, positive and beneficial changes also defined the daily lives of Americans in the 15 years between 1990 and 2005. New technologies accelerated communication, allowing worldwide communication within microseconds. A reasonably prosperous economy brought more Americans into the middle class even as the "super rich" increased their share of the nation's wealth. Access to vastly expanded consumer goods and services made more Americans part of a national culture, developing better lives and opportunities for Americans. Immigration became a renewed aspect of life in America, particularly including arrivals from Asia and Latin America. The new immigrants brought intelligence and energy in a variety of areas from medical expertise to harvesting crops. At the same time, concerns regarding "illegal" or undocumented aliens provoked a debate in American society. Charles Dickens has always made sense when he wrote in *A Tale of Two Cities*, "It was the best of times. It was the worst of times." Americans in the past 15 years have seen both.

Domestic Life

Americans are still responding and reacting to the significant alterations of domestic lifestyles that began in the previous 30 years. The traditional roles of men and women have altered. The raising of children has seen a new focus on their safety and education, as "helicopter parents" hover protectively to safeguard children's interests. At the same time, single-parent and even no-parent households have increased, and parental authority has been challenged by entertainment idols and other competitors for children's attention and allegiance. The increasingly programmed life of middle-class suburban youth contrasts with the less adult-ordered worlds of other classes. Drug use, alcohol, obesity, and sexual experimentation continue to threaten the social and physical health of families. Yet, the "traditional family" remains an important social factor in contemporary American life, and much of the fabric of the domestic life shows little basic difference from the 1950s.

Economic Life

The economic life of Americans, both in terms of micro- and macroeconomics, continues to offer new opportunities and challenges. The nation remains the most powerful economy in the world while facing new competition from rising commercial states like China and India. Much of what Americans buy, from their cotton clothes to raw steel, is imported. The nation remains vitally dependent on foreign oil, an economic concern that has existed since the 1970s. The trade deficit continues to soar. Both the government's debt and Americans' personal debt have risen significantly. Americans spend more money than they collect in taxes or personal savings. Yet, those purchases allow for more material goods and products at a cheaper price. Disparity continues to exist between rich and poor, and critics claim that the middle class has begun to suffer a serious decline in its traditional status as an economic force in the society. Yet, unemployment numbers remain well below double digits, as do inflation and interest rates, the triad evaluators of economic health. As always, economic views and predictions remain complicated. With the stock markets fluctuating between "bull" and "bear" activity, and the Federal Reserve providing cautious, but optimistic, reviews of the economy, American economic life moved into the new millennium with uncertainty.

Intellectual Life

A concept defined as *postmodernism* has offered a new focus for intellectual thought in American life. Perhaps, postmodernists argue, the traditional acceptance of progress, reason, and science as the controlling factors in people's lives has been either overdone or are wrong. Is all progress necessarily beneficial? Are reason and empirical analysis the best methods to examine "truth"? Do science and its method of inquiry provide the best way to advance? Albert Borgman has written about a "postmodern divide" that influences American intellectual thought in the contemporary era, in both serious and popular debate. While traditional methods of inquiry and intellectual endeavor continue to provide ideas and conclusions, those approaches often clash, now, with postmodern contradictions and criticisms. The divide appears both interesting and worth an examination in this encyclopedia.

Material Life

Americans have prided themselves on having the highest standard of living in the world. Certainly, the society has access to more goods and services, and it has indulged in a broad consumerism since the end of World War II in the acquisition of those commodities. Whether that "success" fulfills the "American dream" remains open to question. Millions of Americans benefit from the options available, but millions of others lack real access to them. Both the end result of material acquisition and its availability to the largest possible number of people in the society remain a key issue in the contemporary world of American daily life.

Political Life

A number of political observers and pundits have maintained that a divisive struggle has evolved in the society. A definable, contentious battle between Democrats and Republicans has seen a blue state–red state political nastiness that affects the way Americans see the nation and its goals and objectives. From foreign policy to domestic programs, Americans appear to

A young woman looks at her laptop computer and drinks her coffee. Tobkatrina| Dreamstime.com

disagree emotionally as to the direction the nation should follow. The "culture wars" that began in the 1960s have settled into the broad political debate of the new century. At the same time, however, other students of American political life believe that a mainstream America tends to see things in reasonably similar terms. Americans have more in common, they believe, than the concerns that divide them, at least as far as that divisiveness appears on the nightly television news shows. The political debate that seems to rage in Washington, on radio and television, and among the many new "blog" sites that have entered the arena of public discourse may represent a legitimate political divide. Those involved in the debate, however, may also

The World Trade Center, 1999. Wildbirdimages|Dreamstime.com

A young woman is able to lounge in bed while doing her homework thanks to her cell phone. Duey|Dreamstime.com

overlook a mainstream balance among many Americans who reject the political extremes of both groups.

Recreational Life

Television (with numerous cable channels) and movies, spectator sports, specialty magazines, popular literature, varieties of music, and many other means of personal or communal enjoyment compete for patronage and attention in an ever more crowded and fragmented culture.

Paradoxically, the homogeneity of consumer culture as in the remake of old films and television shows has come at the same time as the variety of forms, styles, and presentations of "culture" proliferate. Music blends from Asia, Latin America, and Africa, with Arabic forms, offer one example of that proliferation. Cell phones, iPods, satellite radios, and other hand-held technologies have continued to democratize entertainment choices as well as access to information. Those tools, however, widen the breach between those with access to the technology and those without. Not all Americans can—or even want to—"hum the same tune." Still, two factors continue to drive the recreational life of Americans in the modern age. First, access to the opportunities remains based in commercial, free-market options. Most recreational sources offer their service for a price, whether tickets at the theater, advertisements on television, or sales in music stores. And the options remain egalitarian. They are available to anyone willing to pay regardless of class, race, or gender. In some regards, American recreational opportunities may provide the finest example of democratic opportunity and access.

Religious Life

Americans remain the most "church-going" people in the industrial world, and the United States boasts the greatest variety of religious groups and practices in the world. Religion continues to occupy the attention and interest of Americans as they go about their daily lives. An increase in Christian fundamentalism has directly influenced both political and social thought in the nation. As Protestant evangelicalism has swelled in its appeal, support for mainstream regular worship has fallen off. Some see the influence of the "Christian Right" as dangerous; others argue it is a positive development. Child abuse scandals in the Roman Catholic Church have brought particular focus to that religious institution, but millions of members of that faith continue to pursue its spiritual and ethical authority with pride and comfort. Ecumenical demands to become more tolerant of other faiths have certainly altered former religious views in the society. Americans seem more aware and accepting of the diversity of religious beliefs that are practiced in the country—or, at least,

Americans say they are more tolerant. In any event, the long-standing influence of religious thought in America remains a key aspect of the nation's interest in and focus on spiritual and ethical options within institutional faiths and religious beliefs.

CONCLUSIONS

Because this volume of *The Encyclopedia of Daily Life in the United States* examines, in detail, the issues discussed in this chapter, it remains important to recall the central purpose of the work. The volume explores broad themes in the American experience, organized in both chronological and topical style. Each section seeks to provide a basic theme, statistical information, anecdotal examples, and a reasonable interpretation of the information. Visual examples such as pictures, photographs, graphs, and other additions will seek to provide additional insight and interest for the reader. A bibliography of both printed and online sources aims to provide readers with other sources of information and analysis to consider and to study. As noted above, no encyclopedia on American daily life can hope to examine every issue, every concern, and every aspect of a people so diverse and complex as the people who have lived in the United States between 1941 and 2005. The volume will, however, attempt to include as much as possible to allow a broader, more careful look at how Americans lived their daily lives in the last half of the twentieth century and the first five years of the twenty-first century.

FOR MORE INFORMATION

Adler, Selig. *The Uncertain Giant, 1921–1941: American Foreign Policy between the Wars.* New York: MacMillan, 1965.

Cole, Wayne S. *Roosevelt and the Isolationists.* Lincoln: University of Nebraska Press, 1983.

Ehrman, John. *The Eighties: America in the Age of Reagan.* New Haven, CT: Yale University Press, 2006.

Goldman, Eric. *The Crucial Decade and After—America, 1945–1960.* New York: Random House, 1960.

Goodwin, Doris Kearns. *No Ordinary Time: Franklin and Eleanor Roosevelt, the Homefront in World War II.* New York: Simon & Schuster, 1999.

Halberstam, David. *The Fifties.* New York: Random House, 1993.

Kaledin, Eugenia. *Daily Life in the United States, 1940–1959: Shifting Worlds.* Westport, CT: Greenwood Press, 2000.

Kennedy, David M. *Freedom from Fear: The American People in Depression and War, 1929–1945.* New York: Oxford University Press, 1999.

Marty, Myron A. *Daily Life in the United States, 1960–1990: Decades of Discord.* Westport, CT: Greenwood Press, 1997.

Millett, Allen, and Peter Maslowski. *For the Common Defense: A Military History of the United States of America.* New York: The Free Press, 1994.

O'Neill, William L. *Coming Apart: An Informal History of America in the 1960's.* New York: Quadrangle-New York Times Books, 1974.

Patterson, J. T. *Grand Expectations: The United States, 1945–1974*. New York: Oxford University Press, 1996.

Schulman, Bruce J. *The Seventies: The Great Shift in American Culture*. New York: The Free Press, 2001.

Terkel, Studs. *The Good War: An Oral History of World War Two*. New York: Pantheon Books, 1984.

Tuttle, Frank W., and Joseph M. Perry. *An Economic History of the United States*. Cincinnati: South-Western Publishing Company, 1970.

2

DAILY LIFE IN THE UNITED STATES, 1940–1959

Timeline

DAILY LIFE IN THE UNITED
STATES, 1940–1959

| TIMELINE |
OVERVIEW
DOMESTIC LIFE
ECONOMIC LIFE
INTELLECTUAL LIFE
MATERIAL LIFE
POLITICAL LIFE
RECREATIONAL LIFE
RELIGIOUS LIFE

1940　Congress passes the Smith Act, making it a crime to support the violent overthrow of the government.

　　　The first multilane superhighway opens—the Pennsylvania Turnpike.

　　　In Pasadena, California, the first McDonald's opens.

　　　January 30: U.S. government issues the first Social Security checks.

　　　February 12: The first episode of the hit radio show *Superman* airs.

　　　July 27: The first *Bugs Bunny* cartoon is shown—*A Wild Hare*.

　　　November 5: President Franklin D. Roosevelt (FDR) defeats Wendell Willkie in the presidential election to win a third consecutive term in office.

　　　November 13: Mickey Mouse debuts, as the sorcerer's apprentice, in his first feature film, *Fantasia*.

1941　Congress passes the Land-Lease Act giving the president power to sell, lend, and lease war material to other nations.

　　　Painter Edward Hopper finishes the painting *Nighthawks*.

　　　May 1: Cheerios is first produced as CheeriOats by General Mills.

　　　May 6: Bob Hope performs in his first USO Show at California's March Field.

　　　August 1: The first Jeep is produced.

　　　October 24: The Fair Labor Act goes into effect, producing the 40-hour work-week.

　　　November 26: Thanksgiving is officially declared the fourth Thursday of every November.

　　　December 7: Japan attacks Pearl Harbor, bringing the United States into World War II.

1942　Bing Crosby releases the song "White Christmas."

The first HMO (Health Maintenance Organization) is founded in Oakland, California.

The Manhattan Project is developed to aid the United States in its efforts to design and build an atomic bomb.

February 9: Daylight saving time is established.

November 26: The movie *Casablanca* premieres in theaters. It is critically acclaimed as one of the best films of all time.

1943   During World War II, the All American Girls' Baseball League is formed to fill empty ballparks with entertainment.

To prevent inflation, President Franklin D. Roosevelt freezes prices, salaries, and wages.

After 15 years the *Amos 'n' Andy* radio show is canceled.

January 15: The largest office building in the world, the Pentagon, is built and located in Arlington, Virginia.

February 27: In Bearcreek, Montana, the Smith mine explodes, killing 74 men.

March 31: Rodgers and Hammerstein's *Oklahoma!* debuts on Broadway.

June 20: Due to an influx of African American workers, a race riot explodes in Detroit.

December 4: The Great Depression ends with wartime production and mobilization, and the Works Progress Administration closes because employment has risen.

1944   Congress passes GI Bill of Rights, providing benefits for armed-service veterans.

The United Negro College Fund develops to aid African American students planning to attend college.

January 5: The *Daily Mail* becomes the first transoceanic newspaper.

August 9: Smokey the Bear is used for the first time in posters by the United States Forest Service and the Wartime Advertising Council.

October 8: *The Adventures of Ozzie and Harriet* radio show debuts.

November 7: President Franklin D. Roosevelt wins a fourth term as president over Republican challenger Thomas E. Dewey.

December 26: The Tennessee Williams play, *The Glass Menagerie,* is first performed.

1945   Thirteen television channels are created by the Federal Communications Commission (FCC) for commercial broadcasting; the agency receives 130 applications.

Grand Rapids, Michigan, becomes the first town to fluoridate its water.

April 12: President Franklin D. Roosevelt dies in Warm Springs, Georgia; Vice President Harry S Truman assumes the presidency.

July 28: The Empire State Building is accidentally struck by a B-52 bomber; 13 people are killed.

August 6: The atomic bomb "Little Boy" is dropped on Hiroshima, Japan, at 8:16 A.M.

August 9: The atomic bomb "Fat Man" is dropped on Nagasaki, Japan, at 11:02 A.M.

October 29: The first ballpoint pen goes on sale for $12.50 at Gimbel's Department Store.

December 4: The United State Senate votes 65 to 7 for the United States to join the United Nations.

1946   The New York City Ballet is founded by George Balanchine and Lincoln Kirstein.

The University of Pennsylvania becomes home to the first automatic electronic digital computer (ENIAC).

April 1: Hilo, Hawaii, is hit by a 14-meter-high *tsunami*.

July 7: The Roman Catholic Church canonizes Mother Francis Xavier Cabrini as the first American saint.

November 12: The first drive-up bank teller windows are opened at the Exchange National Bank in Chicago, Illinois.

December 11: United Nations Children's Fund (UNICEF) is founded.

1947   The Central Intelligence Agency (CIA) is formed.

Tennessee Williams's *A Streetcar Named Desire* debuts on Broadway with Marlon Brando as Stanley Kowalski and Jessica Tandy as Blanche DuBois.

Meet the Press airs for the first time on NBC.

Percy Spencer invents the microwave oven.

June 23: Congress overrides President Truman's veto and passes the Taft-Hartley Act restricting the power of labor unions.

September 18: The U.S. Air Force is formed, combining components of the U.S. Army Air Forces and the U.S. Navy's air arm.

1948   George A. Gamow introduces the "Big Bang" theory to explain the creation of the universe.

Fresh Kills, the world's largest landfill, opens in Staten Island, New York.

January 5: The first color newsreel is shown by Warner Brothers at the Rose Bowl.

March 8: The U.S. Supreme Court rules that religious instruction in public schools violates the Constitution.

March 17: The biker gang Hell's Angels organizes in California.

April 2: Congress passes the Marshall Plan to aid European postwar recovery.

July 26: President Harry Truman signs Executive Order 9981, ending racial segregation in the U.S. armed forces.

November 2: President Truman wins a full term of office against Republican challenger Thomas E. Dewey.

1949   Color TV is introduced to mainstream American society.

The first telethon is aired for cancer research and is hosted by Milton Berle.

The song "Rudolph, the Red-Nosed Reindeer" is released to the public.

January 17: The first Volkswagen is sold in the United States.

January 25: The Emmy Awards for television debut.

March 2: The first nonstop flight around the world is achieved by Captain James Gallagher in a B-50 Superfortress called *Lucky Lady II*.

April 4: The North Atlantic Treaty (NATO) is signed in Washington, D.C.

June 8: George Orwell's book *1984* is released.

1950   *Peanuts* comic strip by Charles Schulz is first released.

Otis Elevators in Dallas, Texas, is the first to install a self-service elevator.

September 3: Publication of the *Beetle Bailey* comic strip by Mort Walker begins.

October 2: Saturday morning children's television programming begins.

November 1: President Truman is the target of an assassination attempt by Puerto Rican nationalists.

November 22: Former child star Shirley Temple retires from show business.

1951   The first coast-to-coast live television broadcast occurs with President Harry Truman giving a speech.

J. D. Salinger releases *The Catcher in the Rye*.

March 12: The comic strip *Dennis the Menace* first appears.

April 5: Julius and Ethel Rosenberg are sentenced to death for treason (they are executed June 19, 1953).

July 14: The George Washington Carver Memorial in Joplin, Missouri, becomes the first U.S. national monument to honor an African American.

September 4: The term "Rock 'n' Roll" is used by radio disc jockey Alan Freed to promote rhythm and blues music to white audiences.

October 3: The so-called "Shot Heard 'Round the World," one of the greatest moments in Major League baseball history, occurs when Bobby Thomson of the New York Giants hits a game-winning home run in the bottom of the ninth inning off Brooklyn Dodgers pitcher Ralph Branca to win the National League pennant after the Giants had been down by 14 games.

October 15: *I Love Lucy* debuts on CBS.

1952   *The Jackie Gleason Show*, which includes "The Honeymooners," debuts on CBS.

56 million watch Richard Nixon's "Checker's speech" on TV.

3,300 die of polio in the United States; 57,000 children are paralyzed.

January 14: The *Today Show* hosted by Dave Garroway premiers on NBC.

May 3: U.S. Lieutenant Colonels Joseph O. Fletcher and William P. Benedict land a plane at the North Pole.

July 25: Puerto Rico becomes a U.S. commonwealth.

December 14: The first successful surgical separation of Siamese twins takes place in Mount Sinai Hospital, Cleveland, Ohio.

1953   Dr. John H. Gibbon performs the first successful open heart surgery in which the blood is artificially circulated and oxygenated by a heart-lung machine.

Alleged communist Charlie Chaplin flees the United States.

January 22: *The Crucible* by Arthur Miller is performed for the first time on Broadway.

April 3: The first issue of *TV Guide* magazine hits the newsstands in 10 cities with a circulation of 1,560,000 copies.

June 30: The Chevrolet Corvette is first produced in Flint, Michigan.

December: *Playboy* magazine is first published with a nude Marilyn Monroe on the cover.

1954   The baseball World Series is broadcast in color for the first time.

The first TV dinner is invented by Gerry Thomas.

William Golding writes the novel *Lord of the Flies*.

J.R.R. Tolkien releases the first book in the *Lord of the Rings* trilogy, *The Fellowship of the Ring*.

January 14: Actress Marilyn Monroe weds baseball player Joe DiMaggio.

January 21: First Lady Mamie Eisenhower christens the first nuclear-powered submarine, the *USS Nautilus*.

February 18: The first Church of Scientology is established in Los Angeles, California.

February 23: Polio vaccine administered for the first time in the United States in Pittsburgh by Dr. Jonas Salk.

April 22–June 17: Senator Joseph McCarthy of Wisconsin begins the "Red Scare."

May 17: In *Brown v. Board of Education of Topeka,* the Supreme Court unanimously bans racial segregation in public schools.

June 14: On United States Flag Day, the words "under God" are added to the Pledge of Allegiance.

August 16: Volume 1, Issue 1 of *Sports Illustrated* is published.

September 11: The Miss America Pageant is broadcast on television for the first time.

1955   *Gunsmoke* debuts on CBS and will go on to be television's longest-running western.

January 7: Marian Anderson becomes the first African American singer to perform at the Metropolitan Opera in New York City.

April 18: Albert Einstein dies from an aortic aneurysm at 1:15 A.M.

July 18: Disneyland opens to the public with admission costing just $1. The cost of attractions ranges from 10 to 35 cents.

September 30: James Dean dies in a car accident at age 26 near Cholame, California.

December 1: Rosa Parks refuses to give up her seat on a segregated bus in Montgomery, Alabama.

1956   *The Wizard of Oz* is first aired on TV.

February 22: Elvis Presley enters the U.S. music charts for the first time with *Heartbreak Hotel*.

March 1: Autherine Lucy, the first black student at the University of Alabama, is suspended after riots protesting her presence there.

June 29: President Dwight D. Eisenhower signs the Federal-Aid Highway Act, creating the interstate highway system.

July 30: A Joint Resolution of the U.S. Congress is signed by President Dwight D. Eisenhower, authorizing "In God We Trust" as the U.S. national motto.

1957   Leonard Bernstein's *West Side Story* debuts on Broadway.

August 5: *American Bandstand* is televised nationally for the first time.

September 4: Orville Faubus, governor of Arkansas, calls out the U.S. National Guard to prevent black students from enrolling in Central High School in Little Rock.

September 4: The Ford Motor Company introduces the Edsel on what the company proclaims as "E Day."

October 4: *Leave It to Beaver* premieres on CBS, ushering in an era of television shows that depict the ideal American family.

December 6: First U.S. attempt to launch a satellite fails when the rocket blows up on the launch pad.

1958   *Billboard* debuts its Hot 100 chart; Ricky Nelson's *Poor Little Fool* is the first No. 1 record.

Truman Capote's *Breakfast at Tiffany's* debuts.

January 8: Bobby Fischer wins the United States Chess Championship at the age of 14.

July 29: U.S. Congress officially creates the National Aeronautics and Space Administration (NASA).

September 29: The U.S. Supreme Court rules unanimously that Little Rock, Arkansas, schools must desegregate.

1959   National Academy of Recording Arts and Sciences presents the first Grammy Awards for music recorded the previous year.

Frank Sinatra wins his first Grammy Award—Best Album for *Come Dance with Me*.

Pantyhose are invented.

Boris Pasternak releases his critically acclaimed *Doctor Zhivago*.

January 3: Alaska becomes the 49th state.

February 22: Lee Petty wins the first Daytona 500.

March 9: The Barbie doll is introduced.

April 25: St. Lawrence Seaway opens, allowing ocean ships to reach the Midwest.

August 21: Hawaii becomes the 50th state.

October 2: Rod Serling's classic anthology series, *The Twilight Zone*, premieres on CBS.

October 21: In New York City, the Solomon R. Guggenheim Museum opens to the public; it was designed by Frank Lloyd Wright.

Overview

An overview of American daily life between 1940 and 1959 should focus on how the nation and its people responded to the unprecedented power and responsibility the United States came to embody during that period of time. Both domestically, and in international affairs, the nation became a great world power in fewer than 20 years. The economic and material growth of America, during and following World War II, made the nation the most potent, wealthiest society in the history of the planet. It made available to Americans, in their daily lives, more goods, services, and products than at any previous period in history. How the people responded to those opportunities and challenges remained an essential aspect of the times. Did access and power bring comfort and satisfaction? Did people realize the promised "pursuit of happiness"? Did Americans recognize that critical changes had occurred in their daily lives? Did success and material satisfaction for the majority cause them to overlook or disregard those who remained unable to achieve those ends? Those, and other questions, serve as the focus for this section.

The Japanese attack at Pearl Harbor on December 7, 1941, ended a decade of debate on the role of the United States in world affairs. The battle between isolationists and interventionists that had occupied national affairs in the 1930s, as the world went to war, ended. The "date which will live in infamy" committed the nation to a global war against Germany, Japan, and Italy. America's economy expanded dramatically to confront the massive material demands that the war created. Millions of Americans entered the armed services. Millions more went to work in factories, shipyards, and businesses. Agricultural demands for food grew, and large farming systems evolved to respond to the need for food. If the 1930s offered a worrisome story of unemployment, economic depression, and social anxiety, the war years witnessed an end to the economic concerns that had frustrated America during the Great Depression.

The nation provided more industrial and agricultural goods and products during World War II than all of the other nations involved in the global conflict. In a real sense, the "arsenal of democracy" played a vital role in ultimate victory. When apprised of America's ship-building capacity in 1943, the German dictator Adolf Hitler remarked to an aide, "We have lost the war!"

The economic revival during World War II set the stage for a postwar commercial boom, even though some observers feared it might not. American industry was able to shift its new technologies, capital, and employees from wartime production to peacetime consumer goods. For reasons examined in the chapter, Americans had money, jobs, and demands for new goods and products, and the prosperity that the wartime economy created continued into the postwar decades. With few commercial rivals in the international community, because of the devastation that the war caused in Europe and Asia, the United States experienced a unique period of almost total economic domination and expansion. In every aspect of American daily life, that basic but profound factor remained a critical consideration. The national expectation of limitless employment, expansion, and opportunity that evolved between 1945 and 1959 was a direct result of the postwar situation that the United States experienced. The unusual ability to control natural resources, methods of production, and distribution of goods and services gave the American people a unique position to take material advantage of their situation.

At the same time, however, that special prosperity would lead the nation to draw stark attention to those Americans who had not benefited directly from the advantages the postwar era seemed to provide for a majority of the people. An "other America" (Harrington 1962) existed even in an age of unparalleled prosperity. How was that possible? What had the country and its people missed or disregarded? In the most prosperous, powerful nation on earth, some Americans still went to bed hungry, children remained uneducated, poverty persisted amid plenty, and traditional forms of racism, sexism, and oppression continued. Critics and social observers drew attention to those conditions and tended to focus on the key point that a nation so prosperous and "blessed" had a special responsibility to address the unresolved problems they identified. The "greatest generation" (Brokaw 1998) that had confronted the Depression and the world war still had major and critical issues to address. While the period 1945 through 1959 often seemed a time of disregard for issues more obviously addressed in the 1960s, the seeds of that social conscience evolved in the immediate postwar era.

In international affairs, the single most dominant issue of postwar America hinged on the development of a Cold War confrontation with the Soviet Union. The two powerful allies during World War II had fundamental ideological and geopolitical differences. Those issues had surfaced during World War II, but they intensified in 1945. The new postwar "balance of power" had created a bipolar environment with two "superpowers" at odds and armed with an increasing array of destructive nuclear weapons. The Cold War directly affected the daily lives of Americans. From a peacetime military draft that saw millions of Americans serving in the armed forces, to a military-industrial complex that developed to influence the economy, to a propaganda war that saw overzealous politicians ("red hunters") like Senator Joseph McCarthy stifle political debate in the country, Americans had to confront a new threat, even as they experienced unheralded prosperity in their personal lives. A bipartisan political consensus among Republicans and Democrats accepted the need for a powerful American response to perceived Soviet threats—a strategy broadly defined as "containment." The Marshall Plan, an extraordinary defense budget, and a growing U.S. commitment to a global containment of the Soviet Union saw few critics between 1945 and 1959. If Americans disagreed concerning the issue, they did so more on specifics than on substance. Whether accurate or not, most Americans saw the postwar confrontation as a struggle between democracy and totalitarianism, capitalism and communism, and freedom and tyranny.

In simple terms, they had not defeated the Depression and fascism to succumb to the "new" threat to their American way of life. That thinking and conclusion would dominate the national mood well into the 1960s and beyond. In modern American popular culture, the singular view of the period portrays American daily life as conservative, limited in perspective, and inherently dull or predictable. The popular television series *Happy Days*, now widely syndicated, presented a bucolic view of American teenagers and their families enjoying good times and almost mindless conformity. Some of that portrait is accurate. Yet, seismic social and cultural changes had begun to take shape during the postwar era, and those issues also remain a major aspect of American life. It is the purpose of this chapter to examine both aspects of the period 1940 to 1959.

Domestic Life

THE WAR YEARS, 1940–1945

World War II had a significant impact on domestic life in America. Children went to school as they always had, but their lives were changed by the war. Millions of men served in the military, many sent "overseas" to fight in North Africa, Europe, or the Pacific theater. Millions of women worked in factories to build the arsenal necessary for the war, and the stereotype of "Rosie the Riveter" (a popular song) came to personify those women. Military service separated parents. Families moved more often to find work in the factories. Transient domestic life became more commonplace in America during the war. The anxieties and uncertainties of war affected families throughout the conflict. Wartime rationing of essential foods and services (gasoline, butter, meat, etc.) also placed a daily strain on families as they went about their lives. Yet, men and women married in greater numbers than ever before. The concern about jobs and income during the Depression had seen a decline in marriages in America during the 1930s. That was not the case during the war.

As jobs expanded and wages rose in the 1940s, economic fears about establishing families seemed to disappear. Men and women also may have married because of the war itself and the personal and emotional separation that the war caused. Whatever the reasons, the U.S. Census Bureau estimated that at least a million more marriages took place between 1940 and 1943 than expected. Marriage rates continued to rise until 1946, and the median age of married couples dropped to less than 21 years of age, an unprecedented low number. With the rise in marriages, incidences of divorce also grew. Some married-in-haste relationships ended with "Dear John" letters to servicemen. Those breakups occurred so often that the government passed legislation protecting service personnel from quick divorces.

POSTWAR AMERICA, 1946–1959

In 1946, the film *The Best Years of Our Lives* won seven Academy Awards, including best picture. An adaptation of MacKinley Kantor's book, the film told a poignant story of three World War II veterans returning to domestic life. It not only focused on their readjustment, but also examined the response of their families, wives, children, and neighbors to the touchy issues that confronted American domestic life at the end of World War II. The transition was not as simple as textbooks often suggest, yet Americans appeared to respond to the opportunities as well as the problems with remarkable resilience. Critics and observers often portray the years from 1946 to 1959 as conservative, orthodox, and dull, a kind of mindless "happy days" reflected in the television sitcom of the 1980s. Other critical writers discuss the *Organization Man* (White 1956) or the *Lonely Crowd* as prototypes of a postwar American society that put men in *Grey Flannel Suits*, working in huge corporate businesses, nine to five, and going home to "little pink houses" in the new suburbs. Children become spoiled youngsters growing into unmanageable teenagers. Their world focused on 45 rpm records, drive-in movies, and rebelliousness. Women, dismissed from their wartime factory jobs, were forced to revert to lives as "Betty Crocker" homemakers, bearing children, baking cookies, and waiting for their husbands to return from a variety of "white-collar" jobs. While those images have some merit, the years from 1946 to 1959 also saw enormous innovation and positive changes in domestic life in America.

In 1944, the United States Congress passed the Serviceman's Readjustment Act—the GI Bill. It provided for a series of grants, loans, and other benefits for veterans returning from military service. In education, the GI Bill awarded monthly stipends for tuition, books, and room and board for veterans who entered colleges or vocational schools. Approximately 10 million veterans took advantage of the opportunity at a cost of $10 billion. The result created a new college-educated, white-collar management population that had access to more lucrative employment and hopefully a better domestic standard of living. At the same time, the GI Bill, operated through the Veterans Administration (VA), provided insured loans for veterans buying homes or investing in their own businesses. The government ultimately spent more than $50 billion in the home loan program. The growth of suburban living following the war came as a result of a boom in single-home construction that the GI Bill helped finance. In 1947, Levittown, using prefabricated construction techniques that lowered housing costs, opened in Hempstead, Long Island, and the move to the suburbs accelerated. By 1950, almost 36 percent of Americans lived in suburban communities. And between 1945 and 1955, families moved into 15 million new homes.

The move to the suburbs and the job opportunities that the GI Bill created altered the domestic outlook and options available to many American families. While most Americans still lived in rural, small-town environments or in large urban centers, a suburban mentality seemed to influence domestic thinking in the country as the 1950s evolved. The idea of a neighborhood changed. In the big cities, it meant one thing. In rural America, that domestic sense of community had another quality. Suburbia focused on single homes constructed in patterned communities, where children went to school and played, families communicated with each other, and men or women worked and adapted to the new patterns of postwar life in a novel suburban setting.

The explosive increase in automobile sales following the war reflected that change in domestic life. In 1945, new car sales reached close to 70,000. A year later, that number climbed to more than two million, and by 1949, car sales had climbed to more than five million. By the middle of the 1950s, the number reached almost eight million sales (Kaledin 2000, 55). Responding to the increasing number of automobiles and the lack of transportation infrastructure to link suburbs, cities, and small towns, Congress passed the Federal Highway Act in 1956. Originally budgeted at $32 billion, by 1972 the United States had constructed more than 41,000 miles of interstate highways at a cost of $76 billion. The combined impact of the GI Bill, other government supports, postwar prosperity, the rise of suburbia, and the institutional systems that developed to support those changes became the linchpins of a domestic environment that changed America's lifestyles.

FAMILY LIFE

Most Americans accepted traditional family values and responsibilities in the period following World War II. Heterosexual marriages, the birth of children, and kinship ties within that social context remained the norm. Whether in suburbs, cities, or small towns, the basic formula remained the same. Men (fathers) went to jobs outside the home, women (mothers) bore and raised children (see the following discussion of birth rates in the section on Children), and youngsters grew up under reasonably strict parental guidelines. While the number of extended families (grand-parents, relatives, etc.) living together declined during the period, American daily life still witnessed a social and cultural commitment to the basic formula of family life that had existed for years. The popular artist Norman Rockwell portrayed that idealized lifestyle in many of his works, and the 1998 movie *Pleasantville* poked fun, and some serious reservations, at the conservative quality of family life in the 1950s. Yet, stereotypes and idealized views often represent a basic truth. Teenagers may have gone to malt shops and hamburger joints after school, but most families ate together, at home. Families gathered for religious and national holidays to share meals, attend local events such as Fourth of July fireworks, and enjoy local outings. The major institutions in American society—religious, political, and economic—supported and encouraged those qualities of family life as righteous and acceptable, even while new ideas and challenges to traditional daily life began to develop.

> **📷 *Snapshot***
>
> **Cost of Living: 1950**
>
> New house, $8,450; Average income, $3,216 a year; New car, $1,511; Gasoline, 18 cents a gallon; Postage stamp, 3 cents; Sugar, 85 cents for 10 pounds; Milk, 84 cents per gallon; Eggs, 24 cents a dozen; Hamburger, 4 cents a pound; Bread, 14 cents a loaf.
>
> *Source: Remember When* (Millerville, TN: Seek Publishing).

In terms of family members and family behavior, no greater revolution took place during the 1950s than the shift in attitudes toward sex. By the end of the decade, all institutional control over individual sexual behavior seemed to melt away. Beginning with the two gigantic Kinsey reports, *Sexual Behavior in the Human Male* in 1948 and *Sexual Behavior in the Human Female* in 1953, and ending with the government's approval of the birth control pill in 1960, the nation's mores were turned upside down within two decades. It was still not possible, however, to get a legal abortion during the 1950s, when Massachusetts and Connecticut even made prescriptions mandatory for birth control devices.

Alfred Kinsey, a distinguished entomologist from the University of Indiana, identified his sudden interest in sexuality with his discovery of playwright Tennessee Williams's fascination with façades. Kinsey had come to appreciate the contrasts Williams presented between "social front and reality." His research into sex patterns, funded by the Rockefeller Foundation, and his books, marketed by Saunders, a respected publisher of medical texts, became the subject of national debate and contention. Kinsey represented himself as a crew-cut, bow-tied, middle-American "square." He saw himself as a serious, if somewhat quirky, professor who remained stunned when his scientific sexual surveys became best-sellers.

What Kinsey revealed, as David Halberstam neatly summarized in his 1993 survey of the 1950s, was that "there was more extramarital sex on the part of both men and women than Americans wanted to admit" and that "premarital sex tended to produce better marriages." Kinsey documented that masturbation also was a normal part of sexual development. Perhaps his most controversial discovery was that more homosexuality existed in the United States than Americans wanted to acknowledge. Scholars continued to question the sources of his homosexual statistics, because he interviewed prison populations, but the immediate effect of his findings was one of shock and then curiosity.

People were outraged at Kinsey's refusal to make moral judgments. His materials were delivered as pure statistics without emotional or moral contexts. Yet, few scientists were willing to come forward to support his work. Although Kinsey poured his book royalties back into the Institute for Sex Research of Indiana University, his funding grew insufficient when the Rockefeller Foundation withdrew support after the book on female sexuality received hostile reviews. Following the spirit of the times, the Rockefellers shifted their money to Union Theological Seminary. On the defensive from then on, Kinsey's health deteriorated. In 1956, at the relatively young age of 62, he died.

Even if the age of the "feminine mystique" (to use author Betty Friedan's term) was not any more eager to sanction women's sexuality than their need for serious education, all such social debate was liberating for women. Institutions began to change. By the end of the decade *Playboy* magazine, publisher Hugh Hefner's "respectable" monthly magazine with nude, female centerfolds, had become a popular addition to the new sexual debate, and the mail censorship of classics like Henry Miller's *Tropic of Cancer* and *Tropic of Capricorn* and D. H. Lawrence's *Lady Chatterley's Lover*, which contained sexually explicit material, would be a memory. Admitted to the United States after protests, Vladimir Nabokov's distinguished novel *Lolita*, about an adolescent and her older lover, published in 1958, sold more than 3 million copies. The big-time best-seller of the 1950s, Grace Metalious's *Peyton Place*, about secret lives and sexual desires in a quaint New Hampshire town—far from Thornton Wilder's Grover's Corners—sold 6 million copies in 1958. It would go on to become the best-selling American novel ever, surpassing 10 million copies.

Even Hollywood modified its restrictive sexual codes by the end of the decade in which *Baby Doll*, a 1956 Tennessee Williams story about a child bride, had been condemned by the Legion of Decency as an evil film. Compassion for alienated, vulnerable heroes like the young men James Dean and Sal Mineo played in *Rebel Without a Cause* was as real as the ongoing cult of the cowboy John Wayne. The Mattachine Society appeared in California in 1951 to promote better understanding of homosexuality as well as to prevent individual harassment. One of the most popular films of the decade, *Some Like It Hot* (1959), featured Jack Lemmon and Tony Curtis in drag (they dressed as women throughout the film to avoid gangsters). With the Food and Drug Administration's marketing approval of the birth control pill in 1960, Claire Boothe Luce declared modern woman had become as "free as a man is free to dispose of her own body."

Until the mid-1960s, the early marriage boom and the Baby Boom continued to define preferences in American life. As long as women were willing to subordinate their ambitions to their husbands', marriages remained stable. But the family did not fully absorb most women's energies for long. The proportion of married women in the workforce rose from 36 percent in 1940 to 52 percent in 1950. At the same time, the divorce rate went back to its steady rise. By the mid-1960s the American family—always more complex than portrayed by media myths like *Leave It to Beaver* or *Ozzie and Harriet*—found different representations in movies. In *East of Eden* (1955), James Dean's role as a misunderstood son became the actor's best performance, and *All That Heaven Allows* (1956) described an older woman who shocked people by loving her gardener. American women, who were now living longer, imagined richer lives outside their families. A useful book on changing images of women in the movies during the 1950s, *On the Verge of Revolt*, suggested that even in the world of media myths a new awareness was taking shape. The seed of rebellion described in Molly Haskell's critical classic *From Reverence to Rape: The Treatment of Women in the Movies* (1973) germinated in the kitchen (Kaledin 2000, 109–11; *Daily Life Online*, "Domestic Life: Family Life," in Kaledin, *Daily Life in the United States, 1940–1959*, http://dailylife. greenwood.com).

CHILDREN

Caring for children proved a key issue during the war. The global conflict separated families, as fathers entered the military and mothers went to work in the factories. The War Manpower Commission estimated that two million children lacked appropriate child care. Federally funded day care programs assisted only about 10 percent of workers' children. Often, extended families saw grandparents and other relatives watching children while their parents were gone. In a real sense, however, the problem of the "latchkey" child developed during the war. It remains difficult to gauge the impact the war had on children. If most grew up in caring families, extended or otherwise, went to schools, played with friends, and helped their families with "victory gardens" or gathering scrap, they probably experienced a collective sense of community and shared commitment to the conflict. Others, those left alone, or who moved on a regular basis, or the victims of divorce, had a different exposure to growing up in wartime America.

Some issues and numbers arose as ominous concerns for American children. Between 1941 and 1944, high school enrollments declined by more than a million students. Juvenile delinquency cases throughout the nation increased. Concern regarding the welfare of teenage children, both male and female, grew to the point that local, state, and federal officials attempted to develop policies and programs to combat the problem of teenage delinquency. The evolution of youth agencies, sponsored recreation programs, and new welfare policies all aimed at confronting concerns regarding teenage children. By 1944, the U.S. Office of Education started a "Back-to-School" initiative, asking local school boards to get on board and requesting that employers hire older workers to force children back to school.

In 1946, 3.4 million babies were born, an all-time record—26 percent more than in 1945. Into the next decade babies poured onto the American scene in record numbers. Indeed, by 1964 two-fifths of America's population had been born since 1946 (a generation known as the Baby Boomers). Having developed a strong sense of their capabilities during the war, women transferred many of their skills to raising large families. It was no longer just religious opponents to birth control or the poor who had large families. The greatest jump in fertility occurred among well-educated white women with medium to high incomes. Just as the war created new jobs and prosperity, so did the Baby Boom. Diaper services, baby food, educational toys and playgrounds, and special furniture for children became big business. Dr. Benjamin Spock's book on common-sense child care became an all-time best seller. For a brief period—for a vast middle class—the sense of prosperity and family solidarity seemed real. Before the next decade ended, the divorce rate would continue to climb again—as it had done before the war—and the family would begin to lose power as a source of community stability in American life.

One source of instability in family life was the introduction of television and worries about its effect on children. Many parents tried to limit young children's programs to cartoons and educational shows. In the norms adults were trying to establish for their own lives, many struggled to provide sensible entertainment for the boom generation of children. Milton Berle even called himself "Uncle Miltie," because so many children enjoyed his slapstick show, *Texaco Star Theater*, that their parents asked for his help in putting them to bed.

In the beginning, gentle programs for preschoolers like *Kukla, Fran, and Ollie, Ding Dong School,* and *Captain Kangaroo* counteracted the vicarious violence of Saturday morning cartoons. Those programs often dealt sensitively with specific problems children experienced, emphasizing rational approaches to conflicts rather than fighting. And there were educational programs for older children about zoo animals and space travel. The amount of airtime given over to shows that would enhance the lives of America's children, however, remained meager. From the beginning television programming showed more interest in the buying power of little people than in their minds. By the end of the 1950s the extreme violence that characterized American television at the end of the century would be available to everyone who switched on a station for news or sitcoms at almost any hour. One waggish critic remarked that more people were killed on television in 1954 than in the entire Korean War. Whether excessive exposure to murder, rape, and bizarre horrors of all sorts could create generations of criminals became an ongoing debate. Statistics indicated that the jail population was increasing, and a few sociopaths credited television with ideas they used for particularly horrible crimes. Children could see almost anything when they turned on the set. The TV spectacle of so much blood and cruelty, many feared, might produce generations of youthful viewers who would grow up completely callous to human suffering. In one of her best reviews on how television seemed to be depriving the young of their childhood, Marya Mannes introduced a Danish scholar who challenged America: "If fifty million children see terrible things like this every day," he said, "do you not think they will feel less about shooting and murder and rape? They will be so used to violence that it does not seem like violence anymore."

Mannes characterized the westerns that flourished for a short time as plays that "concerned good men and bad men who rode horses over magnificent country and decided issues by shooting each other." In clarifying how little educational value there was in such programs, she noted that they "were all very much alike in that they bore no resemblance to what used to be the pioneer west of the United States except in the matter of clothes and horses." What these westerns did most successfully, she perceived, was "to sell a great amount of goods." As children became the most promising group of consumers for televised products, Hopalong Cassidy items boomed. The grandfatherly cowboy became a children's idol, inspiring a line of toys that grossed $100 million in 1950. Howdy Doody, a freckled clown, also inspired quantities of consumer toys at the time. The television portrayal of Davy Crockett seemed capable of putting coonskin caps on every small head in America before overproduction led to warehouse surpluses. Such toys often provided a source of community for children of different backgrounds. Just as adults found a source of identity in discussing their cars or their hi-fi music equipment with each other, children came together with their collections of televised loot designed for young people.

Davy Crockett, a one-hour prime-time western series sponsored by Walt Disney, garnered the highest ratings of the decade. Not only did the show make children eager for coonskin caps, but it also inspired some parents to turn to the simplicity of the old West for housing and furnishing styles. Log cabins and wagon wheels were easy to copy even in suburbia. By the end of the decade the ranch house would become the most popular style among the choices at Levittown. The West brought back echoes of a simpler life and easier living. Dungarees became the classic weekend wear for suburbanites.

The television show *Disneyland* appeared in the early 1950s, testing on air all the American themes that would be incorporated during the next decade into the sparkling California amusement park. At the time, few realized that Walt Disney's construction of that utopian vision would come to represent a worldwide dream of American possibility. In 1954, when *Disneyland* first appeared regularly on TV, it was a source of publicity for the Disneyland theme park Disney was building to represent his dreams. Some critics called the show an hour-long commercial. Fantasyland, Frontierland, Adventureland, and Tomorrowland, with all the star-studded glitz that attended the grand opening of the park, quickly became as real to the American imagination as America itself—perhaps more real. Child viewers eager to participate in the televised adventures Disney conjured up might indeed learn something from the details of the displays, but many reviewers criticized the brash commercialism. One described the theme park as "a giant cash register, clicking and clanging as creatures of Disney magic came tumbling down." Television previews had prepared visitors to Disneyland for necessary compromises, but it was the tension between perfection and reality, Karal Ann Marling suggests, "between the real and the more or less real," that really delighted so many visitors.

On New Year's Eve in 1957, attendance at Disneyland reached 10 million. The kind of entertainment the theme park offered fit perfectly with the togetherness of the car-centered suburban family. For the price of admission, Walt Disney's TV dream worlds conducted everyone from an imperfect present into an idealized past or a thrilling future. And Main Street, USA, like an exhibit at a world's fair, suggested that utopia was already possible in middle-class America. Some children may have been inspired to pursue a study of Disney's themes even if many more were seduced into buying Mickey Mouse Club paraphernalia and other trademarked toys and T-shirts. Eager children often found both pleasure and instruction in Disney's optimistic distortions. In a world of chaotic diversity, Marling points out, "Disney motifs constituted a common culture, a kind of civil religion of happy endings, worry-free consumption, technological optimism and nostalgia for the good old days." Such dreams could define survival.

If parents monitored the hours small children sat before their television sets, they need not have been concerned. And adults did not have to worry about the disc jockeys shaping teenage taste at the time; Dick Clark's decency, as he hosted *American Bandstand* from Philadelphia, charmed everyone. Jukeboxes in popular hangouts still offered songs with inoffensive lyrics in the decade that was still by all contemporary standards quite innocent (Kaledin 2000, 21–22, 69–70, 143–44). Some observers have challenged the idea that children were so easily influenced by the violence and consumer seduction of television, suggesting that they understood the difference between cartoon violence and the real thing. Studies at the Annenberg School of Communication at the University of Pennsylvania continue to debate the issue (*Daily Life Online*, "Domestic Life: Children," in Kaledin, *Daily Life in the United States, 1940–1959*, http://dailylife.greenwood.com).

WOMEN

Although race had emerged from World War II as a clear category, gender was not used in the 1950s to help women define their rights. But the experiences of American women from the end of World War II through the 1960s also reflected an underlying social upheaval. The high marriage and birth rates and the low divorce rate intertwined naturally with the "feminine mystique"—the idea that woman's fulfillment was in the home and nowhere else. Yet, women were already questioning domesticity as a consuming and permanent role. Like many African Americans of both sexes, they needed to make invisible selves visible and valued. They came slowly to realize that sex discrimination could be subtle as well as overt—even as they played the roles of wife and mother that society demanded. Most women were content for a time to make the most of these old-fashioned roles. Yet, although many middle-class 1950s white women are identified in women's magazines with suburban homes and large families, the truth is that many others kept working after the war—not just to help pay the mortgage, but because work outside the home was satisfying. In 1955 that stalwart feminist Eleanor Roosevelt published an article titled "What Are the Motives for a Woman Working When She Does Not Have to for Income?" Self-esteem was Roosevelt's conclusion. She made readers recognize women's right to fulfill all their potential.

In *Personal Politics: The Roots of Women's Liberation in the Civil Rights Movement and the New Left*, a documentary book on radicalism, Sara Evans asserts that throughout the 1950s, "[W]omen from middle income families entered the labor force faster than any other group in the population." By 1956, 70 percent of all families in the $7,000 to $15,000 annual income range had two wage earners. Although women usually took the duller jobs that were offered them and suppressed the higher aspirations provided by better educations, they often saw such jobs as temporary. Instead of regarding themselves as victims—as later feminists often saw them—they just put their professional and working lives on hold while their children were very young. By no means did they accept domesticity, as their mothers might have, as their only choice—any more than they believed the television commercials that made "ring around the collar" the reason for their husbands' failures. American women have never been as gullible as Madison Avenue advertising writers—or as historians—see them. Tupperware may have made life in the kitchen easier for some women, but it also made jobs for the many women who sold the plastic containers.

Nor were women obsessed with the appliances that future president Ronald Reagan and the current Miss America displayed on television. Large refrigerators with freezers allowed people to shop less often. And middle-class women with families made good use of washing machines without wringers and dryers that did away with clotheslines. Some still liked the smell of clothes dried in the wind, and others enjoyed baking as a kind of escape therapy. Prepared foods like soup mixes and cake mixes—and even instant coffee—entered the kitchen slowly. When labor-saving devices like dishwashers appeared, homemakers of childbearing age often took advantage of freed time to explore new opportunities to do volunteer work.

In the 1950s, to be sure, women were denied access, as blacks were, to equal professional education and equal salaries. They were not readily welcomed back into competition with men. In 1963, Betty Friedan, a Smith College *summa cum laude* graduate, published *The Feminine Mystique,* which, based on questionnaires sent to Smith College graduates in 1957, explored the glorification of homemaking. Though the book sold three million copies and made her famous, Friedan was labeled "too old" at age 42 to master statistics for a Ph.D. at Columbia. Most medical schools at the time had quotas to admit fewer than 5 percent women. And a number of prestigious law schools, and some graduate schools, often denied all women admission, asserting that they would be taking places away from more serious men. Too many women grew depressed at being locked out of professions and high-paying jobs. Psychotherapy flourished. But other women found ways to escape confinement. As Friedan discovered, even as she decried the feminine mystique, American women often became ingenious at creating lives that enabled them to be useful citizens outside the home. In the 1950s, however, most women seemed to put family needs first.

A belief in Cold War victimization that shed light on some women's lives at this time by no means captured the energies of vast numbers who defined themselves beyond the narrow confines of one decade. Historians need to adapt interpretive time frames to women's gender roles to value women's achievements more precisely as opposed to those of men. The magazine articles usually cited to describe women's lives during the 1950s suggest little about their vision of society in any depth or about their future goals for themselves. And such articles do little to assert the significance of the many important older women on the scene. The same magazines that celebrated domesticity offered lively journalism by Martha Gellhorn, Dorothy Thompson, Marguerite Higgins, and others. Betty Friedan suggested at one point that mothers be given the GI Bill to compensate for child-rearing years, as men were rewarded for a different kind of social service. Of those women who had been in the armed forces, fewer than 3 percent were able to take advantage of the GI Bill.

Some studies suggest that a good number of women did not envy the lives of middle-income "organization men," advertising executives in gray flannel suits, or even well-paid factory workers creating appliances for the new world of consumers. At a time when there was no organized child care, few suburban families had relatives nearby to help with babysitting, and the jobs offered to women—still advertised in separate sections of the newspapers—were dull and ill-paid, many women willingly stayed home with their children if they could afford to do so. At the time it was still possible for many families to live on just one income. People seemed to have fewer needs or inclinations to possess more.

Even if they did not see themselves fighting the Cold War in the kitchen, many middle-class college graduates seemed to take Adlai Stevenson seriously when he urged the young women at Smith College's 1955 graduation to value the role of nurturing the "uniqueness of each individual human being." Yet, new patterns of domesticity were emerging that were more deeply connected with the human rights of the nurturers. When Dr. Benjamin Spock rewrote his bestseller *Baby and Child Care* (originally published in 1945) for the third time, it was to eliminate sexist biases that perpetuated discrimination against girls and women. Spock acknowledged that his use of the male pronoun and his early childhood gender differentiation might well begin "the discriminatory sex stereotyping that ends in women so often getting the humdrum, subordinate, poorly paid jobs in most industries and professions; and being treated as the second-class sex."

In 1957, when Betty Friedan read the responses to questionnaires sent to her college classmates as the basis of her research on what was happening to women, she discovered a deep restlessness among the respondents. But she also found an attitude different from that of women of earlier decades who saw having children as limiting access to other roles. The "either/or" dilemma—children or career—that had characterized women's lot before the war was changing. Although Friedan herself acknowledged never having known a woman who had both a good job and children, the 1950s brought about a decided change. All the women she interviewed were planning ahead for freedom to be themselves. Postwar actuarial statistics revealed that women lived longer than men and would often have as many as 40 years ahead of them to lead creative lives after their children left the nest. Most women entering the workforce in the 1950s were older. The number of women over age 35 in the labor force had jumped from 8.5 million in 1947 to almost 13 million by 1956. As the median age of women workers rose to 41, the proportion of married women who worked outside the home also doubled between 1940 and 1960.

When she later became a founding member of the National Organization for Women (NOW), Betty Friedan spoke to the needs she had discovered in the lives of 1950s women. NOW's statement of purpose proclaimed, "Above all, we reject the assumption that women's problems are the unique responsibility of each individual woman rather than a basic social dilemma which society must solve."

Bringing about social change is rarely fast or easy. The self-consciousness of the 1950s became essential preparation for the decades of action ahead. Consensus and containment describe much of the postwar era, but history demands that more serious attention be given those—like Betty Friedan—who also worked hard to define and improve the moral quality of American life (Kaledin 2000, 99–106; *Daily Life Online,* "Domestic Life: Women," in Kaledin, *Daily Life in the United States, 1940– 1959,* http://dailylife.greenwood.com).

MEN

As women and children responded to the new opportunities and changes in post-war America, men experienced similar domestic concerns. Their images and realities had also undergone significant challenges. Millions of service veterans had to re-adjust to peacetime life following the war. And, as the film *The Best Years of Our Lives* suggested, that was not always an easy task. When the U.S. government instituted a peacetime draft in 1948 and extended that policy in 1951, it subjected a generation of American men, 18 years and older, to a two-year period of military service. Many of those young men found themselves stationed throughout the world, as the United States developed its global military response to the evolving Cold War. Certainly, the Korean War (1950–1953) dramatically impacted the domestic life of American men. Hundreds of thousands served in the Korean conflict, including veterans of World War II called back to active duty. Often, those men had just settled into new jobs and careers and were starting families and growing accustomed to the postwar prosperity of the new decade.

The Korean conflict came as a shock to the domestic environment, and the heavy casualties served as a rude and tragic reminder that the Cold War would have a serious influence on domestic life in the nation. More than 54,000 Americans died in the war, and more than 100,000 were wounded. Many of the veterans returning from Korea not only faced the same problems with marriage and family that their World War II counterparts had confronted, but the nature of the war itself added to their concerns. Never as easily understood or accepted as World War II, Americans appeared less willing to reward Korean veterans with the adulation and patriotic ardor of 1945. Most veterans who survived the conflict returned to their peacetime lives without fanfare. In American popular culture, Korea became known as the "Forgotten War."

As fathers, husbands, sons, and breadwinners, most American males accepted traditional standards of behavior and attitude. The society expected them to be strong, self-reliant, and responsible heads of their households. Dr. Benjamin Spock's popular book on child care called for a joint effort on the part of mothers and fathers to work as a team in every aspect of rearing their children, from changing diapers to attending Parent Teacher Association (PTA) meetings to monitoring their children's education. At the same time, however, fathers were expected to secure stable, successful jobs and provide an increasing income to support their home and family. The revolution in sexual attitudes and mores confronted American males head on. In 1956, William Whyte's *The Organization Man* sought to define the "new breed" of middle-class, suburban, white males working in the new corporate environment. As the following excerpt from the book's Introduction indicates, he hoped to identify the impact that that world had on their domestic life:

They are all, as they so often put it, in the same boat. Listen to them talk to each other over the front lawns Of their suburbia and you cannot help but be struck by How well they grasp the common denominators which Bind them. Whatever the differences in their organization Ties, it is a common problem of collective work that Dominates their attentions, and when the DuPont man Talks to the research chemist or the chemist to the army Man, it is these problems that are uppermost. The word Collective most of them can't bring themselves to use. except to describe foreign countries or organizations they don't work for—but they are keenly aware of how much deeply beholden they are to organization than were their elders. They are wry about it, to be sure; they talk of the "treadmill," the "rat race," or the inability to control one's direction. But they have no great sense of plight; between themselves and organization they believe they see an ultimate harmony and, more than most elders recognize, they are building an ideology that will vouch-safe this trust. (Whyte, Introduction)

If Whyte correctly identified the new work/domestic role of white men in the postwar society, he did so with concern, and his major themes focused not so much on the business or economic aspects of the stereotype, but rather the influence the thinking had on these men as domestic individuals. His interest hinged on the "new society" of the organization man. Where were their loyalties? How did their jobs conflict with their relationships with wives, children, and the family? He recognized that the character he studied did not reflect the lifestyle of all American males. To be sure, he did not study blue-collar workers, laborers, rural males, or minorities. He focused, however, on what many American observers saw as the "model" of the postwar era. Here, one sees the image of conservative men responding to the pressures and demands of a corporate world that influenced every aspect of their lives.

THE "OTHER AMERICA"

In 1962, Edward Michael Harrington published *The Other America*, a critical study of American life challenging the standard belief that the prosperous, middle-class suburbs of the nation remained the only template to view domestic life in the country. A broad majority of Americans had experienced significant economic and social opportunity since the end of the war, but a noteworthy minority, examined in Harrington's study, had not. His work focused on the millions of Americans, the poor, minorities, and others, who lacked access to the "American dream," so much heralded in the decade following World War II. To those families, single homes in the suburbs, new shopping malls, automobiles, corporate jobs, good public schools, and backyard barbecues remained unattainable. Their standard of living, he argued, had not grown with the rest of the nation. Racism, endemic poverty, and other failures in the richest domestic society in human history had cavalierly bypassed a significant portion of the American population.

Harrington's influence would not be felt until the 1960s when Presidents John F. Kennedy and Lyndon Johnson heralded his study. Yet, Harrington based his work on what he observed during the 1950s. As late as 1947, the government still identified 30 percent of the American people as poor. More than 30 percent had no running water,

40 percent lacked modern toilets, and 60 percent had no central heating (Kaledin 2000, 69). Those numbers certainly declined between 1947 and 1957, but by the end of the 1950s, Harrington and others would argue that 15 percent of the American people still lacked the basic options, services, and domestic needs that their suburban counterparts accepted as normal. That discrepancy, and those who drew attention to it, created one of the key social issues of the 1960s.

How should the nation respond to the obvious concerns of the "other Americans"? What responsibility did the booming free market economy have to attack the problem? What role might the government play in addressing the concerns? What was the root cause of the problem—racism, ignorance of the situation, disinterest, or what? Domestic life in America had expanded, changed, and altered so significantly between 1945 and 1959 that the society had barely stopped to examine the results of that domestic revolution. The new decade of the 1960s would call for that examination.

 *Snapshot*

Cost of Living: 1955

New home, $10,950; Average income, $4,137 a year; New car, $1,910; Gasoline, 23 cents a gallon; Postage stamp, 3 cents; Sugar, 85 cents for 10 pounds; Milk, 92 cents a gallon; Coffee, 80 cents a pound; Hamburger, 56 cents a pound; Eggs, 27 cents a dozen; Bread, 18 cents a loaf.

Source: Remember When (Millerville, TN: Seek Publishing).

FOR MORE INFORMATION

Chafe, W. H. *The Paradox of Change: American Women in the 20th Century*. New York: Oxford University Press, 1991.

Fehrenbach, T. R. *This Kind of War*. Washington, DC: Brassey's, 2000.

Friedan, Betty. *The Feminine Mystique*. New York: Norton, 1963.

Galbraith, John Kenneth. *The Affluent Society*. Boston: Little Brown, 1958.

Goodwin, Doris Kearns. *No Ordinary Time: Franklin and Eleanor Roosevelt: The Home Front in World War II*. New York: Touchstone, 1994.

Harrington, Michael. *The Other America: Poverty in the United States*. Baltimore, MD: Penguin, 1962.

Harrison, C. *On Account of Sex: The Politics of Women's Issues, 1945–1968*. Berkeley: University of California Press, 1988.

Hayes, C. D., J. L. Palmer, and M. J. Zaslow, eds. *Families That Work: Children in a Changing World*. Washington, DC: National Academy Press, 1982.

Kaledin, E. *Daily Life in the United States, 1940–1959: Shifting Worlds*. Westport, CT: Greenwood Press, 2000; also online as *Daily Life Online*, in Kaledin, *Daily Life in the United States, 1940–1959*, http://dailylife.greenwood.com.

May, E. T. *Homeward Bound: American Families in the Cold War Era*. New York: Basic Books, 1988.

Mills, C. Wright. *White Collar: The American Middle Classes*. New York: Oxford University Press, 1951.

Mintz, S., and S. Kellogg. *Domestic Revolutions: A Social History of American Family Life*. New York: Free Press, 1988.

Tuttle, W. M., Jr. *"Daddy's Gone to War": The Second World War in the Lives of America's Children*. New York: Oxford University Press, 1993.

Whyte, William. *The Organization Man*. New York: Doubleday, 1956.

Economic Life

THE WARTIME ECONOMY, 1940–1945

Even before the United States entered World War II in December 1941, the American economy had begun to surge out of the Depression. The Roosevelt administration's commitment to the "great arsenal of democracy" called for a slow but growing industrial and agricultural response. American military supplies came off assembly lines to support nations fighting against the Germans and Japanese, but production numbers remained low compared to what would occur after the Japanese attack at Pearl Harbor.

In 1938, defense appropriations amounted to less than 2 percent of the federal budget. Six months after Pearl Harbor, the government budgeted $100 billion for war materials. In 1942, the president announced a goal of 60,000 airplanes, 8 million tons of ships, and close to 50,000 armored vehicles. The federal government created the War Production Board, in January 1942, to coordinate the economic effort, but federal officials generally left production methods and employment practices in the hands of private business owners.

America's gross national product (GNP) rose from under $89 billion in 1938 to almost $200 billion by 1943, most of that increase a result of government defense contracts. New factories, new tools, equipment and supplies, and novel technology helped revitalize an American industrial system that the Depression had weakened. By 1943, 40 percent of the GNP was tied to military production. Big businesses and corporations benefited most from the government contracts, because they could produce the large amounts of material the government required. The hundred biggest businesses in America produced 30 percent of the contract requirements and gained 70 percent of the defense contracts. Estimates indicate that as many as half a million small businesses closed between 1941 and 1943 as they failed to compete with the larger corporations.

The wartime economy not only benefited the heavy industry of America, it impacted on other businesses as well. Cotton textile factories in the South produced millions of dollars worth of uniforms. A number of southern states saw the opening of large military training bases that provided construction jobs and other supporting work in and around the bases. Agriculture also expanded its production and markets. While the rural population of the nation declined by 20 percent during the war, as people moved to the cities and factories for higher-paying jobs, the demand for food increased. The effort to provide that necessity, however, appeared to have the same impact on small farms as the industrial demands had on small businesses. At the beginning of 1945, large "industrial" farming had doubled profits and production, but thousands of small farms had ceased to exist. Either their people had moved to more profitable work in the factories or the big agricultural combines had made it

An American World War II poster stating the need for women to work, 1943. Chaiba.

impossible for them to compete. Demographically, the nature of wartime production changed regional growth and development. As America prepared for a two-front war, the conflict in the Pacific made California a different place. The state received 10 percent of federal funding during the war. Los Angeles became the second largest production center in the nation, behind only Detroit (Faragher et al. 2000, 757–60).

The wartime economy virtually ended unemployment in America. Seventeen million new jobs developed. Women and minorities found access to work previously closed to them. African American workers in industry jumped from under three million to almost four million. Many black women who had been employed as domestics (housekeepers or cleaning women) left those low-paying jobs for better wages in the factories.

The *bracero* legislation invited 200,000 Mexicans to the United States to work in the vegetable fields and fruit orchards of the Southwest and California. The female workforce expanded by more than 50 percent. In 1945, more than 19 million women were at work, many in positions previously closed to them. Stereotypes, sexism, and racism remained prevalent during the war even as various new employees joined the workforce. Both the government and private employers tended to seek out white males first in their employment practices, but the demands of the war made that more difficult. Ultimately, workers experienced a general rise in wages, as much as 50 percent in some industrial jobs, and a clear escape from the economic anxiety of the Depression. At the same time, most men and women working in America during the war believed they were supporting an important national cause. Certainly, the 16 million servicemen and women of America's armed forces thought so. The general rate of increase in salaries

Two women welders working on ship construction, ca. 1942. Library of Congress.

and wages between 1940 and 1945 varied depending on the type of work and the location. Roughly, however, annual wages in the United States rose from about $1,700 to $2,400 during the war years.

OVERVIEW, 1945 AND BEYOND

With the end of World War II in August 1945, many American economists feared the United States might confront a postwar depression similar in scope to that of the

1930s. As government military contracts ended, as the economy dealt with the debt that the conflict had created, and as millions of servicemen returned to a peacetime economy looking for work, America braced for a recession. The war, critics believed, had created an artificial prosperity that would collapse in peacetime. That dire prediction failed to occur for the following reasons:

1. During World War II, Americans had accumulated personal and investment capital. Full employment had created earnings, and rationing and the inability to buy essential and consumer goods and products led Americans to put their money in banks or savings bonds. That income, protected by the government's Federal Deposit Insurance Corporation (FDIC), ensured a surplus of capital.

2. The nation's industrial system remained able to shift from the production of wartime material to the production of peacetime products. Instead of jeeps and tanks, General Motors could send new automobiles off its assembly lines. DuPont shifted from the production of munitions and chemicals to house paint. The technology that had developed radar and sonar systems for the military had the capacity and the expertise to make new radios, television sets, and record players. The war had revitalized American industry with new plants and factories, new tools and technology, and businesses possessed the innovative skills to shift adroitly from government contracts to consumer "supply-and-demand" interests.

3. World War II had devastated the competing economies of Europe and Japan. Bluntly, the United States confronted few foreign alternatives for consumers looking to buy.

4. The American economy faced a population of consumers eager to purchase new goods and products. The grim days of the Depression and the restricted years of wartime rationing had ended, and American consumers had money to spend and a desire to do so.

As government, business, and economic observers began to recognize the elements working in favor of a prosperous postwar economy, they also looked back at the causes of the Depression and reached an interesting conclusion. Americans, they argued, had perhaps saved too much revenue in the 1920s rather than spending it on consumer goods. That, they maintained, had created a surplus of goods, upset a supply-and-demand market, and plunged the nation into the Great Depression. A healthy free market economy, in their view, depended on some capital savings, but most importantly relied on heavy consumer spending. To avoid a reoccurrence of that flaw, therefore, Americans needed to engage in perpetual consumption. To a degree, the consumer culture of postwar America, the target of a host of critics, served as the best economic method to prevent a future depression. If Americans continued to buy goods and products on a regular basis, businesses would find a ready market for their services. That would guarantee ongoing employment, thus creating wages and salaries, enabling people to spend more money on more consumer items, thus a continued cycle of positive supply and demand. Business would benefit. Workers would have jobs. Consumers could buy all they wanted. The economic thrust of the nation would expand and prosper in a cyclical economic theory of success (Tuttle and Perry 1970, 698–705).

Did it work? Yes! Between 1945 and 1959, the United States created the most powerful, profitable, innovative economy in history. From labor unions to white-collar managers to professionals in supporting work (law, teaching, medicine, etc.), America saw the evolution of a vast middle class, employed, with access to a host of new goods and services, and relatively stable and secure compared to previous decades in the United States.

LABOR UNIONS

Organized labor unions became a powerful and influential part of the American economy following the war. The Roosevelt administration, and the individual commitment and struggle of union leaders and their rank and file members, had created legislation guaranteeing the right of workers to organize and collectively bargain with owners to improve and advance their work and salary conditions. Unions had also provided the Democratic Party with a substantial group of voters. The National Labor Relations Act (Wagner Act) in 1935 set the stage for government support of collective bargaining. It created the National Labor Relations Board (NLRB), and the Roosevelt administration came out squarely in support of union organizers. As early as 1886, Samuel Gompers had created the American Federation of Labor, a skilled workers union. That organization united with John L. Lewis's Committee of Industrial Organizations (CIO) in 1935. The two major industrial unions split during the war years.

In 1933, at the height of the Great Depression, union membership had dropped to fewer than 3 million, but by 1940, it had climbed to more than 10 million, and membership grew during World War II. The postwar era saw an increase in labor union membership, reaching a peak of 17.5 million by 1956 (United States Department of Labor). During the 1950s, the AFL and CIO reunited in an organizational convention in New York in December 1955. George Meany became its new president. At that point, one out of three workers in the private sector belonged to labor unions.

The large unions calculated their demands for increased wages and fringe benefits (health insurance, vacation time, etc.) on the profit and loss statements of the corporations that employed them. Business owners tended to negotiate with the unions based on worker productivity and competition with other similar businesses. That debate dominated discussions, negotiations, and disputes throughout the postwar era. During the war, the National War Labor Board sought to encourage union leaders to avoid strikes in order to confront the national emergency and guarantee full production. It worked for most of 1942, but a number of "wildcat" strikes (unannounced, short work stoppages) did occur throughout the war in a variety of different industries. For the most part, however, organized American workers did their jobs. Following the war, however, union disputes and strikes occurred in increasing numbers. In 1946, the United Steel Workers struck and the United Auto Workers stopped work at General Motors. Those actions led to later labor union strikes in the steel and coal industries. The threat of those strikes so concerned the probusiness Republican Congress that it passed the Taft-Hartley Act in 1947, over President Harry Truman's veto. Under that new law, unions were required to give 60 days notice before considering a strike. Both labor and management then had an obligation to seek a resolution to their dispute during that time period. An 80-day cooling-off period was also added to the Taft-Hartley Act in a clear effort to forestall union actions (Tuttle and Perry 1970, 702–15).

While organized labor clashed with the government during the period, its membership continued to grow and wages and work benefits expanded. At the same time, however, Congress began hearings concerning illegal racketeering activities within the major unions to investigate possible organized criminal involvement in union management and operations. That led the AFL-CIO to expel three of its key unions, including the Teamsters (trucking union), one of its largest groups. While probusiness legislation and criminal investigations threatened the development of labor unions in the 1950s, membership and benefits grew to unprecedented numbers during the decade. It is important to remember that economic growth for Americans following the war did not accrue only to "men in gray flannel suits." The era also witnessed the high point of American industrial blue-collar workers, both men and women.

WOMEN AT WORK

American women had found employment during the war in a variety of jobs previously closed to them. Many wished to continue working. While a standard view of the postwar era saw women returning to their traditional role as homemakers and mothers, and the Baby Boom of that generation was profound, women continued to enter the workforce in significant numbers. Whether expanding consumer spending or a desire to work outside the home encouraged women, they took employment at a quicker rate than men, providing more than 50 percent of the total growth of the workforce following the war. By the beginning of the 1950s, two million more women were working outside the home than had during World War II. Economic necessity or personal interest appeared to have created an increasingly two-paycheck family as the decade progressed.

Critics bemoaned the abandonment of the traditional home and family on the part of women. In *Modern Woman: The Lost Sex* (1947), a best-selling book by Ferdinand Lundberg and Marynia Farnham, the authors warned that working women threatened the stability of the family. Even the popular Dr. Benjamin Spock, whose book on childcare, *Baby and Child Care* (1946), became the "bible" of the era, advised women to stay at home and care for their families. The threats failed to accomplish their goal. The role of American women as a viable and contributive aspect of the postwar economy remained both a commercial and social aspect of evolving life in the United States.

BENEFITS, GROWTH, AND CHANGE

American workers in most jobs and professions experienced a formula of sorts in their daily employment. Five days a week, 40-hour workweeks (with overtime as a bonus), paid two-week vacations, health care and retirement packages, and other fringe benefits became a standard template between 1945 and 1959. Most of those benefits had not existed prior to 1945, yet they became standard practice by the 1950s. Americans believed that if they remained loyal, hardworking employees of businesses and corporations, they could count on lifelong jobs with relatively comfortable working conditions and the promise of a secure retirement after 20 to 30 years of commitment. With that stimulus, the positive promise of American economic life galvanized the nation's workforce following World War II. Essentially, the presumed rewards of the new economic environment far surpassed the anxiety that had existed during the Great Depression and the war.

As a result, American workers experienced an unprecedented period of economic prosperity after World War II. As people settled down to domesticity to compensate for the uprooted anxiety of the war years and the fear of the Cold War, it became a paradox that materialism provided comfort. Americans saw themselves in close-knit nuclear families rather than as a lonely crowd. What is called "the culture of the Cold War" not only had an impact on the growing birthrate—in 1955 as great as India's—but also influenced the increased production of material goods. By the mid-1950s, with only 6 percent of the world's population, the United States was producing and consuming over one-third of all the world's goods and services. The gross national product, considered by many the most important index of economic success, leaped from $206 billion in 1940 to over $500 billion in 1960.

In place for defense reasons at the end of the Korean War, the military budget continued to provide economic stimulus for research and development in fields like electronics and aviation. Easily available credit for installment buying encouraged Americans to purchase consumer durables on budget terms, while the booming public relations industry took note that people spent 35 percent more using credit cards than they would using money.

In 1950, "credit cards" entered the vocabulary of the American financial world with the creation of the Diners' Club card. American Express and credit cards from oil and phone companies and car rental services followed by the mid-1950s. Such installment purchases caused consumer indebtedness to soar during the decade from $73 billion to $196 billion. Madison Avenue advertisers preached immediate personal gratification as a way of life, and manufacturers complied by building "planned obsolescence" into many new products. Along with new lives, people were encouraged to refurbish their personal worlds. The Model T car that still drove and the turreted GE refrigerator still running when given away were treasures from the past. So many additional appliances appeared in new households that the use of electricity nearly tripled during the decade.

As the country's population increased by one-third between 1940 and 1960—in the Pacific states it rose by 110 percent—people needed more basic material goods. Half of the population in the far West now lived in a state different from the one in which they were born. And one-fifth of the nation's new population had settled in California, which by 1963 had surpassed New York as the most populous state. From 1946 to 1958 venture capitalists invested huge amounts of money in mechanization and power. Air conditioning, along with more available water, helped open new regions of the nation for homes and businesses. The electronics industry also began to thrive. Industry experienced a great rise in output per man-hour as automation intensified postwar scientific management.

If many unskilled workers did indeed lose their jobs to machines, economists argued that technology would create many new ones. The first giant computer, built around the time of the invention of the transistor during World War II, was marketed in 1950. IBM, the industry leader, could not turn computers out fast enough to satisfy demand. In 1954, the company produced only 20; by 1957 it produced 1,250; only a decade later it managed to turn out 35,000. Factory sales increased from $25 million in 1953 to $1 billion by the end of the decade, bringing all sorts of new jobs into the marketplace.

The huge spending on research and development still used as much as 50 percent government funding to support the Cold War's defense needs. Long after World War II the electronics industry continued to sell expensive weapons systems. In 1956, military items amounted to $3 billion—40 times the amount spent in 1947.

With the new interstate highway system demanding construction workers, the government remained one of the decade's largest employers. Jobs in the public sector doubled between 1950 and 1970. And incomes rose enough to create an expanded middle class. The proportion of the population enjoying an income of $10,000 or more increased from 9 percent in 1947 to 19 percent by 1968. The proportion of those earning below $3,000 also fell, from 34 percent to 19 percent. As late as 1940, fewer than two million Americans had any education beyond high school, but the GI Bill enabled many ex-soldiers to become professionals. By 1960, college enrollment reached 3.6 million, creating a range of skilled graduates with higher salaries to spend.

Some believed America had experienced a bloodless revolution. But the statistics about personal wealth did not document great changes. The distribution of income or wealth in America remained roughly the same throughout the period. The wealthiest 5 percent of Americans received a bit more than 18 percent of personal income; the richest 20 percent earned 45 percent. The poorest two-fifths of the population earned approximately 14 percent. In basic terms, the rise in wages, salaries, and income had grown for all of the various economic segments of the society, but the actual distribution of that personal capital remained about the same throughout the 15 years following World War II (Faragher et al. 2000, 805).

In 1953, just 1.6 percent of the population, for example, held 90 percent of the corporate bonds. By 1968 only 153 Americans possessed nine-digit fortunes, while millions still lived in want. In 1957, a University of Wisconsin sociologist, Robert Lampman, produced research revealing that 32.2 million Americans (nearly one-quarter of the population) had incomes below the poverty level. And many people still lacked minimal comforts like indoor toilets, hot water, and heating systems. Because there was so much visible well-being it remained easy to ignore the "other America."

Along with all the new homeowners, but not living beside them, grew a varied culture of poverty that included old people of all races, African Americans, Hispanics, and residents of Appalachia as well as many rural citizens who wanted to remain on farms. From 1948 to 1956 the American farmers' share of the wealth fell from 9 percent to scarcely 4 percent. Small farmers could not profit from the mechanization that was creating agribusiness to make the wealthy wealthier. Even during this period of the Baby Boom, the farm population declined by nine million between 1940 and 1960. By the end of the 1960s only 5 percent of the American population remained on farms.

Yet, paradoxically, many unlikely people seemed to have more material goods. In a place as poor as Harlan County, Kentucky, a depressed coal-mining community, 40 percent owned homes; 59 percent had cars, 42 percent telephones, 67 percent TV sets, and 88 percent washing machines. Michael Harrington noted that in the most powerful and richest society the world has ever known the poor remained "the strangest in the history of mankind." An American prophet, Harrington wrote a number of essays during the decade passionately reminding readers that the misery of the poor "has continued while the majority of the nation talked of itself as being 'affluent' and worried about neuroses in the suburbs" (Harrington, *The Other America*).

It was true that more Americans owned their homes in the 1950s than at any other time in the country's history. The 1949 National Housing Act had promised to build 810,000 low-cost homes so that every American family could have "a decent home and a suitable living environment." But by 1964, only 550 units had been built. The Federal Housing Authority made matters worse by refusing to allow integration in public housing projects. Michael Harrington insisted that it would take an effort of the intellect and will even to see the poor.

Many Americans later learned much from Harrington's 1962 book *The Other America*, the collection of his research on the poor. Many more knew about John Kenneth Galbraith's 1958 bestseller on the American economy, *The Affluent Society*. Not just concerned with examining America's newly defined wealth, Galbraith also seriously considered the remaining poverty. He attempted to shatter the argument that increased production would destroy poverty. In his view, distribution of wealth did not eliminate the poor. Although by 1960 per capita income in the United States was 35 percent higher than in the war boom year 1945, the poor were still part of the American landscape.

And public spaces deteriorated as surely as transportation systems decayed. The cities became impoverished as money set aside for low-income housing remained unused or was spent inappropriately on soon-to-be-destroyed high-rise buildings. Not until the social and environmental movements of the 1960s would many Americans begin to recognize that public spaces were as important to a democracy as personal consumer goods. The appeal of a simpler life had always been a powerful force in America's spiritual heritage, but the abundance of the 1950s made it hard to escape the materialism that defined the times.

The following famous passage from Galbraith's *The Affluent Society* epitomizes the dilemma of this period, the implications of which Americans still need to consider seriously:

The family which takes its mauve and cerise, air-conditioned, power-steered and power-braked automobile out for a tour passes through cities that are badly paved, made hideous by litter, blighted buildings, billboards and posts for wires that should long since have been put underground. They pass on into a countryside that has been rendered largely invisible by commercial art.... They picnic on exquisitely packaged food from a portable icebox by a polluted stream and go on to spend the night at a park which is a menace to public health and morals. Just before dozing off on an air mattress, beneath a nylon tent amid stench of decaying refuse, they may vaguely reflect on the curious unevenness of their blessings.

By the end of the decade the hazards of successful free enterprise had become as real as the Cold War anxieties that communism had provoked (Kaledin 2000, 127–30). The bleak assessment that Galbraith, Harrington, and other critics leveled at America's postwar consumer-driven society, however, failed to counter the conclusion that more people had gained economic stability, jobs, access to goods and services, and a measure of security than at any time in the previous history of the United States. Similarly, the American economy that emerged after 1945 became a powerful force in the global community as well. It remains important for students of daily life in America to consider the concerns expressed in *The Affluent Society* and *The Other America*, but it is myopic to see those problems as the single, most significant result of the nation's boom period between 1940 and 1959. Suggestions that some simple life of contentment and comfort existed prior to the consumer culture of the postwar era fail to pass objective scrutiny. Galbraith's "air-conditioned automobiles" and "packaged food," so casually dismissed as harmful to the society at large, reflected more an access, for many Americans, to comforts and benefits unrivaled in the daily lives of men, women, and children anywhere else. Milton Friedman, the Nobel Prize-winning economist at the University of Chicago, would take issue with Galbraith and other critics of the economy in his 1962 book *Capitalism and Freedom*. Friedman became a lifelong advocate of a free market, consumer-driven economic concept.

CONCLUSIONS

The concern regarding postwar unemployment with the return of millions of service personnel to civilian life failed to materialize. In fact, the reverse occurred.

The economy saw an increased demand for employees. Unemployment remained below 4 percent until 1949, spiked to 5 percent in 1949 and 1950, dropped to under 3 percent until 1954, and then remained around 4 percent for the remainder of the decade. Employers found it necessary to offer fringe benefits to attract workers. Paid vacations, health insurance, retirement benefits, and other options became a new aspect of employee packages in the 1950s. Wages for production workers rose significantly between 1946 and 1959, even when calculated against the rise in inflation. In 1946, wage earners in production and manufacturing jobs worked an average of 40.2 to 40.5 hours a week and received a weekly salary of $41.14 to $46.49. By 1950, the hourly workweek remained about the same, but salaries had jumped to between $54.71 and $63.32 a week. At the end of the decade, those wages had grown to between $79.60 and $97.10 weekly (Tuttle and Perry 1970, 711).

The construction industry emerged as one of the nation's largest employers. The suburban housing boom, the expansion of business construction in warehousing and office buildings, and other aspects of commercial growth following the war created a demand for workers. At the same time, the infrastructure of roads and highways needed for the expanding economy created additional demands. So-called complimentary services included public school teachers, college professors, firefighters, police officers, trash collectors, and government employees.

The GI Bill supported an increase in college attendance, and the emerging white-collar graduates of four-year institutions also found a ready job market in expanding professional and administrative fields. The so-called organization man (see William Whyte's view under "Men," in the section on Domestic Life) found some critics concerned, but that new generation of management employees secured career opportunities that promised stable, secure jobs their parents or grandparents had never envisioned (*Daily Life Online*, "Economic Life: Work," in Kaledin, *Daily Life in the United States, 1940–1959*, http://dailylife.greenwood.com).

FOR MORE INFORMATION

Faragher, John Mack, Susan Armitage, Mari Jo Buhle, and Daniel Czitrom. *Out of Many.* Upper Saddle River, NJ: Prentice Hall, 2000.

Galbraith, John Kenneth. *The Affluent Society.* Boston: Little Brown, 1958.

Goodwin, Doris Kearns. *No Ordinary Time: Franklin and Eleanor Roosevelt: The Homefront in World War II.* New York: Simon and Schuster, 1994.

Kaledin, E. *Daily Life in the United States, 1940–1959: Shifting Worlds.* Westport, CT: Greenwood Press, 2000; also online as *Daily Life Online*, in Kaledin, *Daily Life in the United States, 1940–1959*, http://dailylife.greenwood.com.

Lundberg, Ferdinand, and Marynia F. Farnham. *Modern Woman: The Lost Sex.* New York: Harper and Brothers, 1947.

Tuttle, Frank W., and Joseph M. Perry. *An Economic History of the United States.* Chicago: South-Western Publishing, 1970.

Winkler, A. *Home Front U.S.A.: America during World War II.* 2nd ed. Wheeling, IL: Harlan Davidson, 2000.

Intellectual Life

OVERVIEW

In the present world of instant telecommunication with excesses of information in every space, it is hard even to imagine the 1930s, when not every American family owned a radio. In fact, much of rural America lacked the necessary electricity to plug one in. When Franklin Roosevelt gave his fireside chats, often more than one household joined together to listen. During that period, rural electrification had just begun to extend airwaves to allow farmers to hear stand-up comedians like Jack Benny and Fred Allen, sitcoms like *Fibber McGee and Molly* and *Amos 'n' Andy* (stories of blacks played by whites—not heard as racist at the time). Daytime soap operas (which really advertised laundry soap) like *Ma Perkins, My Gal Sunday,* and *Pepper Young's Family* enabled the homebound to imagine that other families' problems could be worse than their own.

A popular radio demagogue and Catholic priest, Father Charles Coughlin, used *The Golden Hour of the Little Flower* to attract as many as 40 million listeners. His original belief in the New Deal turned into hatred for Franklin Roosevelt and support for European fascism, causing his audience to drop away before he left the airwaves in 1940. One sensationalist reporter, Walter Winchell, broadcast gossipy versions of news like the items printed in the *National Enquirer*—even as a few serious journalists, like Edward R. Murrow and H. V. Kaltenborn, felt free to express personal liberal opinions. Lowell Thomas, a daily newscaster, used broadcasting to help isolated families visit remote places like Arabia and Tibet, making more convincing the "One World" advocated by Wendell Willkie, Roosevelt's 1940 Republican opponent, in a best-selling book (*One World,* 1943). In trying to solidify new ideals, Americans have often found it difficult to imagine the vast range of cultural experiences others have had to put aside to become citizens of the United States. More than books or magazines, the radio became a source of public relations for unifying a frequently fractured society. Just as talking pictures took over from the silent films of the 1920s, movies replaced radio as a means of communication and entertainment, becoming one of the few American businesses that flourished in the 1930s.

After World War II, television began to replace movies and the radio as the main means of communication. By the end of the 1950s visual images taught Americans who they were. Although an advertising slogan of the decade boasted that movies were better than ever, and the introduction of drive-in theaters tried to accommodate both car culture and family (many had playgrounds, diaper services, and special foods for kids), the truth was that television was taking over as the main medium of communication. Gimmicks like three-dimensional films and aroma-ramas that puffed scents through the theaters' ventilation systems failed to bring in necessary crowds. Cinerama appeared in 1952, using overlapping cameras for a gigantic screen effect to extend the possibilities of adventure films. Pictorial innovations such as the famous chase across the face of Mount Rushmore in Alfred Hitchcock's *North by*

Northwest (1959) suggested that the excitement of the big screen was far from over, but by then many movies were being created just for the living-room viewer. Weekly movie attendance dropped from 90 million to 47 million in the 10 years after 1946. By 1952, 19 million Americans had television sets, and a thousand new TV appliance stores were opening each month. When Lucille Ball bought the unused RKO film lot in 1955 to film *I Love Lucy,* the most popular sitcom of the decade, she became a pioneer producer in the new industry of making movies specifically for TV.

On its face, *I Love Lucy* might seem another example of a stream of simple plots about a ditzy housewife manipulating a loyal husband to advance her schemes for money and attention. In fact, the show reflected different levels of media liberation. For one thing, Desi Arnaz played himself on the show—Lucy's Cuban bandleader husband, Ricky Ricardo. Far from the suburban organization man, Arnaz offered a vast audience the chance to appreciate Latino culture. He used his accent and charm to introduce viewers who knew nothing about Cuba to a different kind of civilization, while audiences enjoyed the tensions of the mixed-culture marriage. Everyone knew that the slapstick character Lucy Ricardo, played by Ball on-screen, was far removed from the brilliant businesswoman producing the most popular show on television.

Always torn between trying to please her husband and dreaming of being a star, Lucy Ricardo responded to every woman's fantasies while coping with the social mandate of the "stay-at-home" 1950s. Ball insisted on playing the role as a housewife, not a star. Desi and Lucy represented caricatures that helped many—in this most married of decades—laugh at the disasters and peculiarities of marital stress. There was never any suggestion that divorce and extramarital love affairs were realities. Both characters emerged as sympathetic and vulnerable, far from sure of their social status. Their on-screen dealings with their neighbors' points of view offered some exposure to the world of compromise many Americans experienced in new housing arrangements everywhere.

The Monday evening show was such a success that Marshall Field's, the Chicago department store, changed its weekly Monday night clearance sale to Thursday. As early as 1952, 10.6 million households were tuning in to *I Love Lucy,* the largest audience thus far in history. By 1954, as many as 50 million Americans watched. The show allowed CBS-TV to make a net profit for the first time in 1953. No problems emerged with Desi's being Latino—except behind the scenes when one producer argued that Americans would not accept Desi as a suitable TV husband for Lucy.

In 1947, Lucille Ball had been among the Hollywood stars who protested the activities of the House Un-American Activities Committee. On a radio show called *Hollywood Fights Back* she had read excerpts from the Bill of Rights. When the tabloid journalist Walter Winchell accused her of being a communist in 1953, she acknowledged that she had joined the party to please her grandfather. But her television ratings were so high that Philip Morris cigarettes, Lucy's sponsor, refused to withdraw its backing, demonstrating that in a capitalist society the bottom line frequently shapes ideals. Desi had left Cuba when Fidel Castro, the communist leader, was just six years old. He insisted that both he and Lucy were 100 percent American. The only thing "red" about Lucy, Desi claimed, was her hair—and even that was dyed.

The situations played out on the show often challenged audiences to think more about marriage, especially when Lucy's pregnancy took center screen. The on-TV baby was another example of Lucille Ball's power to challenge network stereotypes. Before Lucy's baby all pregnancies had been hidden. CBS wanted her to stand behind chairs. Even the word *pregnant* was not to be used; she agreed to call herself an *expectant mother*. By the time Desi (too busy on-screen to notice the change in his wife) acknowledged the great event, CBS had lined up a rabbi, a priest, and a minister to make sure the script was in good taste. But at the hospital it was Lucy who pushed Ricky in the wheelchair. When the baby was born in January 1953, 68 percent of the television sets in the country were tuned in as 44 million people watched—twice as many as watched the inauguration of Dwight Eisenhower the next day. As time went on Lucy and Desi followed their fellow Americans into suburbia, but their domestic adventures ended at the close of the decade when their real marriage, sympathetic as it seemed, collapsed. Lucille Ball held financial control of the ongoing programs that she developed herself (Kaledin 2000, 30–31, 133–42; *Daily Life Online,* "Intellectual Life: Communication," in Kaledin, *Daily Life in the United States, 1940–1959,* http://dailylife.greenwood.com).

EDUCATION

Albert Einstein. Chaiba.

"No other idea has seemed more typically American," wrote Diane Ravitch, a historian of education, "than the belief that schooling could cure society's ills." In *The Troubled Crusade: American Education, 1945–1980,* she made a list of all the problems—from crime rates to unemployment, to ethnic differences, to health standards, to traffic accidents, to general morality—that most Americans placed at the door of public education. In a society that continued to pay teachers low salaries, and rewarded athletes and media stars with much more money than what scientists and scholars earned, the government began to take greater responsibility for better education. Between 1944 and 1965, the United States was willing to spend $14.5 billion to educate its people.

The disparity between the elementary education offered to the middle classes and that offered to the poor emerged sharply during the war. Community differences in income meant sharp differences in the quality of education, determining whether children had books and paper to write on—or even chairs to sit on. When defense jobs offered new opportunities for better pay, many teachers in poverty-stricken communities simply quit. In the three years following Pearl Harbor, 11,000 out of 20,000 teachers in Alabama left their jobs. In Iowa 800 rural schools had no teachers at all. In 1947, the *New York Times* reported that 350,000 teachers had quit teaching for better jobs. Those who remained worked at salaries lower than those of garbage collectors.

Twelve major teacher strikes took place after 1946, calling attention to the fact that both Russia and Great Britain spent more on education than Americans did.

Federal aid to education began to be considered essential to bringing about equality of opportunity for American children. By the mid-1940s even "Mr. Republican," Robert Taft, senator from Ohio, would agree that "children were entitled not as a matter of privilege but as a matter of right to a decent roof, decent meals, decent medical care and a decent place in which to go to school." Astonishing to many was his conclusion: "Education is socialistic anyway" (remarks made in a stump speech while campaigning against Harry S Truman in 1948).

After the war a variety of new schools—with some experimental programs—grew up in the midst of all the freshly built communities. Although the relaxed ideas of John Dewey's progressive education movement extended in many directions, debates were ongoing on the need for rote learning versus more imaginative programs. The same debates would continue into the 1990s—not only in Walt Disney's utopian town of Celebration, Florida, but in every community where parents became involved in what children needed to be taught to be civilized and productive members of society.

Funding for religious education came under renewed discussion. Because the GI Bill was sending people to all sorts of religiously oriented schools, and because lunches at every elementary school were also subsidized in the mid-1940s, it was hard to argue then that the separation of church and state was clear-cut. A 1947 Supreme Court decision even allowed public funds to be used for transporting children to parochial schools. But a strong anti-Catholic movement arose to limit such funding. Fear of church influence was ongoing. A book by Paul Blanshard (*American Freedom and Catholic Power*, 1949) attacking the intrusion of the Catholic hierarchy into public education went into 26 printings and remained on the national best-seller list for six months. Even Eleanor Roosevelt wrote in her "My Day" column (syndicated in a number of national newspapers) in June 1949, "I do not want to see public education connected with religious control of the schools which are paid for by taxpayers' money." The issue of federal funding for education relating to the separation of church and state remains alive today. The only federal money freely given at the time would be for local schools near military installations, because such bases contributed no real estate taxes to subsidize the education of youngsters on base.

The postwar commitment to educating all the children in a democracy used the vocabulary of John Dewey's progressive education movement to define its goals. Such education stressed training in problem solving more than memorizing historical facts and arithmetic. Modern pedagogy favored projects, field trips, life experiences, and group learning instead of rote memorization and drills to acquire knowledge. Although high school attendance went up by over 50 percent by 1950, such education was broadly attacked for lowering standards. The progressive faith, as Lawrence Cremin, another historian of education, described it, believed that "culture could be democratized without being vulgarized, and everyone could share not only in benefits of the new sciences but in pursuit of the arts as well" (Cremin, *A History of Education in American Culture*). Yet narrow professionalism and anti-intellectualism often impeded such ideal goals. One of the most unfortunate results was a shift to "life adjustment" courses that taught little of substance and kept many young people—especially women and working-class students—in social grooves.

In 1947, the National Commission of Life Adjustment for Youth created state commissions to respond to a general demand for vocational or functional education. Simultaneously, the study of foreign languages and the serious study of the history of past civilizations were considered less significant for everyone. Later decades would call this "dumbing down" education. By the mid-1950s, only 20.6 percent of American high school students would study a second language. And multiple-choice exam questions began to replace essay writing in tests that measured the critical-thinking skills students had mastered. Conservatives began to blame progressive education for all that was vacuous and anti-intellectual in postwar America. Before the decade was over, strong debates would take place all over the country about what students should be taught.

Even *Time* magazine, among several critics, ridiculed the frenzy for "life adjustment education" that seemed to absolve teachers from teaching and students from learning. A famous elite educator, Robert Hutchins, president of the University of Chicago, tried to define the direction general education in the United States should take: "Our mission here on earth is to change our environment, not to adjust ourselves to it." More specifically, Hutchins questioned how minds should be trained. "Perhaps the greatest idea that America has given the world is the idea of education for all," he wrote. "The world is entitled to know whether this idea means that everybody can be educated or only that everybody must go to school."

After World War II, when liberal education—once available only to a privileged few—became available to everyone, at least in principle, educators had to consider attitude changes related to who was being educated, not just what was being taught. The social texture of postwar America no longer resembled Thornton Wilder's small town, Grover's Corners (from his play *Our Town*, 1938). "Our Town" might be a trailer camp or a Levittown more often than a community of elm-lined streets.

The most significant development in higher education related to the GI Bill. Specific entitlements offered returning soldiers the choice of a year of monetary benefits while job hunting or—more important for fulfilling the dream of human potential—a chance for paid higher education or additional training in skills that postwar America needed. As the gross national product expanded from $91.1 billion in 1939 to $213.6 billion in 1945 to $300 billion in 1950, 17 million new jobs had been created. Between 1944 and 1946 also, the six million working women who had done so well during the war were pressured to give up their lucrative jobs; four million either were fired or left voluntarily, offering returning veterans a vast array of work opportunities. But many still chose more education over the immediate possibility of earning a living.

Instead of going to work, almost eight million veterans took advantage of the GI Bill to pursue the higher education they would not otherwise have been able to afford. The creation of a new educated class meant extending professional status to all sorts of ethnic newcomers in law and medicine and in the university. For the first time, colleges and universities became multicultural on a broad scale. Unfortunately, elitist admissions policies continued to work against blacks and women. At the same time, the expansion of all higher education in terms of huge enrollments, new buildings, and new kinds of community colleges also opened doors wider for everyone, preparing the way for a more meritocratic society. Many people going to college after the war would become that first person in the family to get a higher degree. The government gave each veteran $65 a month ($90 to those with families) and $500 a year to cover tuition and books—adequate at most colleges at the time. State institutions felt a special mandate to meet the great need, expanding at new campuses—like Stonybrook in New York—and offering new courses presumably keyed to a modern economy and a more complex society.

Conservative educators predicted the end of quality education in the great tides of mediocrity flowing into America's most famous institutions. They began to give attention to creating more complex entrance exams for the best universities. But after only a few years of experience with GIs in the classroom, many had to concede that maturity, motivation, and hard work often produced scholarship as competent as that of young people trained at preparatory schools. Instead of lowering standards, those older students forced educators to reassess their vision of America's potential. By the 1990s, the State University of New York at Stonybrook, built only 40 years before, was ranked the third best public research university in the country.

The creation of more possibilities to get an education grew out of the great sense of need that was discovered during the war. A 1940 census revealed that only 2 out of 5 people in America had gone beyond the eighth grade; only 1 in 4 had graduated from high school; and only 1 in 20 went on to complete college. During World War II, the government was so concerned about the low level of American education that it set up all sorts of additional training programs for soldiers: to help make illiterates literate, to teach foreign languages, and to train mechanics and builders in new electronics skills. The U.S. Armed Forces Institute set up courses in which more than 6,000 students enrolled during its peak. Many poor young men joined the army as a way to achieve the upward mobility that education promised. Indeed, the U.S. government spent $321 billion on education between 1941 and 1945, twice as much as in the entire preceding 150 years of its existence. Investing in education represented an ongoing belief in America's citizens—an affirmation of faith in the future.

When the army was officially integrated in 1948, such training was clearly extended also to African Americans. As early as 1944, Wendell Willkie, the Republican who ran against Roosevelt in 1940, asserted that the war should make us conscious of the "contradiction between our treatment of the Negro minority and the ideals for which we are fighting." With the congressional establishment of the Women's Armed Services Act, also in 1948, the country acknowledged that women too were entitled to the same educational rewards offered men. Yet, Americans learned slowly that legalization may be just the first step toward achieving broader social goals. Fewer than 3 percent of the women eligible took advantage of this opportunity to educate themselves, and too many African Americans coming out of segregated schools did not have adequate preparation for higher education. Nevertheless, the GI Bill provided education for 50 percent of all the people who served in the armed forces. By 1956, when it ended, 7.8 million veterans had taken advantage of its entitlements: 2.2

million (97 percent men) had gone to college, 3.5 million to technical schools, and 700,000 to agricultural programs. In the academic year 1949–1950, 497,000 Americans received university degrees—over twice as many as in 1940. No longer would higher education be seen simply as the proprietary right of the upper middle class. The quality of cultural experience had begun to change for everyone.

Even women began to see changes in their educational opportunities. Although larger numbers of women had begun to go to college in the 1950s, only 37 percent stayed to graduate, and the number going on for higher degrees was smaller than in the 1920s and 1930s. Yet women, glad to sacrifice careers for family at the beginning of the decade, were eager to get back to school by its end, even though most institutions would not let women with families attend college part-time. One brilliant Wellesley dropout, divorced with four children, was told that to return to college she would have to attend full-time and take gym.

Betty Friedan praised the few enlightened institutions that modified their degree programs to accommodate women with children. In 1955, the New School for Social Research set up a human relations workshop to help the homebound pursue broader goals. In 1959, the University of Minnesota established a revolutionary program to encourage older women to get degrees. By 1962, when Sarah Lawrence College announced a grant to help mature women finish their education or get graduate degrees, the number of eager inquirers put their switchboards out of commission. Most adult education programs during this decade gave no credits and led nowhere—except in fields like nursing and teaching, where there were labor shortages. In those fields, a few programs also met women's needs by scheduling classes during the daytime when children were in school. And some schools tried to make good use of women who already had bachelor's degrees by setting up master of arts programs in teaching.

"Unless we get more women equal education we can't get them equal pay and opportunity," declared the president of the Federation of Business and Professional Women in the *New York Times* in 1952, anticipating the idea of equal rights embodied in the *Brown* decision in 1954. Keeping women undereducated in the 1950s by maintaining quotas for the young and denying older women—often in their early thirties—admission to professional schools was also a way to keep establishment power in the hands of white men. When the Educational Testing Service at Princeton went on to design college-level equivalency exams to enable women students who had followed their husbands' jobs to write off credits, such exams were often not accepted by schools that relied heavily on Scholastic Aptitude Tests—produced by the same company—to evaluate the young. No one wanted to make it easy for women who were also mothers to do anything more with their lives. In 1956, the *New York Times* described a mother and daughter who were both getting degrees at Rutgers. The mother—also still taking care of her house and family and commuting—was permitted to take six courses to catch up. Another mother commuting from New Jersey to Brooklyn College three nights a week so she would not have to leave her children alone managed to graduate with Phi Beta Kappa honors. With a tone of amazement, the *Times* completed this story with her future plans for law school. Such "superwomen" stories made people pay attention to general concerns about what was happening to other bright women with complicated lives.

Perhaps just as embarrassing as the quota systems of the 1950s that kept women out of competition with men for professional jobs was what was called sex-directed, gender-focused education. Mills College in California, trying to compensate for the indifference of Eastern establishment schools to talented women faculty, defined gender education that would cater to women's needs. Unfortunately, like the high schools that fostered functional education, these colleges often ended up emphasizing "life adjustment" rather than intellectual achievement. Categories of experts—sociologists, psychologists, and psychoanalysts—banded together to persuade women to believe they were better off in the role of housewife. As noted sociologist Talcott Parsons described the American woman, her life was as "her husband's wife, the mother of his children." At a time when the Cold War made Americans critical of progressive education designed to foster good judgment and problem-solving skills rather than rote learning, women were urged back into functional feminine molds, not developed as critical thinkers.

Although progressive education, expressing the ideas of the great pragmatic philosopher John Dewey, reached back to the 1920s, it became another target for the paranoia of the 1950s. All sorts of local groups thought such education was responsible for Marxist ideas and juvenile delinquency. In 1951, in Pasadena, California, Willard E. Goslin, a creative progressive educator and president of the American Association of School Administrators, was pressured by organized right-wing groups to resign. In the same year the American Association of School Administrators chose to devote its entire annual meeting to examining widespread assaults on public education. Anxiety produced best-sellers like Arthur Bestor's *Educational Wastelands* (1953) and Rudolph Flesch's *Why Johnny Can't Read and What You Can Do about It* (1955). Few new programs, however, emerged. Successful schools, long influenced by progressive ideas, continued to produce well-trained, creative students. And, Dr. Spock, whose child-rearing classic was in almost every home with children during this era, did not hesitate to label his book a "common-sense" guide to child care. "Trust yourself," he urged new mothers.

In 1957, when the Russians sent two *Sputnik* satellites to circle the globe, a huge outcry went up for more serious education that would improve standards for everyone. Americans confronted the reality that in the Soviet Union 69 percent of the medical students and 39 percent of the engineers were women, whereas in the United States in 1956 three out of five women in coeducational colleges took secretarial, home economics, nursing, or education courses. Only 20 percent of all science and math majors in American colleges were women.

A 1957 book, *Signs for the Future*, prepared by a varied group of educators and edited by Opal D. David, urged greater flexibility in admissions and scheduling and use of educational television, adult education, and refresher courses to enable more women with children to come back into a more high-powered career stream. The Cold War concern that we had fallen behind the Russians inspired Congress to pass the National Defense Education Act in 1958, allotting over $900 million for scholarships and loans to encourage the study of science, math, and foreign languages. That act also provided 12,000 counselors for secondary schools. Although the pendulum seemed to be swinging back to conservative education, with the subsequent creation of a huge number of community colleges (one every two weeks by the mid-1960s), many child-free women as well as young men were given the chance to begin entirely different lives. The flexibility of our institutions was helping us turn away from what Betty Friedan had labeled a culture that educates its most capable women to make careers out of raising their families. Again, the government was helping the individual find human fulfillment.

The importance of the GI Bill in enriching institutions and changing old-fashioned educational environments cannot be overestimated. Not only did the army of new learners not diminish academic standards, as feared, but the presence on campus of older students able to make mature judgments also worked to erode sophomoric customs like fraternity hazings and wearing freshman beanies. Older students were presumed to be wiser. The idea that college discipline replaced the parent—strong before World War II—began to erode by the 1960s, when parietal rules and dress codes became quaint memories. Who could even imagine that women at Radcliffe College, going to classes at Harvard, were not permitted to wear pants on the streets of Cambridge, Massachusetts? Wellesley students had to leave their dormitory doors open while entertaining men. Because so many men everywhere also returned to college with wives, married women were slowly tolerated as part of the learning environment (Kaledin 2000, 64–68, 106–09; *Daily Life Online*, "Intellectual Life: Education," in Kaledin, *Daily Life in the United States, 1940–1959*, http://daily-life.greenwood.com).

FILM

During the 1940s sales of movie tickets soared to 3.5 billion a year. By then, movies would be what embodied American ideas—not just for Americans but for the whole world. Entertaining, informative, and relatively cheap, films reinforced the values the United States wanted to honor, the ideas people would be willing to make sacrifices for. A 1940s classic, *Mrs. Miniver*, that was created to glorify the bravery and ingenuity of America's British ally, personified by the charming Greer Garson, could be seen in New York along with the famous Rockettes' precision dancing stage show at the elegant Radio City Music Hall for 75 cents. The film broke all attendance records for the time, grossing over a million dollars.

One anthropologist, Hortense Powdermaker, referred to Hollywood as a "dream factory" in her book *Hollywood, The Dream Factory* (1950), while the historian Robert Sklar defined the whole country as "movie-made America" (*Movie-Made America*, 1975). The power of the motion picture industry to influence how Americans saw themselves, to turn myths into live traditions, would become increasingly apparent. When the nation elected its first movie star president, critics remarked that Ronald Reagan sometimes seemed to confuse his World War II movie roles with what actually happened. In the 1940s the social and cultural makeup of the movie industry reflected the values of an America concerned with helping people recognize what was worth fighting for.

Hollywood's representation of the American dream has been definitively described by the television movie critic Neal Gabler in a social history of the film industry, *An Empire of Their Own: How the Jews Invented Hollywood* (1989). Examining the lives of Hollywood tycoons as symbolic American successes, Gabler revealed the anxieties of the movie moguls' world as suggestive of the values of most new Americans. In articulating on film their own immigrant dreams of the good life available in America, the filmmakers helped influence how other Americans defined their identities. Most convincingly, Gabler recorded the intense and often uncritical patriotism that shaped the moviemakers' attitudes toward foreign ideologies, like the Nazism so many in the industry had fled and the communism that others believed was a threat to American life. In the 1940s, the movie empire demonstrated unquestioning patriotism—a wholehearted commitment to the war effort that would help both to educate soldiers and to stir up civilian support for the war. Films such as *This Is the Army* (1943), *Yankee Doodle Dandy* (1942), *The Fighting 69th* (1940), and *Lifeboat* (1944) attempted to revitalize the American myths of ethnic success and integrated culture. All groups needed to believe that individuals could do well working together in a pluralistic society for a common goal.

During the war years, attendance at local theaters mounted to over 90 million viewers a week. Commitment to the war effort by the film industry extended to many different levels. Movie houses—palaces of imagination in the 1930s—were used in the 1940s as community centers. In their spacious lobbies, people gathered to buy and sell War Bonds and to collect flattened tin cans and aluminum pots as well as surplus fats for making munitions. Even youngsters worked at selling defense stamps at small tables set up near the ticket takers to remind people of their civic responsibilities. When movie stars joined in the sale of government bonds at American theaters everywhere they sold over $350 billion worth. People did not hesitate to lend their savings to the government.

Teenagers also collected money in movie lobbies to boost the canteens of the United Service Organizations. Many young soldiers stationed all over America in army training camps far from their homes needed wholesome places for entertainment on weekend leaves. Members of the film industry worked with local volunteers to make these Stage Door Canteens represent homey refuges of warmth and hospitality for young strangers. Even though the armed forces were racially segregated during World War II, the canteens for relaxation often made a point of being integrated. Actress Bette Davis, one anecdote records, threatened to sever connection with her local canteen when some officious volunteers questioned the interracial dancing that took place there. Although most of the elegant theaters where such community activities could happen were torn down in the 1960s when television became a more socially isolating way to view movies, a film called *Stagedoor Canteen* (1943) remains a tribute to the idea of innocent entertainment and welcome for out-of-towners under supervision of the movie industry. The Hollywood Canteen, sponsored by 42 craft guilds including both white and African American musicians' locals, fed thousands of meals to eager soldiers and sailors during its first two years. Yet, it is the movies themselves—the "things" that embody the ideas of the 1940s—that students will continue to consider the most important social artifacts of the war. Almost every film made during the war years reveals some social aspect of wartime America.

On the most obvious level Hollywood filmmakers offered the government their resources to create training films for the army—telling soldiers about our allies and introducing our enemies. The public would be offered similar fare. Propagandistic work like *A Yank in the R.A.F.* (1944) and *Journey for Margaret* (1942), about an evacuated English child, were meant to demonstrate our deep connection with the British. Ideological films like *Hitler's Children* (1943) or Charlie Chaplin's *The Great Dictator* (1940) made it easier to dislike Germans. Exaggerated features of treacherous Japanese film characters helped Americans accept the necessity to incarcerate patriotic fellow Americans. Not until after the war, when Japan had become an American friend, was a film made to expose the injustice of the internment camps. Other movies created during wartime to familiarize the American people with our new allies, the Russians—like *Mission to Moscow* (1944)—would haunt their Hollywood producers and writers after the war when the relationship with Russia disintegrated and a blacklist labeled the creators of such sympathetic scripts communist sympathizers.

That distinguished writers like John Steinbeck joined the war effort with *The Moon Is Down* (1943) and *Lifeboat* (1944) suggests the extent of involvement of serious writers and artists in wartime propaganda. A list of Hollywood producers, writers, directors, technicians, and stars that put personal preferences aside to do what was most helpful for their country in fighting the war would fill a small book. Two favorites—the witty movie star Carole Lombard and the bandleader Glenn Miller, who traveled as an enlisted army officer entertaining troops—lost their lives in military air crashes. No one in the movie community criticized the government or questioned the need to get behind the war. A rare pacifist, star Lew Ayres, emphasized his opposition to killing by joining the medical corps. Newsreels—shown in Translux theaters for short subjects—were also included with feature films, recording ugly realities just as TV news did during the Vietnam War. There were honest journalists like Ernie Pyle who described what continuous fighting did to people, but there was also protective censorship—as people on the home front complained if too much brutality was shown. Movies were constructed to show the enemy—not American young men—being blown to bits. Students might consider how much such attitudes shift in different decades by looking at the 1998 film *Saving Private Ryan*, an effort to depict the invasion of Europe with some degree of realism and accuracy.

Glorification of the war experience became essential while the war was being fought. Although films such as *The Story of G.I. Joe* (1943), *A Walk in the Sun* (1945), and *Pride of the Marines* (1945) stressed a wholesome distaste for war as human activity, they made a point of demonstrating the surprising courage of the ordinary individual in the multicultural foxhole. Critics tend to make fun of the Hollywood melting-pot group: black–white, Catholic–Jew, slum kid–stockbroker dependent on each other in submarine or fighter plane; but the need to nourish the myth of equality for those willing to die for it brought about a more realistic exploration of American prejudice in films after the war. A 1939 movie like *Gone with the Wind* could get away with showing blacks to be dully loyal or simply silly. In the name of the national unity forged out of the Civil War, this famous classic praised only the individual spunk of whites enduring social disaster—slavery was not an issue in the film. After World War II, African Americans would be taken more seriously in films, and American prejudice would be discussed in the open. Such movies as *Crossfire* and *Gentleman's Agreement* (both 1947) would also help to alert many to the reality of American anti-Semitism. *Intruder in the Dust* (1949) allowed viewers to appreciate the intelligence of a black hero. In 1948, acknowledging the need for equality of opportunity in an important section of American life, Harry Truman integrated the army. In 1945, during Roosevelt's brief fourth term, the government repealed the 1882 Chinese Exclusion Act, which set quotas on Chinese immigration and denied citizenship to the Chinese.

The 1940s film industry's contribution to pure entertainment to help people escape the tensions of war and the problems of reshaping postwar life also included such classic musicals as *State Fair* (1945) and *The Harvey Girls* (1945). *Film noir* is a term that describes dark Hollywood crime dramas that were often focused on corruption and sex. Masterpieces of *film noir*, such as *The Maltese Falcon* (1941), *Laura* (1944), *Double Indemnity* (1945), *The Postman Always Rings Twice* (1946), and *Spellbound* (1945), often made distraction exciting. Westerns like *The Ox-Bow Incident* (1943) and *My Darling Clementine* (1946) extended the mythology of the West with greater compassion.

Through the 1950s, movies continued to have a link with larger national political issues. The House Un-American Activities Committee (HUAC), designed to ferret out communists in labor unions in the 1930s, became an invigorated source of terror under the control of Congressman J. Parnell Thomas. In 1947, a group of Hollywood screenwriters and directors summoned before the committee to account for past communist beliefs were considered especially dangerous because of their power to influence American opinion through the movies. Called "unfriendly witnesses" because they took the Fifth Amendment to keep from having to name friends, the "Hollywood Ten" were all indicted for contempt of Congress. Although even film star Ronald Reagan testified at the time that he did not believe communists had ever been able to use motion pictures to spread their ideology, the Supreme Court upheld the indictment. Those people were fined a thousand dollars each and sent to jail for a year. Richard Nixon, who would become the most prominent committee member during the 1950 Alger Hiss trial, demanded that new movies be made to spell out "the methods and evils of totalitarian Communism." But the only examples J. Parnell Thomas could find of dangerous old movies were those made during the war, like *Mission to Moscow* and *Song of Russia*—corny propaganda films created to help wartime allies appear sympathetic. Ironically, Chairman Thomas, accused of stealing from the government he had been protecting from communists, would soon find himself in the same prison where he had sent one of the Hollywood Ten, Ring Lardner Jr. As a result of that arrest, Lardner, a particularly talented writer, would not see his name on any list of screen credits for 17 years. But by 1970 his gifts would be valued again; he won an Oscar for work on *M*A*S*H*, an antiwar film ostensibly about the Korean War, but effectively questioning the conflict in Vietnam.

After this trial the atmosphere of fright was so great that a national blacklist was set up not only to deny future employment to the Hollywood Ten but also to keep anyone with questionable political allegiances from working in the media. Loyalty oaths became a part of the American scene, and many less talented and less influential people lost government and teaching jobs—also considered positions of influence. Fortunately for the history of freedom of speech, a panoramic array of gifted writers has recorded many versions of this period of anxiety, labeled "scoundrel time" by playwright Lillian Hellman in her book of the same name (*Scoundrel Time*, 1976). In the future, when scholars and critics collect all such memoirs and compare them, careful research may reveal how much prejudice may have been involved in accusations against intellectuals and New Deal civil servants and whether, indeed, 1930s writers connected with the Communist Party continued to support the Soviet Union.

Although a number of films tried to capture the mood of this decade, two remain classical comments on the emotions of the time. "Friendly witnesses" (the label for those who believed it a patriotic duty to name all the communists they knew) Elia Kazan and Budd Schulberg collaborated on the 1954 prize-winning movie *On the Waterfront*. Awarded eight Oscars, it examined the dilemmas involved in becoming an informer. Kazan acknowledged using his own story in the film to justify his testimony before the House Un-American Activities Committee. In the movie, the informer, whose moral choices are relatively simple, becomes a hero.

A film offering a different viewpoint could be made only at a much later time. In 1976, once-blacklisted artists Walter Bernstein and Martin Ritt wrote and directed the Woody Allen production *The Front*, re-creating the lives of a writer and comedian barred from work during the 1950s. Although there is humor in the delicatessen cashier character who fronts for the talented writer denied his livelihood, the themes of humiliation and loss of self-esteem involved in being blacklisted dominate the film. The comedian, brilliantly played by Zero Mostel, who had himself been a victim of the blacklist, commits suicide. Such despair was real for artists at the time, because their survival demanded audiences. "The great fear," as British scholar David Caute termed the fear of communism in a long book of the same name (1978) on anticommunist purges under Truman and Eisenhower, touched almost every kind of contemporary activity.

To be sure, by the 1990s, when Russian spy files were opened to reveal the Venona documents of deciphered codes passed by the Russian Secret Service, the KGB, to its American agents, there could be no doubt that the American Communist Party had been controlled by the Kremlin. And there was evidence for espionage where many believed none had existed. But the number of actual subversives remained small. In an eloquent 1950 book, *The Loyalty of Free Men*, Alan Barth, a journalist for the *Washington Post*, pointed out that the number of Communist Party members equaled about 1/30th of 1 percent of the population—yet the general hysteria of the late 1940s and early 1950s appeared extreme. In 1954, a famous critic of American civilization, Lewis Mumford, echoed the concerns of some liberals: "In the name of freedom we are rapidly creating a police state; and in the name of democracy we have succumbed not to creeping socialism but to galloping Fascism" (quoted in

Kaledin 2000, 76–78). The "police state" that Mumford feared, however, neither occurred nor persuaded the broad American public (*Daily Life Online*, "Recreational Life: Film," in Kaledin, *Daily Life in the United States, 1940–1959*, http://dailylife. greenwood.com).

HEALTH

During World War II, the huge budget allotted for war—$321 billion from 1941 to 1943—was not focused solely on the creation of weapons. Americans' payroll deductions and defense bonds also went into research that would eventually contribute to the better health of humankind. First, in that research, was a focus on the massive production of antibiotics. Although Sir Alexander Fleming had discovered penicillin in 1928, it was hardly available until a number of scientists and facilities pooled their energies to meet the needs of war. The federal government, using the Department of Agriculture's regional laboratory in Peoria, Illinois, combined the talents of more than 21 companies to produce more than 650 billion units of penicillin a month by 1945—enough to include even some civilian needs. The discovery of streptomycin by Selman Waksman in 1943, subsequently produced by private pharmaceutical companies, demonstrated that cooperation between industry and government remained important during this period, as it had before in the history of American science.

Because private laboratories rarely had adequate money for complex research, government funding given to university laboratories enabled rapid and important discoveries to take place. One historian of medicine commented that the cooperation among university researchers, government support groups, and private industry seemed a unique American phenomenon leading to extraordinary productivity. Other antibiotics produced during the decade included bacitracin, chloramphenicol, polymyxin B, chlortetracycline, and neomycin. By the end of the 1940s almost all known bacterial illness appeared under control. By 1950, John Enders had also succeeded in isolating viruses in tissue culture that would lead to the successful creation of vaccines against polio and other dreaded viral childhood diseases.

Another concentrated wartime effort, the search for synthetic quinine to combat malaria—essential because the Japanese had cut off areas of natural production— also proved successful. Many American troops taking part in the Pacific war became completely disabled by the mosquito-borne illness. One survey from Guadalcanal reported three entire divisions inoperative with malaria. The discovery of the synthetics atabrine and chloroquine alleviated much physical suffering in the South Pacific. Just as important at the time was the mass production of insecticides such as DDT and insect repellents for personal use that wiped out the plague-carrying mosquitoes and body lice. A typhus epidemic may have been averted by those new vermin destroyers. No one thought about disturbing the balanced life cycle involving the other creatures who survived on such insects, nor was there any awareness of other illnesses that human beings could develop from pesticides. What mattered most was saving the lives of soldiers and making their national service as comfortable as possible.

Perhaps one of the most important areas of study to emerge from World War II has been the examination of secondary effects of goal-oriented knowledge. The realization that unforeseen results often arose from the pursuit of focused purposes would become a challenging and legitimate field of study, as well as a source of popular fear—a favorite theme of science fiction.

Along with the antibacterial drugs that for a time ended pneumonia and tuberculosis came the extensive use and production of blood plasma. Death from infection became so rare that between 1945 and 1951, mortality from flu and pneumonia fell by 47 percent. Mortality from diphtheria dropped 92 percent and from syphilis 78 percent. During World War II, research on steroids to relieve arthritic pain also intensified. The discovery of cortisone led to the production of the most complex drug yet manufactured on a large scale. Wartime managerial and production skills became part of the nation's overall approach to health. Along with the 1948 expansion of the National Institutes of Health came the establishment of smaller foundations dedicated to research on specific problems. Only a few days after the bombing of Nagasaki, for example, General Motors—in the names of its directors, Alfred P. Sloan and Charles Kettering—gave $4 million to set up a cancer research center in New York City. Certain kinds of childhood leukemia would be eradicated before the end of the 1950s. Elsewhere new drugs were being discovered to alleviate severe allergies and anxieties and, most important, to combat certain forms of acute mental illness. Chlorpromazine, produced in quantity after the war by Smith, Kline, and French, liberated many individuals who might have spent years in custodial care in mental hospitals.

The rapidity of change can be imagined in the assertion of historian James Patterson that by 1956, 80 percent of all the drugs being prescribed had reached the market only within the past 15 years. Those "miracle drugs" had an immediate impact on the longevity of Americans. Life expectancy reached an average of 69.7 years by 1960, in contrast with 62.9 years in 1940. Women would continue to live longer than men, and whites to live longer than blacks, but wartime medical research unquestionably produced healthier lives for most Americans.

One of the most significant medical breakthroughs of the postwar era occurred when Dr. Jonas Salk discovered an antiviral drug to attack the disease of polio. During the long summers of the 1950s, parents dreaded the potential of their children contracting the disease. Salk, who had spent most of the 1940s working on drugs to inhibit the flu virus, developed an injection to attack polio. In April 1955, that research bore fruit. Initially injected, Salk later found a method to provide an oral polio antiviral pill. By the beginning of the 1960s, one of the most dangerous and debilitating diseases in America had been virtually eliminated. The advances in medicine and drug treatments not only improved public health but also fostered a confidence that technology and science might conquer all maladies and create a utopia (Kaledin 2000, 52–54; *Daily Life Online*, "Intellectual Life: Health and

Medicine," in Kaledin, *Daily Life in the United States, 1940–1959*, http://daily life. greenwood.com).

LITERATURE

Two classic war novels, James Jones's *From Here to Eternity* (1951) and Norman Mailer's *The Naked and the Dead* (1948), remain testimonies to the fighting men of the time as well as skeptical statements about the nature and necessity of war. After *From Here to Eternity* became a movie in 1953, Frank Sinatra, who had been black-listed for using an allegedly communist songwriter, won an Academy Award, which allowed him to make his comeback as a singer. Norman Mailer believed the writer's role was adversarial. As one of America's most gifted authors, he would go on to re-cord a panorama of his country's social dilemmas before shifting to a more allegorical style. Of special interest in connection with the 1950s view of war are the stories of Kay Boyle, whose short fiction documented the rarely articulated lives of members of the occupation army and their army wives.

If Mortimer Adler thought his series of the Western world's great books would continue to determine the best tastes, he was mistaken. Adler perhaps assumed that readers would depend on the classics alone, books that had generally been written by European males. Educated readers began to heed a richer variety of viewpoints. The self-consciousness that emerged from the postwar search for identity no longer neglected the writing of women and people of color—even as talent remained the 1950s criterion for judgment. After the war, a great curtain lifted on the literary scene, revealing a tremendous chorus of new and gifted performers.

The most common generalization about postwar fiction, connecting it with so-cial criticism, is that it was a literature of alienation. Writers of the 1950s depicted individuals who no longer felt part of any community. J. D. Salinger's *Catcher in the Rye* (1951) and Jack Kerouac's *On the Road* (1957) described wayward lives seeking release from the material goals of civilization.

In 1996, some 40 years after its initial publication, Kerouac's *On the Road* sold 110,000 copies, clearly demonstrating that it was not a book for just one decade. In the 1950s, young women writers Carson McCullers, Flannery O'Connor, and Jean Stafford used a growing awareness of independent womanhood to express individual skepticism about social institutions.

Jean Stafford, Eudora Welty, Elizabeth Spencer, and Flannery O'Connor—all proud 1950s writers—made much of place in shaping their characters. During this period many powerful southern writers emerged, following the earlier examples of Allen Tate and William Faulkner, to demonstrate that regional consciousness could teach much about the broader human condition. The plays of Tennessee Williams and Lillian Hellman; the stories of Truman Capote, Gore Vidal, William Styron, Walker Percy, Shelby Foote, and Shirley Anne Grau; and the poetry of Randall Jarrell and Robert Penn Warren helped keep the South a source of creativity. The only defeated section of the United States continued to offer the country impressive talent, adding to the national awareness of class as well as alienation. Searching for different levels of personal identity, the decade's literature offered a rich variety of complex individual worlds rather than established political contexts. The "dissidence from within," as the critic Richard Chase described it, may be "our most useful tradition." "In what other mood," he asked, "has the American mind ever been creative, fresh or promissory of the future?" (1952). Like Norman Mailer, Chase believed that American writers often worked best in opposition to the mainstream culture.

Women writers distinguished by their work in other decades—Edna Ferber, Gertrude Stein, Fannie Hurst, Pearl Buck, Katherine Anne Porter, Elizabeth Bishop, and Marianne Moore—produced some of their best writing during this period. Mari Sandoz's classic biography *Crazy Horse: The Strange Man of the Oglalas* was recognized as one of the best serious books on the West in 1954. Although few women would have labeled themselves feminists during the 1950s, they nevertheless found writing a source of power. Shirley Jackson became a popular writer who managed to capture both the humor and the anxiety involved in domesticity. As her 1947 classic story "The Lottery" was suggestive of the danger of modern witchhunts, so her 1950s stories explored the deep anxieties of homebound women.

In his celebration of the next decade, *Gates of Eden: American Culture in the Sixties* (1977), Morris Dickstein attacked the writers of the 1950s for being too concerned with the "elusive mysteries of personality" and too involved with "craft, psychology, and moral allegory"; yet readers must question whether those qualities do not continue to fortify the human spirit in ways that political attitudes may not. The three-volume unabridged collection of Emily Dickinson's poetry appeared in 1955, suggesting how profound a writer could be without needing to mention the Civil War she lived through. In 1955, another elusive novel of American adventure on the road, Vladimir Nabokov's allegorical classic *Lolita*, was published in Paris. After rejection by five American publishers and much public protest, the story of the older man's obsession with a young girl would be in bookstores in the United States by 1958, on its way to the best-seller list. By the 1990s, *Lolita* would be accepted as a classic. Students of the 1950s fantasizing about what books to take to a desert island or what to read during a long stay in outer space could find a huge variety of satisfying choices to deepen every level of consciousness.

Many of the women writers of the 1950s tackled the social and political issues of the day—even as they delved into personal domestic lives for material. Grace Paley, Tillie Olsen, Hortense Calisher, Harriette Arnow, and Mary McCarthy offered outright challenges to the current definitions of women's roles. The great angry poets of the next decade—Sylvia Plath, Anne Sexton, Adrienne Rich, and Denise Levertov—were all writing away in the 1950s as they took care of their babies. Rich and Levertov would write their roles more specifically as political voices.

Grace Paley and Harriette Arnow made social involvement part of the definition of being human. Gwendolyn Brooks, Ann Petry, Paule Marshall, and Lorraine Hansberry emphasized the distinguished tradition of black women, using their own culture to write about feminism and humanism. Hansberry could imagine a black heroine going to medical school at a time when the idea seemed preposterous. Brooks could write a poem about a journalist witnessing the horrors of Little Rock. In 1950, she won the Pulitzer Prize for poetry. Later Gwendolyn Brooks would be named poetry consultant to the Library of Congress, a job more recently renamed as *poet laureate*.

Strong writers from prewar days were still writing for a large audience. John Steinbeck, John Dos Passos, Eugene O'Neill, and Ernest Hemingway made their opinions heard. In 1952, Steinbeck wrote to Adlai Stevenson, the defeated Democratic candidate, "If I wanted to destroy a nation I would give it too much." In 1954, two years after he published *The Old Man and the Sea,* Hemingway won the Nobel Prize for a lifetime of carefully crafted writing about human courage.

Two of the decade's great men of letters were African Americans; Ralph Ellison and James Baldwin emerged during the 1950s as writers with special evocative skills, not as polemicists. The intensity of their articulation of experiences as black Americans expanded the consciousness of many white readers and inspired a growing tradition of twentieth-century black writing. Playwright Lou Peterson's *Take a Giant Step* opened in 1953 to warm reviews, remaining off-Broadway for 264 performances. Those black artists did not write solely to help African Americans recover their identity. They were well aware of the distinguished writers still on the scene in the 1950s—Richard Wright, Langston Hughes, W.E.B. Du Bois, Zora Neale Hurston, and Jean Toomer. To be sure, many of their insights into the human condition cannot be separated from their racial identity. But as black culture extended into the next decades, black writers spoke to more Americans of every color about the quality of American life. "You are white," Langston Hughes had written, "yet a part of me as I am part of you."

On Broadway a bowdlerized version of Anne Frank's diary helped remind audiences why they had fought World War II. The 1950s became a liberating period for a new generation of American Jewish writers. Saul Bellow, Bernard Malamud, Delmore Schwartz, Philip Roth, and even Isaac Bashevis Singer, who wrote in Yiddish and whose novels were translated into English, spoke to many kinds of Americans in much the same way that Jewish American filmmakers had done at an earlier time. At this moment, when Jews and Catholics were beginning to be accepted on the faculties of elite colleges, gifted Jewish culture critics also emerged to explore their own roles in American civilization. Thinkers like Philip Rahv, Irving Howe, Lionel Trilling, Alfred Kazin, Norman Podhoretz, Diana Trilling, and Leslie Fiedler not only contributed original interpretations of American culture but also celebrated their personal—often ambivalent—success as they became more American than Jewish. They too questioned the good life.

By the 1950s, earlier immigrant consciousness melted into everyone's postwar identity dilemmas. Heroes of contemporary novels, with a sense of ambivalence about all their choices in life, belonged as much to John Updike and John Cheever as to Bellow, Roth, and Malamud. J. D. Salinger's character Seymour Glass is more Buddhist than Jewish. And Kerouac's Catholics also turned to the Zen religions of the East. Norman Mailer would not have been placed with other Jewish writers at the time, nor would Adrienne Rich. Finding out who you were remained one of the exciting mind games of the 1950s, a period when complexity was cherished. The 1947 Broadway musical *South Pacific,* enormously popular throughout the decade and adapted as a movie in 1958, made identity dilemmas seem easy to resolve as *Abie's Irish Rose* (1922), a mixed-culture drama, had done during the vaudeville era. Assimilation remained an attainable ideal in many of James Michener's successful 1950s novels. *Sayonara* (1957) and *The Bridges of Toko-Ri* (1954) also spread Michener's commitment to tolerance to the movies.

A few talented writers opted to drop out of society by becoming part of a drug culture that rejected connections with conventional communities. William Burroughs published *Naked Lunch* in Paris in 1959; Nelson Algren, *The Man with the Golden Arm* in 1947 and *A Walk on the Wild Side* in 1956.

Science fiction writers captured some of the most real social dilemmas of the time in books—as they were doing in original television dramas. Ray Bradbury published his classic on book burning, *Fahrenheit 451,* in 1953—the year before Joseph McCarthy was censured by the Senate. Andre Norton used intergalactic conflict to highlight human values, while Ursula Le Guin and Madeleine L'Engle began writing science fiction that appealed to both children and adults. In 1957, four of the best science fiction writers of the decade—Cyril Kornbluth, Robert A. Heinlein, Alfred Bester, and Robert Bloch—gained respect by lecturing at the University of Chicago.

Writing for young people has been another way for talented individuals to express ideas in a broader context. Helping children adapt to a new postwar world as they developed strong egos and an understanding of democratic choice were a number of distinguished writers who should be honored by the entire society—not just by the readers who award medals to writing for children.

Books for young people, such as Jean Latham's on the doctor Elizabeth Blackwell and the biologist Rachel Carson, not only described women who played roles outside the home but also stressed how they dealt with setbacks. In the 1950s, Ann Petry and Dorothy Sterling both wrote about Harriet Tubman, the fugitive slave who helped many other slaves escape, making the point that black children had too long been deprived of knowledge of the bravery of their own forebears. Elizabeth Yates wrote about Prudence Crandall as a pioneer in school integration at a time when many people, ignorant of the American past, believed such dilemmas began with the *Brown* decision in 1954.

Ann Nolan Clark's long experience in the Bureau of Indian Affairs enabled her to remind 1950s young people of the dignity of the Native Americans' nontechnological civilizations. Rachel Carson introduced children to the wonders of nature by educating their parents in elementary terms about the wilderness resources that many ignored at the time. "When I have something important to say," Madeleine L'Engle wrote, "I write it in a book for children."

During the 1950s, special library rooms for children appeared in many places where mothers worked as library volunteers. Many children discovered E. B. White's *Stuart Little*, which had been a reading pleasure since 1947, and *Charlotte's Web* appeared in 1952 to the delight of Americans of all ages.

The poetry of the 1950s flowered in the midst of consumer delights. Not only did new poetry reflect the expanding consciousness of specific social groups, but a variety of experimentalists appeared, evoking America on many other levels.

Older poets basked in their honors. Robert Frost continued to give readings that celebrated New England as a metaphor for the human soul. T. S. Eliot continued to manicure his British conscience. Marianne Moore, Louise Bogan, and Elizabeth Bishop published collections of distinguished work during the 1950s. William Carlos Williams continued to produce volumes of *Paterson,* comparing a city to a human being. Wallace Stevens, vice president of a Hartford insurance company, managed to offer the decade several magical volumes, and the hospitalized fascist sympathizer Ezra Pound continued to write *Cantos,* a long work of poetic distinction (between 1915 and 1962). e. e. cummings also gathered together a summary of his life and work. John Berryman began to celebrate sonnets.

Gifted young poets emerging at the time included Donald Hall, Richard Wilbur, John Ashbery, Randall Jarrell, Delmore Schwartz, Charles Olson, James Merrill, May Swenson, Denise Levertov, Sylvia Plath, and Adrienne Rich. Frank O'Hara helped shape a school of poets in New York City, and the Poets' Theatre flourished in Cambridge, Massachusetts. Yale University continued to offer gifted unpublished poets the opportunity to see their words in print. Perhaps the general prosperity made it possible for the great variety of new talents to take chances as poets. Visitors to America—chosen home of another great poet, W. H. Auden—could easily assume that this was a country that took poetry seriously.

Indeed, Robert Lowell, the best-known new American poet during the 1950s, quickly made his way into the academic canon, even as he extended his self-awareness into the confessional mode that would characterize much of the next decade's writing. With his solid New England ancestors and obvious talent, Robert Lowell sought a more complex identity in the 1950s. As he exposed his manic depression and his family's quirks in his poetry, Lowell gave permission to a new generation of younger poets to set aside traditions and be themselves.

The most outrageous poet of the decade, Allen Ginsberg would remain identified with the Beat community and its hostility to law and order. As he shocked his listeners Ginsberg insisted on being the heir to Walt Whitman. A poem called "Supermarket in California" addresses Whitman as "lonely old courage teacher" and asks the great poet to tell us where we are going. When Ginsberg read his famous long poem "Howl" in 1955 in a converted auto repair shop, the San Francisco City Lights Bookstore crowd greeted him with foot-stomping enthusiasm. By 1992, the City Lights quarto edition of Ginsberg's *Howl and Other Poems* would be in its 40th edition, with 725,000 copies in print.

The Beats insisted that they stood for more than rebellion against the world of comfort and conformity. They too were trying to define the good life as they expanded America's consciousness. During the 1950s and 1960s, Allen Ginsberg preached love to stunned audiences while taking off his clothes or playing finger cymbals for interminable amounts of time. Identifying with Buddhism even though one of his most famous poems, "Kaddish," was a Jewish prayer for his dead mother, Ginsberg joined Salinger in the long American tradition of looking East for philosophical wisdom. In the dedication to *Howl and Other Poems,* he called Jack Kerouac the "new Buddha of American prose" and asserted that Neal Cassady's biography enlightened Buddha. A distant neighbor in Paterson, New Jersey, William Carlos Williams, wrote a brief introduction to the text, recognizing that "this poet sees through and all around the horrors he partakes of."

Writing of America, wondering if his country would ever be angelic, Ginsberg wanted his love to show. Yet, his disappointments spoke to many of his followers even as his gentle spirit transcended the vocabulary that shocked. By the early 1980s, Allen Ginsberg had become so respected as a representative of America's counterculture that the State Department sent him all over the world as an ambassador of freedom.

When Ginsberg died in 1997, his poetic vigor and personal kindness were honored in every community where poetry mattered. Harvard professor Helen Vendler noted that Ginsberg was a liberator. For many young people, Vendler suggested, Ginsberg offered "the first truthful words ever heard." "How beautiful is candor," his American ancestor Walt Whitman had written—allowing Allen Ginsberg to continue a legacy of free expression touching every social and erotic experience.

"The real question"—asked by a dying friend of writer Grace Paley and included in the dedication to her collected stories—"How are we to live our lives?" was asked many times during this decade. The 1950s offered up no easy answers. Levittowners, black urban migrants, atomic scientists, victims of blacklists and victims of quotas in professional schools—all struggled to define themselves in an affluent world that offered many the freedom Allen Ginsberg represented. Artists in other media also found that this moment offered time to explore new ideas and individual talents (Kaledin 2000, 155–62; *Daily Life Online,* "Intellectual Life: Literature," in Kaledin, *Daily Life in the United States, 1940–1959,* http://dailylife. greenwood.com).

SCIENCE: THE ATOMIC BOMB

After World War II, science and scientists became closely related to the federal government, especially with the development of nuclear science and space exploration. Not only did hundreds of scientists devote their careers to advancing the scientific goals of the federal government, but they also became the subject of government investigation. Anyone involved with specialized military knowledge always needed scrutiny. In the decade after the war, the case that embarrassed the entire country was that of J. Robert Oppenheimer, former director of the Manhattan Project (which developed the atomic bomb). After his success at Los Alamos, America valued Oppenheimer as the man whose energies created the bomb that ended the war. He became a national hero and in 1948 appeared on the cover of *Time* magazine. A new professional journal, *Physics Today,* also displayed his picture on its first issue—in spite of Oppenheimer's having put aside his career as a research physicist to build the bomb. As head of the Manhattan Project, he experienced no doubts about his status, but the intellectual depth that made him question future atomic wars and oppose the development of the devastating hydrogen bomb turned Oppenheimer, in many eyes, into a security risk.

Edward Teller, a physicist enthusiastic about building the "Super"—as the new hydrogen bomb was called—blamed Oppenheimer for alienating the best scientists from working on the project. Because of the witch-hunting atmosphere, the tensions among scientists and government officials in 1954 were extreme. When Oppenheimer went before the House Un-American Activities Committee (HUAC) in 1949, the young Richard Nixon had praised him for his candor. In 1954, however, the government moved to strip Oppenheimer of his security clearance. Always naive about politics, the great physicist had confessed to past left-wing beliefs and communist associates. Yet, those ideas had not been held against him as director of the Manhattan Project. Suddenly, his opposition to the H-bomb made Oppenheimer a target for spy hunters who wanted to define all disagreement as treason. Oppenheimer's trial, a series of hearings before the Atomic Energy Commission, remains a scar on the history of American justice. With abundant personal detail David Halberstam captures its intensity in *The Fifties*: "There hadn't been a proceeding like this since the Spanish inquisition," he quotes David Lilienthal, former head of the Atomic Energy Commission (AEC).

The H-bomb in action. Library of Congress.

The hearings against him left Oppenheimer stunned. Although the most distinguished scientists in America testified on his behalf, the government's judges paid no heed. After a lifetime of eloquence, Oppenheimer wilted. He could no longer be "the powerful witness for freedom of scientific opinion" his friends had expected him to be. At that moment, as one journalist reported, the great scientist appeared sadly as a man "diminished by tiny misdeeds from the past." Edward Teller's calculated praise of Oppenheimer's patriotism ended with implications that he was no longer fit to protect the vital interests of the country. In April 1954, the AEC voted two to one to deny security clearance to the man who had enabled the United States to build the atomic bomb.

Meanwhile Harry Truman had already gone ahead with the construction of the hydrogen bomb. He had never shared Oppenheimer's doubts about using the atomic bomb. He knew he had done the right thing. Moreover, Truman listened to political advisors, not to scientists. In March 1954, the United States made a series of hydrogen bomb tests at Bikini Atoll in the Pacific, spreading radioactive ash over 7,000 square miles and inadvertently harming a boatful of Japanese fishermen 80 miles away (Kaledin 2000, 81–82).

FOR MORE INFORMATION

Barnouw, Erik. *Tube of Plenty: The Evolution of American Television*. 2nd ed. New York: Oxford University Press, 1990.

Caute, D. *The Great Fear: The Anti-Communist Purge under Truman and Eisenhower*. New York: Simon and Schuster, 1978.

Chaplin, Charlie, dir. *The Great Dictator*. 1940.

Chase, R. "Our Country and Our Culture (Part 3)." *Partisan Review* (Sept./Oct. 1952): 567–69.

Cremin, L. *American Education, 1876–1980: The Metropolitan Experience.* New York: Harper and Row, 1988.

Halberstam, David. *The Fifties.* New York: Random House, 1993.

Hart, J. D. *The Oxford Companion to American Literature.* 6th ed. New York: Oxford University Press, 1995.

Jowett, G., and J. M. Linton. *Movies as Mass Communications.* Beverly Hills, CA: Sage, 1980.

Kaledin, E. *Daily Life in the United States, 1940–1959: Shifting Worlds.* Westport, CT: Greenwood Press, 2000; also online as *Daily Life Online,* in Kaledin, *Daily Life in the United States, 1940–1959,* http://dailylife.greenwood.com.

Marling, K. A. *As Seen on TV: The Visual Culture of Everyday Life in the 1950s.* Cambridge, MA: Harvard University Press, 1994.

Patterson, J. T. *Grand Expectations: The United States, 1945–1974.* New York: Oxford University Press, 1996.

Ravitch, D. *The Troubled Crusade: American Education, 1945–1980.* New York: Basic Books, 1983.

Rybczynski, W. *Waiting for the Weekend.* New York: Viking, 1991.

Shorter, E. *The Health Century.* New York: Doubleday, 1987.

Sklar, R. *Movie-Made America: A Cultural History of American Movies.* New York: Vintage Books, 1975. Rev. ed., 1994.

Spring, J. *The American School, 1642–1993.* 3rd ed. New York: McGraw Hill, 1994.

Whitfield, S. J. *The Culture of the Cold War.* Baltimore, MD: Johns Hopkins University Press, 1991.

Material Life

OVERVIEW

Every culture has sought forms of material comfort as a significant aspect of daily life. The basic needs of food and shelter, by definition, require specific expressions of materialism to accomplish those goals. The desire to accumulate material possessions existed in American daily life from the colonial beginnings of the society, and the aspects of evolving materialism are examined in previous volumes in this series. During the Great Depression and World War II, various factors limited the amount of material possessions Americans could acquire. Since free market societies tend to provide basic and superficial possessions on "supply-and-demand" purchasing, people need personal income in order to secure those material goods and products. The 1929 Depression resulted partly from a drop in consumer demand. Wholesale and retail inventories had tripled between 1927 and 1929, leaving warehouses and retail store shelves filled with unsold goods (material). As a result, cutbacks in production to deal with the surplus led to unemployment and a rapid shut-down of the American economy. Effectively, the supply-and-demand curve had produced too much supply and too little demand. While early New Deal efforts to correct that problem sought to control and coordinate production, costs, and employment, the fundamental causes and consequences of the free market system remained unresolved well into Franklin Roosevelt's second term (1937–1941). Unemployment remained high and production had not rebounded from the fundamental impact of the 1929 collapse in the market economy. Much of the success of the New Deal centered on developing programs that accepted the basic concept of supply and demand, recognized that downturns in the economy would occur, and aimed to put in place policies to soften that "natural" condition. Programs like Social Security, the Federal Deposit Insurance Corporation (FDIC), and others did not aim to prevent a depression; they were put in place to assist Americans who might confront a future depression.

WORLD WAR II, 1940–1945

As noted above in the Economic Life section, the beginning of World War II saw a massive government commitment to revitalize American industry in order to wage war. Government defense contracts put the factories, businesses, and people back to work. "Rosie the Riveter," and millions of others, built the largest industrial war machine, to that point, in history. While that effort certainly helped win World War II, and while it ended unemployment in the United States, America's production resources did not aim at material goods and products for daily consumption. The resources of production focused on warplanes, naval vessels, guns, ammunition, and supplies for the U.S. military and America's allies. Between 1940 and 1944, unemployment in the nation dropped from 8 percent to less than 1 percent. For the first time since 1929, Americans could count on paychecks and the ability to purchase needed material items to make their lives better. Ironically, the commitment to military production, not consumer goods, made it difficult, if not impossible, to buy things.

At the same time, the government instituted a series of rationing laws. The Food Rationing Program began in 1942. Americans usually went to their local public school, one person per family, provided some details on family numbers and other information, and received War Ration Books. "Red Stamp" books provided a limited amount of purchases for butter, meat, cheese, and cooking oil. "Blue Stamps" enabled people to purchase frozen fruit and vegetables, canned and bottled food and drink, and beans. Gasoline rationing came through a different book. Some businesses developed novel products to make access to food easier. Oleomargarine became a substitute for butter in many homes. Kraft made a macaroni and cheese product that served as a replacement dinner for hard-to-procure meat and vegetables. In both an expression of patriotism and necessity, many American families began to grow their own fruit and vegetables in "victory gardens" to supplement hard-to-buy commodities. Store owners might keep their businesses open on weekends and for evening hours, which they did during the war, but Americans found little time to shop and rationing imposed limitations in any event. As with all restrictive programs, people inevitably found ways to break the law and get around the system. Black market selling of rationed items began almost as soon as the Food Rationing Program went into operation. When rationing finally ended in 1946, millions of Americans knew where to go to buy goods and products without their ration books, and they had the money to do so.

POSTWAR CONSUMERISM AND MATERIALISM, 1945–1959

The end of the war created a unique series of conditions that impacted significantly on material life in America. Denied access to a broad range of goods and products since the Depression, people were eager to buy new things. Given the full employment of the war years, they had the money to do so. Business, industry, agriculture, and government recognized that demand for material goods now far exceeded supply. Military contracts had provided businesses with the capital to reinvest into the production of consumer products (private materialism), and new technologies enabled them to shift from wartime production to peacetime material goods and services fairly easily. Consumerism and materialism became, then, synonymous terms in the postwar generation. Housing and automobiles tended to take center stage as explosive expressions of the new materialism.

Appliances

When Vice President Richard Nixon challenged Soviet premier Nikita Khrushchev at a trade fair in Russia in 1959, he did not argue that Americans had little poverty, nor did he champion the civic freedoms that define American democracy. Instead he made a big issue of American consumer production for easier living. Later called the "kitchen debate," because the two men hovered about a model American kitchen set up in a model home for fair visitors, the confrontation gave Nixon a chance to bombard the Russians with statistics on American consumption. He boasted that 30 million American families owned their own homes and that 44 million families owned 56 million cars and 50 million television sets—awesome evidence, he insisted, of the success of democratic capitalism. The average working man, Nixon asserted, could easily buy the split-level house on display. He noted also that women bought an average of nine dresses and suits and 14 pairs of shoes a year, trivial statistics that made Khrushchev furiously retort that Americans were just interested in surfaces, gadgets, and obsolescent machines. Khrushchev did not pick up on the fact that America's huge defense industry continued to subsidize many consumer goods. Were Americans just self-indulgent pleasure seekers? Karal Ann Marling, in her challenging book *As Seen on TV: The Visual Culture of Everyday Life in the 1950s* (1994), depicted the kitchen as a symbol of the domestic culture of the 1950s. The model on display in Moscow appeared designed around new family values—even though such values reached deep into a past where oven, hearth, and warm food traditionally suggested security. Marling suggested that the several kitchen models sent to Moscow were more than just gadgetry, providing "a working demonstration of a culture that defined freedom as the capacity to change and to choose." By the end of 1959, women comprised over a third of the American workforce. Whether they worked to pay for new appliances or because new appliances gave them more time for self-fulfillment remains a middle-class issue. It has taken decades for Americans to acknowledge that many women have no choice about working outside the home. Their wages contributed to rent or mortgage payments and helped pay for their children's basic needs.

The escape into different levels of consumerism was real in postwar America for the great number of people with good jobs. Five years after the war was over, the amount spent on household furnishings rose by 240 percent. Four years after the war, Americans bought 20 million refrigerators and 5.5 million stoves. The icemen who once delivered large blocks of ice to put in wooden chests became a memory and part of American folklore. To many people, the well-furnished domestic nest supplied stronger moral protection from the bomb than the official shelters a few continued to buy. In her carefully documented book *Homeward Bound: American Families in the Cold War Era* (1988), Elaine Tyler May used the word "containment"—the same word government officials used to define America's relationship with the Soviet Union—to define the lives locked into the domestic scene during the period from 1946 to 1960, when real income rose by 20 percent.

The advances in air conditioning also enhanced technical materialism in the postwar era, both in homes and businesses across the nation. Willis Haviland Carrier, a Cornell University engineer, had begun to design and patent forms of air conditioning systems in the early 1900s, and by the 1920s and 1930s, factories and even movie theaters had installed various systems. After World War II, it became commonplace for stores and businesses to install cooling units, particularly in the American South and Southwest. Homes and automobiles began to use air conditioning widely in the 1950s. In 1946, Americans purchased 30,000 portable air conditioners, and, by 1953, that number had reached more than a million. Containment, as Elaine Tyler May described homes in America in the 1950s, may have had some ironic reference to the Cold War, but more accurately, air conditioning may literally have protected Americans from hot summers. The broad material impact, both commercial and domestic, that air conditioning had on American daily life was enormous.

Most of the appliances created for the American home during those years—washing machines, blenders, toasters, electric razors, dishwashers, power mowers, even television sets—were simple in design to accord with a world in which people did their own household chores. Although wild colors came into the kitchen, and airplane models influenced some industrial architects, the basic domestic designs of the period reflected functional European modernism. In fact, certain classics of industrial design, like the sleek chairs fashioned by Charles and Ray Eames, became part of a rebirth of aesthetic awareness emphasizing function and simplicity. Distinguished industrial architects and artists like Eero Saarinen and Raymond Loewy began to make their work available on a grand scale. Indeed, the most elegant of the period's new appliances remain in the collections of the Museum of Modern Art in New York City and in the Smithsonian collections in Washington, D.C.

The new emphasis on style in personal material surroundings also made choosing furnishings time-consuming and socially challenging. Taste started to be graded in popular magazines—few people wanted to be middlebrow when either highbrow or lowbrow items could suggest individuality and character. The ubiquitous picture window—sensibly created so that mothers could keep an eye on children from inside—also allowed neighbors to evaluate each other's home furnishings. If prewar furniture manufacturers could not always make the costly new styles available rapidly and cheaply, there was, nevertheless, no shortage of canvas butterfly chairs or curved boomerang coffee tables. As many as five million wrought-iron butterfly chairs were manufactured at the time, copied from the original basic Knoll chair designed as an example of excellence in inexpensive furniture.

Easy portability as well as functional design remained another mark of a period when many Americans moved as often as every year. Historian Thomas Hine remarked that a feature of the "populuxe" age was that everything had handles or appeared easy to lift. The demand for informality and flexibility supported the invention of small portable appliances. Nothing stayed in its traditional place: washing machines were in the kitchen and television sets were in the dining room. Many carried their entertainment to the beach or office. Portable radios, ancestors of the boom box, began to intrude on parks and even on public transportation.

By the end of the decade, push-button products defined a new life. Even if a cook did not know the difference between "puree" and "liquefy," the blender appeared to take over all drudgery. Ads showed women talking on the phone as their wash whirled behind glass in a nearby machine, but they did not urge those women to learn new skills in their free time or offer them more stimulating lives. Too often, "labor-saving" devices led simply to more labor in the home. No-iron fabrics and synthetic casual clothes made it easier for women to do all their own laundry. When market researchers discovered that women also wanted to feel useful, they urged producers to leave out essential ingredients in packaged mixes so that good wives could feel they were adding something of themselves to their family's lives when they baked a cake. Betty Friedan's 1963 classic *The Feminine Mystique* also helped women to recognize how extensively they were being manipulated to consume (Kaledin 2000, 121–23).

Clothing

While Americans found new ways to buy and eat food in the years following World War II, clothing styles also saw a shift in material needs and interests. At the end of the war, traditional clothing saw men in suits, ties, and hats. The "man in the gray flannel suit" seemed to dictate a basic, conservative style of clothing that defined the conservative nature of the 1950s.

Just as hairstyles for men remained short (crew cuts, etc.) and their faces clean shaven, the color of their suits and shirts and shoes offered the same basic style. Certainly, men bought more clothes than in the past. Again, affluence and middle-class employment tended to require more. Materialism was not just something people wanted; it was often something the socioeconomic culture expected. Women wore calf-length dresses and high heels when stepping out, and they enjoyed the ability to purchase nylon stockings, the new synthetic material that was cheaper than silk. The garment industry was able to copy high-fashion women's clothing designs from Paris dress designers like Coco Chanel and Christian Dior and reproduce copies at retail cost in stores like Sears and Roebuck and J. C. Penney's. American women could buy more dresses and other items to fill the closets of their new suburban homes. Shoes and other accessories added to their closets. Marketing clearly encouraged people to buy more, suggesting persuasively that the guarded, anxious years of the Depression and war had ended, at least materially.

The noteworthy change in clothing habits began with the emergence of a teenage culture, with its own spending potential. Prior to the 1950s, parents tended to establish clothing styles for their children. By the beginning of the new decade, with more money, new music, and movie idols of their own and an inclination to rebel, American teenagers heralded a new materialism in their clothing purchases. James Dean's portrayal of an "average" teenager in *Rebel Without a Cause* (1955) served as a sartorial icon of the new generation of young adults.

Gregory Peck stars in *The Man in the Gray Flannel Suit*. 20th Century Fox/The Kobol Collection.

Leather jackets (although Dean wore a red, cotton zippered jacket), Levi's blue jeans, and sneakers or penny loafers adorned the new idols of teen fashion, unless they added motorcycle boots to go with the leather jackets. Hair was longer (ducktails and sideburns), and the young men often kept a pack of cigarettes in the rolled short sleeve of their t-shirts. Teenage girls opted for poodle skirts, blouses, saddle shoes, and ballet slippers. Cardigan sweaters became part of the young high school girl's apparel as well. James Dean and Natalie Wood (his co-star in the film) personified the look and the style, but other teenage heroes also influenced clothing styles. Soon, the influence of casual clothes and styles among American teenagers began to affect the way their parents dressed. The suburban backyard barbecues and the long drives on the new interstate highways made comfortable clothes more appealing. The new washing machines made cotton fabric easier to clean than sending clothes to a dry cleaner. And new casual styles simply became part of a more casual lifestyle in the late 1950s. For these and other reasons, adult men and women began to alter their clothing styles as well and add new types of clothes to their wardrobes.

If James Dean's influence motivated teenagers, Katharine Hepburn's choice to wear slacks in her films influenced American women as well. A style of "preppy" (loosely defined upper-middle-class prep school styles) comfort clothes influenced a different direction in selection. Mail order stores like L.L. Bean in Freeport, Maine, had

Hollywood actress Terry Moore epitomizes 1950s women's fashion. The Kobol Collection.

mailed camping gear and clothing to people who hunted and fished for years. Suburban men and women began to order their khaki slacks and Norwegian fisherman sweaters as a regular addition to their wardrobes. Jean LaCoste, the French tennis star, marketed a new short-sleeved tennis shirt with a unique emblem on its front. The "alligator" shirt (actually it was a crocodile, LaCoste's nickname) became popular with affluent American men who saw their local country club pro shops stocked with the item. At the opposite end of the affluent, preppy, country club set, a "beatnik" culture offered another alternative dress style. The trend in American clothing increasingly suggested a more comfortable, less formal style of dress in every part of the culture. Variety had begun to replace orthodox requirements in dress and fashion, and the changes that began in urban and suburban America spread throughout the country.

Marketing

The high priests of American materialism had established their temples along Madison Avenue in New York. The advertising and marketing agencies on that famous avenue became powerful purveyors of the postwar consumer culture and a dominant force in persuading people what they should purchase. Advertising products had existed in the United States and elsewhere for centuries. During the 1800s, newspaper and periodical advertisements for a broad variety of goods and services helped create more than 20 advertising agencies on Madison Avenue by the beginning of the American Civil War. The business of selling products to consumers grew rapidly in the twentieth century. In the 1930s, United States Steel and General Motors created their own public relations departments to work with ad agencies to sell their products. The War Advertising Council coordinated U.S. public relations programs during World War II, marketing everything from War Bonds to enlistment posters, propaganda, and security messages. By the end of the war, powerful advertising agencies like Young & Rubicam and J. Walter Thompson had established multimillion dollar businesses in New York. Their account executives competed for a host of clients, businesses willing to purchase space in magazines and newspapers or time on radio to sell their products to American consumers.

The Edsel, the car Ford could not sell. Library of Congress.

When television surfaced as a new medium of attraction, advertisers flocked to the sets with their messages. Advertising agencies developed the ads, sold the time or space to print or other mediums, and monitored the effect the ads had on public interest. By 1947, J. Walter Thompson sold $100 million in advertising revenues. CBS radio and television became the largest purchaser of advertisements in the nation. In 1952, advertisers used the new Nielsen ratings to determine what shows Americans watched on their television sets and billed advertising time accordingly. Agencies hired sociologists and psychologists to study market interest and public attitudes. Dr. Ernest Dichter, the president of the Institution for Motivational Research, maintained that a successful agency "manipulates human motivations and desires and develops a need for goods with which the public has at one time been un-familiar . . . perhaps even undesirous of purchasing" (http://www.trivia-library.com/ahistoryofadvertising).

Few American consumers were left out of the message. Children confronted a series of advertisements on Saturday morning television as they watched cartoons. Toys and cereal ads sought to persuade the youngsters to entice their parents to buy particular brands at the new supermarkets or toy stores. Afternoon soap operas encouraged women to use the right laundry detergent or bathroom soaps. Sports programs offered men new brands of razors and shaving cream or beer. As bathroom medicine cabinets filled with a host of new products, kitchen cupboards with cereal brands, and driveways in suburbia with cars hot off the assembly lines from Detroit, Madison Avenue went about its clever and expensive campaign.

While periodicals and newspapers remained a continuing source of advertising revenue, and while radio sought to carve a particular market for advertising dollars, television became the new darling of the industry in the 1950s. Thirty- and sixty-second spots, neatly filmed and produced for television, filled a nice gap in programming. In many cases entire hour-long programs attracted one company's advertising. In 1951–1952, 4 of the top 10 television programs had a single sponsor's title. By the end of the decade, advertising had become too expensive, and businesses could no longer afford the cost of supporting a program alone. In popular, important books like Vance Packard's *The Hidden Persuaders* (1957), the author attacked the advertising industry as a manipulative force in the United States, pushing the materialism and consumer-driven culture of the decade. The powerful ability of ads to form taste and purchasing desires created concern among a host of critics and observers. Yet, Americans seemed able to withhold their dollars and enthusiasm from the most intense advertising when they decided that the product failed to impress them. The classic examples of that marketing calamity emerged during Ford Motor Company's effort to market and sell their new model *Edsel* in 1957. An advertising campaign costing millions of dollars could not attract car buyers to the new model, and it remains a stark example of consumer resistance no matter what the effort to have them buy the product.

Food

If the human need for food remains a necessity, the shift in material access to food products changed significantly following World War II. Traditional neighborhood "mom and pop" grocery stores, in cities and small towns, gave way to a growing demand for supermarkets. In the 1920s, initial self-service stores like Piggly Wiggly and A&P opened their doors to customers looking for convenient, one-stop shopping. The large retail stores offered a variety of food products and household items under one roof, with convenient parking for cars and dependable hours of operation. After the war, with the growing move to the suburbs, supermarket chains expanded rapidly. The addition of frozen and processed foods as convenient items stocked in new systems of refrigeration allowed consumers to select from a broad variety of goods. Meat, produce, and dairy products could be kept cold and displayed in larger volume,

A young boy surprising Santa Claus as he takes a bottle of Coca-Cola from the refrigerator, ca. 1945. Library of Congress.

along with canned and packaged foods. By the 1950s, a number of chain stores had opened throughout America. Wholesale food producers could deliver larger quantities of goods, in refrigerated trucks, to the supermarkets, and customers came to depend on a wide variety and amount of food and other products to purchase in one location.

By 1957, food producers had introduced more than 5,000 new products into the stores. As an example, American consumers purchased 400 million frozen chicken pot pies in 1958. Examining the postwar growth of consumer–material culture in American daily life, it remains essential to consider the abundance of food products available to people living in the United States. Critics have suggested that processed and frozen food diminished both the health and quality content of supermarket selections. Americans settled on quick, tasteless food that lacked nutritional value as they rushed through their local supermarkets doing their weekly shopping. Consumers also saw large corporations enhance their control of the distribution of products and their marketing in everything from boxed cereal to canned goods. Some concern existed as to the ability of the Pure Food and Drug Administration (FDA) and the U.S. Department of Agriculture (USDA) to monitor the safety of the products going into the stores. Yet, by the end of the 1950s, the expansion of supermarkets in America had made more food products available to more people, at less cost, than ever before in history. The system appeared here to stay.

If Americans continued to have their meals at home, they also began to eat out more often in the postwar era. New technology in kitchen appliances and access to supermarket convenience certainly made home food preparation easier, but Americans also exhibited an interest in going to restaurants more often than in the past. Clearly, the affluence of the emerging middle class helped prompt the trend. At the same time, the transient nature of wartime travel and separation from families required Americans to find meals outside their homes. Again, neighborhood restaurants, coffee shops, malt shops, and other types of eating establishments offered people everything from quality dining experiences to hamburgers and sodas. Horn and Hardart had opened its chain stores as early as 1902, serving prepackaged food in slots in glass enclosures that could be retrieved by placing a coin in the appropriate slot.

"Food-to-go" options had developed as early as 1921, when *White Castle* began to sell hamburgers for five cents. A series of *White Castle* chains grew throughout the 1930s and 1940s. The revolution in fast food occurred when Ray Kroc purchased a hamburger and milk shake shop in San Bernardino, California, in 1954. Kroc noted that the store owners, Richard and Maurice McDonald, had ordered milk shake machines in large quantities, suggesting clearly that the owners were doing a lot of business. He recognized the potential bonanza in fast-food sales, bought the name McDonald's from the original owners, and began the history of the McDonald's fast-food empire. Kroc envisioned a systematic preparation of fast food, reasonably inexpensive, ready to go, and predictable in quality. In simple terms, whether you went into a McDonald's in Keokuk, Iowa, or Bangor, Maine, a customer could expect the same hamburger, the same milk shake, and the same French-fried potatoes for the same price. Nutritional value didn't matter. Americans developed a taste for the new fast food restaurant for these reasons. By 1961, McDonald's had established the system of production and preparation, franchised its restaurants nationwide, and made the "Golden Arches" the most ubiquitous and recognized business symbol in the country. Other fast-food franchises followed suit.

At the same time as fast food, food to go, and processed food entered the American market, so too did a variety of "comfort food" and ethnic options. Potato chips topped the list of preferred comfort food for Americans, followed by ice cream, cookies, and candy. Chips probably evolved in the mid-nineteenth century at a lodge in Saratoga, New York, but they were not mass marketed until after World War II. Sealed bags replaced tin cans to hold the crisp potatoes, and, in the 1950s, Joe Murphy developed a method to season the potato chips with salt. Under the brand name Tayto, his small company soon attracted a host of copycats, and supermarkets and restaurants filled with bags of chips. The same type of material marketing developed for other forms of comfort foods as well. Freezers in supermarkets and better refrigerators in homes allowed shoppers to purchase prepackaged ice cream to transport from store to house easily. Bags of candy and cookies, which different companies offered on market shelves, emerged in the 1950s and continued to expand in variety. The popularity of comfort food seemed simple. It tasted good. Critics warned that the food had almost no nutritional benefit and probably was unhealthy for people. Heavy in carbohydrates, refined sugar, and other chemicals, the items did little but please the palate. That was enough! The traditional meat and potatoes diet of Americans (also apparently bad for one) had begun to succumb to a host of options and tastes.

Ethnic food also surfaced after World War II as a varietal form. While urban neighborhoods in cities, and rural and regional recipes elsewhere, had always offered different and unique forms of food, the national marketing of ethnic foods became popular in the 1950s. Pizza and Chinese food topped the list. Tomato sauce and mozzarella cheese oven-baked on flat bread with herbs had existed for centuries in Italy, and the item had come to America with immigrants in the early 1900s. Small pizzerias or pizza shops operated in ethnic neighborhoods throughout America, often developing different styles and types of offerings. In 1943, Pizzeria Uno opened in Chicago to sell deep-dish pizza. It is still in business. Mass marketing and franchise pizza restaurants did not appear until the 1960s, but pizza, as a comfort food, had become a staple of American cuisine in the decade and a half following the war.

Chinese restaurants evolved from the numerous immigrants who came to the United States in the nineteenth century and settled in "Little China" neighborhoods in American cities, particularly in the far West. By the mid-twentieth century, such restaurants existed throughout the United States. Every city and town of size in the country had a version of Chinese food available in small establishments, usually family owned, serving everything from legitimate Chinese food to versions of American Chinese options like chop suey and egg rolls. Boxed containers of rice, noodles, mixed vegetables, and some wok-fried meat became staple take-out food in the 1950s.

Through the broad evolution of different food options in the postwar period, from food-to-go restaurants, to frozen food options in the new supermarkets, to a growing interest in ethnic food, American regional menus and options remained. Southern cookouts and picnics featured fried chicken and corn bread. New Englanders cherished their lobster and clambakes. New Yorkers could relish a corn beef on rye at a Jewish delicatessen, and a wide variety of regional, ethnic, and cultural foods continued to appeal to Americans in the era of consumer-material conventionality. The broad, general affluence of the postwar generation made food consumption a matter of taste and choice as much as a condition of mass marketing and prepackaged convenience.

Housing

Housing and the necessities of life also changed during the war for American families. A dramatic housing shortage developed during World War II, and prices for buying or renting homes and apartments rose significantly. In 1940, the average home cost $3,900 and apartment rentals were $30 a month. Salaries averaged $1,800 a year. By 1945, apartment rents had doubled, housing costs had risen by almost 20 percent, and salaries had only increased by $600. To respond to the housing dilemma, the National Housing Agency developed a "Share Your Home" program, asking Americans to volunteer space in their homes for others. Almost 1.5 million families did so. The federal government also built a number of low-cost housing developments that provided around two million new residences.

 *Snapshot*

Cost of Living: 1940

Sugar, 6 cents for 10 pounds; Milk, 51 cents a gallon; Coffee, 42 cents a pound; Eggs, 19 cents per dozen; Hamburger, 15 cents a pound; Bread, 8 cents a loaf.

Source: Remember When (Millerville, TN: Seek Publishing).

Similar increases in the cost of food, clothing, and other domestic needs had also risen proportionately. Rationing continued to confront Americans with day-to-day problems in their domestic life. Most agreed to the necessity of rationing essential items for the war effort, but the government-issued ration books for such items as meat, butter, sugar, and gasoline made shortages at home a serious concern. The books had to be presented when purchasing items and the tickets inside limited the amount Americans could procure. Certainly, Americans fared better than people experiencing worse access to domestic goods in other countries, but rationing became an inconvenience during the war. As always, people found ways to get around the law and the ration books. A black market economy grew, and many Americans, particularly toward the end of World War II, took advantage of the opportunity (*Daily Life Online*, "Material Life: Housing," in Kaledin, *Daily Life in the United States, 1940–1959*, http://dailylife.greenwood.com).

The "Other America"

African Americans and Hispanics witnessed an ambivalent evolution in their domestic lives during World War II. Certainly job opportunities expanded significantly, and demographic shifts in population became noteworthy. The number of black workers rose from under three million to almost four million in the industrial North and Midwest.

As black Americans moved from the rural South to the urban North, their domestic life changed. Racism continued throughout the war regardless of location. The military services remained segregated as well. Pay, housing, and available domestic services, including schooling for children, never approached the access that white families had. The domestic shift in living conditions for American minorities ultimately led to racial tension and confrontation.

The *bracero* program was a binational temporary labor contract that the United States and Mexico initiated in 1942. The program was designed to increase the number of Mexican workers in the United States. The influx of Mexican workers produced similar racial tensions in the United States. In June 1943, as an example, riots broke out in Los Angeles, as white sailors attacked Mexican Americans, ostensibly because of the clothes the young Latino males wore. The so-called "Zoot-suit" riots lasted five days.

Japanese-American children heading for internment. Library of Congress.

The worst example of domestic differences in America during the war occurred with the internment of Japanese Americans. Certainly, their domestic lifestyle during the war differed dramatically and tragically from other Americans. The December 7, 1941, attack on Pearl Harbor had created a growing demand for the removal of all Japanese Americans from the West Coast of the United States. Under pressure, President Roosevelt signed Executive Order 9066 approving Japanese internment.

More than 100,000 Japanese Americans, men, women, and children, were removed from California, Oregon, Washington, and other states. They lost their property, businesses, and homes. By 1942, the War Relocation Authority had interned the Japanese Americans in 10 camps. The Supreme Court in *Korematsu v. United States* (1944) upheld the constitutionality of the internment. The domestic life of those interned Japanese Americans certainly differed from others living through the war. Ironically, a Japanese American division fighting in Italy during the war received more combat decorations than any other unit in the Italian campaign.

World War II had changed both perspective and practice in American domestic life. It had created jobs and money but also rationing. New opportunities for movement and relocation existed, but the anxiety and tension that arose with that condition evolved. Children may have been caught up in the excitement of the war, with scrap drives and victory gardens, but their lives could be disrupted and devastated by moving, divorce, or the death of a loved one in the war. Women certainly had access to newer, perhaps better, employment opportunities, but the work placed stress on their family lives and called into question their "traditional" or "orthodox" role in marriage and family. Of the 17 million Americans who served in World War II, 405,000 died and 670,000 were wounded. Most of those casualties were men. Those who had lived through the war would be returning relatively quickly to peacetime and domestic responsibilities. The women and children had also changed, confronted with a new world of domestic opportunity, responsibility, and challenge. The war had changed all of them.

The demand for housing to fit new lives—to accommodate all the Americans who moved during the war or needed a place to put a new family—was again eased by financial help from the government. In 1949 congressional subsidies helped build low-income urban housing, and many universities built temporary housing for the huge number of new students coming to school under the GI Bill.

The GI Bill helped returning veterans get mortgages as well as educations. A great variety of developments in single-family homes appeared in the suburbs. Between 1945 and 1955 some 15 million housing units were constructed in the United States, leading to historic highs in home ownership. Before World War II would-be homeowners often had to offer down payments as high as 50 percent to buy a house, promising to pay the rest in periods of as short as 10 years. With the GI Bill some veterans put down nothing at all, and others offered a token one-dollar down payment with long-term mortgages. Also important was the wide-scale adoption of the self-amortizing mortgage that fundamentally altered the lending business and made it possible for millions of Americans to become homeowners in the postwar era.

After 1947 changes brought about by the Federal Housing Administration, working with the Veterans Administration, made available mortgages of up to 90 percent with interest rates as low as 4 percent—and with periods as long as 30 years to pay off the debt. By 1960, 60 percent of all Americans owned their own homes.

By 1950, these two government agencies also insured 36 percent of all non-farm mortgages; by 1955 they handled 41 percent. The suburbs that grew out of governmental generosity became the market for the new consumerism, demonstrating once again the interdependence of public and private forces shaping the lives of every class. Federal income taxes, withheld from salaries for the first time in 1943, continued to be deducted during the postwar period. People gladly maintained the New Deal tradition of tax-provided public services, such as twice-a-day mail deliveries and, at the local level, services such as street cleaning.

The same technological and production skills that fired United States defense efforts were turning 1950s America into a world of new things. Consumerism made it as easy to be distracted from the Russian menace as it was to ignore the one-third of the population that remained outside of the generally flourishing economy, the "other America" Michael Harrington clearly defined in 1962.

In the years between 1950 and 1970 the suburban population more than doubled, from 36 million to 74 million. People enjoyed living in the mortgage- and building-subsidized communities exemplified by Levittown. In the 1950s the "typical

American" lived in suburbia. Everywhere groups of people established new roots with the help of money saved during the war from higher salaries and War Bonds. If people shared no past experiences with new neighbors, they could still manage to focus on the future of the children most of them had in great numbers. Community efforts to build playgrounds, libraries, schools, swimming pools, and baseball diamonds brought many families together who did not know each other before the war.

The flight to the suburbs remained difficult for blacks. Although over a million African Americans managed to move away from the inner cities after 1950, by 1970 the suburban population still remained 95 percent white. Even though it was true that the American dream of family security embodied in home ownership was more possible than ever before, it was clearly not available to everyone. A gifted journalist and historian, Thomas Hine, described the period between 1954 and 1964 in his book *Populuxe* (1986). Hine pointed out that the number of better-paying jobs running or maintaining new machinery was increasing faster than the number of low-paying jobs was declining. The average industrial wage for white men had doubled since pre-Depression days, and health insurance and paid vacations allowed many working-class people to see themselves as middle class. No longer made up of small proprietors, much of this new middle class, which even included service workers, was employed by large corporations. Because of the smaller number of Depression-born adults, more wealth was shared by fewer people.

Liquor

The consumption of alcoholic beverages has seemed a pervasive aspect of American history since colonial times. Europeans brought the cultural and social traditions of drinking to the Americas, and that aspect of daily life has continued to the present day. Evidence suggests that Americans drank more in the eighteenth and nineteenth centuries than they do in modern times. Certainly concerns about the social dangers of excess drinking prompted the rise of the temperance movement in the mid-1800s. By the beginning of the twentieth century, a number of states had banned the sale of alcohol. In 1919, the Volstead Act prepared the way for the 18th Amendment. In 1920, the U.S. government banned the manufacture, transportation, and sale of alcoholic beverages throughout the nation. While the law pleased temperance advocates, it led to some serious unforeseen consequences. The acerbic writer H. L. Mencken reportedly noted that "Americans were the most law abiding people in the world, so long as they agreed with the law." Prohibition apparently did not fall into that category. Speakeasies, bootlegging, and organized crime syndicates became commonplace responses to the law as Americans in the 1920s found a variety of ways to circumvent restrictions.

In 1933, the 21st Amendment repealed the 18th. President Franklin Roosevelt, frankly, enjoyed a martini (gin and vermouth) as a favored afternoon cocktail. Throughout World War II, the nation resumed its cultural affection for alcohol. Beer, wine, and hard liquor resumed a legal presence in local and neighborhood bars and restaurants and in American homes. A number of states retained laws prohibiting the sale and consumption of alcohol, but the "noble experiment," as

1949 Lincoln Convertible. Courtesy of Jolyon Girard.

1956 Ford Victorian. Courtesy of Jolyon Girard.

Herbert Hoover defined national prohibition, had ended. Like food and other material options in American life, liquor followed a similar pattern of postwar development. Mass marketing of beer made it a standard advertised product on radio, television, and magazines, particularly on aired sports programs. The evening cocktail served as a predinner social habit in millions of American middle-class homes. Sophistication, marketed in magazines like Hugh Hefner's *Playboy*, suggested that not only drinking but also what one consumed, defined style and class. Food and drink, in American daily life, became another broad example of materialism as consumers added beer to their refrigerators and more hard alcohol to expanding liquor cabinets. Affluence and variety continued to dictate American material tastes.

Transportation

America's postwar attraction to automobiles seemed both functional and emotional. The growth of suburban living, the government's construction of interstate highway systems, and the simple luxury of owning a car stimulated the automotive industry to produce and sell millions of new cars in the decade following the war. In 1945, Americans bought 69,500 new cars. A year later, purchases topped two million. By 1949, auto makers sold over five million new vehicles. And the numbers kept increasing. The auto industry reported 6.7 million new sales in 1950 and almost 8 million by 1955. Almost 40 million families registered more than 40 million new cars in 1950 (Kaledin 2000, 55). The boom in purchases turned the Detroit-centered automotive industry, both its corporate management and its labor unions, into one of the most powerful enterprises in postwar America. At the same time, it helped create a host of new subsidiary enterprises that became profitable companies. The oil industry, trucking, road construction, motels, shopping malls, even drive-in movies all grew and prospered with the expanding sales of automobiles. At the same time, car use threatened other businesses. Bus and train transportation began to slowly, then rapidly decline as a method of travel for Americans.

Greyhound and Trailways bus companies saw a loss of business and routes as more Americans took to the highways in their $1,300 new Fords or Chevrolets. Trains and busses also lost customers as a result of the new consumer use of air travel as a long-range transportation option. The develop-

1957 Ford Thunderbird. Courtesy of Jolyon Girard.

ment of jet engines at the end of the war, and their application to commercial planes, enabled the planes to fly higher and faster, above the turbulent weather patterns at lower altitudes. That made air travel safer and more comfortable. By the end of the 1950s major American airline corporations provided a method of transportation previously reserved for the wealthy and privileged.

FOR MORE INFORMATION

Evans, S. *Born for Liberty: A History of Women in America*. New York: Free Press, 1989.

Galbraith, John Kenneth. *The Affluent Society*. Boston: Little Brown, 1958.

Harrington, Michael. *The Other America: Poverty in the United States*. New York: Macmillan, 1962.

Hine, T. *Populuxe*. New York: Knopf, 1986.

Kaledin, E. *Daily Life in the United States, 1940–1959: Shifting Worlds*. Westport, CT: Greenwood Press, 2000; also online as *Daily Life Online*, in Kaledin, *Daily Life in the United States, 1940–1959*, http://dailylife.greenwood.com.

Marling, K. A. *As Seen on TV: The Visual Culture of Everyday Life in the 1950s*. Cambridge, MA: Harvard University Press, 1994.

May, E. T. *Homeward Bound: American Families in the Cold War Era*. New York: Basic Books, 1989.

Patterson, J. T. *Grand Expectations: The United States, 1945–1974*. New York: Oxford University Press, 1996.

Tennyson, Jeffrey. *Behind the Arches*. New York: Bantam Books, 1986.

Wright, G. *Building the Dream: A Social History of Housing in America*. New York: Pantheon, 1981.

Political Life

THE ERA OF FRANKLIN ROOSEVELT

Between 1940 and 1945, President Franklin D. Roosevelt (popularly known as FDR) dominated American political life. Most Americans recognized FDR's profound influence on both the Depression and U.S. involvement in World War II. What the New Deal accomplished most successfully was the restoration of faith in the power of government to help individuals—those forgotten men and women who worked hard but could not manage to support their families. No manuscript collection is more moving than the file of letters collected in Eleanor Roosevelt's archives in the Roosevelt Library at Hyde Park from needy people asking for small loans of money until they could get on their feet again. Eleanor Roosevelt acted as Franklin's eyes and ears as she traveled all over the country to help the New Deal become synonymous with concern for human dignity. The creation of Social Security, workers' compensation, and higher income taxes for the rich, along with guarantees that workers could strike for fair wages, among several New Deal programs and reforms, demonstrated respect for the American worker, even if a number of political promises fell short of fulfillment. Called "a traitor to his class," the patrician FDR made his commitments the source of loyalty for many blue-collar workers. The 31 "fireside chats" he gave on the radio made him a father figure to many who thought of the Roosevelts (both Franklin and Eleanor) not as politicians but as moral leaders. Although people at the time never saw pictures of Roosevelt in a wheelchair or realized just how physically helpless he was (no one talked about disabilities), most Americans knew about his bravery in reentering politics after surviving polio. His overpowering smile and his sense of humor won him admirers all over the world, and his aristocratic self-assurance—enriched by Eleanor's great social awareness—proved exactly what the country needed to inspire a national turn from provincial isolationism to global power.

President Roosevelt, as the leader of the Democratic Party, had also created a powerful political coalition of various interest groups in the United States that enabled him and his party to exercise control of the White House and the Congress between 1932 and 1946. He attracted labor union voters, minorities, and ethnic-urban Americans and managed to hold the southern Democrats to the party by providing a number of programs and policies that benefited their interests. Ironically, he shifted African

A sailor and a nurse kiss in Manhattan's Times Square, as New York City celebrates the end of World War II, 1945. AP/Wide World Photos.

American voters to his party while, at the same time, providing few viable benefits in the area of civil rights. That omission enabled him to hold white southern segregationists as Democrats even while Eleanor Roosevelt sought avidly to work with black leaders in support of their causes. Ultimately, African American voters left the Republican Party for the party of FDR largely because they believed that the New Deal programs promised them more in access to jobs, training, housing, and other vital needs than Republicans offered. As a "broker politician," FDR's political legacy remains noteworthy.

In a 1999 prizewinning book, *No Ordinary Time: Franklin and Eleanor Roosevelt: The Home Front in World War II*, Doris Kearns Goodwin documented how amazingly popular FDR's radio speeches were. A May 1941 talk designed to alert the nation to the possibility of a national emergency got a 95 percent favorable response from the more than 65 million people in 20 million homes who listened. When popular comedians such as Bob Hope and Jack Benny appeared thrilled to have a listener rating of 30 to 35 percent, Roosevelt attracted radio audiences of over 70 percent. The only other broadcast that even approached FDR's for listeners was the audience for the Joe Louis–Max Schmeling world heavyweight boxing match in 1938—an encounter that seemed symbolic of battles to come.

Uncle Sam—World War II recruiting poster. Library of Congress.

The paternalism of the New Deal made it easier for many to accept the new constraints on freedom that preparation for war demanded. Price controls and gasoline and food rationing, blackouts and air raid drills, limits on travel, censorship, and security clearances were all part of the war world that took over the New Deal in 1941. "Loose lips sink ships" declared a poster plastered in coastal towns, reminding ordinary people that everyone was involved in winning a war. Along both the East and West Coasts, citizens prepared for attacks from enemy submarines or bombers. Communities set up first-aid stations, and even junior high children trained with Red Cross manuals to learn simple survival techniques. Air raid drills in schools were conducted with buddy systems so that older children became responsible for smaller ones in reaching makeshift shelters or simply hiding under designated tables. Looking back on those moments as the New Deal was replaced by the push to win the war, older Americans found it hard to reconstruct that reality of fear. More often, they cherished the orderliness of the daily tasks that made them feel useful to the country as a whole. The New Deal raised America's self-confidence.

In 1944, Roosevelt broadcast his State of the Union message to Congress as a fireside chat, because so few newspapers would print the entire message. What FDR suggested sought to extend the original commitments of the New Deal into the country's wartime role in the world. A "basic essential to peace," he asserted, "is a decent standard of living for all individual men and women and children in all nations. Freedom from fear is eternally linked with freedom from want." As he went on to define America's role as one that would not repeat the tragic errors of isolationism, FDR made sure that people understood the need for firm inner discipline and well-organized government to control profiteering and social injustice.

In that speech, FDR not only recommended a specific set of new laws to control the cost of living and equalize the burdens of taxation, he also set up what he called a "second Bill of Rights," based on the belief that "true individual freedom cannot exist without economic security and independence." The rights he defined and connected with the war and with the needs of the entire world might not be as "self-evident" as FDR believed in the 1940s, but they will remain worthy of serious consideration. Roosevelt wanted "all" (in his introduction he did not say "all men," but rather "all—regardless of station or race or creed") to have the right to a useful and remunerative job, the right to a decent home and food and clothing, and the right to medical care and a good education. He also included protection for farmers and businessmen from monopolies and unfair competition abroad, and he articulated once again the concern to provide for the economic insecurities of old age. Always the main agenda of Eleanor Roosevelt's articles, lectures, press conferences, and columns, the bill of economic rights FDR wanted to guarantee—the nation understood—also remained his wife's first priority. Seeking to clarify the dreams of the New Deal for the rest of the world, FDR concluded the 1944 chat with a reminder that "unless there is security here at home, there cannot be lasting peace in the world" (Kaledin 2000).

Children who grew up in the midst of World War II gathered a sense of self-esteem from the many small roles they played to help win the peace. In Vermont, schools provided bags for gathering milkweed pods to replace the no longer available kapok fibers used for warmth and padding in jackets; in New York children collected fats used for making explosives. All over America young people saved tinfoil, flattened tin cans, and enjoyed squishing little yellow buttons of color in white margarine to make it look like rationed butter. Many children bought and sold 10-cent defense stamps, purchases that represented real sacrifice at the time, as 10 cents could also pay for an entire matinee at the movies, with short serials, cartoons, and two feature films included.

Mothers who had been convinced that being housewives was their only true profession often did both volunteer and paid work to contribute to the war effort. They labored in hospitals, knitted afghans (blankets), and helped plot and identify aircraft in undisclosed places all over American cities. Many women were proud to take jobs in defense plants doing "men's work" and to find themselves making higher wages than ever before. By the end of the war, a rare group of women pilots were even flying huge bombers to destinations all over the world.

In one of his remarkable collections of interviews with Americans who lived through significant moments of American history, *"The Good War": An Oral History of World War II*, author Studs Terkel recorded the impressions of a number of citizens who for the first time in their lives felt free of intense competition to survive. To a lesser extent, that same experience became true on the home front: "It was the last time most Americans thought they were innocent and good without qualifications." One man noted, "It's a precious memory. . . . That great camaraderie of savin' tinfoil, toothpaste tubes, or tin cans, all that stuff made people part of somethin', that disappeared" (Kaledin 2000).

That sense of community also developed in parts of the army where people felt what it was like to work together for the same goals for the first time in their lives.

One ex-soldier told Terkel they were in a tribal sort of situation where they helped each other without fear. The absence of economic competition and phony standards created for many men a real love for the army. Many defense industries refused to give African Americans higher-paying jobs until Roosevelt issued an executive order mandating equality. Although the armed forces themselves, at the time, were bastions of racism, as several of Terkel's black citizens reported, people *had* to learn to work together. The dream of equal rights became part of the incentive for fighting a war against countries that made national ideals of inequality. Wartime belief in cooperation to win seemed more than simple propaganda. Another man Terkel interviewed remembered that the whole world seemed absolutely mad—people were in love with war.

Feeling they were part of something important enhanced the lives of soldiers of all ages. One man recalled those moments of need when others were there to help him as the high point of his entire life. Civilians felt similar connections. A journalist whose patriotism led him at age 14 to lie about his age to get a job in an arms plant felt that he would have done anything for the president. When he was able to join the navy at 18, he told Studs Terkel he was sure "there was right and there was wrong and I wore the white hat" (Terkel 1984).

HARRY TRUMAN'S FAIR DEAL AND THE MARSHALL PLAN

Harry S Truman, a former Missouri senator, was elected as Roosevelt's fourth vice president and succeeded him in office when FDR died in April 1945. Faced with the monumental challenge of ending World War II (victory in Europe in May 1945) and the particular decision to use the atomic bomb to end the war against Japan (August 1945), the new president confronted a variety of difficult postwar issues. George Kennan, a career foreign service officer in the American embassy in Moscow, alerted the president and his secretary of state, George Marshall, to the new threat of a postwar confrontation with America's World War II ally, the Soviet Union. Between 1945 and 1947, Kennan developed a long-range policy (defined as "containment") to challenge the Russians.

In June 1947, George Marshall announced the new American response at a Harvard University commencement address. The so-called Marshall Plan would commit millions of dollars to revitalize the economies of western Europe and confront the Soviets in that region. It became the initial basis for a growing Cold War strategy against perceived Russian expansion. The plan received the bipartisan support of the Congress, and Senator Arthur Vandenberg (R-Michigan) shepherded the necessary legislation through the Congress. President Truman also sought to continue some of the commitments of the New Deal in his domestic policies. By executive order, he eliminated racial segregation in the military and in all federal offices. He also proposed legislation to provide a new program for medical support for Americans. While Republican majorities in the Congress blocked many of his proposals, Truman did seek to continue his predecessor's drive to "promote the general welfare." President Truman narrowly defeated his Republican opponent, Thomas Dewey, in 1948 in an upset victory that stunned most political pundits. The Korean War (1950–1953), however, harmed Truman's influence and popularity, and the rise of Senator Joseph McCarthy and the "Red Scare" of the 1950s took center stage in American politics.

THE DECADE OF DWIGHT EISENHOWER AND MCCARTHYISM

President Dwight D. Eisenhower and wife Mamie at home in Gettysburg, Pennsylvania, 1952. Library of Congress.

As much as Roosevelt dominated the years from the Great Depression through World War II, Joseph McCarthy, a senator from Wisconsin, seemed to influence the decade of the 1950s. Politically, the period following World War II was different from the New Deal era as government solutions became suspect and as the government sought to destroy communists at home and abroad. The term McCarthyism, which now appears in the dictionary and is defined as "the political practice of publicizing accusations of disloyalty or subversion with insufficient regard for evidence" (*American Heritage Dictionary of the English Language*, 1969), was applied to that battle against leftists, including those who had helped the New Deal. In other words, Senator McCarthy made a political career of attacking the accomplishments of the Roosevelt years. McCarthy shared Richard Nixon's hostility toward those who were running the State Department, which he claimed was infested with communists. He boasted a list of 205 State Department spies, but when challenged to produce proof McCarthy changed his accusation to "bad risks" and lowered the number to 57. Later Senator Millard Tydings of Maryland offered McCarthy $25,000 to convict just one actual employee of the State Department. McCarthy never collected the money.

The country looked for scapegoats to compensate for Russia's Cold War aggression and for the loss of China to communist ideology. McCarthy came up with Owen Lattimore, a Johns Hopkins University professor and China scholar who would call his memoir *Ordeal by Slander*. Lattimore retired to England after being accused of spying for Russia. John Stuart Service, a State Department China desk expert in the 1940s who favored withdrawing U.S. support from Chiang Kai-shek, was fired in 1951 on trumped-up charges. The simple idea that ridding America of communists at home would cure world tension and purify democracy appealed to many. By the end of 1950, Congress had also passed the Internal Security Act, also known as the McCarran Act, to register all communists, strengthen espionage and immigration laws, and set up detention camps for spies and saboteurs in case of emergency. As early as 1947, the *American Legion* magazine boasted that the House Un-American Activities Committee had not summoned any farmer, workman, or "common man." Without exception, the legionnaires pointed out, the suspect people examined were college graduates, Ph.D.s, summa cum lauds, and Phi Beta Kappas from Harvard, Yale, Princeton, or other great colleges. Such dominant populist sentiments made it easy for Dwight Eisenhower to defeat the "egghead" Adlai Stevenson, who ran a sophisticated campaign against him in 1952. A professor at the University of Utah commented on Stevenson's defeat, "A whole era is ended, is totally repudiated, a whole era of brains and literacy and exciting thinking."

Senator Joseph McCarthy. Chaiba.

Most Americans disagreed with that assessment, as Dwight Eisenhower's victory in the election indicated. Eisenhower, the much admired former general who led the Allied victory in Europe, had capitalized on his military credentials to end the conflict in Korea and ensure American security. His campaign also effectively used television to promote the "I like Ike" candidacy. Eisenhower was a man of his time (Kaledin 2000).

After the tremendous Eisenhower landslide in the presidential election of 1952, the Republican-dominated Senate made McCarthy head of his own committee on government operations. He had been reelected by a margin of more than 140,000 votes. Immediately, McCarthy sent two young assistants, Roy Cohn and G. David Schine, on a whirlwind tour of U.S. Information Services abroad that ended with the banning of "books, music, painting and the like" of any communist or fellow traveler. Included were books by Henry David Thoreau and Foster Rhea Dulles, an anticommunist professor who was a cousin of the secretary of state. Ordered to remove dangerous thinkers from libraries, some custodians actually burned books. Many librarians lost their jobs. Eisenhower openly criticized that outrage at a graduation speech in June 1952 at Dartmouth College: "We have got to fight Communism with something better," he declared, "not try to conceal the thinking of our own people." But the president did not countermand McCarthy's directive.

The Wisconsin senator seemed as out of control as a forest fire in a high wind. He made outrageous accusations and bullied innocent people to try to establish guilt by association or past connection. Such irresponsible behavior caused a fellow Republican, Margaret Chase Smith from Maine, to present to the Senate "A

J. Edgar Hoover. Library of Congress.

Declaration of Conscience," signed by six other brave Republicans. She gave her "Declaration of Conscience" speech on June 1, 1950: "I don't like the way the Senate has been made a rendezvous for vilification, for selfish political gain at the sacrifice of individual reputations and national unity," Smith proclaimed. "The American people are sick and tired of being afraid to speak their minds lest they be politically smeared as Communists." She concluded with a common sentiment: "I want to see our nation recapture the strength and unity it once had when we fought the enemy instead of ourselves" (Congressional Record, 82nd Cong., 1st Sess.). In 1952, Smith's name had been put in nomination for vice president by approving Republicans, although she did not receive the nomination.

Yet McCarthy seemed unable to stop. He did not even hesitate to accuse General George Marshall, wartime chief of staff and later secretary of state, of being a longtime communist sympathizer, although it was Marshall's economic plan for rebuilding Europe that kept much of the West out of communist control. Perhaps for party solidarity, Eisenhower tolerated many of McCarthy's antics, but he responded to the attack on Marshall by declaring the general a distinguished patriot—"a man of real selflessness." He went on to assert, "I have no patience with anyone who can find in Marshall's record of service to this country cause for criticism."

By 1951, many Americans began to agree with Harry Truman that Senator McCarthy was an asset to the Kremlin. Adlai Stevenson, twice the Democratic presidential nominee, commented that "perhaps this hysterical form of putrid slander...flourishes because it satisfies a deep craving to reduce the vast menace of world Communism to comprehensible and manageable proportions." Stevenson also noted the damage done to freedom: "We have all witnessed the stifling choking effect of McCarthyism, the paralysis of initiative, the discouragement and intimidation that follow in its wake and inhibit the bold, imaginative thought and discussion that is the anvil of policy."

When McCarthy took on the rest of the army, people speculated it was because his protégé, G. David Schine, had been denied special status when drafted, bringing his flashy political career to an end. Not only did McCarthy once again come up with no proven communists in leadership positions in the U.S. army beyond one sympathizing dentist, but he also flaunted his bullying tactics on camera before the American people. In 1954, the Army–McCarthy hearings provided 35 days of riveting television performances demonstrating the new medium as a strong force for exposing truth. No doubt remained about McCarthy's cruel character as he browbeat witnesses and lawyers alike. A documentary film, *Point of Order,* released in 1964 by Emile De Antonio, shows how offensive McCarthy's performances were. In 1954, after eight years of destructive misuse of senatorial authority, McCarthy was condemned by the Senate by a vote of 67 to 22, for misconduct. Through their representatives the American people made clear that they had had enough of profitless ranting. Three years later McCarthy would be dead of acute hepatitis. Yet the anxiety about communism lingered in underlying fears of what the Russians might be up to in the postwar world. As late as 1958, 300 subscriptions were canceled when *Esquire* magazine published an anti-McCarthy article.

THE ARMS RACE, THE DRAFT, REGIONAL SECURITY, AND THE MILITARY-INDUSTRIAL COMPLEX

The developing bipolar tension between the United States and the Soviet Union following World War II altered seriously the daily lives of Americans as the government created a variety of new policies and initiatives to respond to the tension. As the Russians created their own atomic weapons in the late 1940s, a nuclear arms race began between the two "superpowers." During the decade of the 1950s, more deadly weapons emerged in the nuclear arsenal (hydrogen bombs) to escalate the tension and danger. Both nations, and other states as well, increased their stockpiles of nuclear weapons in an ever-expanding nuclear arms race. Delivery systems became equally important. Bomber aircraft served as the primary source, but technical development of missiles and submarines added a triad (including bombers) of potential delivery options for nuclear weapons. By the end of the 1950s, the United States and the Soviet Union had placed hundreds of nuclear weapons into their arsenals, and Americans confronted the daily danger of a nuclear holocaust.

The Cold War prompted other influences on Americans' daily life. In 1950, the United States instituted a peacetime draft. The law required 18-year-old males to register with the Selective Service Administration as the nation moved to create a large peacetime military force to confront the Soviet Union on a global scale. The National Security Act of 1947 created the National Security Council (NSC), combining the Defense Department, State Department, and Central Intelligence Agency as an advisory body. The NSC had determined that George Kennan's policy of containment and the Marshall Plan were insufficient to confront the dangers of Soviet expansion. The Korean War (1950–1953) also convinced American policy makers that the nation needed to challenge Russia in a global contest that required military as well as economic responses. Accordingly, the United States signed a series of regional security treaties to defend U.S. and Allied interests across the world. The North Atlantic Treaty Organization (NATO) in 1949, the South East Asia Treaty Organization (SEATO) in 1954, and several additional treaties in other regions brought the nation into a number of military defense pacts. Thousands of American servicemen, drafted in the 1950s, became "global police," serving in outposts from Europe to Japan and from the Middle East to the Pacific. Ironically, Secretary of State John Foster Dulles defended the expansion of nuclear weapons in the American arsenal by arguing that they were cheaper, both economically and socially, than drafting more American young men to confront the massive conventional forces of the Soviet Union. In colloquial terms, those deadly weapons provided "more bang for the buck."

The social impact of the draft saw hundreds of thousands of young Americans serving two- and three-year enlistments that required basic training and deployment not only to bases in the United States but throughout Europe, Asia, and elsewhere.

A generation of American families became accustomed to that required service for their young men. The draft did not end until Richard Nixon's administration in the 1970s and the creation of the so-called all-volunteer army.

During the 1950s, the federal budget devoted more than 50 percent of its revenues to defense, an enormous increase in spending and commitment that Americans had never experienced in peacetime. Those demands on the economy placed an increased emphasis on research and development (R&D) in military technology and saw the evolution of corporations and businesses devoted to the production and distribution of military weapons and systems of defense. Traditional peace advocates and other concerned citizens in the United States had begun to question the wisdom of the nation's expanding military and nuclear commitment. The National Committee for a Sane Nuclear Policy (SANE) claimed 25,000 members at the end of the decade. A Student Peace Union organized in 1959, even while Reserve Officer Training Programs (ROTC) existed on most American college campuses to train commissioned officers to serve in the military.

Delivering his Farewell Address in January 1961, President Eisenhower, a lifelong military officer, worried about the evolution of a "military-industrial complex" that had emerged during his administration. He noted that its impact, "economic, political, even spiritual—is felt in every city, every statehouse, every office of the federal government." Eisenhower continued, "The potential for the disastrous rise of misplaced power exists and will persist. We must never let the weight of this combination endanger our liberties or democratic processes" (Faragher 2000, 838).

THE ROSENBERGS: A CASE STUDY

The trial of Julius and Ethel Rosenberg, the final significant communist trial of the McCarthy era, reached beyond the United States. The whole world commented on the capital punishment meted out to the "atomic spies," who were also parents of two small boys. Their execution seized the literary, mythic imagination and continues to haunt the definition of American justice. Even many who believed in capital punishment were appalled at the lack of moderation in the justice system that sent the Rosenbergs to their deaths with so little concrete evidence against them.

The British atomic physicist Klaus Fuchs had acknowledged in 1950 that he stole atomic bomb plans from Los Alamos. He served 9 years of a 14-year sentence in a British prison. Yet, in the United States, anticommunist fervor became so fierce that the Rosenbergs—whose messenger roles for an allegedly similar theft were much less certain—were executed. Later evidence made it clear that Ethel knew almost nothing about her husband's role. The government had arrested her as a bargaining chip to get more information from him. But, the Rosenbergs' refusal to cooperate with the justice system remained their undoing.

Years later, in March 1997, Alexander Feklisov, a retired KGB agent who had had frequent direct contact with the Rosenbergs, told the *New York Times* that the couple had given Russia no useful information at all about the atomic bomb. Although

Julius had given away some military secrets during 50 or so meetings between 1943 and 1946—when Russia was also our military ally—Feklisov claimed that Ethel was completely innocent. He thought she probably knew of her husband's activities but added, "You don't kill people for that" (Benson 1996).

Convicted mainly on the testimony of Ethel's brother, David Greenglass, who had worked on the bomb, the Rosenbergs appeared an affront to the American myth of family solidarity. The press, instead of revealing the couple's affection for each other and their concern for their little boys, dehumanized them as robot-like Soviet ideologues. That practice continued even after the Rosenbergs' executions when their collected letters were edited to exclude homey details like their passion for baseball and music and the sustenance they found in their Judaism. To be sure, the Rosenbergs were unrealistically committed to communism as a means to making a better world, but in 1942, a freer time, a *Fortune* magazine poll revealed that as many as 25 percent of all Americans considered themselves socialists and another 35 percent were open-minded about socialism. Just a few years earlier, the dogmas the Rosenbergs accepted would never have brought about such extreme punishment. Yet, the dogmas of the man who passed judgment upon them seemed equally distorted. Judge Irving R. Kaufman, perhaps afraid of being labeled soft toward fellow Jews, accused the couple of "a crime worse than murder" in putting the atomic bomb into the hands of the Russians. When Eisenhower denied the Rosenbergs clemency, it was because he too believed they had increased the chances of atomic war and "exposed to danger literally millions of our citizens." He ignored the pleas of Pope Pius XII and the 40 members of the British Parliament who had joined the pope in urging leniency. Jean-Paul Sartre, a powerful French philosophic voice, called the executions "a legal lynching that covered a whole nation with blood."

Whether the Rosenbergs' deaths made Americans feel more secure or merely heightened their anxiety is worth debating. What is certain is the role that the Rosenbergs began—almost at once—to play in the literary imagination. They joined abolitionist John Brown, slave rebel Nat Turner, and anarchists Sacco and Vanzetti as characters in the mythology of American martyrs. As scapegoats, as government pawns, as intellectual outsiders, the Rosenbergs would find literary definition in such works as E. L. Doctorow's novel *The Book of Daniel* (1971) and Robert Coover's *The Public Burning* (1977) and in the poetry of Adrienne Rich and Sylvia Plath. The 1990s drama by Tony Kushner, *Angels in America,* would present a confrontation between Ethel Rosenberg and Roy Cohn, Senator McCarthy's aide, who boasted of getting her executed. "You could kill me," Ethel tells him, "but you couldn't ever defeat me."

Prominent liberal culture critics Leslie Fiedler and Robert Warshow reflected the general public's hostile attitude toward the doomed couple. Falling in with the consensus of Cold War intellectuals, they made it clear that there could be little humanity in people who pursued the rigidity of communist ideology. Recent evidence does indicate that the Rosenbergs were involved in minimal espionage, but whether the punishment fit the crime remains an ongoing matter of debate.

In 1990, *Ethel: The Fictional Autobiography* by Tema Nason created a brave characterization. A movie version of *The Book of Daniel* (1983) attempted to make her sympathetic—unfortunately, not by remembering Ethel as she was but by turning her into a compliant blonde. Tony Kushner's Ethel may well have captured her most essential traits. Students trying to evaluate this trial and what it meant for the United States must look into *Invitation to an Inquest: A New Look at the Rosenberg and Sobell Case* (1968) by Miriam and Walter Schneir (Kaledin 2000, 5–8, 83–86).

THE SUPREME COURT AND *BROWN V. BOARD OF EDUCATION*

While Americans may have focused their attention on news dealing with the Cold War, Joseph McCarthy's rants against "pinkos" and other subversives in the government, and the Rosenberg case, the United States Supreme Court issued a powerful opinion against segregation in the *Brown v. Board of Education* case (1954). It served as the most significant judicial opinion regarding race and segregation since the late nineteenth century. In 1896, in *Plessy v. Ferguson,* the justices had agreed to permit "separate but equal" accommodations for white and black Americans in a Louisiana issue involving public transportation. As a result, racial segregation became commonplace, especially in the South, in a variety of public venues, including schools, theaters, restrooms, and even water fountains in public parks. In the postwar South, still populated by more than half the nation's 15 million African Americans, segregation remained an oppressive, sometimes violent issue. The lawyers of the National Association for the Advancement of Colored People (NAACP), led by Thurgood Marshall, had begun a series of legal challenges questioning the laws of segregation. The cases tended to focus on examples of less than equal conditions, but Marshall sought to attack the entire concept of segregation regardless of equality of available services.

The *Brown* case involved six challenges to racially segregated schools, brought together in the federal docket. Brown referred to a suit that Oliver Brown filed on behalf of his daughter, Linda, with the local NAACP office in Topeka, Kansas. The youngster had to walk past a white school to attend her segregated school. Combining the issue with other earlier cases, Marshall went before the Supreme Court in 1952. Chief Justice Fred Vinson and the associate justices seemed interested but unconvinced. When Vinson died, President Eisenhower appointed Earl Warren, the former governor of California, to his place. Marshall found a more sympathetic ally in Warren.

Using evidence that Professor Kenneth Clark (an African American psychologist) provided Marshall, he argued that the very nature of segregation developed a negative self-image among black children. Clark had used a collection of black and white dolls as examples. He showed them to schoolchildren, and, in virtually every instance, both black and white youngsters identified negative stereotypes when shown black dolls and positive ones when shown white dolls. Along with other social science evidence and arguments, Marshall persuaded the justices, and Earl Warren utilized his political skills to convince all members of the court to issue a 9–0 decision on May 17,

1954, so as to give the decision collective force and encourage its acceptance. The chief justice summed up the majority report as follows: "Does segregation of children in public schools solely on the basis of race . . . deprive the children of minority groups of equal educational opportunity?" He answered, "We believe that it does" (Faragher 2000, 854).

Effectively, the *Brown* decision had struck down *Plessy v. Ferguson* and challenged institutional segregation as a violation of civil rights in America. In *Brown II*, in 1955, the court left it to local school districts and federal judges to work out desegregation plans "with all deliberate speed." While southerners seized on that vague timetable to stall any real compliance, they also organized resistance to prevent voluntary desegregation. Still, with the imposition of the *Brown* decision, its method and purpose encouraged other groups to push for civil rights and respect.

The Supreme Court joined the postwar African American civil rights movement with full force. During the next decade, the nation would engage in a critical, often violent struggle over the implementation of the law. President Eisenhower, less than supportive of the decision, felt compelled, however, to send federal troops to Little Rock, Arkansas, in September 1957, when that state's governor, Orval Faubus, defied a court order to integrate Little Rock's Central High School. The issue at every level of government and politics dwarfed the concern Americans had shown over Cold War concerns like McCarthyism and the Rosenberg trial. By the end of the 1950s, the fight for civil rights for African Americans had become a central factor in American political life (*Daily Life Online*, "Political Life: Government," in Kaledin, *Daily Life in the United States, 1940–1959*, http://dailylife.greenwood.com).

FOR MORE INFORMATION

Benson, Robert Louis. *The Venona Story*. Washington, DC: National Security Agency, 1996.

Coover, R. *The Public Burning*. New York: Viking Press, 1977.

Doctorow, E. L. *The Book of Daniel*. New York: Random House, 1971.

Faragher, John Mack, Susan Armitage, Mari Jo Buhle, and Daniel Czitrom. *Out of Many: A History of the American People*. Upper Saddle River, NJ: Prentice Hall, 2000.

Goodwin, D. K. *No Ordinary Time: Franklin and Eleanor Roosevelt: The Homefront in World War II*. New York: Simon and Schuster, 1999.

Kaledin, E. *Daily Life in the United States, 1940–1959: Shifting Worlds*. Westport, CT: Greenwood Press, 2000; also online as *Daily Life Online*, in Kaledin, *Daily Life in the United States, 1940–1959*, http://dailylife.greenwood.com.

Kennedy, David M. *Freedom from Fear: The American People in Depression and War, 1929–1945*. New York: Oxford University Press, 1999.

Kushner, T. *Angels in America: A Gay Fantasia on National Themes*. New York: Theatre Communications Group, 1993.

Patterson, J. T. *Grand Expectations: The United States, 1945–1974*. New York: Oxford University Press, 1996.

Saville, P., dir. *Fellow Traveler*. 1989.

Terkel, Studs. *"The Good War": An Oral History of World War II*. New York: Pantheon Books, 1984.

Recreational Life

OVERVIEW

A variety of recreational options had developed for Americans throughout the twentieth century. Mass culture, egalitarian and commercial, became readily available to the public throughout the first three decades of the century. New technologies expanded the influence of movies, and radio programming became a major home entertainment option by the 1930s. New musical forms replaced ragtime as jazz and blues pieces filled the speakeasies and new record shops. Many sports historians consider the 1920s the golden age of spectator sports. George Herman Ruth, "The Babe," swatted home runs for the New York Yankees. College football grew into a powerful force in athletics. Bobby Jones even popularized golf, formerly an elite, private country club sport. Gertrude Ederle became the first woman to swim the English Channel, and the new sports heroes created a host of athletic idols for Americans to admire.

The Great Depression may have reduced the time and money available for Americans to spend on such trivial pursuits, but throughout the 1930s, popular culture remained a powerful attraction and escape for the people. Radio shows were free and the soap operas, sitcoms, and melodramas drew millions of listeners. Movie attendance remained high. Spectator sporting events still attracted patrons. Life during the Depression years still appeared to warrant forms of recreation and entertainment to balance the serious economic concerns that faced the nation. By the beginning of the 1940s, and for the next 20 years, American recreational life experienced a new surge of interest in and involvement with the mass culture of American recreation.

FILM

Orson Welles, the famous director and actor, had defined motion pictures as a "ribbon of dreams," a fantasy and escape for Americans in the dark theaters of the United States. A visual medium and form of entertainment, movies became the single most important commercial enterprise in twentieth-century U.S. history, eclipsed only by television by the end of the century. By the beginning of the World War II, major corporate studios, centered in Hollywood, California, controlled the movie industry. Warner Brothers, Metro-Goldwyn-Mayer, RKO, Paramount, and 20th Century Fox contracted actors, directors, scriptwriters, and technical people. They produced movies, usually 40 to 50 a year, which went to theaters throughout the country, theaters that they owned. In 1940, a movie ticket cost 30 cents and weekly attendance topped 80 million. While the movie industry remained big business for its studio executives, films provided a broad variety of quality and technical innovation to enhance the status of the art form as well as to bring more patrons into the theaters.

From its early years of silent movies and grainy black-and-white options, Hollywood had developed "talkies" in the 1920s (*The Jazz Singer,* 1927) and movies in color by the 1930s (*The Wizard of Oz,* 1939). In a period of only three years, the studios produced four of the great, classic films in American history: *Gone with the Wind* (1939), *The Grapes of Wrath* (1940), *Citizen Kane* (1941), and *Casablanca* (1942). The 1940s also saw the production of Walt Disney animated movies. In 1937, Disney had created *Snow White and the Seven Dwarfs.* Three years later, he produced *Pinocchio* and *Fantasia.* At the same time, studios cranked out Saturday morning serials (which lacked the style and substance of classic westerns) and melodramatic *Buck Rogers* science fiction fare for youngsters to enjoy in a pretelevision era. Newsreels, shorts, travel films, and documentaries added to the rich lode of film fare available to moviegoers. The movie industry appeared capable of providing a broad variety of films for a huge audience, both young and old.

Hollywood joined the war effort in 1942. The movie industry created a host of training and propaganda films for the military and for the nation as a whole. Between 1942 and 1945, the famed director Frank Capra (an army major) produced seven films for the War Department entitled *Why We Fight.* John Ford's *Battle of Midway* became one of the most famous docudramas of the war. Those movies offered a powerful defense of America's war effort. At the same time, the studios made a series of commercial movies that portrayed the nation's commitment to World War II in heroic terms. A quintessential hero of many of those films, John Wayne (who never served in the military) confronted the Japanese in *Flying Tigers* (1942), *The Fighting Seabees* (1944), and *Back to Bataan* (1945). Other Hollywood stars joined in the effort. Errol Flynn, Cary Grant, and Robert Taylor, to name a few, gave American audiences a stirring portrait of Americans at war. Critics have argued, correctly, that the popular films portrayed ugly stereotypes of the nation's enemies during the war. Almost without exception, the Japanese and Germans appeared as caricatures, evil and oppressive, even racially offensive in the case of the Japanese. The movies also enhanced a mythical community of soldiers serving in the American armed forces, a team of young men and women from every walk of life and ethnic, racial, and religious background fighting and dying to preserve democracy and freedom. Audiences flocked to theaters to enjoy the options.

While Hollywood continued to produce movies in support of the war effort, thousands of actors, directors, and others joined the armed services, encouraged the sale of War Bonds, and traveled on United Services Organization (USO) tours to visit and entertain the troops serving in the war. Marlene Dietrich, a German actress who moved to the United States, returned to Europe to entertain soldiers throughout the war years. Bob Hope became a notable celebrity and continued his USO visits during the Korean and Vietnam wars. The movie industry believed it had done its part to secure America's victory in World War II, and it emerged from the conflict with pride and profits intact.

In 1938, the United States Congress created the House Un-American Activities Committee (HUAC) to investigate the influence and threat of communist subversion in America. HUAC became a permanent committee in 1945, and by 1947, it cast, oddly, a baleful eye on Hollywood. Searching for left-wing communist sympathizers in the movie industry, the committee subpoenaed 41 witnesses to testify before Congress. A number of those witnesses were jailed for "contempt of Congress," and many more were blacklisted by the studio executives and failed to find work in the industry as a result of their public support for the convicted members of their professional community. Whether any of those involved had legitimate ties to the Communist Party remains dubious at best, but as in other areas, the commercial world of the studios feared the backlash of the anticommunist sentiment of the postwar era and responded accordingly.

While the movie industry responded shabbily to the HUAC assault on its colleagues, it continued to produce profitable films for the American audience. In 1946, *The Best Years of Our Lives* provided a brilliant, poignant view of three servicemen returning from the war and the effects the conflict had on them and their families. Movie attendance continued to thrive until the 1950s. In 1946, attendance reached its highest numbers—90 million a week.

Minorities continued to appear as racial stereotypes in most American movies even while Hollywood had begun to make some effort to address the issue of racism in the country. Sydney Poitier starred in *No Way Out* (1950), an example of that shift in attitude, but black Americans and other minorities still had to wait for the civil rights movement of the postwar era to challenge the traditional roles they were forced to accept as secondary, stereotyped characters in movies made primarily to attract white audiences.

Like other recreational options, movies offered Americans a variety of entertainment during the period. Prices for movies rose from 30 cents a ticket in 1940 to 65 cents in 1950 to $1.00 in 1960. People could attend their local theater in small towns or cities, buy a variety of refreshments like popcorn or candy, watch previews of coming attractions, a *Movietone* news clip, and perhaps even sing along with "bouncing ball" lyrics of popular songs of the day. Often the theater showed double features, with two studio films for the price of one. Major urban centers offered large, impressive theaters with similar fare. Drive-in movies became popular in the 1950s as a more private way for young people to view films (critics referred to them as "passion pits") or as a baby-sitting alternative for married families. The first drive-in theater opened in Camden, New Jersey, in 1933. By the 1950s, more than 4,000 drive-in theaters, mostly in rural areas in America, served patrons.

An ominous Supreme Court decision in 1948, the antitrust *Paramount Decree*, ordered the studio to divest ownership of theater chains and forbid "block booking" (studios, in the past, could require theaters to take all of their films whether or not theater owners wanted to do so). The court's decision signaled the end of a monopoly of the business that the major studios had enjoyed for years. The times appeared to be changing as the movie industry moved into the 1950s, yet the business went on as before, apparently content to deliver the same products to a happy audience of postwar Americans. Television offered the new and dangerous alternative. By the mid-1950s, movie attendance began to decline as more Americans turned on their television sets rather than head for the local theater. By 1956, movie attendance had dropped to 46 million a week. Jack Warner, a top Hollywood executive, flying cross-country from California to New York, appeared stunned by the television antennas he saw in the neighborhoods below. At the same time, a number of European directors and films had begun to enter the American market. Federico Fellini and Ingmar Bergman offered new, subtle film interpretations that attracted so-called highbrow viewers. While television appeared to attract a mass culture audience, formerly dependent on the movies, the European films drew the other side of the aisle.

The movie industry felt compelled to respond. New technology enabled Hollywood to produce Cinemascope (wide-screen) color epics and spectacles like *The Ten Commandments* (1956) to challenge television. Additionally, the movie studios began to purchase rights to produce their own television programs, ultimately moving the whole business of television programming from New York to Hollywood. By the end of the decade, the movie industry had also become the television industry.

MUSIC

The music of the 1940s and 1950s shaped significantly the rest of the twentieth century. The special music of the war years became popular for dancing on 78 rpm vinyl "platters" even when the leaders of the big bands—such as Tommy Dorsey, Benny Goodman, and Glenn Miller—were either in uniform or entertaining troops. Middle-class teenagers often held weekend dances with records in neighborhood homes as well as in high school gymnasiums. Some coastal towns inaugurated curfews. Although not every community had complete blackouts, walking about at night in streets with dimmed lights was unwise. Older high schoolers, imitating many movie stars and draftees, might smoke a cigarette or two at such record parties. Often, their parents gave consent to smoking. But drinking and drugs remained unfashionable. Soft drinks and non-alcoholic cider prevailed. Potato chips, pretzels, and popcorn were the only junk food available.

Everyone could sing along with wartime favorites like "Don't Sit under the Apple Tree with Anyone Else but Me," "Praise the Lord and Pass the Ammunition," and the Andrews Sisters' sensational "Boogie Woogie Bugle Boy." "Rosie the Riveter" became a particular swing favorite on the home front. Young people—themselves often lonely at home—enjoyed the yearning in sad songs of separation like "I'll Walk Alone" and "Saturday Night Is the Loneliest Night in the Week."

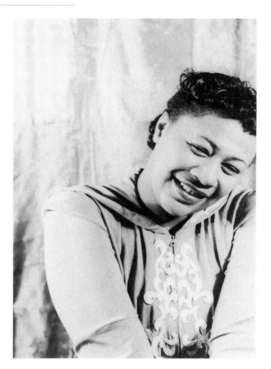

Ella Fitzgerald, "the first lady of jazz." Library of Congress.

The 1950s may have been the richest decade in American history for African American music. All the great classical jazz musicians and singers, including Louis Armstrong, Duke Ellington, Billie Holiday, and Ella Fitzgerald, performed during this decade. As the LP (long-playing 33 rpm records) brought back the early sounds of King Oliver, Ma Rainey, and Bessie Smith, the new Motown sound began to shape itself in Detroit. In a different cultural genre, Marian Anderson, in 1955, became the first black woman to sing at the Metropolitan Opera, opening the stage for a great parade of superb African American singers. And although Paul

Chuck Berry. Library of Congress.

Elvis Presley, the "King of Rock 'n' Roll." Photofest.

Robeson—because of his communist sympathies—had his request for a passport denied along with opportunities to sing and act, many recordings of his rich, deep voice remained to be transferred to the new vinyl LP recordings.

African American musicians also led the wave of new rock and roll music (a term that came from a black slang term for sex) that swept the nation in the 1950s and began to attract teenage fans. Chuck Berry, Little Richard, and Fats Domino became popular performers, not only with African American audiences, but with white teenagers as well. Joining with white performers, black rock and roll singers and bands breached the racial barrier in popular music entertainment. Richie Valens, a Hispanic performer from California, joined the diverse entourage and created a major hit record with an upbeat, rock version of a traditional Mexican folksong—"La Bamba." Buddy Holly, a white guitar player from Lubbock, Texas, entertained at the Apollo Theatre in Harlem, and signs of a new integrated music became evident. Quickly, radio disc jockeys like Allen Freed put together rock concerts that engaged a host of black and white stars who performed on the same stage to mixed racial audiences. The new music and the racial overtones shocked and alarmed many older Americans, but teenage record buyers (now purchasing new 45 rpm records) supported the growth of rock and roll with millions of dollars in record purchases. The commercial implications of the new music led to a serious "payola" scandal in the 1950s. Agents and record company executives often paid disc jockeys to play particular artists and songs—a form of bribery. Alan Freed, one of the most popular disc jockeys of the era, became involved in one of the major payola scandals of the decade and lost his job and influence. Yet, in the phrase of a contemporary lyric, "Rock and Roll Is Here to Stay!" (Danny and the Juniors, 1956).

The 1950s was also the decade of Elvis Presley, the rockabilly performer from Tupelo, Mississippi. Entertainer Steve Allen first focused discussion on Elvis Presley's pelvic gyrations by making him stand still as he serenaded a tethered hound dog on Allen's popular TV show. But Jackie Gleason deserves credit for pushing Presley's talents on the 1956 *Tommy and Jimmy Dorsey Stage Show* in spite of the Dorsey brothers' protests. Gleason rightly recognized Elvis as another hero of working-class culture, labeling him a guitar-playing Marlon Brando who had "sensuous, sweaty, T-shirt and jeans animal magnetism." Elvis managed to step forward—in between the quaint clowns and trained animal acts—to send rock and roll music into affluent suburban America. Although Dick Clark was on *American Bandstand* every afternoon in Philadelphia with well-groomed youngsters and modest songs, Elvis's ability to attract huge audiences suddenly put him in great demand. Milton Berle even hired him to inject life into his dying show—at what was then the outrageously high salary of $50,000 a week.

Like the rebel James Dean portrayed in 1950s movies and the exposer of phonies Holden Caulfield represented in J. D. Salinger's 1951 classic *Catcher in the Rye*, Elvis Presley became a symbol of youthful independence and teen rebellion. By the singer's third appearance in 1957 on America's most popular variety show, *The Toast of the Town*, host Ed Sullivan defended Elvis as "a real decent, fine boy." The press began to stress his patriotism and how good he was to his mother. Estimates suggest that over 82 percent of the American viewing audience saw Elvis on the Ed Sullivan show—54 million people watched as the cameras shot him only from the waist up.

Fifty years later Elvis Presley would be esteemed by music critics not for his sensationalism but for the agility of his voice and for the variety and range of his ballads. The accusation that he borrowed much from African American gospel music and from black blues had to be understood in the same way that blending of cultural currents must always be explained in a country made up of complex energies. Elvis's rock and roll and rockabilly represented in music the integration of black and white folk cultures that the law attempted to bring about on the social level. Greil Marcus in his classic *Mystery Train: Images of America in Rock 'n' Roll Music* (1975) attributes Elvis's great popularity to the self-respect he offered people who were only on the edge of the new affluence. Marcus believed Presley managed to stabilize country music even as he pulled away from it. The power of his music stems from such tensions.

If Elvis remained "king" after the 50 intervening years since appearing with Ed Sullivan, it may be because the tensions he communicated are still part of an upwardly mobile society. The country music Elvis Presley offered America in his own extreme forms continued to celebrate traditions people were losing in the decade after the war. To many, Elvis suggested how much Americans remained trapped by fate. Often his message seemed to be simply that his music passed on lost values from many different roots. Marcus's belief that Elvis embodied "the bigness, the intensity, and the unpredictability of America itself" may well be true. Although many black musicians complained that Elvis stole their material, his African American audience endured.

It is important to remember that the new music that teenagers in America supported continued to compete with other styles. Big band and swing orchestras still entertained audiences at resorts and nightclubs. Frank Sinatra, Doris Day, Nat King Cole, and other crooners still sang their ballads to adoring fans. Broadway and a host of regional theaters offered excellent musicals like *South Pacific* and *Oklahoma*. Innovative new forms of jazz evolved during the era. Dizzy Gillespie, Miles Davis, and numerous black and white musicians pursued a whole new genre of interpretive jazz that brought a different group of record buyers to the stores. Folk music also offered an alternative. The Depression songs of Woody Guthrie would encourage a generation of singers. Joan Baez, Peter, Paul, and Mary, and Bob Dylan topped the list of new recording artists who began to work in the late 1950s. Part of the key to understanding the commercial and cultural quality of American music between 1940 and 1959 should focus on the broad variety of musical forms that became available to men, women, and children living in the United States. By the end of the decade, record stores had begun to divide their options into many different styles, subjects, and tastes. The egalitarian and commercial quality of American mass culture permeated the music business and its entertainers and fans.

The evolution of modern, popular music also created new forms of dancing for Americans. In the 1940s, people would foxtrot to the big band, swing orchestras, but jitterbugging emerged as a wartime option. Teenagers in the late 1940s and throughout the 1950s invented their own styles to complement the evolution of rock and roll. Dick Clark's *American Bandstand*, an afternoon television show from Philadelphia, encouraged young viewers to copy the latest dance crazes they saw their peers performing for the cameras. High school "sock hops" and proms followed suit (*Daily Life Online*, "Recreational Life: Music," in Kaledin, *Daily Life in the United States, 1940–1959*, http://dailylife.greenwood.com).

RADIO

Popular radio programs continued to offer the best home entertainment recreation for Americans throughout the 1940s. Television technology had existed much earlier, but the commercial switch to that new visual medium failed to occur until the 1950s. The same basic format for commercial radio that had emerged in the 1920s continued to drive the programming and ownership. The National Broadcasting Corporation (NBC), the American Broadcasting Corporation (ABC), and the Columbia Broadcasting System (CBS) dominated the airways. Their local affiliate stations throughout the country broadcasted programs and formats developed at the national level, with some time set aside for local news and ads. The commercial structure operated on the sale of advertising time to a variety of businesses. Listener interest determined how or whether sponsors would continue to support programs with their money. The Federal Communication Commission (FCC) issued station licenses to operate and assigned radio frequencies on the Air Modulated bands (AM). The advent of television changed the impact of radio and forced it to change its format. Yet, the same major corporations owned television rights of broadcast, and they adopted the same style of organization and format for the visual, home entertainment systems as black-and-white televisions began to enter American homes in the decades following World War II.

While radio remained an important entertainment option, with traditional programming into the 1950s, the advent of television slowly began to erode the former medium's influence with advertisers. As networks shifted to television in the mid and late 1950s, radio altered its approach and appeal as well. A new option for automobiles included AM radios, and the stations began to program music and news as primary forms of programming for car owners. The increase in car sales enhanced that genre for radio programmers and radio bowed to the new "giant" while retaining its entertainment value for Americans through another alternative.

TELEVISION

The rise of television as both a technical and recreational medium following World War II remains a dominant factor in the daily lives of Americans. Erik Barnouw's study, *Tube of Plenty* (1990), offered a thorough and sound history of television's influence. As a technical innovation, television had existed since the 1920s, but it failed to develop as a commercial option until the end of World War II. The dominance of radio, the problems of the Depression and the war, and other factors led network executives and others to conclude that people would not buy the product. That changed after 1950. In 1940, 28 million households owned radios (80 percent). In 1950, almost 41 million homes had radios (93.6 percent). Yet, only four million households had purchased television sets (9 percent). The explosion of television purchases and viewing rose between 1950 and 1960. By the end of that decade, almost 46 million American homes had purchased television sets (87 percent), and the new age of the visual medium had become the home entertainment phenomenon of the postwar era (Faragher 2000, 830).

The three national radio networks, ABC, CBS, and NBC, also controlled the commercial and technical development of television programming, and they made an easy transition into the new medium. The FCC provided licensing and technical support for the networks, advertisers flocked to television with commercials, and program directors transferred traditional forms of radio entertainment to the black-and-white television sets that took center stage in American living rooms. Radio advertising often saw a single sponsor underwrite an entire program, but the expanded costs of television advertising made that prohibitive. Instead, advertisers bought 30-second "spots" and spread their advertising dollars to different programs accordingly. As had been the case with radio, the sponsors generally left types of programs to the networks and their affiliated stations. In 1947, net advertising revenues amounted to $2 million. In 1959, that number had reached close to $1.5 billion.

Radio programs had depended on a basic format of offerings: comedy–variety shows, melodramas, and soap operas during the daytime hours. Television easily followed suit. The contention that advertisers foisted those less-than-quality shows on an unwary public is a tenuous one. Both advertising and network executives provided the entertainment that the public appeared to want, often slavishly so. At its worst, the new medium programmed hackneyed, simple shows like *I Remember Mama*. At its best, it produced teleplays written by serious playwrights like Paddy Chaevsky. His 1952 teleplay *Marty* served as example of early television drama at its best. As with all commercial enterprises, supply and demand remained the key factors in television programming, and the networks and advertisers remained quick to respond.

The popularity of particular television shows changed more often than radio shows. If *Amos and Andy*, a comedy about the African American Sunshine Cab Company, remained the top radio show throughout the late 1930s and early 1940s, television audiences appeared more fickle in their selections. In 1950, variety shows like *Texaco Theater* and *Fireside Theater* were numbers one and two in television ratings. Five years later, the *$64,000 Question* (a quiz show that became part of a major television scandal in 1957, when the "selected" contestant, Charles Van Doren, was given answers to help him win the top prize) was number one, and *I Love Lucy*, a comedy program with Lucille Ball and Desi Arnaz, took the second spot. In 1959, westerns commanded top ratings. *Gunsmoke* and *Wagon Train* led the list (http://www.ClassicTVHits.com).

Top Ten Shows in 1954/1955

1. *I Love Lucy*
2. *The Jackie Gleason Show*
3. *Dragnet*
4. *You Bet Your Life*
5. *The Toast of the Town*
6. *Disneyland*
7. *The Chevy Show* (Bob Hope)
8. *The Jack Benny Show*
9. *The Martha Raye Show*
10. *The George Gobel Show* (Steinberg)

It is easy to make fun of amateur hours like Ed Sullivan's. Fred Allen, a witty radio comedian who did not survive on television, said that Sullivan would stay on the air as long as other people had talent. But there was talent—a prodigious amount. In the 1950s Sullivan offered the public artists as varied as the violin prodigy Itzhak Perlman and the great black musical performers Ella Fitzgerald, Duke Ellington, and Lena Horne.

At a time when black singer Nat King Cole could not get a sponsor for a television series because of his race, Sullivan made a vast audience aware that talent had nothing to do with race or ethnicity. As the nation's leading TV impresario for 23 years, Sullivan shaped American values and taste. Money spent for music lessons and musical instruments soared from $86 million in 1950 to $149 million in 1960. During those early years, Sullivan's Sunday night show brought families and neighbors together in living rooms to watch and discuss new talents.

How much television influenced national values remains a "chicken-and-egg" dilemma. The new medium allowed many Americans to appreciate, for the first time, the best of the national pastime as big-league baseball appeared on the screen. TV also exhibited cultures and countries never thought about in isolationist pre–World War II America. The video screen revealed aspects of nature never imagined before and expanded viewers' visions of what the global village contained. Such images could dispel fear (Kaledin 2000, 18, 138–39, 165).

SPORTS

The 1940s and 1950s witnessed the dawn of televised sports in America, but the full effect of televised sports would not be felt until later in the twentieth century. Following World War II, as television gained popularity across the country, professional team owners and the National Collegiate Athletic Association (NCAA) made efforts to limit the availability of televised games. Owners and NCAA schools correctly feared that televised games would depress attendance figures. In 1946, Major League owners adopted a rule that prevented teams from broadcasting games into another team's territory, but they repealed that rule in 1952 under the threat of an antitrust lawsuit from the Justice Department. In 1951, the National Football League (NFL) adopted its blackout rule—home teams could not broadcast their games within their own markets. For example, whenever the Philadelphia Eagles played home games, they could not televise those games within the Philadelphia area. In 1952, the NCAA negotiated a deal with Westinghouse to sponsor a limited number of events on NBC. Although attendance at major sporting events declined from the late 1940s to the late 1950s, the availability of televised sports skyrocketed during the ensuing decades, because networks paid increasing amounts of money for the rights to broadcast games. Ultimately, television harmed the popularity of Major League baseball, increased the "win-at-any-cost" attitude within college football and basketball, and sparked the emergence of professional football as America's most popular sport.

—*Courtney Smith*

Sports and Race

Racial discrimination represented another problem plaguing college sports, as most southern schools stubbornly clung to segregation policies. Until the 1960s, most southern schools refused to recruit black players and instructed integrated northern teams to leave their black players at home when they played in the South. Prior to World War II, northern schools bowed to the demands of southern schools, but after the war, the attitude of northern schools began to change. The biggest controversy over integrated northern football teams flared during bowl season, since segregated southern cities hosted three of the most popular postseason bowl games. To remain relevant, southern bowl committees and host cities gradually modified and even removed their segregation guidelines to accommodate integrated northern football teams. By the end of the 1950s, the Sugar Bowl in Louisiana, the Cotton Bowl in Texas, and the Orange Bowl in Florida had held games featuring white southern teams and integrated northern football teams. Despite that progress, racial discrimination remained a persistent problem in American college and professional sports.

In the early 1940s, most American professional sports remained rigidly segregated. Since the 1934 season, professional football owners had maintained almost exclusively white rosters, but by the late 1940s, the National Football League had several black players. Major League baseball's racial segregation policies dated back to the late 1800s. Several early Major League teams had employed a few black players, but all of those black players had disappeared by 1890. Until 1945, Major League owners adhered to a gentleman's agreement, an unwritten rule barring all black players. Due to the gentleman's agreement, black Americans created their own baseball leagues, collectively known as the Negro Leagues. By 1940, the Negro Leagues consisted of the Negro National League with teams in the Northeast and upper South and the Negro American League with teams in the Midwest. After suffering through years of financial losses, the leagues enjoyed a period of economic prosperity during World War II. The war, however, also intensified the movement to integrate Major League baseball, a movement that would unintentionally lead to the demise of the Negro League baseball.

Wendell Smith of *The Pittsburgh Courier*, a black newspaper, initiated the movement to integrate Major League baseball in the late 1930s. Smith wrote columns comparing the statistics of black and white players and petitioned Major League owners to hold tryouts for Negro League players. He also conducted surveys among Major League players and coaches and discovered that most of them were open to the idea of signing black players. During World War II, Smith and other antisegregation activists started their own "Double Victory" campaign, equating victory on the battlefields with victory over segregation on the home front. Antisegregation activists compared American racial segregation laws to Nazi Germany's treatment of the Jews and even staged protests outside Major League ballparks.

Jackie Robinson of the Brooklyn Dodgers and Larry Doby of the Cleveland Indians, the first two African American major leaguers. AP/Wide World Photos.

Much to the worry of Negro League owners, Smith intensified his efforts to secure tryouts for black players with Major League teams. Negro League owners did not assist Smith, because they correctly recognized that the integration of the Major Leagues would mean the end of the Negro Leagues.

Smith's efforts resulted in a handful of sham tryouts, since the vast majority of Major League owners remained opposed to integration. At a press conference in early 1945, Smith briefly met with Branch Rickey of the Brooklyn Dodgers and urged him to scout a promising young player, Jackie Robinson of the Kansas City Monarchs. Unbeknownst to Smith, Rickey had already resolved to sign a black player. Following that meeting, Rickey instructed his most trusted scout, Clyde Sukeforth, secretly to investigate Robinson and determine whether he was a good candidate to break the color barrier. Robinson's personal and athletic background made him the ideal person for this role. He came from a middle-class family, had played on integrated college teams at the University of Southern California (UCLA), and had served in the army during World War II. Most importantly, in secret meetings with Rickey, Robinson promised not to fight back when he faced racial taunts or slurs when he played in the Major Leagues. Consequently, Rickey stunned the baseball world in October 1945 when he signed Robinson to a contract and assigned him to play for the Dodger's minor league club, the Montreal Royals.

Robinson spent one very successful season with the Royals before making his Major League debut with the Dodgers on April 15, 1947. Around the same time as Robinson's debut with the Dodgers, professional football and basketball teams also began to sign black players. Unfortunately, the integration of Major League baseball destroyed Negro League baseball. When he signed Robinson, Rickey neither consulted with the owner of the Kansas City Monarchs nor offered the franchise any kind of financial compensation. As other Major League owners signed black players, they followed Rickey's example and essentially stole the best talent from the Negro Leagues. Consequently, black baseball teams suffered steep financial declines, and the Negro National League disbanded following the 1948 season. During the 1950s, the need for all-black baseball teams eroded as young black players completely bypassed black teams on their way to predominantly white major or minor league teams.

Despite facing a torrent of racial taunts and slurs from fans as well as opposing teams, Robinson enjoyed another successful season and even won the inaugural Rookie of the Year Award. Before retiring in 1956, Robinson added a Most Valuable Player award, a batting title, and a World Series championship to his impressive resume. Unfortunately, the pace of integration proceeded very slowly in the Major Leagues. When Robinson retired, two teams, the Philadelphia Phillies and Boston Red Sox, still had all-white rosters; the Phillies finally started a black player in 1958, and the Red Sox followed suit in 1959. Moreover, spring training facilities in Florida remained segregated, so black players could not live at the same hotels or eat at the same restaurants as their white teammates. Blatant racial discrimination persisted in the Major Leagues through the end of the 1950s and would represent a source of controversy between more assertive black players and conservative white baseball officials in the 1960s.

Sports and Gender

Since the early twentieth century, American social mores had discouraged women from playing competitive sports. In the 1920s, the Women's Division of the National Amateur Athletic Federation passed a series of resolutions that required all female college teams to engage in noncompetitive "play days" instead of competitive intercollegiate contests. During the 1940s, however, white American women enjoyed their first opportunities to play professional sports. In 1943, concern over the World War II-induced manpower shortage in the Major Leagues led Philip Wrigley, owner of the Chicago Cubs, to establish the All-American Girls Professional Baseball League (AAGPBL). During its inaugural season, the AAGPBL maintained four franchises in small Midwestern cities—the Rockford Peaches, the Racine Belles, the South Bend Blue Sox, and the Kenosha Comets. Interest in the AAGPBL peaked in 1948 and then declined sharply in the early 1950s; the league disbanded after the 1954 season. In addition to having female players, the AAGPBL differed from the Major Leagues in several ways. AAGPBL players used a slightly larger baseball, and for the first season, the rules allowed softball-style pitching. Additionally, the base paths in the AAGPBL were only 85 feet long, and the pitcher's rubber was located only 55 feet from home plate.

Penny Marshall's 1992 movie, A League of Their Own, starring Geena Davis and Madonna, included some factual errors, but it captured wonderfully the stereotypes AAGPBL players endured. All AAGPBL players had to be beautiful; the players had to maintain feminine appearances, meaning they had to wear make-up and have long hair, or else they were expelled from the league. The players also had to regularly attend charm classes, wear uniforms that resembled miniskirts, and obey their female chaperones. In 1988, the Baseball Hall of Fame in Cooperstown, New York, finally recognized the league by creating a permanent exhibit, Women in Baseball, that honored all AAGPBL members.

The life and career of Mildred "Babe" Didrikson Zaharias, the most famous female American athlete in the 1940s and 1950s, best exemplified the stereotypes facing white female athletes. At the 1932 Summer Olympics in Los Angeles, Babe captured the nation's attention by winning two gold medals and one silver medal in track and field events. Since she had very short hair and wore "masculine" clothes, many sportswriters wrote unflattering articles about her and openly questioned her sexuality. The constant criticisms and questions took their toll on Zaharias and, by the early 1940s, she had very dramatically altered her public persona. She always posed for pictures while wearing dresses or performing domestic tasks, abandoned track and field for golf, and married a professional wrestler named George Zaharias. After dominating the women's amateur golf circuit, Babe worked with other female golfers to establish the Ladies Professional Golf Association (LPGA). Much to the dismay of other female golfers, Babe also dominated early LPGA tournaments and quickly became the tour's biggest financial draw. Sadly, cancer shortened Babe's spectacular career; she died in 1956 at the age of 45. Following those humble beginnings, opportunities for American women to play sports would increase in the 1960s and 1970s.

Sports and Athletics

The American sporting world of the early 1940s differed greatly from the American sporting world of the early twenty-first century. For example, Major League baseball represented America's national pastime, but all of its franchises remained confined to the Northeast and Midwest. The popularity of college football vastly overshadowed the popularity of professional football, the National Hockey League had only four American teams, and the National Basketball Association did not exist. Teams traveled by train, and sports fans followed their favorite teams through the daily sports pages or through game broadcasts on the radio. In their dealing with owners, professional athletes suffered from a lack of bargaining power. Major League baseball owners restrained their players' power through the reserve clause in every player's contract that permitted owners to "reserve" his services indefinitely. Consequently, professional athletes earned comparatively meager salaries, and they usually remained with one team for their entire careers.

The end of World War II unleashed powerful forces that drastically altered American society and transformed the nature of American sports. As a result of a postwar economic boom, many Americans joined an increasingly affluent middle class that enjoyed both greater leisure time and discretionary income. Consequently, many Americans devoted more time to playing and watching sports. Attendance at Major League baseball games and college football games skyrocketed, with several teams establishing new attendance records. Middle-class Americans also participated in a larger number of sports; hundreds of new golf courses and tennis courts dotted the landscape, and sporting goods manufacturers rushed to meet surging demands for new and better products. The postwar sporting boom also touched America's growing youth population, as parents enrolled their sons in Little League baseball and Pop Warner football teams.

Professional sports, particularly Major League baseball, mirrored the changing geographic patterns of middle-class Americans. As a result of the postwar economic boom, the affluent white middle class moved out of urban areas and settled in newly emerging suburban communities. Old industrial cities in the Northeast and upper Midwest suffered the most from that population shift, and new Sunbelt communities in the South and Southwest benefited the most. More significantly, "white flight" decimated those older industrial cities and compelled many Major League owners who had teams in those cities to look for new homes. Since the early twentieth century, Major League baseball had teams in only 10 cities—Boston, New York, Philadelphia, Washington, D.C., Pittsburgh, Cleveland, Cincinnati, Detroit, Chicago, and St. Louis. The movement of Major League franchises began in 1953 when the Boston Braves moved to Milwaukee. In the following year, the St. Louis Browns moved to Baltimore and became the Orioles, and in 1955, the Athletics moved from Philadelphia to Kansas City.

The most shocking and significant relocations occurred after the 1957 season, when the Brooklyn Dodgers moved to Los Angeles and the New York Giants moved to San Francisco. Dodgers owner Walter O'Malley engineered the relocation of both franchises. The Brooklyn Dodgers played at Ebbets Field, an aging ballpark that lacked the facilities to accommodate an increasingly suburban fan base. O'Malley worked with Brooklyn officials to build a new, modern ballpark, but behind the scenes, he also successfully negotiated with officials from Los Angeles to build a new ballpark on a site known as Chavez Ravine. To make the relocation palatable for his fellow National League owners, O'Malley brokered a stadium deal between the city of San Francisco and the New York Giants. With two franchises on the West Coast, O'Malley soothed his fellow owners' concerns about long road trips, and he maintained the long-time fierce rivalry between the Dodgers and Giants. The relocation of the Dodgers and the Giants foreshadowed the era of "franchise free agency" and the appearance of more professional franchises in Sunbelt communities later in the twentieth century. Moreover, those relocations also established a pattern of cities using lucrative stadium deals to attract professional sports franchises, often to the detriment of their local economies.

The rapid growth of youth sports also exemplified both the promise and problems present within postwar American sports. Since the late 1800s, organizations like the YMCA had sponsored organized youth sports programs under the premise that sports fostered good character and discipline. Following World War II, the economic boom and the newly affluent middle class triggered a Baby Boom, which in turn sparked a surge in sports programs. For example, from 1945 to 1959, the number of Little League teams skyrocketed. Parents enrolled their children in Little League baseball, because they believed that it instilled sportsmanship, patriotism, and character in their children. Unfortunately, an insatiable desire for victory at any cost often plagued Little League baseball and negated the program's beneficial qualities. Critics of Little League baseball disliked its adult-controlled bureaucracy and accused adult coaches of placing too much stress on children to win games and championships. Those critics believed that children should organize their own teams, write their own rules, and structure their own games so that everyone, not just the athletically gifted stars, had chances to participate. Little League officials ignored those criticisms and continued to insist that their teams offered many benefits to young boys. Criticisms of Little League baseball would increase after the 1950s as the League expanded its annual World Series and even made games available on national television.

Criticism and the victory-at-any-cost attitude also plagued post–World War II intercollegiate athletics, particularly the big-time sports of football and basketball. Since football's emergence as the predominant intercollegiate sport in the late 1800s, critics had accused coaches and athletic departments of sacrificing academic priorities in favor of athletic victories. In 1906, American colleges had created the National Collegiate Athletic Association (NCAA) in response to concerns about falling academic standards and increasing brutality in college sports. As a cooperative organization of member institutions, the NCAA relied on individual schools to police themselves and consequently lacked any real authority to punish schools for rules violations. In October 1929, the Carnegie Foundation for the Advancement of Teaching published a report, *American College Athletics*, that highlighted widespread abuses present within most intercollegiate athletic programs. The report criticized schools for recruiting potential athletes, lowering academic standards for those athletes, and offering illegal athletics-based scholarships. The report also criticized alumni and athletic boosters for establishing slush funds and for giving talented athletes jobs that did not entail any actual work. The Carnegie Foundation suggested reforms, but it lacked authority to enforce those reforms or to punish schools for their illegal tactics. Additionally, any uproar over the Carnegie Report quickly became lost amid concerns about the stock market crash and the subsequent Great Depression. Consequently, most colleges and universities openly ignored the Carnegie Report and continued to bend academic guidelines to achieve athletic success.

In 1948, the NCAA tried to implement reform by establishing the Sanity Code, which limited the amount of financial aid schools could offer athletes and required that all jobs given to athletes demand actual work. The Sanity Code, however, quickly fell apart since NCAA member institutions refused to adhere to the new regulations. Seven schools, including the Citadel and the University of Virginia, emerged as the Sanity Code's most vocal opponents, arguing that most schools would find ways to work around the new regulations. Two years later, a shocking and embarrassing scandal erupted when the prestigious U.S. Military Academy (USMA) had to dismiss all but two members of its football team for cheating on exams. The USMA's football team had ranked among the top national title contenders for most of the 1940s and had engaged in a very popular rivalry with another national powerhouse, Notre Dame.

Although college basketball lagged behind the popularity of college football, it also endured a widespread and very embarrassing scandal in the early 1950s. Since Madison Square Garden in New York City hosted most important intercollegiate basketball games, gamblers and mobsters frequented the arena and enticed key players to shave points or even throw games. Alerted to the problem by a local sportswriter, District Attorney Frank Hogan launched an investigation that ultimately indicted 32 players and a handful of professional gamblers. Schools implicated in the scandal included the City College of New York, Long Island University, Manhattan, Bradley, Toledo, and the University of Kentucky; Kentucky had won national championships in 1948 and 1949. In addition to convictions on charges of bribery, conspiracy, and gambling, most of the 32 indicted players also received lifetime bans from the newly created National Basketball Association (NBA). In response to the cheating and gambling scandals, NCAA schools moved to give the association more credibility and authority. At the 1952 convention, member institutions gave the NCAA power to impose sanctions, passed legislation governing postseason competition, and named a full-time executive director. During that same convention, however, NCAA schools formally repealed the Sanity Code and approved the awarding of athletic scholarships, or full scholarships based solely on athletic ability. Despite the increased power of the NCAA, the win-at-any-cost attitude continued to grow, and the gap between academics and athletics widened.

—*Courtney Smith*

FOR MORE INFORMATION

Barnouw, Erik. *The Golden Web: A History of Broadcasting in the United States from 1933–1953.* New York: Oxford University Press, 1968.

———. *The Image Empire: A History of Broadcasting in the United States from 1953.* New York: Oxford University Press, 1970.

———. *Tube of Plenty: The Evolution of American Television.* New York: Oxford University Press, 1990.

Cayleff, Susan E. *Babe: The Life and Legend of Babe Didrikson Zaharias.* Urbana: University of Illinois Press, 1995.

Davies, Richard O. *America's Obsession: Sports and Society since 1945.* Belmont, CA: Wadsworth Publishing, 2007.

DeCurtis, A., and J. Henke, eds. *The Rolling Stone Illustrated History of Rock & Roll: The Definitive History of the Most Important Artists and Their Music.* New York: Random House, 1992.

Faragher, John Mack, Susan Armitage, Mari Jo Buhle, and Daniel Czitrom. *Out of Many: A History of the American People.* Upper Saddle River, NJ: Prentice Hall, 2000.

Kaledin, E. *Daily Life in the United States, 1940–1959: Shifting Worlds.* Westport, CT: Greenwood Press, 2000; also online as *Daily Life Online,* in Kaledin, *Daily Life in the United States, 1940–1959,* http://dailylife.greenwood.com.

Kenney, W. H. *Recorded Music in American Life: The Phonograph and Popular Memory, 1890–1945.* New York: Oxford University Press, 1999.

Marcus, Greil. *Mystery Train: Images of America in Rock 'n' Roll Music.* New York: E. P. Dutton, 1982.

Olson, James, and Randy Roberts. *Winning Is the Only Thing: Sports in America since 1945.* Baltimore: Johns Hopkins University Press, 1991.

Presley, Elvis. *30 No. 1 Hits.* CD, 2002.

Rader, Benjamin G. *American Sports: From the Age of Folk Games to the Age of Televised Sports.* Englewood Cliffs, NJ: Prentice Hall, 1998.

Sklar, Robert. *Movie-Made America: A Cultural History of American Movies.* New York: Vintage Books, 1975; rev. ed. 1994.

Steinberg, Cobbett S. *TV Facts.* New York: Facts on File, 1980.

Tygiel, Jules. *Baseball's Great Experiment: Jackie Robinson and His Legacy.* New York: Oxford University Press, 1997.

Religious Life

OVERVIEW

Institutional religion and belief have played a key role in American daily life since the colonial beginnings of the nation. Many of the initial European settlers who arrived in America in the seventeenth and eighteenth centuries immigrated to pursue some form of religious practice that they could not follow securely in their country of origin. At the same time, an evolving sense of exceptionalism developed in the American character as generations of immigrants concluded that God had provided a special place and opportunity for them to pursue their lives, both secular and religious. Concepts like Manifest Destiny were colored by that sense of exceptionalism and had strong antecedents in religious belief. At the same time, the eighteenth-century Enlightenment created a more secular commitment to reason rather than faith as a guiding principle in human behavior. Institutional religions remained a major factor in American daily life, as did the creation of more religions in the ferment of America's open religious climate, where there was no state church. Religions grew on the ability to attract and hold believers through persuasion and service. Yet, the Constitution's First Amendment, prohibiting Congress from favoring any religion, and early interpretations of its meaning created ambivalence in American religious life that has remained to the present. Thomas Jefferson wrote of a "wall of separation" between church and state, and Americans have wrestled with that issue ever since. Overall, American religions expanded dramatically so that the United States became the most "churched" nation in the modern world by the twentieth century.

MORALS, MEMBERSHIP, AND ANTICOMMUNISM

Statistically, America has remained a predominantly Christian nation. The vast majority of Americans claimed Protestant Christianity, in a variety of denominations, as their institutional faith. Roman Catholic immigration in the nineteenth century helped to make Catholics the second largest group. Judaism claimed a distant third. Cultural diversity in immigration in the twentieth century saw small groups of other faiths come to the country, but Buddhists, Hindus, Muslims, and others have always remained a small percentage of the population. Effectively, Christianity dominated religious life and cultural overview within the American society. At the same time, religious prejudice, often expressed in the form of nativism against immigrants, remained an aspect of American daily life well into the 1900s. Anti-Catholic and Anti-Semitic attitudes were expressed in many different forms, political, economic, and social, throughout the century. Yet, the First Amendment provided a significant legal protection for free religious expression. And the clash of faith and reason continued to occupy the sometimes emotional debate over the role of religious life in American society.

One aspect of that clash emerged in the Scopes Trial in 1925. Fundamentalist Christians vigorously denied the work of Charles Darwin's theories of evolution, which contradicted, in their view, the creation message of the Bible in the book of Genesis. By 1925, five states banned the teaching of evolution in their school systems. In Tennessee, a biology teacher, John Scopes, broke the law, taught Darwin's theories, and was arrested and tried in the small town of Dayton, Tennessee. The American Civil Liberties Union (ACLU) hired Clarence Darrow to defend Scopes, and the prosecutor had William Jennings Bryan, a nationally known politician and fundamentalist, join his team. The resultant "Monkey Trial" called into question the entire religious debate and the role of the First Amendment and made national headlines. The sensational trial, wonderfully portrayed, if grossly distorted historically, in the film *Inherit the Wind* (1960), set the table for religious ambivalence in

America for the remainder of the twentieth century. What was the role of religion in a secular state? How should the First Amendment apply to religious conviction in a society with broadly different points of view? The expanding role of federal courts in making judgments about those questions would serve as a key factor in the last half of the twentieth century.

During World War II, most Americans came to believe that God was on their side in the conflict against Nazi Germany and Imperial Japan. "Praise the Lord and pass the ammunition" and "there are no atheists in foxholes" provided glib, supportive clichés to Americans engaged in the "good war." Nostalgic songs and music like Irving Berlin's *White Christmas* and Norman Rockwell's patriotic paintings portrayed religious messages in their responses to why Americans fought the World War. Movies about the war even sought to project a religious message of ecumenical sacrifice in an effort to underplay the religious prejudice that still existed in the nation. Virtually every infantry or Marine squad of soldiers had a stereotyped Protestant, Catholic, and Jew fighting together to preserve the "Four Freedoms" that Americans believed they were in defending.

Notable institutional changes took place within the religious establishments in the years 1945 to 1950. Americans felt the need to protect their children from "godless communism." It was a time when atheists and agnostics were sometimes fired from jobs that earlier inspired anticommunists to take work away from liberals. An American skeptic, Elinor Goulding Smith, published an article in *Harper's* magazine in 1956 titled "Won't Somebody Tolerate Me?" Smith could not believe the extent of hostility she experienced as an agnostic during the Cold War. She felt it her duty to champion respect for diversity of opinion.

The rise in church membership during the 1950s astonished those who identified America with the Enlightenment spirit that defined the Founding Fathers. During his administration, Eisenhower even had himself baptized in the White House. In 1954, inspired by Eisenhower's minister, Congress added the words "under God" to the Pledge of Allegiance to the United States. And, beginning in 1955, "In God We Trust" was engraved on all U.S. currency. Statistics revealed that although only 49 percent of Americans were church members in 1940, just before the war, membership rose to 55 percent in 1950. And by 1959 an all-time high of 69 percent of polled Americans acknowledged church membership. The generalized breakdown was 66 percent Protestant, 26 percent Catholic, and 3 percent Jewish. No other Western culture was so religious, at least as measured claims of membership in a church or synagogue.

In 1952, the Revised Standard Version of the Bible sold 26.5 million copies in its first year of publication. For two years in a row—1953 and 1954—it was on the best-seller list. The religious enthusiasm of the 1950s, unlike that in other periods of American history, involved every class and economic division. A 1954 survey revealed that four out of five people would not vote for an atheist for president, and 60 percent would not permit a book by an atheist to remain in a public library.

Will Herberg's popular 1955 book *Protestant-Catholic-Jew: An Essay in American Religious Sociology (1955–1960)* characterized the spiritual mood as "religiousness without religion." He saw the new affiliations not as a way of reorienting life to

God, but as a way to sociability. In his view, churches provided social communities for a nation of uprooted individuals. What might seem more disillusioning about the 1950s was the degree to which American religion—committed to fighting the materialism of communism—was also involved with marketing itself. In 1957, Billy Graham, an enormously popular evangelical preacher, reported a $1.3 million budget, a tremendous amount for the time.

Television provided a new arena for evangelism. Billy Graham, Fulton J. Sheen, and Oral Roberts became important leaders in the religious Cold War, and the evolution of the contemporary Christian Fundamentalist movement probably had its origins during the 1950s. Norman Vincent Peale sold over two million copies of *The Power of Positive Thinking* (1955); Joshua Loth Liebman's *Peace of Mind* (1946) found thousands of readers beyond his own Jewish community. In California a drive-in church—"pews from Detroit"—matched the excitement of drive-in movies and fast foods. A dial-a-prayer service offered solace for those who could not get out. Religious movies such as *The Robe* (1953), *The Silver Chalice* (1954), and *The Ten Commandments* (1956) dramatized Christian struggles in terms easily translated into Cold War images. Spiritual biographies such as Catherine Marshall's *A Man Called Peter* (1952) and Jim Bishop's *The Day Christ Died* (1957) provided personal inspiration.

J. Edgar Hoover's minister preached that communism was really just secularism on the march. Detective fiction writer Mickey Spillane quit writing corpse-strewn best-sellers to become a Jehovah's Witness. The well-endowed actress Jane Russell called the Lord a "livin' doll," Elvis Presley offered up a special Christmas record, and the notorious gangster Mickey Cohen joined Billy Graham's Crusade for Christ. Commitment did not have to be associated with any special religion, nor did religious choice necessarily involve social action. The focus, as in all else during the decade, was on the individual family—the personal, not the civic. A popular slogan claimed that "the family that prays together stays together." Both Billy Graham and Norman Vincent Peale emphasized personal salvation and improvement and downplayed social activism, too readily identified with socialism.

POSTWAR RELIGIOUS SOCIETY

While some of the social and political quality of religious resurgence in the 1950s stemmed from fear regarding communism and the Cold War confrontation with the "godless" Soviet Union, other factors also influenced the quality and style of religious life. The swift and significant changes in postwar lifestyles impacted on religious commitment in the United States. Prosperity, consumerism, demographic movement to the suburbs, new technology, and the influence of the "new science" of the postwar era also confounded Americans even while providing them with a host of new options and opportunities. Institutional religious faith and regular church attendance provided a traditional "sanctuary" for Americans seeking to understand the broad revolutionary trends that faced Americans in the postwar era. Billy Graham and others may have been less interested in communism and more concerned about secular humanism and self-indulgence, which they perceived as the result of a society more concerned with the acquisition of goods and products than serious religious conviction. Most of all, they were concerned with saving souls and used modern instruments of mass appeal, including radio, film, and television. They also utilized carefully staged revivals with inspirational music to get their message out to millions of people.

Socially committed groups like those affiliated with the Catholic Worker and Quakers called attention to the needy. And the black civil rights workers depended on African American churches and ministers as much as on lawyers to back their efforts toward change. For many, peace of soul and mind still centered on ideas of patriotism and community.

In Levittown, Herbert Gans noted that 13 houses of worship—including two synagogues—sprang up during the first two years. Controlled by outside organizations, these religious establishments met local social needs by providing nursery schools, couples' clubs, and associations to bring about civic improvements. Gans saw no social hierarchies among churches. A Levittowner described the most common attitude: "Religious differences aren't important as long as everyone practices what he preaches."

Memories of the Depression and World War II and nightmares of the Holocaust and the H-bomb made the turn to religion often more than just social or material. The great power of the African American churches during this decade demands ongoing respect and study. In his recent detailed work on the civil rights movement, *The Children* (1998), David Halberstam pays special homage to James Lawson, admitted to Vanderbilt Divinity School in 1959 in a token gesture. Along with John Lewis and James Bevel, Lawson helped connect religious faith—as Martin Luther King did—with social justice. He taught his followers to move beyond the passivity of their elders, yet to remain nonviolent as they became the next decade's freedom riders. Black preachers spread their deep religion among people risking their lives for a better society, not for easy salvation. But they too were often invisible at the time.

Women who were denied access to power through careers and institutions also began to play a greater policy-making role in organized religion. Their great enrollment as church members demanded attention on other levels. As early as 1951, the first woman Methodist minister was ordained. And women deacons were encouraged by Southern Presbyterians to help in the fight against communism. Mary Lyman, ordained a Congregational minister in 1950, became the first woman to hold a faculty chair at Union Theological Seminary. Before her retirement as dean of women students in 1955, she played a vigorous advocacy role for other women in the ministry. She also wrote about women's concerns for international accords through the World Council of Churches in a 1956 book, *Into All the World*. In 1957 New York City boasted its first woman Presbyterian minister and also its first Episcopalian "vestry person."

On the West Coast, Georgia Harkness of the Pacific School of Religion published three books during the 1950s emphasizing Christianity's need to create greater meaning for the people in the pews, a belief designed to make better use of women's social gifts. Edith Lowry—an example of such outreach as a Protestant minister to migrant workers—in 1950 took over the directorship of the Home Mission for the National Council of Churches. "Golden Rule Christians" emerged in many church organizations to guide members toward ethics—lived religion—in everyday life (Kaledin 2000, 111–13).

RELIGION AND THE COURTS

As noted above, the federal courts had become critically involved in debates on American religious life, particularly with regard to the First Amendment and the "establishment clause" in the U.S. Constitution. In 1943, in *West Virginia State Board of Education v. Barnette,* the justices ruled that the school could not require students to salute the American flag during Pledge of Allegiance ceremonies if it contradicted their religious beliefs. In 1947, the Supreme Court considered the question in *Everson v. Board of Education.* The court concluded as follows:

Neither a state nor the Federal Government can set up a church, Neither can pass laws which aid one religion or aid all religions, Or prefer one religion over another...Neither a state nor the Federal Government can, openly or secretly, participate in the affairs of any religious organizations or groups and vice versa. In the words of [Thomas] Jefferson, the clause against establishment of religion by law was intended to erect "a wall of separation between Church and State." (McCarthy and Cambron-McCabe 1987, 26, 39)

The court's decision made clear, utilizing the First and Fourteenth Amendments, that the issues that had created the Scopes Trial debate in 1925 had no basis in law. Neither individual states nor the federal government could legislate the kind of laws that Tennessee and others had in the 1920s. Critics would continue to challenge the court's conclusions, but the battle was joined. Future Supreme Court decisions in the 1960s would reaffirm, in more detail, the conclusions reached in *Everson v. Board of Education.*

Any effort to portray American religious life in the period 1940–1959 as simply orthodox, conservative, and focused on fear of communism lacks credibility. Religion in the United States remained a complex, often divisive issue even as it also was a means of bringing people together and meeting not only spiritual needs but also social ones. Just as there were families that attended weekly services for social reasons, there were others deeply committed to social justice. For fundamentalists who demanded orthodoxy and unquestioning faith, other Americans challenged the status quo and called for sweeping changes in the role that women should play in institutional religious life. The federal courts assumed an active role in examining the separation of church and state during the period even while other branches of government sought to imprint religion more obviously on American currency. To some degree, the very nature of the emotional debate in America defined the seriousness with which people in the country approached the issue. Elinor Goulding Smith's article in *Harper's* called clear attention to her concerns about intolerance and her desire for more diversity. Yet, the magazine published the piece, and a variety of champions and supporters joined her call for acceptance (*Daily Life Online*, "Religious Life: Religion," in Kaledin, *Daily Life in the United States, 1940–1959*, http://dailylife.greenwood.com).

FOR MORE INFORMATION

Barton, B. *The Man Nobody Knows*. Indianapolis, IN: Bobbs-Merrill, 1925.

Herberg, W. *Protestant-Catholic-Jew: An Essay in American Religious Sociology*. Garden City, NY: Doubleday, 1955.

Kaledin, E. *Daily Life in the United States, 1940–1959: Shifting Worlds*. Westport, CT: Greenwood Press, 2000; also online as *Daily Life Online*, in Kaledin, *Daily Life in the United States, 1940–1959*, http://dailylife.greenwood.com.

Marty, M. E. *Pilgrims in Their Own Land: 500 Years of Religion in America*. Boston: Little Brown, 1984.

McCarthy, Martha M., and Nelda H. Cambron-McCabe. *Public School Law: Teachers' and Students' Rights*. Newton, MA: Allyn and Bacon, 1987.

3

DAILY LIFE IN THE UNITED STATES, 1960–1990

Timeline

DAILY LIFE IN THE UNITED
STATES, 1960–1990

|
TIMELINE
OVERVIEW
DOMESTIC LIFE
ECONOMIC LIFE
INTELLECTUAL LIFE
MATERIAL LIFE
POLITICAL LIFE
RECREATIONAL LIFE
RELIGIOUS LIFE

1960 The movie *Psycho* by Alfred Hitchcock becomes one of the most famous
      psychological thrillers of all time.

      Ninety percent of U.S. homes have a television set.

      Democrat John F. Kennedy defeats Republican Richard Nixon in a closely fought
      presidential race.

      Harper Lee publishes *To Kill a Mockingbird*.

      February 1: Four black college students are denied service at a Woolworth's lunch
      counter in Greensboro, North Carolina; the students refuse to leave their seats,
      thus initiating the civil rights movement protest tactic known as a sit-in.

      July 4: Following Hawaii's admission as the 50th state in August 1959, the 50-star
      flag of the United States is introduced in Philadelphia, Pennsylvania.

      September 26: The two leading U.S. presidential candidates, Richard M. Nixon
      (Republican) and John F. Kennedy (Democrat), participate in the first televised
      presidential debate.

      October 29: In Louisville, Kentucky, Cassius Clay (who later will take the name
      Muhammad Ali) wins his first professional fight.

1961 January 26: Wayne Gretsky, a future professional hockey player, is born.

      March 1: President John F. Kennedy establishes the Peace Corps.

      April 17: U.S. forces unsuccessfully attempt to invade Cuba in what becomes
      known as the Bay of Pigs invasion.

      May 5: Alan Barlett Shepard Jr. becomes the first American in space.

      July 2: The writer Ernest Hemingway commits suicide.

1962 February 20: John Glenn becomes first American astronaut to orbit the earth.

      June 25: In *Engel v. Vitale*, the U.S. Supreme Court rules that mandatory prayer in
      public schools is unconstitutional.

July 6: Nobel Prize-winning American writer William Faulkner dies.

August 5: The famous actress Marilyn Monroe is found dead after a sleeping pill overdose.

October 14: A U-2 plane photographs Soviet nuclear arms positioned in Cuba.

October 22: President John F. Kennedy announces the Cuban missile threat to the American public.

October 28: After a tense standoff between the United States and the Soviet Union, Soviet leader Nikita Khrushchev announces the removal of nuclear warheads from Cuba.

1963   January 11: *Whiskey a Go Go* opens in Los Angeles as the first disco club in the United States.

June 17: In the case *Abington School District v. Schempp*, the U.S. Supreme Court declares mandatory Bible reading in public schools to be unconstitutional.

August 28: Martin Luther King Jr. delivers his "I Have a Dream" speech in Washington, D.C.

November 22: President John Kennedy is assassinated in Dallas, Texas.

November 24: Dallas nightclub owner Jack Ruby murders Lee Harvey Oswald, the suspected assassin of President John F. Kennedy, on live television.

1964   February 9: The Beatles make their first appearance on the *Ed Sullivan Show*, sparking "Beatlemania."

July 2: President Lyndon B. Johnson signs the Civil Rights Act of 1964.

July 31: Ranger 7 sends back the first close-up photographs of the moon.

August 28–30: Race riots erupt in Philadelphia.

September 24: The Warren Commission's report on the assassination of President Kennedy is published.

1965   February 25: Malcolm X, the founder of the Organization of Afro-American Unity, is shot to death.

March 8–9: President Lyndon B. Johnson sends first U.S. troops to Vietnam.

September 6: Cesar Chavez and the United Farm Workers (UFW) Union launch a boycott of table grapes.

October 30: A march in support of the Vietnam War draws 25,000 to Washington, D.C.

December 9: "A Charlie Brown Christmas" airs on CBS for the first time.

1966   June 13: The U.S. Supreme Court rules in *Miranda v. Arizona* that police must inform suspects of their rights before questioning.

August 1: Sniper Charles Whitman kills 13 people at the University of Texas.

August 29: The British rock band the Beatles play their last concert.

October: Bobby Seale and Huey P. Newton found the Black Panther Party.

December 15: American animated film producer Walt Disney dies.

1967   January 15: The Green Bay Packers of the National Football League defeat the Kansas City Chiefs of the American Football League in the first Super Bowl.

February 10: Ratification of the 25th Amendment establishes the succession to the presidency.

August 30: Thurgood Marshall is confirmed as the first African American justice of the U.S. Supreme Court.

October 2: Thurgood Marshall is sworn in as a justice of the U.S. Supreme Court.

December 19: Professor John Archibald Wheeler uses the term *black hole* for the first time to describe an object in space characterized by a gravitation field strong enough to even prevent the escape of light.

1968   January: Viet Cong troops attack Saigon, Hue, and other provincial capitals in Vietnam; the action is known as the Tet Offensive.

March 18: The U.S. Congress repeals the requirement for a gold reserve to back U.S. currency.

April 4: Civil rights leader Martin Luther King Jr. is assassinated in Memphis, Tennessee.

April 11: President Lyndon B. Johnson signs the Civil Rights Act of 1968.

June 1: Helen Keller, the famous deaf-blind inventor and activist, dies in her sleep in Connecticut.

June 5: Robert Kennedy, brother of the late President John F. Kennedy and a candidate for the Democratic presidential nomination, is shot at a campaign rally in Los Angeles; he dies on June 6.

November 5: Republican Richard Nixon defeats Democrat Hubert Humphrey to become the 37th president of the United States.

1969   June 27: Police storm a Greenwich Village gay bar, the Stonewall Inn, sparking three nights of riots in the area; the Stonewall riots are widely accepted as the beginning of the gay rights movement.

July 20: Neil Armstrong and Edwin "Buzz" Aldrin Jr. become the first men on the moon.

August 9: Members of the Charles Manson cult, on orders from Manson, murder actress Sharon Tate and others in her home in Los Angeles.

August 15–18: The Woodstock Music and Art Fair is held on a dairy farm near Bethel, New York.

September 26: The pilot episode of *The Brady Bunch* airs.

1970   April 17: Apollo 13 safely lands in the ocean after experiencing a burst air tank on its mission to the moon.

April 22: Earth Day is observed for the first time in the United States.

May 1: Four students are shot to death by National Guardsmen during an antiwar protest at Kent State University in Ohio.

October: The Public Broadcasting Service (PBS) begins broadcasting.

October 4: Janis Joplin dies of a heroin overdose.

1971   January 1: Cigarette advertisements are banned on national television.

June 13: The *New York Times* begins publishing the Pentagon Papers.

June 30: The movie *Willy Wonka and the Chocolate Factory* is released in theaters.

July 1: Ratification of the 26th Amendment gives 18-year-olds the right to vote.

July 3: Doors musician Jim Morrison is found dead in his Paris apartment.

1972   February 1: First handheld scientific calculator (HP-35) is introduced (price $395).

March 22: Equal Rights Amendment is passed by Congress and submitted to the states for ratification.

June 14–23: Hurricane Agnes kills 117 along U.S. East Coast.

September 1: American Bobby Fischer becomes the world chess champion.

November 7: President Richard Nixon is reelected by a landslide over Democratic challenger George McGovern.

November 8: Home Box Office (HBO) is launched.

1973   January 14: Elvis Presley's "Aloha from Hawaii" television special is seen around the world by over one billion viewers.

January 22: In its *Roe v. Wade* decision, the U.S. Supreme Court makes abortion legal in the first trimester.

March 29: U.S. troops are removed from Vietnam.

August 13: The Houston mass murders occur; 3 men kill 27 boys.

September 2: Fantasy writer J.R.R. Tolkien, the author of the *Lord of the Rings* trilogy, dies.

October 10: Vice President Spiro Agnew, facing charges of tax evasion and money laundering, resigns from office.

December 6: Gerald Ford, President Nixon's nominee, is confirmed as vice president of the United States.

1974   May 19: The Philadelphia Flyers defeat the Boston Bruins, becoming the first expansion team to win hockey's Stanley Cup.

August 8: Facing likely impeachment as a result of his involvement in the Watergate cover-up, President Richard Nixon becomes the first president to resign from office; Gerald Ford assumes the presidency effective August 9.

September 8: Gerald Ford grants a presidential pardon to Nixon.

October 4: American poet and writer Anne Sexton dies from inhaling carbon monoxide.

November 20: The U.S. Department of Justice files its final antitrust suit against AT&T.

1975   *Jaws* becomes the first movie to gross $100 million dollars in North America.

March 10: *The Rocky Horror Picture Show* opens in New York City with four performances.

May 5: The Busch Gardens Williamsburg Theme Park opens in Virginia.

July 31: Labor leader Jimmy Hoffa is reported missing in Michigan.

October 1: First *Saturday Night Live* episode is aired in New York City.

1976   March 27: The first 4.6 miles of the Washington, D.C., subway system open.

July 4: Americans celebrate the U.S. Bicentennial, the 200th anniversary of the Declaration of Independence.

July 29: In New York City, the "Son of Sam" kills his first victim and seriously wounds another, marking the beginning of a reign of terror unleashed by his serial killings.

July 31: NASA releases the famous Face on Mars photo.

November 2: Democrat Jimmy Carter of Georgia defeats Republican Gerald Ford to become the first candidate from the Deep South to win the presidency since 1848.

November 26: Microsoft is officially registered with the Office of the Secretary of the State of New Mexico.

1977 The book *The Amityville Horror* by Jay Anson is released.

January 21: President Jimmy Carter pardons all Vietnam War draft evaders.

July 28: The first oil piped through the Trans-Alaska Pipeline System reaches Valdez, Alaska.

August 16: Elvis Presley dies in Memphis, Tennessee, at the age of 42.

December 14: The film *Saturday Night Fever* is released.

1978 First Sundance Film Festival is held.

Artificial insulin is invented.

February 15: Serial killer Ted Bundy is captured in Florida; he later confesses to over 30 murders.

April 10: Volkswagen becomes the first non-American automobile manufacturer to open a plant in the United States.

April 18: The U.S. Senate votes 68–32 to turn the Panama Canal over to Panama on December 31, 1999.

1979 January 13: The YMCA sues the Village People for libel because of their song of the same name.

January 29: Brenda Ann Spencer opens fire at a school in California, killing two teachers and wounding eight students.

March 28: Three Mile Island nuclear reactor in Pennsylvania experiences a near meltdown.

September 1: The *American Pioneer 11* becomes the first spacecraft to visit Saturn.

November 4: Iranian students storm the U.S. embassy in Tehran, holding 66 people hostage; the hostages will remain in Iranian custody for the next 444 days.

1980 January 20: The United States announces that its athletes will not attend the Summer Olympics in Moscow, unless the Soviet Union withdraws troops from Afghanistan.

January 27: Six American diplomats, posing as Canadians, manage to escape from Tehran, Iran.

February 22: Team U.S.A. beats the Soviet Union in what would later be called the "Miracle on Ice" at Lake Placid, New York, thus ending the Soviet Union's chance for five consecutive gold medals in hockey.

April 24: A failed attempt to rescue the American hostages in Iran results in the deaths of eight rescuers.

April 24: In the Pennsylvania lottery scheme, the state lottery is rigged by six men, including Nick Perry, the host of the live TV drawing.

November 4: Republican challenger Ronald Reagan defeats incumbent Democratic President Jimmy Carter, winning 44 of the 50 states.

December 8: John Lennon is murdered outside his New York apartment.

1981   January 20: The U.S. hostages in Iran are given over to American custody only minutes after Ronald Reagan is sworn in as president of the United States.

March 19: Walter Cronkite signs off from the *CBS Evening News* for the last time.

March 30: President Ronald Reagan is shot and wounded by John Hinckley.

June 12: Major League Baseball begins a 49-day strike over the issue of free agent compensation.

August 12: IBM releases its first personal computer.

September 25: Sandra Day O'Connor is sworn in as the first woman justice of the U.S. Supreme Court.

1982   February 10: *Das Boot* is released in the United States.

July 13: Montreal hosts the first Major League Baseball All-Star game held outside the United States.

September: The first episode of *Cheers* premieres.

December 2: Barney Clark becomes the first person to receive an artificial heart.

December 9: Norman Mayers threatens to blow up the Washington Monument before being killed by U.S. Park Police.

1983   February 28: The final episode of M*A*S*H is aired, becoming the most watched episode in TV history.

March 23: President Reagan introduces the Strategic Defensive Initiative (SDI).

April 4: Space shuttle *Challenger* makes its first voyage into space.

August 9: Peter Jennings hosts the first broadcast of ABC's *World News Tonight*.

November 10: Microsoft announces the release of Windows, an extension of MS-DOS that allows for a graphical operating environment for PC users.

1984   February 3: Space shuttle *Challenger* is sent on its tenth mission into space.

March 29: The Baltimore Colts of the National Football League move to Indianapolis.

April 24: Apple Computers introduces the Apple IIc portable computer.

July 12: Geraldine Ferraro becomes the first woman on a national political ticket when she is selected by Democratic nominee Walter Mondale to be his vice presidential running mate.

August 6: Prince releases his blockbuster album *Purple Rain*.

October 7: Walter Payton of the Chicago Bears breaks Jim Brown's National Football League rushing record.

November 6: President Ronald Reagan wins a landslide reelection victory over Democratic challenger Walter Mondale, winning 49 of the 50 states.

1985   March 11: Mikhail Gorbachev is elected leader of the Soviet Union.

April 23: New Coke is introduced.

July 3: *Back to the Future* is released in theaters.

September 11: Pete Rose gets his 4,192nd hit, breaking Ty Cobb's record.

October 18: Nintendo releases *NES* to limited American markets.

October 19: The first Blockbuster video store opens in Dallas, Texas.

1986   January 28: Space shuttle *Challenger* explodes just over a minute after takeoff; the entire crew is killed.

April 3: IBM releases the PC convertible, the world's first laptop.

July 18: The motion picture *Aliens* is released in the United States.

October 25: Thanks to Bill Buckner's error, the New York Mets defeat the Boston Red Sox to win Game 6 of the World Series; the Mets go on to win the Series two days later.

September 8: The *Oprah Winfrey Show* hits national television.

November 21: The Iran-Contra scandal breaks out.

1987   January 4: Amtrak train heading from Washington, D.C., to Boston collides with Conrail engines, killing 16 people.

January 5: President Ronald Reagan undergoes prostate surgery; many question the health of the president, who is nearly 76.

May 11: First heart-lung transplant takes place in Baltimore, Maryland.

June 12: President Reagan gives his "tear down this wall" speech in Berlin.

July 11: The United Nations announces that Earth's population has exceeded 5 billion.

August 11: Alan Greenspan becomes chairman of the U.S. Federal Reserve.

August 13: President Reagan admits his role in the Iran-Contra scandal.

1988   April 4: Republican Governor Evan Mecham of Arizona is convicted in his impeachment trial and removed from office.

April 14: The USS *Samuel B. Roberts* strikes a mine in the Persian Gulf, sparking U.S. retaliation against Iran; known as Operation Preying Mantis, the resulting encounter is the world's largest naval battle since World War II.

August 6: Police riot in New York City's Tompkins Square Park.

September 24: Ben Johnson sets a record of 9.79 seconds in the 100 meters at the Summer Olympics.

November 8: Republican George H. W. Bush, who was vice president under Ronald Reagan, defeats Democrat Michael Dukakis to become the 41st president of the United States.

December 7: Yasser Arafat recognizes the right of the state of Israel to exist.

1989   March 24: The *Exxon Valdez* tanker spills more then 10 million gallons of oil after running aground in Prince William Sound, Alaska.

April 26: The beloved American comedienne Lucille Ball dies at age 78.

June 23: *Batman* is released in movie theaters.

July 5: *Seinfeld* debuts on NBC.

August 22: Nolan Ryan becomes the first pitcher in baseball history to reach 5,000 strikeouts.

August 24: Pete Rose is banned from baseball for illegal gambling.

October 15: Wayne Gretzky becomes National Hockey League's all-time leading scorer.

December 17: *The Simpsons* debuts on Fox and becomes an instant hit.

1990   January 13: L. Douglas Wilder, the first African American elected governor of a U.S. state, takes office in Virginia.

February 7: The Soviet Communist Party agrees to give up power in the Soviet Union.

June 30: East and West Germany unite their economies.

August 6: The United Nations orders a global trade embargo against Iraq for its invasion of Kuwait.

November 13: The world's first known World Wide Web page is written.

Overview

IMPACT OF THE "AGE OF PROTEST AND CHANGE" ON AMERICAN DAILY LIFE

Changes in the everyday life of Americans usually occur so gradually that often they are discovered only after they have gained momentum and resulted in new structures and patterns of living. Looking back on the years 1967–1974, we see continuities in everyday life being broken. Lines between private and public lives became so blurred that it became virtually impossible to draw distinctions between them. The descriptive term *modern* fit less well than before, although *postmodern* did not fit well either. Thoughtful men and women of all ages had reason to ponder the meaning of what they saw around them.

They could ask, for example, where idealism had got them: personal insecurity still existed. Some continued to suffer from hunger or a lack of decent clothing or shelter. Some were unemployed or lacked the skills for economic advancement. Distribution of wealth remained unequal. Some Americans still experienced discrimination in their quest for housing, jobs, and education and as producers and consumers in the marketplace. Some were politically powerless; some who had power abused it. They could wonder whether the Voting Rights Act of 1965 did much to change the circumstances of the African Americans who were previously denied the right to vote, or whether lowering the voting age from 21 to 18 (achieved through ratification of the 26th Amendment in 1971) conferred significant power on American youth.

How long did the forces driving the cultural changes of the 1960s last? Did the counterculture leave a permanent mark on America? Many of the changes of these years were most visible among youth on college campuses, so one way to answer those questions is to compare life and ideals there in the early 1970s with what they had been in the late 1960s. Polling studies done by Daniel Yankelovich between 1967 and 1974 and reported in *The New Morality* showed, among other things, that by the early 1970s what might be called the everyday life on campuses was different in these ways:

- the campus rebellion was moribund;
- new lifestyles were scarcely connected to radical politics;
- students sought self-fulfillment within conventional careers;
- criticism of America as a "sick society" had lessened;
- campuses were free of violence;
- gaps between generations in mainstream America had narrowed on values, morals, and outlook;
- the new sexual morality prevailed in both mainstream college youth and main-stream working-class youth not enrolled in college;
- the work ethic seemed stronger on campuses but was growing weaker among noncollege youth;
- criticisms of major institutions were tempered on campus but taken up by noncollege youth;
- criticism of universities and the military had subsided;
- although campuses were quiet, signs of latent discontent and dissatisfaction appeared among working-class youth;
- concerns for minorities had lessened;
- the number of radical students was significantly smaller and there was greater acceptance of requirements for law and order;
- public attitudes toward students showed few signs of anger and little overt concern about them. (Yankelovich 1974, 3–5)

Obviously, the revolt of the 1960s had ended. "Youth no longer appeared as a major force on the national political scene, in search of new institutional patterns and interpersonal relationships," wrote David Chalmers in *And the Crooked Places Made Straight: The Struggle for Social Change in the 1960s.* Even though the war in Vietnam was over, "military budgets escalated. No organization spoke for black America. Preachments about radically changing America were more likely to be heard from the Right than the Left. The poor were still poor, particularly the children." Although it may not be proper to blame the 1960s and the consumer culture, he adds that "three of the saddest developments in the following decades derived from both too little and too much affluence and freedom. By the eighties, teen-age pregnancy among the poor, and drugs among the young, had become national epidemics, while the dark shadow of AIDS hovered over sexual liberation" (Chalmers 1991, 144–45).

By 1974, the times of one kind of troubles were over. Other troubles remained, however, as America entered a period of readjustment. At the same time, the period 1960–1990 had created as many new opportunities as it had problems. American daily life responded to both the problems and opportunities with a new set of values and experiences. The cultural transitions we have considered became cultural stand-offs that intensified throughout the years. Given their multiple causes and terrains, the term *standoffs* is intentionally used here in the plural. If the opposing sides in the standoffs wish to find common ground, it will be necessary to learn that fixing blame for what went wrong and claiming credit for what went right will not accomplish that (*Daily Life Online*, "Not Ready for New Times," in Marty, *Daily Life in the United States, 1960–1990*, http://dailylife.greenwood.com).

PROSPECTS AND LATENT EVENTS

When the 1980s drew to a close, there were few signs that sources of discord would soon fade away. Moreover, what historians call the latent events of the 1960s through the 1980s meant that discord was likely to broaden and deepen. Latent events—in contrast to events that are seen as they occur and have immediate, observable consequences—are generally unnoticed, partly because their consequences are postponed. Latent events of the decades treated in this book, particularly the 1980s, carry prospects of consequences awaiting future generations of Americans. Some latent events merit mention here. Interpretations of their meaning, speculation on the nature of their consequences, and ideas on how they should be dealt with are left to readers (*Daily Life Online*, "Prospects: Latent Events," in Marty, *Daily Life in the United States, 1960–1990*, http://dailylife.greenwood.com).

FOR MORE INFORMATION

Carr, Edward Hallet. *What Is History?* New York: Alfred A. Knopf, 1963, pp. 42–43.

Chalmers, David. *And the Crooked Places Made Straight: The Struggle for Social Change in the 1960s.* Baltimore, MD: Johns Hopkins University Press, 1991.

Hughes, H. Stuart. *History as Art and as Science: Twin Vistas on the Past.* New York: Harper & Row, 1964, p. 107.

Marty, Myron A. *Daily Life in the United States, 1960–1990: Decades of Discord.* Westport, CT: Greenwood Press, 1997; also available online as *Daily Life Online*, in Marty, *Daily Life in the United States, 1960–1990*, http://dailylife.greenwood.com.

Yankelovich, Daniel. *The New Morality: A Profile of American Youth in the 70s.* New York: McGraw-Hill, 1974.

Domestic Life

OVERVIEW

If the 15 years following World War II appeared to create a clear template for American domestic life, the 30 years between 1960 and 1990 saw major alterations in that domestic lifestyle for men, women, and children. While changes occurred in family life with regard to marriage, divorce, the perception of the roles of men, women, and children, and other factors, many fundamental domestic concepts re-mained the same. American families continued to pursue the acquisition of material goods and services, and those families came to expect a continued quality of life that offered variety, options, and benefits to improve their standard of living. In the 30-year period between 1960 and 1990, regardless of economic conditions or new per-ceptions about families, American domestic life witnessed an increasing expansion of access to products and services designed to equate quality of life with consump-tion. That basic domestic reality had existed since the end of World War II.

By the beginning of the 1960s, 70 percent of women had married by age 24. That contrasted with only 42 percent just two decades earlier. By 1990, only 50 percent of women that age were married. The birth rate had also grown significantly between 1945 and 1960. Over 4 million children born in 1960 contrasted with the 2.3 mil-lion born in 1940. Many families had three and four children. The popular culture suggested an iconic family lifestyle assuming that males had the financial ability to provide sufficient income to manage the growing families, while women could suc-cessfully raise children and maintain domestic life with success and pride. The cul-ture also appeared to lavish more time and attention on children than it had in the past. The so-called Baby Boom era had a definable framework for American families, a broad social perception of how domestic life in America ought to proceed. As the economy continued to expand, and the cultural norm continued to present a clear image of American domestic life, the patterns remained reasonably static. Divorce rates also remained historically low. At a bit more than 2 divorces per 1,000 popula-tion, the new decade of the 1960s saw divorce rates rise to 2.5 divorces per thousand in 1966 and reach more than 5 per thousand by 1981. The 1960 census noted that a "typical" American family included a father, mother, and three children. The times were about to change.

By 1972, the birth rate in the United States began to decline as numbers dropped below 2.1 children per mother. Those numbers continued to fall throughout the 1970s and 1980s. During those years, two major commissions began to analyze what the data might suggest. The President's Commission on Population Growth and the American Future and the Select Commission on Population both considered the long-term impact and considerations regarding population and American society. While observers saw the studies as primarily aimed at demographic and statistical concerns relating to overpopulation, critics argued that the studies appeared to be subtle but profound assaults on the American family and traditional Baby Boom era thinking. Certainly, the decline in the birth rate signaled some significant change in American domestic life. A subtle, but apparent, shift took place beginning in the 1960s. The daily lives of Americans, as they viewed family relations, home life, and other aspects of domesticity, altered perceptibly in the 30 years that followed.

THE "OTHER AMERICA"

It remains important to remember that a segment of the American domestic population did not have full access to the goods, services, and opportunities that continued to expand for most people in the years between 1960 and 1990. Poverty levels in the nation tended to remain steady at between 10 and 15 percent depending on how various agencies calculated the data. While suburban expansion benefited the middle class, still the largest percentage of Americans, inner cities and rural areas continued to see the loss of jobs and revenue. As urban areas lost businesses and tax revenue, school systems suffered, unemployment rose, crime increased, family structure broke down, and domestic life in much of the inner cities did not match the style and substance discussed previously. Similar problems had also occurred in rural areas. The Great Society and War on Poverty programs, initiated in the mid-1960s, certainly had a long-term positive impact in a variety of measurable ways. Yet, the domestic crises that confronted a significant portion of America's people remained an unresolved concern. The fact that middle- and upper-class Americans continued to enjoy a comfortable, secure domestic environment with more options and variety may even have exacerbated the situation. The disparity between the shopping malls of Shaker Heights, Ohio, and Cherry Hill, New Jersey, and the ghettos of Detroit and Camden, New Jersey, drew stark attention to a disturbing reality.

There were two Americas, and that condition remained unresolved. In some ways, it seemed worse. As early as 1965, Daniel Patrick Moynihan, a sociologist working as assistant secretary in the Department of Labor, published *The Negro American Family: The Case for National Action*. The book created a fire storm of controversy. Moynihan's statistics indicated that African American family life in the urban ghettos of northern cities had broken down. One of four children was illegitimate. The divorce rate among black families was higher than for their white counterparts (5.1 percent to 3.6 percent). Crime rates among young black men had risen dramatically. Urban blacks lived, predominantly, in single-parent environments, invariably matriarchal, and the nature of domestic life for African Americans in the cities had become a national disgrace. Intended for internal review and study within the Department of Labor, the book became known publicly as the *Moynihan Report*. It made national headlines, and it drew a host of supporters and critics throughout the late 1960s and for the next two decades. Critics saw the report as an attack on African Americans and characterized the study as embodying a blame-the-victim mentality. They believed the report played into the hands of racists who would use the statistics to justify segregation and discrimination. Supporters saw the data as evidence that a trend had developed based on long-standing racism and discrimination. Those "facts" had to be addressed and corrected if positive changes could occur. As a drug culture began to grow in the inner cities in the 1980s, the situations described in Moynihan's report worsened. More studies, more statistics, and more recrimination continued to spark the debate.

📷 *Snapshot*

Average Cost of Living Examples, 1960 and 1980

	1960	1980
Average Income	$5,199	$19,100
New Car	$2,600	$7,200
Gasoline	$0.25 per gallon	$1.19 per gallon
Milk	$1.04 per gallon	$2.02 per gallon
Movie Ticket	$1.00	$2.25

Source: Remember When (Millersville, TN: Seek Publishing).

CHILDREN

The postwar generation of parents focused more time and lavished more attention on children than had any previous generation in American history. From birth to adolescence, children were perceived as unique and deserving of special consideration and were provided with as many resources and opportunities as possible to help develop their potential. From public schools, to organized sports, to television programming, to access to money, children experienced a wave of attention. Perhaps, themselves denied stability and security during the Depression and the war, American parents, and the society that supported them, encouraged a new view of children. Local Parent Teacher Associations (PTAs) witnessed a more direct involvement between parents and their children's schoolteachers and administrators. If recreation and sports activities had been spontaneous and child controlled in the past, the 1960s saw an evolution of parent-run organizations designed to sponsor and direct their children's play time. The 1976 film *Bad News Bears* offered a wonderful critique of the harmful influence such organized activities could have in a less-than-subtle knock at Little League baseball. Organizations like the Boy Scouts and Girl Scouts of America grew into large, administrative systems with paid professionals running the organizations while using volunteer parents to operate the day-to-day activities for their children. Advocates of the adult involvement argued that it made recreation safer and more beneficial. Critics contended that the trend toward such organization and control ruined the pure fun and innovation that spontaneous recreational activity provides children. The debate continues, but the shift to adult-controlled and -supervised activity for young people has remained a standard since the 1960s.

The influence of television on children also grew during the 30-year period between 1960 and 1990. As television technology provided better, bigger color sets, and as advertisers and program directors expanded viewing options for children, kids simply watched more TV. The adolescent "couch potato" evolved in the 1960s and provoked another explosion of commissions and studies examining the impact of too much television on America's youth. From Newton Minnow's warnings as head of the Federal Communication Commission to scholarly work at the Annenberg School of Communication at Pennsylvania University, critics worried that children watched too much television (six to eight hours a day), saw too much violence, and remained subject to ill-advised advertising. Clearly, the medium, to its critics, had a harmful impact. To combat the negative image, new positive shows for children began to compete. *Sesame Street, Romper Room*, and *Mr. Roger's Neighborhood* offered instructive and interesting alternatives to previous options, and they certainly became long-standing parts of television's effort to present wholesome entertainment. Critics, however, continued to point out that "plopping" a young child in front of *Sesame Street* may have been better than having them watch competing commercial programs for kids, but it remained a technological "baby-sitter" that freed parents from direct supervision. In any event, the studies, critiques, and concerns failed to diminish the time children spent watching television, nor did it impact fundamentally on the types of programs they viewed.

If American children watched more television between 1960 and 1990, they also had the purchasing power to indulge in a broad variety of technological entertainment options that began to appear in the 1960s and 1970s. Traditional vinyl records (78 rpm) fell victim to new 45 rpm and 33 rpm long-playing records that encouraged teenagers to purchase new record players and records. By the beginning of the 1960s, they dominated the market. Abruptly, tape recorders, stereophonic hi-fidelity components, and other innovations offered another source of entertainment. Between 1965 and the early 1970s, 8-track cassettes became standard fare in automobiles and homes. Sony Walkman portable tape systems entered the market in 1978–1979. As the sale of new records and record players swelled, American children (as well as their parents) could indulge their consumerism in an increasing technological supermarket of items.

Video games also drew the attention of children during the era. Between 1958 and 1962, *Pong* and *Space War* were the first video games developed. Initially devised for use in arcades, the number of video games expanded to more than a hundred in the early 1970s. *Atari* and *Odyssey* pioneered video entertainment systems for children, and, in 1972, they produced home consoles for television sets. By 1980, *Death Race*, *Space Invaders*, and *Pac-Man* became three of the most popular video games, and children had become enthralled with the games, spending hours in front of their consoles and millions of dollars on the systems. Critics saw the same dangers in the video games as they had with television programming. While one could argue that video games provided children with interactive involvement in contrast to the passive influence of television, the new games still tied young people to sedentary recreation, often violent and clearly commercial. Children had become the victims of a consumer-marketing barrage of new technology that stole time from their formal education and healthy outdoor recreation. Glued to their television sets or record players, America's children had become captive to unhealthy alternatives. The President's Council on Youth Fitness had warned as early as 1961 that America's children lacked sufficient physical activity to maintain healthy lives.

Coupled with new technologies that appealed to children, toy manufacturers expanded their businesses to appeal to American families. Mega-toy stores like *Toys "R" Us* expanded from a furniture store for children in Washington, D.C. to a franchised retail store for toys in the 1960s. Large toy companies like *Mattel* and *Hasbro* added hundreds of new options to the market, and a billion dollar annual industry developed around the business of selling toys to children of all ages. Increasingly, the Christmas holiday focused as much on toy buying for children as it did on religious observance for Christians. Hanukkah, a traditional but minor Jewish religious holiday, also drew parents to the toy stores as sales rose and children came to expect more and more gifts. Saturday morning television commercials not only encouraged youngsters to have parents buy this or that breakfast cereal, they also bombarded children with the latest toys and games to consider.

Education occupied the attention of adults throughout the 30-year period between 1960 and 1990. On the political and social level, the era often focused on civil rights and integration. The Great Society programs of President Lyndon Johnson included massive new education bills to support every level of public education from grade school through college. At the same time, however, educators and parents had begun to rethink the role of education and its domestic purpose for young people. The traditional separation of school and family as dual educators of children began to blur in the public mind. The view that "reading, writing, and arithmetic" were the sole purpose of schools changed. Public education began to accept a social and domestic function as well. Building esteem and self-confidence became important components of the "new education." Sex education in the schools, the subject of a heated social debate, became a standard aspect of the curriculum. Special education legislation developed throughout the public school systems in America, as did new options for underprivileged children that included breakfast programs and after-school care centers. Increasingly, a broad public debate began as to the limits of authority in child rearing. Parents had traditionally controlled subjects and interests now assumed in schools. The domestic role of families in child rearing remained fundamental, but public policy increasingly transferred key aspects of that function to professional educators.

Certainly, the "decades of discord" that marked the period had a direct influence on the attitudes and behavior of children. High school and college-age young people not only questioned the role of government in public issues like civil rights and the war in Vietnam, they also challenged parental authority. In 1955, James Dean's *Rebel Without a Cause* became a popular movie depicting the problems high school students confronted in the immediate postwar era. Their concerns appeared mild by the 1960s and 1970s. Alcohol, drugs, sex, and rebelliousness among teenagers dominated the news and concerned educators and parents. Traditionalists claimed that permissiveness and the decline of family influence had created a trend of defiance and disobedience among young people in every area from clothing styles to outright aberrant behavior. Too much money, self-indulgence, and a lack of social discipline, they argued, had created a generation of ill-behaved adolescents. Other observers argued that the problems confronting young people had become so complex and difficult that their responses to the times were understandable. It was not their fault. It was society's failure.

MEN

Any social change regarding domestic life in America included the role of men. If the previous era had prescribed specific roles for women as mothers and homemakers, that same social conditioning had determined the responsibilities of males as well. Conditioned as breadwinners, patriarchal heads of families, and hardworking, responsible leaders in community standards and behavior, males certainly held power positions within the domestic environment. Just as children and women began to respond to new conditions and options, however, so, too, did American men. Those alterations provoked a variety of responses. Because half of American marriages remained stable, and because many married women began to work outside the home, men had to respond to changes in their home life. The anecdotal world of women changing diapers, cooking meals, and cleaning the house, while men cut the grass, took out the trash, and changed light bulbs required some rethinking. A new division of labor within the family began to surface in American domestic life. Shared responsibilities became more commonplace in the 1970s and 1980s.

While divorce laws certainly made marital separation easier for men and women, the issue of child custody continued to pose a critical problem. Divorce court judges almost invariably awarded custody to women, and they required men, still financially better off than their spouses, to provide alimony and child support payments. Court decisions regarding child visitation policy hinged on narrow options. Men complained that divorce settlements cost too much, they were granted too little access to their children, or some variety of other concerns. Yet, a number of divorced males failed to comply with court orders regarding alimony and child support. "Deadbeat dads" became a catch phrase for men who disregarded their court-ordered responsibilities. At the same time, however, significant numbers of divorced men did pay required alimony and child support but began to question a legal system that seemed to automatically award child custody to their former wives. The complex issues that surrounded the domestic impact of divorce on men, women, and children have remained a major problem.

An area of domestic responsibility that had always confronted American men hinged on their required military service. More than 30 million men served in the U.S. military during World War II (1941–1945), the Korean War (1950–1953), and the conflict in Vietnam (1965–1975). Millions of others were drafted to serve in peacetime assignments overseas and in the United States between 1940 and 1971. The Selective Service System, initiated after World War II and retained until 1971, required all males 18 years of age to register for a military draft. If a man was called to active duty, military service demanded two years of active military duty and, often, additional service in the National Guard. In simple terms, American males could be asked to leave their homes and families and provide military service for the United States. The domestic impact on the men and their families is often overlooked in studies of military history. How that military service shaped men's attitudes and pre- and post-service roles in the domestic environment remained a key aspect of their lives. In 1971, President Richard Nixon, facing increasing political pressure regarding the war in Southeast Asia, announced the end of the military draft. By 1973, conscription into military service ended. While 18-year-old males were still required to register, the U.S. government had determined to create an all-volunteer military force (Millett and Maslowski 1994).

SUBURBS, CITIES, AND RURAL AMERICA

In Richard Hofstadter's award-winning book, *Age of Reform,* he noted that "America was born in the country and moved to the city." If urbanization dominated the first half of the twentieth century, the move to America's suburbs influenced domestic life in the last half of the century. While that movement began following World War II, it accelerated after 1960, and suburban living became more complex. By 1990, a majority of Americans lived in the suburbs. Both rural and urban populations had declined in relation to the suburbs, and demographics also showed a shift in population from the South and East to the Southwest and the Pacific Coast. Suburban living no longer had the look of early Levittown communities, isolated from urban centers. The growth of the American population, the increasing development of land resources for housing, and the rising income of American middle-class workers had begun to create the "megalopolis." Highways and transportation systems tied suburb to city in an expanding network of homes, businesses, shopping centers, and government offices. From Washington, D.C., to Boston, Massachusetts, a massive domestic complex of cities, towns, and infrastructure had emerged as an example of the American megalopolis. Suburban downtowns like those in Tyson's Corner, Virginia, and Costa Mesa, California, were often centers of commerce and business that were as large as many former urban areas. At the same time, utilization of living space in suburban areas required a new form of development. If single homes built on quarter-acre lots had dominated housing construction in the 1950s and 1960s, townhouses and condominiums emerged as an option in the 1980s. The cost of housing and space allocation demanded a more confined suburban option, and those new complexes answered the problem.

Cities suffered in the 1960s and 1970s as more middle-class families and businesses moved to the suburbs. Observers of the accelerating shift saw a variety of reasons for the move. Racial unrest in the 1960s, often punctuated by inner-city riots, prompted "white flight." Businesses found better tax incentives to locate in suburban industrial parks and corporate centers. The decline in industrial production, centered in major urban locations, also influenced the loss of jobs, revenue, and people. The resultant drop in tax revenue placed cities in the impossible situation of providing services with decreasing funds to do so. As a result, unemployment, urban blight, and the slow deterioration of the inner city became common problems in the 1970s and 1980s. Attempts to regenerate the health and prosperity of American cities remained an issue. Baltimore, Maryland, developed an Inner Harbor complex to attract tourists and business. Cleveland, Ohio, began a similar revival, as did other cities. How to bring money back to urban areas became a driving concern by the beginning of the 1990s. Tax incentives, gentrification, and regional responsibility all became strategies to redress urban decline.

Rural America suffered a similar loss of people, revenue, and farms. The number of farms dropped from around 4 million in 1960 to fewer than 2.5 million by 1980, and to fewer than 2 million by 2000. While large corporate agricultural businesses continued to reduce the number of small family-owned farms, a process that had occurred throughout the century, other factors changed the nature of rural living. Rural locations close to cities and suburbs saw the sale of small farms to real estate developers, and the former farming communities became increasingly tied to the burgeoning megalopolis complex of the 1980s. It became more profitable for a farmer to sell his land to developers than continue to compete in an increasingly difficult enterprise. Former farming communities, as diverse as the eastern shore of Maryland and the Amish counties of Pennsylvania, had become tied to the expanding demands and domestic structure of the suburban lifestyle.

Traditionalists argued that two distinct and unique domestic ways of life had been altered dramatically. The great hope of many Americans in the twentieth century had centered on its thriving urban centers. The long-standing value of farmers and rural living had also been part of the nation's mystical, exceptional past. In lore and reality, urban and rural life had defined the American experience. From small town picnics and Fourth of July celebrations to big-city ball games, skyscrapers, and ethnic diversity, domestic life in America had tended to focus on the two traditional templates. Suburban living altered that way of life and created a new way for Americans to assess their domestic environment (Jackson 1985).

TECHNOLOGY, GADGETRY, AND DEBT

Americans continued to use the consumer options of a successful middle-class economy to improve or expand the products and household items brought into their homes. Even while economic observers indicated, and the recession in the 1970s proved, that the expansion of the postwar economy had begun to slow down, Americans continued to improve aspects of their standard of living. If income levels had begun to remain steady in the 1960s and 1970s, American consumers purchased more domestic goods and products on credit. Using credit cards, reducing family savings, using mortgage loans on their homes, or buying big-ticket items on credit, family indebtedness grew substantially between 1960 and 1990. In 1957, family debts made up 47 percent of income. By 1969, that number had reached 55 percent, by 1981 62 percent, and by 1990 it had climbed to 90 percent (U.S. Census Report, 1990). In simple terms, Americans continued to buy things, but they paid for them on credit and appeared comfortable doing so. The consumer-driven economy of the postwar, free market system had convinced most Americans that their "keep up with the Joneses" lifestyle remained a necessity and not an indulgence. What did the increased spending and personal debt provide? Larger or newer homes, two-car families, new domestic technology, clothes, food, and other consumer items expanded dramatically between 1960 and 1990.

Most middle-class homes included clothes washers and dryers, large refrigerators with built-in freezers, dishwashers, microwave ovens, electric garage door openers, two or more color television sets, stereo and component sound systems, and other domestic conveniences that would have seemed incredible a decade or more earlier. By the 1970s and 1980s two-car families were commonplace in suburban America. Conspicuous consumption had replaced basic home needs as a fundamental aspect of domestic life in America, and while critics had worried about the consumer culture of the 1950s, the three-decade period between 1960 and 1990 dwarfed the purchasing demands of that early domestic public. Advertisers and producers continued to encourage families to keep acquiring goods, but those forces had a relatively easy sell. American middle-class society had become addicted to material consumption. They could argue, reasonably, that the products, gadgets, and items in their homes made life easier and more enjoyable and provided additional time for recreation and relaxation. Women could defend the many new household appliances as time-saving devices that allowed them more time with children or the opportunity to pursue careers and other professional or social options outside the home. As a final addition to the growing list of gadgets and resources, the Federal Communications Commission authorized the private, commercial sale of cellular telephones in 1982. Five years later, a million Americans had purchased the new communications device (U.S. Census Report, 1990).

WOMEN

The role of women in American domestic life may have witnessed the most significant change during the 30-year period from 1960 to 1990. Rising divorce rates and the decline in the birth rate during the period reflect a broader issue. The role of women as wives and mothers remained important but was no longer a domestic imperative. Betty Friedan, a graduate of Smith College, published *The Feminine Mystique* in 1963. The popular, best-selling book argued that the traditional role of American women as mothers and homemakers had become a stifling stereotype limiting female fulfillment. Friedan and other feminist advocates encouraged women to seek careers and satisfaction outside the home, and a new wave of women's rights issues entered the mainstream of America's social debate. Women's rights had concentrated on voting and other political and economic issues in previous generations. The new feminism struck at psychological and social concerns, much of it tied to the domestic role of women in American society.

In the past, women had been tied to marriages because divorce laws in the nation made divorce difficult. In the early 1960s, state law generally accepted adultery and abandonment as the only two legal reasons for separation. The *National Association of Women's Lawyers* began to advocate a new position in that decade arguing the need for "no-fault" divorce laws in the various states. By 1977, only nine states accepted no-fault divorces. By the beginning of the 1990s, almost every state in the nation had passed laws allowing them. In 1966, Christopher Lasch published an article titled "Divorce and the Family in America." Lasch challenged the hypothesis that the rising divorce rate reflected simply a breakdown or decay of the family. He argued that it indicated a major cultural shift in American society. Child raising, Lasch argued, had been the central obsession of the previous generation. The times, however, had changed. The sexual revolution, including the increasing use of birth control pills, freed women from the danger of unwanted pregnancy and the need to seek marriage as a safety net. Industrialism and the new technology gave rise to enhanced professional opportunities for women. It also reduced the traditional demand for large families. The modern feminist movement encouraged women to seek personal satisfaction in areas and arenas outside the home. The option of contributive lives beyond their traditional roles as wife and

Gloria Steinem—feminist activist. Chaiba.

mother existed, and women knew it. They could seek equal education, find rewarding, successful careers, and achieve self-fulfillment in other arenas. In simple terms, women's "obligation to family and society" could be replaced by their "obligation to self" (Whitehead 1997).

More liberal divorce laws and a growing social perception of obligation to self may have played key roles in the changing status of women in domestic American life, but other issues also influenced women's positions in family life. Economics had begun to increasingly demand two family incomes. If divorce rates reached numbers close to 50 percent of American marriages by the 1990s, the numbers still suggest that a majority of Americans remained in two-parent households. Yet, women in increasing numbers sought employment outside the home, whether married, divorced, or single. The emerging debate regarding women's rights and opportunities tended to hinge on the dual issue of home and career. Could or should women try to manage both? Did men have more of a responsibility as homemakers and caregivers for children? Were there broad sociological, even biological factors that separated the roles of men and women in domestic life? The fundamental focus of the women's rights movement in the era argued those domestic questions, even as they branched into other arenas and issues. For the first time since the end of World War II, American society faced a serious discussion regarding the role of the family and the primary responsibility that women had in that regard.

FOR MORE INFORMATION

Jackson, Kenneth. *Crabgrass Frontier: The Suburbanization of the United States*. New York: Oxford University Press, 1985.

Marty, Myron A. *Daily Life in the United States, 1960–1990: Decades of Discord*. Westport, CT: Greenwood Press, 1997; also available online as *Daily Life Online*, in Marty, *Daily Life in the United States, 1960–1990*, http://dailylife.greenwood.com).

Millett, Allen R., and Peter Maslowski. *For the Common Defense: A Military History of the United States of America*. New York: The Free Press, 1994.

U.S. Department of Justice Report. 1991.

Whitehead, Barbara. *The Divorce Culture*. New York: Alfred Knopf, 1997.

World Health Organization. "Global Status Report on Alcohol." 2004.

Economic Life

OVERVIEW

The American economy began to experience significant changes between 1960 and 1990, and those alterations had a key influence on American daily life. While the nation's Gross Domestic Product (GDP) continued to expand, economic variables began to alter American lifestyles. Personal or household debt rose from 25 percent to 45 percent of GDP between 1950 and 1964, then remained steady at around 45 percent into the 1980s. Unemployment rates had averaged between 4 and 6 percent during the decades of the 1960s and 1970s, spiked to 7.2 percent in the 1980s, and then declined to about 5 percent by 1990. Interest rates had also remained at around 5 percent during the 1960s, began to climb slowly, and then accelerated in the 1970s to reach double-digit numbers. By the 1980s, those rates had dropped to 5 percent and by the beginning of the 1990s had dipped to 4 percent. Inflation experienced a similar pattern: single-digit numbers in the 1960s, a significant increase to double digits in the 1970s, and then a decline in the 1980s, leading to 3 to 4 percent inflation by the beginning of the 1990s (U.S. Department of Labor). Those numbers indicate that the 1970s saw a clear shift in the American economy, one that did influence the day-to-day lives of Americans. Economic statistics may be uncertain and debatable, but the economic changes suggested by those broad numbers remain important.

Competition with newly emerging economies in Europe and Asia challenged a virtual American economic monopoly that had existed since 1945. By the 1960s, U.S. businesses were competing with a variety of foreign products. The rise in household debt signaled that Americans were buying more goods and services on credit. The spike in interest and inflation rates in the 1970s also placed Americans in a position in which home mortgages, car payments, and big-tag appliances cost more. The 1970s energy crisis, which saw petroleum prices rise dramatically, also had a key influence on the American economy and daily life in the nation. What had become clear during the 30-year period between 1960 and 1990 was an American economy that was still the strongest in the world but now in competition with a variety of external conditions that the nation had not faced in the 15 years following World War II.

NUTRITION

Food continued to be plentiful for most of the American population, but concerns regarding nutrition appeared well founded. A report by a Senate committee in 1977 estimated that deaths in the United States caused by heart disease could be reduced by 25 percent through better diets. In addition, improved nutrition would reduce infant mortality by half and eliminate or minimize the effects of other diseases. Healthful diets included more fruits, vegetables, whole grains, poultry, and fish and smaller quantities of meat and salty, high-fat, high-sugar foods. It is not surprising that meat, dairy, and egg producers took issue with the report. Word that the American Medical Association questioned the report's scientific justification lessened its impact, but it nonetheless gave the American people reason to be more conscious of the nutritional content of foods they consumed. Such consciousness, furthered by heavy advertising campaigns, resulted in modest dietary changes. For example, sales of bran cereals and breads with higher fiber content increased significantly (*Daily Life Online*, "Cares of Daily Life: Nutrition," in Marty, *Daily Life in the United States, 1960–1990*, http://dailylife.greenwood.com).

CHANGING POPULATION PATTERNS AND CIVIL RIGHTS IN THE ECONOMY

The daily lives of most Americans may not seem to have been directly affected by what came to be known as the unrest of the 1960s, but the changes wrought by protests in those years rippled across America. The most striking changes were the fruits of the civil rights movement, which had gained significant force since World War II. At that time the cruel irony of asking African Americans to risk their lives for a country that denied them constitutionally guaranteed rights became glaringly obvious. Several Supreme Court decisions set precedents for the 1954 landmark case of *Brown v. Board of Education*. In *Brown* the court ruled that schools designed to be "separate but equal" were inherently unequal and therefore unconstitutional.

Armed with the conviction that the Supreme Court's decision outlawing separate but equal schools extended to other aspects of their lives, and frustrated by resistance to calls for change, African American activists adopted a strategy of nonviolent, direct action that at first baffled those seeking to thwart them: They defied laws that denied them rights but refused to respond in kind against physical and verbal attacks. On February 1, 1960, four students at North Carolina A&T College in Greensboro took the first nonviolent action of the 1960s. Those students, the 66 who joined them the next day, the 100 the next, and the 1,000 by the end of the week, sat down at a "whites only" lunch counter in a Woolworth's store in Greensboro. The Greensboro "coffee party," which historian William Chafe (1995) says "takes its place alongside the Boston Tea Party as an event symbolizing a new revolutionary era," infuriated segregationists. Television cameras captured the segregationists' resistance and broadcast it nationwide, thereby creating support for blacks who were ready to take further direct actions (*Daily Life Online*, "Changing Population Patterns: Civil Rights for African Americans," in Marty, *Daily Life in the United States, 1960–1990*, http://dailylife.greenwood.com).

LABOR IN THE ECONOMY

Like the period 1940 to 1959, from the 1960s to the 1990s, many homes and families throughout America enjoyed a general prosperity. But if migration to the suburbs remained a sign of affluence, the city neighborhoods and the people left behind soon showed the many faces of poverty. Poverty was abundantly evident in rural America as well, particularly in Appalachian regions of West Virginia, Kentucky, Tennessee, and North Carolina. Although industries had moved from the North to the South, particularly in textile and furniture manufacturing, it was the prospect of paying lower wages that lured them, so increases in living standards were slow in coming. Most African Americans who earlier had migrated from the South to what they saw as the promised land in northern cities found poverty rather than promise there. Slums and derelict housing projects populated almost exclusively by blacks became common in major cities, and racial discrimination posed barriers as formidable as those existing in the South.

Some economists and social activists who had studied the conditions faced daily by America's poor proposed strategies for economic development to ameliorate them, but action did not come quickly. John F. Kennedy's slight margin of victory in the 1960 presidential election would have hobbled any major reform efforts he might have proposed, and his conservative instincts probably discouraged him from recommending ambitious plans anyway. His measures to stimulate the economy had some positive effects, as the gross national product (GNP) grew at an average annual rate of 5.3 percent between 1961 and 1964, compared to the 3.2 percent annual average of the 1950s. But problems of unequal distribution of wealth—indeed, of outright poverty—persisted.

Just as Rachel Carson's *Silent Spring* (1962) and Ralph Nader's *Unsafe at Any Speed* (1965) had stimulated interest in environmental and product safety concerns, Michael Harrington's passionate book *The Other America* (1962) changed what many people thought about problems of poverty. Although Harrington sprinkled statistics throughout the book, it was his description of the "invisible poor," particularly the elderly, the young, and minorities, that gave the book its power. "In a sense," he wrote,

one might define the contemporary poor in the United States as those who, for reasons beyond their control, cannot help themselves. All the most decisive factors making for opportunity and advance are against them. They are born going downward, and most of them stay down. They are victims whose lives are endlessly blown round and round the other America.

There were 40 to 50 million of them, he estimated. Harrington asked his readers

to respond critically to every assertion, but not to allow statistical quibbling to obscure the huge, enormous, and intolerable fact of poverty in America. For, when all is said and done, that fact is unmistakable, whatever its exact dimensions, and the truly human reaction can only be outrage.

Although Harrington chose not to use statistics to dramatize the condition of the "other Americans," one can see in the numbers of the early 1960s that daily life differed dramatically according to where one stood on the nation's economic ladder. The 20 percent of Americans on the top rungs of the ladder owned more than 75 percent of the nation's wealth; the 20 percent on the bottom rungs owned only 0.05 percent. Those on the bottom rungs received 23 percent of the total money income; those on the top, 77 percent.

In 1968, 13 percent of the American population still lived below the poverty line as defined by the federal government. That compared with 20 percent at the beginning of the decade. Twenty percent of African Americans remained below the poverty line, down from 40 percent eight years earlier. These improvements meant that the Great Society's War on Poverty could claim only a partial victory.

When Richard Nixon became president in 1969, he supported modest growth in the size and cost of a few Great Society programs, went along with legislation that increased Social Security benefits, and approved construction of subsidized housing and expansion of the Job Corps. More significant, he offered a bold and ambitious plan for welfare reform. The Family Assistance Plan (FAP) would have ended piecemeal allowances and guaranteed every family of four an annual income of $2,400, with a maximum of $3,600 for a family of eight or more. The FAP passed the House of Representatives but died in the Senate, caught between liberals who thought it too conservative and conservatives who thought it too liberal.

Mostly left out of the political debates of the 1970s, the American poor suffered even more in the 1980s. Hit especially hard by economic circumstances and policy decisions in the mid-1980s were those Americans affected by the reductions in various welfare programs. President Reagan's inaugural address dramatically revealed his intentions: "Government is not the solution to our problem," he asserted, as he had throughout his campaign; "government *is* the problem." Government generosity and good intentions, he believed, were out of control; he called for "new federalism," a plan to make the down-and-out in society a local and state responsibility. Reductions in federal welfare programs caused worries about whether there would be a safety net to catch those losing government assistance.

Statistics on poverty in 1984 reveal the plight of many Americans. More than 33 million people, about one-seventh of the nation's population, lived below the poverty level, reversing trends set in motion by the Great Society. The percentage of children living in poverty was higher than that of adults. Among both blacks and persons living in female-headed households, the ratio was one in three. Monthly payments to the 3.7 million families covered by the Aid to Families with Dependent Children (AFDC) program averaged $338. About 21.5 million persons received services funded by Medicaid, with average annual costs of $1,569 per person. Nearly 20 million people were eligible for food stamps, a four-year low resulting from more stringent eligibility requirements.

From time to time Congress attempted to reform the welfare system, with specific measures aimed at giving the poor the job training or education needed to get off welfare. In 1988 Congress passed a law requiring parents on welfare whose children were past the age of three to enroll in appropriate education, training, job search, or work programs. The new law, which had an estimated cost of more than $3 billion over five years, allowed for a long lead-in time, reflecting awareness of the difficulty of moving welfare recipients into independence: By 1995, 20 percent of those eligible for welfare would be required to enroll in an appropriate program.

At the very bottom of society were those who lived with no place called home. Estimates of homeless Americans reached a record high in 1986, but the numbers were still rising. New York counted 10,000 single people and 5,500 families as homeless. In Chicago the number of homeless was somewhere between 9,000 and 22,000; in Newark, New Jersey, 4,000–7,000; in Atlanta, 5,000; in Philadelphia, 13,000; and in Los Angeles, 40,000. Included in the tallies were higher proportions of women, children, and younger men than in previous decades.

More than a sluggish economy and a tight employment market accounted for the increased numbers of homeless persons. As noted earlier, in the 1960s and 1970s state and local governments had released mentally ill people from medical facilities. As a result of those deinstitutionalization policies, the population in state mental hospitals dropped from more than 550,000 in the 1950s to fewer than 150,000 three decades later. Community-based programs were intended to help those former patients, but the programs were never sufficiently funded. Those who lacked the mental, physical, financial, and familial resources to cope with life in the outside world, particularly the ability to find and keep jobs, ended up on the streets. Cities grappled in various ways with the problem of caring for them, none with notable success.

Compounding government failures to handle poverty was the decline in the labor movement that in the early 20th century had helped poor working-class people emerge from poverty. From the mid-1930s until the 1960s labor unions had played an important part in improving the economic security of many working-class Americans. By 1970, however, the unions' influence had begun to erode, not only in the workplace but in politics too.

In only two respects did unions maintain or increase the strength they had enjoyed in the 1950s and early 1960s. First, as women entered the workplace, they formed two organizations—the National Association of Working Women (known as Nine to Five) and the Coalition of Labor Union Women. Recognizing the potential power of women in the labor movement, the AFL-CIO, labor's largest organization, endorsed the Equal Rights Amendment in 1973. In subsequent years unions provided support on what came to be called women's issues, such as affirmative action, child care, and pay equity.

Second, unions representing uniformed and nonuniformed public employees at all levels gained power and influence. By 1970, membership in public employees' unions exceeded four million, making it 10 times larger than it had been 15 years earlier. Particularly powerful were the American Federation of State, County, and Municipal Employees; the American Federation of Teachers; and the National Education Association, along with unions of police officers, firefighters, nurses, and postal workers. Yet, their power remained limited by the fact that work stoppages—some legal, some illegal—by public servants directly affected the lives of those whom they served, thereby arousing public resentment.

The recruitment of women and the growth of government workers' unions were insufficient to offset the decline of industrial unions. That decline reflected many changes in economic processes that attracted little attention until their consequences were widely felt. One was the increased automation of manufacturing processes, making assembly-line workers dispensable. Another involved the rising aspirations of families that had moved to the suburbs and worked their way into white-collar jobs. They sent their children to college with expectations that the children could reach even higher rungs on the employment ladder through individual rather than collective effort.

More significant was the process known as deindustrialization. In the 1970s, the United States became an exporter of raw materials and an importer of more cars and steel as well as electronics, and other manufactured goods. The U.S. share of global manufactured exports declined significantly and trade deficits ballooned. Large corporations invested their money in mergers, so much so that in 1968 the Federal Trade Commission launched a sweeping investigation of the causes and consequences of runaway conglomerate mergers. The chairman of the commission referred to those conglomerates—the joining of companies engaged in unrelated or remotely related businesses—as a virus threatening the health of the American economy. Corporations also acquired related business enterprises and invested in overseas operations. Consequently, workers found themselves competing more strenuously against one another for jobs in the United States and against poorly paid workers in other countries. That competition allowed businesses to call for concessions, or "givebacks," as they were known. They included reductions in pay, elimination of formerly protected jobs, and the scaling back of such fringe benefits as medical insurance.

Also affecting unions' effectiveness was something unseen by most Americans, that is, the development of more than a thousand consulting firms that specialized in advising corporations on how to keep union organizers and sympathizers out of the workplace. Those firms also showed how to defeat a union when elections could not be avoided and helped employers find ways to decertify unions that had won elections.

The 1980s got off to a bad start for labor unions when President Reagan fired 12,000 members of the Professional Air Traffic Controllers Organization (PATCO) on August 5, 1981. PATCO had rejected the final bargaining offer made by the Federal Aviation Authority (FAA), and the traffic controllers had gone on strike a week earlier. Because the strike violated federal law, the firings were legal. "Dammit, the law is the law," Reagan said to his aides, "and the law says they can't strike. By striking they've quit their jobs." With the firing of the professional controllers, the FAA had to use military controllers, nonstrikers, and supervisors to keep the nation's planes in the air. The immediate results included a cutback in services, loss of business from people who were reluctant to fly in uncertain skies, and, according to the International Air Transport Association, a $200 million loss by the airlines in the month of August alone.

The symbolic effects of the firings lasted longer. Unions could not expect cordial or deferential treatment from the new administration, particularly the increasingly restive unions of government employees. Those effects, along with the changing nature of workplaces across the nation, made it natural for the decline in union membership to continue. Fear of company shutdowns or permanent layoffs weakened individual union members' readiness to support aggressive tactics by unions in dealing with employers. For ordinary workers, union membership had once symbolized a mutual commitment between themselves and their employers, even in times of difficult negotiations. That sense of commitment gave way to anger and humiliation in the 1980s when unions were compelled to accept distasteful provisions in bargaining agreements. These included such things as lump-sum payments based on company profits rather than permanent wage increases; givebacks of benefits and wage increases that were won in earlier bargaining; and systems of pay with two tiers, allowing for lower wages for new employees.

In the early 1980s, organized labor represented about one worker in four; by the end of the decade it represented one in six. With the decline in membership and the disadvantaged positions in which union workers found themselves, the use of work stoppages in disputes with management declined. In 1988, according to the Bureau of Labor Statistics, the 40 stoppages involving 1,000 or more workers was the lowest number since it began keeping records 40 years earlier (Marty 1997, 43–44, 100–103, 268–69, 271–72; *Daily Life Online*, "Economic Life: Class and Caste Experience" in Marty, *Daily Life in the United States, 1960–1990*, http://dailylife.greenwood.com).

MALLS AND SHOPPING CENTERS

Consumers attending to their material needs went shopping, and by the 1960s that meant going to shopping centers. The rise of such centers went hand-in-hand with the increased use of automobiles and the growth of suburbs. The first—including such well-known and distinctive ones as the Country Club Plaza in Kansas City, Missouri—were built in the 1920s and 1930s. Construction accelerated rapidly following World War II, and by the end of the 1960s there were more than 10,000 shopping centers of all sizes and descriptions. Most notable were the new creations of the 1960s, the enclosed shopping malls. Only homes, schools, and jobs claimed more of the American people's time than did shopping malls.

The malls, developed in the 1960s, had features that have since been refined. By today's standards, the early malls seem unsophisticated. Although each shopping mall had distinctive architectural features and each sought to set itself apart from others, a monotonous predictability prevailed. In mall after mall, the climate-controlled interiors with replanted landscapes blurred indoor and outdoor sensations. Few sounds could be heard—only Muzak, music intended to remove silence without requiring listening.

In Disneyesque fashion, malls reproduced images of the small town. Missing, however, as one scholar has noted, were pool halls, bars, secondhand stores, and the kind of people who patronize them. From one mall to the next, even the shoppers seemed to look the same: white, middle-class, suburban. So did those who were there just to hang out, or to meet over a cup of coffee and a doughnut, or to walk routes where rain and snow, cold and heat, never interfered.

A main purpose of malls was to create a community of shoppers so as to make time at the mall a regular part of everyone's day. Walk in, they seemed to say, and feel at home. Listen to the folksingers. Visit Santa Claus. See the temporary art gallery in the center court. Give blood. Gather around the automobile on display. Spend a few minutes at the antique fair, the science fair, or the history fair. Forget about the elements. Slip into a store and buy something. Feel safe. Malls have never been free of crime, of course, but they are intended to make shoppers feel that they are (*Daily Life*

Online, "Consumers in the Material World: Shopping Centers and Malls," in Marty, *Daily Life in the United States, 1960–1990*, http://dailylife.greenwood.com).

ENVIRONMENTAL ISSUES AND CONSUMER PROTECTION

The American people in the 1960s had reasons to worry about the air they breathed, the water they drank, the food they ate, and the hazardous wastes found in their communities or transported through them. Industrial processes that produced much-desired consumer goods also produced waste that was dumped into streams or blown into the atmosphere. Automobiles consumed huge quantities of natural resources and pumped substantial quantities of pollutants into the air. The streets and roads on which automobiles traveled and the space required for parking took up large parts of the landscape. Tankers that brought petroleum to the United States burst open when they ran aground, and offshore oil wells were susceptible to leaking, as happened in the Santa Barbara channel in 1969.

A spokesman for the Public Health Service (PHS) reported in 1970 that annual household, commercial, municipal, and industrial wastes totaled 360 million tons. Only 6 percent of the nation's 12,000 landfill disposal sites, according to the PHS, met even less-than-minimum standards for sanitary landfills. Of the 300 incinerators used for disposal of waste, 70 percent were without adequate air pollution control systems. Consumers' preference for disposable cans, bottles, and other packaging, as well as their general resistance to recycling, caused the bulk in landfills to multiply.

Survival may not have been an immediate concern, but the welfare of generations to come caused worries. When the sources of worry were specific and close to home, men and women who had never before plunged into political action organized and took steps to protect themselves. Even when immediate concerns were absent, Americans faced the hard question of how to preserve and improve the natural environment at the same time that their rising standard of living posed serious threats to it (*Daily Life Online*, "Environmental and Consumer Protection: Environmental Worries," in Marty, *Daily Life in the United States, 1960–1990*, http://dailylife. greenwood.com).

GASOLINE, PETROLEUM, AND THE ENERGY CRISIS

America and other Western industrial nations depended on a steady and increasing use of fossil fuels to supply the heavy demands of energy, transportation, home heating, and industrial production. For years, a consortium of Western oil companies had controlled the drilling and refining process to bring crude oil to consumers. The Arabian-American Oil Company (ARAMCO), a business relationship between American oil producers and Saudi Arabia, had dominated the energy field since the 1930s. The price of crude oil on the world market remained at about $3.00 a barrel between 1957 and 1970, but a major shift in control of the market occurred in 1960. In that year, five oil-producing nations (Iran, Iraq, Kuwait, Saudi Arabia, and Venezuela) created the Organization of Petroleum Exporting Companies (OPEC). They established their headquarters in Vienna, Austria, in 1965 and added five more nations to the organization. The goal of OPEC was to take control of the important energy market from ARAMCO. Prices remained steady at $3.00 until the mid-1970s. During the October 1973 Yom Kippur War in the Middle East, OPEC embargoed the sale of petroleum to any nation that supported Israel in that conflict against Arab states.

The Alaska Pipeline. Mangionej|Dreamstime.com.

Abruptly, OPEC raised the price of oil to $12.00 a barrel. Arab oil accounted for 37 percent of all the petroleum consumed in the West. The embargo and price increase hurt the American economy. A 1974 Department of Energy report argued that the five-month embargo cost 50,000 jobs and close to a $20 billion loss in gross domestic product. Gas lines formed at stations around the nation. Another war in the Middle East, between Iran and Iraq, added to the cost of petroleum, and by 1981, the cost of a barrel of crude oil had risen to $35.00 (Girard 2001, 236–37).

While prices dropped significantly in the late 1980s, it had become clear that an energy crisis had evolved, and it affected every aspect of American daily life. Alternate sources of energy, such as nuclear, solar, wind power, and so on, seemed unlikely to diminish the nation's deep dependence on fossil fuels, and Americans made only a minimal effort to reduce consumption of gasoline and heating oils. The demand for oil from foreign resources not only impacted on the daily cost of those resources, it also altered America's export–import balance as the nation paid more for foreign resources.

INDUSTRIAL COMPETITION: AUTOMOBILES AND STEEL

During the period 1945–1960, Detroit automakers had become the stars of America's postwar industrial boom period. The "Big Three" automakers, Ford, General Motors, and Chrysler, had dominated both the American and global market. As Europe and Japan began their slow postwar economic recovery, competition in the auto industry developed. In 1958, two Japanese firms, Toyota and Nissan, exported fewer than 2,000 automobiles to the United States. German car manufacturers like Volkswagen and Mercedes Benz had also begun to sell cars in America, but consumers

The Jeep Wrangler, 1980s. Mshake|Dreamstime.com.

had grown accustomed to the large, eight-cylinder, gas-consuming automobiles that the Detroit manufacturers had sold for years.

The oil embargo and gas crisis in the 1970s, however, appeared to make smaller, four-cylinder, Japanese and German options more desirable. By the 1980s, Japanese cars made up 22 percent of the American market. In 1981, Detroit automakers laid off 215,000 employees, almost 25 percent of its workforce. A year later, another 50,000 auto workers became unemployed. The impact on the American automotive industry influenced steel, rubber, parts, and other industrial product sales in the United States. Foreign competitors appeared able to produce better or similar items more cheaply and efficiently than their U.S. counterparts. As Detroit automakers sought to respond to the foreign imports, they developed new styles and options for American car buyers.

As fuel costs dropped in the 1980s, manufacturers turned to the production of minivans and sport utility vehicles (SUVs). More upscale and consumer versions of former World War II jeeps, the new models began to attract consumers. The Jeep Wagoneer had been on the market since 1963, was replaced by the Jeep Cherokee in 1984, and drew an increasing number of car buyers. Chevrolet developed the Blazer and Ford the Bronco. Built on light truck chassis, often with four-wheel drive, SUVs became increasingly popular items in the 1980s. Minivans experienced the same popularity, as suburban families appreciated the larger space and passenger room as well as raised bodies that allowed a better view of the road. The fact that the new models consumed more gasoline seemed to fly in the face of increased gasoline prices, a factor in the impact of Japanese and European imports, but the 1980s saw a dramatic drop in gas prices. Additionally, consumer advocates warned that SUVs had a tendency to flip over in a number of roadside accidents. Neither energy costs nor safety issues seemed to concern consumers. By the beginning of the 1990s, more than 50 percent of the drivers of SUVs were women. The Chrysler minivan had become one of the most popular vehicles on the road for suburban families, and Detroit automakers appeared to have staged a major comeback in the auto market with the development of the two new consumer options.

With the exception of the SUV and minivan market, the nation began to experience a serious economic recession as production declined and unemployment rose. Shortly, Japanese automakers also produced their SUV versions to compete with American products. Management blamed excessive labor costs. Labor unions blamed inefficient owners who drew unrealistic salaries. The new models of efficiency and product design appeared to reside in Japan and Europe, and critics and pundits proclaimed that America's genius in the free market, industrial global community had ended. While the industrial economy of the United States began to rebound toward the end of the 1980s, it remained clear that in traditional industries, the nation's domination of the world marketplace had come to an end.

I'll Buy That!, published in 1986 by *Consumer Reports* magazine, identified and described "50 Small Wonders and Big Deals That Revolutionized the Lives of Consumers" during the magazine's 50-year history. The attention that the book's pictures and essays give to the automobile reveal the important role this technological wonder has played in American life. Through the

A man enjoys ice fishing thanks to his SUV, which became very popular in the 1980s. Iofoto|Dreamstime.com.

years, American-made cars grew bigger and more technologically complex. In the 1960s, automatic transmissions became standard on cars of all sizes. Power brakes, power steering, and air conditioning came first in larger cars, then in cars of all sizes. In 1966, Oldsmobile introduced the Toronado, the first domestic car with front-wheel drive. Before long, that innovation, too, became a standard feature.

I'll Buy That! pointed to the 1965 Mustang as a symptom of change in Americans' buying habits. The editors described the Mustang as neither a sports car nor a family car but a "personal car." A 1962 version was a two-seater, but then, say the book's editors, there was a further corporate vision. "Put a young couple in something as romantic as a Mustang and they might just be fruitful and multiply and three into two doesn't go." So the design was scrapped in favor of "two-plus-two"—that is, two seats in front, plus a small rear seat for two children. Of course, not by chance did the Mustang gain popularity. The Ford Motor Company launched it with a $10 million publicity campaign, calling it a "school bus," a "shopping cart," and a "dream boat." "Join the tide of history," one advertisement said, "with a car that scoots through traffic . . . hoards gas . . . and sports a low price tag." Creating the sense of need for the Mustang was just as important as creating the car itself.

The Volkswagen (VW) Beetle, a tiny German-made import with its engine in the rear, established its own popularity through unconventional advertising: "Think small" and "Ugly is only skin deep," for example. Despite the car's many inconveniences and crudities, VW owners drove their Beetles with immeasurable pride. Still, the Beetle was not a family car. The Toyota Corona, introduced in 1965, was. Its acceptance as an economical but comfortable car encouraged other Japanese manufacturers, particularly Honda, Toyota, and Nissan (known then as Datsun), to enter the American market; within a decade the three Japanese companies claimed about 20 percent of the U.S. market. This jeopardized the very existence of Chrysler

Corporation and dented the prosperity of General Motors and Ford, the other two manufacturers in the Big Three. The popularity of smaller cars had implications for automobile safety, as tests showed that their drivers were more vulnerable to accidental injury or death than drivers of larger vehicles. Also affected by the increasing popularity of imported cars were the thousands of families whose breadwinners worked in manufacturing plants that now faced cutbacks caused by declining sales of American-made automobiles.

Ever since its invention, the automobile had played an important role in the development of America. By 1960, wrote historian Kenneth Jackson, "the best symbol of individual success and identity was a sleek, air-conditioned, high-powered personal statement on wheels" (1985). The presence of plain, low-powered, low-prestige foreign vehicles did not threaten that symbol. The imported vehicle often served as a family's second car, providing transportation rather than luxury. Nonetheless, it contributed to a phenomenon noted by Jackson: between 1950 and 1980 the American population increased by 50 percent, but the number of automobiles increased by 200 percent.

Americans' reliance on the automobile had led President Dwight D. Eisenhower to propose and Congress to approve the Interstate Highway Act in 1956, providing for a 41,000-mile system of limited-access highways. Construction proceeded rapidly, with little regard for the farmland and urban neighborhoods that lay in the highways' paths or for the consequences of highway-spawned sprawl. Connecting urban highways to the interstate system meant the construction of spaghetti-like interchanges and resulted in the loss of more neighborhoods and the migration of more residents to suburbia. In the 1960s, factories, offices, and shopping centers also migrated to the suburbs, so that by 1970, according to Jackson, in 9 of the 15 largest metropolitan areas the suburbs were the principal sources of employment. In some cities, such as San Francisco, almost three-fourths of all trips to and from work were by people who did not live or work in the core city. Similar patterns in other cities explain why extensive public transportation systems were usually hopeless dreams.

Romance with the automobile helped create a drive-through culture. The drive-in restaurants, where carhops served patrons who ate in their cars, disappeared rather quickly as new technologies had customers shouting their orders into a loudspeaker and passing a window to pick up their orders. Drive-through banking was its counterpart, along with drive-through cleaners and drive-through pharmacies. Eventually there were even some drive-through funeral homes, where friends could pay their respects to the deceased without getting out of their cars. A drive-through bridal chapel was yet to come.

In 1970, although one family in five had no automobile, Americans' reliance on automobiles showed no signs of diminishing. Nor did the automobile industry escape numerous technological problems. One had to do with air pollution caused by automobile emissions. The California legislature, responding to complaints about the smog that pestered cities, became the pacesetter in setting emission control standards. It imposed limits on the amount of carbon monoxide and hydrocarbons permitted from automobile exhausts. The federal laws that followed permitted California to enforce stricter ones, as atmospheric conditions there differed from other parts of the country. Had mass transit—buses, subways, streetcars, and trains—held greater appeal, pollution problems might have been less severe, but mass transit could not compete with the convenience, power, and pride derived from automobiles. Nationwide between 1945 and 1967, mass transit rides fell from 23 billion to 8 billion.

More vexing for the American makers of big cars was consumers' growing preference for small ones, caused mainly by rising fuel costs resulting from the oil crisis. Japan's Datsun (known later as Nissan) and Toyota were serious about doing business when they entered the U.S. market. By 1968, they had been joined in the American market by other Japanese manufacturers (principally Honda, Mitsubishi, and Mazda), and Japan had passed Germany as the world's second-largest producer of motor vehicles.

In response, American makers marketed what were called captive imports. Mitsubishi made the Dodge Colt and Mazda made the Ford Courier pickup. General Motors owned 35 percent of Isuzu, maker of the LUV, marketed by GM. When imports reached 10 percent of all sales of passenger cars, the American automakers began producing their own subcompacts. The Ford Maverick and American Motors Hornet, introduced in 1969, and the Chevrolet Vega, Ford Pinto, and American Motors Gremlin in 1970 did not distinguish themselves as high-quality vehicles, but they positioned the American automobile industry to take on the greater challenges to come.

Those challenges arrived with the petroleum crisis that began in 1973, a crisis resulting from a situation President Nixon described in an address to Congress on June 29: "While we have 6 percent of the world's population, we consume one-third of the world's energy output." He continued, "The supply of domestic energy resources available to us is not keeping pace with our ever growing demand." The demand for petroleum in the United States was 17 million barrels per day, but domestic output was little more than 11 million barrels per day.

The situation worsened in October 1973. The Yom Kippur War between Israel and its Arab neighbors prompted Middle Eastern oil-producing countries to impose an embargo on exports to countries regarded as sympathetic to Israel. Included were the United States, Canada, all of western Europe, and Japan. While the embargo remained in effect, until the spring of 1974, panic buying caused long lines at gas stations. To keep their tanks full, drivers would fill up when they needed as little as three gallons. In January 1974, President Nixon signed into law a 55-mile-per-hour speed limit act, after having asked Congress to set the limit at 50 miles per hour. The reduced speed limit conserved an estimated 3.4 billion gallons per year, and highway fatalities in 1974 fell to 45,196 from 54,052 in the previous year. They soon climbed again as motorists flouted the unpopular law. Some states imposed limits on quantities of gas that could be purchased, causing drivers to go from station to station. Others restricted days on which cars with even- or odd-numbered license plates could fill up. Many communities organized carpools, and state highway departments provided lots to enable drivers to park their cars and share rides with others.

Anger over the problems the 1970s oil shortage caused was plentiful. After all, a way of life seemed in jeopardy. Those who suspected conspiracies believed that oil companies seeking to raise prices were responsible for the shortages. They claimed there were loaded tankers waiting offshore and supplies of gas hidden in the tanks of abandoned stations, all ready to be released when the price was right.

The gasoline energy crisis caused Americans to look to technological developments to decrease reliance on crude oil and provide other ways to power the nation. What could be done to guarantee that electricity, the lifeblood of America, would continue to flow without interruption? Government experts and utilities executives knew that demand for electrical power would increase dramatically in coming years. The threat of blackouts and brownouts, which occurred when power had to be cut back because reserves had fallen too low, demanded answers. Electricity generated by nuclear power plants seemed to provide them. The Atomic Energy Commission estimated that by the year 2000 half the electrical power consumed in the United States would be generated by nuclear fuel. Building more nuclear-powered plants made sense.

Consequently, by 1966 half the new generators planned or being built were nuclear powered, even though serious but unpublicized accidents in nuclear reactors had occurred since testing first began on nuclear generators in 1949. (No American has died as a result of any nuclear plant accident in the United States.) In January 1966, the first nuclear-powered plant, the Enrico Fermi, located on Lake Erie between Detroit and Toledo, went into operation. The following October a malfunction caused the reactor to overheat. Safety devices and extraordinary efforts by plant workers averted a potentially enormous disaster. The Detroit police were able to call off their plans to evacuate the city, thus avoiding something that would have been much more than a mere interruption in daily life. After being out of commission for several years, the Enrico Fermi reactor was eventually dismantled.

Thus, nuclear power brought the American people a new environmental worry. Problems with other nuclear reactors—mainly accidents and difficulties in finding ways to store wastes that would remain radioactive for thousands of years—dashed hopes that nuclear power would be safe and relatively inexpensive. Nuclear power was not going to be the ultimate technological fix, the cure-all for energy shortages, at least until new technologies dealt with the problems and concerns that emerged in the initial ventures.

Finally, in the period 1960 to 1990 there were also technological developments in the home. In 1974, the Amana Refrigeration Company began to market small microwave ovens for home use. Because meals cooked in them, however, seemed less attractive and less tasty than those prepared in regular ovens, microwaves did not catch on for general use. Rather, they became "heat-things-up" devices, increasingly useful for families that found it impossible to gather around the dinner table at the same time. Also, as Baby Boomers headed off to their own apartments and as childless families became more numerous, microwaves proved useful for heating prepackaged dinners and leftovers. Another small but important technological device that was installed unobtrusively in many homes deserves mention: smoke detectors became household necessities after their introduction in 1970 (Marty 1997, 57–61, 145, 149–51, 153–54, 222–23, 305–6; *Daily Life Online*, "Material Life: Technology," in Marty, *Daily Life in the United States, 1960–1990*, http://dailylife.greenwood.com).

TECHNOLOGY

Computers

Personal computers (PCs) had been manufactured since 1977, but the market for them did not come of age until 1981, when IBM produced its first one. IBM's size enabled it to market its PCs aggressively, and sales climbed in three years from 25,000 to 3 million, although its experiment with a low-cost model, the PC jr., failed. The Apple Corporation, famous for development of the Apple II, introduced the Macintosh (Mac) in 1984. By 1987, its Macintosh II and SE models were the most powerful personal computers on the market. The Mac was also regarded as more user-friendly than personal computers with disk operating systems, and debates over Mac versus DOS continued for years. The Mac's mouse for moving the cursor on the screen made it even more user-friendly, and eventually other lines of computers also made the mouse a standard feature.

Sales of personal computers stood at 1.4 million in 1981. Sales doubled in 1982, on their way to 10 million in 1988, at a profit of $22 billion. A number of other computer developments made news that year. One was the "virus," a mischievous small program planted in an operating system with the intent of altering or deleting data throughout the network as the virus spread. Another was the expanded capacity and speed of laptop computers, with sales exceeding $1 million. A third concerned possible health hazards posed by computer monitors, known as video display terminals. Studies showed that many people who worked at monitors for six hours or more each day developed difficulties in focusing their eyes. Long hours spent at keyboards also caused injuries to hands and arms, sometimes to a disabling extent (*Daily Life Online*, "Technology: Personal Computers," in Marty, *Daily Life in the United States, 1960–1990*, http://dailylife.greenwood.com).

Benefits and Costs

Technology plays an important part in almost every aspect of American life: business and industry, farming, urban development, health care, law, politics, banking, courtship, marital relationships, child rearing, schooling, religion, housekeeping and home maintenance, cooking and dietetics, shopping, social interactions, the spending of leisure time, and more. But the benefits of technology often have a price. For example, its relentless quest for the new necessarily makes our present possessions obsolete. Determination to keep up with the better or the different imposes challenges on both bank balances and human emotions. Technology encourages uniformity and predictability, thereby erasing the distinctiveness of communities and cultures.

Technology's solutions to one generation's problems often create new ones for the next. Disposable diapers are an example. Widespread use did not begin until around 1970, when increasing numbers of mothers of infants and small children found employment outside the home. But since their introduction, there have been concerns about their effects on the environment. By the early 1990s, soiled diapers amounted to 1.4 percent of the bulk in landfills, according to a study conducted in Arizona. Was that too much? And, whatever the quantity, should disposable diapers be banned for other environmental reasons—for seepage of waste into groundwater, for example? Not necessarily. Debates over comparative environmental costs and benefits of using disposable as opposed to laundered diapers typically end in a draw. Washing diapers consumes energy and puts both human waste and detergents—another technological advance with harmful environmental consequences—into sewer systems and larger bodies of water where the wastewater flows (*Daily Life Online*, "Technology: Personal Computers," in Marty, *Daily Life in the United States, 1960–1990*, http://dailylife.greenwood.com).

In 1974, the Amana Refrigeration Company began to market small microwave ovens for home use. However, probably because meals cooked in them seemed less attractive and less tasty than those prepared in regular ovens, microwaves did not catch on for general use. Rather, they became "heat-things-up" devices, increasingly useful for families that found it impossible to gather around the dinner table at the same time. Also, as baby boomers headed off to their own apartments and as childless families became more numerous, microwaves proved useful for heating pre-packaged dinners and leftovers. Another small but important technological device that was installed unobtrusively in many homes deserves mention: smoke detectors became household necessities after their introduction in 1970 (*Daily Life Online*, "Technology's Small Steps and Giant Leaps: Technology in Homes" in Marty, *Daily Life in the United States, 1960–1990*, http://dailylife.greenwood.com).

THE "OTHER AMERICA"

The preceding chapters might create the impression that the general prosperity enjoyed throughout America reached into all homes and families. But, if migration to the suburbs was a sign of affluence, the city neighborhoods and the people left behind soon showed the many faces of poverty. Poverty was abundantly evident in rural America as well, particularly in Appalachian regions of West Virginia, Kentucky, Tennessee, and North Carolina. Although industries had moved from the North to the South, particularly in textile and furniture manufacturing, it was the prospect of paying lower wages that lured them, so increases in living standards were slow in coming. Most African Americans who earlier had migrated from the South to what they saw as the promised land in northern cities found poverty rather than promise there. Slums and derelict housing projects populated almost exclusively by blacks became common in major cities, and racial discrimination posed barriers as formidable as those existing in the South.

Some economists and social activists who had kept an eye on the conditions faced daily by America's poor proposed strategies for economic development to ameliorate them, but action did not come quickly. President Kennedy's slight margin of victory in 1960 would have hobbled any major reform efforts he might have proposed, and his conservative instincts probably discouraged him from recommending ambitious plans anyway. His measures to stimulate the economy had some positive effects, as the gross national product (GNP) grew at an average annual rate of 5.3 percent between 1961 and 1964, compared to the 3.2 annual average of the 1950s. But problems of unequal distribution of wealth—indeed, of outright poverty—persisted.

Just as *Silent Spring* and *Unsafe at Any Speed* had stimulated interest in environmental and product safety concerns, Michael Harrington's passionate book *The Other America* (1962) changed what many people thought about problems of poverty. Although Harrington sprinkled statistics throughout the book, it was his description of the "invisible poor," particularly the elderly, the young, and minorities, that gave the book its power. "In a sense," he wrote, "one might define the contemporary poor in the United States as those who, for reasons beyond their control, cannot help themselves. All the most decisive factors making for opportunity and advance are against them. They are born going downward, and most of them stay down. They are victims whose lives are endlessly blown round and round the other America." Forty to 50 million of them, he estimated. Harrington asked his readers "to respond critically to every assertion, but not to allow statistical quibbling to obscure the huge, enormous, and intolerable fact of poverty in America. For, when all is said and done, that fact is unmistakable, whatever its exact dimensions, and the truly human reaction can only be outrage" (Harrington, 15).

Although Harrington chose not to use statistics to dramatize the condition of the "other Americans," one can see in the numbers of the early 1960s that daily life differed dramatically according to where one stood on the nation's economic ladder. The 20 percent of Americans on the top rungs of the ladder owned more than 75 percent of the nation's wealth; the 20 percent on the bottom rungs owned only 0.05 percent. Those on the bottom rungs received 23 percent of the total money income; those on the top, 77 percent (*Daily Life Online*, "The Other America: The Other America," in Marty, *Daily Life in the United States, 1960–1990*, http://dailylife. greenwood.com).

URBAN AND RURAL ISSUES

One of the major urban developments from the 1960s was the building of thousands of city shopping centers or malls to attract consumers (and their dollars) to urban and suburban areas. Before shopping centers, discount stores, and specialty mail-order houses became plentiful, most consumers shopped in locally owned stores. Even big department stores were owned by hometowners, or at least by local businesspeople from nearby towns. One study reported that in each decade after 1950, more than three-fourths of the towns with populations under 2,500 suffered net losses of such retail and service businesses as gas stations, farm implement dealers, and lumberyards as well as grocery, hardware, and furniture stores. Population decline accounted for some of the losses, but the readiness of small-town residents to drive 50 miles or more for the variety and savings offered in shopping malls and discount stores made a bigger difference.

In cities, stores on main thoroughfares served people in their neighborhoods while big department stores lured them downtown. Competition from malls and grocery supermarkets put many neighborhood stores out of business and emptied the downtowns. Ironically, mall developers eventually discovered that the vacant spaces they had helped create in America's downtowns might be ideal for malls, so that is where, in the 1970s and 1980s, they began to build them (Marty 1997, 134–35; *Daily Life Online*, "Economic Life: Urban and Rural Experience," in Marty, *Daily Life in the United States, 1960–1990*, http://dailylife.greenwood.com).

WORK AND EMPLOYMENT

The transformation of work during the 1980s had both encouraging and discouraging features. By the end of the decade, more than 35 million persons did part-time or full-time income-producing work at home. Increasing most rapidly among them, to a total of more than five million, were telecommuters, that is, employees of companies who did part of their work at home during business hours, most typically involving the use of computers. The trend toward telecommuting was so strong that it seemed likely that it would soon be regarded as unexceptional. Telecommuting served the needs of dual-career families particularly well, in that it reduced the need for child care outside the home. Twice as large a number as telecommuters were those who worked at home as freelancers, earning extra income during hours away from their regular jobs—if they had regular jobs.

Yet another change of the 1980s was the growing resistance of employees to management-dictated relocations. Dual-career families found uprooting particularly difficult, even when it involved promotions or pay increases. The costs involved in buying and selling homes also accounted for the reluctance, as did the sense that accepting a move in the new economic times would not necessarily guarantee job security. Employers had increasingly come to regard their employees as a contingent workforce, to be retained or dismissed depending on immediate circumstances. Employees responded by regarding themselves as entrepreneurs seeking advancement where it best served their interests (Marty 1997, 272–73; *Daily Life Online*, "Economic Life: Work," in Marty, *Daily Life in the United States, 1960–1990*, http://dailylife.greenwood.com).

FOR MORE INFORMATION

Barnouw, E. *Tube of Plenty: The Evolution of American Television*. 2nd ed. New York: Oxford University Press, 1990.

Boyer, P. S. *By the Bomb's Early Light: American Thought and Culture at the Dawn of the Atomic Age*. Chapel Hill: University of North Carolina Press, 1994.

Brumberg, J. J. *The Body Project: An Intimate History of American Girls*. New York: Random House, 1997.

Chafe, William H. *The Unfinished Journey: America since World War II*. 3rd ed. New York: Oxford University Press, 1995.

Comstock, George S. *Television in America*. Beverly Hills, CA: Sage Publications, 1980.

Consumer's Union. *I'll Buy That! 50 Small Wonders and Big Deals That Revolutionized the Lives of Consumers: A 50 Year Retrospective*. Mount Vernon, NY: Consumer's Union, 1986.

Cremin, L. *American Education, 1876–1980: The Metropolitan Experience*. New York: Harper and Row, 1988.

"Downsizing of America." *New York Times*.

Ehrenreich, B. *The Worst Years of Our Lives: Irreverent Notes from a Decade of Greed*. New York: Pantheon Books, 1990.

Flink, J. J. *The Car Culture*. Cambridge, MA: MIT Press, 1975.

Girard, Jolyon. *America and the World*. Westport, CT: Greenwood Press, 2001.

Grmek, Mirko D. *History of AIDS: Emergence and Origin of a Modern Pandemic*. Princeton, NJ: Princeton University Press, 1993.

Halberstam, D. *The Fifties*. New York: Ballantine Books, 1994.

Hallowell, E. M., and J. J. Ratey. *Driven to Distraction*. New York: Pantheon Books, 1994.

Harrington, M. *The Other America: Poverty in the United States*. Baltimore, MD: Penguin, 1962; New York: Penguin, 1981.

Harris, Neil. "American Space: Spaced-Out at the Shopping Center." *The New Republic* (December 13, 1975): 23–25.

Hart, J. D. *The Oxford Companion to American Literature*. 6th ed. New York: Oxford University Press, 1995.

Jackson, Kenneth T. *Crabgrass Frontier: The Suburbanization of the United States*. New York: Oxford University Press, 1985.

Jowett, G., and J. M. Linton. *Movies as Mass Communications*. Beverly Hills, CA: Sage Publications, 1980.

Kaledin, E. *Daily Life in the United States, 1940–1959: Shifting Worlds*. Westport, CT: Greenwood Press, 2000.

Kennan, E. *Mission to the Moon: A Critical Examination of NASA and the Space Program*. New York: Morrow, 1969.

Kowinski, William Severini. "The Malling of America." *New York Times* (May 1, 1978): 35.

Lemann, N. *The Promised Land: The Great Black Migration and How It Changed America*. New York: Vintage Books/Knopf, 1991.

Marty, Myron A. *Daily Life in the United States, 1960–1990: Decades of Discord*. Westport, CT: Greenwood Press, 1997; also available online as *Daily Life Online*, in Marty, *Daily Life in the United States, 1960–1990*, http://dailylife.greenwood.com).

Miller, Z. L. *The Urbanization of Modern America: A Brief History*. New York: Harcourt Brace, 1973.

Moore, Michael, dir. *The Big One*. 1998.

Moore, Michael, dir. *Roger and Me*. 1989.

Newman, K. *Falling from Grace: The Experience of Downward Mobility in the American Middle Class*. New York: Free Press, 1988.

Patterson, J. T. *Grand Expectations: The United States, 1945–1974*. New York: Oxford University Press, 1996.

Ravitch, D. *The Troubled Crusade: American Education, 1945–1980*. New York: Basic Books, 1983.

Rybczynski, W. *Waiting for the Weekend*. New York: Viking, 1991.

Shorter, E. *The Health Century*. New York: Doubleday, 1987.

Spring, J. *The American School, 1642–1993*. 3rd ed. New York: McGraw Hill, 1994.

Tichi, Cecelia. *Electronic Hearth: Creating an American Television Culture*. New York: Oxford University Press, 1991.

Whitfield, S. J. *The Culture of the Cold War*. Baltimore, MD: Johns Hopkins University Press, 1991.

Williams, T. I., ed. *Science: A History of Discovery in the Twentieth Century*. New York: Oxford University Press, 1990.

Williamson, J. *The Crucible of Race: Black-White Relations in the American South since Emancipation*. New York: Oxford University Press, 1984.

Winn, M. *The Plug-In Drug*. New York: Viking Press, 1977.

Intellectual Life

ART AND FILM

Television did not bring about the demise of the motion picture industry, as some had predicted years earlier that it would. The industry held its own partly by producing made-for-television films and selling broadcast and videotaping rights of movies after they had run in theaters. Sales in foreign countries also helped. Most of the industry's revenue, however, poured in through box offices, as going to movies remained a popular social activity. People were still willing to pay more to see a film on a big screen. In 1975, box-office revenue broke the record set the previous year. Higher admission prices accounted for part of the increase, but the average weekly attendance of 21 million, up 10 percent from the previous year, was the main reason. Those figures were notable mainly because they represented a reversal of the 25-year downward spiral from the average attendance of 80 million in pretelevision days.

Blockbuster films brought in much of the industry's revenue. In 1975, Steven Spielberg's spine-tingling *Jaws* was the big moneymaker. The violence and terror wrought by a huge man-eating white shark in a resort community evidently appealed to the tastes of vast numbers of the reading and movie-going public. Like other popular films, it was based on a novel; when the film was released, there were 5.5 million copies of Peter Benchley's novel in print. Another film based on a novel, *One Flew over the Cuckoo's Nest* (1975), did very well at the box office and achieved critical acclaim with its portrayal of life and medical treatment in mental institutions. In 1977 came another blockbuster: *Star Wars*, a movie saturated with special visual and sound effects. Some of that film's appeal lay in its depiction of the romance of fighting a just war in the melodrama of science fiction.

The diverse tastes of producers and audiences were evident in the variety of films winning honors each year. In 1982, for example, *Gandhi*, the story of the man who led India's struggle for independence, won an Oscar for best picture. Several years later the Oscar went to *Amadeus* (1984), which treated the life of the great composer

Wolfgang Amadeus Mozart. Then came *Out of Africa* (1985) and *The Last Emperor* (1987), the latter the story of a bygone China. Named best picture in 1988 was *Rain Man*, starring Dustin Hoffman, named best actor for his performance. The film introduced audiences to autism, a baffling mental disorder. It was followed by *Driving Miss Daisy* (1989), with Jessica Tandy playing the role of an eccentric but lovable elderly woman and winning best actress for it. Then came *Dances with Wolves* (1990), directed by and featuring Kevin Costner (best director) in a romanticized story of the Lakota Sioux nation.

Award-winning films were often bested at the box office by those featuring daring themes or techniques. That explains the success of the 1981 blockbuster *Raiders of the Lost Ark*, and another in 1982, *E.T.—The Extra-Terrestrial*, the story of love between an Earth boy, lonely in suburbia, and a stranded alien from space. Both movies were directed by Steven Spielberg. *E.T.* grossed $228 million at the box office and demonstrated the commercial success that lay in embedding a film's vocabulary ("Elliot," "ouch," and "phone home") into the language of everyday life and in marketing a film's images on such things as lunch boxes, bicycles, and even underwear. Another blockbuster success was Tim Burton's *Batman* in 1989. Although it did not match the revenue produced by *E.T.*, the "Batmania" it inspired paid dividends to marketers of products bearing the image or logo of the Batman.

Sylvester Stallone's *Rambo: First Blood, Part II* (1985) was a good example of a popular film featuring violence. Stallone played the role of a Vietnam veteran who freed prisoners of war, thereby exposing the alleged indifference of the U.S. government. The film's prowar perspective drew complaints from those who thought it tried to revise truths about the war, but the complaints did not keep Rambo from becoming a folk hero or Rambo guns and knives from becoming popular children's toys.

In 1984, the Motion Picture Association of America (MPAA) added a new rating, PG-13, the first change since the introduction of the rating system 16 years earlier. The new rating placed films between PG (parental guidance suggested) and R (restricted). It was advisory in that it did not exclude viewers under age 14, but it informed parents that violence or other content in the film might not be suitable for their children. In 1990 the MPAA replaced the controversial X rating, which had come to be regarded as synonymous with pornography, with NC-17. The new rating was intended for movies that despite depictions of explicit sex or extreme violence, such as *Henry & June*, were regarded as serious artistic efforts (Marty 1997, 209–10, 281–82; *Daily Life Online*, "Recreational Life: Film," in Marty, *Daily Life in the United States, 1960–1990*, http://dailylife.greenwood.com).

COMMUNICATION: TELEVISION AND COMPUTERS

There were two major themes in the history of communication during the period 1960 to 1990. The first was the continued dominance of television and the second was the rise of the computing age. The 1960s was the second decade of television's

Home computers like Apple's IIg revolutionized communications among Americans. Here, Apple Computer founder Steven Wozniak demonstrates a new Apple IIg in Cupertino, California, September 16, 1986. AP/Wide World Photos.

dominance of home life. The average number of hours of viewing per home per day increased from just over five in 1960 to almost six in 1970, nearly 18 percent. With more channels, there were more programs to watch. Although virtually no homes were hooked to a cable television system in 1960, the increase to 8 percent in 1970 was the beginning of an accelerating trend. The 2,350 cable systems, up from 640 a decade earlier, principally served isolated areas; but when the Federal Communications Commission allowed cable channels to enter major markets, they began to increase program options for viewers in urban areas, too.

Television did not become, as some had expected, a theater in the home with featured attractions being the center of attention. Although a set might be on most of the time, it did not interfere with the activities of people in the room. One study showed that about one-fifth of the time it played to an empty room. For another fifth, those in the room did not look at it at all. That study reported that children "eat, drink, dress and undress, play [and] fight . . . in front of the set," and that is where adults "eat, drink, sleep, play, argue, fight, and occasionally make love." Almost always, the viewing was discontinuous. Hours spent in front of television sets were greater among persons of lower income and lesser education than among the wealthier and better educated, for whom other activities were within reach and within budgets.

By the mid-1970s, the affordability of televisions increased, and about half of American households had two or more television sets. The sets had become, in historian Cecelia Tichi's words, the home's "electronic hearth," the focal point in a room. Viewers absorbed their radiating warmth and flickering images. They were also a home's window to the world, as the programs and commercials shaped viewers' needs, interests, habits, and values. Television's manipulated portrayals of reality became indistinguishable from reality itself. "As seen on TV" validated claims and opinions.

Given television's dominant role in American life, it is not surprising that its images altered viewers' ways of apprehending the world. In contrast to the way one reads—from left to right across a line, top of the page to the bottom, page after page—television follows no predictable or essential lines. Viewers move quickly, not necessarily randomly but seemingly so, from one scene to another with subtle transitions or no transitions at all. Reading is another matter: one *learns* to read books, magazines, and newspapers, typically going through reading-readiness exercises and then moving from elementary to more complex material.

No one *learns* to watch television. Many programs, and particularly commercials, are designed to simultaneously hold the attention of 6-year-olds, 16-year-olds, and 60-year-olds. As television holds viewers' attention hour after hour, it becomes what Marie Winn has labeled "the plug-in drug." Viewers may not be in a perpetual state of stupor—perhaps they cheer about what they see or talk back to those they hear— but they are addicted to viewing nonetheless. In her book *The Plug-In Drug* (1977), Winn described how the addiction changed viewers' ways of learning, thinking, and being, as well as their relationships with others and their environment. She focused particularly on television's narcotic effects on children, but adults suffered from them as well. Those effects had become widespread.

Television communication changed significantly in 1975 with Sony's video-recording system known as Betamax. At first the system could be purchased only in a console package containing a videocassette recorder (VCR) and color TV that cost as much as $2,295. Even though the price soon dropped almost by half, JVC's Video Home System (VHS) soon displaced Betamax. The systems were incompatible, and VHS eventually won out (partly because of its longer recording time and lower cost), leaving Betamax owners with technology that was almost instantly obsolete.

But VCRs quickly overcame consumers' misgivings, and by the end of the 1980s about two-thirds of American households with television sets owned at least one unit. With a VCR connected to their set, viewers could for the first time arrange to watch whatever they chose, whenever they chose. Television schedules no longer controlled mealtimes and evening activities. Appreciated just as much was the ability to fast-forward through commercials as viewers watched programs they had recorded. Knowing how to program VCRs for recording, however, remained a challenge. VCRs were used most frequently for watching rented VHS videocassettes. Within a decade, consumers were spending almost $2 billion on rentals and purchasing about 50 million videocassettes.

In addition to television, another important technological and communication development in the 1960s was the advent of computers. The first electronic digital computers, built in the 1940s, were huge machines usually dedicated to a single purpose. The development of the transistor, in the early 1950s, made possible integrated circuits, and old vacuum tubes swiftly became obsolete. Texas Instruments's patenting in 1961 of a silicon wafer, known as a chip, opened the way for further changes in computer technology. No bigger than a postage stamp, the silicon chip eliminated the miles of wires required in earlier machines.

Although personal computers did not become common in American households until several decades later, IBM's production of a primitive word processor in 1964 was a first step in that direction. IBM failed, however, to anticipate what was to come as far as personal computers were concerned. Not until 1981 did it market its first one.

As computer technology came to play a larger role in American life, it was not limited to such obvious processes as financial record management, credit card accounting, airline reservation systems, and word processing. In 1966, it took a small first step into the daily lives of users who were unaware of how it worked and even of its existence, as British technologists developed the first computer-controlled, fuel-injection automobile engine. Such advances, while making life easier in some respects, also made it more confusing—as backyard mechanics would soon discover.

The computerization of America accelerated rapidly in the late 1960s and early 1970s, with each step affecting more directly the lives of Americans. Until the mid-1960s, most computer applications were found in large businesses and the military, but they spread quickly to smaller settings. Office secretaries who had learned to use the IBM Selectric typewriter when it was introduced in 1961 struggled with electronic typewriters by the end of the decade. Soon they faced the intricacies of primitive word processors.

In 1971, when Intel of California introduced the microprocessor—essentially a computer on a silicon chip—a whole new industry opened up. That meant new jobs in the production of both hardware and software. Boom times came to places like "Silicon Valley," the 25-mile strip in California between Palo Alto and San Jose.

As computers entered the workplace, those who used them did not need to understand how they worked. Previously, processors of data worried about stacking and storing the punch cards or magnetic tapes carrying the data they worked with. Now, they simply used hard drives and floppy disks to enter, manipulate, store, and retrieve data, all in unprecedented amounts and with impressive speed. But the picture was not all rosy for computer users. The repetitive nature of their work, as they sat in the same position hour after hour with their eyes focused on a screen with moving images, made them vulnerable to new physical maladies, particularly something called repetitive strain injury or cumulative trauma disorder.

As computer users became more adept and productive, they unwittingly caused the underemployment and unemployment of other employees who were displaced. Their work also unwittingly increased the prospects that confidential financial, legal, medical, military, and other records would be vulnerable to invasion by persons who had no right or reason to see them. Another worry was that records would be improperly transferred, scrambled, destroyed, or simply lost in the system. Another problem that persisted resulted from the perpetual introduction of new generations of hardware and software. Data generated and stored in obsolete generations cannot be retrieved in the next and can be lost. That might not affect the immediate operations of an organization, but it is a concern to those who attempt, years later, to retrieve original records.

Aside from affecting business life, the computer, by the 1970s, had changed personal and home life. A technological device with a large impact had small beginnings in 1976, when Steven Jobs and Stephen Wozniak, college dropouts, founded the Apple computer company. They designed the Apple I, a crude personal computer (PC) most notable for paving the way for Apple II. The Apple II, introduced in 1977, caught on quickly in both homes and schools and set in motion four important processes. The first led to the development of personal computers by IBM, the big company in the computer business. Before long many companies were manufacturing machines more important for the description "IBM-compatible" than for the name of the manufacturer.

The second came side-by-side with the first: the rapid expansion of Microsoft, founded in 1975 by software whiz Bill Gates, a 19-year-old Harvard dropout (who had scored a perfect 800 on his math SAT), and his 22-year-old partner, Paul Allen. Before long, Microsoft dominated the software market and Gates was on his way to becoming the richest man in America. Third, costly, complicated mainframe systems gradually came to play a different role in computer operations in businesses, as they accommodated increasingly flexible workstations connected through telephone networks. Fourth, the miniaturization of personal computers led to the development, in the 1980s, of battery-powered laptop models.

In anticipation of the PC's arrival, a scarcely noticed event occurred in 1976 when the German manufacturer of the slide rule presented the last one it produced to the Smithsonian Institution in Washington. For 350 years that venerable device had been the handheld calculator of mathematicians, scientists, and engineers and a mystery to many in the general public who never mastered it. Electric, battery-operated calculators quickly replaced the outmoded tool.

The development of personal computers and desktop workstations accompanied other trends begun earlier. By 1980, computer technology had established itself in manufacturing and business processes and touched the daily lives of producers and consumers in many ways, from automated assembly lines to banking and credit-card operations, for example, as well as in the operating systems of automobiles and the most intricate surgical devices.

Personal computers had been manufactured since 1977, but the market for them did not come of age until 1981, when IBM produced its first one. IBM's size enabled it to market its PCs aggressively, and sales climbed in three years from 25,000 to 3 million, although its experiment with a low-cost model, the PC jr., failed. The Apple Corporation, famous for development of the Apple II, introduced the Macintosh in 1984. By 1987, its Macintosh II and SE models were the most powerful personal computers on the market. The Mac was also regarded as more user-friendly than personal computers with "disk operating systems," and debates over Mac versus DOS continued for years. The Mac's "mouse" for moving the cursor on the screen made it even more user-friendly, and eventually other lines of computers also made the mouse a standard feature.

Sales of personal computers stood at 1.4 million in 1981. Sales doubled in 1982, on their way to 10 million in 1988, at a profit, then, of $22 billion. A number of other computer developments made news that year. One was the "virus," a mischievous small program planted in an operating system with the intent of altering or deleting data throughout the network as the virus spread. Another development was the expanded capacity and speed of laptop computers, with sales exceeding $1 million. A third concerned possible health hazards posed by computer monitors, known as video display terminals. Studies showed that many people who worked at monitors for six hours or more each day developed difficulties in focusing their eyes. Long hours spent at keyboards also caused injuries to hands and arms, sometimes to a disabling extent (Marty, 59–60, 115–18, 151–53, 205–9, 221–22, 303–4; *Daily Life Online*, "Intellectual Life: Communication," in Marty, *Daily Life in the United States, 1960–1990*, http://dailylife.greenwood.com).

EDUCATION

As the Great Society changed the political and economic face of America through legislative and presidential actions, and as the civil rights movement and technology brought other changes in American life, additional forces transformed American culture. With college youth drawing the most attention for their challenges to established practices in American life and rejection of conventional sexual mores and practices, they were joined in quieter ways by men and women of all ages (*Daily Life Online*, "Cultural Transformations," in Marty, *Daily Life in the United States, 1960– 1990*, http://dailylife. greenwood.com).

The most striking changes in education in the early 1960s affected adults, who enjoyed new opportunities in higher and continuing education. A burst of enrollment in higher education had followed the GI Bill in the years after World War II. Of 14 million persons eligible, 2.2 million veterans jumped at the chance to have their college tuition paid as partial compensation for their military service. Eventually, nearly eight million took advantage of the bill's educational benefits. That set the stage for the continued growth of colleges and universities in the 1960s. In states with rapid population growth the expansion appeared breathtaking. In Florida, for example, where in the early 1940s there had been one university for men, one for women, and one for blacks, along with one public junior college, by 1972 there were nine public coeducational universities and 28 community colleges.

The demand for such institutions increased in part because of the enrollment of women. Nationwide, the proportion of women in college populations grew from around 33 percent in 1960 to more than 40 percent a decade later. The increased enrollment of both women and men was served mainly by the establishment and enlargement of public institutions. In 1940, about 47 percent of the 1,494,000 students enrolled in colleges and universities studied in private, denominational, or sectarian institutions. By 1970, the enrollment reached 7,136,000, with nonpublic institutions serving only 28 percent of the total.

The establishment of community colleges—160 between 1960 and 1966— opened doors for many young people and brought back to school adults seeking to acquire new knowledge and skills. In the five years preceding 1968, enrollment of full-time students in community colleges increased from 914,000 to 1,909,000, and part-time enrollment

Mario Savio, a founder of the Free Speech Movement, leads a campus protest at the University of California, Berkeley, 1966. AP/Wide World Photos.

rose from 489,000 to 888,000. Priding themselves on the comprehensiveness of their offerings, community colleges enabled students to lay the groundwork for transferring to four-year institutions or to equip themselves for better jobs by enrolling in two-year vocational programs. Community colleges also provided credit and noncredit continuing education courses of almost limitless variety, some of them designed to improve job opportunities, some for intellectual and artistic growth.

In those same years of educational growth, school administrators, board members, and teachers wrestled with such issues as minimum competency testing, community advisory councils, programs in values clarification, bilingual education, and questions about textbooks. In their student populations were some judged to be at-risk, others gifted and talented, and still others learning disabled (a term used initially in 1963). For those judged to be learning disabled, that designation most likely meant separate classrooms, in that mainstreaming (integrating designated disabled students into regular classroom settings) was not yet a part of schools' responses or vocabularies.

Moreover, until the 20 years of enrollment growth ended in 1970, school administrators faced overcrowded schools and classrooms. Predictably, but with seeming suddenness, enrollment problems shifted into reverse in 1971, as a long downward spiral began. Soon decisions over what schools to close became battles between neighborhoods within school districts. Convenience of location served as one issue. The perception that an empty school building signaled neighborhood decline remained another.

School administrators as well as teachers, students, and parents had to deal with schools' perennial scarcity of funds. A snapshot of the budget picture of schools in 1970–1971 reveals their plight. In that year, about 52 percent of the $39.5 billion spent to operate public elementary and secondary schools was raised by local taxes, typically on property; 41 percent came from state taxes on sales, income, and property; and 7 percent came from the federal government under a variety of programs. A report on school finance showed that in 1970 voters approved only 48 percent of school bond issues, compared with 81 percent a decade earlier. In other words, as the public increased its demands on schools, it also became more reluctant to foot the bill. Unequal distribution of dollars among schools and school districts caused another budgetary problem: where the tax base was low, so was tax revenue, and the schools suffered. Poor children attended inferior schools. Court decisions over the next several years achieved only limited success in equalizing the resources of school districts.

The other major issue educators, parents, and students confronted was school desegregation. In some parts of the country, school districts with racially segregated schools had, for more than a decade, defied the Supreme Court's 1954 ruling in *Brown v. Board of Education* that such schools had to be eliminated. They changed school boundaries, redrew bus routes, and offered voluntary choice programs to perpetuate segregation. A series of Supreme Court rulings, however, particularly one in 1968, declared that the federal courts would insist on proof of racial integration in areas that formerly had segregated their schools by law. In 1971, the court upheld busing of schoolchildren as a means to achieve racial balance where segregation still had official local sanction and where school authorities had not offered acceptable alternatives to busing. By 1976, as a result of court orders, 77 percent of black schoolchildren in the South attended schools that had at least 10 percent white students.

In 1972, the court ruled that segregated schools resulting from residential segregation must be treated as the result of deliberate public policies, just as if they had been segregated by law. Such schools were judged in violation of the Constitution, and remedies to eliminate segregation were required. Busing and the creation of magnet schools—schools offering special programs in the arts or the sciences, for example—were the most common remedies. Pairing schools was another remedy, with a portion of black students bused to a predominantly white school and vice versa. School desegregation proceeded slowly, partly because many families moved to avoid sending their children to newly desegregated schools. So-called white flight meant that neighborhood populations changed swiftly and dramatically, and desegregation plans had to be updated almost yearly. Thoughtful persons wondered aloud why the task of desegregating society was being given mainly to children, but where they were given a chance, the children showed they were capable of making desegregation work.

Desegregation posed many challenges. Children of both races found themselves in classrooms with other children from whom they had been taught, or even required, to keep their distance. Teachers encountered children who had been denied solid educational opportunities and who, therefore, had difficulty meeting their expectations. Administrators were compelled, often against their personal wishes, to design desegregation plans and make them work. Parents worried about the effects of desegregation on their children and often resisted it passionately. In Charlotte, North Carolina, for example, the Parents Concerned Association vowed to boycott schools if busing plans were implemented. "I'm willing to go to jail if I have to," one parent said. Even if board members and community leaders supported school desegregation, they had to cope with the resistance of citizens who did not.

But the simple and obvious truth was that the only way to eliminate schools attended solely by black children was to enroll those children in schools with whites. Controversies over school policies, court decisions, and legislative and executive actions at both state and federal levels aimed at desegregation continued throughout the 1970s. Some of them became violent. A much larger effect of the Supreme Court's decisions, as well as of decisions by lower courts, was that color consciousness and sensitivity to group identities came to permeate virtually all decisions in schools, particularly in urban districts.

By the 1980s, conservatives had found a way to challenge school desegregation plans that required children to attend schools in neighborhoods other than their own. Since the *Brown* decision in 1954, some Americans saw desegregation as a threat to a seemingly sacred neighborhood-school concept. By the 1980s, however, some parents wanted to choose their children's school with less regard for its location. *School choice* became a popular phrase. For some, it meant giving parents tax monies to send their children to private schools. Others simply wanted to send their children to schools across district boundaries. The practice of allowing students to attend out-of-district schools gained acceptance, but using tax funds for sending children to private schools was tried on a very limited basis and almost always challenged in the courts.

Conservatives also challenged school textbooks. In a number of school districts, particularly in southern states, parents identifying themselves as Christian and conservative found certain textbooks objectionable. In Hawkins County, Tennessee, for example, a number of parents removed their children from public school reading classes because the textbooks offended their religious beliefs. A lower court ruled in their favor, but an appeals court asserted in 1987 that neither the books nor the classes violated religious freedom guaranteed by the First Amendment. A district court in Alabama allowed the banning of 44 history, social studies, and home economics textbooks on the grounds that they promoted "the religion of secular humanism." Promoting moral behavior without reference to God, claimed the lower-court judge, made humanism a religion, and using books that lacked information on Christianity and other religions advanced godless principles that also amounted to a religion. The judge's rulings were reversed by a court of appeals, also in 1987, but that did not change the sentiments of the 600 fundamentalist parents, students, and teachers (or those of Alabama's former governor, George Wallace) who had initiated or supported the lawsuit that brought the case to trial (Marty 1997, 51–52, 159–67, 309–13; *Daily Life Online*, "Intellectual Life: Education," in Marty, *Daily Life in the United States, 1960–1990*, http://dailylife.greenwood.com).

HEALTH AND MEDICINE

Technology has always been the essential link between science and the practice of medicine, and between 1960 and 1966 technological innovations evolved rapidly. A list of those innovations seems truly impressive, but the items in it take on particular meaning for the countless individuals and families who benefited from them at the time and the many more who have since been affected by the further medical progress those innovations made possible. In these years, among many other things, the following events occurred:

- Lasers were used for the first time in eye surgery.
- The first liver and lung transplants occurred, made possible in large part as a result of improvements in anesthesia.
- A prominent cardiac surgeon used an artificial heart to sustain his patient during surgery.
- Pacemakers allowed persons with heart conditions to live normal lives.
- Home kidney dialysis became possible.
- Vaccines proved to be effective against German measles and rubella (which, if contracted during pregnancy, could injure the fetus).
- Methods were perfected for dealing with the Rh factor, a blood condition that threatened the survival of babies at birth.
- An improved polio vaccine led to virtual eradication of the disease.

- The key antigen for development of a hepatitis B vaccine was discovered.
- Development of antibiotics continued.
- Radioactive isotopes were used widely in the diagnosis and treatment of diseases.
- More sophisticated forms of chemotherapy for cancer treatment showed improved effectiveness.

Meanwhile, scientists engaged in basic research laid the groundwork for technological innovations that would arrive in later years.

During these years, the technological developments in medicine of the preceding decades were refined, but stunning new medical procedures captured the headlines. Although they were initially rare, just as organ transplants had been at first, new procedures offered hope to victims of various conditions. Perhaps the best example is the "test-tube baby" as an answer to problems of infertility. The first test-tube baby was born in London in 1978. She had been conceived when an egg extracted from her mother was fertilized in a laboratory by her father's sperm. The fertilized egg remained in a Petri dish until it had developed into an eight-celled embryo; it was then implanted in the mother's uterus, where it developed as a fetus until delivered as a healthy 5-pound, 12-ounce baby. Other such conceptions and births followed as use of the procedure spread.

Technological advancements in medicine and science ranged from those that seemed distant and exotic to those that affected the daily lives of millions of people. Sometimes the speed with which a rarity became commonplace seemed stunning. Within a decade of the first implantation of pacemakers to control irregular heartbeats, those devices enabled thousands of men and women to enjoy longer and happier lives. The same remained true of coronary bypass surgery.

Sometimes medical miracles captured worldwide attention, as when Christian Barnard, a South African surgeon, transplanted the first human heart on December 3, 1967. That it could be done was amazing; whether it was worth the time and expense required to extend one's life for 18 days, as happened in this instance, was debatable. Four days later, the first transplant patient in the United States lived only a few hours.

Though there was no shortage of patients waiting to receive transplanted hearts, the number of hearts available for transplant was always very low. However, the shortage of organs available for transplants—of hearts, livers, lungs, kidneys, and corneas—was not the main obstacle to making transplants routine. Nor was it a lack of surgeons with technical skills for performing transplants. Rather, it was the limitations of drugs to prevent rejection of the implanted organs. In the seven years after Dr. Barnard's feat, more than 250 patients received transplanted hearts, but only about 20 percent lived more than a year after the surgery. For them, life each day was a reminder that the medical miracle performed by their surgeon was worth it, but general questions about transplant surgeries continued to raise ethical, medical, and financial questions.

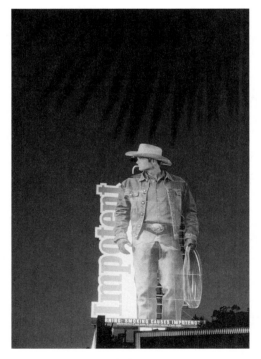

Revenues generated from the 1998 voter-approved antismoking Proposition 10, which added a 50-cent tax on tobacco products, helped fund antismoking programs such as this billboard. Tom Stoddart/Getty Images.

Many changes in health care that made headlines during these years resulted from these technological advances. Less newsworthy than changes in technology, but undoubtedly more significant in the daily lives of the American people, were the dramatic reductions in infectious diseases occurring between 1960 and 1970, continuing a trend that had begun in the postwar years. Reported cases of measles, for example, which had increased from 319,124 in 1950 to more than 440,000 in 1960, dropped to 47,351 in 1970. Between 1960 and 1990, cases of diphtheria declined from 918 to 4, and poliomyelitis from 3,190 to 7. On the other hand, while deaths per 100,000 population from infectious diseases continued to decline, the decade-to-decade increase in deaths caused by cancer also continued, as it would further in subsequent decades. Deaths from cardiovascular and kidney-related causes began to decline for the first time in the 1960s, although they remained 10 times as high as deaths caused by infectious diseases and 3 times as high as those caused by cancer.

Technological advances still did not solve some of the basic problems of the medical profession, such as a shortage of doctors and the rising costs of health care. The federal government took steps to deal with shortages of physicians caused partly by the broadened availability of health care resulting from the instant popularity of Medicare and Medicaid. In 1971, Congress enacted legislation offering government funding for medical schools that increased their enrollments. Two years later it passed a law encouraging the development of health maintenance organizations (HMOs). Those HMOs, consisting of groups of physicians and other medical providers, offered comprehensive health care to members of groups who paid fixed monthly premiums.

Decades earlier, physicians had stopped making house calls. Now the medical profession made other changes affecting doctor-patient relationships. Patients with acute illnesses and serious injuries were more likely to be referred by their primary doctors—family practitioners, pediatricians, obstetricians/gynecologists, and internists—to persons in specialized fields. Hospitals preferred having only board-certified physicians on their staffs, and health insurers paid higher fees to board-certified specialists, so the American Medical Association and other medical societies began to insist that every physician be certified in a specialty. Family practitioners, the primary care physicians who gradually replaced those known as general practitioners, also required certification. After 1970, therefore, almost all physicians-in-training served multiple-year residencies to be certified.

As medical specialization increased, physicians seemed more inclined to form group practices. Some groups included physicians with the same specialty, such as orthopedics or obstetrics/gynecology. Some included individuals or groups from a broad range of specialties, making it possible for them to provide comprehensive medical care through in-group referrals. In 1970, more than 93 percent of the nation's physicians were men. By 1990 women physicians were beginning to claim a larger place in the profession, as the percentage of male physicians declined to below 83 percent.

In the period 1960 to 1990, there were several health issues that doctors struggled to solve. Among the biggest were the illnesses caused by smoking. Most aspects of health care depend on the willingness of individual Americans to exercise responsibility for their own health. The most persistent preventable health problems were caused by smoking. By 1967, the surgeon general's warning on the hazards of smoking had induced many smokers to tackle the difficult challenge of quitting, and smoking-withdrawal clinics appeared across America.

It is difficult to estimate the numbers of persons whose attempts to quit smoking succeeded. Many quit for short periods, but their addiction to nicotine was so powerful that they ultimately returned to their old habits. Nevertheless, it appears that between 1966 and 1970, 13 million Americans gave up smoking. The percentage of adult men who smoked dropped from 52 to 42, and of women from 34 to 31, although smoking among teenagers increased. The decreases and increases seem to have evened out the per capita consumption of cigarettes, for the figures for 1960 and 1970 were almost identical. By 1980, however, there had again been a slight increase in total consumption. The National Association of Broadcasters announced a plan in 1969 to phase out cigarette advertising on radio and television over a three-year period beginning on January 1, 1970. Publicity accompanying that announcement may have influenced some smokers to quit.

Smoking came to be regarded as a more serious threat to health and a greater social stigma after the surgeon general issued a warning in 1972 that secondhand smoke—that is, other people's cigarette smoke—might pose health hazards for nonsmokers. Gradually thereafter restaurants began to provide nonsmoking areas, and hotels sometimes honored requests by hotel guests for rooms where smoking was not permitted. Meetings and social gatherings that would once have been held in smoke-filled rooms began to be smoke-free. Laws calling for smoke-free workplaces and lawsuits demanding them carried restrictions against smoking even further. Tobacco companies fought the laws and challenged the evidence on the damaging effects of smoking, but they could only slow the imposition of restrictions.

The surgeon general of the United States, Julius B. Richmond (1977–1981), continued the efforts of his predecessors to publicize findings about the relationship between smoking and health. In 1979 he called smoking the "most important environmental factor contributing to early death." In 1980, he reported that cases of lung cancer in women had increased rapidly and that lung cancer soon would lead to more deaths than breast cancer. In March of the same year came reports on research at the University of California at San Diego that produced the first scientific evidence that breathing secondhand smoke harmed nonsmokers. That report and others boosted efforts to limit smoking in public places.

The surgeon general's reports caused some smokers to fight their addiction and sometimes to win. Between 1970 and 1980 smoking dropped 28 percent among men age 20 and older, 13 percent among adult women, and 20 percent among teenage boys. Among teenage girls, however, it increased 51 percent in the dozen years preceding 1980.

Whether from eating too much, eating the wrong foods, or failing to adequately exercise, many American men and women also jeopardized their health and appearance by being overweight. Diet plans promoted on television, in books, and through programs like Weight Watchers all attracted believers and followers. Some nutritionists placed the emphasis on healthful, balanced diets. Others called for drinking nutritious concoctions in place of solid foods. The range of gimmicks for losing weight appeared impressive, but then, as later, most who managed to lose weight by following one plan or another quickly regained it when they returned to their predieting habits.

During these years a number of psycho-physiological eating disorders began to receive greater attention. The most common were anorexia nervosa and bulimarexia, or simply bulimia, whose victims were typically women. The symptoms of anorexia include an abnormal fear of being fat, a distorted image of one's appearance, aversion to food, and, consequently, extreme weight loss. Victims of bulimia go on eating binges followed by periods of depression and guilt. To deal with their insatiable appetites, they try extreme diets, fasting, and self-induced vomiting and diarrhea. For persons suffering from these disorders, the problem is not unavailability of food but inability to cope with its presence.

More and more people, faced with increasing complexity in their lives, sought counseling from psychologists and psychiatrists. Many received effective treatment through counseling and medication. At the same time, there was an increase in so-called pop psychology, that is, do-it-yourself approaches to coping with stress, depression, and other troubling conditions. Doctors and counselors on radio programs provided ready-made answers for questioners seeking help, but probably more significant were books promoting self-help. The first best-seller in what was to become a self-help industry was *I'm OK, You're OK* (1969), a popular rendition of the principles of a field of treatment known as transactional analysis, by Thomas Harris, M.D. Transactional analysis was used widely by psychiatrists, although not without controversy, and it became something of a game, a means for people to discover much about themselves and others. One practitioner remarked, "Tom Harris has done for psychotherapy the same thing Henry Ford did for the automobile: made it available to the average person."

Reliance on medication by persons suffering from stress and physical pain had grown rapidly in the 1960s and early 1970s, so much so that drug manufacturers began to worry about dependence on it. They endorsed warnings to physicians by the Food and Drug Administration that tranquilizers not be prescribed for the stress of everyday life. Perhaps in response to such warnings, legally filled prescriptions for tranquilizers (the most widely used of which was Valium) dropped from 88.3 million to 62.3 million between 1975 and 1979.

Treatment of mentally ill persons changed in other ways as well, the most notable being that fewer of them were confined in institutions. In earlier times, persons judged to suffer from mental illness could be institutionalized without their consent. To gain their release, they had to prove their sanity and ability to handle freedom. In 1975, the Supreme Court ruled that mental patients could not be confined against their will unless they were a danger to others or could not care for themselves. As a result, and also in reaction to worries inspired by reports of mistreatment in mental institutions (as depicted in Ken Kesey's 1962 novel *One Flew over the Cuckoo's Nest*, made into a film in 1975), mental wards emptied. Mental patients, in many cases, were simply put out on the streets to become homeless.

Through the 1980s and into the 1990s, mental health remained a concern for millions of Americans. Such illnesses as schizophrenia were the subject of ongoing research, as were depressive illnesses that prevented their victims from functioning well in daily life. Antidepressant medications, along with electroconvulsive therapy, had been used for a number of years to bring about recovery from bouts of manic depression, but the quest continued to find something that would prevent recurrences. In 1970, lithium carbonate became available by prescription for treatment of acute depression and maintenance of relatively normal lives by manic-depressive patients. This required close monitoring of side effects. Lithium is regarded as the first successful preventive medication in the treatment of psychiatric patients.

People in the 1980s complained frequently about pressures of time, family responsibilities, earning a living, and adjusting to change, among other things. The fact that many were indeed affected by stressful conditions could be documented by psychologists and psychiatrists. Moreover, a survey conducted by the National Institute of Mental Health in 1984 concluded that almost 20 percent of adults in the United States suffered mental disorders. Women, according to the study, appeared more prone to depression and phobias, while men to drug and alcohol abuse and antisocial behavior.

Decades earlier the quest for relief from mental conditions often involved psychoanalysis. Patients poured out tales of their past to persons trained to listen and, by asking questions, help them understand themselves and deal with their problems. By the 1980s, neither the pace of life nor the terms of medical insurance allowed for protracted psychoanalytical treatment, and psychoanalysts had few patients. Nonetheless, counseling—both individual and in group therapy sessions—remained important in dealing with mental and emotional problems.

At the same time, the growing belief that mental disorders were often caused by such physical problems as chemical imbalances led psychiatrists increasingly to prescribe medications. That may explain the popularity of Prozac, introduced in 1988 as an apparently effective treatment for depression. Before long, it was also used to treat problems associated with obesity, gambling, and anxiety over public speaking. Although many benefited from it and its side effects were few, some physicians and psychologists voiced concern that Prozac and similar drugs were substitutes for dealing directly with what was wrong in the lives of their users. There were reasons to wonder, too, whether medications might inhibit creative powers in those dependent on them.

Another mental condition that received considerable attention in the 1980s was attention-deficit disorder (ADD); sometimes the term *hyperactive* also describes an aspect of the condition, known then as ADHD. Although physicians and psychologists made many of the diagnoses of ADD and ADHD, many other cases were self-diagnosed. In fact, most people could see in themselves varying degrees of ADD's most common symptoms: a tendency to be easily distracted from tasks at hand, a low tolerance for frustration or boredom, an inclination to act impulsively, and a fondness for situations of high intensity. When diagnoses were made by professionals, they were followed by counseling and sometimes by medication, such as Ritalin. Indeed, overuse of Ritalin for children suffering from attention-deficit and hyperactive disorder worried parents and teachers. Persons who diagnosed their own condition apparently compensated for it by doing such things as establishing demanding schedules or setting goals that required them to work obsessively.

If there was in fact an ADD epidemic in the United States, it was probably related to the hyperactive nature of society. Edward Hallowell and John J. Ratey, both psychiatrists, wrote in *Driven to Distraction* (1994) that "American society tends to create ADD-like symptoms in us all. We live in an ADD-ogenic culture." In the following excerpt, they identify some of the hallmarks of American culture that are typical of ADD as well as of postmodern times:

The sound bite. The bottom line. Short takes, quick cuts. The TV remote-control clicker. High stimulation. Restlessness. Violence. Anxiety. Ingenuity. Creativity. Speed. Present-centered, no future, no past. Disorganization. Mavericks. A mistrust of authority. Video. Going for the gusto. Making it on the run. The fast track. Whatever works. Hollywood. The stock exchange. Fads. High stim.

It is important to keep this in mind, he suggested, or you may start thinking that everybody you know has ADD. The disorder is culturally syntonic—that is to say, it fits right in.

Americans in the 1980s also witnessed two major epidemics. First, in March 1981, the Centers for Disease Control (CDC) determined that cases of the sexually transmitted disease known as genital herpes had reached epidemic proportions in the United States. Victims suffered painful, recurring sores on their genital organs. Between unpredictable outbreaks, the virus withdraws into nerve cells, where it remains out of the reach of the body's immune system. A medication existed to relieve the symptoms when initial outbreaks occurred, but there was no means as yet to prevent or relieve the symptoms in subsequent recurrences, making it the first incurable sexually transmitted disease since the introduction of antibiotics. Research continued for medications to prevent outbreaks for those afflicted with the disease and for vaccines to protect others from contracting it.

At the same time a more deadly disease, usually transmitted sexually, crept into the nation's consciousness. In June 1981, the CDC reported five cases of a strain of pneumonia among previously healthy homosexual men in Los Angeles hospitals. This strain, *pneumocystis carinii*, usually occurs in infants or in adults receiving immunosuppressive drugs, as in the chemotherapy treatment of cancer patients. Reports of other cases of strange illnesses appeared elsewhere, most commonly among homosexual men. Initially labeled GRID (for gay-related immunodeficiency), the name was changed when the victims included recipients of blood transfusions, female prostitutes, intravenous drug users, and heterosexual Africans and Haitians. The disease became known as AIDS (acquired immunodeficiency syndrome).

By the end of 1982, 750 AIDS cases had been reported in the United States and almost 1,600 worldwide. A year later the number of reported cases reached about 3,000. With the number of cases growing daily, the AIDS crisis became one of the big stories of the decade. Other factors also made it so, such as movie star Rock Hudson's revelation in 1985 that he battled AIDS and his death later that year. The dedication of an AIDS hospice in New York by Mother Teresa, a nun renowned for her work with the poor and suffering, also increased public awareness. Close-to-home reminders of the dangers posed by AIDS came in 1987 and 1988, when patients began to see their doctors and dentists slip their hands into latex gloves before treating them.

When the CDC reported the first cases of AIDS in June 1981, it opened one of the decade's big stories. Awareness of AIDS spread slowly, but within five years just about everyone knew that scientists, physicians, hospitals, and the victims and their friends and families faced dreadful challenges. In 1986, the Department of Health and Human Services (DHHS) estimated that the number of cases and deaths would increase tenfold in the next five years. In 1991, predicted HHS, some 50,000 Americans would die of AIDS—more than the number killed in most years in automobile accidents. That prediction may have been too grim. In 1990, there were 29,781 deaths, bringing the total since the center began keeping records in 1981 to 98,350. With about 140,000 cases known, however, the CDC made another grim prediction: that the AIDS death total could reach 340,000 by 1993.

Reporting on the spread of AIDS in 1986, HHS noted that about 70 percent of the victims of AIDS were homosexual or bisexual men. That prompted those who regarded homosexuality and bisexuality as sinful to call AIDS God's punishment. They judged the 25 percent of the victims who were intravenous drug users infected by contaminated needles in much the same way. The fact that more than one-third of the known cases were in New York and San Francisco gave those hostile to homosexuality an opportunity to condemn the cities as centers of wickedness.

Wherever cases appeared, AIDS victims were kept at arm's length, even though it was well established that the virus that caused AIDS could not be spread by casual contact. In well-publicized instances that caused controversy across the nation, even children who had been infected through blood transfusions were kept out of the schools they had been attending. The gravity of the AIDS epidemic, lack of information about the disease, and attitudes about it compelled the federal government to educate the American public concerning its nature and consequences. In May 1988, the government took the unprecedented step of mailing an explicit eight-page booklet, *Understanding AIDS*, to 106 million households.

An often controversial search continued for vaccines to prevent the further spread of AIDS and cure existing cases. In 1989, two studies showed that the drug AZT offered hope as a treatment for AIDS. Initially AZT had been used to treat severely ill patients, but the studies indicated that it could delay the onset of symptoms if it was administered when early signs of damage to the immune system appeared. But AZT was not without side effects. The National Cancer Institute reported in 1990 that persons with AIDS who received it stood a nearly 50 percent chance of developing lymphoma after three years on the drug. The cost of $7,000 to $8,000 per year for those being treated with AZT also inhibited its widespread use. Although other therapies began to develop, it remained too early to determine their effectiveness. Understandably, the slow progress in AIDS research, coupled with homosexuality as a culturally divisive issue, made this an emotional political subject.

Technological advances in developing treatments for diseases such as AIDS played a part in pushing health care costs upward. So did the increased longevity of the population. Another contributor, medical malpractice insurance, had grown in significance for a decade and reached crisis levels in the mid-1970s. Doctors and hospitals purchased malpractice insurance as protection against justified and unjustified claims of mistakes or negligence. Insurance funds were used to investigate the claims, provide legal defenses against them, and pay damages to patient-victims in court judgments or out-of-court settlements. Between 1969 and 1975, according to authoritative estimates, claims had increased by about 180 percent. One doctor in 10, on average, was sued, and the size of awards by juries rose during those years.

A number of factors played a part in the increase, including sharply rising doctors' fees, patients' beliefs that they failed to receive personal attention, lack of personal relationships between specialists and patients, and, apparently, the conclusion that greater sophistication in medical techniques should make doctors and hospitals infallible. The popularity of the television program *Marcus Welby, M.D.* seems to have encouraged notions of medical infallibility. The fact that awards in court cases and settlements were reaching into the millions of dollars also encouraged avaricious patients and lawyers to file claims. Even though the plaintiffs lost about 80 percent of the cases that went to trial, the cost of defending them was often so high that insurers frequently agreed to pretrial settlements. In the decade prior to the mid-1970s, insurance premiums for neurosurgeons and orthopedic surgeons increased more than 10-fold, and practitioners in less-risky specialties also saw sharp increases. Where state insurance commissions refused to approve rate increases, insurance companies withdrew coverage. In such instances, some doctors declined to perform anything but emergency procedures. Even as solutions to the insurance problems proved elusive, most states tried to find them. Meanwhile, patients covered the cost of increased premiums when they paid the larger fees charged by their doctors.

In the 1980s, the portion of the gross national product devoted to health care increased from 9.1 percent to 12.2 percent, on its way to more than 14 percent by the mid-1990s. The rate of increase in the total health bill for the nation soared to double the inflation rate. Not only did the annual increases have implications for state and federal budgets, but they also had significant effects on family budgets. Insurance premiums and payments made directly to doctors and hospitals multiplied several times between the late 1970s and 1990. Employers felt the squeeze, too, as the cost of providing health care insurance for their employees skyrocketed.

In the absence of a national plan guaranteeing health insurance for all Americans, some simply accepted the spiraling costs of individual and group coverage, some did without coverage and hoped that hospitals' emergency rooms or charity policies would meet their needs, and some hoped to control costs by joining health maintenance organizations (HMOs). Although the relatively lower costs of HMO coverage made them popular, to compete with other forms of coverage they had to relax their initial limits on patients' rights to choose their doctors. Even so, the less-restricted choices left many of their members unsatisfied.

That dissatisfaction no doubt reflected a cynicism about providers of health care in general. One survey reported that only 29 percent of its respondents believed that physicians performed important services. Another 27 percent said that few physicians perform such services. In another survey, respondents expressed much greater confidence in pharmacists than in physicians and were more satisfied with their services. The changing health care scene prompted changes in the education of pharmacists, who were taught to counsel persons about their prescriptions. Their pill-counting role was being taken over by more accurate and efficient technological devices.

Despite the superior training of doctors and the breakthroughs in research, health problems were far from solved. The National Cancer Institute reported that cancer deaths continued to rise. Between 1973 and 1987, for example, occurrences of cancer increased by 14 percent. Melanoma (skin cancer) showed the greatest increase (83 percent), followed by prostate cancer (46 percent), lung cancer (31 percent), and breast cancer in women over age 50 (30 percent) and under age 50 (20 percent). Incidents of stomach, uterine, and cervical cancer declined. Heart disease also remained a major cause of death, with coronary disease or heart attacks accounting for more than 25 percent of the deaths occurring annually (Marty 1997, 62, 135–38, 155–57, 217–19, 295–99, 321; *Daily Life Online*, "Intellectual Life: Health and Medicine," in Marty, *Daily Life in the United States, 1960–1990*, http://dailylife. greenwood.com).

LITERATURE

Newspapers had difficulty competing with television for readers' time. The *Washington Star* shut down in 1981 and the *Philadelphia Bulletin* in 1982; also in 1982 nine newspapers located in all parts of the country merged their morning and evening papers into single morning or all-day publications, resulting in the loss of one kind of coverage or another. In 1985 the 131-year-old *St. Louis Globe-Democrat* folded when a new owner could not rescue it from bankruptcy. At the end of the decade the *Los Angeles Herald Examiner* and the *Raleigh Times* (North Carolina) ceased publication, and the morning edition *Kansas City Times* (1867–1990) was absorbed by the morning *Kansas City Star*. In a basic sense, many Americans turned to other mediums, particularly television, and often morning "drive time" radio, for their news.

Perhaps the biggest change in the newspaper business occurred in 1982 when the Gannett Company, owner of a chain of dailies, launched *USA Today*. The national newspaper made explicit attempts to compete with television as a primary source of news. Boxes dispensing it on street corners displayed the front page in windows that looked like television screens. News reports and features were brief and crisply written, and pictures, often in color, appeared more plentiful than in other newspapers. The fast-glimpse qualities of *USA Today* inspired critics to compare its fare with that offered in fast-food restaurants. "McNews," they called it. Within the next several years Gannett also acquired a number of major newspapers, including the *Detroit News*, the *Des Moines Register*, and the *Louisville Courier-Journal* and *Louisville Times*. Although Gannett-owned newspapers maintained individual identities, they also reflected traits displayed most prominently by *USA Today*, such as the shortened news reports. Some readers detected a loss of local flavor in the papers' coverage.

Following *USA Today*'s lead, other newspapers printed more pictures in color and abbreviated their reporting. Perhaps that enabled them to remain a staple in the life of the two-thirds of American adults who read them daily. Only one in five of the readers spent more than 30 minutes with the daily paper, and they tended to be older and better educated. Meanwhile, television continued to grow as the main source of news for the American people, partly because the network anchors seemed like authoritative guests in many homes and partly because of the news coverage of CNN. Ted Turner founded the Cable News Network in 1980.

Big-circulation magazines intended for general audiences saw their sales slump as their traditional readership was aging and dying. Smaller, more precisely targeted magazines fared better, as did some fashion magazines. The wide range of choices, symbolic of postmodern conditions, no doubt encouraged browsing rather than selecting one magazine and staying with it. Reflecting the get-rich climate of the times, *Forbes*, one of the nation's leading business magazines, saw its circulation grow and the median age of its readers move downward.

By the end of the 1980s, total book sales approached $15 billion, double the amount recorded at the beginning of the decade. Much of publishers' revenues came from the works of best-selling authors. Stephen King landed 10 horror novels on best-seller lists during the decade, and Danielle Steele eight romances. Sometimes outstanding works like Umberto Eco's *The Name of the Rose* and Toni Morrison's *Beloved* also became best-sellers, promising to become classics.

In 1982, readers of established classics by American writers welcomed the appearance of eight handsome, sturdy, meant-to-last volumes in the new Library of America series. Published in the first year were works by Walt Whitman, Herman Melville, Harriet Beecher Stowe, Nathaniel Hawthorne, Jack London, Mark Twain, and William Dean Howells. Admirers of such best-sellers as Robert Fulghum's *All I Really Need to Know I Learned in Kindergarten* (1988) would contend that they were classics, too. The very fact that such best-sellers existed alleviated fears that books would be crowded out of people's lives by television and computers. So did the continued popularity of children's books—longtime favorite writer Theodore Geisel published two more Dr. Seuss best-sellers. Children who grow up with books are more likely to be serious readers as adults (Marty 1997, 280–81; *Daily Life Online*, "Intellectual Life: Literature," in Marty, *Daily Life in the United States, 1960–1990*, http://dailylife.greenwood.com).

SCIENCE AND AMERICA'S SPACE PROGRAM

In the United States, space exploration reflected not only the close relationship between scientists and the government but also the strong desire to beat the communists in the space race. American scientific technology propelled the United States into space. Computer technology, in particular, played an essential role in America's first flights into space. In 1961, navy commander Alan Shepard and Air Force captain Virgil Grissom each piloted space capsules in suborbital flights of just over

300 miles, preparing the nation for the big moment to come the following winter. At 9:47 A.M. on February 20, 1962, with schoolchildren bunched around television sets in their classrooms and their parents interrupting tasks at work and at home, an Atlas missile at Cape Canaveral, Florida, launched the space capsule *Friendship 7* into orbit around the earth, with Colonel John Glenn aboard. Minutes short of four hours later, CBS newsman Walter Cronkite narrated Glenn's reentry into the atmosphere and his splashdown in the Caribbean Sea. In orbit, the capsule had reached a velocity of 17,500 miles per hour, and in the four hours between launch and recovery from the water Glenn had seen three sunrises. Viewers cheered what they saw and buzzed with excitement as they talked about it. Still, the way it was carried out was so precise that it looked routine, matter-of-fact, and predictable. It had all the marks of a choreographed theatrical production. Surely this was American progress, the success of modern times.

There was more to come: Three months later, astronaut Scott Carpenter repeated Glenn's feat, this time taking control of functions done by computerized instrumentation in the first flight. The following October, navy commander Walter Schirra completed a nearly perfect flight of more than nine hours, circling the earth six times and making a pinpoint landing in the Pacific Ocean. Television viewers began to take success for granted, but even bigger things would occur in the developing space program.

Based on the counsel of the National Aeronautics and Space Administration (NASA) and his advisors, and at the urging of Vice President Lyndon Johnson, President Kennedy declared in a speech before Congress on May 25, 1961: "This nation should commit itself to achieving the goal, before this decade is out, of landing a man on the moon and returning him safely to earth." President Kennedy concluded. "No single project . . . will be more exciting, or more impressive to mankind, or more important for the long-range exploration of space; and none will be so expensive to accomplish."

The cost? Likely $30 to $40 billion, with those dollars contributing little to economic growth. The Cold War explained why American taxpayers were willing to pick up the tab. Johnson was correct in saying he did not believe "that this generation of Americans is willing to resign itself to going to bed each night by the light of a Communist moon" (remarks made during a news conference). Anyone doubting that the Soviet Union saw the contest in the same terms should remember that every day thousands of Russians pass a statue of Yuri Gagarin mounted on a pedestal 40 meters tall on a main thoroughfare in Moscow. Gagarin was the Russian hero whose single-orbit flight on April 12, 1961, three weeks before Alan Shepard's suborbital flight, showed America that the Soviet Union could beat the United States in launching a man into spatial orbit.

The only immediate benefit of the space flights for the American people seemed bolstered pride in the nation's technology. The flights had been accomplished in full view of the American people, via television. So what if comparable feats had occurred earlier in the Soviet Union? They had been done in secret. How could we know, Americans asked, how many failures had preceded the Russians' successes?

More tangible benefits were to come, space scientists claimed, as by-products of space exploration reached into many quarters of daily life. One such benefit became apparent by mid-1962, with the placement in orbit of AT&T's Telstar communications satellite. The satellite permitted transmission of the straight-line waves of television, unhampered by mountains or oceans. When more orbiting stations were launched later, continuous transmission via satellites became possible. Television networks and weather forecasters soon came to rely on satellite transmissions, and eventually homeowners willing and able to mount a "dish" in their yards or on their roofs enjoyed the benefits too. Meanwhile, the American people maintained their interest in space flights, particularly those with two men tucked tightly into the Gemini capsules. In a period of 20 months, 20 astronauts in Project Gemini conducted a variety of experiments in space. Despite scary moments, NASA called each one of them an unqualified success.

As the Gemini space capsules scored successes in the mid-1960s, it became only a matter of time before a moon landing would occur. In May 1969, *Apollo 10* astronauts took their lunar module into orbit within nine miles of the moon before reconnecting with the command module. On July 20, hundreds of millions of Americans listened to communications preceding the landing on the moon of the Eagle, *Apollo 11*'s lunar module, by astronauts Neil Armstrong and Edwin Aldrin. When it touched down, their television sets enabled them to watch events as they occurred. Speaking the first words on lunar soil, Armstrong called the venture "one small step for a man, one giant leap for mankind." The astronauts conducted experiments on the lunar surface, collected about 45 pounds of rock and soil samples, and returned safely to the command module for the journey back to earth.

"After centuries of dreams and prophecies," wrote *Time* magazine, "the moment had come. Man had broken his terrestrial shackles and set foot on another world." The magazine continued, "Standing on the lifeless, rock-studded surface he could see the earth, a lovely blue and white hemisphere suspended in the velvety black sky." One of the six remaining missions, *Apollo 13*, survived a near-disaster without a moon landing, but the other five were successful, the last one in December 1972. In that year, NASA began a space shuttle program to provide means for further scientific exploration, and possibly future colonization and commercial activities. In the meantime, though, NASA faced deep budget cuts. Some were caused by the costs of waging war in Vietnam, others apparently by the belief that the big goal, reaching the moon, had been accomplished. By 1970, NASA's workforce of about 136,000 was roughly half of what it had been five years earlier.

The dividends of the space program for the American people, the payoff on the $25 billion it cost them, seemed difficult to calculate but included photographs of the lunar surface, rock samples of great geological interest but no known practical significance, considerable knowledge concerning how to maneuver vehicles in space, improved technological bases for telecommunication via satellites and weather surveillance worldwide, and information that would prove useful in advances in medicine. Most important, perhaps, was the restoration of American morale that had been damaged when the Russians sent *Sputnik* into orbit 12 years before the moon landing. Never mind that the Soviet Union used unmanned moon landings to accomplish many of the same results as the manned landings of NASA. Of the tangible benefits of space technology, one cited frequently, sometimes sarcastically, is Velcro. That material had been designed to help space travelers keep track of pencils and other handheld objects in the zero gravity of space. The prototype of video cameras that later came into common usage was developed for space missions, as were electronic stethoscopes, fire-resistant fabrics, lightweight insulation materials, dehydrated foods, computer technology for automated control of highly sophisticated equipment, and many other things.

Early fascination with television spectaculars featuring the accomplishments of the space program had seduced viewers into ignoring its cost. So what, they seemed to say, if with each launching a $200 million Saturn rocket sank into the ocean? As the consecutive launchings and returns blurred together, however, viewers' interest waned. The technical and political milestone represented by the linking of an *Apollo* spacecraft and the Russian *Soyuz* on July 17, 1975, attracted only passing attention. Television showed the exchange of visits by the American astronauts and Russian cosmonauts during the nearly 44 hours their spacecrafts were linked, but viewers seemed to take this historic occurrence for granted. The same was true when two *Viking* spacecraft landed on the planet Mars in 1976 and sent back spectacular pictures.

The 1980s saw more technological feats in space. The decade began on a promising note for the space program when the *Columbia,* the first reusable spacecraft, touched down at Edwards Air Force Base in April 1981. Its landing in the Mojave Desert concluded a flight begun more than 54 hours earlier when the spaceship launched as a rocket. In 36 orbits of the earth, it operated like a typical spacecraft, and it landed like an airplane on a runway. An amazingly successful mission, it gave Americans a renewed sense of pride and raised the prestige of the nation worldwide.

The goals of the space program, though, went beyond pride and prestige. NASA hoped to make orbiting in space a profitable venture. The communications industry was its early client, but NASA wanted to encourage advancements in medicine and other technologies. It faced competition from other nations as well as from private companies trying to break into space travel.

The American people took success in space exploration for granted until January 28, 1986. On that day the space shuttle *Challenger* exploded 73 seconds after liftoff from Cape Canaveral, Florida. Six astronauts died, along with a teacher on board, Christa McAuliffe. Her presence had attracted special attention to the flight, and millions of schoolchildren saw the explosion on television. News reporters could say nothing to set the children at ease, and the entire nation was stunned.

Failures of other spacecraft occurred in subsequent months, but none so dramatically as the *Challenger.* Almost three years passed before the launching of *Discovery* again put a shuttle in space. Things went well for a while, but an event in 1990 that should have been a spectacular achievement turned out to be tarnished. The space shuttle *Discovery* launched the $1.5 billion Hubble space telescope into orbit, only to find very soon thereafter that an incorrectly made mirror blurred the images it was to transmit back to earth. The Hubble telescope was later corrected and went on to provide valuable data that changed the thinking about the scope and nature of the galaxy and beyond.

Another shuttle disaster, again resulting in the loss of the seven-person crew, occurred on February 1, 2003, when the *Columbia* broke up upon reentry. The new tragedy again resulted in the grounding of the shuttle fleet. Nevertheless, despite the disasters and mistakes, the scientific-government complex, as one might call it, remained firmly intact and hard at work developing more scientific and technological breakthroughs that helped to advance humanity in general and the U.S. government and people in particular (Marty 1997, 60–61, 153–54, 222–23, 305–6; *Daily Life Online,* "Intellectual Life: Science," in Marty, *Daily Life in the United States, 1960–1990,* http://dailylife.greenwood.com).

FOR MORE INFORMATION

Barnouw, E. *Tube of Plenty: The Evolution of American Television.* 2nd ed. New York: Oxford University Press, 1990.

Boyer, P. S. *By the Bomb's Early Light: American Thought and Culture at the Dawn of the Atomic Age.* Chapel Hill: University of North Carolina Press, 1994.

Brumberg, J. J. *The Body Project: An Intimate History of American Girls.* New York: Random House, 1997.

Cremin, L. *American Education, 1876–1980: The Metropolitan Experience.* New York: Harper and Row, 1988.

Grmek, M. D. *History of AIDS: Emergence and Origin of a Modern Pandemic.* Princeton, NJ: Princeton University Press, 1990.

Halberstam, D. *The Fifties.* New York: Ballantine Books, 1994.

Hallowell, E. M., and J. J. Ratey. *Driven to Distraction.* New York: Pantheon Books, 1994.

Hart, J. D. *The Oxford Companion to American Literature.* 6th ed. New York: Oxford University Press, 1995.

Jowett, G., and J. M. Linton. *Movies as Mass Communications.* Beverly Hills, CA: Sage Publications, 1980.

Kaledin, E. *Daily Life in the United States, 1940–1959: Shifting Worlds.* Westport, CT: Greenwood Press, 2000.

Kubrick, S., dir. *Dr. Strangelove.* Tri-Star Home Video, 1964.

Marty, Myron A. *Daily Life in the United States, 1960–1990: Decades of Discord.* Westport, CT: Greenwood Press, 1997; also available online as *Daily Life Online,* in Marty, *Daily Life in the United States, 1960–1990,* http://dailylife.greenwood.com).

Parker, A., dir. *Mississippi Burning.* 1988.

Patterson, J. T. *Grand Expectations: The United States, 1945–1974.* New York: Oxford University Press, 1996.

Ravitch, D. *The Troubled Crusade: American Education, 1945–1980.* New York: Basic Books, 1983.

Ritt, M., dir. *Norma Rae.* 1979.

Rybczynski, W. *Waiting for the Weekend.* New York: Viking, 1991.

Shorter, E. *The Health Century.* New York: Doubleday, 1987.

Sklar, R. *Movie-Made America.* Rev. ed. New York: Vintage, 1994.

Spring, J. *The American School, 1642–1993.* 3rd ed. New York: McGraw Hill, 1994.

Tichi, Cecelia. *Electronic Hearth: Creating an American Television Culture*. New York: Oxford University Press, 1991.

Whitfield, S. J. *The Culture of the Cold War*. Baltimore, MD: Johns Hopkins University Press, 1991.

Williams, T. I., ed. *Science: A History of Discovery in the Twentieth Century*. New York: Oxford University Press, 1990.

Winn, M. *The Plug-In Drug*. New York: Viking Press, 1977.

Material Life

OVERVIEW

American daily life continued, in most instances, to pursue a consumer-driven material commitment during the 30-year period from 1960 to 1990. While new economic and political concerns had altered the expansive productive growth of the immediate postwar period, the middle class, in the United States, still had money to spend and an urge to do so. New products, broader options, and technological innovations had created a marketplace of goods and services to attract American consumers. While critics, particularly in the youth movement, began to question the materialism evident in American society, the trend that had begun following World War II persisted.

ALCOHOL AND DRINKING HABITS

Champagne to toast newlyweds, a martini at a cocktail party, wine with dinner, a bottle of beer at a picnic, a gin and tonic at a bar—such customs came to America with immigrants from diverse backgrounds and became standards. Drinking establishments, from the corner tavern to the bar in exclusive clubs, have long been fixtures in the American social landscape. With the drinking goes friendly conversation, political arguments, television watching, and "hanging out." The other side of the story is also part of daily lives: poor schoolwork done during repeated hangovers, tragedies caused by drunk drivers, families ruined by alcohol-related conflicts, jobs lost because of excessive absences caused by drinking binges, homeless men and women clutching bottles barely concealed in giveaway brown bags, and illness and death caused by excessive drinking.

Although the effects of excessive drinking are well known, knowledge alone does not restrain those who are tempted to drink too much. By the mid-1960s, the National Institute of Mental Health began to encourage research into the causes and consequences of alcoholism, and in 1966, two federal appeals court decisions supported contentions that alcoholism was a disease. Two years later, the Supreme Court, in the 1968 case *Powell v. Texas*, took note of those decisions, observing that experts were divided on the matter; the court then ruled that arrests for public intoxication were permissible. The next logical step was for Congress to establish an agency to direct federal efforts to deal with alcohol-related problems. President Richard Nixon and Congress developed the Hughes Act in 1970, creating the National Institute on Alcohol Abuse and Alcoholism (NIAAA), making it possible for treatment, research, and educational activities to be conducted at new levels. One result was a recommendation that states remove many alcohol-related legal infractions from the criminal justice system, substituting medical treatment for punishment.

Researchers at the University of Iowa confirmed the increasingly popular theory that a tendency toward alcoholism might be inherited. Children of alcoholics had a high incidence of alcoholism even when they had been adopted and raised by non-alcoholics. Theories aside, the reality of the 1960s and 1970s was clear: Between 1960 and 1975, the annual per capita consumption of alcoholic beverages increased by one-third. Did that signal a return to earlier times? Not quite, given that the average consumption remained at a level half as high as in 1830. The increase came in part from the fact that teenagers began drinking at earlier ages and in larger numbers. Further, with liberation of women from old constraints, their drinking levels approached those of men. As far as consumption of hard liquor (distilled spirits) was concerned, 1978 was the peak year in recent times. Then came a steady decline, continuing to the mid-1990s.

Excessive drinking harmed the health of the drinkers, but it also did damage to others—particularly when accidents resulted from drunk driving. Between World War II and 1980, drunk drivers were involved in half of the 45,000 fatalities caused annually by automobile accidents. Mothers against Drunk Driving (MADD), founded in 1980, became the most powerful organization striving to reduce drunk driving, particularly among the young. As a result of health and drunk-driving concerns a slight decline in consumption of alcoholic beverages occurred in the later 1980s.

At the same time, the consumption of soft drinks increased by almost 20 percent. Diet drinks got a boost in 1983 when the Food and Drug Administration approved the use of *aspartame*, an artificial sweetener. Although critics warned that aspartame's effects on certain chemicals in the brain could cause behavioral changes, diet-conscious consumers ignored the warnings and the sweetener quickly became popular. Much sweeter than sugar, aspartame has the advantage of not causing tooth decay. While diet and regular soft drinks continued to attract consumers, they also began to use a variety of bottled water options. The use of bottled water doubled in the latter half of the 1980s.

Consumers of soft drinks were ready for a new sweetener, but millions let the Coca-Cola Company know they were not ready for a new taste. In 1985, a year before its 100th birthday, Coca-Cola decided to change its formula for Coke, the world's most popular soft drink, by making it sweeter. A $100 million advertising campaign promoting the new Coke attracted overwhelming attention. A survey by the company claimed that 81 percent of Americans heard about the change within 24 hours of its announcement—higher than the percentage who were aware in the same length of time of the 1969 moon landing. The campaign, however, failed to persuade angry protesters that the new formula was better than the old, so within three months the company brought back the original formula, now labeled Coca-Cola Classic. Some preferred the new taste, however, so the company produced both the old and the new. The controversy gave the Coca-Cola Company valuable free publicity, boosting sales of both old and new Coke and arousing suspicions (that the company denied) that creating controversy had been the plan all along. The episode provided a dramatic demonstration of corporate America's responsiveness to consumers (Marty 1997, 130, 216, 291–92; *Daily Life Online*, "Material Life: Drink," in Marty, *Daily Life in the United States, 1960–1990*, http://dailylife.greenwood.com).

NUTRITION

Eating and drinking practices frequently did not match the heightened awareness of the need for healthful foods. Advertising for such foods abounded, and labels became more honest and explicit in reporting the contents of food packages, especially after a law passed in 1990 required it. But even with accurate labels, food products and repeated warnings concerning the health hazards posed by cholesterol, fats, salt, and sugar, and junkfood, consumption increased. Reports that poultry was healthier than pork and beef led to increased poultry consumption, although not sufficiently to catch up with either of its competitors. Nutritional concerns led to other healthful changes, including increased consumption of fruits and vegetables and reduced intake of fats and oils. The food industry encouraged the trend. In 1988, it spent more than $1 billion on advertising that included some type of health message, although critics contended that the messages were both confusing and misleading. Nutrition and the eating habits of Americans remained a major aspect of their material life throughout the era and into the new millennium. Particularly the impact of eating habits on heart disease and the growing issue of obesity in American life would make nutrition a high-profile concern as the century came to an end (*Daily Life Online*, "Concerns of Daily Life: Nutrition" and "Cultural Reflections/Cultural Influences: Home Life and Television," in Marty, *Daily Life in the United States, 1960–1990*, http://dailylife.greenwood.com).

FOOD

Since World War II, eating and drinking have amounted to more than meeting bodily needs. In *Eating in America*, published in 1976, Waverly Root and Richard de Rochemont summarized as follows their observations on practices that were well under way by the early 1960s:

Americans are consuming, along with unheard-of amounts of valuable proteins in their meats and cereals, and along with vast quantities of fruits and vegetables full of good nutrients and vitamins, tens of billions of dollars' worth of packaging, additives, and advertising, as part of their total estimated two hundred and fifty billion dollar contribution to the food industry, agribusiness, and the conglomerate corporations that decide what we will be allowed to eat.

What was new in this "great glob," as the writers called it, that made up the American diet? By the early 1960s, what nutritionists called junk food had claimed a big place in the fare American people consumed. Promoted by Saturday-morning cartoons for children, the options included sugared breakfast foods and synthetic "fruit" drinks containing little fruit juice. Added to those items were much of the fatty, salty, and sugary goods passed over the counter at fast-food restaurants. If Americans were improperly nourished, they were at least not underfed.

Just as important as the quantity and quality of what the young and old in America ate is when and where they ate it. In 1965, one meal in four was eaten outside the home, with that number on the rise. When meals *were* eaten at home, they were less likely to be occasions for families to come together. That is not surprising, given the many commitments to jobs, school, and leisure and cultural activities of all generations in the typical family.

Fashion consciousness, particularly that inspired by the super-thin "Twiggy" look that came into vogue in the 1960s, and health concerns made many Americans sensitive to being overweight, so it is not surprising that dieting became something of a national pastime. The most prominent organization in the weight-loss industry was Weight Watchers, begun in 1961 and incorporated for granting franchises in 1963. It gained adherents using a combination of group therapy in weekly meetings and menus that prescribed foods low in fat and high in protein; the diet prohibited foods not fitting that description. Although Weight Watchers changed its prescriptions and prohibitions through the years and the character of its approach evolved with the times, it continued to attract followers. Other diet formulas and plans have enjoyed bursts of popularity and then faded away as new ones took their place. But diet books and articles published in magazines catering to women especially filled store racks at supermarket checkout aisles.

Dieters had more than mere weight loss as their concern. Reports on relationships between nutrition and health appeared regularly. For example, the Food and Nutrition Board of the National Academy of Sciences published a calorie table showing dietary allowances based on one's age and desired

McDonald's famous golden arch. Courtesy of Jolyon Girard.

weight. The American Heart Association recommended that people reduce the amount of fat they eat and begin "reasonable substitution" of vegetable oils and polyunsaturated fats for animal fats. Previously the association had suggested dietary changes for persons judged to be vulnerable to heart attacks. Now, for the first time, it called for changes in the eating habits of the general public. Sharp controversy followed, with representatives of the dairy industry leading the attacks on the recommendations.

Despite dieting fads, the American people were, in the words of historian David Potter, "people of plenty." Even so, many were distressed by the high prices of foods—so much so that in 1966 and again in 1970 and 1973 consumers in various parts of the nation organized boycotts of supermarkets. A Gallup poll showed that the 1973 boycott involved 50 million people, or 25 percent of all consumers. Boycott participants acknowledged that the increases in per capita spending on food resulted in part from their demand for more meat, bakery products, delicacies, and easy-to-prepare foods, but those were matters within their control. Beyond their control were such things as the amount of money producers and retailers spent on advertising, promotions, and trading stamps. Buyers earned trading stamps with their purchases, placed them in savings books, and exchanged them for such premiums as toasters, can openers, and electric blankets. Enthusiasm for stamps peaked in the early 1960s, but by the end of the decade most consumers regarded them as a nuisance. Some consumers, however, remained passionate stamp collectors who would shop anywhere to get them.

In the midst of plenty, well fed does not always mean well nourished. In recent decades, consumers have gained more knowledge about nutrition than in earlier times, but increased knowledge has not always led them to better eating habits. Appealing advertisements aimed especially at children, catchy promotional jingles, and attractive packaging have often had more to do with choice of food than did its nutritional content.

The Fair Packaging and Labeling Act, passed in 1966, intended to assure consumers that packages and labels told the truth. So powerful was the lobby opposed to the act, however, that it required only that manufacturers print their name and address on the label, display the net weight prominently, state the size of servings, and stop using terms like *giant* and *jumbo*. Several packaging mandates came later, one requiring that a label list all the ingredients in a packaged product and another that package sizes be standardized. Those requirements were poorly enforced, however, and by the end of 1969 the commissioner of the Food and Drug Administration (FDA) could only guess that 70 percent of the packages were in line with the law.

Had the labels been required to list all of a package's ingredients, what might have caught the consumer's eye? The list likely would include artificial flavoring and sweeteners and such

Readily available electricity radically changed the American kitchen and its appliances. This kitchen had the most advanced cooking tools of the day. Library of Congress.

natural flavorings as salt and sugar to change food's taste, food colorings to change its appearance, chemical preservatives to lengthen its shelf or refrigerator life, thickeners and thinners to change its texture, and ingredients such as caffeine to change its effects. Revelations about the effects of some 3,000 food additives, many of them poorly tested, gradually led to new labeling requirements. In 1973, the FDA required standardized nutrition information on food labels and began to require the listing of such things as calories and grams of protein, fat, and carbohydrates per serving. As the printing of that information on labels became more widespread, competition induced some marketers to include information that the regulations may not have explicitly required.

Just as important in changing the nutritional qualities of foods with additives were practices that removed important ingredients. Refining processes often removed fiber, now considered important in preventing certain diseases. Canning, freezing, heating, and dehydrating destroyed at least part of such water-soluble nutrients as thiamin and various vitamins, enzymes, and proteins. Here, too, consumers heard wake-up calls and began to change their eating habits. Perhaps those changes reflected a change in the character of the American people, for, as anthropologists contend, to know what, where, how, when, and with whom people eat is to know the character of that society.

Advertising for foods thrived on ambiguities. Foods were called "natural" without particular attention given to what that meant. Restaurants served "shakes" containing no dairy products. Producers of imitation "chocolate" bars synthesized from various agricultural products, made tasty with an artificial flavor, mixed with bulking agents, and given the appearance of chocolate, could describe them as "all natural." Such developments, along with the profusion of foods to which chemical fertilization and pesticides had given a misleading appearance of wholesomeness, encouraged interest in organically grown foods. In their growth and processing, these foods were not touched by chemical fertilizers, pesticides, or additives. Whether those organic foods are any safer or healthier remains a matter of debate, but such foods served to heighten the debate regarding food consumption in American material life.

Despite quickened lifestyles and changes in family structures, much good cooking continued to be done at home. Would-be gourmet cooks used high-tech food processors and cookbooks filled with nutritious and tasty recipes. Newspapers and women's magazines had long contained recipes, but now, as more and more men helped out with home cooking, sometimes taking over completely, food sections in newspapers moved from women's sections to lifestyles pages, and special magazines devoted to cooking began to appear. Television programs also featured cooking ideas, examples, and recipes.

According to estimates in 1973, one meal in three was eaten outside the home—many of them hastily at fast-food restaurants, the number of which doubled between 1967 and 1974. McDonald's, described by *Time* magazine as "the burger that conquered the country," had fewer than 1,000 restaurants in 1967 and more than 3,000 in 1974. New ones opened at the rate of one every day. In 1972, McDonald's passed the U.S. Army as the biggest dispenser of meals; by then it had served more than

12 billion burgers. Numbers like that are only part of the story. McDonald's managers' greatest achievement, according to *Time*, was the following:

taking a familiar American institution, the greasy-spoon hamburger joint, and transforming it into a totally different though no less quintessential American operation: a computerized, standardized, premeasured, superclean production machine.

The fact that its menu items were loaded with fats and calories—almost 1,100 in a meal consisting of a Big Mac, a chocolate shake, and a small order of fries—did not keep customers away.

In 1969, it was difficult to avoid news reports of possible hazards in food, even in mothers' milk for breast-fed children. The Sierra Club reported that mothers' milk contained four times the amount of the pesticide DDT that was permitted in cows' milk sold in stores. High concentrations of DDT in coho salmon in Michigan lakes and streams led the state to restrict the spraying of crops with DDT. Baby food producers discontinued use of monosodium glutamate (MSG), a flavor enhancer, when tests showed that mice fed large amounts suffered brain damage. Test rats given excessive amounts of artificial sweeteners known as cyclamates developed cancer in their bladders. The FDA then removed cyclamates from its "generally recognized as safe" list and revealed plans to remove products sweetened with it from stores. Later, however, serious doubts were raised about the validity of the tests. The next year the FDA ordered the recall of large quantities of canned tuna because the mercury levels were thought to be too high. Despite the scare, it turned out that only 3 percent of canned tuna exceeded the FDA-prescribed limit.

It seems somewhat ironic that in the midst of plenty, hunger was as serious a problem in the United States as it was at the time. Throughout the nation's history there have been people who have gone hungry, particularly in times of depression. A 1968 CBS documentary, *Hunger in America*, revealed how serious the problems of hunger could be, even in relatively prosperous times. In the same year, a nutrition investigator claimed that malnutrition in some parts of the United States was as grim as any he had seen in India or any other country. At one school, he reported, children had vitamin A deficiencies worse than those who had gone blind as a result of that deficiency.

Buying food stretched the budgets of many beyond their limits. To help such persons, the government established a program to provide food stamps to purchase certain items in grocery stores. By Thanksgiving 1967, three years after that Great Society program was launched, 2.7 million Americans received food stamp assistance. That was just the beginning. By 1969, the number of participants climbed to 7 million, on the way to 19.6 million in mid-1975. Between 1969 and 1974, funding for the program increased from $4 million to $3 billion. Urban food stamp recipients typically had to pay more for food than more affluent suburbanites, because their parts of town had no supermarkets and prices in the small stores located there were higher. When government programs provided free or reduced-cost meals for schoolchildren in areas where feeding a family was difficult, the meals were often the best, if not the only, meals some children ate. The programs also benefited farmers and helped reduce government-financed food surpluses (Marty 1997, 37–38, 127–30; *Daily Life Online*, "Material Life: Food," in Marty, *Daily Life in the United States, 1960–1990*, http://dailylife.greenwood.com).

DINING OUT AND COOKING

Americans ate more and drank more between 1960 and 1990 than in previous generations, and they did so with greater variety, both in and out of their homes. Calorie consumption climbed from an average of 3,000 a day in 1960 to 3,300 in 1970 to 3,600 a day by 1990. In 1960, the Department of Agriculture reported that 23 percent of Americans were overweight and 13 percent were defined as obese (30 lbs. over average). Twenty years later those numbers had doubled to 46 percent and 27 percent. Oddly, while Americans seemed to be getting heavier, they were actually spending a lower percentage of their income on food than they had in the past. In 1971, Americans spent 13.4 percent of their disposable income on food. In 1981, it was 13 percent, and by 1990, the percentage had declined to 11.6. At the same time, Americans spent more of those food dollars away from home—dining out. In 1990, families spent 40 percent of their food dollars eating out (U.S. Department of Agriculture Report, 1990).

Nutritionists and others have consistently questioned what American families eat, with particular concern about both amount and food value: too few fruits, vegetables, and whole grains and too many meat, sugar, and dairy products with high fat content. While the domestic response to those warnings influenced some families and led to a more healthy awareness, most American families either added only a little healthy food to their diets or disregarded the concerns. Oddly, while Americans had begun to exhibit more anxiety about their weight and physical condition, and while different forms of dieting systems emerged to respond to the concern, people continued to eat more and gain more weight. Junk food in the home contributed to the problem as did the growing inclination to eat out. By 1981, families consumed some type of meal outside the home 3.7 times a week—38.4 billion meals a year. Lunch made up more than 50 percent of those meals, mostly eaten by men in the workforce. Women, children, and families, however, had also begun to eat more meals at fast-food chains and ethnic, neighborhood, and "four star" restaurants. The explosion of restaurant options during the period indicated how broad the experience had become. McDonald's, as a franchise, had appeared as a phenomenon in the 1950s. By the 1960s and 1970s, the fast-food giant competed with a host of others. Kentucky Fried Chicken (KFC), Genos, Wendy's, Burger King, and others all established businesses. National pizza franchises like Domino's and Pizza Hut challenged small, local pizzerias, and the trend continued. If Howard Johnson's had served as a nationally known family restaurant along America's turnpikes, it faced competition with new family-style restaurants like Bob Evans and Jimmy Dean. By the end of the 1990s, American families had so many dining-out options, in so many rural, urban, and suburban locations, that the experience became an issue of choice, not availability.

As American families spent more of their time eating out, they also purchased a host of new cookbooks and began to watch popular cooking shows on television. Betty Crocker's famous home cookbook had been on most American brides' gift lists for years and served as a basic "how-to" for home cooking. While a variety of regional and specialized cookbooks had always been part of domestic kitchen libraries, the home kitchen changed in 1961, when Julia Child (1912–2004) published *The Art of French Cooking*. A graduate of Smith College (1934), Child had worked for the Office of Strategic Services (OSS) during World War II and studied at the famous French cooking academy—Le Cordon Bleu—after the war. She lived in Cambridge, Massachusetts. Her book became a best-seller, and Child began a half-hour television show on PBS—Boston (WGBH) in 1963, titled *The French Chef*. The sophisticated, witty chef became an instant hit as she doled out equal amounts of good humor and good menus, arguing that Americans did not have to eat bad food. Although she liked McDonald's French fries, Child hoped to convince American families to add a simple, but gourmet quality to home cooking that she believed did not exist in America. Her popularity led to other chef and cooking shows Graham Kerr's *Galloping Gourmet* became an equally popular program. Men and women visited gourmet shops to purchase cooking utensils and other items shown on television. Family cooks began to experiment with a variety of new herbs, spices, and foods that had only seemed the privilege of experienced chefs. Supermarkets added gourmet aisles to their stores and began to import exotic fruits and vegetables for their produce sections. As with many of the domestic trends in American life, variety and options continued to expand, both in and out of the home.

In a similar fashion, America's drinking habits changed, not just in the consumption of alcoholic beverages, but in general terms. Families tended to serve coffee, water, and occasionally homemade iced tea or lemonade as staple drinks at meals and for snacks. Children drank orange juice and milk as healthy options or limited choices of soft drinks like Coca Cola or Pepsi. Between 1960 and 1990, those staples became part of an expanding option. Mass-produced, pasteurized, and bottled forms of iced tea, lemonade, soft drinks, and a variety of fruit drinks hit the supermarket shelves. At the same time, health concerns about whole milk led to fat-free milk with the ability for families to select anything from 0 percent to 2 percent alternatives. Alcoholic beverages saw a similar increase in variety.

While Americans had always consumed liquor as a cultural habit, the amount and options grew significantly after 1960, even while actual consumption began to decline. Average American alcohol consumption amounted to approximately six quarts a year in 1960 and dropped to four quarts by 1980. That continued until the 1990s. By comparison, Europeans on average consumed 17 quarts in 1960 and 10 quarts in 1980. Concerns about health, drunk driving, family abuse, and alcoholism all contributed to the decline. Adolescent drinking also increasingly concerned the public. A Justice Department report suggested that the largest percentage age group drinking in the United States was between 18 and 25. Eighty-eight percent of college students indicated that they drank alcohol. Beer remained the beverage of choice for all Americans. Beer sales accounted for more than 40 percent of liquor sales throughout the period. Beginning in the 1960s, wine became an increasingly popular choice for American families as well as individuals. With less alcohol than hard liquor and with an expanding amount of choices, both foreign and domestic, wine purchases made up around 30 percent of the market. The liquor industry had voluntarily removed their advertisements from radio in 1936 and television in 1948, unlike cigarette advertising. The 1965 Surgeon General's Report on the harmful effects of tobacco had led the FCC to place enormous pressure on television advertisers to remove cigarette ads. They did so, voluntarily, in 1971. Liquor manufacturers, however, had already done so, with the notable exception of beer advertisements. Still, the industry remained a multibillion dollar business as Americans chose between increasing varieties of drinks. In 1990, a World Health Organization study indicated that 40 percent of the American public were nondrinkers, 30 percent light drinkers (five drinks a week), 25 percent moderate drinkers (10 or more drinks a week), and 5 percent heavy drinkers or alcoholics.

Whether drinking the newest varietal wine from Napa Valley in California or mixing some rum or vodka concoction in a blender or drinking dozens of optional beer brands, the domestic expansion of brand, option, and variety continued to present the same commercial theme and practice that had developed so clearly beginning in the 1960s (World Health Organization, "Global Status Report on Alcohol," 2004; U.S. Justice Department Report, 1991).

CLOTHING AND STYLE

In 1980, Lisa Birnbach edited *The Official Preppy Handbook*, a tongue-in-cheek view of domestic habits and styles for "prep" families and their social set. The book identified the proper places to shop, what to wear, how to behave, and what to eat and drink. While humorous and irreverent in tone, many of its readers took the styles seriously, even slavishly, rushing out to buy Norwegian fisherman sweaters from the L. L. Bean catalog or lime-and-pink patterned skirts from Lilly Pulitzer resort wear. The trend and the response to it signaled a phenomenon in American domestic style. People of different backgrounds, incomes, and regions appeared to associate almost in tribal adherence to styles. In a real sense, the clothes one wore, one's hairstyle, even a person's speech and language served as forms of social and domestic identity. To a degree, that had always been true in the daily lives of most cultures. Modern American styles, however, offered a broad variety of "tribes" to join, and commercial observers sought to appeal to whatever the market would bear. Young people certainly aided the evolution of informal clothes and style in American daily life. During the 1950s, with their own allowances, jobs, and so on, teenagers began to shape their own clothing styles, and they became less and less formal. Jeans, t-shirts, and sneakers became questionable styles in public and at school, and many local institutions passed ordinances and rules restricting the so-called delinquent styles.

In the 1960s, however, those orthodox rules came tumbling down, as young people rejected the restrictive style requirements as part of a general rebellion against the stodgy 1950s. Not only did teenagers challenge the conservative rules of that decade, but many adults followed suit. By the beginning of the 1960s, women became more accustomed to wearing slacks and shorts in public rather than dresses. Men rarely wore coats and ties, let alone suits, outside of professional white-collar businesses. Blue jeans or denims became ubiquitous in the 1960s and 1970s for every age and both genders. The former alternatives of more traditional clothing existed, but a wide variety of casual clothes filled department stores and specialty shops, appealing to the new tastes. And brand-name logos that had been rare in the 1950s became commonplace in the 1960s and 1970s. Virtually every polo shirt sported a LaCoste, Ralph Lauren, or some other purveyor's identification so that their wearers could make clear whose shirt they had purchased. Style identified with stylist. Just as haute couture designers like Givenchy or Prada identified their expensive gowns, blue jean designers did the same with noticeable labels on millions of rear ends. The same demand for variety, name brands, and more casual dress also influenced domestic attitudes about hairstyles, cosmetics, and other fashion concerns. Shopping in the modern American middle-class environment became a form of consumer entertainment, and the marketplace could provide so much variety.

Certainly, alternative lifestyles emerged in the 1960s and 1970s to challenge the trends discussed above. The youth-led hippie movement, or counterculture, rejected the consumer culture in a variety of ways but specifically questioned the broad domestic framework of American life that had existed since the end of World War II. Family, suburbs, conventionalism, free market economics, and other aspects of American domestic life served as targets for a number of young critics during the era. Just as protesters questioned U.S. policy in Southeast Asia or joined a growing chorus of dissent regarding the racism and poverty they saw in the society, many of those same critics rejected how American families lived, what they ate, what they wore, and how they had made material consumption so much a part of their lives. When Timothy Leary, a Harvard professor, encouraged young people to "turn on, tune in, and drop out," his advice became a catch phrase for a generation of hippies rejecting the domestic lifestyle. Sex, drugs, love beads, and communes appeared to replace suburban living as the rebellious option. While the number of young men and women committed to the new movement always remained a small minority within the general population, their criticisms of a society infatuated with consumerism and advertising style bore some merit. Ironically, the movement became as much a parody of itself as the very conservative domestic world it criticized. It finally provided another domestic "tribe" that had access to its own goods and products and its own lifestyle.

HOUSING

Before long, changes in economic conditions, partly due to the drain caused by the war in Vietnam, meant the end of concerted efforts to eliminate poverty. But poverty persisted. A good way to comprehend the dilemmas involved in dealing with poverty is to consider a specific project that represented the hopes, failings, and ultimate destruction of a major effort supported by both parties to improve conditions for the poor. In St. Louis, in 1958, the federal government constructed housing that, on first impression, would seem to have answered the needs of families looking for a good place to live. Known as Pruitt-Igoe, the housing project consisted of 33 towers, each 11 stories high.

Pruitt-Igoe and other projects like it concentrated a large number of poor people in a small geographic area. That would have been bad enough, but design flaws made matters worse. Inadequate wiring made installation of window fans or window air conditioners impossible, causing the apartments to be miserably hot in the sweltering summers of St. Louis. Elevators stopped only on the 4th, 7th, and 10th floors. Residents on other floors had to walk up or down a level from the one where the elevator stopped. Children were not always able to judge the time it would take to make a bathroom run from the playground to their apartments, and before long the elevators were filled with wretched odors and filth. The best intentions for those involved in the project had failed to address the post-construction problems.

Perspectives of those who lived in Pruitt-Igoe differed from those who did not. To a resident, "A project ain't nothing but a slum with the kitchen furnished and an absentee landlord; except we know who the landlord is—it's the city and government." To an outsider, "Whether it is a pig pen or not isn't important. When people have done nothing to contribute to the society but make an application for welfare, a housing project is more than they deserve." Either way, Pruitt-Igoe had no future. Poor management, poor maintenance, too heavily concentrated living arrangements, and crime made the apartments uninhabitable within a decade. Judged to be beyond repair and too poorly conceived to justify salvage efforts, the buildings were imploded with dynamite in 1972 (Marty 1997, 103–4).

While the Pruitt-Igoe project construction concept points to the problems that many inner-city Great Society programs faced, it does not define the general condition of housing options in the United States during the period. The development of single-family housing availability in the suburbs continued to attract buyers. New condominium growth offered smaller and cheaper home-buying options, both urban and suburban, to homeowners. Home designers and architects played with a wide variety of new housing styles. Split level and ranches (one-story options) had remained traditional in the postwar era, but other, alternate ideas had emerged in the 1960s and 1970s to attract home buyers. Inflation and interest rates soared in the 1970s and 1980s, making home ownership a

In the 1970s, cities tried to improve the quality of available housing by destroying old, run-down apartment complexes. © CORBIS/Bettmann.

tenuous prospect, yet Americans continued to search for alternatives and methods to purchase the home of their dreams (*Daily Life Online*, "Material Life: Housing," in Marty, *Daily Life in the United States, 1960–1990*, http://dailylife.greenwood.com).

FOR MORE INFORMATION

Clark, W. B., and M. E. Hilton, eds. *Alcohol in America: Drinking Practices and Problems*. Albany: State University of New York Press, 1991.

Farb, P., and G. Armelagos. *Consuming Passions: The Anthropology of Eating*. Boston: Houghton-Mifflin, 1980.

Levenstein, H. *Revolution at the Table: The Transformation of the American Diet*. New York: Oxford University Press, 1988.

Martin, J. K. *Drinking in America: A History*. New York: Free Press, 1982.

Marty, Myron A. *Daily Life in the United States, 1960–1990: Decades of Discord*. Westport, CT: Greenwood Press, 1997; also available online as *Daily Life Online*, in Marty, *Daily Life in the United States, 1960–1990*, http://dailylife.greenwood.com.

Patterson, J. T. *Grand Expectations: The United States, 1945–1974*. New York: Oxford University Press, 1996.

Root, Waverly, and de Rochemont, Richard. *Eating in America*. New York: HarperCollins, 1981.

Schlosser, E. *Fast Food Nation: The Dark Side of the All-American Meal*. New York: Houghton-Mifflin, 2001.

U.S. Justice Department Report. 1991.

Waverly, L. R. *Eating in America: A History*. New York: Morrow, 1976.

World Health Organization. "Global Status Report on Alcohol." 2004.

Wright, G. *Building the Dream: A Social History of Housing in America*. New York: Pantheon, 1981.

Political Life

OVERVIEW

A major shift in American political life took place between 1960 and 1990. At the beginning of the 1960s, Democrat John F. Kennedy won a narrow victory in the presidential election against his Republican opponent Richard M. Nixon. Kennedy pledged a "New Frontier" that he suggested would alter the bland conservativism of the Eisenhower administration. In domestic affairs, the new president indicated a commitment to the concerns that Michael Harrington and other critics had identified. The "other America" of poverty, racism, and injustice required, Kennedy argued, federal involvement and concern. With a Democratic Party majority in Congress, it appeared likely that programs and policies would be forthcoming. In fact, that failed to occur. Southern Democrats blocked Kennedy's efforts regarding civil rights as that issue continued to heat up in the 1960s. Additionally, major programs regarding education, poverty, and other social justice issues did not emerge as full-blown policies while President Kennedy occupied the White House. After he was assassinated in Dallas, Texas, on November 22, 1963, Vice President Lyndon Johnson aggressively turned to the problems that his predecessor had been unable to attack successfully.

Results of 1960 Presidential Election

Candidate	Popular Vote	Electoral Vote
John F. Kennedy (Dem.)	34,227,096 (49.7%)	303 (56%)
Richard M. Nixon (Rep.)	34,108,546 (49.5%)	218 (41%)
Harry F. Byrd (Ind.)	501,643 (.7%)	15 (3%)

Lyndon Baines Johnson, a former U.S. senator from Texas, personified the liberal tradition of New Deal and Fair Deal politics and government that Franklin Roosevelt and Harry Truman had championed during their administrations. With a strong belief that the federal government had a clear responsibility to "promote the general welfare," Johnson, tough, knowledgeable, and politically savvy, instituted a Great Society "War on Poverty" crusade that dominated the political debate for the remainder of the 1960s. Many of the programs and policies his administration initiated are examined below. Effectively, however, Johnson's presidency defined the quintessential liberal belief that government, specifically at the national level, could identify, address, and correct the social and economic inequities that existed in American daily life. That view has remained a key aspect of American political thinking for liberals. His critics argued that the private sector, the free market, and state and local government served as the best methods to address America's major domestic concerns. Those conservative arguments served to define the alternative ideology of government that continues to the present day.

Using every asset and ability at his command, President Johnson created the most impressive liberal social and economic agenda in American political history. His domestic policies, supported increasingly by a Democratic Congress, surpassed any of the New Deal and Fair Deal efforts of his predecessors. In civil rights, the Civil Rights Act (1964) and Voting Rights Act (1965) created a dramatic legal advance for African Americans. The variety of aid to education programs enhanced federal involvement in that arena. And the federal government, under Johnson's leadership, developed a host of poverty programs to address those concerns.

President Johnson apparently had the support of the American people in those efforts, for he easily defeated his

Jacqueline Kennedy, the President's popular and elegant First Lady, 1961. Library of Congress.

Republican rival in 1964. Senator Barry Goldwater certainly provided a conservative alternative, but his arguments appeared unpersuasive.

Results of 1964 Presidential Election

Candidate	Popular Vote	Electoral Vote
Lyndon B. Johnson (Dem.)	44,127,041 (61.1%)	486 (90.3%)
Barry M. Goldwater (Rep.)	27,175,754 (38.5%)	52 (9.7%)

It proved the most lopsided presidential victory in American history; President Johnson interpreted it as a popular mandate to pursue his Great Society programs. Unfortunately, he lost his influence as America's increasing involvement in the Vietnam War overshadowed and then undercut his domestic efforts. Additionally, growing racial confrontation and issues of discord in American daily life drained his political capital. In 1968, Johnson announced that he would not run for a second term. The high point of liberal, Democratic presidential leadership had occurred.

Richard M. Nixon's election in 1968 returned a Republican president to the White House, but the former senator and vice president was no conservative ideologue. A political realist faced with the crisis of war in Southeast Asia, Nixon experienced a reasonably successful first term in office. He dramatically reduced American troop presence in Vietnam, began negotiations with the North Vietnamese government, and opened a new diplomatic dialogue with the Soviet Union and China, hoping to ease some of the Cold War tensions of the past. He and his top advisors, however, had begun a murky and illegal slide into questionable political actions against their perceived enemies. While he easily defeated his opponent for reelection in 1972, the Watergate scandal exploded during Nixon's second term. On August 9, 1974, after a long, painful period in American political history, Richard Nixon became the first president to resign his office. That scandal and the frustrating and tragic end to the war in Vietnam (1975) seemed to indicate a low point in American political life. Until 1980, a transitional era of politics offered the nation little in the way of vision or optimism, either left or right, in the political spectrum. Gerald Ford (Republican), 1974–1977, and Jimmy Carter (Democrat), 1977–1980, had to confront a nation soured and despondent with the political system and reeling from "stagflation" and uncertain

President Ronald Reagan and the First Lady Nancy Reagan, c. 1980s. Photofest.

of its place in the world. It was an unpleasant period in American politics and government that neither leader could successfully combat.

In 1980, Ronald Reagan, a California governor and former movie actor, easily defeated his incumbent opponent, Jimmy Carter. Reagan's political conservativism and optimism would alter the nature of American political life. For two terms, Reagan's views on government, foreign policy, and American exceptionalism dominated the political landscape. Even while serious critics questioned his tax cuts, heavy defense expenditures, and the rising federal deficit and debt, he remained a popular, admired leader. Reagan and his supporters also appeared to have rejected the liberal commitment to social justice that had been so much a part of the Great Society in the 1960s. During the 1980s, Republicans regained control of the U.S. Senate for the first time since 1952. Shortly, the House of Representatives would experience a similar Republican majority. A clear conservative ascendancy had led American voters to select candidates following President Reagan's lead to the forefront of day-to-day political thinking. The ideological pendulum had swung dramatically from left to right between 1960 and 1990. That shift would define America's daily political thinking during the "decades of discord."

CAPITAL PUNISHMENT

In the post–World War II era, the United States is the only Western nation where capital punishment remains legal. Several cases examining the constitutionality of the death penalty came to the courts in the mid-twentieth century. In 1967, the death penalty was suspended so that federal appellate courts could decide if it was constitutional. In 1968, in the case *U.S. v. Jackson,* the U.S. Supreme Court denounced the federal kidnapping law, which stated that only a jury could prescribe the death penalty. The court ruled that the practice encouraged defendants to waive their rights to a jury trial in hopes of avoiding a death sentence. Also in 1968, the court ruled in *Witherspoon v. Illinois* that a juror could not be dismissed simply because he or she had reservations about the death penalty. Prosecutors must illustrate that the juror's beliefs would prevent him or her from making an unbiased decision on a death sentence.

Throughout the 1970s, the Supreme Court ruled on several important capital punishment cases. In *Furman v. Georgia,* the court ruled that the death penalty was unconstitutional because it amounted to "cruel and unusual punishment." However, in 1976, the Supreme Court ruled in *Gregg v. Georgia* that states could enact death penalty laws and not necessarily violate the Constitution. By 1977, the Supreme Court ruled that the only crime that constitutionally can be punished by death is murder. Executions began again in 1977.

A variety of important capital punishment cases came before the Supreme Court in the 1980s. In 1986, the court ruled that execution of persons deemed legally insane is unconstitutional. Two cases addressing the age at which a person could legally be sentenced to death were brought to the court at the end of the 1980s. In

Thompson v. Oklahoma, which made it to the Supreme Court in 1988, the court ruled that it was unconstitutional to recommend a death sentence for persons who were 15 years old or younger when they committed their crimes. In 1989, however, the court ruled that the death penalty could be considered in cases with defendants age 16 and older (*Daily Life Online*, "Capital Punishment in the United States" by Heather Stur, in Marty, *Daily Life in the United States, 1960–1990*, http://dailylife. greenwood.com).

CIVIL RIGHTS AND GROUP IDENTITY: AFRICAN AMERICANS

By the late 1960s, it appeared obvious that if enacting civil rights laws remained difficult, changing practices remained even harder. Still more difficult appeared changing American attitudes. For example, despite the passage of antidiscrimination laws, job bias was still all too common. Growing impatience by blacks seemed understandable. A year after his speech at the Lincoln Memorial in 1963, when he spoke hopefully of his dream that someday freedom would ring in America, Martin Luther King Jr. published a book titled *Why We Can't Wait*. Challenges to his leadership by more radical figures—Malcolm X, Stokely Carmichael, and the Black Panthers, among others—and changing circumstances in 1967 compelled him to become more radical too.

Television networks that year brought the nation live coverage of riots in Detroit. Scenes of looting, fires, injuries, and deaths reminded viewers of the riots in Watts two years earlier. The next year a commission appointed by President Johnson to investigate the causes of civil disorders formally reported that the United States was moving toward two societies, "one black, one white—separate and unequal."

Did it have to be that way? In the year that Martin Luther King Jr. spoke passionately of his dream for America, novelist James Baldwin acknowledged that creating one nation had proved to be "a hideously difficult task." The past that blacks had endured, a past "of rope, fire, torture, castration, infanticide, rape; death and humiliation; fear by day and night, fear as deep as the marrow of the bone," had forced them each day to "snatch their manhood, their identity, out of the fire of human cruelty that rages to destroy it." In so doing, Baldwin wrote in *The Fire Next Time*, they achieved their own unshakable authority. Blacks had the advantage, he claimed, of never having believed the myths to which white Americans cling about the heroism of freedom-loving ancestors, about American invincibility, about the virility of white men and purity of white women. They were free to take on the problems they faced. But they could not do it alone.

If we—and now I mean the relatively conscious whites and the relatively conscious blacks, who must, like lovers, insist on, or create, the consciousness of the others—do not falter in our duty now, we may be able, handful that we are, to end the racial nightmare, and achieve our country, and change the history of the world. If we do not now dare everything, the fulfillment of that prophecy, re-created from the Bible in song by a slave, is upon us: "*God gave Noah the rainbow sign, No more water, the fire next time!*" (Baldwin, quoted in Marty 1997, 88)

By 1968, it looked as though the fire was coming. The assassination of Martin Luther King Jr. on April 4 led to more urban riots. Before the decade had ended, riots occurred in more than 100 cities and resulted in at least 77 deaths. Thousands suffered injuries, and property destruction was incalculable. The well-publicized purpose of a civil rights law that was passed one week after King's death was to prohibit racial discrimination in housing policies and practices. However, a provision insisted on by Senator Strom Thurmond of South Carolina showed the ambivalence of white politicians toward militant blacks. That legislature made it a crime to use the facilities of interstate commerce "to organize, promote, encourage, participate in, or carry on a riot; or to commit any act of violence in furtherance of a riot." Robert Weisbrot, a historian of the civil rights movement, has observed that the bill's priorities were clear: "modest federal involvement in black efforts to flee the ghetto, but overwhelming force to curb all restiveness within it."

Before his death, Martin Luther King Jr. had planned a "poor people's march on Washington" to shift the focus of the civil rights movement from racial to economic issues, believing it might attract broader support. Leadership of the campaign fell to his successor in the Southern Christian Leadership Conference, Ralph David Abernathy. Even under ideal conditions, the prospects of success seemed limited, but the weather in Washington at the time of the march was miserable. The political climate the campaigners faced was even worse, and their well-intentioned efforts seemed only to call attention to the powerlessness of poor blacks and their isolation from poor whites.

Martin Luther King Jr., civil rights leader. Chaiba.

The death of King, the riots, and exhaustion took much of the impetus out of the civil rights movement. The election of Richard Nixon in November 1968 appeared an additional blow. Nixon's "southern strategy" (a policy devised by Nixon's campaign strategists in 1967) played on the resentments of whites. At the same time, supporters of civil rights turned to Congress for laws calling for affirmative action policies in hiring and protective measures of other kinds. The notion of establishing race-conscious policies and preferential treatment for blacks to remedy past injustices caused strains among supporters, both black and white. Some contended that the struggle should be for a color-blind society, with neither advantages nor disadvantages resulting from the color of one's skin. Race-conscious policies also intensified the backlash by those who thought the movement had already gone too far too fast. Pursuit of civil rights goals in the courts also encouraged the backlash, particularly on the matter of busing to achieve school desegregation. A period that had begun on a note of gloom ended on an even gloomier one.

Hoping to serve the interests of African Americans more effectively, black leaders sought to increase their representation in executive positions at the local level and in state legislatures and the Congress of the United States. By 1971, 12 African Americans held seats in the House of Representatives, and a number of cities had African American mayors, but that did not have much effect on the daily lives of

African Americans. Policy changes to achieve success would require that they hold more political power.

With that in mind, the Congressional Black Caucus, formed in 1971, cooperated tactically with more militant blacks in planning the National Black Political Assembly in Gary, Indiana, in March 1972. The assembly was the largest black political convention in U.S. history. About 3,000 official delegates attended, representing almost every faction and viewpoint. An additional 9,000 persons attended as observers. Historian Manning Marable referred to the assembly as a marriage of convenience between the aspiring and somewhat radicalized black petty bourgeoisie and the black nationalist movement. The collective vision of the convention, he says, "represented a desire to seize electoral control of America's major cities, to move the black masses from the politics of desegregation to the politics of real empowerment, ultimately to create their own independent black political party."

The fiscal, social, and demographic problems urban blacks faced were awesome, for as the affluent populations of cities had fled to the suburbs, the tax base declined sharply. Racial conflicts over dwindling job opportunities remained common. Civil service laws protected the jobs of insensitive or racist city bureaucrats. States and the federal government lost interest in coming to the cities' rescue. At the national level, President Nixon made no moves to increase the voting power of African Americans. He supported only voluntary efforts to integrate schools, did little to push integration of federal housing programs, and failed to provide adequate funding for black entrepreneurs seeking to start businesses.

The laws passed in the 1960s with the intention of making things better, or at least of offering hope that things would change, instead magnified African Americans' sense of hopelessness. Ending discrimination in the workplace provided one major test for the federal government's new commitment to civil rights.

In 1965, President Johnson, applying the principles of the 1964 Civil Rights Act, issued an executive order requiring federal contractors "to take affirmative action to ensure that applicants are employed...without regard to their race, creed, color, or national origin." A series of court cases followed that dealt with the barriers to affirmative action principles. In a 1971 decision involving a standard written examination for employment, *Griggs v. Duke Power Co.*, the U.S. Supreme Court ruled that so-called objective criteria for hiring employees could in fact be discriminatory. Specifically, the court said that the aptitude tests being challenged were illegal, because they resulted in a relative disadvantage to minorities without at the same time having a compelling business interest. To be permissible, the knowledge and skills they evaluated had to be directly applicable to the jobs for which the employers used them. The court later extended the principles of this ruling to recruitment practices, job placement, transfers, and promotions. The court rulings made it possible for women and minorities to get jobs from which they had previously been excluded, but unequal pay remained a problem (Marty 1997, 88–91, 101–2).

Between the 1954 *Brown v. Board of Education* Supreme Court decision and the 1964 Civil Rights Act, the United States experienced a momentous shift in the government's position on civil rights. The successful Montgomery, Alabama, boycott in 1956, sparked by Rosa Parks's famous refusal to give up her seat on a segregated bus, gained national attention. With support from other black civil rights leaders, Martin Luther King Jr. formed the Southern Christian Leadership Conference (SCLC) in 1957 and began a series of nonviolent protests in the South. As the 1960s began, the African American effort to address the injustice of segregation was in full swing. John Kennedy's administration had to face the issue. The new president offered verbal support for the movement, because he did not want to buck powerful white southern Democrats, but remained concerned regarding the impact his position would have with white southern Democrats. While he balanced the political dilemma, Kennedy managed to win 70 percent of the black vote in 1960. Since the Roosevelt era, African American voters had shifted their allegiance from the Republican Party to the Democrats. Lyndon Johnson not only recognized the political implications of that shift, he also legitimately supported King's movement and made civil rights a key aspect of his Great Society. The August 1963 March on Washington, highlighted by Reverend King's "I have a dream" speech, crystallized the nation's political position. Less than three months later, President Kennedy was assassinated in Dallas, Texas, and after he took office Lyndon Johnson addressed the issue. Using every political skill and exploiting every political leverage in Congress, Johnson worked with black civil rights leaders to pass the Civil Rights Act of 1964. He signed the law on July 2, 1964. The Voting Rights Act would follow a year later.

Ironically and tragically, a series of racial riots and unrest began at the same time, from Watts in Los Angeles to Detroit. For many African Americans, the civil rights movement had provided too little and come too late. The new laws had done little to change living conditions for black Americans. In Mississippi, African Americans made up more than 40 percent of the population, but only 5 percent were registered to vote. Their median family income was one-third of white income in that state. By the late 1960s it was obvious that if enacting civil rights laws was difficult, changing practices was going to be even harder. Still harder was changing attitudes. Growing impatience by blacks was understandable. A year after his speech at the Lincoln Memorial in 1963, when he spoke hopefully of his dream that "someday" freedom would ring in America, Martin Luther King, Jr. published a book entitled *Why We Can't Wait*. Challenges to his leadership by more radical figures—Malcolm X, Stokely Carmichael, and the Black Panthers, among others—and changing circumstances in 1967 compelled him to become more radical too. Many white Americans who had supported Martin Luther King's "moderate" civil rights activism became alarmed and frightened by the changing nature of the debate. Television networks that year brought the nation live coverage of riots in Detroit. Scenes of looting, fires, injuries, and deaths reminded viewers of the riots in Watts two years earlier. The next year a commission appointed by President Johnson to investigate the causes of civil disorders formally reported that the United States was moving toward two societies, "one black, one white—separate and unequal." One political result of that concern led white voters to support Republicans candidates, and it also helped create a "white flight" to the suburbs. Ironically, the series of laws passed in the 1960s to attack de jure segregation and racism saw the evolution of de facto racism and segregation in ways that were as harmful as before (*Daily Life*

Online, "Economic Life: Discrimination," in Marty, *Daily Life in the United States, 1960–1990,* http://dailylife.greenwood.com).

EDUCATION AND GOVERNMENT

In April 1983, Secretary of Education Terrell H. Bell released a report entitled *A Nation at Risk.* It was the work of an 18-member National Commission on Excellence in Education appointed to "make practical recommendations for action." The appointment had been inspired in part by concern over the nationwide decline in scores on the Scholastic Aptitude Tests (SAT) that had begun in 1963 and continued in 17 of the next 20 years. Coincidentally, a slight improvement in the scores occurred in 1982, as well as in 1983 and 1984, but that did not alleviate concerns about the quality of the nation's schools.

A 1981 Gallup poll and a study by the Charles F. Kettering Foundation had shown that the majority of Americans wanted more demanding curricula, more control over student behavior, and more attention to ethical concerns. But the surveys also detected a growing feeling that parents were more deficient than schools in the upbringing of their children. Polls also showed a continued decline in the public's willingness to support schools financially. Rejection of proposed tax increases to support school improvements was common.

A Nation at Risk presented a comprehensive indictment of American education, citing high rates of adult illiteracy, declining SAT scores, and poor performance on 20 international academic achievement tests. On none of those tests had American children ranked first or second. The "educational foundations of our society," the report contended, "are presently being eroded by a rising tide of mediocrity that threatens our very future as a nation and a people." The tragedy, it continued, was that no unfriendly power was responsible for what had happened to the nation's schools, but rather that "we have allowed this to happen to ourselves."

The report made five recommendations. The first was that all students seeking a high school diploma be required to have four years of study in English, three years in mathematics, three in science, and three in social studies, as well as half a year in computer science—fields identified as "the New Basics." The second was that all educational institutions expect more of their students and that requirements for admission to four-year colleges and universities be raised. Third was that significantly more time be devoted to learning the New Basics through more effective use of the existing school day or that the school day or year be lengthened. Fourth was that the preparation of teachers be strengthened and that teaching be made a more rewarding and respected profession. Fifth was that citizens require elected officials to support those reforms and provide funds necessary to accomplish them. The report concluded by urging parents to expect much from their children and for students to put forth their best efforts in learning (National Commission on Excellence in Education 1984, 5, 69–79).

Although critics of *A Nation at Risk* insisted that many schools were doing a good job, the report struck a responsive chord in the general public. A flurry of other reports that appeared shortly after the release of *A Nation at Risk*, such as *Making the Grade*; *Academic Preparation for College: What Students Need to Know and Be Able to Do*; *Action for Excellence*; *A Policy Framework for Racial Justice*; and *Educating Americans for the 21st Century* also had significant influence. Each of these reports had a different theme, and each reflected the interests of a specific constituency (*Daily Life Online*, "More Discord: Education," in Marty, *Daily Life in the United States, 1960–1990*, http://dailylife.greenwood.com).

GOVERNMENT AND THE GREAT SOCIETY

In the 1960s, much of what the federal government did became synonymous with the War on Poverty. Attacking poverty first became a priority in the 1960s when Michael Harrington's book *The Other America* captured President John Kennedy's attention and stirred him and other national leaders to face the issues it raised. His administration was developing proposals for action when he was assassinated. Taking up more aggressively where Kennedy left off came naturally to Lyndon Johnson. His origins in rural Texas had included few of the material advantages that had been Kennedy's from childhood. On his first full day as president, Johnson asked his advisors to come forward with specific proposals, which reached him in time to permit him to declare "unconditional war on poverty in America" in his 1964 State of the Union address. "The richest nation on earth," he said, "can win it. We cannot afford to lose it."

Circumstances were right in the mid-1960s for the nation to attack poverty through legislation and executive and other actions. Kennedy's assassination seemed to have inspired national leaders to believe that if they could not undo that wrong, they could at least right other ones. In President Johnson, who had been majority leader in the Senate until he became vice president in 1961, they had someone who knew how to pull legislative strings and mobilize public sentiment more effectively than most presidents before him. Unrest stirred by the civil rights and student movements promoted the kind of introspection that leads nations as well as individuals to change what they can while they can do so on their own terms. The space race with the Soviet Union led schools across the country to insist that teachers teach better and students learn more and learn it faster. More extensive homework assignments and more demanding instruction, particularly in the sciences, were widespread, demonstrating a national mood to not let the Soviets win. That mood made it natural for education to be a weapon in the War on Poverty as well.

Besides, these were times of economic expansion, and with no major military conflict being waged; a War on Poverty could be a war of choice. In August 1964, responding to Johnson's War on Poverty proposals, Congress enacted the comprehensive

Equal Opportunity Act. Although conservatives in both parties opposed it (185 in the House and 34 in the Senate), the opponents were largely soft-spoken, fearful that opposition might be taken as indifference to poverty. The act was a noble effort, almost a heroic one, to solve the problems Harrington and others had identified. Each of its major parts held potential for changing the daily lives of countless Americans: It provided job training for the poor, programs to teach marketable skills to unemployed youths in inner cities, arrangements for recruiting middle-class volunteers to work in programs in poverty-stricken areas, funding for public works projects in poor areas, and structures for making loans to indigent farmers and small businesses. The Head Start program gave disadvantaged preschool children training in basic skills—more than 500,000 youngsters in 2,400 communities participated in 1965, the first year of operation. The 1965 Elementary and Secondary Education Act sought to stimulate innovation in schools and make educating America's poor children a priority. Upward Bound helped youth from poor families attend college. The Office of Economic Opportunity served as the operational center in the War on Poverty, and the Community Action Program encouraged grassroots involvement in program development. It hoped to empower the poor to better look after their own interests.

Although that seemed a boon to cities, big-city politicians and state governors did not like the Community Action Program at all. They resented what they took to be loss of control to tenant unions in public housing. They opposed organized voter registration drives and resisted other efforts by activists to give poor people the power to deal effectively with their own problems. The Community Action Program therefore became the target of hostility and attacks. That, in turn, created fear that the War on Poverty would lead to class warfare, and it neutralized the effectiveness of other programs.

But troubles in the War on Poverty failed to dampen President Johnson's enthusiasm for shaping what he called the Great Society. Proposals poured forth from the White House in 1965 and 1966, and Congress enacted laws at a pace not seen since the famous Hundred Days at the beginning of Franklin Roosevelt's first term in 1933, when Congress enacted 15 major laws between March 9 and June 16. Although the effectiveness of the Great Society legislation was mixed, the impact on daily lives of the intended beneficiaries and those who implemented the programs was considerable.

The Housing and Urban Development Act of 1965, for example, offered reduced interest rates to builders of housing for the poor and elderly, thus benefiting builders and construction workers as well as those who would live in the units they built. It also provided funds for health programs, beautification of cities, recreation centers, and rent supplements for the poor. The new cabinet-level Department of Housing and Urban Development assumed responsibility for coordinating the creation of urban and regional planning agencies. The Urban Mass Transportation Act of 1966, establishing the cabinet-level Department of Transportation, provided funds and structures for development of mass-transit systems in urban areas. The Model Cities Act of 1966 provided over $1 billion for slum clearance and urban renewal.

The Elementary and Secondary Education Act, passed in 1965, designated more than $1 billion for educationally deprived children. Because the funds were ultimately under the control of local school districts, however, they were frequently diverted to other purposes. The Higher Education Act of 1965 established a scholarship and low-interest loan program for financially needy college students and provided library grants to colleges and universities. The Immigration Act of 1965 eliminated the discriminatory quotas designed to exclude certain national groups, or to admit them on a restricted basis, that had been in effect for 40 years and reaffirmed just 13 years earlier.

As life expectancy increased, resulting in growth of the elderly population that continues to the present day, provisions for caring for the elderly became more critical. Elderly persons worried about that, as did their children, whose houses and urban apartments did not have space for additional dwellers and whose incomes were typically not sufficient to provide for institutional care. After the Democratic landslide in the 1964 election, sentiment for new laws providing for medical care for the elderly enabled those who backed them to surmount the opposition, including that of the American Medical Association.

The Medicare program, enacted by Congress in 1965, provided insurance to cover most hospital charges, diagnostic tests, home visits, and in some instances nursing home costs for the elderly. Participants in Medicare could volunteer to purchase supplementary coverage, subsidized by the government, to take care of other medical expenses, including visits to doctors' offices. Prescription drugs, eyeglasses, and hearing aids were not covered. At the end of Medicare's first year of operation, approximately 17.7 million elderly persons (93 percent of those eligible) enrolled in the voluntary medical insurance program. Also included in the Medicare bill were funds for nursing schools, medical schools, and medical student scholarships, all intended to train personnel to provide health care services.

The Social Security Act of 1935 was the first federal government step toward providing the elderly with means to be cared for by others if they were unable to care for themselves. Sometimes the care was given in not-for-profit nursing homes. The more extensive benefits provided through Medicaid—a companion program to Medicare that provided funding to states to pay for medical care for the poor of all ages—quickly spawned a lucrative for-profit industry. Nursing homes, one observer noted, "changed from a family enterprise to big business. Major corporations, including several hotel/motel chains, purchased large numbers of facilities and nursing home issues became the hottest item on the stock exchange." Between 1960 and 1976, nursing homes increased in number from under 10,000 to 23,000; the number of residents more than tripled, to one million. The number of employees increased during the period from 100,000 to 650,000. Impressive though those numbers were, they do not compare in magnitude with the 2,000 percent increase in revenues received by the industry. Almost 60 percent of the more than $10 billion in revenues was paid by taxpayers through Medicare and Medicaid. While those numbers were all skyrocketing, the population of senior citizens increased by only 23 percent.

Who were the elderly in nursing homes? In the mid-1960s they were moving toward the profile that existed a decade later: more than 70 percent were over 70 years of age; women outnumbered men by 3 to 1; 63 percent were widowed, 22 percent had never married, 5 percent were divorced; only 1 in 10 had a living spouse; more than 50 percent had no close relatives. More than 60 percent had no visitors at all. Fewer than 50 percent were able to walk. The average stay in nursing homes was 2.4 years, and only 20 percent of the residents ever returned to their homes. The vast majority died in the nursing homes, with a small number succumbing in hospitals.

Such a profile meant that in addition to worries over health and finances and fear of being a burden to others, many elderly people lived in dread of having to move to a place other than their own home. "It is a time of no tomorrows," wrote former senator Frank Moss in 1977, "a time of no hope. Death lurks like a mugger in a dark alley. The elderly await the inevitable, when they are reduced to the simple act of breathing and eating—and less."

An initial appropriation of $6.5 billion got Medicare started, and increased Social Security payroll deductions were to provide for its long-term funding. Medicare and Medicaid planners, however, underestimated the rate at which increases in doctors' fees and hospital charges, as well as the longer lives of the elderly, would create spiraling costs.

To celebrate the enactment of Medicare, President Johnson traveled to Independence, Missouri, where he signed the new bill into law in former president Truman's presence. Truman then became the first person to hold a Medicare card. What the two presidents celebrated, however, was a limited victory, for the American Medical Association had succeeded in restricting Medicare to bill-paying functions. The government had virtually no role in redesigning health care systems or controlling costs. By the 1990s, with expenditures for both Medicare and Medicaid having multiplied more than 10-fold, problems continued that might have been dealt with better when the programs were first created.

Programs in the War on Poverty had significant effects on the daily lives of millions of beneficiaries and benefit providers. The proportion of Americans recorded as being below the federal poverty line dropped from 20 to 13 percent between 1963 and 1968, and the ratio of African Americans living in poverty declined from 40 percent in 1960 to half that figure in 1968, but the problems of poverty remained an ongoing challenge for Americans.

In attempting to account for the bursts of optimism that inspired the War on Poverty and public confidence in it, it is useful to reflect on the words of Lyndon Johnson, the war's mastermind. Speaking to Howard University students on June 4, 1965, Johnson laid out his vision for America, and particularly for the black students he was addressing. Members of their race were disproportionately represented among the poor, and he was sensitive to their circumstances. The breakdown of the family, President Johnson said, flowing from "the long years of degradation and discrimination, which have attacked [the Negro man's] dignity and assaulted his ability to produce for his family," was the main cause. So strengthening families was essential. To accomplish that and to solve all the other problems society faced, Johnson said, there was no single easy answer. Jobs were part of it, as were decent homes, welfare and social programs, and care for the sick. But another part of the answer is what moved President Johnson: "An understanding heart by all Americans" (Marty 1997,

44–49; *Daily Life Online*, "Political Life: Government," in Marty, *Daily Life in the United States, 1960–1990*, http://dailylife.greenwood.com).

REFORM

Through the 1960s, civil rights remained a paramount reform issue in America. The daily lives of most Americans may not seem to have been directly affected by what came to be known as the unrest of the 1960s, but the changes wrought by protests in those years rippled across America. The most striking changes were the fruits of the civil rights movement that, in its modern form, traced its origins to before World War II. During World War II, the cruel irony of asking African Americans to risk their lives for a country that denied them constitutionally guaranteed rights became glaringly obvious. Several Supreme Court decisions set precedents for the 1954 landmark case of *Brown v. Board of Education*. In *Brown* the Court ruled that schools designed to be "separate but equal" were inherently unequal and therefore unconstitutional.

Armed with the conviction that the Supreme Court's decision outlawing "separate but equal" schools extended to other aspects of their lives, and frustrated by resistance to calls for change, African American activists adopted a strategy that at first baffled those seeking to thwart them: they defied laws that denied them rights but refused to defend themselves against physical and verbal attacks. The practice of holding sit-ins at lunch counters and other whites-only establishments spread, and before the end of the year an estimated 70,000 activists put pressure on white business leaders by challenging segregation laws and practices in more than 150 cities. In 1961 came Freedom Rides, organized by James Farmer of the Congress on Racial Equality (CORE). The Freedom Riders, small interracial groups who traveled by public buses into the Deep South to test whether federal court orders on integration of bus depots were being honored, encountered hostile and often brutal treatment. Again, television cameras brought the bloody scenes into homes throughout America. More important, the spreading public outrage provoked by those scenes forced the federal government to take sides, and only one side it could take made both moral and political sense.

In 1962, the nation watched the violence erupt when James Meredith, a black Mississippian, enrolled at his state's university under a court order to admit him. The next year, federal marshals led black students past Governor George Wallace as he attempted to block entrance to the University of Alabama. Television carried that, too, across the nation. With each such incident, awareness of the civil rights movement reached into the lives of viewers throughout the United States. Children, particularly, seemed impressed by what they saw. "They can do what they want to," a former principal of a southern black elementary school remarked, "but millions of little eyes are watching, and they're making plans."

Along with the Freedom Rides came protests and marches with locally organized civil rights protesters working with Martin Luther King Jr. and the Southern

President Johnson signs Civil Rights bill into law. Library of Congress.

Christian Leadership Conference in Birmingham and other cities in the South. Stressing nonviolence as essential in the practice of civil disobedience, efforts led by King laid the groundwork for the now-famous March on Washington in 1963. At that event, King spoke from the steps of the Lincoln Memorial to a crowd of 250,000. Carried by television to millions more—perhaps the first civil rights demonstration to capture the attention of the entire nation—Dr. King departed from his prepared text to speak of his dream. "I have a dream," he said, "that one day this nation will rise up and live out the true meaning of its creed: 'We hold these truths to be self-evident; that all men are created equal.' " Rhythmically he intoned the next seven sentences with "I have a dream." Two sentences said simply: "I have a dream today." With the audience stirred by his eloquence and passion, King urged the nation to "let freedom ring." Eight times he repeated that line, concluding with the following:

When we let freedom ring, when we let it ring from every village and every hamlet, from every state and every city, we will be able to speed up that day when all of God's children, black men and white men, Jews and Gentiles, Protestants and Catholics, will be able to join hands and sing in the words of the old Negro spiritual, Free at last! Free at last! Thank God almighty, we are free at last!

Just a month later, the Sunday-morning bombing of a church in Birmingham in which four black girls were killed was a sobering reminder that not everyone shared King's dream.

Despite the resistance that acts like the church bombing exemplified, modern America seemed ready for some of the changes demanded by civil rights leaders. In fact, the resistance helped build momentum for enactment of a civil rights law in 1964 that, among other things, prohibited racial discrimination in public accommodations in any business engaged in interstate commerce and in most employment situations. It soon became apparent that the Democratic Party's position on civil rights would cause it to lose its dominance in what had been known as the "solid South" since the Civil War. Indeed, when Lyndon Johnson signed the 1964 Civil Rights Act, he remarked to an aide: "I think we just delivered the South to the Republican Party for a long time to come." By the time of the presidential election that year, the phenomenon known as white backlash came into evidence not only in the South but in all quarters of America. Johnson's opponent, Senator Barry Goldwater of Arizona, had voted against the Civil Rights Act. Although he lost the election, his followers adhered to his convictions on civil rights in rebuilding the Republican Party, and Goldwater ran well in southern states.

In 1965, responding to the leadership of President Johnson (himself a southerner), Congress passed the Voting Rights Act, aimed at removing barriers that had long kept African Americans out of polling places, particularly in the South. For decades thereafter, the new voters generally supported the Democratic Party, although not in sufficient numbers to offset the loss of white voters. Through their actions on racial matters, both parties prompted ordinary citizens to ask themselves where they stood on matters of race and access to jobs, housing, and social opportunity. As voters answered these questions, both parties gained and lost supporters in regions outside the South as well as in it, although party affiliation continued to rest on much more than one's position on racial issues.

Laws and court decisions were not alone in pushing and pulling the American people one way or another on racial matters. Two other things came into play: violent behavior and increasingly militant language by blacks. The most extreme example of the former was the riot in Watts, a black ghetto in Los Angeles. On August 11, 1965, just five days after President Johnson signed the Voting Rights Act, a confrontation between white police and a black man stopped for a traffic violation sparked a six-day riot. When it was over, 34 people were dead, 900 were injured, 4,000 were under arrest, and property damage amounted to more than $30 million. Despite the presence of 1,500 police officers and 14,000 National Guardsmen, rioters destroyed entire city blocks. Seething black resentment of white police (in the 98 percent black Watts district, 200 of the 205 police officers were white) had set the stage for the riot, but the rioters lost whatever sympathies they might have inspired among whites, both in Watts and elsewhere, by chanting "Burn, baby, burn!" Riots in other cities, frequently sparked by confrontations between blacks and police, blurred the sense of progress that the court decisions and new laws had seemed to create.

Rachel Carson's *Silent Spring* helped forge a new environmental movement in the United States. Library of Congress.

The militant language of some black leaders dismayed many Americans, both white and black. Speeches by Malcolm X, a preacher formerly associated with the Nation of Islam, struck many as hateful and scornful of whites for the treatment of his people through the years. By stressing racial pride and dignity, he inspired his followers in ways whites had difficulty understanding. The assassination of Malcolm X by Black Muslims, followers of Elijah Muhammad, on February 21, 1965, failed to silence his message.

Advocates of Black Power, led by Stokely Carmichael and the Student Non-violent Coordinating Committee (SNCC, known as Snick), used language just as harsh. Working closely with the powerless and disadvantaged victims of discrimination, they understood the daily suffering of members of their race. As were the followers of Malcolm X, the activists in SNCC were driven by deep cynicism about the honesty and good faith of America's white leaders and the entire country's white population.

The division between Stokely Carmichael and those who stood with him on one side, and Martin Luther King Jr. and his followers on the other, became starkly clear in June 1966. James Meredith was again a key figure in an event that once more drew Americans to their television sets. While he marched alone across Mississippi to give blacks the confidence to register and vote, a shotgun fired by an assassin from roadside bushes cut him down, planting 60 pellets in his body. With Meredith's family's consent, civil rights groups converged on the scene to complete the march.

At rallies along the way, King continued to advocate nonviolence, but Carmichael spoke more militantly. Finally, in Canton, Mississippi, Carmichael exhorted his hearers as follows:

The only way we are going to stop them from whuppin' us is to take over. We've been saying freedom for six years and we ain't got nothin'.... The time for running has come to an end.... Black Power. It's time we stand up and take over; move on over [Whitey] or we'll move on over you.

"Black Power!" chanted the crowd. "Black Power! Black Power!" The call for Black Power shattered the façade of unity among civil rights leaders and their followers. Martin Luther King Jr. still wanted to preserve a national coalition of blacks and whites committed to the cause of civil rights, but Carmichael refused to limit his efforts to stir black people to action.

By the late 1960s, it was obvious that if enacting civil rights laws appeared difficult, changing practices was going to be even harder, especially by 1968. The assassination of Martin Luther King Jr. on April 4 led to more urban riots. Before the decade was over, riots occurred in more than 100 cities and resulted in at least 77 deaths. Thousands suffered injuries, and property destruction was incalculable. The well-publicized purpose of a civil rights law passed one week after King's death was to prohibit racial discrimination in housing policies and practices. However, a provision insisted on by Senator Strom Thurmond of South Carolina showed the ambivalence of white politicians toward militant blacks. This provision made it a crime to use the facilities of interstate commerce "to organize, promote, encourage, participate in, or carry on a riot; or to commit any act of violence in furtherance of a riot." Robert Weisbrot, a historian of the civil rights movement, has observed that the bill's priorities were clear: "modest federal involvement in black efforts to flee the ghetto, but overwhelming force to curb all restiveness within it."

Before his death, Martin Luther King Jr. had planned a "Poor People's March on Washington" to shift the focus of the civil rights movement from racial to economic issues, believing that this might attract broader support. Leadership of the campaign fell to his successor in the SCLC, Ralph David Abernathy. Even under ideal conditions, the prospects of success were limited, but the weather in Washington at the time of the march was miserable. The political climate the campaigners faced was even worse, and their well-intentioned efforts seemed only to call attention to the powerlessness of poor blacks and their isolation from poor whites (Marty 1997,

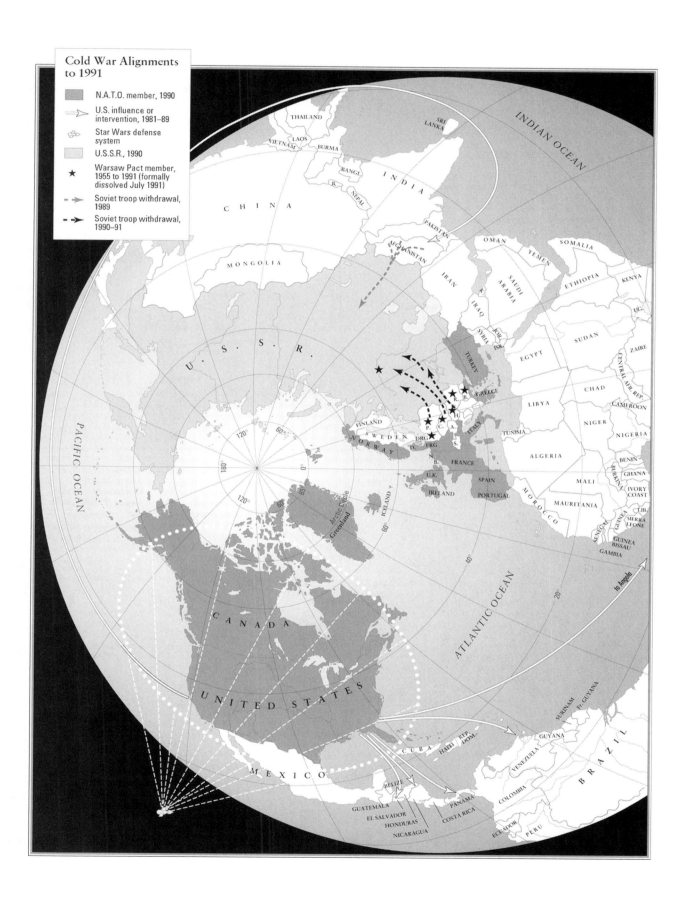

Cold War Alignments
to 1991

N.A.T.O. member, 1990

U.S. influence or
intervention, 1981–89

Star Wars defense
system

U.S.S.R., 1990

★ Warsaw Pact member,
1955 to 1991 (formally
dissolved July 1991)

Soviet troop withdrawal,
1989

Soviet troop withdrawal,
1990–91

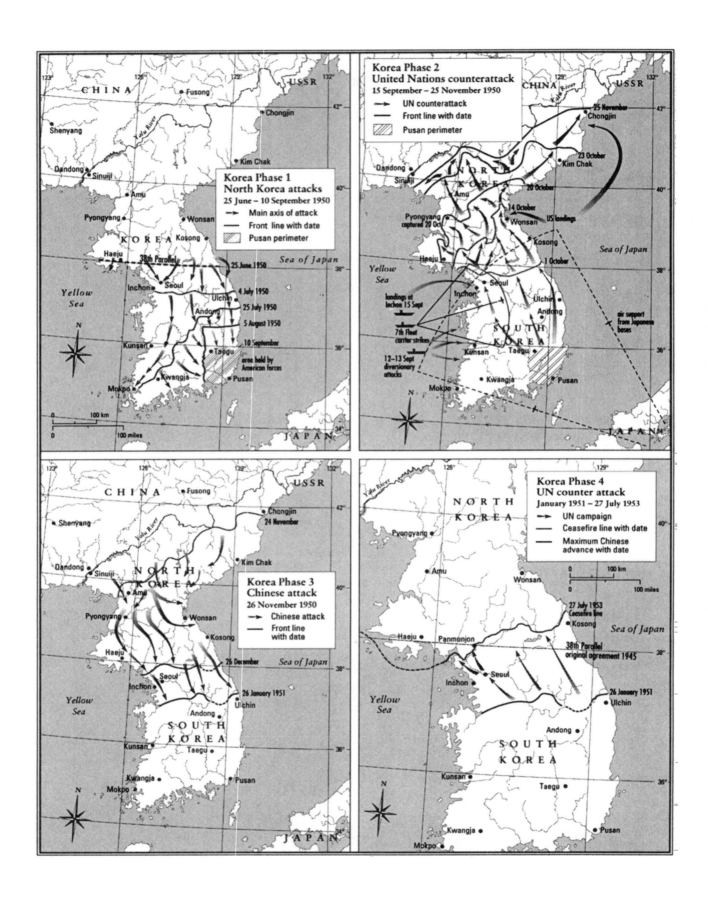

Korea Phase 1
North Korea attacks
25 June – 10 September 1950

→ Main axis of attack
— Front line with date
▨ Pusan perimeter

CHINA

Fusong
Chongjin
Shenyang
Kim Chak
Dandong • Sinuiji
Amu
Pyongyang • Wonsan
KOREA Kosong
Haeju 38th Parallel
Inchon Seoul 25 June 1950
Ulchin 4 July 1950
Andong 25 July 1950
5 August 1950
Kunsan 10 September
Taegu area held by
Kwangja American forces
Mokpo Pusan

Yellow Sea
Sea of Japan

100 km
100 miles

JAPAN

Korea Phase 2
United Nations counterattack
15 September – 25 November 1950

→ UN counterattack
— Front line with date
▨ Pusan perimeter

CHINA USSR
Yalu River
25 November
Chongjin
Dandong
Sinuiji Kim Chak 23 October
NORTH
KOREA 20 October
Amu 14 October
Pyongyang US landings
captured 20 Oct Wonsan
Kosong
Haeju 1 October
Yellow Sea
landings of Seoul
Inchon 15 Sept Inchon Ulchin
Andong air support
7th Fleet SOUTH from Japanese
carrier strikes KOREA bases
12–13 Sept Kunsan Taegu
diversionary
attacks Mokpo Pusan
Kwangja
Sea of Japan
JAPAN

Korea Phase 3
Chinese attack
26 November 1950

→ Chinese attack
— Front line with date

CHINA
Fusong
Shenyang
Chongjin
24 November
Dandong Kim Chak
Sinuiji NORTH
KOREA
Amu
Pyongyang Wonsan
Kosong
Haeju 26 December
Inchon Seoul 26 January 1951
Ulchin
Andong
Yellow SOUTH
Sea KOREA
Kunsan Taegu
Kwangja Pusan
Mokpo
USSR
Sea of Japan
JAPAN

Korea Phase 4
UN counter attack
January 1951 – 27 July 1953

→ UN campaign
— Ceasefire line with date
— Maximum Chinese advance with date

NORTH
KOREA
Pyongyang
Amu
Wonsan
100 km
100 miles
27 July 1953
Ceasefire line Kosong
Haeju Panmunjon Sea of Japan
38th Parallel
original agreement 1945
Inchon Seoul
26 January 1951
Yellow Ulchin
Sea
Andong
SOUTH
KOREA
Kunsan
Taegu
Kwangja
Mokpo Pusan

11–16, 87–89; *Daily Life Online,* "Political Life: Reform," in Marty, *Daily Life in the United States, 1960–1990,* http://dailylife.greenwood.com).

WARFARE: VIETNAM

The United States engaged in several major shooting wars and in an ongoing ideological conflict with the Soviet Union known as the Cold War. The Cold War is the popular name applied to the deterioration of U.S.–Soviet relations after the end of World War II in 1945. The rivalry between the two nations was marked by a series of diplomatic and military incidents that frequently threatened but never actually led to open warfare. Each nation sought to limit the influence its rival exercised around the world. The United States sought to check the extension of Soviet power in central and eastern Europe, where Soviet-dominated communist governments came to power in the late 1940s, by economically, politically, and militarily rebuilding western Europe. Initiated in 1947 and lasting until 1951, the Marshall Plan sent more than $12 billion in economic assistance to help the countries of western Europe rebuild basic industries, increase trade, and raise basic standards of living. In Germany, which had been divided after the war into zones of occupation controlled by the Americans, French, British, and Soviets, the U.S. Air Force thwarted Soviet attempts to blockade the Allied sectors of Berlin, which were surrounded by the Soviet sector of Germany, by airlifting supplies into the city in 1948 and 1949.

The focus of the Cold War shifted to Asia in 1950, where a shooting war commenced on the Korean Peninsula. The armies of Soviet-influenced North Korea invaded South Korea, a U.S. ally, on June 25. A United States–led coalition, authorized by the United Nations, came to the defense of South Korea, while China, which had become a communist state in 1949, eventually entered the war on the side of the North Koreans, who were also supplied by the Soviets. The war ended with a cease-fire in 1953. It left the peninsula divided between the communist North and the democratic South. Over 33,000 Americans died in the Korean War. At the start of the twenty-first century, U.S. forces were still stationed in South Korea.

The Cold War continued until 1989–1990, when the collapse of the Soviet Union and of the Soviet-controlled regimes of eastern Europe left the United States without a significant rival as a world superpower. In the years since 1960, however, the United States had fought two other major wars. The first of those was the Vietnam conflict. The numbers of persons directly involved in the war in Vietnam provide a sense of the war's broad and powerful impact in America. Of the almost 27 million men of draft age during the war, 11 million were drafted or enlisted. The remaining 16 million who never served included some who enlisted in the National Guard or were granted conscientious objector status. Some were exempted for physical reasons. Others had educational, vocational, marital, or family hardship or other reasons for exemption. An estimated 250,000 men, many from urban ghettos, did not register at all. Fifty thousand evaded the draft or deserted the military by exiling themselves to Canada and other places.

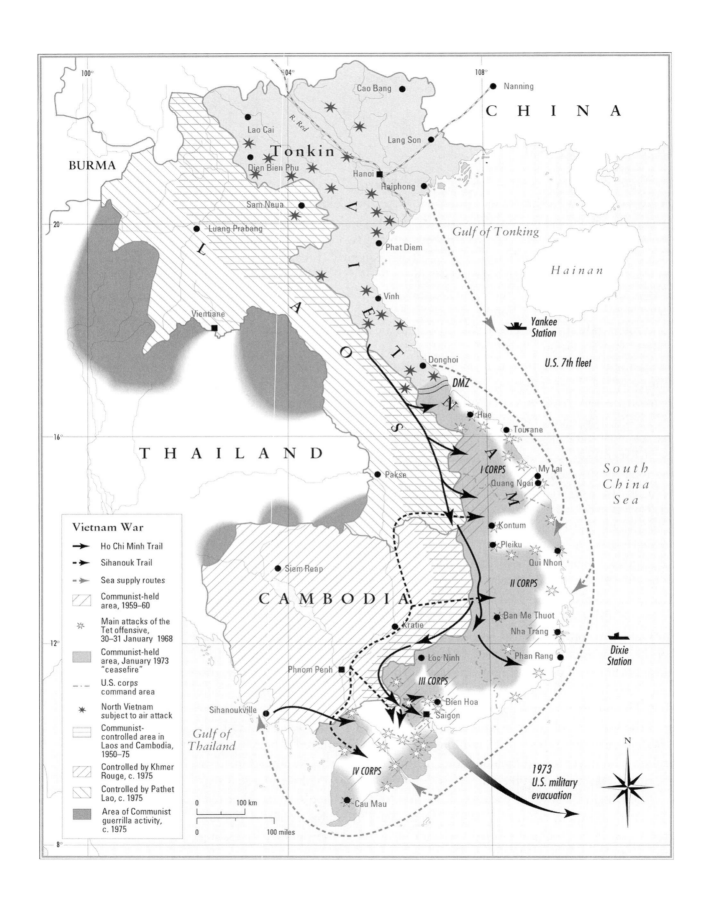

Vietnam War

→ Ho Chi Minh Trail

⇢ Sihanouk Trail

⇠ Sea supply routes

▨ Communist-held area, 1959–60

✳ Main attacks of the Tet offensive, 30–31 January 1968

▦ Communist-held area, January 1973 "ceasefire"

–·–· U.S. corps command area

✶ North Vietnam subject to air attack

▤ Communist-controlled area in Laos and Cambodia, 1950–75

▨ Controlled by Khmer Rouge, c. 1975

▨ Controlled by Pathet Lao, c. 1975

▦ Area of Communist guerrilla activity, c. 1975

Of the 2.7 million persons who served in Vietnam, 300,000 were wounded and 58,000 died. For their parents, spouses, siblings, and friends, the pain caused by the loss of loved ones was indescribable. Even though the flow of daily life in the United States seemed in some respects to be undisturbed, the loved ones of those who served and returned, those who evaded service, and even those who were exempted from it endured anxiety and heartache. For the rest, the daily reports on casualties, the commentaries on the war, and the protests the war inspired meant that happenings far away were affecting the lives of everyone.

U.S. Army flamethrower in action, Vietnam, 1966. POPPERFOTO/Alamy.

Protests against U.S. involvement in the war between North and South Vietnam began in the early 1960s. As troop levels went up, so did the numbers and vehemence of the protesters. On April 15, 1967, 125,000 Americans gathered in New York to rally against the war. More than 55,000 joined in a comparable event in San Francisco. Organized by a coalition known as the Spring Mobilization to End the War in Vietnam, the demonstrations had the support of a broad range of groups and such prominent individuals as Martin Luther King Jr. and Dr. Benjamin Spock, whose book on baby and child care had been relied on by the parents of many of the protesters.

The efforts of antiwar protesters, many of them college-educated and middle class, initially met with indifference. As the protesters became more insistent and more vocal, however, they increasingly alienated working-class people who knew that those fighting the war came primarily from their ranks. In December 1967, a Louis Harris poll reported that more than three-fourths of American people polled believed the protests encouraged the enemy to fight harder. Seventy percent of the respondents expressed the belief that antiwar demonstrations were acts of disloyalty to the soldiers fighting the war. A poll several weeks later showed that 58 percent favored continuing the war and stepping up military pressure on the communists. Sixty-three percent

Leading the march against the Vietnamese conflict are Dr. Benjamin Spock (center, with white hair) and Dr. Martin Luther King Jr. (third from right), in a parade on State Street in Chicago, March 25, 1967. AP/Wide World Photos.

opposed halting the bombing of North Vietnam as a tactic to see if the communists would be willing to negotiate a peace settlement.

Yet, the demonstrations showed that opposition to the war could not be taken lightly. The antiwar sentiment of some demonstrators sprang from moral outrage over the loss of American lives in what seemed to be a lost cause, of others from long-standing pacifist commitments. Still other demonstrators believed it made sense to cut losses in a war that was simply an imprudent endeavor.

Even though the antiwar movement failed to attract multitudes of followers, televised reports on marches and acts of civil disobedience created widespread uneasiness about the war. Critics of the news media, particularly Presidents Johnson and Nixon, were outraged by what they considered to be antiwar bias. Since then, other critics have claimed (contrary to persuasive evidence) that the United States could have won the war if the media had reported more fully and accurately the U.S. military successes in Vietnam, rather than embracing the antiwar arguments.

Careful analyses show that most of the media, at least until 1968, held positions sympathetic to President Johnson's policies. Most continued to support the government's actions well into the Nixon presidency. On the other hand, the media's reports on antiwar activities tended to focus on violent or bizarre behavior by the protesters. *Time* magazine, for example, dismissed the April 1967 protests as a "gargantuan 'demo'" that was "as peaceful as its pacifist philosophy, as colorful as the kooky costumes and painted faces of its psychedelic 'pot left' participants, and about as damaging to the U.S. image throughout the world as a blow from the daffodils and roses that the marchers carried in gaudy abundance."

Henry Kissinger. Library of Congress.

By failing to give serious attention to the arguments advanced by the protesters—admittedly difficult to do in collages of short clips and sound bites—the media failed to give viewers and readers insights into the ideas and ideals of those who genuinely thought the war wrong.

The agony caused by an offensive launched by the Vietnamese communists in January 1968 did more to turn sentiment against continuing U.S. involvement in Vietnam than anything the antiwar movement might have done. The media provided uncensored coverage of that offensive, named for Tet, the Vietnamese New Year. The North Vietnamese and Viet Cong attacked at many points, but the focus of American news coverage was on a siege at the combat base known as Khe Sanh. The siege lasted from January 21 until April 14 and included fierce battles, reported daily. At one extreme, television viewers saw hand-to-hand combat with knives, rifles, and grenades. At the other, they saw the dropping of 100,000 tons of bombs by American planes in the area. By the time the siege ended, about 300 U.S. Marines had been killed and 2,200 wounded, but estimates of enemy casualties ranged from 2,500 to 15,000.

Military and political leaders in the United States claimed that the Tet Offensive had failed. Tactically, they were correct. Even North Vietnamese political and military leaders saw their offensive as a failure in military terms. Yet, Tet served as a turning point in the minds of many Americans who had previously supported the war effort or were neutral about it. Savagely fought contests struck raw nerves. Perhaps even more so did a photograph showing South Vietnam's police chief shooting a Viet Cong suspect in the head on a Saigon sidewalk, or hearing a U.S. major say about the fighting at Ben Tre, a city of 35,000, "It became necessary to destroy the town to save it." When CBS anchorman Walter Cronkite, in his "Report from Vietnam" on February 27, 1968, expressed doubts about prospects for U.S. success, those doubts spread. They spread further when the Business Executives Move for Vietnam Peace, which claimed 1,600 members, said that "as businessmen we feel that when a policy hasn't proved productive after a reasonable trial it's sheer nonsense not to change it." Even the *Wall Street Journal*, always a spirited antagonist of the antiwar movement, published an editorial on February 23, 1968, stating that "everyone had better be prepared for the bitter taste of a defeat beyond America's power to prevent."

In subsequent months, more and more people expressed opposition to the war. They wrote letters to members of Congress and the president, placed advertisements in newspapers, signed petitions, and joined in vigils in public places, including military installations. They supported candidates who took antiwar positions, most notably presidential candidates Eugene McCarthy and Robert Kennedy in 1968 and George McGovern in 1972. A few refused to pay taxes, register for the draft, or be inducted. A few burned draft cards and participated in strikes on campus and occasionally in workplaces. By engaging in nonviolent civil disobedience, they became subject to arrest, jailing, and court trials. More extreme actions included raids on offices of draft boards to destroy records by burning or pouring blood on them, as well as trashing, burning, or setting off bombs in buildings and, in several instances, committing suicide.

In the aftermath of the Tet Offensive, and two weeks after a weak showing in the New Hampshire primary, President Lyndon Johnson announced, on March 31, that he would not seek reelection. Vice President Hubert Humphrey, who hoped to be Johnson's successor, had been reluctant to question Johnson's policies, thus making himself the object of bitter and ferocious criticism by the war's opponents. The assassination of Robert F. Kennedy, Humphrey's leading rival for the nomination, added to the Democratic Party's turmoil. The Democratic National Convention in Chicago was a nasty affair. Protesters made the conventioneers angry, and Chicago police officers attacked the protesters, resulting in what came to be called a police riot.

As opposition to the U.S. role in Vietnam increased, Republican presidential candidate Richard Nixon implied that he had a secret plan for ending the war. Humphrey gradually let his opposition to the war be known, and his strong campaign finish made the results of the election surprisingly close: Nixon received 43.4 percent of the popular vote, Humphrey 42.7 percent, and George Wallace 13.5 percent.

After the election, the antiwar movement lost whatever coherence it had had and fell into general public disfavor. The Nixon administration's questionable statements about its intentions and its denunciations of the movement's leaders, along with divisions within the movement, were partly responsible. Probably more important were the excesses displayed by radical campus groups, such as the Weathermen, and the news media's willingness to be influenced by Nixon's foreign policy advisor,

Henry Kissinger. Still, opponents of the war mobilized for a Vietnam Moratorium Day on October 15, 1969. An organization of Republicans known as the Ripon Society, the liberal Americans for a Democratic Society, the United Auto Workers, and the Teamsters union, along with many political and religious leaders, endorsed the moratorium. A number of Vietnam War veterans were among the millions of participants in local protests across the nation.

Conflicts between supporters and opponents of the war continued into 1970, most notably on university campuses. During the academic year ending in the spring of 1970, there were nearly 250 bombings and about the same number of cases of arson, resulting in at least six deaths. The event that brought into sharp focus the conflict between those who opposed the war and those who defended U.S. policies and actions occurred on May 4, 1970. Five days earlier Nixon had shocked the nation by announcing that U.S. troops had invaded neutral Cambodia to wipe out enemy strongholds there. Ohio National Guardsmen, apparently in panic as they faced protesters of this action at Kent State University, fired 61 shots into a crowd of students, killing four and wounding nine. Students around the nation, reacting to what they had seen on television, threw their own campuses into turmoil, forcing some 400 colleges and universities to end the semester prematurely.

By mid-1970, the lines between opposing sides in the conflict over the war in Vietnam seemed fixed. While casualties mounted, protests continued. In April 1971, Vietnam War veterans marched in Washington, D.C.; some came on crutches, and others rode in wheelchairs. Thousands of veterans gathered at the U.S. Capitol, removed medals awarded them for bravery, and threw them away.

The demonstrations changed few minds. The imposition of a draft lottery system defused some of the antiwar protesters' charges about class and racial biases in calling Americans to serve. More importantly, Nixon's policy of Vietnamization—that is, of turning the fighting of the war over to the Army of the Republic of Vietnam—meant that more U.S. troops returned home. The number of U.S. troops in Vietnam dropped from 536,000 in 1968 to 156,800 by the end of 1971. By March 1972, troop strength was down to 95,000, including only 6,000 combat troops. Those coming home made difficult reentries into the routines of everyday life, and the lives of those who remained in Vietnam changed. Estimates of drug use by troops in 1970 stood at about 50 percent. By March 1972, nearly 250 underground antiwar papers were circulating among U.S. troops. Reenlistment rates dropped sharply, and desertions spiraled upward, as did combat refusal incidents. Officers feared rebellion in their ranks, and some found their very lives in jeopardy.

Many Americans greeted skeptically Secretary of State Henry Kissinger's announcement on October 26, 1972, that "peace is at hand." Even so, the nation was not ready to oust Richard Nixon from the presidency. His bold moves in pushing détente with the Soviet Union and opening talks with communist China won him many supporters who otherwise criticized his Vietnam policy. Similarly, Nixon's southern strategy on civil rights issues and willingness, at the same time, to endorse new federal programs to relieve problems of urban decay and joblessness made him seem a moderate able to appeal to middle-class, white, suburban voters. He easily defeated Democrat George McGovern, a staunch antiwar opponent, in the presidential election the following month. The next month, December 1972, peace talks made no progress, and Nixon again ordered bombing of North Vietnam. That prompted some who had not previously joined in protests to attend services of prayer and repentance, believing that as citizens they were party to morally indefensible actions. One such service, attended by persons of all ages, was led by Francis B. Sayre Jr., who had been dean of the Washington National Cathedral for 21 years. He was the son of a diplomat, the grandson of Woodrow Wilson, and the last then-living person to have been born in the White House. After the service, most in attendance marched silently with Dean Sayre to the White House, where they were ignored.

Despite the strength of their feelings, protesters found it hard to sustain the momentum of protests against the war. When Richard Nixon was inaugurated for a second term on January 20, 1973, a counter-inaugural demonstration drew a crowd of more than 60,000 persons at the Washington monument. The mood there, write Nancy Zaroulis and Gerald Sullivan, was "one of witness. Most were there because they were unable not to be. They had come to manifest silent concern for a war in which, as Lincoln's [second inaugural address] had put it, 'Neither party expected . . . the magnitude or the duration which it had already attained.' " But "the stale rhetoric from the monument platform on a day when little remained to be spoken that had not already been said many times before could not hold the audience. Most wandered off in the direction of Pennsylvania Avenue to watch, unbelieving, the inaugural parade and its anticipatory bicentennial theme of 1776." (No one knew then, of course, that by 1974 both President Nixon and Vice President Spiro Agnew would have resigned in disgrace.)

Two days later Nixon announced in a televised statement that representatives of the United States and North Vietnam had initialed the Agreement on Ending the War and Restoring Peace in Vietnam. "Peace with honor," he declared, had at last been achieved. A cease-fire began several days later. Withdrawal of the remaining 23,700 troops was to be accomplished in 60 days, and all American prisoners of war were to be released. The agreement left South Vietnam, known as the Republic of Vietnam, at the mercy of North Vietnam. The South Vietnamese managed to continue their struggle for two more years, but as American aid dwindled, they saw their capital, Saigon, fall on April 30, 1975. It was left to President Gerald Ford to issue a proclamation stating that May 7, 1975, was the last day of the "Vietnam era."

Whether any actions on the part of war protesters through the years accomplished the results they sought was debatable then and remains so. Attempts, then as well as more recently, to portray those opposed to the war as irresponsible anti-Americans who committed treasonous acts under orders from communist leaders run contrary to facts. Like every mass movement, the one opposing the war in Vietnam included some radicals, and the radicals engaged in bizarre, violent, destructive acts. But the movement was homegrown and eventually included persons of all ages from across the political spectrum. Leaders and followers in the movement, with rare exceptions, believed deeply in their American heritage as defined in the Constitution and built into their political traditions.

The second significant American military action (smaller U.S. armed intervention took place in Granada in 1983 and Panama in 1990) was the liberation of Kuwait. In

August 1990, the United States began a massive deployment of troops in response to Iraq's invasion of Kuwait. By January 1991, the total number of American personnel in Iraq had reached 540,000. For troops already on active duty, being sent to a possible combat zone in a desert in the Middle East was not exactly all in a day's work, but they were expected to be prepared for such a contingency. For the more than 125,000 reservists and members of the National Guard who were called to active duty by the Pentagon, readiness for war was another matter. Among them were men and women from all walks of now-disrupted lives. Not all were sent overseas, because some were needed to fill positions vacated by the full-time troops who had been deployed, but the abrupt changes in their lives and the lives of those they left behind were considerable.

The effects on most Americans of preparation for war had little to do with strategies or ethics, or even with disruption of their personal lives by calls to service. Rather, their concerns were with what it cost to fill the tanks of their cars with gasoline. Before Iraq's invasion of Kuwait on August 2, the price of gasoline in the United States averaged $1.09 per gallon. By mid-October it had risen to $1.40, even though only about 9 percent of imported oil had come from Kuwait. Various maneuvers by the government brought the price down again, but the episode brought three reminders: First, the reliance of Americans on automobiles was enormous. Second, the vulnerability of the nation's oil supply was something Americans would rather not think about. Third, oil and automobiles are so central to the American economy that anything threatening their place shakes the stock market badly. Worries about the war and its implications caused investors to be so jittery that the market lost 20 percent of its value from August to mid-October (Marty 1997, 105–12, 265–66; *Daily Life Online*, "Political Life: War," in Marty, *Daily Life in the United States, 1945–1990*, http://dailylife.greenwood.com).

FOR MORE INFORMATION

Baldwin, James. *The Fire Next Time*. New York: Dial Press, 1963.

Banner, Stuart. *Death Penalty: An American Story*. Cambridge, MA: Harvard University Press, 2001.

Brandon, Craig. *Electric Chair: An Unnatural American History*. Jefferson, NC: McFarland and Company, 1999.

Cremin, Lawrence A. "Grading America's Public Schools." *The 1984 World Book Year Book*. Chicago: World Book, Inc., 1984.

Hering, G. C. *America's Longest War: The United States and Vietnam, 1950–1975*. New York: Wiley, 1979.

Karnow, S. *Vietnam: A History*. New York: Viking, 1983.

Lemann, N. *The Promised Land: The Great Black Migration and How It Changed America*. New York: Vintage Books/Knopf, 1991.

Marty, Myron A. *Daily Life in the United States, 1960–1990: Decades of Discord*. Westport, CT: Greenwood Press, 1997; also available online as *Daily Life Online*, in Marty, *Daily Life in the United States, 1960–1990*, http://dailylife.greenwood.com).

Matusow, A. J. *The Unraveling of America: A History of American Liberalism in the 1960s*. New York: Harper and Row, 1984.

National Commission on Excellence in Education, USA Research, ed. *A Nation at Risk: The Full Account.* Cambridge, MA: USA Research, 1984.

Pakula, D., dir. *All the President's Men.* 1976.

Patterson, J. T. *Grand Expectations: The United States, 1945–1974.* New York: Oxford University Press, 1996.

Sitkoff, H. *The Struggle for Black Equality, 1954–1992.* New York: Hill and Wang, 1993.

Steelwater, Eliza. *Hangman's Knot: Lynching, Legal Execution, and America's Struggle with the Death Penalty.* New York: Basic Books, 2003.

Williamson, J. *The Crucible of Race: Black-White Relations in the American South since Emancipation.* New York: Oxford University Press, 1984.

Zaroulis, N. L. *Who Spoke Up? Americans Protest the War in Vietnam, 1963–1975.* Garden City, NY: Doubleday, 1984.

Recreational Life

OVERVIEW

By the beginning of the 1960s, American interest in and commercial development of recreational options in the nation had begun to result in previously unimagined choices. An evolving form of popular culture, egalitarian and commercial, provided Americans with a broad selection of entertainment, both as spectators and participants. Television dominated the domestic landscape, with nearly 90 percent of American homes owning sets by 1960, and other types of recreation expanded as well. If radio lost its monopoly on household entertainment, more than 50 million families still had radios in their cars or kitchens. New stereo record players and tape decks replaced earlier forms of home musical entertainment. Those components would become commonplace in American homes. Hollywood and the film industry continued to draw audiences into theaters, and a new rating system sought to respond to a growing concern regarding appropriate standards. Youth sports grew increasingly organized and directed, and Title IX of the Educational Amendments of 1972 finally drew attention to the issue of women's participation in interscholastic and intercollegiate athletics. At the same time, professional sports, both their expansion and commercial ties with television, changed the nature of all the major sports franchises and their players. As an example, the National Football League (NFL) became a billion dollar industry, and its unique relationship with television broadcasting made professional football the new darling of spectator sports in America.

Variety appeared the key concept in popular culture, from amusement parks to ballparks. American popular culture continued to search for new forms of entertainment, and the commercial nature of the various options in recreation responded in classic supply-and-demand profitability. In journalism and periodical literature, Americans saw the same move toward variety. The traditional weekly or monthly magazines like

The first issue of *Playboy* magazine featuring Marilyn Monroe, left, and a boxed DVD set of *Playboy* magazines from the 1950s are shown in New York, 2007. AP/Wide World Photos.

Look and *Life* began to lose audiences and advertisers after 1960. Magazines became more focused, appealing to specific audiences with specific interests. The era also witnessed an increase in participation in sports and recreation in American daily life. Youngsters had always played games; now adults began to join them. From bowling to skiing, and from golf and tennis to jogging and health clubs, there was a surge in adult participation in recreational activity. If the term "couch potato" defined Americans sitting in recliners watching prime-time television and weekend sports, millions of Americans had added exercise and recreation to their daily lives to challenge that stereotype.

Critics of popular culture complained that its lowbrow quality had created a lowest common denominator in American cultural life, and they certainly had numerous examples to support their charge. On the other hand, every major city in the nation offered symphony orchestras, ballet, opera, art museums, and sophisticated magazines and journals to counter these concerns. Important and serious films still came to movie screens for discerning audiences, and a generation of new writers like Joseph Heller, Norman Mailer, Kurt Vonnegut, William Styron, and others created novels that rivaled an earlier generation of novelists who spoke to their times and their issues. To be sure, Harlequin romances, detective and spy novels, science fiction, and other popular fare commanded the largest readership, but Americans made their daily choices and did so with little or no interference from political or social institutions seeking to guide those choices. Whether they chose to buy *Catch-22* or *Peyton Place*, the option remained theirs.

DANCE, MUSIC, AND THEATER

Changes in sexual mores and practices were just one part of the interwoven forces that created an American culture quite different from that of a generation earlier. Rock music, with its increasingly explicit sexual themes, was another. Herbert London contended that "like the inscriptions on the Rosetta stone that solved the mystery of hieroglyphics, rock music provides a key record of the Second American Revolution that may unlock its inner logic." Not wishing to overstate the case, he added that "rock is a spectator at the cultural storm, not its ruler. It may rekindle the ashes with a spark, but it cannot make the original fire" (*Closing the Circle: A Cultural History of the Rock Revolution*).

Historians trace the origins of rock music to several sources. One was the rock and roll craze of the 1950s, featuring black musicians like Chuck Berry and Little Richard as well as white ones, including Elvis Presley, Jerry Lee Lewis, and Buddy Holly. The new phenomenon, wrote historian Edward P. Morgan, "represented a merging of such traditional strains as black blues, jazz, gospel, and white country music." A second source, Morgan (1991) said, lay in "traditional folk music—protest songs from the labor movement, anti-war tradition, ballads, and folk-blues." By the mid-1960s, a gentler phase of

The Beatles, 1964. Library of Congress.

folk music, with Bob Dylan, Joan Baez, and Peter, Paul, and Mary as leading artists, yielded to more critical variations. Those variations reflected the alienated perspectives of the Beat movement characterized by the poetry of Allen Ginsberg and musings of Jack Kerouac and the countercultural lifestyle of the 1950s that was called Beatnik.

As rock music evolved with its merged traditions, some of it expressed the political sensitivities of the civil rights movement and antipathy to the arms race with the Soviet Union. Performers also attacked what they regarded as repressive social mores. In other words, like music of earlier eras, it reflected the times. The lifestyles of the rock musicians and their most devoted followers were countercultural, at least in style, but the ingredients of rock music gradually infiltrated the larger culture. That may explain why it became the subject of so much scholarly analysis, such as that provided by James Haskins and Kathleen Benson, who, in *The 60s Reader* (1988), outline three distinctive characteristics of rock music.

First, rock's sexually explicit lyrics revealed society's new sexual permissiveness. Those who found it offensive contended that its sexual themes also fed that permissiveness, something those who "dug it" could hardly deny. *Second*, not only did rock music belong to the youth culture, but youth's elders could scarcely tolerate it. To them, it seemed raucous and incoherent, its lyrics unintelligible. Television shows like *Hit Parade*, starring Rosemary Clooney and appealing to audiences across generation lines, disappeared. *Third*, rock broke down the barriers between white musicians and their black counterparts. By the 1960s, the new music, aimed at both blacks and whites, was well established, and a distinctive, affluent teenage market wanted more.

Leonard Bernstein. Library of Congress.

A generation gap, encouraged if not created by the sound, lyrics, and staging of rock music, soon became a matter of concern to older generations. Indeed, Haskins and Benson wrote that "nowhere did that gap present itself more clearly

The Woodstock Music Festival and Art Fair had about 450,000 participants in August 1969. Photofest.

than in the controversy over rock 'n' roll and over its most popular purveyor at the turn of the decade, Elvis Presley. He rode in a gold Cadillac, he dressed in gold lamé suits, he gyrated his hips so sensuously that when he appeared on television the cameras never showed him below the waist. Parents were enraged; young people were delighted. A generational tug-of-war resulted." Attempts at censoring rock music on the radio and banning rock stage shows failed to reduce its seemingly inevitable appeal to the younger generation.

Three developments of the 1960s proved wrong any thoughts that American performers would be unable to sustain enthusiasm for rock and roll or that the appeal of its performers might wear thin. One was the enduring strength and adaptability of folk music. Continuing the tradition of Woody Guthrie and Pete Seeger (whose music had been inspired by social conditions of the 1930s and 1940s), Joan Baez, Bob Dylan, Judy Collins, and others, as well as groups like the Kingston Trio and Peter, Paul, and Mary, now appealed to millions with their songs of alienation and protest.

The second was the arrival of groups from England, particularly the Beatles in 1964 and the Rolling Stones a year later, to be followed by others such as The Who. Those performers, Morgan says, bypassed "the more tepid rock and roll imitations" and "reached back to the blues roots of rock and roll and figures like Chuck Berry. Together with a kind of working-class stance and each group's distinctive signature—the Beatles's pathbreaking chord combinations and harmonies, the Rolling Stones' swaggering alienation—resulted in a burst of new energy in popular music." David Chalmers described the appearance of the Beatles on *The Ed Sullivan Show* in 1964 as "electrifying" and said

British pop singers Phil Collins, left, and Sting are shown onstage during the Live Aid concert held at London's Wembley Stadium, England, July 13, 1985. AP/Wide World Photos.

that their "well-scrubbed look, their Teddy Boy dress and the hair down over their ears, their wit, their ensemble performance that did not submerge the individual personalities, their compelling but not overwhelming acoustical beat, and their lyrics of love and holding hands created a powerful personal chemistry. They came across as real."

The very power of the Beatles, Jeff Greenfield observed in 1987, "guarantees that an excursion into analysis cannot fully succeed." Even so, he writes, "they helped make rock music a battering ram for the youth culture's assault on the mainstream, and that assault in turn changed our culture permanently."

The third was the success of Motown Productions, a Detroit-based music empire closely tied to the civil rights movement of the mid-1960s. Its success lay in grooming, packaging, marketing, and selling the music of black performers, such as the Supremes, to masses of white Americans. Using methods practiced by the Detroit automobile factories in which he had worked, its founder, Barry Gordy, according to David P. Szatmary (1991), "ensured the success of the Supremes by assembling the parts of a hit-making machine that included standardized songwriting, an in-house rhythm section, a quality-control process, selective promotion, and a family atmosphere reminiscent of the camaraderie fostered by Henry Ford in his auto plant during the early twentieth century." The Temptations and other groups assembled later were all part of the Motown machine. The machine itself enjoyed success from 1964 until things came apart in 1967, but the sounds and the stars it got started continued.

The sudden burst in popularity of rock music should not obscure the fact that other forms of popular music—jazz, country, and traditional folk music, for example—also thrived. As rock and roll evolved in the later 1960s, many groups of performers sprang up, some of them attracting huge followings. Listing and describing those groups in any detail is unnecessary, but several happenings in the world of rock music demonstrate what an important part the performers played in the cultural transitions of the late 1960s and early 1970s.

Among the most striking was that a number of rock and roll superstars—leaders of protests against the establishment—became big moneymakers. According to *Forbes* magazine, in 1973 at least 50 superstars earned an estimated $2 million to $6 million annually. Overlooked in that report were the sums earned by mainstream American businesses through production and sale of the superstars' records and promotion of their concerts. By the early 1970s, seven corporations accounted for 80 percent of all sales, and those sales were enormous. In 1950, record companies' sales totaled $189 million. Five years later they reached $277 million. By 1971, sales of records and tapes amounted to $1.7 billion in the United States alone. In two more years, sales stood at $2 billion (compared with $1 billion in network television and $1.3 billion in the film industry). That was only part of the story: In 1973, sales of records and tapes reached $555 million in Japan, $454 million in West Germany, $441 million in the Soviet Union, and $384 million in the United Kingdom.

The stars and superstars may have paid a high price for the money and adulation they enjoyed. Heavy performance and recording schedules and frenetic lifestyles, saturated with drugs and alcohol, sometimes ruined them. Janis Joplin, whose intense performances were laced with obscenities, died of an overdose of heroin in 1970. Jimi Hendrix, one of the most talented and extreme acid-rock guitarists, died of an overdose of sleeping pills in the same year. And Jim Morrison, whose dialogues with the audience were filled with raw sexuality, died of a heart attack in 1971, his body ravaged by the excesses of his lifestyle. Joplin, Hendrix, and Morrison were all 27 years old when they died. Elvis Presley died at age 42, in 1977, the victim of a dissipated life.

As rock music gained wider acceptance, not by moving closer to mainstream America, but by drawing mainstream America closer to it, some performers gained critical acceptance with their distinctive styles and sounds. The lyrics of Bob Dylan, set to folk melodies, were ambiguous enough to express the protests of almost anyone. Mostly, though, the performances of his touring group, the Band, reflected the outlook of his own Baby-Boom generation. Some consider Dylan's style as marking the beginning of the use of the term *rock* instead of *rock and roll.*

Other performers helped extend the influence of rock music. As young people played the record albums of Simon and Garfunkel, for example, their parents picked up both the lyrics and the tunes. Perhaps they shared the performers' concern over the "sounds of silence," of "people talking without listening"; or perhaps they too hoped to find a "bridge over troubled waters." The Beatles had caught on quickly with youth in the United States, and they attracted older listeners by experimenting with exotic instruments, melodies from classical music, and sophisticated recording techniques, creating something called studio rock. Although the Beatles disbanded in 1970, their records continued to gain in popularity. Until the death of John Lennon in 1980, and even thereafter, rumors of a comeback persisted.

The wider acceptance gained by Bob Dylan, Simon and Garfunkel, and the Beatles, among others, displayed the adaptability of rock music and the swiftness with which it changed. The folk-based performers' style came to be known as soft rock. Some groups, such as the Rolling Stones, drew fans with a blues-based, hard rock style. In the late 1960s, as experimentation with drugs moved through the counterculture and permeated the youth culture, acid rock gained popularity with its dissonant, glass-shattering sounds. Jefferson Airplane and the Grateful Dead were the two best-known acid-rock groups. Also gaining fans in those years were groups modeled on Led Zeppelin, whose loud, blues-based music combined with a macho stage show was called heavy metal.

Consciousness-raising, a popular term in the late 1960s, was applied to almost anything that enabled people to see things in different ways. Rock music's main consciousness-raising events were the festivals staged by promoters in various parts of the country. Although those who attended—perhaps as many as 2.5 million fans between 1967 and 1969—often displayed boundless enthusiasm, media coverage of the biggest festivals attracted much unfavorable attention to the music, the performers, and the fans.

The Monterey International Pop Festival in 1967 was the first large gathering of rock bands and superstars. The event that let the whole nation know that a new phenomenon had arrived, however, was the Woodstock Music and Art Fair. Held in a large pasture in the Catskill Mountains at Bethel, New York, for four days in August 1969, it appeared to be an event of young people simply coming together for a good time. But it was not a spontaneous happening. Rather, like other rock festivals, it was a well-calculated business venture. It was planned by John Roberts, a young millionaire who had graduated from the University of Pennsylvania, and his partner, Joel Rosenman, a Yale Law School graduate. Working with Michael Lang and others who gave the event stronger connections with the counterculture, they intended to make money from the performances by rock stars but also from the sale of food and souvenirs (such as posters of the late Che Guevera, the revolutionary ally of Cuba's Fidel Castro, who had been killed in 1967). They also sold movie and recording rights to the festival. One of the promoters observed that although those who came "fancied themselves as street people and flower children," he and his partners were in fact "a New York corporation capitalized at $500,000 and accounted for by Brout Issacs and Company, tenth largest body of CPAs in New York City."

Despite careful planning, events at Woodstock were so chaotic that no one was certain how many people were there. Estimates ranged between 300,000 and 460,000. They came from all over America to hear Jimi Hendrix, Joan Baez, Jefferson Airplane, The Who, the Grateful Dead, and other rock stars and groups. Traffic jams were horrendous. Torrential rains, accompanied by intense heat, made mud bathing and nude parading a natural pastime. Shortages of food, water, and medical facilities contributed further to making Woodstock a mess. In the midst of the mess, loving and sharing went on everywhere, and everywhere folks were using marijuana, LSD, barbiturates, and amphetamines. Yet, round-the-clock entertainment helped maintain a measure of orderliness—and even peacefulness. Supporters of Woodstock hailed it as an example of the better world to come. There were no signs of violence. Looking at it from a distance, mainstream America could not imagine a place for such things in their everyday lives. The generation of youth that thrived on such events wore the term *Woodstock* proudly. Others regarded it with contempt.

Four months after Woodstock, a rock festival at a stock-car racetrack near Altamont, California, was the climax to an American tour by the Rolling Stones. With about 300,000 in attendance, promoters hired members of a motorcycle gang known as Hell's Angels to keep order. From the outset the crowd appeared rough and rude. When a naked, obese man climbed on the stage and began to dance, the cyclists triggered a melee by beating him to the ground. By the end of the festival, an 18-year-old black youth had been stabbed to death, and three other people died from accidents, drug overdoses, and beatings. If that, too, was the wave of the future, a sign of cultural transitions in the making, it seemed an unsettling one.

Nonetheless, the back-to-nature notions of rock music conveyed by the festivals continued to strike a responsive chord in urban youth. At the same time, a brief turn to a gentler, more reflective style enabled rock music to continue its progress across generational lines and into the American mainstream. The evolution of rock was not over, however, as it continued to blend with folk, blues, and country music.

The big names in rock music in the mid-1970s included Elton John (the first performer to fill Dodger Stadium in Los Angeles since the Beatles had done so in 1966);

Billy Joel; and Stevie Wonder, to whom Motown Records offered contracts guaranteeing $13 million over seven years. New performers occasionally hit it big. Critics compared one of them, Bruce Springsteen, to Bob Dylan, Elvis Presley, and Buddy Holly, claiming that his style demonstrated the power that had characterized rock music in the 1960s. Springsteen's appearance on the cover of both *Time* and *Newsweek* showed the mainstreaming of rock music. So did the sale of two million Elvis Presley records within a day of Presley's death in 1977.

The evolution of rock continued, with blues-based hard rock and heavy metal increasing in popularity. Punk rockers, most notably the Sex Pistols, took things in another direction, emphasizing rebellion and featuring such things as screaming obscenities and hair dyed orange. Pop rock offered a softer sound that was more appealing to middle-of-the-road audiences. Art rock attempted to mix classical sounds with rock and jazz.

Disco was another music phenomenon of these years. Regarded initially as dance music by black singers, it captured attention with *Saturday Night Fever*, a 1978 movie starring John Travolta. The Bee Gees' album of its soundtrack sold 30 million copies worldwide. Disco blended pop, rock, and black styles, accompanied by repetitive rhythms and dance beats. Discotheques attracted dancing revelers of all ages. Disco garb, including skintight Lycra jeans and dresses slit thigh-high, appeared everywhere. The disco beat filled the airwaves. Disco record sales zoomed upward. *Newsweek* described disco as "rhythm without blues; a body trip, not a head trip. It is relentlessly upbeat and unabashedly embraces the consumer society's latest trendy goods." Disco's popularity soon faded, but for a time it was all the rage.

Popular music—rock, jazz, soul, traditional pop, country, and disco—was big business getting bigger. In 23 countries, sales of recordings totaled $8.6 billion in 1977; the U.S. share, $3.5 billion, was 28 percent higher than the previous year. Sales increased by 18 percent in the next year. Revenues surpassed the receipts of movies, the theater, and professional sports, sometimes several times over. In 1979, however, sales spiraled downward by as much as 40 percent. One reason, the Recording Industry Association of America complained, was radio's growing practice of playing record albums without commercial breaks; that encouraged listeners to tape-record new releases on their units at home.

Contemporary music accounted for nearly two-thirds of the records sold. Who bought them? Not just teenagers. Teenagers from earlier times had grown up and kept on buying. Three studies reported that in the late 1970s about 40 percent of the buyers were in their 30s and another 36 percent in their 20s; teenagers accounted for less than 25 percent of sales. Buyers of records spent large sums attending concerts, too, as big-name performers drew large, enthusiastic, and often boisterous crowds. The Rolling Stones, for example, grossed $13 million on their 1975 tour.

Stressing the moneymaking aspects of popular music obscures the fact that bands across the country were playing in clubs and bars, and sometimes just for themselves, simply because they liked the music and they liked to play. Their musical energy found a good partner in the energy of the music.

Classical music offered another creative leisure activity, and concertgoing was popular, at least among older persons. Most symphony orchestras and opera companies, however, faced annual deficits, caused not by poor attendance but by high labor and production costs. In their 1976–1977 season, the 200 largest performing arts organizations had deficits totaling an estimated $125 million. Some, such as the New York City Opera Association, were threatened with bankruptcy. After failing to reach agreements with its various unions, the association canceled its 1980–1981 season, but two months of mediation and compromise made it possible to salvage part of the season. Similar problems shortened the seasons for the North Carolina, New Jersey, Denver, and Kansas City symphonies. Because admission receipts covered only a small part of arts organizations' costs, the more performances they gave, the greater their losses. These woes extended to the lives of individual artists, for whom chronically low pay alternated with unemployment. As performers sought to better their individual lots by demanding higher wages, they put in jeopardy the organizations with which they performed.

By the 1980s, the rock music young people had found so appealing and their elders so appalling in earlier decades enjoyed a large measure of acceptance in mainstream America. Indeed, it became a standard feature of mainstream advertising. One reason was that the teenagers of the 1960s did not forsake their earlier tastes in music when they reached their thirties. Another reason is that rock music lost much of its shock quality. A third is that the varieties of rock music were so plentiful that persons who did not like one variety had plenty of other choices. The same was true of performing groups. Fans could love one and detest another. Consequently, variations of rock music thrived alongside country music, surf music, jazz, disco, and a new arrival, Jamaican reggae.

Music continued to be big business. Bruce Springsteen's *Born in the USA* sold more than 13 million copies within 18 months of its 1984 production, and his concert tour, lasting from July 1984 to October 1985, attracted some five million fans. Respondents to a *Rolling Stone* poll placed him first in six categories, and one of his singles, "Dancing in the Dark," earned him American Music Awards and Grammys. He was not alone among rock stars, as many others also enjoyed large followings.

On occasion, rock music became more than big business. It joined the big business of fund-raising. In the mid-1980s, Live Aid concerts featuring many of the most prominent stars and bands were broadcast by satellite to raise money through telethons in some 30 nations. People in need around the world benefited from millions of dollars raised by these events. In the United States, some Live Aid concerts were held for the benefit of farmers facing hard times.

Rock music's lyrics, with themes of sex and violence, worried many. The National PTA and the Parents' Music Resource Center (a group based in Washington, D.C.) urged the Recording Industry Association of America to rate its records in a system similar to the one used for motion pictures. The association refused to do so, but it recommended that its members label some of their records "Explicit Lyrics—Parental Advisory." Such measures did not appease rock music's harshest critics. Allan Bloom, a professor at the University of Chicago, seemed to reflect their sentiments in his attack on rock music in his best-selling *The Closing of the American Mind*. He contended that rock music "has one appeal only, a barbaric appeal, to sexual desire—not love, not *eros*, but sexual desire undeveloped and untutored....Rock gives children, on a silver platter, with all the public authority of the entertainment industry, everything parents always used to tell them they had to wait for until they grew up and would understand later."

Those who worried about rock music had more to worry about when rap became popular in the late 1980s. Initially rappers mixed bits of songs, repeated passages, and added rhythmic scratching sounds as background for recited lyrics, or raps. At first rap was a street phenomenon accompanied by acrobatic displays in break dancing and a hip-hop look featuring, among other things, fancy sneakers, caps turned backward, and heavy gold jewelry. Soon it made its way into recording studios, and by the 1980s it gained considerable popularity for its protests (typically as insults) against poverty, violence, and racism. Sales surveys found that the biggest market for rap was among suburban white youth.

Before the end of the decade the lyrics of several rap groups, such as Slick Rick and 2 Live Crew, drew sharp criticism for their explicit description of sexual organs and activities and for seeming to encourage violence against women. To many, the lyrics were offensive or unintelligible. When a sheriff in Florida brought an obscenity complaint against a store owner for selling records of 2 Live Crew, a U.S. district judge convicted the owner after months of hearings. The leader of 2 Live Crew and two band members were arrested and brought to trial too, but a jury found them not guilty of obscenity charges. The jury foreman acknowledged that members of the jury found it difficult to understand the key piece of evidence, a tape recording of the performance that had led to the defendants' arrest.

The difficulties faced by symphony orchestras, opera companies, and composers suggested that classical music was no longer a central feature of American culture. Operating deficits were common. Listening audiences had never been diverse, but in the words of an anonymous administrator quoted by the *New York Times*, they were now "white, rich, and almost dead." Portions of their audiences were tired of the standby classical pieces by great composers of the past; other portions had no use for the avant-garde works of contemporary composers. Imitations of classical forms by contemporary composers did not work either.

Moreover, as younger generations matured they generally failed to replace their popular tastes, which were so different from those of previous generations of youth, with classical ones. Linda Sanders explained it as follows in her 1996 article in *Civilization:*

It was one thing for educated adults to tell hormone-crazed teenagers back in the 1950s that "Blue Suede Shoes" was worthless trash. It was quite another for educated adults to try to tell other educated adults in the 1980s that blues, reggae, and minimalism (or, for that matter, the Beatles, Bruce Springsteen, and Prince) were either musically or spiritually inferior to Bach and Beethoven.

Add to that the maturing generations' opinion that classical music was for the intellectual and social elite, and it is easy to see why classical music was losing its appeal and its audiences.

Technology also caused problems for performers of classical music. The intensity and spontaneity of live performances were unmatched, but if precision and purity were what mattered, these could be found by listening to compact disks through high-quality sound systems. For the price of a ticket, a music lover could purchase a couple of choice compact discs and listen to them repeatedly, without the hassle of attending a concert.

Performing groups therefore had to change their programming, the staging of performances, promotion methods, and general understandings of themselves. They had to find the balance between perpetuating a sacred classical canon and being a community center for the enjoyment of music and advancement of musical knowledge (Marty 1997, 67–70, 120–21, 210–12, 283–86; *Daily Life Online*, "Recreational Life: Music," in Marty, *Daily Life in the United States, 1960–1990*, http://dailylife.greenwood.com).

SPORTS AND ATHLETICS

In keeping with his image as a young and vigorous president, John F. Kennedy urged the American people to get out of their armchairs and do something to get in shape. In fact, he charged the President's Council on Youth Fitness with developing a program to improve the physical condition of the nation's schoolchildren. The council proposed standards for measuring fitness and urged schools to provide children with at least 15 minutes of vigorous activity daily. Running became a popular activity, even an obsession, for many people, and the commercial world encouraged a running craze. German shoes imported to meet new demands included Adidas, designed by Adi Dassler, and Puma, the product of his brother Rudi. From Japan came Tiger Marathons. New Balance, a Boston manufacturer of orthopedic footwear, designed a new type of shoe for runners. Before long other companies produced their own versions. Reports on testing and rating of shoes appeared as regular features in magazines on running, and shoes became status symbols.

Other sports such as tennis and golf also flourished, as did spectator sports. Major League Baseball gained fans in cities through the expansion or relocation of franchises. In the process, other fans were left behind or left out. The process began in 1953, when the Boston Braves moved to Milwaukee; the St. Louis Browns to Baltimore in 1954, becoming the Orioles; and the Philadelphia Athletics to Kansas City in 1955. The bigger news came in 1958, when the Brooklyn Dodgers moved to Los Angeles and the New York Giants to San Francisco, reflecting the westward shift of the population in general. Over the next dozen years, a fan-boggling shuffling of franchises occurred. Three more existing franchises moved: the Kansas City As to Oakland, the Milwaukee Braves to Atlanta, and the Washington Senators to Minneapolis–St. Paul, becoming the Minnesota Twins. Eight new ones were created: the Los Angeles/Anaheim Angels; the Washington Senators, becoming the Rangers when the team moved to Dallas–Fort Worth; the Houston Astros; the New

York Mets; the Montreal Expos; the San Diego Padres; the Kansas City Royals; and the Seattle Pilots, which became the Milwaukee Brewers. The expansion prompted the American and National Leagues to form two divisions each in 1969, with league playoffs determining competitors in the World Series.

Baseball fans had new records to talk about during those years: The Yankee's Roger Maris hit 61 home runs in 1961, breaking Babe Ruth's 34-year-old record. The fact that his teammate, Mickey Mantle, was close on his heels made the race for the record all the more exciting. The next year Maury Wills stole 104 bases for the Los Angeles Dodgers, breaking Ty Cobb's previous record of 96. His teammate, Sandy Koufax, struck out 18 batters in a nine-inning game. In 1965, Koufax struck out a record 382 in the season and pitched a perfect game, his third no-hitter. Television's coverage of such feats made them nationally celebrated events.

Developments in football made it possible for that sport to challenge baseball's dominance as the national pastime. The National Football League (NFL) and the American Football League (AFL) merged in 1966 and agreed to a playoff game between the leagues. Thus, in 1967, the Super Bowl was born. At first the NFL dominated, with the Green Bay Packers winning the first two Super Bowls. In 1969, however, Joe Namath, the charismatic quarterback of the New York Jets, led his AFL team to victory over the Baltimore Colts.

These were interesting years in boxing, too, as much outside the ring as inside it. A young athlete from Louisville gained fame by his actions in the ring and notoriety by his words outside of it. Cassius Marcellus Clay, the 1960 light-heavyweight gold medal winner in the Olympics, came into his heavyweight title match with Sonny Liston four years later as an 8-to-1 underdog, but he won. Then, he announced that he had joined the Nation of Islam, renounced his "slave name," and, following the lead of another black Muslim, assumed the name of Cassius X. A few weeks later he said that henceforth he would be known as Muhammad Ali, adding another dimension to controversies about him. More than any other heavyweight champion, except possibly Joe Louis in the 1940s, Ali became the subject of conversations across the land, and controversies involving him would become more intense later in the decade.

The popularity of bicycling increased tremendously during the 20th century. Lionandblue|Dreamstime.com.

Despite Kennedy's push for fitness and the importance of professional sporting evenings in the daily lives of many Americans, it is hardly accurate to say the nation was immersed in a fitness craze by the late 1960s. Many Americans continued to lead sedentary lives. Still, running claimed the interest and time of millions of Americans. Many runners became insatiable consumers of running gear, causing rapid growth of new companies. Nike, a company founded in 1972, soon gained a dominant role in many sports.

Bicycling reached new levels of popularity in the early 1970s, when for the first time since 1897 Americans purchased more bicycles annually than automobiles; 60 percent of the bicycles were purchased by adults. Other nonteam sports such as golf and tennis held their appeal, and multitudes were hooked on team sports made for the occasional athlete, such as slow-pitch softball.

Spectator sports, however, particularly as they were carried into homes on television, consumed far more of the ordinary American's time. Regular-season games drew substantial audiences, but playoff games hooked viewers to a much greater extent. The playoffs that gained enormous popularity in the 1960s and 1970s were the NCAA men's basketball tournaments played each March and April. The astonishing success of the UCLA teams, coached by John Wooden, was particularly intriguing. After winning the championships in 1964 and 1965, UCLA missed the next year, but, then, for seven consecutive years, 1967 to 1974, they were the big winners.

Other records, especially those established over long periods, gripped sports fans—especially if they contained an element of controversy. When Hank Aaron broke Babe Ruth's career home run record by hitting his 715th on April 8, 1974, some wondered if he could have done it if he had not played about 25 additional games as a result of the lengthening of the Major League Baseball season from 154 games to 162 in 1962. Denny McLain's 31-victory season for the Detroit Tigers in 1968 was made more interesting by McLain's reckless lifestyle, which ultimately cut short his career and landed him in jail. Other events in sports proved controversial, such as the decision of the American League to install a gimmick advocated by the unconventional owner of the Oakland Athletics, Charles Finley: The designated hitter, known as the DH, became the regular pinch hitter for pitchers in 1973. The National League refused to use the DH, creating odd situations when teams from the two leagues met annually in the World Series and All-Star games.

Most controversial among sports fans was heavyweight champion Muhammad Ali, whose request for conscientious objector status on the basis of his adherence to Muslim teachings was denied. For refusing to be inducted into the military, Ali was arrested on April 28, 1967, given a five-year prison sentence, and fined $10,000. Boxing authorities had earlier stripped him of his title. An outrage, said some. Just what he deserved, said others. Ali, always a fountain of words on any subject, had his own say.

The power structure seems to want to starve me out. I mean, the punishment, five years in jail, ten-thousand-dollar fine, ain't enough. They want to stop me from working. Not only in this country but out of it. Not even a license to fight for charity. And that's in this twentieth century. You read about these things in dictatorship countries where a man don't go along with this or that and he is completely not allowed to work or to earn a decent living. (Ali, press conference in May 1967)

By the 1970s and early 1980s, physical fitness had taken a more important place in American lives. In particular, running continued to be a popular activity, so much so that Jim Fixx's *The Complete Book of Running* found 620,000 buyers in 1978. Health clubs, with their elaborate exercise equipment, prospered by attracting men and women who spent their days behind desks. Stock-car racing, widely regarded as a blue-collar sport, attracted many participants and fans, particularly in the South.

Around home, skateboarding gained in popularity, particularly among teenagers. Sometimes skateboards were used for stunts, sometimes simply as a sporting way to get to school. Before long skateboarding became competitive, with cash prizes awarded in regional events. Parents who held their breath or turned away as their offspring performed daring stunts must have been surprised when a study by the Consumer Product Safety Commission in 1975 showed that skateboarding ranked 25th in danger among activities measured, whereas bicycling was rated the most dangerous. An alternative to skateboards made a quiet arrival in 1980 when Rollerblade, Inc., a Minneapolis firm founded by a 20-year-old Canadian hockey player, perfected the design for in-line roller skates with "blades" of polyurethane wheels and molded boots like those worn by skiers.

Sporting events, such as Muhammad Ali's regaining the heavyweight title by beating Joe Frazier in 1975 and losing it to Leon Spinks three years later, gave sports fans something to talk about, even if these matches were carried only on closed-circuit television. Other subjects of conversation were the skyrocketing salaries of athletes made possible when they gained free agency rights. Fans began to get a taste of things to come when O. J. Simpson agreed to a three-year, $2.9 million deal to complete his football career with the Buffalo Bills and when baseball player Jim "Catfish" Hunter left the Oakland As to sign a contract with the New York Yankees in 1975 for $2.85 million. Hunter led the Yankees to championships in 1977 and 1978.

A different kind of conversation began at the 1976 Super Bowl, when television cameras panning the sidelines focused on the Dallas Cowboys cheerleaders. Dressed in tight-fitting, low-cut, skimpy outfits, they drew oohs and ahhs from male television viewers and complaints from those who considered this another instance of sexual exploitation for commercial purposes. But then, everything done in professional sports—and much of what occurred in college sports, too—was designed to have consumer appeal. Highly paid stars in professional sports played the same role as did the stars in the movie industry: their success at the box office mattered more than their success on the field, although the two were usually inseparable.

Major League Baseball tested its place in the hearts of many Americans when a seven-week players' strike interrupted the 1981 season. The strike caused the middle third of the schedule to be canceled, resulting in the Major Leagues' first split season. The origins of the discord between players and management lay in legal actions taken by players in the mid-1970s to gain the right for veteran players to sign with other teams as free agents. When the owners' absolute power over players was broken, they established a system that required the loss of a free agent to be compensated in the form of a player from the team with which the free agent had signed. In the impasse that followed, fans were caught in the middle and left with a gameless midsummer.

In 1982, the National Football League (NFL) faced a similar situation. No games were played during a 57-day strike. In 1987, though, when the season was interrupted by a 24-day strike by players over rules surrounding free agency, management canceled games on the first weekend but then fielded teams made up of replacement players and regulars who drifted back. When the players decided to go back to work, the owners told them they could not play immediately and would not be paid. The National Labor Relations Board ruled in the players' favor and ordered the NFL to pay striking players more than $20 million in lost wages and incentive bonuses for the game they had missed. As with baseball, the fans were on the sidelines—mostly disgusted with both players and management.

The United States hosted the 1984 Summer Olympics in Los Angeles. Broadcast by ABC, the event's 168 hours on the air drew ratings higher than expected, and it produced several heroes: Carl Lewis won gold medals in the 100-meter dash, the 200-meter dash, the 400-meter relay, and the long jump, duplicating what Jesse Owens had done in 1936 in Berlin. In contrast to earlier times, the rules of the Olympics allowed Lewis to earn about $1 million yearly and still compete as an amateur. Another hero was the Olympics' real crowd-pleaser, Mary Lou Retton, a 16-year-old whose five medals included a gold in all-around gymnastics. Her feat gained her many commercial endorsements.

By 1988, the Olympics were greeted as welcome television fare by millions of viewers. To accommodate their interests, the Winter Games, held in Calgary, Canada, were extended to 16 days. But ratings were disappointing, partly because the United States won only 2 of the 46 gold medals, in addition to silver and three bronzes. The Summer Games, held in Seoul, Korea, also lasted 16 days. Although the competition provided enjoyable viewing, much of the attention went to controversies concerning the use of drugs that had been banned—particularly anabolic steroids. Taking steroids makes athletes stronger and enables them to train harder, putting them at a competitive advantage, but it also has harmful side effects. Altogether, 18 athletes were disqualified before or during the games, including Canada's Ben Johnson, who had defeated Carl Lewis in the 100-meter dash.

Physical fitness participants in this decade wanted to look good, feel good, lose weight, have fun, make friends, develop personal discipline, and, above all, stay well. Avid runners claimed that running gave them more daily energy, sharpened their mental edge, kept them in good physical condition, and increased their resistance to illness. Tennis players were just as avid about their sport, although they made fewer claims for its benefits. Bowlers, golfers, skiers, bikers, and participants in other sports were avid, too, but their fitness claims were less audible. Many of them considered their participation as recreational rather than fitness-driven.

Private health clubs eagerly exploited the fitness interests of many Americans. The number of clubs increased from 7,500 in 1980 (not including YMCAs or golf, tennis, and other sport-specific clubs) to more than 20,000 by the end of the decade. Membership in health and fitness clubs reached about 40 million before the end of the decade. The quest for fitness could be satisfied in one's home, too, as the popularity of *Jane Fonda's Workout Book* (1981) bears witness. In addition to providing an exercise regimen, this book by an actress turned political activist and now fitness promoter included dietary advice and musings on ways for women to maintain good health. A best-seller, it opened the way for Fonda's further commercial ventures—exercise studios, cassette tapes with music to accompany workouts, and an exercise video. Other exercise promoters, such as Richard Simmons, also produced videos for use at home, and sales of home exercise equipment by Nordic Track, Nautilus, and other companies boomed. So did sales of improved equipment for outdoor sports (Marty 1997, 38–40, 123–25, 213–14, 286–89; *Daily Life Online,*

"Recreational Life: Sports," in Marty, *Daily Life in the United States, 1960–1990*, http://dailylife.greenwood.com).

TELEVISION, MOVIES, AND MORE

On May 9, 1961, Newton Minnow, the new head of the Federal Communication Commission, spoke at the National Association of Broadcasters. As the following excerpt indicates, he stunned the audience of television executives, advertisers, and producers with a devastating attack on the medium and its impact on American daily life:

But, when television is bad, nothing is worse. I invite you to sit down in front of your television set when your station goes on the air and stay there without a book, magazine, newspaper, profit-and-loss sheet, or rating book to distract you—and keep your eyes glued to that set until the station signs off. I can assure you that you will observe a vast wasteland.

You will see a procession of game shows, violence, audience-participation shows, formula comedies about totally unbelievable families, blood and thunder, mayhem, violence, sadism, murder, western bad men, western good men, private eyes, gangsters, more violence, and cartoons. And, endlessly, commercials—many screaming, cajoling, and offending. And most of all boredom. (*Chicago Tribune*, April 24, 2001, 17; a reprint of Minnow's 1961 address)

Minnow threatened to review station licenses when they came up for renewal unless the broadcasters and advertisers took a serious look at their programming. Although little ultimately changed in broadcast options, primarily because of public demand for the shows, television producers did begin to offer other forms of programming and actually aired shows with more appeal and substance. Some of the best, most provocative shows did appear in the decades that followed.

A more ominous challenge to the major broadcast corporations and their subsidiaries than Minnow's threats, however, emerged in the 1970s and 1980s. Cable television existed as early as the 1940s but did not become a successful alternative to the major networks until Home Box Office (HBO) sold viewing options to subscribers in 1972. By 1975, local cable operators had begun to provide services to an expanding audience of viewers. Coaxial cables could now feed directly into individual homes and connect potential audiences to a whole new set of viewing options. By the 1990s, close to 150 channels became available and millions of Americans had added the option to their television sets. The impact of cable television affected everything from news programs to specialty shows.

Although Americans in the 1980s enjoyed a cafeteria of entertainment possibilities, the main fare for most remained television. Thanks to the Federal Communications Commission (FCC), what they watched on TV underwent certain changes. Mark Fowler, appointed by President Reagan to head the FCC, regarded television as just another appliance, "a toaster with pictures," that should be treated like a business, nothing more nor less. Under Fowler's leadership, the FCC in 1981 discontinued rules limiting the number of minutes per hour that could be devoted to advertising and stopped requiring television stations to play a public service role.

A 1990 Gallup poll showed that the percentage of persons who considered watching television as their favorite way to spend an evening declined from 46 percent in 1974 to 24 percent in 1990, no doubt reflecting their complaints about the quality of programming. During those years, dining out, going to movies or the theater, playing cards and other games, dancing, and listening to music showed comparably sharp declines in popularity. Taking their places were activities not included in the 1974 survey, such as jogging, working in crafts, and gardening. Reading and spending time at home with the family showed slight increases. Nonetheless, the average American spent some 28 hours in front of a television set each week. Many of those were daytime hours, as soap operas and talk shows remained popular (*Daily Life Online*, "Diversions: Television," in Marty, *Daily Life in the United States, 1960–1990*, http://dailylife.greenwood.com).

By the mid-1970s about half of American households had two or more television sets. The sets had become, in historian Cecelia Tichi's words, the home's "electronic hearth," the focal point in a room. Viewers absorbed their radiating warmth and flickering images. They were also a home's window to the world, as the programs and commercials shaped viewers' needs, interests, habits, and values. Television's manipulated portrayals of reality became indistinguishable from reality itself (Tichi 1991, 8–9). "As seen on TV . . ." validated claims and opinions.

Given television's dominant role in American life, it is not surprising that its images altered viewers' ways of apprehending the world. In contrast to the way one reads—from left to right across a line, top of the page to the bottom, page after page—television follows no predictable or essential lines. Viewers move quickly, not necessarily randomly but seemingly so, from one scene to another with subtle transitions or no transitions at all. Reading is another matter: One *learns* to read books, magazines, and newspapers, typically going through "reading-readiness" exercises and then moving from elementary to more complex material.

No one *learns* to watch television. Many programs, and particularly commercials, are designed to simultaneously hold the attention of 6-year-olds, 16-year-olds, and 60-year-olds. As television holds viewers' attention hour after hour it becomes what Marie Winn has labeled "the plug-in drug." Viewers may not be in a perpetual state of stupor—perhaps they cheer about what they see or talk back to those they hear—but they are addicted to viewing nonetheless. In her book *The Plug-In Drug* (1977) Winn described how the addiction changes viewers' ways of learning, thinking, and being, as well as their relationships with others and their environment. She focused particularly on television's narcotic effects on children, but adults suffered from them as well. These effects were by now widespread (Winn; *Daily Life Online*, "Television, Movies, and More: Television," in Marty, *Daily Life in the United States, 1960–1990*, http://dailylife.greenwood.com).

FOR MORE INFORMATION

Bloom, Allen. *The Closing of the American Mind*. New York: Simon & Schuster, 1987.

Deardorff, D. L. *Sports: A Reference Guide and Critical Commentary, 1980–1999*. Westport, CT: Greenwood Press, 2000.

DeCurtis, A., and J. Henke, eds. *The Rolling Stone Illustrated History of Rock & Roll: The Definitive History of the Most Important Artists and Their Music.* New York: Random House, 1992.

Greenfield, J. "They Changed Rock, Which Changed the Culture, Which Changed the US." In *Rock Music in America,* ed. J. Podell. New York: H. W. Wilson, 1987.

Haskins, J., and K. Benson. *The 60s Reader.* New York: Viking Kestrel, 1988.

Kenney, W. H. *Recorded Music in American Life: The Phonograph and Popular Memory, 1890–1945.* New York: Oxford University Press, 1999.

London, H. *Closing the Circle: A Cultural History of the Rock Revolution.* Chicago: Nelson-Hall, 1984.

Marcus, G. *Mystery Train: Images of America in Rock 'n' Roll Music.* New York: E. P. Dutton, 1982.

Marty, Myron A. *Daily Life in the United States, 1960–1990: Decades of Discord.* Westport, CT: Greenwood Press, 1997; also available online as *Daily Life Online,* in Marty, *Daily Life in the United States, 1960–1990,* http://dailylife.greenwood.com).

Morgan, E. P. *The 60s Experience: Hard Lessons about Modern America.* Philadelphia: Temple University Press, 1991.

Rader, B. C. *American Sports: From the Age of Folk Games to the Age of Spectators.* Englewood Cliff, NJ: Prentice-Hall, 1983.

Sanders, L. "Facing the Music." *Civilization* (May/June 1996): 38–39.

Szatmary, D. P. *Rockin' in Time: A Social History of Rock and Roll.* 2nd ed. Englewood Cliffs, NJ: Prentice Hall, 1991.

Tichi, Cecelia. *Electronic Hearth: Creating an American Television Culture.* New York: Oxford University Press, 1991.

Winn, Marie. *The Plug-In Drug.* New York: Viking Press, 1977.

Religious Life

OVERVIEW

Matters of faith and religious practice cannot be ignored if we wish to understand everyday life in America. Jewish children had *bar mitzvahs* and *bas mitzvahs*, Christian children celebrated first communion and confirmation, and Muslims learned early in life the place of prayer in their daily routines. Dozens of religious denominations and sects flourished. Leaders continued to strive for church unity, even though their efforts had few discernible effects on individual lives. Similarly, they advocated positions on social issues of war and peace, racial and civil strife, economic justice, and world hunger. Issues of social activism, theology, and missionary efforts gave religions increased visibility and new congregants. They also divided religious bodies.

Many Americans found inspiration, guidance, and fellowship in their churches, synagogues, mosques, and meetinghouses; but because those were human institutions, they were also places for contests over doctrine and practice, and disputes over budgets, programs, personnel, and facilities. Many longtime church members could recount strife with fellow members in their congregations, and official and unofficial schisms within denominations remained common. That may explain why many who claimed to have religious convictions had no formal religious affiliations and why polling data on church membership and attendance fluctuated (*Daily Life Online*, "Spiritual Matters: Religion in Everyday Life," in Marty, *Daily Life in the United States, 1960–1990*, http://dailylife.greenwood.com).

BY THE NUMBERS, 1960s

A revival of interest in religion as the 1960s approached was another sign that many had come to regard religion as important to the needs of their daily lives. Church membership and participation seemed less likely than in the past to be traditions continued from generation to generation. In the later 1950s, church membership increased at a rate slightly higher than the growth of the population, reaching an all-time high in 1960. Nearly two-thirds of the U.S. population claimed church membership.

Did increases in membership mean that church-related activities were a part of the daily life of large numbers of Americans? Polls taken in the 1960s revealed a relatively high measure of participation, but the picture was mixed. A Louis Harris poll in 1965, for example, showed that roughly half the U.S. population claimed to attend church weekly. The numbers for Protestants were substantially lower than for Catholics. Another poll reported that regular weekly church attendance declined from 49 percent in 1958 to 45 percent in 1965. A third poll indicated that in 1957, 69 percent of those polled believed the influence of religion was growing, but that figure dropped to 33 percent in 1965. In fact, 45 percent thought religion's influence had declined.

Numbers aside, religious ferment in those years was noteworthy. A spirit of ecumenism (promoting unity among religions) became evident. At the very least, interdenominational rivalries cooled. The editor of a Lutheran periodical probably spoke for many when he wrote near the end of 1963 that "some of the expressions Protestants have long been using about Roman Catholics will necessarily and in all fairness have to be drastically qualified. Wince though we might at first, we won't be able to escape thinking and speaking of Romans in much more deliberate and 'defrosted' tones."

Nonetheless, although desires for unity led to discussion of mergers and collaborative efforts, church denominations maintained their identities and distinctive practices. Individual members did not witness sweeping changes in their own places of worship. To a greater extent than their churches' leaders, they had probably always been more open to acceptance of religious pluralism—that is, to the sense that rivalries between denominations were self-defeating. Supporters of pluralism believed that allowing the free practice of religion and avoiding the concentration of power and authority in one church was in accord with American ideals and preserved the freedom of all.

Members of the Christian group "Children of God" sing before sitting down for lunch at their headquarters in Los Angeles. AP/Wide World Photos.

Sometimes powerful forces caused church members to ignore denominational lines. Protestants, no matter what their formal affiliations were or their views on evangelist Billy Graham's methods or message, could not ignore him or the movement he represented. In the years following his huge rally in Madison Square Garden in New York in 1957, Graham intertwined his message of the Christian Gospel with expressions of faith in American progress. The fact that he became a favorite of presidents and the news media helped to establish him as an important public figure. At the same time, his rallies broadcast over television brought him into the private lives of millions of Americans. Other evangelists built followings by emulating Graham. Going further, adapting their preaching styles to the settings of show business, these televangelists carried on lucrative ministries (*Daily Life Online*, "Religious Life: Religion," in Marty, *Daily Life in the United States, 1960–1990*, http://dailylife.greenwood.com).

BY THE NUMBERS, 1970s

In 1967, Gallup polls showed that 98 out of every 100 Americans had a preference for some church. About two-thirds called themselves Protestants and one-fourth said they were Catholics. Jews accounted for 3 percent, and "all others" the same. The slight changes in the next eight years might lead one to believe that not much changed in the world of religion, in that the total expressing some preference dropped by only four percentage points. The numbers claiming to be Protestant or Jewish declined slightly, and Catholic and "all other" preferences showed slight increases.

But, as early as 1968, evidence began to grow that the American people were pessimistic about the state of religion and morality. A Gallup poll that year showed that 50 percent of those polled believed life was worse as far as religion was concerned, and 78 percent said morals had declined. A series of five polls conducted over a period of 11 years showed a decided increase in the number of persons who saw religion's influence as waning. The 67 percent in the polling sample who believed religious influence was diminishing matched almost exactly the 69 percent in 1957 who saw it as increasing. Between 1968 and 1970, the respondents believing religious influence was being lost increased from 67 to 75 percent. By 1974, however, that figure had dropped to 56 percent, confirming notions that those were years of real uncertainty about the status of religion.

There were other signs of an uncertain future for mainstream religions. Total attendance in churches and synagogues declined, reaching the point where only 4 in 10 claimed to be regular members. Whereas regular church attendance reported by Protestants declined from 39 to 37 percent during these years, among Catholics the decline was from 66 to 55 percent. Financial contributions also declined, and, measured in constant dollars, money spent on church construction decreased in five years by more than one-third from the $1 billion spent on it in 1970. Yet another worrisome matter was a sharp decline in the numbers of persons studying in seminaries to be pastors and priests.

One explanation for the uncertain state of church membership lay in changes in the age distribution within the population. The disproportionately youthful population apparently felt less need for religious affiliations, or perhaps they believed churches failed to serve their needs. Changes in family structures and commitments and increased demands on family time also had affected involvement in religious activities. Some individuals probably became dropouts to protest against their churches and denominations for positions taken on social issues, whether too liberal or too conservative.

Perceptions of decline must also take into account the search by many for alternatives to the religions they had come to question. In almost all denominations, there were underground movements of individuals who believed that traditional places of worship had become stagnant and unresponsive. They sought to create a different kind of worshipping community, simpler in structure and free of trappings and traditions. Often those communities were simply groups of men and women who gathered in the homes of their members. Few lasted more than a year or two (*Daily Life Online*, "Religious Life: Religion," in Marty, *Daily Life in the United States, 1960–1990*, http://dailylife.greenwood.com).

BY THE NUMBERS, 1980s

Polls showed that the religious involvement of the American people remained relatively constant throughout the 1980s. About 92 percent of the American people had a religious preference, 68 percent said they were members of a church or synagogue, 40 percent said they attended church or synagogue in a given week, and 56 percent claimed religion to be very important in their lives. Mainstream denominations suffered general declines in membership, however, whereas more conservative ones held their own or gained.

Alongside traditional religious commitments, something described loosely as New Age gave expression to spiritual sentiments. Its basic doctrine, according to *Time* magazine, was "you can be whatever you want to be."

Defining New Age, though, is difficult. It includes, says *Time*, "a whole cornucopia of beliefs, fads, rituals; some subscribe to some parts, some to others. All in all, the New Age does express a cloudy sort of religion, claiming vague connections with both Christianity and the major faiths of the East, plus an occasional dab of pantheism and sorcery. The underlying faith is a lack of faith in the orthodoxies of rationalism, high technology, routine living, spiritual law and order."

It is not surprising that in the postmodern 1980s there were organizations, publications, radio stations, and some 2,500 bookstores to serve the growing number of persons attracted to the sort of spirituality New Age offered.

Conflict was common within religious denominations. In some instances, as in the Southern Baptist Convention, conservatives faced off with moderates over interpretation of the Bible. Year after year, the conservatives consolidated their power and began to place limits on what seminary professors could teach. Some, whose teaching did not meet their standards, were removed. Here and there, and from time to time, moderates made modest gains in efforts to keep the conservatives from controlling everything in the church body, but before the decade ended, it was apparent that moderates would soon have little power.

In other denominations—the United Presbyterian Church in the United States, for example, and the Episcopal Church—differences over policies and practices created discord. As earlier, ordination of women and the churches' positions on Latter-Day Saints (LDS), whose members are known as Mormons, found itself at sharper-than-usual odds with the Reorganized Church of Jesus Christ of Latter Day Saints (RLDS) over a document purporting to show that Joseph Smith, founder of the LDS, had wanted his son to be his successor. Joseph Smith III had led his followers to Missouri and formed the RLDS, whereas Brigham Young had persuaded many Mormons to go with him to Utah and establish a new kingdom there. The document, "discovered" by an accomplished forger, did nothing to keep the LDS from being the fastest-growing denomination in the United States.

Despite long-standing opposition by Protestant denominations to diplomatic recognition of the Vatican, President Ronald Reagan appointed an ambassador to that political state and ecclesiastical entity in 1984. A coalition of Protestant groups responded by filing a lawsuit to nullify the new relationship, claiming it violated guarantees of separation of church and state.

In the United States, discord existed within the Roman Catholic Church, too, providing further evidence that the church once run with unquestioned authority now had to cope with dissent and disobedience. In 1986, the Vatican ordered Father Charles E. Curran, who taught moral theology at the Catholic University of America, to retract his statements on the moral authority of the church on such matters as birth control, abortion, homosexuality, premarital sex, and divorce. When Curran said that for reasons of conscience he could not change his positions, the Vatican withdrew his credentials for teaching as a Catholic theologian. Around the same time, the Vatican reassigned some of the authority of Seattle's Archbishop Raymond G. Hunthausen. It considered his teachings on birth control, homosexuality, and nuclear arms to be too liberal.

Though the discord in those instances involved a scholar and an archbishop, there was little doubt that the views of Curran and Hunthausen were shared widely among Catholic laity. Perhaps that was why the Vatican felt it necessary to censure them, hoping its action would keep discord from spreading. To reinforce the church's position on its authority—as well as on such matters as birth control, medical procedures using artificial means in human reproduction (in vitro fertilization), and abortion—Pope John Paul II undertook a highly publicized tour of the United States in September 1987. His reception appeared enthusiastic in the nine cities he visited.

Around the same time, however, charges of sexual misconduct made against prominent members of the clergy brought Catholicism unfavorable attention. Most prominent among those charged was the archbishop of Atlanta; revelations of his intimate relationship with a woman led him to resign. Accusations against parish priests, popular in their own communities, caused greater concern. Accusations of misconduct gained credibility by reports of a 25-year celibacy study done by a former priest, now a psychotherapist, that reported significant degrees of heterosexual and homosexual involvement among priests. Church officials claimed that because the study was based on interviews with persons who were in treatment for sexual misconduct or who had been touched by such misconduct, it was distorted. The issue of sexual abuses by clergy, however, refused to go away. The church faced lawsuits and clergy were indicted in the 1990s (see the section on Religion in Daily Life in Chapter 4) and after on sexual abuse charges. Various dioceses paid out millions of dollars to settle lawsuits and claims.

For television evangelists, 1987 was a bad year. It started when Oral Roberts, one of the best known among them, announced that God would call him "home" unless his followers contributed $8 million to a medical fund he had started. The money arrived, but Roberts's fellow evangelists thought his announcement had tarnished fund-raising practices for all of them. They all depended on contributions from viewers and could not afford to have their lifelines jeopardized.

The more widely publicized scandal occurred in 1987 when other televangelists accused Jim Bakker, the leading public figure in an organization known as PTL (Praise the Lord, or People That Love), of an extramarital sexual encounter. In addition, they claimed, Bakker had paid more than $250,000 to silence the person with whom it occurred. One of the accusers, the Reverend Jimmy Swaggart, remarked that "the gospel of Jesus Christ has never sunk to such a level as it has today." When the scandal forced Bakker to resign, PTL leaders asked televangelist Jerry Falwell to rescue the organization. Despite strenuous fund-raising efforts, PTL soon declared bankruptcy. The entire scandal placed under further scrutiny the practices televangelists used to raise funds and called into question their high incomes and lavish lifestyles. Eventually Bakker was convicted of 24 counts of fraud, sentenced to a prison term of 45 years, and fined $500,000. In the next year, Jimmy Swaggart himself was forced to confess to his Baton Rouge, Louisiana, congregation that he had committed a "sin," later reported as involving sexual misconduct. His denomination, the Assemblies of God, suspended him from preaching for a year, and when he refused to comply, it removed him from the ministry. Before long he was preaching again as an independent minister.

Attempts continued by what came to be known as the New Christian Right to change American institutions. For example, it sought to have public schools teach theories concerning the origins of the universe and humankind based on a literal interpretation of the Bible. Advocating what it called scientific creationism, the New Christian Right argued that schools taught theories of evolution as though they were a religion and that their own theories merited equal time. Laws in Arkansas and Louisiana requiring schools to teach "creation science" were ruled unconstitutional in both instances, but that did not deter leaders of the New Christian Right from trying to find new ways to accomplish their goals—ways that usually met the same fate in the courts.

The New Christian Right also pushed for a constitutional amendment that would have allowed voluntary individual or group prayer in public schools, overturning the 1962 Supreme Court decision it judged objectionable. President Reagan sent a proposed amendment to Congress in 1982, but it died in committee. The intensity of the Christian Right's commitment to an amendment increased when a Supreme Court ruling in 1985 seemed to put more mortar in the wall of separation between church and state by invalidating an Alabama law that permitted a one-minute period of silence daily "for meditation or voluntary prayer" in public schools (Marty 1997, 52–56, 169–73, 230–34, 317–20; *Daily Life Online*, "Religious Life: Religion," in Marty, *Daily Life in the United States, 1960–1990*, http://dailylife.greenwood.com).

CHRISTIANITY REVITALIZED AND FUNDAMENTALISM

Some who sought alternatives to traditional forms of religious practice found it in the Jesus movement that sprang up in California in the late 1960s. The first ones in the movement were known to the bemused public as "Jesus freaks," young persons claiming to be born again. Their lives had lost meaning and purpose, they said, and finding it neither in drugs nor in the counterculture, they responded emotionally to calls to focus everything on Jesus. Their ecstatic version of faith resembled that displayed in earlier Christian revivals. For many, it was the "ultimate trip." The apparent innocence, simplicity, and spirit of community displayed by the Jesus people helped the movement to spread rapidly, often through campus networks. In 1971, the Religious News Writers Association called the Jesus movement the news event of the year in religion.

The most radical members in the Jesus movement formed highly disciplined "families" and repudiated everything they regarded as "establishment." Typically living communally, sharing everything, they required their members to renounce their biological families and the churches where they had been raised. Distraught parents, believing their offspring to be the victims of mind control, sometimes tried to retrieve them with the aid of deprogrammers. In less radical ways, the Jesus movement broadened its boundaries. The emotions of the movement drew favorable responses from persons in established Christian churches who would not have considered joining it in its informal communal or coffeehouse days. Just as effects of the counterculture had seeped into the lives of people in mainstream America at the very time when it was itself vanishing from the scene, so it happened with the Jesus movement. Its effects, particularly its born-again themes, continued after the movement itself was gone.

The continuation resulted in part from the work of musicians such as Pat Boone and Johnny Cash, who fused Christian lyrics with rock music to reach vast numbers with the Jesus movement's message of sin and salvation. Families playing the musicians' tapes learned the words and tunes without connecting them to their origins. Church youth groups that went to see *Godspell*, which opened a long run on May 17, 1971, had, by then, no reason to connect the lyrics to the movement that inspired it. Nor, as moms and dads sang along with their records of Andrew Lloyd Webber's popular musical *Jesus Christ Superstar*, which opened on October 10 of the same year, did they think about the emotion-filled movement that had popularized the message it carried.

The spirit and practice of the Jesus movement had counterparts among Pentecostals, who believed they were restoring and maintaining practices neglected since Christianity's early days. Prophesying, interpreting prophecy, speaking in tongues, and performing miraculous acts of healing played an important part in Pentecostal ministries. Their distinctiveness did not prevent Pentecostalists from finding a place in the American religious scene, alongside the growing evangelical and fundamentalist churches. Regarded as either evangelical or fundamentalist or both were Baptists, Assemblies of God, Seventh-Day Adventists, Nazarenes, and various churches known simply as Christian. At the same time, mainline Protestant churches suffered declining membership, among them the Methodist, Lutheran, Presbyterian, and Episcopalian churches; the Disciples of Christ; and the United Church of Christ.

Although people identifying themselves as fundamentalists and evangelicals have much in common (indeed, many claim to be both), it is useful to draw distinctions. Fundamentalists stress a belief in the inerrancy of the Bible, meaning that the Bible is free of error. They regard the Bible as the absolute authority on religious matters. Many fundamentalists apply biblical authority to secular matters as well. Evangelicals stress their born-again conversions, their acceptance of Jesus as their personal savior and the Bible as the authority for all doctrine, and their obligation to spread the faith through personal witness and by supporting missionaries. Billy Graham, the best known of the evangelicals, embodied these convictions. Graham's eloquence as an evangelist and the efficiency of his organization enabled him to maintain national prominence and respect throughout the 1960s and 1970s and into the 1980s and 1990s (*Daily Life Online,* "Religious Life: Religion," in Marty, *Daily Life in the United States, 1960–1990,* http://dailylife.greenwood.com).

CONTENTIOUS RELIGIOUS ISSUES

The fact that churches could no longer ignore or evade questions of homosexuality was not surprising, for homosexuals would not allow them to do so. Most of the major denominations experienced turmoil as they grappled with the issue of homosexuals in their churches. Some sought ways to minister to them without condoning homosexuality, but militant conservatives, who regarded gays as blatant sinners, opposed openness and efforts to support them. Whether gay men and lesbians could be ordained into the ministry, even in churches less antagonistic toward them, was a particular source of discord. Indeed, homosexuality was potentially the single most divisive issue facing churches since the time of slavery. Religious denominations in the United States also considered and debated the question of the ordination of women as ministers, priests, and rabbis.

A decade earlier, religious conservatives had criticized the political actions of mainstream religious leaders on behalf of civil rights or against the Vietnam War. Now, reacting to changes in society that they found objectionable, they became politically active themselves. Besides opposing protection of rights and opportunities for homosexuals, they called for legislation against pornography, worked to defeat the Equal Rights Amendment, and demanded laws to counter the effects of the 1973 Supreme Court decision allowing abortion.

A large part of evangelicals' and fundamentalists' success in political action resulted from their use of radio and television to raise money for promoting their causes. Evangelist Oral Roberts, broadcasting from Tulsa, Oklahoma, showed that it was possible to build an expansive television ministry by combining evangelical preaching with faith healing—healing by placing the healer's hands on the believer and praying fervently. Based in Louisiana, Jimmy Swaggart reached huge audiences, as did Jim and Tammy Bakker's PTL (Praise the Lord; later People That Love) broadcast from South Carolina. Pat Robertson's *700 Club*, featuring interviews with evangelical leaders and carried on the Christian Broadcasting Network (CBN) he founded in 1961, became a powerful force in conservative political causes.

In 1979, televangelist Jerry Falwell used his *Old Time Gospel Hour*, broadcast on more than 300 television stations, to launch an explicit political movement, the Moral Majority. Falwell, pastor of the Thomas Road Baptist Church in Lynchburg, Virginia, claimed that the moral ills of society—reflected in such things as sex education in the schools, the Equal Rights Amendment, and abortion—could be corrected through the political mobilization of moral people. Joining forces with other well-funded conservative organizations, he aimed to register millions of new conservative voters for the 1980 election. Success gave him reason to say, "We have enough votes to run the country. And when the people say, 'We've had enough,' we are going to take over."

Conflict within denominations also affected church members. The Southern Baptist Convention, the largest Protestant body in the United States, came under the control of organized conservative forces in 1979. Much the same thing had happened in the two-million-member Lutheran Church–Missouri Synod a decade earlier, resulting in strife and schisms. The principal issue dividing Baptists was inerrancy, the teaching that the Bible was without error in all respects. Conservatives claimed that students in Baptist seminaries were taught that the Bible may not be completely accurate in scientific, historical, and geographic details. Further, they charged, this doubting of scriptural inerrancy had made its way into pulpits in Baptist churches and was threatening the purity of Baptist teachings. Their opponents held diverse views of biblical authority. Although they also regarded the Bible as the inspired Word of God, they were willing to apply scholarly interpretive methods to discover its meaning. The division over this and other issues continued throughout the 1980s and into the 1990s (*Daily Life Online*, "Religious Life: Religion," in Marty, *Daily Life in the United States, 1960–1990*, http://dailylife.greenwood.com).

CROSS-DENOMINATIONAL ISSUES

The Roman Catholic Church maintained its vitality as its members adapted to changes initiated by the Second Vatican Council. The aggressive mission practices of the Church of Jesus Christ of Latter-Day Saints (Mormons) resulted in its rapid growth.

The astonishingly swift triumph of Israel in the Six-Day War with Arab states in 1967 revitalized Jewish communities in the United States, but problems resulting from assimilation and dispersal of Jewish people in America continued to threaten Jewish identities.

Also during these years, groups sometimes described as cults claimed a share of public attention. Hare Krishna followers, for example, handed out literature, tried to sell books, and begged for contributions in major airports. The Unification Church of the Reverend Sun Myung Moon was an aggressive recruiter of new members (known as Moonies for their absolute subservience to the leader). Various Eastern religions, transcendental meditation, and quasi-religious "technologies of the spirit" also attracted followers, but they represented such minute slivers of the population that their impact on mainstream America was negligible.

Religious bodies also found themselves in unsettled circumstances. Although the Jesus movement described earlier faded away rather quickly, a new one just as quickly succeeded it. Focusing on a new birth through faith in Jesus, those swept up in the born-again movement sought to convert others to beliefs in personal salvation. "I found it!"—a catchy phrase displayed on bumper stickers and billboards—provided a theme for sermons, particularly by televangelists, as well as for pamphlets and person-to-person testimonies. Christians critical of the "I found it!" theme claimed that those using it got it wrong. The message, they said, should be, "He found me"; in other words, it was God who did the finding. Such criticism did not slow the movement. The aggressive bearers of the born-again message, particularly those in the Campus Crusade organization led by evangelist Bill Bright, gained many converts. Complaints that the movement used high-pressure tactics did not faze its followers.

The born-again movement represented part of the upsurge of evangelicalism in the 1970s. Between 1963 and 1978, the percentage of Americans claiming to have been born again and personally experienced salvation rose from 24 to 40. By the end of the 1970s, more than 50 million Americans claimed to be evangelicals. Local congregations played a part in evangelicalism's growing strength, as did church-related colleges, publishing firms, and the denominations sponsoring or supporting them. Evangelicals regarded their gospel-centered emphasis and clear-cut moral codes, along with their belief in conversion experiences, as standing in sharp contrast to what they perceived to be the consequences of secular humanism. Evangelicals and fundamentalists, who were more rigid in their biblical literalism than other Christians and harsher in their criticisms of societal changes, blamed secular humanism for increases in teenage sexual activity, alcohol and drug abuse, and discipline problems in public schools.

CULTS

A phenomenon that worried members of all mainline, evangelical, and fundamentalist churches was the appearance of religious groups labeled cults by their critics and the media. Typically, those groups sprang up around leaders who based their teachings on claims of revelation beyond traditional religious teachings and scriptures. They guaranteed salvation and satisfying lives to all who submitted to their absolute authority and severed all ties with families, jobs, schools, and friends. Indoctrination and repetitive rituals, some of them emotionally and physically dangerous, played important parts in the leaders' tactics, designed to break down followers' loyalties to and habits from their families and communities before joining a particular group.

Willingness of a group's followers to surrender unquestioningly to their leaders was demonstrated most dramatically in November 1978, when the People's Temple, founded in California by Jim Jones, came to a tragic end. By then, Jones had led his followers to Jonestown, Guyana, where they engaged in a mass murder and suicide. The deaths of more than 900 People's Temple members made headline news as television networks carried the story into homes across the nation.

Although members of such groups claimed to belong to them voluntarily, many former members contended that they had been converted by deception and subsequently compelled to endure treatment designed to destroy their egos. In addition to indoctrination, tactics included limiting members' sleep, changing their diet, controlling all conversations, and doing other things to disorient them and make their alienation from society complete. Although the number of people who joined groups with such practices was small, the lives affected by them—the members and the families of members—remained profound. Consequently, discussions were widespread about ways of protecting particularly the young from such groups' advances.

ROMAN CATHOLICISM AND PAPAL IMPACT

Catholics around the world mourned the death in 1978 of Pope Paul VI, who had had the task of dealing with the changes brought by the Second Vatican Council called by Pope John XXIII. Those changes affected church members in many ways.

Liturgical practices continued to evolve, moving farther away from the rituals of the traditional Latin Mass. Traditionalists regretted the abandonment of the distinctive black habits nuns had worn and objected to seeing priests without clerical collars. Vatican II encouraged greater lay involvement in religious, managerial, and pastoral roles within the church. Particularly disturbing to Catholic parishioners was the departure in unprecedented numbers of priests, brothers, and sisters who sought dispensation from their sacred vows and left their religious orders or diocesan positions. Men and women entering the orders were far too few in number to replace them. Perhaps more serious for the church's future, the Catholic parochial schools that had long been an important instrument in carrying out the church's mission faced cutbacks and closings. For the hierarchy, managing church affairs became more difficult. Although the pope remained supreme and bishops wielded considerable authority, grassroots assertiveness and practical necessity meant that power was decentralized. In other words, the people in the church had greater influence in church matters than ever before.

Upon the death of Pope Paul VI, his successor honored the two preceding popes by taking the names of both, becoming Pope John Paul I. However, he died just 34 days after his election. His successor, Karol Cardinal Wojtyla from Poland, took the name John Paul II. When the new pope traveled to the United States in October 1979, he was greeted by huge, enthusiastic crowds in New York City, Philadelphia, Des Moines, Chicago, and Washington, D.C. His warm and gentle manner pleased the throngs who came to see and hear him. The pope's pilgrimage had more than creating goodwill as its purpose, however, for he used the occasion to stress human rights and speak on behalf of the poor. If this meant opposing abortion and criticizing the consumerist culture of the United States, the pope was not reluctant to be candid. One effect of his visit was to give a boost to the claims of religion to a legitimate place in American life.

Certain changes in organized religion begun in the 1960s, such as allowing the ordination of women into the ministry in several Protestant churches, proved to be deeply divisive. Although women were ordained with little or no controversy in some denominations, the ordination of 15 women in the Episcopal Church created fierce controversy among Episcopalians. Because the church officially opposed the ordination of women, those who participated in ordination ceremonies were censured or admonished and sometimes subjected to formal canonical trials. Some Episcopal priests and members of that denomination were so antagonistic to allowing women to be ordained that they led their local parishes into a separate, conservative Episcopal body. Opposition to changes in emphasis and language, along with alternative versions of central rites in the updated version of the *Book of Common Prayer*, added to the resentments of dissenters and gave them another reason for separation.

The Roman Catholic Church continued to take strong positions against the ordination of women, with Pope Paul VI and Pope John Paul II speaking forcefully against it. Nonetheless, stirrings for change were evident among lay Catholics and some clergy, who claimed that there were no substantial theological reasons to deny women ordination. The role of women also became a point of controversy in the three strands of Judaism. Several were ordained as rabbis in Reform Judaism, and one became a presiding rabbi in Pennsylvania in 1979. A survey among Conservative rabbis showed that a majority favored ordination of women. Orthodox Jews called for expanded roles for women but only in keeping with their understandings of religious law.

The work of Father John Courtney Murray, the principal figure in leading American Catholics to understand the meaning of religious freedom, prepared them for the changes in church practices that came from the Second Vatican Council. The council, held in Rome in four sessions between 1962 and 1965, was convened by Pope John XXIII to reassess the role of the church in the modern world. Continued by his successor, Pope Paul VI, the council issued a number of documents, the most important for American Catholics being the Declaration of Religious Liberty. That document asserted one's right not to be coerced by individuals or society into acting contrary to one's conscience or into not following one's conscience in religious matters. By that time, the election of a Roman Catholic to the presidency of the United States and the conduct in office by John F. Kennedy had persuaded many Americans that Catholicism posed no threat to American democracy.

As Pope John XXIII intended, the council "threw open the windows" of the church. Changes in practices among American Catholics resulting from the council were striking. Regular attendance at Mass remained an integral part of life for many Catholics, but after November 29, 1964, priests offered the liturgy in English rather than Latin. Removal of restrictions in everyday life, such as one prohibiting the eating of meat on Fridays, gave Catholics a greater sense of being in mainstream America. So did the church's softened opposition to easing civil divorce laws. At the same time, the church's official opposition to the use of contraceptives of any kind—affirmed formally by Pope Paul VI in 1968 in the encyclical *Humanae Vitae*—kept it at odds with Catholics and non-Catholics who accepted birth control as morally right. Also at odds with the church were those who advocated birth control because of fears that a "population bomb" would explode if growth was not kept under control.

The Vatican Council's Declaration on the Church's Relations with Non-Christian Religions had considerable significance for Jews as well as Catholics. It condemned displays of anti-Semitism and denounced all prejudice and discrimination on the basis of race, religion, nationality, or tribe.

JUDAISM IN AMERICAN LIFE

Will Herberg, author of *Protestant-Catholic-Jew* (1960), helped Jews come to understand and strengthen their place in the religious scene in America. At the same time, their assimilation into the cultural mainstream posed a threat to their distinctive identity, as wartime and postwar Jewish immigrants established themselves in America and joined migrations to suburbs, leaving behind their enclaves in the city. So, too, did the growing frequency of interfaith marriages. Jewish leaders recognized that even though the practice of religion among Jews as measured by synagogue attendance and religious observances in their homes was minimal, their identity was inherently associated with religion. Consequently, they encouraged establishment of Hebrew day schools and after-school religious studies programs. Nearly two-thirds of the nation's one million Jewish children engaged in formal study of religion. Jewish leaders also supported efforts to increase the number of programs in Jewish studies in American colleges and universities. The number of such programs increased from 10 to 70 in the 20 years preceding 1965.

Jewish leaders also participated in interfaith conferences aimed at combating prejudice and implementing the Vatican Council's Declaration on the Church's Relations with Non-Christian Religions. These conferences affirmed the acceptance of Jews in the trio of faiths Herberg had described in *Protestant-Catholic-Jew*. Mainstream Protestants began to purge their Sunday school materials of portions that seemed to justify anti-Semitism. As Protestants, Catholics, and Jews gradually felt more secure in the pluralistic religious scene, they were more ready to accept into it believers in Islam, Buddhism, and other religions.

Perhaps religious denominations lowered their voices in speaking of one another because they recognized the need to work together against forces in American life that ran contrary to beliefs they shared. The leadership that black churches in the South provided in civil rights struggles compelled their white counterparts to examine their own teachings and practices. Such self-examination almost always led to formal and informal support of those seeking an end to racial segregation.

Some church members believed that decisions of the U.S. Supreme Court in 1962 (*Engel v. Vitale*) and 1963 (*School District of Abington Township v. Schemp*) finding school-sponsored prayer and devotional Bible reading in public schools to be unconstitutional were signs of the power of antireligious forces. In the first case (involving the recitation of a prayer composed by the New York Board of Regents) Justice Hugo Black, writing the opinion for the majority, observed that the daily classroom invocation of God's blessings as prescribed in the prayer was a religious activity. The opinion stated the following:

[W]e think that the Constitutional prohibition against laws respecting an establishment of religion must at least mean that in this country it is no part of the business of the government to compose official prayers for any group of the American people to recite as a part of a religious program carried on by government.... When the power, prestige and financial support of government is placed behind a particular religious belief, the indirect coercive pressure upon religious minorities to conform to the prevailing officially approved religion is plain.

So intense in some quarters was the reaction that the U.S. Congress held hearings on a proposed amendment to the Constitution that would permit such religious activities. In these hearings and in additional statements by church leaders, it became clear that there were good reasons for drawing a line between private and public devotional practices. Mainly, it protected children from having imposed on them teachings that were at odds with their own beliefs. Besides, the greater forces in the secularization of America were found in the commercial and entertainment worlds, and they were not likely to be turned back by reinstatement of school-sponsored prayers and devotional Bible readings in the schools (*Daily Life Online*, "Religious Life: Religion," in Marty, *Daily Life in the United States, 1960–1990*, http://dailylife. greenwood.com).

FOR MORE INFORMATION

Herberg, W. *Protestant-Catholic-Jew: An Essay in American Religious Sociology*. Garden City, NY: Anchor Books, 1960.

Marty, Myron A. *Daily Life in the United States, 1960–1990: Decades of Discord*. Westport, CT: Greenwood Press, 1997; also available online as *Daily Life Online*, in Marty, *Daily Life in the United States, 1960–1990*, http://dailylife.greenwood.com.

Marty, M. E. *Pilgrims in Their Own Land: 500 Years of Religion in America*. Boston: Little Brown, 1984.

Marty, M. E., and R. Scott Appleby. *The Glory and the Power: The Fundamentalist Challenge to the Modern World*. Boston: Beacon Press, 1992.

4

DAILY LIFE IN THE UNITED STATES, 1991–2005

Timeline

1991   January 12: The U.S. Congress votes to use force to remove Iraq from Kuwait.

January 16: The Persian Gulf War begins.

February 4: Baseball Hall of Fame votes to ban Pete Rose because he gambled on baseball games as a player and coach.

March 31: Warsaw Pact is dissolved.

April 6: Iraq accepts UN resolution ending Persian Gulf War.

April 17: Dow Jones Industrial Average goes above 3,000 for the first time.

July 31: The United States and the Soviet Union sign the Strategic Arms Reduction Treaty (START I), further limiting strategic nuclear arms.

November 7: Basketball star "Magic" Johnson announces that he has tested positive for HIV and is retiring.

December 2: First version of QuickTime is released.

December 25: Mikhail Gorbachev resigns as president of the Soviet Union; the USSR dissolves the next day.

1992   February 1: President George H. W. Bush and President Boris Yeltsin of Russia meet at Camp David and formally end the Cold War.

April 29: Rioting takes place in Los Angeles following the acquittal of four police officers involved in the Rodney King beating incident.

April 30: Last episode of *The Cosby Show* airs.

May 22: Johnny Carson signs off as the host of the *Tonight Show* and is replaced by Jay Leno.

August 24: Hurricane Andrew devastates South Florida.

November 3: Democratic challenger Bill Clinton defeats incumbent Republican President George H. W. Bush in a three-way race that saw independent candidate Ross Perot win almost 19 percent of the popular vote.

December 4: President George H. W. Bush orders 28,000 troops to Somalia.

1993 January 3: President George H. W. Bush signs the second START treaty to further limit nuclear arsenals.

January 14: David Letterman announces his move from NBC to CBS.

February 26: Terrorists explode bomb in the basement garage of the World Trade Center.

March 13: The "great blizzard" hits, leaving record snowfall across the East Coast.

April 19: Almost 80 cult members, 21 of them children, die in a fire that ends an FBI and ATF siege of the Branch Davidian headquarters outside Waco, Texas.

May 20: TV show *Cheers* ends an 11-year run on NBC.

December 8: President Bill Clinton signs the North American Free Trade Agreement (NAFTA).

1994 January 1: North Atlantic Free Trade Organization is formed.

January 6: Nancy Kerrigan is clubbed on the leg by men acting on behalf of rival figure skater Tonya Harding.

June 7: After a highway chase and an attempt at suicide, O. J. Simpson is arrested for the murders of his wife Nicole Brown Simpson and her friend Ronald Goldman.

September 19: The pilot episode of *ER* airs on NBC.

November 8: As a result of a 54-seat swing, the Republicans win control of the House of Representatives for the first time since 1954.

December 8: President Bill Clinton signs a bill enabling the United States to participate in the General Agreement on Tariffs and Trade (GATT).

1995 January 24: Opening statement is delivered by prosecution in the O. J. Simpson murder trial.

February 23: Dow Jones Industrial average peaks at 4,000.

April 19: The Alfred P. Murrah Federal Building in Oklahoma City is bombed; 168 people are killed.

September 2: The Rock and Roll Hall of Fame and Museum opens in Cleveland, Ohio.

September 6: Cal Ripken Jr. of the Baltimore Orioles breaks Lou Gehrig's record of playing in 2,131 consecutive games.

September 9: Sony Playstation is released in the United States.

October 3: O. J. Simpson is found not guilty on murder charges.

October 16: The Million Man March takes place in Washington, D.C.

November 21: The Dow Jones Industrial Average climbs above 5,000.

1996 January 7: One of the worst blizzards in American history hits the East Coast, killing more than 100 people.

July 27: A pipe bomb in the Centennial Olympic Park kills one person and injures 111, but the Olympic games continue in Atlanta, Georgia.

August 1: Michael Johnson breaks the world record in the 200 meter at 19.66 seconds.

September 13: Rap entertainer Tupac Shakur dies after being shot six days earlier in Las Vegas, Nevada.

October 2: Biker Lance Armstrong is diagnosed with testicular cancer.

November 5: Democratic President Bill Clinton is reelected, defeating Republican challenger Bob Dole; third-party candidate Ross Perot wins just over 8 percent of the vote.

November 16: Mother Teresa receives an honorary American citizenship.

1997　March 13: Golfer Tiger Woods becomes the youngest player to win the Masters.

June 2: Timothy McVeigh is convicted of 15 counts of murder in his involvement with the Oklahoma City bombing.

June 26: J. K. Rowling releases *Harry Potter and the Sorcerer's Stone*, the first book in the Harry Potter series.

December 19: *Titanic* is released in movie theaters across the United States, on its way to becoming the highest-grossing movie of all time at over $600 million.

1998　March 24: Jonesboro Massacre takes place in Jonesboro, Arkansas, when two boys fire on students at Westside Middle School, killing 4 students and 1 teacher, leaving another 11 wounded.

May 14: An estimated 76 million viewers watch the last episode of *Seinfeld*.

August 19: President Bill Clinton admits to an "improper physical relationship" with White House intern Monica Lewinsky.

September 8: Mark McGwire hits home run number 62, passing Roger Maris's single-season home run record.

September 27: Google is launched.

October 7: University of Wyoming student Matthew Shepard dies after being attacked by two assailants for being homosexual.

December 19: President Clinton is impeached by the House of Representatives for perjury and obstruction of justice.

1999　February 12: President Bill Clinton is acquitted of impeachment charges.

April 20: A school shooting at Columbine High School in Colorado leaves 14 students and 1 teacher dead, and 23 others wounded.

July 25: Lance Armstrong wins his first Tour de France.

November 5: The U.S. Supreme Court rules that Microsoft is a monopoly.

December 31: The Panama Canal is transferred to the control of the Panamanians.

2000　January 3: The last *Peanuts* comic strip is written by Charles Schulz.

January 10: America Online announces an agreement to buy Time Warner for $162 billion, the largest corporate merger to date.

May 31: *Survivor* is first aired on television.

October 26: Playstation 2 is released in the United States by Sony.

November 7: The extremely close presidential election contest between Republican George W. Bush and Democrat Al Gore ends in controversy as both candidates claim victory in Florida and thus in the election.

December 12: The U.S. Supreme Court rules against a manual recount of ballots from Florida, effectively awarding George W. Bush the presidency.

2001   April 21: Dennis Tito becomes the first space tourist.

September 11: Two hijacked jetliners fly into the World Trade Center, one flies into the Pentagon, and one crashes in rural Pennsylvania; carried out by Islamic extremists, the terrorist attacks leave over 3,000 dead.

October 7: The United States invades Afghanistan, launching a campaign that leads to the overthrow of the extremist Taliban regime.

October 26: President George W. Bush signs the U.S. PATRIOT Act.

November 2: *Monsters Inc.* debuts with the biggest tickets sales ever for an animated film.

November 11: Microsoft releases Xbox to compete with Sony's Playstation 2.

November 14: Afghan Northern Alliance troops take the capital of Kabul.

December 11: People's Republic of China joins the World Trade Organization (WTO).

2002   January 22: Kmart Corp. becomes the largest retailer in American history to file for chapter 11 bankruptcy.

February 19: NASA's Mars Odyssey probe begins to map the surface of Mars.

May 12: Former president Jimmy Carter arrives in Cuba to meet Fidel Castro, becoming the first American president to visit the island since the 1959 Revolution.

June 4: The planetoid Quaoar is discovered orbiting the sun in the Kuiper Belt.

2003   January 24: U.S. Department of Homeland Security begins operations.

March 20: The United States and allied forces invade Iraq.

April 28: iTunes Music Store launches, selling one million songs in the first week.

May 22: Annika Sorenstam becomes the first woman golfer to play in a PGA event in 58 years.

November 5: The final installment of the *Matrix* movie series is released worldwide.

December 17: The final installment of *Lord of the Rings* trilogy is released in movie theaters.

2004   May 6: The final episode of *Friends* airs on NBC.

June 5: Former President Ronald Reagan dies in California.

June 11: Ronald Reagan's funeral is held at Washington National Cathedral.

July 25: Lance Armstrong wins his sixth consecutive Tour de France.

November 2: Republican President George W. Bush defeats Democratic challenger John Kerry.

December 2: Brian Williams succeeds Tom Brokaw as host of *NBC Nightly News.*

December 26: A massive tsunami strikes Indonesia, Thailand, and other Indian Ocean coastal regions, leaving upwards of 219,000 dead.

2005   February 16: The National Hockey League (NHL) decides to cancel the entire 2005–2006 season after a prolonged labor dispute.

March 23: The 11th Circuit Court of Appeals, in a 2–1 decision, refuses to order the reinsertion of coma patient Terri Schiavo's feeding tube.

April 2: Death of Pope John Paul II.

April 19: German Cardinal Joseph Alois Ratzinger is elected pope, taking the name Benedict XVI.

July 29: Astronomers discover a 10th planet in the Solar System.

November 22: Xbox 360 debuts in the United States.

Overview

Francis Fukuyama published *The End of History and the Last Man* in 1992. Printed in 22 languages, the book hinted that the end of the Cold War and the rise of the United States to the position of a lone superpower had changed the global society and the future of America. While positive in its intent, the author neglected to foresee, as did many others, the complex issues that would continue to confront the daily lives of Americans in every aspect of their existence.

Politics and government, always a contentious factor in American life, witnessed a growing gap between liberals and conservatives over every aspect of life, from foreign policy to social values. The division of so-called blue states and red states into divisive electoral votes and voters led to the 2000 presidential election that ended with the U.S. Supreme Court intervening to settle issues of recounting votes. Political rancor regarding U.S. foreign policy from Bosnia to Somalia to Iraq divided political loyalties and saw an increasing harshness to the rhetoric of political opponents. The terrorist attacks of September 11, 2001, drew the nation together for a brief period, but the serious debate about how to fight the new war on terror shortly divided the two main political parties, and the 2003 war that began in Iraq sharply split the nation over its purpose and prolonged nature.

Domestic issues also divided American political opinion and fired serious partisan debates. Along with the long-standing concerns regarding education, crime, poverty, and health care, newer forms of social and cultural concerns have joined the mosaic of American domestic debate. Gay rights, stem cell research, church-and-state relationships, pornography, violence in the media, and other adroitly named "family values" often dominated the campaign trail as candidates vied for votes.

Television pundits and political observers tended to focus on the deep divisions that existed between the

Homes in Chester, Pennsylvania. Courtesy of Jolyon Girard.

extreme wings of the Democratic and Republican Parties, and the tone of political discourse in Washington, D.C., and elsewhere, seemed more shrill and caustic than ever. AM radio talk show hosts, mostly conservative, vied with what Rush Limbaugh, one of the more popular conservative hosts, called the "drive-by" or mainstream media, with the clear implication that they pursued a liberal agenda. Computer bloggers have joined the battle with both liberal and conservative sites. Scholarly analyses and even many public opinion polls, however, continued to suggest that there was a "middle American political view" that saw neither left nor right extreme as acceptable or desirable. By 2004, a Republican president, George W. Bush, had been reelected to a second term in an election less dramatic than in 2000. At the same time, the Republican Party controlled both houses of Congress. In Washington and around the nation, the battle for votes and voters continued.

The American economy saw clear and positive economic growth in the 1990s. The standard barometers of economic health: unemployment, inflation, interest rates, stock market numbers, gross domestic product (GDP), trade balance, and the national debt all impressed economists and the business community. Between 1992 and 2000, the nation created 12 million jobs as unemployment fell to 4 percent. Inflation stayed in low single digits, as did interest rates. The GDP grew reasonably, and the national debt began to decline as new taxes and increased revenues, as well as low interest rates, fueled the federal government's effort to reduce the debt and deficit. Revamped businesses, new technology, and other corporate and labor rethinking made American commerce more competitive in the global economy. There was much to applaud.

At the same time, problems also continued to demand attention and consideration. In 2001–2003, the stock markets crashed in a style reminiscent of, if not so tragic as, the Great Depression of 1929. The major investment markets, like the Dow Jones Industrial Average, dropped significantly, while the new tech-stock markets, like NASDAQ (National Association of Securities Dealers Automated Quotations), felt even more intense declines. By 2005, the investment picture had returned to pre-2001 numbers and the market looked healthy. The 2001–2003 crash, however, had harmed many investors. Group retirement funds, individual programs like 401k accounts, and other forms of savings were severely weakened. Coupled with a series of business scandals—Enron, WorldCom—the period produced a mixed set of emotions for Americans looking for economic security. The nation's continued dependence, in fact, growing dependence on foreign goods and products, also presented an economic issue for Americans as they went about their daily lives. If the nation was becoming increasingly a service economy, and if the traditional industrial power of the United States, so much a part of the postwar society, had declined, what did that shift mean? Americans bought their cotton clothes, "the fabric of our lives," in stores nationwide, but they were mostly produced in foreign countries. Were Americans losing jobs because of that? The price of petroleum seemed the classic example of U.S. dependence on foreign products, and that

Condominiums in the Philadelphia suburbs. Courtesy of Jolyon Girard.

price continued to rise, as did American consumption. Statistics would show that the price of a gallon of gasoline in 2005 was actually cheaper than 1959, adjusted for inflation, but most car owners had little interest in the comparison.

Housing prices rose steadily, even dramatically, from 2003 to 2005, so that the "paper wealth" of homeowners grew. A housing boom fueled economic growth, and easy and abundant credit encouraged many people to enter the housing market—upgrading or downsizing, moving further into new suburban developments or heading to center city areas to take up condo living and enjoy urban amenities in culture and entertainment. Despite the highest levels of personal indebtedness in American history, the middle class felt rich as they tallied up the worth of their home and possessions.

Domestic Life

OVERVIEW

Family life in the United States during the past 15 years has both experienced noteworthy changes and, at the same time, retained many of the traditional values, concerns, and interests of earlier generations in American daily life. Parents, whether single parents, or gay couples, or married men and women, worried about their children's education and safety. They remained concerned with the security of their homes and neighborhoods. They sought to enhance the quality of their lives, and they wanted to do so in +safety and comfort. As recent national elections suggested clearly, Americans often expressed significant interest in so-called family values. While definitions of the meaning of family values differed broadly in the United States, domestic life remained a critical concern, not only at the ballot box, but in day-to-day living. Did Americans have a better lifestyle than their parents or grandparents? How did one define that phrase? Were Americans healthier, wealthier, and wiser? With significant alterations in regional life, ethnic diversity, and other recent trends, was it possible to reach a clear and broad conclusion concerning domestic life in the United States? For years, concern about the "other America" tended to focus on the failure of America to confront the racism

Rural America contemporary barn in Lancaster County, PA. Courtesy of Jolyon Girard.

and poverty that impacted the domestic life of African Americans. At the same time, however, the substantial increase in the Latino population in the United States (now the largest minority) required another subject to evaluate and consider.

As the nation became more aware of its cultural diversity, an examination of domestic life in the United States demanded that one look at all of the people who live in the country. While white Americans of European heritage remain the majority and require the broadest attention, it is important to consider other people living in the nation. In a similar fashion, suburban, domestic life has tended to define an emerging postwar domesticity that occupies the attention of scholars and general observers. Since 1945, American domestic life was often viewed in the template of split-level suburbia. Yet, urban and rural life also offered a picture of life in the United States that was different in many ways.

The population of the United States approached 300 million as the century came to its conclusion. While many of the domestic aspects of American daily life remained the same, significant alterations took place within the 15-year period. Census numbers indicated that Hispanic Americans had become the largest minority in the United States. (The term *Hispanic* is a government or popular catch-all for persons of Spanish-speaking cultures in the Western Hemisphere. It suggests a greater unity of identity and interest than the diverse Hispanic people have.) Even as immigration and ethnic diversity continued in the nation, the growth of the Latino population prompted renewed interest and controversy. The following overview of immigrant or minority numbers suggests the importance of the changes.

📷 Snapshot

Average Daily Cost of Living

	1990	1995
New House	$123,000	$113,000
Annual Income	$29,000	$36,000
Gasoline	$1.34/gal.	$1.12/gal.
New Car	$16,000	$15,500
Movie Tickets	$4.00	$4.35
Milk	$2.78/gal.	$2.55/gal.

Source: Remember When (Millersville, TN: Seek Publishing).

	1960	1990
Native Americans	0.5 million (.3%)	2.5 million (.9%)
Asian-Pacific Islanders	1.1 million (.6%)	3.7 million (3.7%)
African Americans	18.9 million (10.5%)	34.7 million (12.3%)
Hispanic Americans	No data	35.3 million (12.5%)

Source: Goldfield et al. 2001, 900.

CHILDREN

As of 2002–2003, 21.4 percent of Americans were younger than 15 years. Since Benjamin Spock wrote his famous book on child care, Americans have devoted significant time and effort to understanding and responding to the lives of children. A recent attempt to understand and analyze how American children have developed occupied a broad spectrum of views. Many critical observers see today's young people as spoiled, dependent, and ill-informed. In a 2006 article in *Philadelphia* magazine, Amy Donohue Korman, a local social pundit, suggested that parents had lost control of their children. "It's as if an entire generation has overreacted to what felt like too-controlling parents and ended up with a society-wide inability to serve as authority figures in the home." She continued, "At one time, kids were beloved extensions of the parent, but now [parents are] the satellites revolving around the sun that is our children" (Korman 2006, 68–69). Korman's contentions focused on a middle-class absorption with today's children that has failed to teach them responsibility, so-called helicopter parents who indulged every child's whim without consideration for their need to learn life's demands and considerations. Child psychologists, educators, and other experts have chimed in with similar evaluations of America's young people, citing a variety of statistics and anecdotal evidence to support their conclusions. Scholastic Aptitude Test (SAT) scores were down. Both major and minor crime statistics showed an increase in violence and vandalism among young people. A recent piece on CBS's *Sixty Minutes* highlighted the rising incidence of young people assaulting homeless men. Korman finished her article with the warning, "Worried yet?" Other observers, however, challenge the pessimistic conclusions regarding today's children.

In his study, *"Why Do I Love These People?" Understanding, Surviving, and Creating Your Own Family* (2005), Po Bronson, a national author and critic on American social issues, suggests a quite different idea. Bronson maintained that coddling of contemporary children was not the epidemic the society had been led to believe in a host of books, articles, and television reports. Additionally, she believed that the protective "supermom" syndrome was an affectation of the upper middle class. Nearly a third of 16-year-old youngsters had jobs. Most college students worked to support their tuition costs. The intense drive on the part of upper-middle-class American parents to place their children in "the right schools," often starting as early as kindergarten, was, in Bronson's view, abnormal in the society. He argued that access to education, at every level, remained readily available for most children. Only a very few, high-profile colleges and universities rejected student applications for admission. Children did not move home after college in the numbers critics suggested. In fact, evidence indicated that more 18-year-olds lived at home in the 1980s than in 2005.

Bronson interviewed 700 families across the United States to obtain evidence for his book and concluded that the "hyperachieving, supermom" protective interpretation of American children remained inaccurate and inappropriate. Most popular analysis of recent trends in the behavior and issues surrounding American children seemed to focus on upper-middle-class white children, often in suburban environments. It has failed to account for the lives of young people who live in rural or urban areas. A stereotypical image sees children as frozen in front of their X-Boxes or Play Station video games, oblivious to anything else but the most recent sports or adventure option. That picture overlooks the more complex quality of American daily life that took place throughout a nation with 300 million people. And, as Bronson suggested, many American children practiced a different lifestyle than that portrayed by the "couch-potato" image.

DRUGS, LEGAL AND ILLEGAL

Americans in the past 15 years have increased significantly the amount of prescription drugs they purchase and consume. In 2002, Americans filled 3,340,000,000 outpatient prescriptions for drugs, 12 drugs for every man, women, and child in the United States. Drug sales in America amounted to $219 billion, an average 12–18 percent increase each year since 1995. Drug costs have doubled since 1999, and volume in purchases has increased by 25 percent. Cholesterol-lowering, ulcer, reflux-corrective, and antidepressant drugs remain the leading prescriptions. Both the medical establishment and social observers remain divided on the growth of drug use in America. Many believe it provides a beneficial solution to a variety of medical problems people face. Critics argue that the United States has become a drug-dependent society. The debate continues (http://www.MedicationSense.com).

A debate even rages regarding illegal drug use. Should drug policy focus on the source of drugs and try to eliminate where they are made and imported into the United States? Or should the nation concentrate on eliminating the use of drugs domestically? Some observers argue that drugs should be legal to purchase in order to reduce the criminal and violent drug culture that permeates much of the inner cities in the United States. Recent surveys indicate that more than 50 percent of teenagers have smoked marijuana, 10 percent have taken stimulant drugs, 8 percent try inhalants, 2 percent have used crack cocaine, and 1 percent have used heroin. Those percentages are slightly less than drug consumption in the late 1980s. At the same time Americans in 2000 spent an estimated $36 billion on cocaine, $12 billion on heroin, and $11 billion on marijuana (Office of National Drug Control Policy). The continued plague of illegal drug use, particularly the insidious rise of crack cocaine consumption, has added to the crisis that confronts urban and suburban America and has reached into rural areas, even among the Amish. Beyond the health and safety issues involved with the use of illegal drugs, evidence suggests clearly that illegal drugs have created a major crime problem, particularly in urban society. Most criminal offenses in the inner city revolve around the drug culture. The large percentage of young African American males in prison or awaiting trial were involved in some aspect of drug trafficking. Domestic life in the United States, in every area of the society, is tragically affected by the insidious underworld of the illegal drug culture.

MEN

Domestic life for American men has changed as well in the modern era. No longer simply perceived as father and breadwinner, men have adapted to the broad changes in the society that impacted on American daily life in the 1990s. While some studies evaluate the role of men in society in less-than-flattering terms, the broad evidence indicates that they have adapted well to new perspectives and responsibilities in the new century.

A negative image of American males portrays them as irresponsible, often violent, and less social than women. Recent academic studies suggest that the performance of male students in colleges falls below the accomplishments of their female colleagues. Violence among young males in America continues to draw analysis and concern. Television sitcoms often portray men as silly and self-indulgent, a popular cultural image that has existed for years in that medium. Yet, men continue to exercise a major and contributive impact on American daily life, from the boardrooms of businesses, to the emergency rooms in hospitals, to the battlefield in the nation's conflicts. All 18-year-old men are required to register for the draft, even while the United

The Home Depot. Courtesy of Jolyon Girard.

States maintains an all-volunteer military. At the same time, men have also adjusted to the demands of married life and parenthood in America. Little statistical information exists to indicate that American males, in general terms, have failed to respond to their traditional domestic roles as husbands, fathers, and breadwinners. Men have tended to assume more domestic responsibilities within the family structure. Just as women have expanded their options, opportunities, and responsibilities in American domestic life, so, too, have men. Men also adjusted to new forms of households and even living alone as adults for long periods.

PETS

Pets have been a part of American domestic life since colonial times. But in contemporary domestic life, Americans devote more time, attention, and money to animal companions than ever before. In 2005, more than 60 percent of households in the United States owned pets—64 million households. Americans spend between $31 billion and $34 billion annually on their pets; $14 billion for veterinary care, $13 billion for food, $1.3 billion for toys, gadgets, and so on, and $2.3 billion for grooming and boarding their animals. Cats and dogs dominate numbers. In 2005, Americans owned 77 million cats and 65 million dogs. Other animal pets, however, also draw attention and affection. A variety of birds, hamsters, gerbils, and other small animals join the list. The United States imported more than two million reptiles as pets in 2004–2005. Polls on the subject suggest that 92 percent of pet owners consider their animals part of the family. Seventy-eight percent say their pets greet them at the door when they come home in the evening (one presumes those are not pet lizards). And 43 percent of pet owners have their pets sleep with them (one presumes not snakes).

The American Society for the Prevention of Cruelty to Animals (ASPCA), founded in 1866, and the Humane Society have worked diligently to create an atmosphere of care and consideration for animals. Animal cruelty is against the law in all 50 states, and it is a felony in 34 states. The humane treatment of animals in the United States remains a major issue and concern, and although the details cited tend to suggest that Americans sincerely love and care for their pets, some people are not doing so (Grier 2006).

THE "OTHER AMERICA"

The United States has made significant strides since the 1940s to attack the overt issue of racism in American society. Supreme Court and federal court judicial decisions, presidential policies, and congressional legislation have basically removed the de jure (legal) aspects of racism that marked previous history. It would be foolish, however, to suggest that de facto (factual) forms of racism do not continue to divide American daily life. In some ways, things may have actually gotten worse. In 1890, 80 percent of African American families had two parents. By 1990, that percentage had dropped to 39 percent. The largest drop took place between 1980 and 1990. By 1994, 57 percent of all black children lived in single-parent homes, mostly female-headed. Sixty-eight percent of all African American children born in 1994 were born to single women.

The numbers continue to warrant concern. In 2000, according to U.S. census data, 12 percent of African American children lived in homes under the supervision of grandparents. That compares to 6 percent for Hispanic Americans and 4 percent for white children. Thirty percent of poor families, defined by the Census Bureau as living on income below the poverty level, are headed by African American women. Crime statistics paint an equally bleak picture of the "other America" for black children and families.

During the 1990s and early 2000, the crime rate for African Americans as victims was 20 percent higher than for the general population. Homicide remained the leading cause of death for young black males between the ages of 15 and 34. In 2002, 10.4 percent of African American males between the ages of 15 and 29 were incarcerated in state or federal prisons. Specialists in the area of criminology have predicted that close to 30 percent of black men in the United States will be jailed before they reach their 30th birthday. Compared to Hispanic and white statistics, the numbers are higher in virtually every category. Concerns regarding unemployment, single families, drugs, and the decline of both urban and rural opportunity suggest clear reasons for the staggering statistics and problems that confront many black Americans. The society has addressed many of those concerns but clearly not resolved them.

While news media and other pundits often focus on the problems that confront African Americans, other data suggest that a black middle class has also evolved in the United States. Those families are not part of the statistical tragedy discussed above. In 1960, only 20 percent of African Americans graduated from high school, and 3 percent graduated from college. By 2005, 86 percent graduated from high school and 13 percent graduated from college. The median income of African Americans in 1997 amounted to $25,050, placing 40 percent of black families in the middle class by general income standards. Although those numbers and statistics remain lower than comparable white percentages and figures, the information suggests that a sizable black middle class has emerged since the beginning of the 1960s (Harris 1999; http://www.worldandi.com; Billingsley 1992).

The 1990 U.S. Census listed the population of Native Americans as just fewer than 1,900,000 people. Although Native Americans make up a small percentage of the total population in the United States, they confront many similar issues and problems. Poverty, alcoholism, higher incidences of disease, unemployment, and racism also play a major role in Indian daily life in America. At the same time, a variety of Indian tribal councils, reservations, and individual families have managed to advance the domestic world of Native Americans. The development of gambling casinos on some reservations has added income for tribes. In 1991, a Wisconsin reservation opened the first gaming casino in the United States. By 1993, 17 more casinos had opened in the state. The federal government has recognized 557 Native American reservations in the United States. By 2005, more than 33 percent had opened some form of gaming operation, and others are in the process of developing the option. While critics have questions about where the profits from the gambling casinos go, most tribal governments contend that the resources from casino gambling have provided a new source of income for their people (Fixico 2006).

WOMEN

In and out of the home, American women have continued to make positive strides since the modern feminist movement began in the 1960s (see Chapter 3, Daily Life in the United States: 1960–1990). Both public policy and changing social and cultural awareness have helped American women pursue careers, families, and recreational options in ways not possible in the first 20 years following World War II. Many observers believe that middle-class, educated, white women have benefited most directly and clearly as a result of the civil rights movements of the 1960s. The median age for women in America has increased slightly since the 1980s. In 1997 it was 34.1. In 2003, the median age was 36.5, the highest in 100 years. Women still outnumber men in the United States by a ratio of 100–96.3. In the workforce, women currently make up 46.5 percent of employed Americans (U.S. Department of Labor Report). The statistical factors that look at education and careers indicate that American women have gained access to a broad variety of opportunities. Since 1980, they make up a majority of the students enrolled in undergraduate education.

As of 2005, 40 to 52 percent of law school students are women and 33,445 women attend medical school, an increase of more than 5,000 since 1996. In 1980, only 11.6 percent of licensed doctors were women. By 2004, that percentage increased to almost 27 percent (American Bar Association and American Medical Association).

Since the government changed to an all-volunteer military, the role of women in that profession has also increased and shifted even to combat duty. In 2004–2005, 212,000 women served on active duty, and 149,000 served in the National Guard, 20 percent of the American military. Fifteen percent of the women are commissioned officers, roughly the same percentage as men. Women also find assignments in a greater variety of positions. Short of some limited combat assignments in the infantry and armor units, women are assigned to virtually every other option (U.S. Department of Defense).

The role of women as wives and mothers has changed little in modern American domestic life. Marriage rates have dropped by almost 50 percent since 1970, from 76.5 per thousand unmarried women to 39.9 percent. The divorce rate, however, has also declined from 22.6 per thousand married women in 1980 to 17.7 in 2005 (U.S. Census Report 2000). In 2005, 2,230,000 marriages took place between men and women in the United States. What do the data suggest? More couples, both heterosexual and homosexual, may be living together without being married, perhaps a majority, with 8.1 percent of heterosexual couples living together without marrying. While statistics regarding gay and lesbian numbers vary widely, some sources indicate that 10 percent of the adult gay population lives together as couples. Given the data, women still remain principally responsible in heterosexual marriages as homemakers and child care providers even while their work outside the home has expanded. That dual responsibility has created both ambivalence and concern for many American women. Managing both a career and marriage and family can become a complicated juggling act, and recent studies indicate that many women have found it a troublesome consideration.

An interesting offshoot of domestic life in the United States, and the role of women, has emerged in the growth of direct marketing and home sales of household products and cosmetics. Avon, founded as the California Perfume Company in 1886, had become, by 2005, an $8.1 billion business with more than 2.5 million sales people, almost all of them women. Selling more than 800 cosmetic products, the self-designated "Company for Women" has pursued a direct marketing business that dominates the field. Mary Kay Ash (1915–2001) founded her company, Mary Kay Cosmetics, in 1963 in Dallas, Texas, with nine sales people selling door to door. By 2005, 1.6 million sales consultants generated sales over $1 billion with 200 products ranging from perfume to suntan lotion. The owner became famous for awarding pink Cadillacs to top sales personnel.

Earl Tupper sold airtight, plastic sealed containers beginning in 1946. In 1948, he initiated Tupperware Home Parties to sell his products in a direct marketing scheme. By 1951, Tupperware removed its items from retail stores and sold only at Tupperware parties in homes throughout America. Revenues reached $1.2 billion in 2005. Most of the employees held full-time jobs elsewhere but added income by hosting those gatherings. Millions of women in the United States enhanced their incomes working for one of the three businesses (Bailey and Ulman 2005).

Given many of the career changes and opportunities, women are still subject to overt displays of sexism in the society. Again, de jure legislation, like Title IX in the field of education and sports, does not always eliminate de facto disregard for equal treatment. The National Organization for Women (NOW) and other organizations continue to document violence perpetrated against women, spousal abuse, rape, and other assaults. Critics still argue about fair salaries and wages for women, "glass ceilings" that block executive promotions, and other forms of subtle or often blatant sexism. Minority women in American society may confront even greater examples of sexism in their daily lives. The factors often examined in an encyclopedia tend to look at generational change. Is it better now than it was 10, 20, or 50 years ago? In most instances, the answer regarding women in American domestic life is yes. In some instances, clearly there remains a long way to go.

FOR MORE INFORMATION

Bailey, Maria, and Bonnie Ulman. *Trillion Dollar Moms: Marketing to a New Generation.* Chicago: Kaplan, 2005.

Billingsley, A. *Climbing Jacob's Ladder: The Enduring Legacy of African-American Families.* New York: Simon & Schuster, 1992.

The Endocrine Society Weighs In: A Handbook on Obesity in America. http://obesityinAmerica. org/endoedge/archive/2005_apr_endoedge.html.

Faragher, John Mack, Susan Armitage, Mari Jo Buhle, and Daniel Czitrom. *Out of Many: A History of the American People.* Upper Saddle River, NJ: Prentice Hall, 2006.

Fixico, Donald. *Native Americans in the Twentieth Century.* Westport, CT: Greenwood Press, 2006.

Goldfield, David, et al. *The American Journey.* Upper Saddle River, NJ: Prentice Hall, 2001.

Grier, Katherine C. *Pets in America: A History.* Durham: University of North Carolina Press, 2006.

Harris, Robert L. Jr. "The Rise of the Black Middle Class." *The World and I Online* 14:2 (February 1999): 40. http://www.worldandi.com.

Korman, Amy Donohue. "The Death of the Chore." *Philadelphia* 97, no. 10 (2006): 68–69.

Office of National Drug Control Policy. http://www.whitehousedrugpolicy.gov/.

U.S. Department of Defense. http://www.defenselink.mil/.

Economic Life

OVERVIEW

From 1992 through 2000, Americans experienced almost a decade of economic growth and broad prosperity. Unemployment dipped from 7.2 percent in 1992 to

4.0 percent at the beginning of 2000. Business enterprise and expansion helped to create more than 12 million new jobs. At the same time, the stock market and financial investments also indicated signs of a healthy and expanding economy. Retirement funds, pensions, and other forms of personal investment swelled during the decade of the 1990s as the percentage of middle-class families with a financial stake in the stock market grew significantly. Statistics and government estimates on Americans living in poverty showed a decline to less than 12 percent by the end of the 1990s. Disparity between wealthy Americans and the poor also narrowed slightly in the 1990s, and more American middle-class families experienced an expansion of their personal income. Inflation and interest rates remained in manageable single digits, as the Federal Reserve Board, under the cautious leadership of Alan Greenspan, monitored the nation's economy with careful attention. Greenspan and others took particular pains to watch inflation trends in the American economy. So long as the rate of inflation remained low, between 2 and 4 percent annually, interest rates could also remain low, and both those conditions fueled a prosperous economy.

The statistical evidence of a growing economy defined a free market system that had become more efficient and productive, particularly in smaller businesses, throughout the nation. During the 1970s and 1980s, critics of the American economy heralded Japanese and European models of industry and commerce as more proficient. From their new technologies to their labor and management styles, Japan and Europe appeared to produce, and market, better goods. Observers argued that labor unions in the United States cost owners too much in salaries and benefits for what their employees produced. At the same time, management, particularly large corporation boards of directors and CEOs, received astronomical salaries, benefits, and stock options that went well beyond their value. Middle management also seemed bloated, underutilized, and inefficient. The business infrastructure, both in manufacturing and planning, had become lax and old-fashioned and appeared to lack the competitive edge to challenge the new products and innovative labor-management methods of America's foreign competitors.

Business leaders at all levels in the United States responded to the criticism and flaws that observers of the economy had noted. Throughout the 1970s and 1980s, a tough, perceptive restructuring and downsizing of businesses took place. Labor unions agreed to contracts that provided lower salaries and fewer benefits. Management streamlined its white-collar payrolls and cut jobs. Businesses also updated and upgraded their use of computers, new production design and equipment, high-tech electronic communication systems, and other innovative and efficient tools to replace the aging technology of the previous generation. That robust response to the perceived problems of the 1970s and 1980s helped create the 7.2 percent unemployment figure in 1992 as corporations and businesses downsized their workforce. It set the stage, however, for the revived, expanding economy of the 1990s, and, as people found new jobs in a more competitive and flexible free market system, unemployment numbers dropped, although individual income for many people declined or did not keep pace with inflation.

GLOBALIZATION

The influence of the new electronic world of economics and commerce also impacted directly the growth of a global economy and America's role in that development. The interconnection of world business—globalization—has had a lasting effect on American economic life. In 1965, the worth of U.S. imports and exports accounted for 7 percent of the country's Gross Domestic Product (GDP). By the 1990s, that number had climbed to 16 percent. Americans saw a major shift in the balance of trade as the nation imported far more goods and products than it exported. The issues concerning globalization have a number of facets, both economic and cultural. Critics maintain that global corporations and managers have created a commercial world that exploits the developing world's population for profit. They argue that the low wages paid in those countries, even in exploding economies like China's, are a key aspect of that exploitation. At the same, critics of globalization believe that the evolving high-tech, commercial Western economy stifles independent growth and even cultural traditions, as developing societies succumb to Western (U.S.) commercial influence. Those who defend global markets maintain that a cooperative, interconnected global economy makes goods and services available to more people worldwide. They suggest that even though the United States consumes a huge portion of global products, without American demands for those goods, people in the developing world would have no jobs, nor would their economies have products to sell. One example of that position emerged clearly when the United States negotiated two commercial treaties in the 1990s. In 1993, America signed the North American Free Trade Agreement (NAFTA) that created an open commercial border with Mexico and Canada. A year later, the government signed a worldwide treaty, General Agreement on Tariffs and Trade (GATT).

The two agreements sparked a heated political and economic debate in the United States regarding free trade and protectionism, the support of American jobs, and the export of those positions to other countries. Labor unions, environmentalists, and other critics gained support from the Democratic Party as NAFTA went into effect. GATT provoked a similar debate. In 1996, GATT became the World Trade Organization (WTO). A wave of protests in Europe and the United States believed that the WTO was controlled by international business conglomerates that showed no interest in poor countries, the people who lived there, or the environment that protestors believed globalization threatened. When the WTO held its annual meeting in Seattle, Washington (November 30–December 4, 1999), close to 50,000 people arrived to protest the meeting. A small number of activists became violent and vandalized portions of downtown Seattle. The police responded, and the expected CNN and Fox coverage followed with divergent views of the protests. Those who supported the protestors claimed that the police overreacted. Others thought the activists epitomized the spoiled generation of "Birkenstock" young people with no serious concerns to confront. The debate continues, as do the protests, now a standard, expected event at WTO meetings.

INVESTING

American families invest billions of dollars annually in the stock market. Personal investments have grown dramatically in the past 20 years, as have the variety of options for investors. Traditionally, the Dow Jones Industrial Average listed leading industrial, utility, and transportation stocks as a barometer of the nation's investment trend. Founded in 1882, the Dow Jones became the bellwether indicator of the nation's financial health. To compete with Dow Jones stocks options, Standard and Poors 500 (S&P 500) opened for business in 1963 as an alternative list of companies for investment. In 1971, NASDAQ provided an investment resource in the rapidly expanding electronics and Internet businesses. NASDAQ became so popular in the 1980s and 1990s, as the Internet market exploded, that it merged with AMEX.

Throughout the twentieth century, banks, businesses, and individuals in the United States purchased stocks on the New York Stock Exchange (NYSE) and the American Stock Exchange (AMEX), hoping to see those investments grow as the general prosperity of the economy expanded. Most Americans, however, had little direct involvement in the stock market except through their bank savings (banks invested savings to enhance their profits and help pay interest to individuals with money in savings accounts). That changed with the rapid expansion of the American economy in the last decades of the twentieth century. The development of 401k retirement funds encouraged employees to create private retirement accounts, and money set aside in 401k accounts was invested in stock markets. Large mutual funds, like TIAA-CREF, Fidelity Investments, and the Vanguard Group, invested billions of dollars in the stock market for millions of American employees who directed a portion of their salaries to company-supported retirement programs.

By the 1990s, more than 45 percent of American families had some form of financial investment in stocks. The buying and selling of stocks no longer remained an economic option only for wealthy and upper-middle-class Americans; it had become a standard means for people in the country to invest their life savings in hopes of a growing return on their savings (*The Wall Street Journal*).

During the 1990s, the faith in the stock market bore profitable fruit. The Dow Jones Industrial Average jumped from 3,000 in 1991 to 5,000 in 1995, to 8,000 in 1997, to 11,000 by 1999. On January 14, 2000, the NYSE listed the Dow Jones at 11,722.98, almost four times the value of stock a decade earlier. It was the largest decade gain in history. The NASDAQ saw a similar growth in investment profits. In 1994, the NASDAQ was less than 1,000 points. By 2000, it had climbed to 5,000. Effectively, the value of investments had quadrupled. In simple terms, an American family that had invested $10,000 in the variety of stock types available would have increased the worth of their money to over $40,000; factoring in inflation, that suggested a huge financial gain. Americans studied the financial news nightly on their television sets to witness the growing value of their retirement funds. In an earlier 1987 movie, *Wall Street*, its star Michael Douglas proclaimed, at a stockholders meeting, "greed for the lack of a better word is good" to advance the broad national faith in market investment.

The rapid growth of the stock markets, however, concealed a potential problem. In some degree, similar to the 1929 stock market crash, the value of financial investments exceeded the pragmatic value of companies and businesses. The market reflection of economic health had increased far beyond the actual strength and real growth of the institutions where that money was invested. A "bubble" had developed, and, in 2000, that bubble popped. Large mutual funds and investment firms sold their stocks, and the markets plunged. The Dow Jones dropped to 10,305 in April 2000, and it reached a low point of 7,702 by July 2002, a 34 percent decline. The NASDAQ collapsed as well. Its stock fell from 5,000 to 1,500 by 2001. Between 2000 and 2002, the markets lost more than $8.5 trillion in investments. American families saw their retirement savings eliminated or drastically reduced, and the nation witnessed a financial crisis, the "Crash of 2000–2002" seeming like a repeat of the stock market collapse during the Great Depression (Securities and Exchange Commission Report 2003).

During the same period, the revelation of a series of investment and accounting scandals became public knowledge. In 1989, Charles Keating, the Chief Executive Officer of Lincoln Savings and Loan Company, a California-based business, came under investigation by the Securities and Exchange Commission (SEC) for illegal securities acts. In a $200 million fraud case that took a decade to unfold, Keating was convicted of securities fraud and sentenced to four years in prison. In 2001, the Enron Corporation, a large Houston, Texas, energy company, also came under SEC scrutiny. Ken Lay, its founder, his key executives, and the company's accounting firm Arthur Anderson were also accused of falsifying over $100 billion in revenues. The firm declared bankruptcy in December 2001, 21,000 employees lost their jobs, and a series of trials to uncover the facts resulted in convictions and prison terms for top executives. WorldCom, a telecommunications corporation, also filed for the largest bankruptcy in American history in June 2001, another case of securities fraud. Again, the SEC began an investigation in March 2002.

Coupled with the stock market crash, a rise in unemployment, a negative trade balance, and the outsourcing of jobs to foreign countries, the crisis in the American economy in the early twenty-first century created a serious loss of faith for millions of families who had seen the 1990s as a decade of prosperity and security. Just as millions of Americans had lived in the 1920s with a positive view of the economy and seen that faith destroyed in 1929, many Americans reacted to the economic news in 2000 and 2001 with the same anger, frustration, fear, and cynicism about the integrity of the business establishment.

The situation had a key political impact on the 2004 presidential election and the 2002 and 2004 congressional elections. Democrats accused President George W. Bush and the Republican Congress of being too cozy with unscrupulous business owners. They attacked their opponents for creating the worst economic crisis since the Depression. John Kerry, the Democratic presidential candidate, accused George Bush of stewarding the worst economy since 1929 and announced that more Americans were unemployed than in 1932. His attack was clear. The incumbent president cared more about CEOs than he did their employees.

It seemed an odd charge for anyone interested in statistics, since the American population had more than doubled since the 1930s, making the comparison questionable.

At the same time, unemployment numbers amounted to 5.4 percent, far fewer than the numbers in 1932. In real numbers, Senator Kerry was correct; as a percentage, he was not (United States Department of Labor Report 2006). The political/economic debate also centered on President Bush's initiative to allow Americans the option to invest some portion of their Social Security payments in the stock market. Had that idea been forwarded in the mid-1990s, while the stock markets soared, it might have appeared more appealing to American families. In the early years of the new century, however, given the crisis in the market and the additional fraud cases, it provoked a heated debate and won few supporters.

MADE IN AMERICA

America's traditional economic strength in the twentieth century had resided in the growth and expansion of its industrial economy. During and immediately following World War II, the industrial capacity of the United States had defined its economic character, both as a domestic force and in the world marketplace. That basic industrial strength, however, changed in the last half of the century. By 1965, half the jobs in the United States were in the service economy. By 2000, 75 percent of employed Americans worked in service-related jobs. Service employment includes a wide variety of positions, some high paid, others low wage and tenuous. A gas station attendant or fast-food employee provides a service. Those positions tend to be low-wage or minimum-wage jobs. At the same time, teachers, government employees, lawyers, doctors, and research specialists often enjoy well-paid and secure positions in the service economy. At the high end, professional athletes, rock stars, and movie idols derive enormous salaries from their service-related professions. The service economy has expanded in the United States as American society demands more of those services and has the ability to pay for them. One clear example of that growth exists in the health care economy. In 1960, health care costs accounted for only 5 percent of the nation's gross domestic product (GDP). In 2000, that number had increased to 15 percent (Goldfield et al. 2001, 922–24).

As industrial production provided a smaller percentage of the U.S. GDP, Americans imported more industrial goods and products. In 1979, the U.S. workforce employed 21 million industrial employees. By 1990, that number had dropped to 19 million. Economists continue to debate the positive and negative aspects of an economy that has shifted so clearly to a service system. It remains important to remember, however, that Detroit still manufactures millions of cars, and while the American industrial workforce lost two million jobs between 1979 and 1990, the actual production of industrial goods increased. American agriculture, a form of production, continues to harvest the greatest food supply of any nation. While agriculture accounted for less than 8 percent of the GDP throughout the 1990s and into 2000, U.S. food production continues to provide a powerful economic sector of the economy.

Thousands of small businesses nationwide also manufacture a variety of goods and products that bear the mark, "Made in America." More often, however, one sees that the clothes and products Americans purchase on a regular basis are made outside the United States. Those imported goods are generally cheaper than similar items manufactured in America. From a consumer's perspective, that has an obvious appeal. A pair of sneakers made in China has labor costs far below what one would pay similar workers in the United States, thus reducing the price of the product in a retail store. Critics maintain that it fosters slave labor wages for the foreign workers, often as little as the equivalent of 25 cents an hour (United States Department of Labor Report 2006). At the same time, it eliminates American jobs, as they are outsourced to other countries.

Outsourcing has become both an economic and political issue in the United States. During presidential debates in 2004, John Kerry accused President Bush and his administration of allowing the outsourcing of thousands, if not millions, of American jobs overseas, from high-tech computer work to low-wage positions. What he failed to mention was the "insourcing" of thousands of employment opportunities for Americans as foreign companies built plants and businesses in the United States and hired Americans to work in those businesses. The Japanese car manufacturer Toyota builds many of its high-end Avalon models in Alabama. Hyundai, the Korean automobile maker, has a production facility in Tennessee. Statistics indicate that Americans have seen more insourcing of jobs than outsourcing in the first decade of the twenty-first century (United States Department of Labor Report 2006). The debate, however, remains a key economic issue.

PAPER VS. PLASTIC

Credit and debit cards have emerged, in the last two decades, as a major factor in the economic structure of daily life in America. Currently, Americans possess 641 million cards, and the use of the cards to purchase goods and services amounted to $1.5 trillion in 2005. The average American family owes $8,000 on credit accounts. The use of "plastic money" has exploded in the modern age. In 1950, the Diners Club issued a small number of cards that people could use to eat in 27 restaurants. American Express also began to issue charge cards in the 1950s to a limited number of users. In 1958, the Bank of America mailed 60,000 cards to residents in Fresno, California. Less then twenty years later, after some title changes in the name of the credit cards, Visa and MasterCard entered the market. Gas stations issued cards, and retail stores provided their own options. American consumers had access to a variety of credit systems that banks and credit companies made available to eager customers. Americans could purchase any number of products with their credit cards (the amount of purchase generally limited to a certain dollar figure). They, or their bank accounts, would pay for that charge at a later date based on a statement of account. In 1980, the government deregulated the amount of interest credit card companies could charge and rates reached as high as 20 percent. In that same year, credit companies also began to charge a fee of $20 or more to own a credit card. Between 1980 and 1990, the use of "plastic money" doubled, and spending per person increased fivefold, from $518 to $2,700 annually.

If credit card users paid their monthly bills on schedule, the system worked well for consumers and retailers. Deferred payment provided a simple and easy way for American families to make basic purchases without using cash. Problems arose, however, when card users chose to pay only a portion of their debts and fell victim to late fee or penalty fee charges. Charging interest and penalty rates as high as 18 and 20 percent, credit card companies earned $30 billion in profits in 2005. And, since 1990, credit card debt for American families has risen from $2,700 to $8,000.

The expansive use of credit cards has created a subindustry in credit reporting companies. Currently, three major credit firms evaluate the credit rating of American families. Equifax, Experian, and TransUnion study millions of credit accounts to determine the credit rating of Americans who use the service. Using a system termed FICO (Fair Isaac Corporation) they use a point system, from 300 to 850, to indicate a credit user's rating—the higher the number, the better the rating. The number 700 signals a moderate approval rating; 750 and above is excellent. Credit card companies, banks, and other lending agencies can track credit ratings to determine the risk regarding loan applications for everything from credit cards to automobile purchases. A recent survey indicated that only 2 percent of Americans knew about the credit rating system or what their status indicated (http://www.shoppbs.org).

American consumers in the twenty-first century depend on the use of credit cards for a large portion of their purchases. The option presents both benefits and dangers. If users pay their account bills promptly and avoid late and penalty fees, plastic money is a much safer and easier way for families to use their finances to obtain the necessary and enjoyable goods and services that are part of economic satisfaction. While a surge in credit card fraud and criminal abuse of the options remains an issue of concern, credit cards are still safer and easier than cash. When users, however, fall victim to late fees and penalty fees, the financial impact can become devastating to family incomes and finances. If credit card companies made $30 billion in interest profits in 2005, that excess came out of the pockets of Americans. When the personal debt of American families rises to almost five figures on average, most of it credit card debt, this generates an unstable financial situation, both to the families themselves and to the general health of the economy. Specialists conclude that the answer to the problem lies in credit card users paying their balances promptly. Yet, the seductive ability in a consumer-driven, material-demand society encourages many Americans to continue the process of buying now and paying later even if later draws them into severe debt.

POVERTY

While problems with the American economy continued to concern observers, the investment market rebounded from the 2000–2002 recession. By the end of 2005, the Dow Jones Industrial Average regained its 11,000 number and the NASDAQ responded accordingly. Unemployment numbers dropped below 5 percent, and the

Federal Reserve kept a careful eye on inflation and interest rates, which remained in the low single digits. Consumer confidence indexes also showed a positive trend, and the economy continued to grow at a steady rate. Problems, however, persisted. Public and personal debt soared in the 1990s and early years of the new century. The American trade balance also continued to show that the nation, once the most powerful creditor in world commerce, had become the globe's largest debtor. And the continual concern of poverty in the wealthiest society on earth drew stark attention to unresolved problems in the economy.

Poverty remains a most persistent and serious concern in the United States. The nation spends more than $500 billion a year, a bit less than 12 percent of its GDP, on public assistance and social insurance projects. Those include Social Security, Medicare, Medicaid, food stamps (which ended in 1997), and other projects. That commitment, however, has failed to eliminate the severe economic and social tragedy of poverty, the fundamental focus of Lyndon Johnson's Great Society program in the 1960s. Fixing a family income for four at $13,359+ per year as at the poverty line, census figures indicated that 14 percent of the population (33.6 million people) fell below the poverty line in 1990. By 2000, the poverty line number was raised to $20,000+, altered for inflation. The percentage number dropped to 11.3 percent. In 2004, the percentage climbed slightly to 12.7 percent (37 million people) (United States Health and Human Services Department Report 2005).

Some analysts argue that looking at wages alone creates an imprecise view of poverty. Net worth includes additional measures of economic substance. As an example, 31 percent of those listed as poor, by wage standards, own their homes. Forty-eight percent own cars and other high-end durable goods, such as televisions, refrigerators, washers, and dryers. When those net worth values enter the equation, the poverty rate drops by as much as 3 percent. Comparisons with previous time periods in America also create divergent viewpoints. Using the standards of 2000 to judge poverty, even given inflation as a factor, 67 percent of the American population in 1939 would be considered poor by today's standards. Numbers and comparisons, however, fail to fully confront the issue. Many researchers conclude that poverty will always exist in some form in a free market, democratic economy, particularly one as large and diverse as that of the United States. Relative deprivation remains a key consideration in any analysis of poverty in the United States.

Some argue that poverty is a state of relative economic deprivation, that it depends not on whether income is lower than some arbitrary level, but whether it falls far below the income of others in the same society. (Isabell Sawhill, Brookings Institute, "Domestic Entitlements and the Federal Budget," February 15, 2006, 1)

If that defines the essence of poverty in the United States, then no matter how wealthy the society becomes, some portion of the society will perceive itself as poor.

Given those issues, poverty as a factor in American economic life also has demographic characteristics. Poverty among young people under the age of 18 fluctuated from 16.2 to 17.8 percent between 1990 and 2004. Elderly Americans aged 65 and over saw their percentage numbers decline from 35.2 percent in 1959 to a little more than 12 percent by 1990. The impact of retirement accounts, Social Security, Medicare, and other benefits has played a significant role in that shift. The poverty rate among African American families has also declined during the past 30 years. At 32 percent, however, in 1990, it remained three times higher than for white families.

Inner-city poverty in large urban centers occupies the current attention of those who study the issue of poverty in America. The concept of an underclass of families or individuals living in urban ghettos continues to suggest a demographic and racial component to the complex problem. Critics, both for and against government or social responses to the problem, cite symptoms of poverty: welfare dependence, joblessness, crime, out-of-wedlock pregnancy, and other issues as causal factors. In a number of urban areas, poverty levels exceed 40 percent, a significant growth when compared to the 1950s and 1960s. Statistically, however, those numbers account for only 7 percent of Americans families defined as living in poverty (Sawhill, 5).

Any review of the American economic condition and its impact on daily life centers on how observers interpret economic data. So many issues determine the fundamental health of an economy that it becomes a matter of continual debate. Those concerned with modern economic conditions in the United States can certainly point to a host of problems. The significant rise of personal and public debt remains a major concern. The trade balance provides another problem, particularly America's dependence on foreign oil resources. The slow and steady decline of industrial production adds another element to the equation, and that combines with the outsourcing of much of that production to other countries. At the same time, however, the traditional barometers of national economic health appear positive. Unemployment, inflation, and interest rates, the noted "misery index" criteria that politicians have used since Jimmy Carter and George H. W. Bush campaigned, have remained historically low. GDP figures also suggest moderate but steady growth. Consumer confidence in the economy is also high. The stock market indicators, from the Dow Jones to NASDAQ, have seemingly recovered from the crisis of 2001–2002. Yet, in a broad, volatile global market, often influenced by economic forces beyond the nation's control, the world's largest economy still faces any number of issues related to access to vital resources, energy, costs of pollution and environmental degradation, technological innovation, protection of intellectual property, productivity, education, uneven distribution of wealth, and complicated and contradictory public policy on taxation, debt, and support for research and development.

RECHARGED ECONOMY

The economic boom of the 1990s also helped to influence the federal budget. The huge federal budget deficit that had developed in the 1980s disappeared in the 1990s. Higher taxes brought more revenue into the treasury, and government expenditures dropped as well. As the economy grew, personal and corporate income generated increased tax revenues and the deficit disappeared. President Clinton signed a deficit-reduction bill in 1997 that aimed to stabilize the federal budget and reduce the debt and deficit. For the next three years, the effort produced positive results as the federal government's annual deficits turned to surpluses. As interest rates lowered, the Treasury Department had to devote less of the federal budget to account for interest paid on the federal debt.

A look at the federal budget between 1991 and 2005 indicated key trends in federal spending and the impact of that spending on the economy. With the exception of 1967, the federal government spent more money than it collected until 1998. Between 1998 and 2001, the government collected a surplus in revenue. Since federal spending accounted for 18 percent of the nation's GDP, government finances played a major role in the nation's economic health. In 1991, the government spent 1,324 billion dollars and collected 1,055 billion in tax revenues. It ran a deficit of 269 billion dollars. In 1995, it collected 1,352 billion in taxes and spent 1,516, adding 164 billion dollars to the deficit. Then, between 1998 and 2001, the federal budget saw more revenue than expenditures. As an example, in 2000, federal expenditures amounted to 1.8 trillion dollars while the government had 2,025 trillion in revenue, a surplus of 236 billion dollars. In basic terms, throughout the early 1990s, the federal government expended around $20,000 per family in the United States. Then, as surpluses increased in the mid-1990s and into early 2001, spending per family dropped to under $19,000. As of 2005 that number has climbed to $22,000 per family (U.S. Office of Management and Budget [OMB] Report 2006).

TAXES

Federal income taxes remain the subject of intense discussion and debate, and they serve as a major factor in examining the impact of the American economy on the daily lives of families. In 2004 the Internal Revenue Service established the following tax rates for married couples filing a joint return. The statistics do not take into account a variety of deductions, such as dependents, medical expenses, and so on.

Income	Tax Rate
Up to $14,300	10%
$14,300–$58,100	15%
$58,100–$117,250	25%
$117,250–$178,000	28%
$178,000–$319,000	33%
Over $319,000	35%

Those figures changed only slightly between 1993 and 2004, even considering the tax reduction bill that the administration of George W. Bush and the Republican Congress legislated in 2003. In 1990, the tax rate for the highest 20 percent of earners was 28 percent. It climbed to 39.6 percent in 1993, dropped to 38.6 percent in 2002, and settled at 35 percent in 2003.

FICA (Federal Insurance Contribution Act, or Social Security) and Medicare payments create additional revenue for the government and increase costs to American employees, employers, and families. The FICA tax adds 12.4 percent of income, and Medicare an additional 2.9 percent. Employees pay half those amounts from their wages, while their employers pay the other half.

Distribution of tax responsibility and revenue collection based on income indicates that the wealthiest 20 percent contribute the largest percentage of revenue to the federal government. The following 1995 sample of revenue collection, by income, indicates the figures.

Highest 20% of earners	78% of revenue
Second highest 20%	16%
Middle 20%	7%
Second lowest 20%	1%
Lowest 20%	–2%

The Internal Revenue Service also evaluates the number of American families who file their tax returns in those five income brackets: 22.2 million in the highest bracket, 21.2 in the second, 21.2 in the third, 21.8 in the fourth, and 21.2 in the bottom 20 percent. While wealthy earners have access to a variety of tax deductions and tax laws that help protect their earnings, the data suggests clearly that the central object of a graduated income tax works. The wealthiest Americans pay the most revenue. At the same time, the numbers indicate that almost two-thirds of American families had earned incomes that defined middle- and upper-middle-class financial status (U.S. Internal Revenue Service).

While politicians and economists debate the various statistics and their day-to-day impact on Americans, the numbers remain an interesting factor to ponder. Free market defenders believe that tax reduction, even for the wealthy, places more money in the hands of individuals and families, encourages them to save or spend their own money, ultimately generates more jobs and income, and therefore creates more income that can be taxed. Critics believe that the tax reduction legislation in 2003 provided a special benefit for the wealthiest Americans and harmed the middle- and lower-income earners. In simple terms, the rich got richer, while other Americans saw little or no benefit. At the end of 2005, the impact of the pro-growth supply side tax reduction created a new debate. Because the economy expanded and personal income rose, tax revenue increased by almost 15 percent and federal revenues jumped to $249 billion. The federal deficit dropped from $318 billion to $260 billion.

Besides federal income taxes, FICA, and Medicare payments, Americans are also subject to a variety of state and local taxes. Forty-one states impose income taxes on their residents. New Hampshire and Tennessee tax only dividends and stock earnings. Alabama, Florida, Nevada, South Dakota, Texas, Washington, and Wyoming have no state income taxes. Thirty-five states base their taxes on federal income returns and charge a smaller percentage than the central government to taxpayers. Maine and New York have the highest state tax rates. Alabama and New Hampshire require the lowest taxes based on income. Besides income taxes, states also have sales taxes to enhance their revenues. Only five states have no sales tax: Alaska, Delaware, Montana, New Hampshire, and Oregon. In most states with sales taxes, which range from 4 to 7 percent, food, clothing, and medicines are exempted. Both states and the federal government derive additional revenue from liquor, cigarettes, and gasoline. The federal government taxes on gasoline amount to 18.4 cents a gallon. Each state imposes its own tax on gasoline, diesel, and other fuels. "Sin taxes," on liquor and cigarettes, also enhance state revenues. Minnesota, as an example, has added a tax of 75 cents to each pack of cigarettes Americans purchase. While supporters of the tax increase applaud the higher sin taxes as a method to reduce consumption, critics charge that the fewer people who purchase the products, as a result of increased costs, the fewer dollars states will derive to respond to health care costs and other necessary social services (http://www.retirementliving.com).

Local property taxes make up a third part of American taxation for families. Real estate taxes account for almost all of local taxation. Most of that revenue, more than 50 percent, goes to public education. The rest supports a variety of services, including police, firefighters, emergency medical response, trash collection, and other essential local demands. On average, Americans pay about 35 percent of their gross incomes, annually, to the three areas of government, federal, state, and local, that require those revenues. Certainly, the amount of income that individuals derive, the amount of consumer purchases they make, and the states where they live alter the percentage. If Americans complain about being over-taxed—"I must work from January to May to pay the government, then from June to December for my own and my family's benefit"—total tax demands are much less than in European countries. Recent figures compiled in the European Union estimate that European families pay tax revenues in excess of 40 percent at the national level (http://www.finfacts.com/Private/tax/taxationeuropeanunion25.htm).

Increased taxes alone did not create the budget surpluses of the late 1990s. An expanded economy, lower interest rates, and reduced inflation also impacted on federal revenues and expenditures. A look at the federal budget indicates the significance of interest rates and the general influence those rates have on the nation's finances.

Federal Budget: Example from 1997 Budget

Medicare/Medicaid—23.25%	Interest on debt—15.2%
Social Security—22.45%	Discretionary—17.3%
Defense—16.8%	Other programs—9.3%

As the interest rates in the nation declined as a whole, the amount of money the government had to allocate to pay the interest on the federal debt declined accordingly. That one factor alone reduced the federal budget by billions of dollars. At the end of the 1990s, the government seemed to have gained control of its expenditures and eliminated the massive deficit that had weakened the economy in the previous decade.

TECHNOLOGY

The evolution and growth of high-tech electronics and computer businesses developed after World War II, partly tied to the defense industry. Early computers were used as code-breaking machines during the war. International Business Machines (IBM) developed computer guidance systems and other sophisticated military hardware for the air force. During the 1950s, half of IBM's revenues came from defense contracts. As scientists and technical specialists looked for ways to bring computer technology into the civilian marketplace, the impact on the American economy grew dramatically. In 1971, scientists created the first microprocessors (microchips) for computers that reduced the size, enhanced the capacity, and lowered the cost of the machines. Just north of San Jose, California, computer businesses established offices in what came to be called Silicon Valley. By the beginning of the 1980s, more than a quarter of a million people worked in the area, and 3,000 businesses dealing in electronics and computers had offices there. Related businesses spread throughout the western United States.

Microprocessors enabled users to store huge amounts of data in relatively small, portable computers (desktop and eventually laptop). Computer programmers continued to work on systems that would make the everyday use of computers easier to comprehend. Bill Gates founded Microsoft in 1975, whose corporate goal aimed at "putting a computer on every desktop." In 1976, Steven Jobs and Stephen Wozniak, college dropouts, founded the Apple Computer Company. IBM joined shortly in the home computer business. The high-tech companies continued to market their products to government, businesses, and home users. By 1988, sales of computers had reached 10 million. By the 1990s they had become an integral aspect of everyday American life. In 1996, 14 percent of adults reported they used Internet access in their homes or businesses. By 2003, 79 percent used the service. By comparison, it took almost four decades for radios to attract 50 million American users, and 13 years for television sets to reside in 50 million homes. It took computers fewer than four years to reach the same numbers of Americans using the equipment.

Computer technology and its everyday use in homes and businesses during the 1990s accelerated the development of Internet services like the World Wide Web. Essentially, the high-tech computer industry had developed a three-part business process as the market expanded. Hardware, software, and the Internet formed the triad. As an example, Apple computers sold hardware, the actual machines. Bill Gates's Microsoft Company sold the software

"Soccer mom" and family. Courtesy of Jolyon Girard.

packages that a corporation, such as IBM, could purchase and put in their computers (hardware). Internet services, like the World Wide Web, could then utilize both hardware and software systems to go online with a variety of informational and commercial systems to make the computers more appealing to consumers. At the technical level, microprocessors (microchips) enabled everyone, from producer to consumer, to use smaller, cheaper, and faster equipment.

The high-tech boom translated into other commercial options. The Internet, e-mail, cell phone (wireless telephones), iPods, and other electronic devices became essential aspects of an expanding electronic economy. The initial concept of Internet connections with computers derived from a national defense and academic demand. During the late 1970s and the 1980s, ARPAnet (Advanced Research Projects Administration of the Defense Department) developed a communication system to respond to a nuclear attack against the United States. During the 1980s, academic institutions, science labs, and other technical facilities also employed Internet services. The Department of Defense released control of the service in 1984, opening the option to private and commercial use. Then, in 1991, the World Wide Web inaugurated Internet services that encouraged commercial and private users to develop their own Web sites. That enabled the users to place commercial, political, economic, and social information online for anyone with Internet ownership to access. At the same time, technology allowed the Internet services to expand their bandwidth, and that innovation enabled Web sites to fill their pages with pictures, designs, and graphic creations. By the beginning of the new century, almost 80 percent of Americans indicated that they used computers and Internet systems as part of their personal or business life (Goldfield 2001, 924–25).

That instant information and communication commerce also witnessed the rapid growth in the use of personal cell phones. Phone companies in the 1980s sold a small number of cell phones (mobile phones) for emergency use. The businesses exploited underused radio bands and satellite systems to provide the wireless service. As consumer interest expanded, the companies began to build a series of wireless microwave broadcasting towers. Government deregulation also encouraged competition as more wireless systems came online and could advertise their products. In 1990, 5 million Americans had purchased cell phones. In 2003, nearly 160 million people owned the wireless option, more than half the population.

Critics of the exploding electronic economy wrote extensively about the "Instant Society." Consumers wanted rapid communication and information. Whether that data was accurate or even necessary remained a subject of debate. Some observers predicted that the Internet would doom published books and magazines as more people typed "www.whatever" on their computers and waited for the information. Would libraries and book publishers go out of fashion and out of business? Would students, at every level of education, forsake books for electronics? How would the new source of information impact on intellectual property rights?

The use of cell phones became both a subject of serious concern and the butt of numerous cartoons and jokes. The stereotyped "soccer mom" in her suburban van, with a cell phone "welded" to her ear, became a commonplace theme for comedians and cartoonists. At the same time, police agencies worried about the increase in automobile accidents, the result, evidence often indicated, of people using cell phones while they drove. The state of New Jersey passed laws prohibiting the use of handheld cell phones in order to alleviate the problem. Drivers cavalierly disobeyed the law and continued talking. It reminded one police officer of H. L. Mencken's comment in the 1920s regarding prohibition—"Americans are the most law abiding people on earth, so long as they agree with the law."

Ultimately, the high-tech economic boom of the 1990s provided consumers with a vast array of products and services to make their lives easier and more beneficial. Other sections of the chapter will examine the influence of high-tech economics on domestic and material life for Americans as they pursued their day-to-day existence. As an economic factor, however, the high-tech boom created a whole new field of commerce that created millions of jobs, billions of dollars in profits, and a major impact on research and development technology.

FOR MORE INFORMATION

About.com. "Globalization." http://globalization.about.com.

Beck, Millie Allen. *Labor Relations*. Westport, CT: Greenwood Press, 2005.

Federal Trade Commission. http://www.ftc.gov/credit/.

Goldfield, David, et al. *The American Journey*. Upper Saddle River, NJ: Prentice Hall, 2001.

North American Free Trade Agreement. http://www.dfait-maeci.gc.ca/nafta-alena/menu-en.asp.

Sawhill, Isabel V. "Poverty in the United States." *The Concise Encyclopedia of Economics*. http://www.econlib.org.

Securities and Exchange Commission. http://www.sec.gov.

Shop PBS. http://www.shoppbs.org.

"Taxation in the EU from 1995 to 2002. Tax Rates." *Income and Corporate Tax Rates 2004*. http://www.finfacts.com/Private/tax/taxationeuropeanunion25.htm.

"Taxes by States." http://www.retirementliving.com/RL taxes.

U.S. Department of Labor. http://www.dol.gov.

U.S. Internal Revenue Service. http://www.irs.gov.

U.S. Office of Management and Budget. http://www.whitehouse.gov/omb.

The Wall Street Journal. http://online.wsj.com/public/us.

Intellectual Life

OVERVIEW

Two main currents continued to influence intellectual life in the United States. The evolution of a popular, mass culture and the continued growth of a classical commitment to more traditional forms of intellectual and cultural interest defined those two trends in modern American intellectual life. Urban, egalitarian, mass interest in a broad variety of popular options from literature to movies to art has generated interest among an increasing number of Americans, and these forms remain a widely popular and diverse aspect of the culture's intellectual attraction. At the same time, however classical modes of intellectual curiosity also attract and continue to influence American thought and practice. Serious, provocative novels compete with melodrama and pulp fiction for the attention of American readers. Symphony orchestras in most American cities offer an alternative to rock concerts. Seventy percent of living Nobel Prize winners live in the United States, most working at major American universities. In the fields of science, medicine, and other intellectual disciplines, the nation still attracts top professionals. Those men and women provide an ongoing creativity of thought and progress.

Ultimately, free societies create an atmosphere of free thought. In contemporary American society, daily life exposes the public to a multitude of intellectual options, both simple and complex. The dichotomy of "lowbrow" versus "highbrow" intellectualism in the United States has often sparked a curious dialogue and debate, both in the United States and abroad. The contemporary era seems to suggest no specific school of thought or viewpoint as dominant on the American landscape. If individual authors, artists, and intellectuals spoke for a particular idea or theme in previous decades in American life, that is not the case in the past 15 years. As one observer noted, American intellectual life currently has no hegemonic view. So many different forms of expression now exist that it remains difficult to point to individuals or styles to define various expressions in intellectual life.

In the 1920s, H. L. Mencken, the noted newspaper iconoclast, remarked that "nobody ever went broke underestimating the taste of the American public." Current critics of U.S. intellectual life might argue that that jab at the culture's substance is still valid. They often point to the great wasteland that they see in American culture. They perceive a people besotted by bad television shows, mass sporting events, overt commercialism, and the dumbing down of intellectual curiosity and substance. As an example, public education in the United States is often challenged as less than productive when compared to other Western, industrialized nations. Test scores in math and reading skills often indicate that American elementary and secondary students fall well below the standards set in a number of other countries. Particular concern exists with regard to minority Americans who fall victim, in Jonathan Kozol's words, to "savage inequality" in their access to sound, stimulating education (from the title of Kozol's 1991 book on American education).

An alternative view sees a robust intellectual climate in the United States. In the midst of lowest-common-denominator arguments, American daily life continues to offer variety that runs the gamut of substance. While that gives critics the opportunity to select appropriate examples to support their claims, and they should, it overlooks the substance they choose not to consider. Education in the United States confronts problems at every level, and the issues are serious and profound. Yet, American education continues to provide more people with access to higher education than any other nation on earth. Thousands of colleges and universities open their doors to millions of students each year, offering an advanced education and intellectual pursuits. Many of those institutions of learning are the finest in the world, where provocative and creative intellectual thought and accomplishment occur every day. One could hardly argue that Yale, the Massachusetts Institute of Technology, and Stanford fail to challenge the best minds in the nation. And hundreds of other colleges and universities do the same.

One can arrange the same debate in all of the topics discussed below, and it remains the goal of the section to examine both aspects of American intellectual life as daily life in the United States entered the twenty-first century. A main theme throughout the encyclopedia continues to stress the idea that a society as complex and broad as the United States offers so many options, both positive and questionable, that it remains difficult to develop a single, simple explanation. Certainly, intellectual life in American daily life sees that same challenge.

ART AND ARCHITECTURE

In the years following World War II, much American art reflected the realism of artists like Andrew Wyeth, but American painters increasingly turned more to abstract art by the beginning of the 1960s. Jackson Pollock, Willem de Kooning, and other abstract artists began to create bold imagery that defined a new abstract expressionism that elevated American painting to a new level of respect in the artistic world. Sculpture saw a similar development, with David Smith and Herbert Ferber using abstract forms of light and space in their creations. Pop art also emerged in the 1960s and 1970s. Andy Warhol's famous Campbell Soup Can epitomized the style, but other artists joined the new fields of pop art, minimalism, and color-field painting to add variety to the expanding field. Traditional observers often criticized the new forms as simplistic or childish, but they became standard and popular by the 1980s.

During the 1970s, the increased creativity of female and minority artists also changed the nature of artistic expression in American life. Artists focused their work on their distinctive heritage or social circumstance. Judy Chicago and Jenny Holzer suggest examples of the individualism in the art of the period. By the end of the 1980s, no single genre of artistic expression seemed to dominate or influence America's scene. As with many other intellectual venues, American art has gone off in a variety of directions. The growing use of words in art, as a statement and an image, and the increased use of photography, collage, and other media also influence contemporary artistic expression. The field has also shown a resurgence of realism and what one critic called "borrowings" from other periods and works of art. American art and architecture in the new century shows broad style and interest that continue to fill the numerous galleries in America with expressive work. Popular commercial artists also influence the field. Howard Behrans and Thomas Kinkade produce mass-consumption landscapes that remain widely popular. Folk, local, and regional art have also added to the healthy and varietal expressions of American life. One person's graffiti is another's art, and the regional Amish barn art continues to attract attention. In every area, rural and urban, in the United States, local artists create for local audiences. They add to the wide quilt of American artistic life.

EDUCATION

Since the U.S. Department of Education published *A Nation at Risk* in 1983, Americans have struggled with concerns regarding the benefits and problems in public education. In that 1983 report, the National Commission on Excellence in Education claimed that American "students were not studying the right subjects, were not working hard enough, and were not learning enough. Their schools suffered from slack and uneven standards. Many of their teachers were ill-prepared." The report concluded with a grim prediction that the nation's elementary and secondary schools would soon be engulfed in a "rising tide of mediocrity." Since the publication of that sobering document, concern about public education and its impact on the intellectual lives of young people has occupied the attention of local and state governments, primarily concerned with public education. At the same time, two presidential administrations have cited "educational excellence" as a major aspect of their agendas. Business executives and human resource departments in the business world have joined a chorus calling for students better able to compete in a global economy, with the basic educational skills to do so. During the 1990s, an increase in drug use, gun violence, gangs, teenage pregnancies, and numerous other concerns seemed to center around a failed public educational system, with lip service paid to other social factors that may have contributed to those issues. One could not disagree, however, that national test scores (Scholastic Aptitude Test) and other evaluations evidenced declining scores and skills, especially when compared to other Western industrial nations. Even worse, minority student scores showed steeper declines. By the end of the decade of the 1990s, half of America's African American students had dropped out by their senior year in high school. One critic defined the education of those black students who stayed in school as a "yawning achievement gap" compared with white students in affluent suburban schools (Williams 2006, A 15).

In a recent ABC story, "Stupid in America," John Stossel attacked the education system in even more stark language. The variety of criticisms has certainly influenced government attention. The administration of President George W. Bush developed the "No Child Left Behind" legislation with Congress in January 2002 to address the growing chorus of concerns. The federal government created standards to measure learning accomplishments in the state systems and seeks to enforce those standards through the Department of Education. Charter schools, home schooling, the growth of private and faith-based schools, and other alternative types of education have also evolved in the past 20 years to offer alternative methods of education. The criticisms of American public education have existed throughout the twentieth century and at various times have drawn significant public attention. In 2005, more than 77 million Americans attended schools, from kindergarten through undergraduate college. In the same year, 85 percent of the general population had earned high school degrees. Twenty-seven percent had earned undergraduate degrees. The literacy rate in the United States for 15-year-olds ranged between 86 and 98 percent depending on the region of the country. A recent UN analysis of American education gave the country a 99.9 rating, the highest it provides, placing the United States with 20 other nations as the top systems throughout the world (U.S. Department of Education Report 2007). Higher education in America, both undergraduate and graduate, still offers a large and impressive opportunity for enhancing intellectual growth in the nation, and the number of college graduates is the highest per capita in the world. As noted in the overview, 70 percent of Nobel Prize recipients live in the United States, and most teach or do research in American universities. While the debate and dialogue concerning the role of education in the United States remains a heated and often divisive issue, daily access to a broad and varied educational experience remains a major aspect of life in the United States.

FILM

During the 1990s, the American Film Institute asked 1,500 members to rate the best 100 films in American movie history. *Citizen Kane* (1941) and *Casablanca* (1942) topped the list. A quick review of decade-by-decade evaluations since World War II offers an interesting look at the number and type of movies that the members considered worthy of merit. Twelve films from 1940, 19 from 1950, 18 from 1960, 18 from 1970, 6 from 1980, and 8 from 1990 made the list. In "movie-made" America, the culture often reflects its stereotypes and attitudes in the films that its people admire and frequent. Outside the United States, many foreign observers identify their views of America based on the nation's exported films and television shows. Movies have become such a profound aspect of America's intellectual climate that they deserve particular scrutiny. Listed below are the films of the 1990s that appeared in the top 100 films, with their rank:

Schindler's List (1993) #9
Silence of the Lambs (1991) #65
Forrest Gump (1994) #71
Dances with Wolves (1990) #75
Fargo (1996) #84
Goodfellas (1990) #94
Pulp Fiction (1994) #95
Unforgiven (1992) #98

All of the films honored in the 1990s explored serious topics, from the Holocaust, to crime, to relations with American Indians. While no single theme or particular genre dominated films in the 1990s, the public could experience a continuing commercial film commitment to quality production and performances. Additionally, the contemporary era has seen major innovations in film technology. Computer graphics and other new forms of technology have had a major impact on movie production. J.R.R. Tolkien's classic trilogy *Lord of the Rings* came to the screen in epic form during

2001–2003 and utilized the new technology brilliantly. The initial use of that form may have begun with George Lucas's *Star Wars* in 1977, and its use has remained a major factor in contemporary films that require digital-graphic production scenes. Special effects technology has changed dramatically.

New concepts in animation have also influenced American movies. Pixar Animation Studios invented new techniques for producing animated films, video games, and other graphics in the 1970s and 1980s and came to the wide screen in the 1990s with *Toy Story*. The company began a long negotiation with Walt Disney Productions to work on additional animated movies like *The Incredibles*. Eventually they would join the Disney family as a subsidiary corporation in 2006.

Commercially, the American movie industry continues to enjoy financial success, although the old studio system has long given way to independent production, release, and profit sharing. Weekly movie attendance remained in the mid-$20 million range throughout the period 1991 to 2001 and climbed to $30 million weekly in 2002. Americans remained willing to pay between $4 and $6 per ticket to see their choices. It is interesting to note that Americans spent 23 percent of their recreation dollars on movies between 1942 and 1945, while they spent only 2 percent in 2000. While attendance figures are far below the record 80 million numbers in the 1940s, it remains important to remember the variety of other media available to Americans today (Pautz 2002). Options in home technology, such as DVD players, have enabled families to rent or purchase films at stores like Blockbuster, which had close to 3,000 stores nationwide by 2004.

Likewise, cable, more channels, and pay-per-view options brought movies into millions of American homes. Reflecting the trend, movie makers regularly adapted their big-screen productions for home viewing.

LITERATURE

No single author or literary style speaks to the contemporary American society, but America's current literary genres have produced a number of exciting and accomplished writers. Douglas Coupland, a Canadian novelist, published *Generation X: Tales for an Accelerated Culture* in 1991. Generation X became the name for those who reached adulthood in the late 1980s. The characters in the novel, often seen as accurate portrayals, shun the fast-paced commercialized world in an effort to find themselves.

This self-exploration is also one of the themes in both Brett Easton Ellis's *American Psycho* and Charles Michael Palahniuk's *Fight Club*. In *American Psycho*, the protagonist, Patrick Bateman, must battle his inner demons as he balances his daytime yuppie *persona* in corporate America and his evening endeavors as a serial killer. *Fight Club*, on the other hand, features a protagonist on the edge of sanity. That schizophrenic character has imaginary conversations and battles with his alter ego. In the Coupland model, this story represents a deep-seated desire to break from normality and delve into the psyche. Both *American Psycho* and *Fight Club* have achieved a cult following and were made into motion pictures starring Christian Bale and Ed Norton, respectively.

The exploration of personal demons also appeared in Edna Annie Proulx's Pulitzer Prize winning novel *The Shipping News* and short story "Brokeback Mountain" and Michael Cunnigham's Pulitzer Prize–winning novel *The Hours*. As with other key works of literature from this era, all were turned into blockbuster motion pictures starring some of the era's finest actors.

In addition to influential novels, several notable writers have produced collections of their short stories and poetry. Dominican-born Junot Diaz became an overnight success in 1996 when his short stories were published in the anthology *Drown*. Edwidge Danticat also rose to fame with the 1995 publication of her short stories in the anthology *Krik Krak*. Only 26 years of age at the time, Danticat was considered one of America's most celebrated new writers. *Krik Krak* was a finalist for the 1995 National Book Award. Two poets who enjoyed notoriety before the 1990s continued to garner accolades throughout the era. New York native Billy Collins published highly recognized collections of poetry, *Questions about Angels* and *The Art of Drowning*, in 1991 and 1995 respectively. Pennsylvania native Gerald Stern's 1998 collection *This Time: New and Selected Poems* won that year's National Book Award.

The period from 1991 through 2005 has seen great diversity in literature. Americans continued to find meaning and diversion in novels, short stories, and poems. Age, level of education, and household income had a tremendous effect on people's reading habits. Of the books sold between 2000 and 2004, the highest percentage, 24.2 percent, were sold to Americans between the ages of 45 and 54. Also of note is the fact that another 20.5 percent of books went to people over the age of 65. Lagging far behind, Americans under the age of 25 bought only 5 percent of the books sold in the United States, although people of that age have access to books in school and online. In that regard, the book-owner count may be deceiving concerning readership.

With regard to education, 54.3 percent of the books were sold to high school graduates. This figure is much larger than the 17.2 percent of books sold to Americans with a college degree and the 16.5 percent of books sold to people with education beyond college. Interestingly, even those American who did not have a high school diploma bought 12 percent of the books sold in the country, and those with a household income less than $30,000 bought 34.7 percent of the books purchased in America (U.S. Census Bureau Report 2000, *Book Purchasing for Adults*).

MEDICINE

Americans saw amazing advancements in the field of medicine during the era. Physicians and patients benefited from the rise in pharmacological research. Drug companies invested billions of dollars in finding new ways to treat common diseases.

In the wake of the HIV/AIDS crisis of the 1980s, Americans became more concerned with health care. Growing concerns regarding health and the health care industry also emerged as an aging generation of Americans considered their own possible problems with heart disease, cancer, and other potential health problems. Yet, the HIV/AIDS concern attracted great interest in American life. Contributing to that was the fact that celebrities like Magic Johnson, the NBA basketball star, were diagnosed HIV positive. His infection suggested that HIV/AIDS threatened more than homosexuals and intravenous drug users. Johnson continued to be one of the most inspirational survival stories. Much of that was due to the experimental medicine to which Johnson has had access.

As the drug industry grew, new companies arose that dedicated themselves to pharmaceutical research. Drug companies often conducted their own research on new medication; however, in order to ensure impartiality, outside organizations called Contract Research Organizations (CROs) began to take the reins. Those CROs contracted out to the drug companies and conducted necessary clinical research trials in order to have a drug or medical device approved by the Food and Drug Administration (FDA).

Drug companies dedicated much time and resources to developing medications to combat the most deadly illnesses in American society. Trials focused on new medication to fight cancer, heart disease, and diabetes. With those advancements, however, Americans also saw setbacks. In 2004, the pharmaceutical company Merck stopped distribution of their popular drug Vioxx. That anti-inflammatory medication, geared toward arthritis patients, allegedly created an increased risk of heart disease and stroke. In the wake of the scandal, Merck faced numerous lawsuits and falling stock prices.

A major change in medicine was the solidification of managed care within the medical insurance industry. In many ways, managed care changed health care from a nonprofit to a for-profit business. Although there were several forms of managed care, including HMO, PPO, and POS, all managed care set regulations on patient–physician interaction. Many of the managed-care companies set limits on the amount of time a physician should spend with a patient, regulated the types of medications (usually favoring cheaper generic drugs) that physicians prescribed, and required referrals from primary care physicians before the insurance company would pay for a patient to see a specialist. Managed care did not succeed in cutting the cost of health care, and as of 2005 medical inflation was two to three times that of the country's overall inflation rate. Health care costs remained a major concern of employers and workers, and proposals for various government-run health care plans became regular fare in political campaigns across the country.

Also complicating the picture was the new practice of drug companies advertising particular prescription drugs directly to potential consumers, on TV and in magazines. The advertisements targeted particular audiences, especially the graying Baby Boomer generation. The wide availability of over-the-counter medicines and drugs, combined with the aggressive promotion of drugs as providing miracle relief from many real, and some imaginary, ailments and health problems contributed to the profits of drug companies. The marketing concept also implied that science could cure all.

MUSIC

As was the case with other forms of intellectual and artistic expression, there is no consensus in recent American music. The past decade and a half continued the trend toward so-called individualism in music. Alternative sounds gained increasing play on radio and on CDs. From 1991–1993, the music from garage band grunge culture coursed through the airwaves. Seattle-based bands like Nirvana, Alice in Chains, Pearl Jam, and Sound Garden created a unique sound that countless others attempted to emulate. That grunge music, a fusion of traditional punk, heavy metal, and idle rock, featured gritty guitar riffs and heavy drums. Those bands expressed their emotions through their heavy-hearted lyrics, sullied appearance, and edgy music.

At the same time the grunge movement was taking the country by storm, other artists were reviving and fusing musical genres. Rhythm and blues (R&B) artists like Boyz II Men, who debuted in 1991, resurrected soul music in their love ballads and joined those songs with more contemporary upbeat R&B tunes. Boyz II Men literally put Philadelphia, Pennsylvania, back at the top of the music industry, calling their music "Motown Philly." That rebirth of music in Philadelphia brought the City of Brotherly Love back to the 1970s glory achieved by "Philly soul" artists like Teddy Pendergrass, the O'Jays, the Spinners, and Patti LaBelle. Other Philadelphia natives, namely Musiq Soulchild and Jill Scott, have since capitalized on the renewed interest in Philadelphia musicians.

With grunge firmly entrenched on the West Coast in cities like Seattle, and soul resurfacing on the East Coast in cities like Philadelphia, the vanguard musical cities of New York and Los Angeles needed to reassess their dominance in the music industry. In both cases, rap became the vehicle for continued influence. West Coast rap, born out of the style of 1980s rap group Niggaz with Attitudes (NWA), featured cavalier attitudes along with forceful racial messages.

Not to be outdone, East Coast rappers, centered in New York City, developed their own version of the genre. While the music samples, often taken from 1960s and 1970s soul and R&B hits, were less intense than in West Coast rap, the lyrics carried a similar message of dissatisfaction with the state of race in this country. Both groups of rappers also spent a great deal of time talking about survival in the urban setting. Christopher Wallace (Biggy Smalls or Notorious BIG) was the most famous of the East Coast rappers. His two albums, *Ready to Die* and *Life after Death*, released posthumously, defined the musical style, and a generation of rappers looked up to him.

Surely, the only things that could have slowed the success of East Coast and West Coast rap were the rappers. In the late 1990s, a feud developed between rappers from the two coasts. The prime example of this was the battles between Californian Tupac Shakur and New Yorker Christopher Wallace. Both men were shot to death, likely as part of the ongoing East Coast vs. West Coast feud. Despite the fact that the leading faces on both coasts died, the music lives on. Wallace's producer Sean "Puffy" Combs (P. Diddy or Diddy) began a solo career after the death of his star artist and, through his record label (Bad Boy), his clothing line, and his television fame, he is one of the most successful musical personalities of the day.

Today, rappers continue presenting politically charged messages as they talk about the conditions of their everyday lives. Curtis James Jackson III (50 Cent) burst on the scene in the late 1990s. He continued the gangsta rap style of Shakur and Wallace. Other regions in the country now also boast a version of the rap genre. Cornell Haynes Jr. (Nelly) put Missouri on the map with his *Country Grammar*, and cities like Memphis, Atlanta, New Orleans, and Miami showed off their "Dirty South" style through rappers like Maurice Young (Trick Daddy), Timothy Mosley (Timbaland), and Katrina Taylor (Trina).

Not all music in the era offered such statements of anger and disillusionment. Popular artists like Whitney Houston, Madonna, Sheryl Crow, and Celine Dion sang sweeping ballads that captured the country's imagination. Throughout the era, their music was featured in motion pictures like *The Bodyguard, Austin Powers: The Spy Who Shagged Me,* and *Titanic.* Additionally, unisex bands like the Spice Girls, the Backstreet Boys, and N-Sync and solo artists like Britney Spears and Christina Aguilera led a revival of teenybopper culture reminiscent of the 1980s New Kids on the Block, Menudo, and New Edition crazes.

Whether an expression of anguish or a celebration of youth, music in the era was typified by individual messages and collective audiences. That merger of the personal and the communal was also the model for the distribution of music. With advancement in technology Americans experienced the rise of online music sharing. By the end of 2001, it was estimated that as many CDs were burned and copied from the Internet as were bought. Internet sites like Morpheus and Limewire allowed people to access millions of songs for free. Anyone who chose to do so could log on to those Web sites and share all of the music on their computer with everyone else. It was the ultimate communal experience, but more importantly, it was cutting into the music industry's bottom line. Over the past several years, the industry has attempted to cut down on this piracy. Following lawsuits for alleged copyright infringements, Napster, the father of the file-sharing industry, began requiring a subscription in order to obtain music. Apple's iPod and Microsoft's proposed Zune require specific file formats to play music on their devices. That, too, cut down on illegal file sharing; however, revenues in the music industry have been dragging, and industry executives blame this solely on online piracy.

PHILOSOPHY AND SCHOLARSHIP

Scholars throughout the era produced a great deal of theory-laden work following poststructuralism models. Theorists dealt with issues like race, class, gender, and sexuality. The so-called "other Americans" became the focus of writers who attempted to break down the alleged white male domination of their respective disciplines and develop works that celebrate diverse American experiences.

Drawing on advancements made since the mid-1950s, historians, anthropologists, literary critics, and sociologists took pains to analyze the lives of nonwhite Americans. Key historical works, like Matthew Frye Jacobson's *Whiteness of a Different Color* and Grace Elizabeth Hale's *Making Whiteness*, challenged ideas of what it meant to be white in American society and who historically was able to claim whiteness. Furthermore, critical race theorists provided a more nuanced picture of the white privilege in American society and culture.

Other scholars took the critical theory model and utilized it in a more global analysis. The 1990s and 2000s saw the proliferation of postcolonial studies. Always wary of language and meaning, those poststructuralists refused to use terms like Third World and Developing Nations to describe non-Western countries, because Third World implied that those nations were inferior to the First and Second World. Developing Nations implied that those countries aspired to be like the West. Instead, to them, the term postcolonial more accurately described the fact that the countries were economic, political, social, and cultural products of Western colonization.

As part of that growing concern for underrepresented groups, scholars have increasingly focused on the plight of women both in the United States and abroad. In fact, much of critical theory and poststructuralist thinking had its roots in gender theory. Prominent scholars like Michel Foucault, who studied power relationships in social institutions, and Jacques Derrida, who focused on deconstructing the language to allow the audience to better understand the presenter, included some discussion of gender in their analyses. Julia Kristeva added to that and focused her attention almost exclusively on women. While those three scholars were not American, their research and theories influenced a generation of American intellectuals.

More recently, scholars, particularly those interested in gender theory, have turned their attention to the study of sexuality. Those intellectuals challenged traditional gender conventions while also questioning the notion that male/female relationships represent the natural order. Rather than touting the male/female relationship, the scholars argued that America suffered from a compulsory heterosexuality, where it was assumed that everyone would find the opposite sex attractive and settle into a heterosexual relationship. The research emboldened a generation of nonheterosexual Americans, and gay pride celebrations, "queer" groups, grassroots activism, and movements to allow gay marriage became staples in American society.

SCIENCE AND TECHNOLOGY

Many of the advances in science and technology since 1991 came in the areas of entertainment. In 1991, Americans watched their favorite sitcoms via cable television or television antennas, viewed blockbuster movies on VCR tapes, communicated via bulky cellular and house phones and researched information in the closest library. All of that changed in subsequent years.

In 1996, small digital satellite dishes (18 inches in diameter) hit the market, and they became the second best-selling electronic item in history. The only better-selling product was the VCR. For many Americans, the dishes allowed satellite television providers to compete with local cable companies.

Although the VCR was a popular item in the 1990s, by the year 2000, DVD movies became as common as VHS tapes. In the next year, the DVD took over the home entertainment industry, and by 2004 DVD sales outpaced VHS tape sales. Adding to the digital phenomenon, in 2003, the first DVD camcorders were released. They allowed individuals to record their own movies in digital format.

To view the new DVDs and home movies, by 2005, almost all of the televisions sold in the United States were flat screen. The prices of large-screen plasma and LCD televisions dropped, and by 2005 a 42-inch plasma television retailed for as low as $1,400. The sales of high-definition televisions, with their greatly improved picture quality, were also on the rise as prices dropped. All of that led to more people watching movies on their state-of-the-art home theater systems. Attempting to capitalize on the recent development, motion picture companies began to decrease the time between when movies appeared in the theater and when they were released for sale to the general public.

Also available for ready consumption was popular music. Cellular phones decreased in size to the point where the Motorola Razr came as small as 13.9 millimeters thick, 53 millimeters wide, and 98 millimeters long. At these decreased sizes, cellular phones still had the capability to store and play music, thus making music readily available. Additionally, cellular phone owners could communicate using text messaging and e-mailing in addition to making a basic phone call.

Another medium for portable music began in 2001 with the introduction of the Apple iPod. That tiny music player revolutionized the music industry. With a sleek design and easy use, the iPod became a market phenomenon. Over its first five years, 67 million iPods were sold, and Apple controlled 75 percent of the music download industry (*Morning Edition*, October 23, 2006).

Of course, the expansion of the Internet provided the forum for music downloading. Over the 15-year period, Internet use skyrocketed. Cellular phones, home computers, laptops, and countless other devices gained Internet capability. High-speed connections made surfing the Web easier and more enjoyable. By 2005, having a good Web site became a must for most businesses in the United States.

Y2K: The Millennium Scare

In the 1960s and into the 1980s, computer software applications had used two-digit number systems to indicate calendar years rather than four-digit designations (81 rather than 1981). A concern grew as the year 2000 (the millennium) approached. The two-digit system could interpret '00 as 1900 rather than 2000. That held the potential to create a computer glitch or bug that might threaten a host of major computer applications in software and firmware. In finance, telecom, aviation, and even government, the flaw held the possibility to impact severely records and sensitive data.

Companies and institutions around the world spent billions of dollars as their computer specialists responded to the potential threat, seeking methods to correct the possible crisis. Some institutions switched off their systems as January 1, 2000, approached and others went to back-up systems. Pundits and experts debated the possible impact, some predicting an international catastrophe. Bank records might disappear, communication systems could fail, and an American society dependent on computer technology could face a major calamity. As the new year began, however, no major problems occurred, and the "Y2K" scare passed without any significant consequences (http://www.y2ktimebomb.com).

TELEVISION

The era saw the rise and fall of countless television shows. In the age of hundreds of channel options, few shows lasted for more than five or six years. Television programs that defied that trend vary in genre. Half-hour sitcoms like *Friends* and *Seinfeld* were the most notable examples. *Friends*, a comedy about six young adults living in New York City, aired from 1994 until 2004. The program dominated the Thursday evening airwaves along with *Seinfeld*. The brainchild of its namesake Jerry Seinfeld, that show aired from 1989 to 1998. Also set in New York City, the creators of *Seinfeld* boasted that it was a show about nothing. Members of the cast, from both of the sitcoms, moved on to spin-off shows, but none of them boasted the fan base of *Friends* and *Seinfeld*.

Hour-long shows also had success during the time period. The part science fiction, part detective drama *X-Files* developed a cult following from 1993 through 2002. That television series was so popular that it inspired a movie released in 1998. When it launched in 1993, *X-Files* became a major hit for the relatively new Fox Broadcasting Company.

Other hour-long programs, geared largely to a young adult audience, thrived during the period. *Beverly Hills 90210* obtained a large following while it aired from 1990 to 2000. The show, about a group of friends in Beverly Hills, California, followed their lives from the teenage years to adulthood and from high school to college life. *Charmed*, a show about three sisters who were also witches, aired from 1998 to 2006. Vampire-themed shows like *Angel* and *Buffy the Vampire Slayer* also enjoyed success in the late 1990s and early 2000s.

Some animated programs enjoyed success over the era. Leading the way were shows like *Futurama*, *Family Guy*, *South Park*, and the favorite, the *Simpsons*. The latter was an Emmy and Peabody Award–winning show that had the distinction of being the longest-running animated program and the longest-running sitcom in American history. First aired in 1989, in 2005 the *Simpsons* was in its 17th season.

At the same time, Americans gained increased access to the world with the spread of 24-hour news networks. By 1991, CNN and Fox News Network already existed;

however, MSNBC entered the news race in 1996. The arguably more conservative Fox News Network enjoyed particular success in the Republican-dominated political environment of the era. Throughout the era viewers watched as the Columbine High School massacre, the O. J. Simpson trial, the events of 9/11/2001, and both Gulf Wars unfolded on their favorite news channels.

FOR MORE INFORMATION

Altbach, Philip G., Robert O. Berdahl, and Patricia J. Gumport. *American Higher Education in the Twenty-First Century: Social Political and Economic Challenges*. Baltimore, MD: Johns Hopkins University Press, 1999.

Basile, Carlo, et al. "The U.S. HDTV Standard: the Grand Alliance." *IEEE Spectrum* 4 (1995): 36–45.

Cocker, Cheo Hodari. "Unbelievable: The Life, Death, and Afterlife of the Notorious B.I.G." *Vibe* (June 15, 2005).

Copeland, C., and J. M. De La Croix. *Encyclopedia of Contemporary American Art*. New York: Elite Associates International, 1987.

Davis, Rocio G. "Oral Narrative as Short Story Cycle: Forging Community in Edwidge Danticat's 'Krik? Krak!'" *MELUS* 26, no. 2 (2001): 65–81.

Derrida, Jacques. *The Post Card: From Socrates to Freud and Beyond*. Translated by Alan Bass. Chicago and London: University of Chicago Press, 1987.

Doss, Erika. *Twentieth-Century American Art*. New York: Oxford University Press, 2002.

"Fiction Is the Poor Man's Cinema: An Interview with Junot Díaz Diógenes Céspedes; Silvio Torres-Saillant; Junot Díaz." *Callaloo* 23, no. 3 (Summer 2000): 892–907.

Finler, Joel W. *The Hollywood Story*. New York: Wallflower Press, 2003.

Foucault, Michel. *The History of Sexuality*. Vols. 1–3. Paris: Gallimard, 1976, 1984.

Gitlin, Todd. *Media Unlimited*. New York: Henry Holt, 2002.

"High-definition (HD) TV: What It Is, Why You'd Want It." *Consumer Reports* (February 2006).

"Ja Rule Calls Beef with 50 Cent 'Studio Bangin.'" *Vibe* 1, no. 10 (2005).

Mardorossian, Carine M. "From Literature of Exile to Migrant Literature." *Modern Language Studies* 32, no. 2 (1996): 15–33.

McCrisken, Trevor B., and Andrew Pepper. *American History and Contemporary Hollywood*. New Brunswick, NJ: Rutgers University Press, 2005.

Morning Edition, National Public Radio (October 23, 2006).

Pautz, Michelle. "The Decline in Average Weekly Cinema Attendance: 1930–2000." *Issues in Political Economy* 2 (2002).

Petersen, Melody. "2 Big-Selling Arthritis Drugs Are Questioned." *New York Times* (June 4, 2002).

Saltzman, Arthur. "Avid Monsters: The Look of Agony in Contemporary Literature." *Twentieth Century Literature* 45, no. 2 (2004): 236.

Spring, Joel H. *American Education*. New York: McGraw Hill, 2004.

Stossel, John. "Stupid in America." ABC News (January 13, 2006).

U.S. Census Bureau Report. *Book Purchasing for Adults*. 2000.

Williams, Juan. *Enough: The Phony Leaders, Dead-End Movements, and Culture of Failure That Are Undermining Black America—And What We Can Do about It*. New York: Crown Publishers, 2006.

———. "Where Are Today's Civil Rights Leaders?" *The Philadelphia Inquirer* (September 26, 2006): A 15.

Woodin, Karen E., and John C. Schneider. *The CRA'S Guide to Monitoring Clinical Trials.* Boston: Thompson, 2003.

Darryl Mace

Material Life

OVERVIEW

In a diverse, broadly prosperous free market economy, Americans continue to purchase increasing amounts and varieties of material goods and products. They have also shown an expanded commitment to material consumption that their grandparents and parents might find both indulgent and excessive. Clear examples emerge when one examines the widening divergence between necessity consumption and discretionary buying. In 1950, for example, Americans spent 29.7 percent of their income on food, 27.2 percent on housing, and 11.5 percent on clothes—the necessity consumption items. They spent 31.6 percent on discretionary items. In 1997, by contrast, Americans spent 49 percent of their income on discretionary items, an 18 percent increase (U.S. Department of Labor 2006, 27, 55).

Materialism remains tied to the economic condition of the society, and, during the 15 years between 1991 and 2005, the American economy has maintained low unemployment numbers, low inflation rates, and low interest rates. Those commercial barometers indicate a healthy economy (see Economic Life section). Except for a brief recession at the beginning of the new century, Americans have continued to support a consumer-driven economy by buying furiously, sometimes beyond their means. To compete for customers in a variety of markets, businesses seek variety and quality to entice consumers. Whether in the expanding arena of electronic products or the traditional big-ticket goods like automobiles, American consumers find access to more, often better, mostly more expensive, but readily available products from retail stores, catalogs, and online computer sites. Whether their shoes come from China, their cars from Japan, or their petroleum from Canada, Mexico, or Venezuela, Americans continue to buy in record amounts. That purchasing power serves as one of the key factors in the nation's economic growth.

AUTOMOBILES

Cars have been a significant material acquisition for Americans since the end of World War II. The automotive industry, centered in Detroit, has provided a multibillion dollar industry that remains one of the key economic indicators within the American economy. In 2002–2003, 88 percent of American families owned at least one car. The average family had purchased two automobiles. Americans spent a little less than 20 percent of their income on transportation, an average of $7,770 yearly (U.S. Department of Labor 2006, 58). A number of foreign competitors have entered the market in the past 30 years. The "big three" American automakers (General Motors, Chrysler, and Ford) no longer dominate the industry—in fact, Toyota sold the most cars in America in 2005. Japanese, German, and Korean manufacturers offer more variety to consumers. More than 40 models of foreign cars, made in U.S. factories, rolled off assembly lines in 2005. In 1985, American plants produced 460,000 foreign automobiles. In 2005, they

2005 Hummer H2. Courtesy of Jolyon Girard.

manufactured 3.7 million cars, 300,000 more than actual foreign imports. And, as of 2005, 57 percent of cars purchased in the United States are American, and 43 percent are foreign. Those numbers indicate a 10 percent decline in American purchases since 1990. Such figures can be deceptive. American and foreign cars are literally composite hybrids, with parts from different sources and assembly in the United States or elsewhere (Center for Automotive Research: www.mergentonline. com). One factor in the increase of foreign purchases has appeared to hinge on gas consumption. American consumers still pay less for gasoline than other industrial, Western nations, but concerns regarding oil prices have witnessed an emphasis on mileage for many consumers. While sport utility vehicles (SUVs) and vans provide a significant portion of the market, the new century has seen an emphasis on hybrid vehicles (battery and gasoline powered) to reduce consumption.

CLOTHING AND STYLE

Americans have become a culture of blue jeans and t-shirts. Fact or fable? As discussed previously, clothing style has changed since the postwar era of the "man in the gray flannel suit." Most people in the country have adopted a more casual style of dress for every aspect of their lives, both work and play. Coats and ties for men, dresses for women, and similar options for young people are no longer the norm in the United States. Americans spent less on clothes per capita in 2000 than they did in 1950, after taking inflation into account. In 1972–1973, families spent 7.8 percent ($647) on clothing. In 1996–1997, Americans spent 5.1 ($1,741) percent of income on clothes. And in 2002–2003, that percentage had declined to 4.2 percent ($1,694) (U.S. Department of Labor 2006).

With the percentage of annual family income allocated for clothing reduced by almost half between the 1970s and the new century, a suggestive trend clearly emerges. In a free society, clothing style remains a matter of cultural choice. Many observers still argue that "clothes make the man (or woman)" in the sense of defining class and status in American life. Yet, the growing trend has been toward casual dress. In the new century, Americans simply spend less than they have in the past and appear to demand a wider variety of casual clothes and style to define their daily lives.

Because a significant portion of clothing sold in America is imported, much of it produced cheaply, with cheap labor, critics have expressed concern that the trend hurts American business and exploits labor in other countries. The "fabric of our lives" (quoted from an ad for cotton)—cotton clothes—may provide Americans with a vast array of choices, but it continues to spark debate and concern among observers who worry about the commercial trends. Still, Americans remain freer, in the new century, to purchase a broad variety of options, both designer expensive and supermarket cheap. A stroll through a suburban American mall suggests the options in clothing available. Large retail stores maintain significant inventories of men's, women's, and children's clothing. American consumers may opt for upscale retail giants, like Nordstrom or Neiman Marcus, for their selections. Or they can visit Wal-Mart, Sears, or J. C. Penney and find similar varieties. Numerous retail outlets specializing in different types and styles of clothing also exist to attract American consumers. Those options include styles based on age, gender, ethnicity, regionalism, and numbers of other considerations. Catalog purchases also offer Americans a wealth of clothing options. Companies like Lands End and L. L. Bean appeal to a certain socioeconomic market, but other catalogs seek similar forms of customer identification.

ELECTRONICS: CELL PHONES

Mobile or cellular telephones have been available since the 1940s, but they were too large and heavy to serve consumers unless installed in automobiles. By the mid-1980s, however, handheld, miniaturized cellular phones that connected to a rapidly expanding system of base stations or cell sites made the option far cheaper and more desirable to users. During the 1990s, technological advances enabled the cell phones to add text messaging (SMS), e-mail service, camera phones (in 2005, 85 percent of the market), and other functions to expand the services cell phones provide. In 1992 only 1 percent of the population owned cell phones. By 2002, that number had jumped to 18 percent. Over 1.14 billion cell phones are in operation worldwide. Americans have already purchased and discarded 500 million used cell phones (http://www.worldwatch.org).

FOOD AND BEVERAGES, DINING OUT, AND COOKING

Americans eat out more than they did in previous generations, yet they buy more home cooking items and utensils, buy more cookbooks, by different authors and about food both generic and esoteric, and watch a number of cooking shows on cable television, with whole channels devoted to cooking. If Julia Child and McDonald's introduced domestic America to home cooking and fast-food chains, Americans have carried those to almost limitless options in the new century.

In 2002–2003, the average American family spent 13.1 percent of its income on food ($5,357). They spent 41.9 percent of that amount ($2,243) eating out. Average consumption of alcoholic beverages amounted to less than 1 percent of expenditures for families, data that call into question the broad concern that Americans, as a whole, remain heavily involved in the use of liquor. Legitimate concern exists regarding drunk driving, and organizations such as MADD (Mothers Against Drunk Driving) perform a valuable service helping to prevent traffic-related tragedies. There is also statistical evidence to suggest that alcoholism and other diseases related to alcohol consumption continue to create health problems in the United States. In broad daily life, however, most Americans appear to consume alcohol on a limited social basis for social and recreational reasons. Many Americans do not drink alcoholic beverages at all (U.S. Department of Labor Report 2006).

Wegman's supermarket in Cherry Hill, New Jersey, part of a national chain of popular upscale stores. Courtesy of Jolyon Girard.

That American families have broad and ready access to food seems a given when one strolls through any of the numerous large supermarkets in virtually any area or region of the United States. Certainly, an identifiable percentage of Americans living in poverty are subject to a different standard, and hunger in certain situations remains a national concern and disgrace. The concern, however, in American daily life seems less focused on those who have little food, and more on those who eat too much. Obesity has become a serious national problem in the United States. While a variety of factors including exercise, physiology, and genetic makeup impact on weight, most experts agree that Americans overeat, both at home and when they go out. Portions of food are larger now than in the past, and the type of food, high in fat and calorie content, has also changed.

Body Mass Index (BMI) is the most current measure to determine whether individuals are overweight or obese. The measurement calculates height and weight and suggests the following: a number less than 18.5 is underweight, 18.5–24.9 is normal, 25–29.9 is overweight, and 30 or more is obese. Since 1995, obesity among children ages 6 to 11 has doubled. Between the ages of 12 and 19, the rate has tripled. Between 1991 and 2001, white Americans have seen an increase in obesity from 11.3 percent to 19.6 percent. African American obesity, in that same period, increased from 19.3 to 31.1 percent. Hispanic rates of obesity have grown from 11.6 to 23.7 percent. The Endocrine Society has also studied rates of obesity regionally in the United States. In the Northeast, rates have risen from 9.9 to 17 percent. The highest rates of obesity exist in the South, where rates have climbed from 13.1 to 23 percent in that 10-year period between 1991 and 2001 (http://www.endo-society.org). The issue of obesity has become a national health problem in the United States for both adults and children, enhancing the risk of heart disease, diabetes, and other medical concerns. If excess consumption remains a major factor in the rising numbers of overweight and obese Americans, that domestic aspect of American daily life needs serious evaluation. Health experts tend to conclude that "two Americas" seem to be emerging in the modern era. One has a percentage of people exercising, concerned with their diet, and involved in calorie counting and weight loss. The other America is profoundly harmed by a problem with obesity.

No consideration of American eating habits would be complete without a brief mention of the nation's love affair with hot dogs. Whether people call them frankfurters, franks, weenies, wieners, or hot dogs, Americans consume 60 to 75 of the national sausage per person annually. They probably arrived in the United States from Vienna, Austria (hence wiener), or Frankfurt, Germany (hence frankfurter), in the nineteenth century and became nationally popular by the end of the 1800s. Generally, Americans bought them, placed in a bun, at fairgrounds, ballparks, and other amusement centers well into the twentieth century. Nathan's opened an establishment at Coney Island in New York in 1916. In 1936, the Oscar Meyer Company marketed its hot dogs by creating the famous "Wienermobile" in Chicago, Illinois. As it drove through the city advertising the item, the gimmick caught on and has gone through a number of additions and changes during the past 60 years. At present, dozens of the remodeled, 27-foot-long vehicles roam nationwide advertising the product. In 1942, at the Texas World Fair, vendors introduced the corn dog, a hot dog fried in a coating of cornmeal.

While most Americans continued to eat hot dogs in large quantities into the postwar era, the expanded use of home refrigerators helped move the food item from amusement area to home where they became standard fare with hamburgers during backyard barbecues in suburbia. Slathered with mustard, onions, relish, or any variety of condiments, Americans showed little concern for the content of the hot dog, either its calories, fat content, or health benefits. It seemed to be an easy option and it apparently tasted good. In 1963, Nicholas McClellan Vincent entered an Oscar Meyer jingle contest and produced one of the most popular advertisements in United States marketing history. His "I wish I were an Oscar Meyer wiener" still ranks as one of the most famous jingles of all time and rocketed the company to top sales.

Since that time, dozens of companies produce numerous varieties of the product and supermarkets are stocked with the options. Dieticians and health experts continue to question the wisdom of consuming the ubiquitous hot dog, but Americans pay little attention. Hot dogs remain one of the nation's most popular and enjoyed junk foods.

The most popular sandwich food for Americans remains the hamburger. The origin of the ground beef meal remains shrouded in myth, but most historians believe the Mongols placed slabs of beef beneath their saddles to tenderize the meat as they rode their horses. German immigrants from Hamburg brought the ground beef to America, and the popularity of the food grew through the late 1800s. While many sources claim credit for placing fried ground beef patties on bread or buns, the popular history suggests that the 1904 St. Louis World's Fair introduced the idea nationwide. During the 1920s, White Castle sold five-cent burgers from a chain of fast-food stores, and in 1934, Whimpy Burger (named for the cartoon character Popeye's friend) opened its doors. Bob's Big Boy opened its doors in the late 1930s. During the Depression and World War II, hamburgers increased in popularity as a cheap on-the-go sandwich for traveling workers and servicemen and women. McDonald's remains the most famous fast-food hamburger franchise (see Chapter 3), but numerous chain restaurants offer the hamburger as their main option. It is also important to remember that thousands of burger joints, regular restaurants, and outdoor barbecues at home add to American consumption of the product.

Between 1990 and 2005, on average, Americans ate three hamburgers a week, accounting for 60 percent of all sandwiches consumed in the United States. Like the hot dog, hamburgers encourage a variety of additions to the basic ground beef on a bun. Cheeseburgers (pick your variety) add to the offering. Ketchup, onions, relish, lettuce, tomatoes, and so on can all sit atop the basic sandwich. Often served with French fried potatoes, a burger and fries provide the most popular fast food in American daily life. Regional or local alternatives also enhance the basic hamburger. In California and Hawaii, avocado slices and pineapple top the burgers. In Texas and areas of the Southwest, chili is added. A slice of bacon tops burgers nationwide. The options are endless. Like hot dogs, hamburgers are heavy in fat content and high in calories. A basic eight-ounce burger amounts to 275 calories. McDonald's Quarter Pounder is 430 calories, and Burger King's Whopper is 760 calories. Add cheese, and it is another 100 calories. Larger, more ambitious cheeseburgers account for more than a thousand calories (Edge 2005).

HEALTH, HYGIENE, AND COSMETICS

Americans spent $133 billion on pharmaceutical purchases in 2004, a business that includes major corporations like Pfizer, Johnson & Johnson, Merck, and Bristol-Meyers Squibb. In conjunction with the $1.7 trillion Americans spent on health care in 2004, the material demand for those services has become a major new aspect of American daily life. Beyond what families set aside for health care and health care products, Americans also spend a significant amount on personal care products.

From toothpaste and deodorant to cosmetics, aftershave lotion, and perfume, the average family devotes 1.5 percent ($520) of its budget to personal care purchases. The people not only want to be healthy, they also hope to smell good and look good. The American cosmetic and care product industry is eager to provide the material resources to meet that goal (U.S. Department of Labor 2006, 50–51).

HOUSING

After World War II, the growth in the construction of homes and the exodus to the suburbs of America altered the demographic landscape. Home ownership became a significant material goal for many families. That trend has continued into the new century. In 1996, 64 percent of American families owned their homes, while 36 percent rented. The estimated average value of homes in the United States was $74,835, while monthly rental averages amounted to $521. Less than a decade later, in 2002, home ownership had risen to 67 percent. The estimated value had reached $114,522 with a commensurate rise in rental value. Current federal administrations, both Democrat and Republican, have also indicated that minority home ownership has increased by 15 percent during the past decade (U.S. Department of Labor 2006, 49, 56).

INDEXING: THE CONSUMER CONFIDENCE INDEX

BJ's Wholesale Club. Courtesy of Jolyon Girard.

Americans spend money on material goods and products partly based on their confidence in the economy, both as employees and as consumers. The Consumer Conference Board, an independent body, publishes the *Consumer Confidence Index* (CCI) on a regular basis. That index takes into account a number of economic variables, both regionally and nationally, to determine how American households view the nation's economy and their confidence in it. Setting an arbitrary number of 100 in 1985, the CCI looks at both current consumer confidence (40 percent of the measurement) and future confidence in the economy (60 percent). The CCI polls 5,000 American households to obtain its number. A number above 100 suggests a positive conclusion, and numbers below, the reverse. The index regards two quarters with numbers below 100 as a potential or actual economic recession. In February 1992, the CCI had reached an all-time low of 50. That number climbed into positive figures throughout the 1990s and reached an all-time high of 144 in January 2000, just before the stock collapse of 2001–2003, when the number dipped below 100. By August 2005, the CCI was back at 123 (http://www.conference-board.org).

As complex as the system and the numbers seem to be, they do provide a set of statistics that give some indication of how American families determine how much money they will spend and in what direction that money will go. Producers, whole-sale and retail providers, and advertisers base much of their response to consumers on their analysis of the CCI. Through all of the economic vagaries of the past 15 years, American consumers continue to buy.

STORES, CATALOGS, AND E-COMMERCE

Americans continue to purchase most of their material goods and products from a variety of retail stores, both small and large. While large shopping malls, such as the Mall of the Americas in Minnesota or King of Prussia Mall outside of Philadelphia, attract thousands of consumers, smaller retail outlets in shopping centers, strip malls, and along main streets in towns and cities in America continue to draw customers. The nation's and world's largest retail business is Wal-Mart. Sam Walton established the retail giant in 1962, and it has since expanded to become a $300 billion annual sales megastore. Wal-Mart employs close to two million people. As new Wal-Marts open throughout the nation, the retail giant has created a great deal of controversy as a threat to local businesses with which it competes and which it often puts out of business. Critics also complain about where the store purchases its retail products (http://www.retailindustry. about.com).

Wal-Mart Stores, Inc.—the world's largest megastore. Courtesy of Jolyon Girard.

Catalog purchasing has offered another method for families to satisfy their material needs. Sears and Roebuck and other stores had catalogs in the 1800s, but the use of mail shopping has grown dramatically. L. L. Bean, Lands End, and Eddie Bauer have sent their quarterly (sometimes monthly) catalogs to buyers for years, but they now compete with thousands of other options and companies. Shipping businesses like Federal Express (FedEx) and United Parcel Service (UPS) have become major businesses bringing items to homes throughout the nation. Catalog sales to consumers amounted to $69.5 billion in 1996, with 42.8 percent of those sales to homes rather than businesses. By 2001, catalog sales jumped to $120 billion with 73.3 percent of sales going to homes. E-commerce (buying products through online computer businesses) has expanded dramatically in the past decade. Whether through eBay, Amazon, or any number of growing options, American consumers are buying more through e-commerce systems. In 2000, consumers spent $37 billion on e-commerce purchases. A year later, that number jumped 20 percent to $53 billion (http://www. retailindustry.about.com; http://www.comscore.com).

If American consumers have found new ways to buy goods and products and have expanded the size and number of traditional retail businesses to address their material needs, the data and evidence suggest that consumer purchasing remains strong. What Americans buy has also shown evidence of both traditional material needs and new options and opportunities.

TELEVISION

When KDKA radio in Pittsburgh broadcast the results of the 1920 presidential election, few Americans could have foreseen the explosion the marketplace would experience in electronic materialism. Radios dominated the pre–World War II era, and television sets emerged as the modern marvel of postwar America in the 1950s and 1960s. Americans own, on average, two televisions per household, many of which are now connected to cable network systems that provide hundreds of channels for viewing. The rapid expansion of cable systems has changed the nature of television, and the introduction of Home Box Office (HBO) and other cable options alters significantly both the variety and style of television viewing. Technological changes in television sets have also broadened consumer options. The shift from black-and-white to color television occurred in the 1960s, and color sets have come to dominate the market. But newer sets now offer consumers the ability to select high definition (HDTV) and digital viewing, which began in 1987. Those new systems provide clearer pictures for consumers. Most networks now broadcast in high definition. Plasma television and other innovations in the technology have also enhanced interest for Americans (Flaherty).

VIDEO GAMES

Video games offer an additional home electronic component for American consumers. As early as 1952, A. S. Douglas created the first home video game—Naughts and Crosses—a version of tic-tac-toe. The Atari company produced Pong (a tennis game) in 1975. The revolution in home consumption, however, began in the 1990s when various companies not only designed a broad variety of games for in-home use but also easier methods to load games into their mini-computer systems. By 1995, PlayStation had sold two million home computer games. The computer gaming industry had become so prolific that the U.S. Congress held hearings on game violence, and the business developed a rating code, by the Entertainment Software Rating Board (ESRB), to alert consumers to the type of games they or their children might be purchasing (http://www.inventors.about.com).

FOR MORE INFORMATION

About.com. "Business and Finance." http://www.inventors.about.com.

About.com. "Retail and Industry." http://www.retailindustry.about.com.

Center for Automotive Research. http://www.mergentonline.com.

ComScore Networks—A Global Internet Provider. http://www.comscore.com.

Consumer Confidence Board. http://www.conference-board.org.

Edge, John. *Hamburgers & Fries: An American Story.* New York: Putnam, 2005.

The Endocrine Society Weighs In: A Handbook on Obesity in America. http://www.endo society.org.

Flaherty, Joseph. "A Perspective on Digital TV and HDTV." *HDTV Magazine.* http://hdt vmagazine.com/history/2005/06/a_perspective_o.php.

U.S. Department of Labor. "100 Years of United States Consumer Spending." May 2006.

Worldwatch Institute. www.worldwatch.org.

Political Life

OVERVIEW

The two-term presidency of conservative Republican Ronald Reagan (1981–1989) signaled a shift to a conservative agenda for the decade of the 1980s. As faith-based, white, and suburban voters gave Republicans new electoral power in state and national politics, the so-called domestic revolution of the decade saw a shift away from traditional Democratic Party majorities in Congress and Republican control of the White House. Since 1940, American voters had elected only two Republican Presidents, Dwight Eisenhower (1953–1961) and Richard Nixon (1969–1974). Gerald Ford, a Republican, had served out Nixon's unexpired term after the Watergate scandal led to Nixon's resignation, but the election of Jimmy Carter (1977–1981) returned a Democrat to the executive office. In similar fashion, the Democratic Party had controlled both the House of Representatives and the Senate since before 1940. Only briefly, following World War II, did the Republican Party have a majority in either House or Senate. That situation changed later in the century.

Republican George H. W. Bush defeated his opponent Michael Dukakis in the 1988 presidential election. As Ronald Reagan's vice president, Bush had adopted

Jessie Jackson, civil rights leader. Chaiba.

many of Reagan's views. Bush won 53 percent of the popular vote and 40 of the fifty state's electoral votes. Effectively, President Bush hoped to continue the Reagan Revolution into the 1990s. The collapse of the Soviet Union and America's emergence as the world's hyperpower had convinced many observers that, as the twentieth century ended, the administration, in the last decade of the century, could concentrate on addressing domestic issues. At the end of the 1980s, those hot-button issues included on crime, illegal drugs, taxes, the national debt, and health care.

Crime and drugs were interrelated. By 1990, 50 percent of prison inmates were incarcerated for drug-related crimes, many of them young African American, inner-city males. A number of states had adopted "three-strikes" laws requiring heavy sentences for criminals convicted of third offenses. Prisons swelled with new inmates, both in state and federal prisons. For example, in 1980, 316,000 prisoners occupied cells in federal penitentiaries. In 1990, that number jumped to 740,000. By 2002, it reached 1,368,000.

In some states, construction of new prisons and maintenance of old ones became major budget items. New get-tough-with-criminals attitudes and sentencing reflected popular views on how to curb crime and antisocial behavior. At the same time, civil rights and civil liberties groups challenged new sentencing guidelines and treatment of persons accused and convicted of crimes.

The issues of crime, drugs, and the people that those problems impact remain a major political and social concern in American daily life. Political responses, at both the national and local levels of government, have, to date, failed to provide a responsible or effective resolution to the crisis (Goldfield et al. 2007, 920).

DEBT, TAXES, AND THE POLITICS OF THE ECONOMY

The problem of debt and taxes had also become a key concern. In 1980, debt accounted for 50 percent of personal savings. A decade later, it had swelled to 125 percent. The United States had become a debtor nation dependent on foreign imports. In 1980, foreigners owed the United States and its citizens an amount comparable to $2,500 per family. By 1990, American families owed foreign creditors an average of $7,000.

While the Reagan administration's income tax cuts had promised to help middle-class families by providing more income, those cuts had also lowered government revenues. At the same time, Reagan's defense budget swelled in the 1980s, adding to the increased cost of government. Coupled with expanded spending on foreign goods and products, Americans confronted a growing debt and deficit. President Bush had told the public that he would not raise taxes to address the growing deficit in a noted "read my lips, no new taxes" speech, but the fiscal problems that the deficit and debt created led him to alter his position. In 1990, he accepted a compromise tax increase package with the Democratic-controlled Congress. Conservative critics considered his actions a betrayal of Reagan's agenda, and some pundits suggested that it could cost him reelection in 1992.

While the Bush administration tended to follow the Reagan model of limiting federal programs and expenditures, it did support major health care and other social legislation that led to the 1990 Americans with Disabilities Act. That law sought to prevent discrimination against people with physical handicaps. It led to a host of laws at every level of government, expanding access to public accommodations for Americans and serving as one of the significant pieces of legislation that occurred at the beginning of the new decade. As such, it was a logical extension of the civil rights movement of the 1960s and 1970s, with the promise of a more open, equitable society.

IMMIGRATION

Immigration also emerged as a key political, social, and cultural concern during the 1990s. Much of the public concern focused on immigrants coming from Mexico, Central America, and the Caribbean. The 1990 census revealed that the Latino immigrant population had increased by almost 50 percent since the 1980 census, from 13.6 to 22.4 million people. By the 2000 census, Hispanic Americans had become the largest minority population in the United States. Sixty percent of those immigrants had arrived from Mexico. In the Southwest states and California, sizable minorities of Latino immigrants worked, raised families, and joined the mainstream of American daily life. At the same time, significant numbers of illegal or undocumented immigrants caused ongoing concern (U.S. Census, 1990, 2000).

American society possessed an ambivalent attitude regarding immigration. Great waves of immigrants had arrived periodically in the United States since its founding. At once welcomed and necessary as economic assets and positive cultural additions to the melting-pot society, immigration had also produced negative backlash. Nativist sentiments, racism, "Red Scares," religious bias, and a host of factors had led to anti-immigrant attitudes throughout the nineteenth and twentieth centuries, but the numbers of people coming to America continued through a

The U.S./Mexico border near El Paso, Texas. Courtesy of Jolyon Girard.

variety of laws and legislation that welcomed, restricted, defined, or structured their arrival. In 1986, the Reagan Administration proposed, and Congress passed, the Immigration and Reform Control Act, specifically reacting to the increase in Hispanic immigration. The bill legalized thousands of immigrants and established employer sanction programs for business owners who hired illegal aliens. It appeared an effort to resolve the concern that many Americans had regarding the cost of social services (health care, education, etc.) for undocumented immigrants, by bringing them into the society as legitimate citizens. It failed to resolve the problem.

In 1994, California citizens passed Proposition 187, a ballot initiative that denied illegal immigrants public services such as health care and public education. The battle over immigration policy, broadly dealing with Hispanic immigration and specifically with Mexican immigration, remained a major political, social, and economic issue into the new century. Immigrants and various organizations, such as La Raza, asserted the human right to dignity and pointed to the wealth and production immigrants provided to the United States. By 2000, food choices, music, and other aspects of Latino culture had spread throughout the United States. Prominent Latino athletes, especially in Major League Baseball, where they played a major role, helped lead the way in asserting their cultural heritage, making Latino culture more mainstream. The appeal of the culture paradoxically was a reason opponents of unrestricted immigration worried about continued influxes of immigrants.

EUROPE AND THE END OF THE COLD WAR

If the Bush administration believed the conclusion of the Cold War would provide a respite from foreign policy crises, events proved them wrong. The end to the United States–Soviet confrontation in Europe witnessed a dramatic change in governments and society throughout the continent. Communist regimes disappeared throughout eastern Europe. Germany, divided since 1945, reunited in October 1990. Former Soviet troops stationed in Europe withdrew their forces. Both the American and Russian nuclear arsenals had also begun a drastic reduction in numbers and targeting locations. The end of half a century of confrontation appeared a positive beginning to the last decade of the 1900s. The two former enemies looked to an era of cooperation and friendship. The end of the Cold War, however, created a new dynamic in American foreign policy and in the response of Europeans. Would the continent require mutual, regional security pacts like NATO if the Soviets no longer posed a threat? If European nations no longer required U.S. nuclear protection against the possibility of a Russian attack, might they begin to rethink their relationship with America? Involved in the creation of their own European Union, many leaders in Europe no longer saw the need to follow blindly America's foreign policy positions. Many Americans saw that attitude as a slap in the face for the United States, the nation that had defended Europe from the Soviets and helped generate a successful, prosperous postwar society on the continent. Trade, tradition, and mutual aspects of society and culture still tied Europe and America. NATO officials looked to redefine the necessity for maintaining the regional alliance, even including several of the former Soviet bloc nations. Yet, in 2005, U.S.–European relations remained a major concern on both sides of the Atlantic.

THE PERSIAN GULF WAR AND IRAQ

On August 2, 1990, Saddam Hussein, the Baathist president of Iraq, ordered his military forces to invade the small, neighboring country of Kuwait. Quickly, they seized the vast oil resources in Kuwait, commanding 20 percent of the world's petroleum reserves. Hussein's military also threatened to attack Saudi Arabia, the Middle East's largest oil producer and a vital if also tenuous ally of the United States. Iraq had just concluded a deadly and expensive decade-long war with Iran. Hussein's government needed financial resources to recover from the conflict. He also believed that critical oil reserves in Kuwait belonged to Iraq. Based on conversations with the American ambassador in Baghdad (April Glaspie), he concluded that the United States would not respond aggressively if he seized that country. Hussein misjudged the reaction of President Bush.

The United States had been increasingly involved in Middle East affairs as a nation-builder and buyer of oil since the end of World War II and the emergence of Israel as a sovereign state in 1947. The increasing need for foreign oil and America's evolving support of Israel created a dangerous foreign policy problem. Most of the nations in the Middle East, Arab and Islamic, had waged war, at one time or another, against Israel and saw U.S. support of that nation as a threat to their interests. At the same time, the U.S. government had often supported tyrannical regimes in the region (the Shah of Iran) as part of its Cold War agenda. American policy was resented, and the so-called Arab street (a term often used to indicate public opinion in the Middle East) tended to express an anti-American attitude. President Jimmy Carter had struggled with that issue during his presidency, when Iranians seized the American embassy in Teheran in 1979 and held embassy employees hostage for almost two years. Ronald Reagan suffered a similar but more deadly failure when terrorists exploded a bomb at a U.S. Marine barracks in Lebanon in 1983. Two hundred forty-one servicemen died in the explosion. Carter's earlier efforts at Camp David (1978) to broker some form of lasting peace in the Middle East had not succeeded. It helped achieve an Egyptian–Israeli modus vivendi, but little else. The Iraqi invasion of Kuwait, coupled with the growth of terrorism both in and beyond the Middle East, made the region the new American foreign policy hotspot. The Iraqi invasion of Kuwait added a dangerous wrinkle to the troubled region and U.S. involvement in the area.

President Bush responded to the Iraqi attack by building a military coalition of European nations, and even Arab states, to challenge the Kuwait invasion. America pressured the United Nations to invoke powerful resolutions requiring Iraq to leave Kuwait, and, while discussions continued in the United Nations, a growing American military force arrived in Saudi Arabia to confront Saddam Hussein. In November

1990, the United Nations passed Security Council Resolution 678, authorizing "all necessary means" to liberate Kuwait. The French government attempted to delay the resolution and Iraq proposed some last-minute concessions, but the American-built coalition chose to disregard those overtures. By the beginning of 1991, close to 600,000 U.S. forces were poised along the Saudi border. By the end of the year, British and French troops had joined the growing coalition. Germany and Japan pledged billions of dollars in financial support. Egypt, Saudi Arabia, and Syria added regional military forces, and the Iraqis faced a massive armed alliance.

The United Nations had established a January 15, 1991, deadline for Iraq's withdrawal from Kuwait. When that failed to occur, Operation Desert Storm began the next day. Massive air attacks destroyed Iraqi communication systems, command-and-control leadership, and logistical support for Iraq's frontline troops. For more than a month, the air forces of the coalition used their dominance of the air (most of Iraq's air force had fled to Iran for sanctuary) to devastate Iraq's military infrastructure. On February 24, United States–led ground forces, with Saudi, Egyptian, and Syrian troops engaged, swept into Kuwait and Iraq and quickly defeated Hussein's military. Five days after the invasion, the war ended with a cease-fire and Iraqi forces ousted from Kuwait. Estimates suggested that more than 100,000 Iraqi military and civilian casualties resulted. American forces suffered 240 service personnel killed in action.

A number of critics had initially questioned both U.S. motives and the potential for massive American casualties as the Bush administration prepared for the war. They saw the possibility of another Vietnam, questioned the motives as purely economic and oil driven, or generally believed that the United States should allow diplomatic resolve and economic sanctions to force Hussein to withdraw from Kuwait. American military planners were well aware of public concerns about the use of its armed forces under any circumstances, a legacy of the Vietnam conflict. Leaders like Colin Powell, who served as chairman of the Joint Chiefs of Staff during the Iraq war, had developed post-Vietnam military doctrine calling for swift, massive use of American military power to destroy an enemy. The so-called Powell Doctrine was designed to avoid the kind of lengthy counterinsurgency conflict that had occurred in Southeast Asia. With new weapons and technology, and U.S. military personnel part of an all-volunteer force, military commanders believed they had the necessary components to pursue the doctrine successfully. The 1991 Gulf War proved their planning successful. The 24-hour news services, like CNN, produced military-approved video of precision bombing attacks, positive morale, and new weapons to highlight the success of the war. At the same time, military policy carefully controlled what news organizations could show the American public.

Ironically, as the cease-fire began, the United States witnessed the outbreak of a civil war in Iraq. A Shi'ite majority, extensively oppressed by Hussein's Sunni Muslim minority, rebelled in the southern part of the country. In the north, Kurdish groups also attacked the government, one that had long oppressed them. The Americans did not want to become involved in an internal conflict, it appeared, nor did President Bush want to leave large numbers of U.S. troops in the country as occupiers. Essentially, they allowed Saddam Hussein to suppress the rebellions in his own country and hold onto power in Iraq. The Bush government maintained that it had accomplished its goals the removal of Iraq from Kuwait, and it had followed UN mandates. Public opinion in America tended to agree. The president emerged from the conflict with a positive approval rating, and numerous political pundits predicted that he would be unbeatable in the 1992 presidential election. As a result, a number of popular, well-known Democratic political figures appeared wary of throwing their hat in the ring to challenge President Bush. William Jefferson Clinton, a young, little-known governor from Arkansas, however, bucked the trend.

THE RODNEY KING INCIDENT: THE CONTINUING ISSUE OF RACE AND POLITICS

One of the most tragic domestic political issues to confront the nation during the 1990s centered on the Rodney King incident in Los Angeles in April 1992. A private citizen, using a handheld camcorder, filmed Los Angeles police officers beating an African American motorist, Rodney King, on March 3, in what appeared an obvious abuse of physical force. The incident became a national cause celebre. When the subsequent trial of the police resulted in a not-guilty verdict on April 29, four days of rioting exploded in south-central Los Angeles. African American and Latino residents stormed into stores and businesses, attacked white passersby, and confronted police in a violent upheaval that reminded Americans of the 1965 racial riots in Watts. The relatively new 24-hour cable news programs (CNN had begun broadcasting in 1980) provided a continual coverage with film, review, and analysis. America was reminded, once again, of one of the central problems of its modern age: the divisiveness that race continued to create in the society.

THE CLINTON YEARS, 1993–2001

Bill Clinton, Arkansas governor and candidate for president, and his advisors concluded that most Americans were more concerned with their everyday domestic life than they were with foreign policy issues. As much as the Gulf War had occupied U.S. attention, the day-to-day affairs of working American families mattered more. Using the internal campaign phrase "it's the economy, stupid," the Clinton presidential campaign in 1992 went after President Bush's failure to resolve the basic economic issues that confronted the nation. A kind of political/social/economic divide seemed to confront political leaders. Conservatives, like Reagan and Bush, had attracted a group of voters disillusioned with the discord that had developed in the 1960s and 1970s. They believed that market forces should respond to the social and economic concerns in American daily life, while the government used its power and influence to respond to foreign policy agendas. Liberals had always contended that the social and economic concerns that confronted the nation remained a priority for the federal government. The legacy of Franklin Roosevelt and Lyndon Johnson remained strong in the Democratic Party. Bill Clinton, however, appeared to represent some combination of both, a more centrist view of American politics and government responsibility. He appealed to a new generation of voters, popularly termed Generation X.

Hillary Clinton. Library of Congress.

Mounting a careful, polished campaign, the young Baby Boomer governor chose another young political leader, Albert Gore, as his running mate. Gore, a two-term senator from Tennessee, had written a popular book on the environment, *Earth in the Balance*. The two men appeared likeable candidates, willing to challenge an older generation of political leaders with new ideas and options. Concerns arose during the 1992 campaign regarding Clinton's personal life and his possible relations with other women. His wife, Hillary Rodham Clinton, defended her husband on national television and seemed to deflate those private matters as a key aspect of the campaign.

President Bush defeated his Republican rival, Patrick Buchanan, to win his party's nomination, but that primary campaign revealed a potential split among Republicans. A number of cultural concerns had entered the debate within the party, including issues about gay rights, the Christian right, and a religious undertone to the right wing of the party. In the end, President Bush controlled the nomination, but conservative ideology remained an essential aspect of his campaign, now not simply economic, but social as well.

To add to the complexity of the 1992 election, H. Ross Perot, a billionaire from Texas, joined the fray as an independent candidate. Flamboyant and feisty, Perot bought television time to explain to the American people what the two-party system had done wrong in Washington and how his common-sense approach would clean things up. The election proved a surprise to those who had predicted that President Bush's Gulf War victory would assure his reelection. Instead, an economic recession, his "no new taxes" lapse, and Perot's third-party candidacy saw Bill Clinton steal the 1992 election.

Bill Clinton (D)	370	43,728,275 (43.2%)
George H. W. Bush (R)	168	38, 167,416 (37.7%)
H. Ross Perot (I)	0	19, 237,247 (19.0%)
(Goldfield et al. 2001, 996)		

The focus of the Clinton administration hinged on strengthening the American economy, making it more equitable for American families and more competitive in the international arena. Defining himself as a New Democrat, or a neoliberal, the president sought to make government a leaner, more efficient institution and the private sector more productive and energetic. The government cut jobs in the federal system and increased taxes for the wealthiest 1.2 percent of households.

The administration also expanded the Earned Income Tax Credit, a program that Richard Nixon had initiated in the 1970s. He also sought to recreate a form of domestic, public service with the National and Community Service Trust program. The government expanded the student-aid system by creating direct federal loans for college students. Additionally, and importantly, in 1993, Clinton shepherded the Family and Medical Leave Act through Congress. It provided a maximum of 12 weeks of unpaid leave for employees with newborn children or because of family emergencies.

During his first term, the president suffered a key policy failure when he sought to develop comprehensive health care legislation. At the time, roughly 83 percent of Americans under age 65 had access to health care. Clinton hoped to increase that to 100 percent, and, at the same time, he wanted a bill that would reduce health care costs. The president had delegated his wife, Hillary Rodham Clinton, to oversee work on the new health care plan, and the end result was a proposal that consisted of more than 1,300 pages of complex plans and regulations. Opponents of the idea attacked every aspect they could, even complaining about the first lady's involvement in the process. Insurance companies balked at increased regulations. Taxpayers worried about increased federal taxes to pay for the program. Senior citizens saw the possibility that the new health care proposal would limit their access to Medicare benefits. The proposed program stalled, as its critics continued to find faults and problems. By the midterm election in 1994, President Clinton had initiated several successful pieces of legislation, but he and his wife also faced a powerful opposition surrounding the health care bill.

The continuing base of Republican conservative voters and reaction to the health care issues and other factors concerning the Clintons in office saw a resurgence of Republican power in the Congressional elections of 1994. Voters defeated a number of incumbent Democrats and the Republican Party gained control of the House of Representatives. In 1995, the new Republican speaker of the House, Newt Gingrich, moved to enact the conservative Contract with America, proposing a broad agenda to reduce federal spending, cut taxes for wealthy and middle-class Americans, and pass other legislation that challenged the president. A testy battle developed between the White House and the Congress over the federal budget. When congressional Republicans blocked an interim spending bill in late November 1995, the president shut down the government for more than three weeks and blamed Newt Gingrich and his colleagues for the situation. While both sides were grandstanding on the issue, the American public sensed a widening gap between political ideologies, left and right, often exhibited in personal and bitter political attacks. The budget confrontation and the health care issue seemed to exhibit the worst aspects of partisan politics in the 1990s.

The president finished his first term in office with a bill that altered a major aspect of welfare legislation in America. In 1996, Congress, with President Clinton's support, passed the Temporary Assistance to Needy Families (TANF) law. It replaced a long-standing Aid to Families with Dependent Children (AFDC) program. The new legislation provided for more strict accountability, required recipients to be seeking work or be enrolled in school, and established a time limit on assistance. Effectively,

TANF reduced welfare aid by close to 60 percent between 1994 and 2000. While critics saw it as an attack on welfare mothers, supporters claimed that it finally addressed the out-of-control welfare boondoggle that had created and sustained generations of poor families, perpetually dependent on the federal government.

The presidential election in 1996 pitted Clinton against Robert Dole and, again, H. Ross Perot. The first Democrat since Franklin Roosevelt to win reelection, the incumbent president won 70 percent of the nation's electoral votes and 49 percent of the popular vote. Claiming traditional areas of Democratic strength, the industrial Midwest, the Northeast, and the far West, Clinton also won the support of minority voters. African Americans, in huge percentages, supported the president, and a significant number of Hispanic Americans also voted for him.

A variety of public issues occupied the attention of the American people during the last four years of the twentieth century. As President Clinton began his second term, gun control, crime, drugs, the death penalty, and acts of random violence within the society drew public attention and debate. A series of isolated and unrelated incidents in the 1990s provided tragic examples of the seeming insecurity that existed. In April 1993, federal law officers had raided a fortified compound near Waco, Texas, occupied by a religious/social cult, the Branch Davidians. After a lengthy siege, the agents attacked the compound and more than 80 people died in the ensuing fire. Two years later, Timothy McVeigh loaded a truck with high explosives and detonated the vehicle in front of a federal office building in Oklahoma City, Oklahoma. In what appeared a revenge action for Waco, 196 people died. In 1997, federal authorities finally arrested Ted Kaczynski, a solitary man accused of sending mail bombs to various people between 1978 and 1997. The "Unabomber" targeted college professors and airline employees as a protest against industrial, free market economies. Then, in April 1999, two students at Columbine High School in Littleton, Colorado, walked into their school, heavily armed, and proceeded to kill 12 students and a teacher.

While statistical evidence indicated that crime and violence had declined in the 1990s, the public seemed unconvinced. Rates of violent crime (murder, rape, robbery, and assault) declined by 33 percent between 1991 and 2000. Murder rates fell by 36 percent, and crimes against property dropped 30 percent. Yet, Americans seemed more anxious about crime than ever before. Perhaps the "24/7" cable news networks drew unusual attention to the issues. Having in their daily lives come to expect comfort, security, and stability as natural, Americans saw isolated incidents of violence as too disturbing to accept. For whatever reason, a broad social debate began regarding the causes for such incidents. The decline of family values, a coarsening of behavior in language and dress, a loss of religious conviction, and other factors became issues of serious discussion on television talk shows, in a variety of magazine articles, from religious pulpits, and in political rhetoric (http://www.ojp.usdoj.gov).

Gun control was one aspect of the growing debate in America. The Brady Handgun Violence Prevention Act (1994) established a waiting period and background check for Americans seeking to purchase firearms. The law provoked a heated controversy between those who defined the Second Amendment in a different fashion. The National Rifle Association (NRA), a powerful lobbyist for gun own-ers and manufacturers, argued that the amendment gave citizens an absolute right to own firearms, as many and whatever type they wanted. State and federal courts, however, had ruled consistently that the "well-regulated militia" clause in the amendment indicated that weapons ownership applied to citizen service in a gov-ernment-organized militia. Most states and the federal government had acted to limit open and unrestricted purchases. The argument became a divisive aspect of the growing social and political divide among Americans. Conservatives tended to support the NRA's position; liberals did not. Regionally, southern and western rural Americans raised where hunting is a traditional right of passage defended the right to own weapons. And they also tended to support political candidates who agreed. The antigun movement tended to reside in the suburban, middle-class areas of the Northeast and far West.

The use of the death penalty as criminal punishment became another issue of po-litical and social concern. While a majority of Americans supported the concept of capital punishment and 38 states had the death penalty as an ultimate punishment, the issue continued to provoke heated controversy. Critics argue that the use of capi-tal punishment too often is applied to minorities who lack access to adequate defense attorneys. Additionally, they maintain that there are too many mistakes regarding guilty decisions that lead to innocent people being executed. In 2005, more than 3,300 people were on death row in state or federal prisons. In 2005, 60 people were executed, 59 men and 1 woman. Of this number, 41 were white and 19 were black. Texas executed the most people in 2005—19 (http://www.ojp.usdoj.gov).

The rising tide of drug use and the crime associated with the social condition has become one of the major concerns of Americans during the last decade of the twen-tieth century. While forms of narcotics use have always been an aspect of modern American society, the 1960s witnessed a profound shift in thinking regarding drug use. The youth culture of the 1960s and 1970s saw the use of marijuana as little dif-ferent than the legal consumption of alcohol. Drug use served as one of many forms of rebellion against the previous generation of conformity that young people experi-enced in the 1950s. It also became big business, as casual users were willing to spend sizable sums of money to purchase so-called party drugs. By the 1970s and 1980s, cocaine had evolved as a socially popular drug among wealthier users, and Latin American producers were shipping the narcotic into the United States at a profit of billions of dollars. Drug cartels in Colombia had made "narco-trafficking" a powerful business enterprise. The television series *Miami Vice* and movies like *Scarface*, with Al Pacino, glamorized the world of drug crime, use, and business. Many people who bought and used cocaine saw the drug as another socially acceptable (if criminal) turn-on. The 1990s, however, saw the increasing use of a more virulent and addic-tive cocaine derivative known as crack. In a relatively short time, it became the less expensive, more addictive drug of choice for many inner-city users. As drug gangs fought for control of the market in numerous urban neighborhoods, and as the drug producers in Latin America continued to move the cocaine in its various forms into the United States, the impact of crack cocaine changed the nature and impact of the debate.

Prostitution, crime, violence, and the government's response to those issues all seemed to center on the drug trade and, most specifically, the expanding use of crack. From Ronald Reagan's administration to Bill Clinton's presidency, attempts to limit production in Latin America and distribution in the United States became a major political concern. Appointed federal "drug czars" sought to devise methods and policies to reduce or eliminate the use of drugs. Should citizens addicted to cocaine be treated as criminals or victims? Should they be sentenced to heavy prison terms or considered a medical problem? Should government policy focus on eliminating the narcotics at their source in Latin America or should it concentrate on eliminating the demand in the United States? The debates and the policies continue, but the use of narcotics does as well, and it has played a major role in filling prisons with users and sellers and damaging the day-to-day life of Americans in many inner-city and also suburban neighborhoods.

While the issues and debates regarding gun control, the death penalty, and drug use served as key concerns during President Clinton's second term, Americans also confronted the unfolding drama of the president's own personal life. In January 1998, evidence emerged that President Clinton had engaged in sexual relations with a White House intern, Monica Lewinsky. Rumors regarding Clinton's extramarital behavior had surfaced when he ran for the presidency in 1992. One woman, Paula Jones, had filed a lawsuit for sexual harassment against him. Another woman, the former Miss Arkansas (Sally Perdue), alleged that she had had an affair with Clinton while he was governor. While the president had dodged those claims, he could not dismiss the allegations regarding Monica Lewinsky.

Many opponents of the administration had taken a personal dislike to both Bill and Hillary Clinton. They saw the couple as representative of social values and beliefs that were too liberal and permissive. Critical pundits sought to find evidence or examples in their personal lives of illegal or questionable behavior throughout the 1990s. While that has occurred throughout American political history, it became excessive during the Clinton era and would continue into the contemporary decade.

In 1994, Republicans in Congress appointed a special prosecutor to examine possible fraud that allegedly had involved the Clintons in Arkansas. The Whitewater Development Corporation, an Arkansas real estate promotion gone bad, had seen the Clintons deeply invested in the scheme. Most Americans found the issue complex and confusing, but the independent counsel, Kenneth Starr, pursued the issue and began to expand his investigation of the Clintons. A broadening review of other alleged improprieties included firing White House travel-office staff (1993), the suicide of Vincent Foster, a White House aide and personal friend of the Clintons, and, increasingly, the sexual behavior of the president. The Lewinsky scandal exploded in the midst of Kenneth Starr's investigation. President Clinton denied the allegations, claiming in a public statement, "I did not have sex with that woman." Evidence, however, shortly challenged that remark, and the president found himself open to charges of perjury. Clinton finally admitted the relationship with Monica Lewinsky, apologized, and pledged to move on with the business of running the government. While the public debated and argued whether his personal behavior should have any influence on his public performance, the Republican-controlled Congress, in December 1998, recommended four articles of impeachment against President Clinton. Those articles centered on the president's alleged perjury and obstruction of justice during his sworn depositions.

Once again, debate raged throughout the nation. Defenders of the president, although disappointed with his personal behavior, claimed that his personal life had nothing to do with his public role as chief executive and did not qualify, in any way, as impeachable offenses. Critics considered his perjury an impeachable offense as well as his outrageous personal behavior as a stain on the presidency. While partisan politics played a key role in the whole issue, the Lewinsky affair also drew clear focus to the culture wars that had evolved in American daily life since the 1960s. In the end, the House of Representatives voted to impeach President Clinton and sent two charges to the Senate. The Republicans in the upper house lacked the necessary votes to convict President Clinton, and the matter ended when the Senate failed to garner the two-thirds majority necessary to impeach the president. The incident, however, tarnished the remainder of President Clinton's term of office.

Foreign policy during President Clinton's presidency saw a reevaluation of the nation's role as the only superpower. With the end of the Cold War, which had dominated U.S. policy since 1945, a host of new concerns and issues arose. President Clinton appointed Madeline Albright as secretary of state, the first woman to hold the office. During his first term, the administration brokered an accord between Israel and the Palestine Liberation Organization (PLO) that would give the latter self-government in Gaza and the West Bank, two demands that organization had claimed for years. The deal failed as extremists on both sides challenged its conclusions with violence. In 1994, American diplomats traveled to North Korea, to convince its dictator, Kim Il Sung, to suspend development of nuclear weapons technology. The Americans thought they had a deal. As it turned out, they did not. A food rescue mission to the East African country of Somalia ended in an American military confrontation with Somali warlords that resulted in the death of a number of U.S. military personnel and hundreds of Somalis. The president removed American forces from the region.

In the early 1990s, the European nation of Yugoslavia, in the Balkans, fragmented into five separate nations—Yugoslavia, Bosnia, Macedonia, Slovenia, and Croatia. A civil war erupted in Bosnia when Christians and Muslims fought for control of the area. Serbian nationalists in Yugoslavia supported Christian Serbs in Bosnia in a conflict that became increasingly brutal and vicious. A campaign of "ethnic cleansing" included Serb massacres and deportations of Bosnian Muslims. Under U.S. and U.N. urging, NATO finally intervened in Bosnia in 1995. Four years later, American forces entered the Balkans to bring an end to violence in Kosovo, a province of Yugoslavia. Mostly Albanian, the province began an independence movement that the Serb-Yugoslav leader Slobodan Milosevic acted to brutally repress. As in Bosnia, international response came late, but in March 1999, United States–led NATO forces began a bombing campaign against Yugoslavia that ended in that nation's decision to withdraw its troops from Kosovo and allow a NATO peacekeeping force to enter the region. Foreign policy issues and events in the post–Cold War era did not appear so simple to solve as the American people had expected.

THE NEW MILLENNIUM

The 2000 presidential election proved one of the most contentious and problematic in modern American history. Clinton's vice president, Al Gore, secured the Democratic Party nomination. George W. Bush, the governor of Texas and son of George H. W. Bush, won the Republican nomination. During the campaign, they appealed to moderate voters and argued about tax cuts, the economy, the environment, education, and other traditional concerns. Both, however, also sought support from their liberal (Gore) and conservative (Bush) base, and that continued the culture war politics that had surfaced earlier. The November election created an explosive conclusion. Victory for the candidates hinged on the electoral votes in Florida. In a key media mistake, CBS-TV predicted that Al Gore had won Florida's electoral votes, and with a lead in the popular vote (over 300,000), Democrats celebrated another four years in the White House. Then, the television pundits changed their prediction claiming Florida had gone for Bush. Florida's votes, however, became more controversial as recount demands led to claims of fraud, racism, and other irregularities. The emotional and political controversy ended in the U.S. Supreme Court when the court assumed authority to decide about Florida's electoral process. On December 12, 2000, the Court ruled in a 5–4 decision that Florida's electoral votes belonged to the Republican candidate. President Bush secured the office in a nation divided over the outcome of the election and the method in which the outcome had been resolved.

The election also showed the regional differences that existed in American politics in the evolution of the "blue state–red state" allegiances. Democratic support centered in the Northeast, the industrial upper Middle West, and the Pacific Coast. The Republicans held the South, the plains states, the Ohio Valley, and the Rocky Mountain voters. While pundits focused on the cultural and political divide among American voters, others contended that a "middle America" tended to be less ideological and more centrist in its views. While the intellectual debate still raged, the closeness of elections had clearly narrowed.

The new administration brought a conservative agenda to the White House, and it had the luxury of a Republican majority in Congress. Tax cuts highlighted the first actions of the administration as the government reduced federal taxes by billions of dollars. Following a Ronald Reagan agenda, the new president also moved to deregulate the economy, leaving the private sector more freedom to pursue its production and profits (see the section on Economics). In the foreign policy arena, Bush appointed Colin Powell as secretary of state, and he relied heavily on the advice of his vice president, Dick Cheney, and his national security advisor, Condoleeza Rice. That team tended to support a unilateral approach to diplomacy, and it wanted the

United States to use its power sparingly to support broad global issues like the Kyoto Energy Accords (the United States chose not to sign the accord). On September 11, 2001, the broad focus of American policy, and the responses of the Bush Administration, changed.

TERRORISM AND 9/11

In hindsight, the evolution of forms of Middle Eastern or Islamic terrorism had been evident since the 1976 assault on the Israeli Olympic team in Munich. Aircraft and cruise lines had been hijacked or blown up by terrorists. American Marines had died in a terrorist attack in Lebanon during Ronald Reagan's presidency. In 1993, terrorists exploded a bomb in the World Trade Center garage in New York. In 1996, 19 U.S. soldiers died in an attack in Saudi Arabia. Bombs exploded in the U.S. embassies in Kenya and Tanzania in 1998, killing over 200 people. Terrorists attacked the destroyer *USS Cole* while it anchored in Yemen. Americans were certainly aware of the terrorism emanating from the Middle East. Public opinion tended to view the issue as an ongoing struggle between Israel and the Palestinians and Arab anger over U.S. support of Israel. Increasing American military presence in the Middle East also created tension in the region. So, too, did a broad cultural difference between a freer, more open society in the West, and the goal of many Islamic fundamentalists to reject and even change that behavior.

One of those who opposed America, Osama Bin Laden, a Saudi Arabian businessman, had created Al-Qaeda as a network of terrorists. That group was responsible for the September 11, 2001, attacks in the United States. Four hijacked airliners aimed at three targets, the World Trade Center in New York, the Pentagon outside Washington, D.C., and either the Capitol building or the White House. Two planes hit the World Trade Center between 8:46 and 9:30 A.M. Eastern Time. By 10:30, the two buildings had collapsed. A third aircraft plowed into the Pentagon shortly afterwards. The final hijacked plane exploded on the ground in central Pennsylvania when passengers attacked the hijackers and diverted the plane from its intended target. Everyone on board the four airplanes died, and more than 2,000 people died in the collapse of the World Trade Center buildings and the Pentagon crash (http://www.9–11commission.gov/report/911Report.pdf). If specialists, in and out of the government, had been warning about the possibility of such attacks, and if previous terrorist attacks had certainly alerted people to the intent and seriousness of the terrorists, the American public was still profoundly shocked by the events on September 11.

The following day, President Bush, himself shaken by the events, called the attacks an act of war and pledged to respond accordingly. On September 15, Congress passed a Joint Resolution giving the president power "to use all necessary and appropriate force against those nations, organizations, or persons he determines planned, authorized, committed, or aided the terrorist attacks that occurred on September 11, 2001." At the end of October, Congress passed the USA PATRIOT Act, providing broader ability for the federal government to investigate and examine evidence in pursuit of terrorist activity. While civil liberties advocates worried and cautioned against the legislation, public support remained substantial.

In an additional response to the terrorist attack, Congress also reorganized federal agencies to deal with the new threat. In November 2002, the government created the Department of Homeland Security, which shortly became the second-largest federal agency after the Department of Defense. By 2004, further legislation sought to improve the Central Intelligence Agency and other antiterrorist agencies in the government. Average Americans saw evidence of the responses in security lines at airports, and the calling to active duty of National Guard and Reserve military units. Public response to the attacks failed to produce a violent backlash against Islamic or Arab citizens in the United States. While some incidents occurred, neither the government nor the public reacted in any way comparable to the Japanese-American incarceration during World War II or the suppression of dissent during World War I. If there were violations of individual civil rights, those affected specific people, and rarely did that happen.

America's military response to the September attacks focused initially on Afghanistan, where a ruling Taliban government supported and allowed Al-Qaeda terrorists to train. Osama Bin Laden also had his headquarters in the country. By early October 2001, American air attacks began in Afghanistan, followed shortly by an armed invasion of the country, with a number of European nations supporting the United States–led attack. Anti-Taliban forces in Afghanistan joined the coalition, the Taliban government was ousted by December, and, in 2002, a new government formed. The coalition forces failed to capture or kill Bin Laden, who apparently went into hiding along the Pakistan-Afghan border in a mountainous region where local tribespeople offered him sanctuary.

While the Afghan conflict raged, a debate emerged in the Bush administration as to the next steps in the war on terrorism. Neoconservatives (neocons) in the Defense Department, led by the Secretary of Defense David Rumsfeld and one of his assistant secretaries, Paul Wolfowitz, argued that the United States should use its power and influence to remodel the Middle East into pro-Western, pro-United States democratic governments, by persuasion if possible, by force if necessary. A power struggle developed between Colin Powell in the Department of State and the neocons over the issue, with Secretary Powell remaining cautious and less than supportive about the idea. George Bush had identified Korea, Iraq, and Iran as national governments supporting terrorism, threatening the interests of the United States, and creating an "axis of evil." Increasingly, his administration focused on Iraq and its leader Saddam Hussein.

If Bush's father had been able to develop U.N. and broad coalition support for the 1991 war in Iraq, his son failed to generate that wide backing. Using the possibility of Hussein's development and possession of weapons of mass destruction (WMD) as a major pretext for the conflict, the president tried diplomatic means to have the United Nations support a second war to oust Hussein. During 2002, the United States continued to prepare for war, while U.N. inspection teams failed to find clear evidence that Iraq possessed the WMD that the Bush administration and others insisted it had. Lacking U.N. support and European approval, an American–British military force, with some help from Italy, Spain, Poland, and other states, invaded Iraq on March 19, 2003. In fewer than two months, the Hussein government collapsed and formal military resistance ended. As the United States moved to create a new government in Iraq, the success story became an increasing problem. President Bush's "Mission Accomplished" flight onto the deck of an American aircraft carrier proved tragically premature and a major political gaffe. Violence, terrorist attacks, and pro-Hussein insurgents challenged the peaceful resolution of the Iraq war, and the country descended into an ongoing guerilla conflict (or civil war) that cost the lives of thousands of Iraqi citizens, and, by 2005, more than 2,000 American servicemen and women were killed in the continuing conflict.

While Iraqis voted to create a new government and constitute a resolution to domestic infighting among Kurds, Shiites, and a Sunni minority that had ruled the nation under Hussein, American public support for the conflict dwindled. The war in Iraqi also became a political issue that divided Republicans and Democrats. While other domestic and international issues also influenced the 2004 presidential election, Iraq took center stage. George Bush ran for a second term against John Kerry, a Vietnam veteran and U.S. senator from Massachusetts. Kerry presented an expected "blue state" liberal record as a senator, while Bush defended his position as tough on terrorism and a "red state" supporter in the culture wars. His political advisor, Karl Rove, played heavily on concerns about gay marriage, moral values, and other divisive concerns. In the November election, Bush defeated his opponent with a clear majority in the Electoral College and a narrow win in the popular vote. Many observers believed that the election turned on the public's view that President Bush would remain a more stringent defender of American security.

While absorbed with the national security concerns that confronted the nation, an unexpected natural disaster added to the problems Americans confronted in 2005. Hurricane Katrina swept into the Gulf Coast in August 2005 and devastated communities in Alabama and Mississippi. The hurricane also created catastrophic damage in New Orleans, Louisiana. The response of the Federal Emergency Management Office (FEMA) and state and local agencies charged with alleviating the problems that Katrina caused fell far short of public expectations. Another flurry of political criticism exploded between Democrats and Republicans. Issues of racism centered on New Orleans, where many African American residents waited for days before help arrived in any substantial way. At the same time, however, areas in Mississippi and Alabama, equally hurt by the hurricane, were predominantly white, and they received no quicker or better response. Ultimately, the president bore the brunt of the criticism. The head of FEMA, a Bush appointee with little experience in emergency management, resigned. The president flew to New Orleans to offer a televised pledge to rebuild the city.

By the end of the year, a majority of the American people no longer approved of the president's conduct of the war in Iraq, nor did they give the administration positive ratings in other key areas. Ironically, many public polls indicated that Americans also had little faith in Congress or the Democratic Party alternative. While the American economy seemed to offer positive numbers in employment, inflation, and interest rates, the traditional barometers of health, the growing deficit and debt also bothered Americans. In mid-decade, the nation possessed a powerful economy, potent military strength, and other positive political and governmental assets. A growing number of Americans, however, appeared disenchanted and concerned about the future direction of the nation's political agenda.

FOR MORE INFORMATION

Freidman, Thomas. *The World Is Flat*. New York: Farrar, Straus, and Giroux, 2005.

Fukuyama, Francis. *The End of the World and the Last Man*. New York: Avon Books, 1992.

Goldfield, David et al. *The American Journey: A History of the United States*. Upper Saddle River, NJ: Prentice Hall, 2007.

Gore, Al. *An Inconvenient Truth*. New York: Rodale, 2006.

Mooney, Chris. *The Republican War on Science*. Cambridge, MA: Perseus Book Group, 2005.

The 9/11 Commission Report. http://www.9–11commission.gov/report/911Report.pdf.

U.S. Census. 1990, 2000. http://www.census.gov/population/www/censusdata/hiscendata.html.

U.S. Department of Justice. www.ojp.usdoj.gov.

Recreational Life

OVERVIEW

Americans in their daily lives continued to devote time, attention, and money to recreational activities. Indeed, historians and sociologists have characterized the age as much by how people spend their leisure time as how they work, especially for the middle class. In the widest variety of pursuits, Americans sought enjoyment, relaxation, and physical and mental pleasure from their recreational life. Two key themes tended to dominate the topic. First, Americans enjoy the widest variety of options, choices, and endeavors as they engage in recreational activity. So much variety exists that it becomes difficult, if not impossible, in an encyclopedia, to discuss those activities in any detail. While large sections of the subchapter deal with college and professional sports, a major aspect of spectator recreation, thousands of other types of activity also draw attention and involvement. From fly-fishing to parachute base jumping, Americans find so many different ways to enjoy their leisure time that the volume of options would require its own encyclopedia. The second theme focuses on the commercial aspects of recreational life in the United States. It remains essential to understand that people generally pay for their recreation options in a variety of ways. As spectators they buy tickets to events, they purchase a host of products to support their own recreational activities, and, in the case of gambling, they expend billions of dollars annually on casino games or sports betting. Whether one pays for season tickets to a college or professional sports program or buys the latest golf or tennis equipment, commercialism plays a major role in recreational life in the United States.

CARDS AND BOARD GAMES

Americans have enjoyed a variety of card games and board games since colonial times, and those options for recreation and enjoyment have expanded dramatically in the modern era. When Edmond Hoyle supposedly created the rules for card playing in England in the eighteenth century, he could not have imagined the potential number of card players or variety of card games that would emerge. Americans play literally hundreds of card games with the so-called standard deck of 52 cards, four suits (clubs, diamonds, hearts, and spades, ranked ace through deuce). They include trick-taking games like bridge, rummy-style options, solitaire, and gambling games. Recently, poker, particularly a variation called Texas hold-em, has become a popular option for million-dollar competitions in Las Vegas, online gambling, and social gambling among friends. Poker has always been one of the most widely played and enjoyed card games in American life. Bridge, whist, canasta, pinochle, hearts, and variations of rummy games also attract fans and players. Solitaire remains a standard option for single players. In the standard phrase "according to Hoyle," each of those games has its particular rules and conventions.

In the modern era, older Americans seem, reasonably, to play more traditional card games than younger people. Few teenagers or young adults still find bridge, pinochle, and canasta interesting. They remain popular among Americans over the age of 40. Poker, however, has recently seized the imagination and commitment of youthful players. Across the board, however, some form of card playing has continued to occupy the time and avid attention of millions of Americans, young and old, and the various options continue to provide recreation and social entertainment in every region of the United States.

Board games have grown significantly in popularity since the end of World War II. While a host of video games appear to distract Americans from the more traditional options, millions of people still enjoy games with dice, boards, player pieces, simple and complex rules, and intense competition. When Parker Brothers introduced Monopoly in 1935, it served as a social response to the Depression. Players moved their pieces around a board buying various properties in an effort to win rent from other competitors. The various properties, named for avenues in Atlantic City, New Jersey, attracted immediate commercial success. To date, an estimated 500 to 700 million people have played the game, and a host of variations (different properties) have added to the popularity of Monopoly. Scrabble, a word game, attracts players to national and international competition, as experts compete for monetary prizes. Toy stores stock dozens of different board games for children of all ages and for adults as well. Risk and other strategy games challenge similar video game options for attention and interest.

Games Magazine has included a Hall of Fame list of board games in its regular publication during the past few years. In 2005, it cited BuyWord as the board game of that year. More than 50 games are included on the magazine's list of Hall of Fame choices. Whether designed to inform toy companies of their importance (a multi-million dollar business) or simply to alert consumers to popular games for their own enjoyment, the health and prosperity of traditional board games has remained a popular and important aspect of American recreational life into the first decade of the twenty-first century.

A final look at games would be remiss if one did not include games like chess, checkers, and dominos. Those, too, some dating back centuries, attract players, young and old, social and serious. The life and times of Bobby Fischer, America's iconoclastic world chess champion (1972–1975), draw attention to the popularity of that challenging, classic, and esoteric board game. More simple enjoyment has always focused on a pair of players hunched over a competitive game of checkers (Parlett 1999).

COLLEGE SPORTS

During the last two decades of the twentieth century, money emerged as the primary driving force within American college and professional sports. From 1961 to 1984, the National Collegiate Athletic Association (NCAA) negotiated package contracts with the major television networks. During that time period, the total value of the television contracts increased from $3 million to $74.3 million per year. In 1984, the Supreme Court ruled that those package television contracts violated federal antitrust laws, thereby undermining the NCAA's authority and leaving individual athletic conferences and schools free to negotiate their own television contracts. The University of Notre Dame, which enjoyed an enthusiastic national following, signed a lucrative television contract with NBC to broadcast all of the "Fighting Irish's" home football games. Since other schools did not have Notre Dame's sizable fan base, they opted to negotiate lucrative television contracts through their athletic conferences. The Big Ten, adding an eleventh team with the inclusion of Penn State in 1994, developed contracts with ABC and ESPN, the all-sports cable network. From 1996 through 2000, CBS broadcasted Big East football games; beginning in 1996, both the Pac-10 and Big 12 games enjoyed contracts with Fox Sports Network.

As colleges negotiated new television contracts, the number of postseason bowl games proliferated, and the amount of money associated with those bowl games escalated due to corporate sponsorships. From 1987 until 1995, USF&G Financial Services served as the Sugar Bowl's official sponsor; Nokia sponsored the Sugar Bowl from 1996 through 2006. FedEx began sponsoring the Orange Bowl in 1989. During the 1980s and 1990s, Sunkist and Tostitos sponsored the Fiesta Bowl, and AT&T and SonyPlaystation2 sponsored the Rose Bowl. In 1998, to maximize revenue and to ensure that the top two teams played for the national championship, Notre Dame joined with the six leading football conferences to create the Bowl Championship Series (BCS). As part of the BCS agreement, the site of the annual national championship game rotated among four sites—the Rose Bowl, the Sugar Bowl, the Orange Bowl, and the Fiesta Bowl. An elaborate ranking system that included computer polls and the two traditional Associated Press and USA Today Coaches' poll determined the participants in the BCS bowl games. From 1998 until 2006, ABC enjoyed the exclusive right to televise the BCS bowls, paying a $400 million broadcasting fee between 2001 and 2006.

One effect of college football's playing for television was to stretch the season with more games into January. To satisfy television needs, colleges also scheduled games on Thursday and Friday nights, away from the traditional Saturday schedules. For fans, students, and viewers, the elongated football season and the several game days a week made college football more central in people's lives. Similar extensions of seasons and postseason play, and games on virtually any day of the week, in other sports such as professional football, baseball, and basketball also increased the fan base of the sports, via television. The amount of time Americans devoted to viewing sports events grew. The marketing of sports clothing with team logos both attested to the popularity of sports and also affected everyday fashion.

In the late twentieth century, the popularity of and amount of money associated with men's intercollegiate basketball also skyrocketed. The NCAA began sponsoring a men's basketball championship tournament in 1939; until the 1960s, however, the National Invitation Tournament (NIT) overshadowed the NCAA's tournament. Started by the Metropolitan Basketball Writers Association in 1938, the NIT annually attracted the country's top teams for a series of championship games at Madison Square Garden. To entice better teams and better television deals, the NCAA tournament gradually expanded its field from 8 teams in 1950 to 64 teams in 1985. In 2001, the NCAA added another team and an opening round game to determine the 64th-ranked team in the tournament. During the 1990s, the tournament's Final Four surpassed the World Series in television ratings, and its television revenue rose from $49 million to $150 million. In 1994, CBS agreed to the biggest sports contract in television history, paying the NCAA more than $1 billion for the exclusive rights to televise the men's basketball tournament through the 2002 season.

The lucrative television contracts led many Division I-A schools to devote more time and resources to their athletic programs. During the regular seasons, football and basketball athletes devoted almost 40 hours every week to practices, team meetings, and traveling; during the off-seasons, those athletes maintained extensive exercise programs. Lucrative television deals also led Division I-A athletic programs to circumvent NCAA guidelines in order to attract the best recruits, receive high national rankings, and participate in postseason bowl games or tournaments. Legally, college athletic programs enticed top prospects by offering athletic scholarships and by highlighting the possibilities of playing in nationally televised games and of playing at the professional level once their college careers ended. Expensive facilities—including weight rooms, locker rooms, modern stadiums or arenas, and even special dormitories reserved for varsity athletes—also served as important legal inducements. Illegal inducements typically came from powerful alumni and athletic booster clubs who offered top prospects free cars, free apartments or houses, jobs entailing little or no work, and large cash payments. Coaches occasionally facilitated contact between top prospects and athletic booster clubs, and they often recruited athletes with little regard for their academic capabilities. In order to keep their athletes academically eligible, coaches directed their athletes toward football- or basketball-friendly professors and sometimes even taught classes specifically designed for their athletes.

As a result of those intensive recruitment efforts, the late twentieth century witnessed a series of embarrassing scandals within Division I-A intercollegiate athletics. Reports surfaced that football players at Arizona State University received academic credits for unattended, off-campus extension courses. Half of the schools in the Pac-10 conference admitted that they tampered with academic transcripts and granted false course credits to student athletes. College athletic programs throughout the country regularly protected their academically ineligible athletes by hiring special tutors and lowering standards. In the early 1980s, only one-third of the NFL players and even fewer NBA players earned college degrees; some high school basketball stars, such as Kobe Bryant and Kevin Garnett, avoided college and entered the NBA after graduating from high school. Ultimately, in the late twentieth century, Division I-A football and basketball programs developed into free minor-league systems for the NFL and the NBA. Some scholars, most notably John Hoberman, argued that the overemphasis on athletics within Division I-A programs had a particularly devastating effect on the African American community. According to Hoberman, the overemphasis on athletics perpetuated a myth that professional athletics represented the only avenue for success for young African American men.

The biggest scandal in Division I-A intercollegiate football occurred at Southern Methodist University (SMU). SMU's troubles began in the late 1970s when head coach Ron Meyer established a system that allowed his players to sell their complimentary tickets and pocket the profits. Meyer gave money to his players' parents so they could attend games; he subsidized flights home for his players whenever they wanted, a form of assistance that clearly violated NCAA's guidelines. Following the 1981 season, the NCAA placed SMU on probation for two years, thereby prohibiting the team from playing on national television or in bowl games; Meyer left to coach the New England Patriots in the NFL. Despite Meyer's departure, problems persisted within SMU's football program since school President L. Donald Shields chose to pacify the athletic boosters and refused to take any action that would undermine the team's success. From 1980 to 1984, SMU's football team enjoyed the highest winning percentage in the nation, and in 1982, it represented the only major football program to enjoy an undefeated season. SMU boosters, working through the football coaches, provided players with monthly payments, free cars, and free apartments. The monthly payments increased as the players matured and as their roles on the team became more important. When President Shields discovered the depth of the violations within the football team, he unsuccessfully tried to cover up the scandal and avoid another round of NCAA sanctions.

In June 1985, the NCAA imposed a three-year probation on SMU for 38 violations of the association's guidelines. The terms of the probation prevented SMU from awarding any football scholarships during the 1986–1987 academic year and limited the school to only 15 football scholarships during the 1987–1988 academic year. Moreover, the terms of the probation forbade SMU from appearing on national television for one year and from playing in bowl games for two years. The NCAA had never imposed such a severe penalty, but SMU boosters and football coaches continued to deliver illegal cash payments to the football players. In November 1986, newspapers in Dallas began reporting on the continued violations within SMU's football program, and the school quickly launched an internal investigation in a vain attempt to fool NCAA investigators and avoid the dreaded "death penalty." The NCAA, however, delivered the death penalty to SMU's program in February 1987—the association suspended the football team for the entire 1987 season. Since the NCAA forbade the school from awarding football scholarships and from hosting any football games for two seasons, the association's actions effectively suspended SMU for both the 1987 and 1988 seasons. Once it resumed play in 1989, a severely weakened SMU football team struggled against Division I-A competition, and in the early 1990s, school officials seriously considered dropping to Division I-AA. School officials, however, decided to remain in Division I-A and made serious efforts to eliminate the environment of corruption that had plagued the football team. The graduation rate for football players rose from 30 percent to 70 percent, the new school president implemented a mandatory ethics course for all student athletes, and the school remained free from NCAA sanctions.

The shocking scandal at SMU, combined with reports of student athlete lawlessness at Oklahoma and other Division I-A schools, sparked a wave of reform aimed at restoring a proper balance between athletic success and academic concerns. In 1986, two new athletic conferences—the Patriot League and the University Athletic Association—formed. Members of those conferences vowed to hold athletes to the same academic standards that applied to the entire student body. During that same year, the NCAA implemented Proposition 48, which established minimum SAT and ACT scores and high school grade point averages for prospective student athletes. Three years later, trustees of the Knight Foundation offered $2 million toward the creation of a special commission to study intercollegiate athletics and to create new strategies for preventing scandals. In 1991, the Knight Commission, composed primarily of college presidents and former college athletic stars, proposed a "One-Plus-Three" model for governing intercollegiate athletics. According to the Knight Commission, college presidents should exercise control over athletic programs, conferences, and the NCAA. To accomplish that goal, college presidents needed three kinds of support—academic integrity, financial integrity, and a system of certification. For the remainder of the decade, many colleges gradually adopted the Knight Commission's suggestions, and the NCAA began certifying and auditing athletic programs. Only time will tell whether American colleges will continue to adopt the Knight Commission's suggestions or whether they will continue to evade NCAA guidelines.

—*Courtney Smith*

GAMBLING

Americans spend billions of dollars annually on both legal and illegal gambling, most of that in casino and sports betting. Gambling casinos, legal in a variety of areas, take in $60 billion annually. In Las Vegas, Nevada, Atlantic City, New Jersey, and elsewhere, the casino business flourishes. The profits from Mohegan Sun's (a Native American–operated casino in Connecticut) are used to benefit the tribal society, and other Indian reservations are creating similar businesses, under treaty rules that allow tribes to regulate their own areas and remain free of state laws on gambling and related activities.

As of 2005, horseracing has 150 operating tracks in the United States and generates $16 billion in betting revenue. Customers may bet both at the track and in off-track locations. While the "sport of kings" has always attracted American attention and interest as a sporting event, it has also always remained tied to betting.

Sports betting in America appears difficult to quantify, because it operates both legally and illegally. Estimates place betting in the multibillion dollar range in every area from professional and college football and basketball to minor sports activities. Sports and casino betting plays a major role in American recreation and has created a significant debate in the society regarding its harm and value.

GOLF, TENNIS, AND INDIVIDUAL SPORTS

Most Americans do not engage in team sports. They, do, however, participate in a variety of individual recreational sporting activities that include golf, tennis, bowling, and other options. Bowling remains one of the most popular sports activities for Americans despite the decline in the number of bowling lanes over the past quarter-century. Since the 1980s the number of people who bowl has increased by more than 10 percent, while sponsored bowling leagues throughout the United States have increased by more than 40 percent. Professional bowling has long attracted spectators and participants. The Professional Bowling Association (PBA) sponsors more than 40 tournaments. The Women's Professional Bowling Association (WPBA), founded in 1960, also provides a series of tournaments for its professional athletes. The development of all-sports cable channels and programming in the 1990s opened the door to televised bowling matches, which had been a staple of early television but lost network coverage in the 1970s to other sports (Professional Bowling Association).

Tennis, at every level of competition, also draws both participants and spectators. Thousands of local recreation departments provide tennis courts for public use. Private clubs include tennis facilities as recreational options for their members. Schools, colleges, and universities provide tennis as a recreational option for students and as an organized competitive sport. Professional tennis in the United States has evolved as a spectator sport throughout the twentieth century. From the golden age of Bill Tilden in the 1920s to the modern era, tennis remains a popular spectator sport. While a number of European stars, both men and women, have challenged

American tennis pros for top spots in the tennis hierarchy, players like the Williams sisters, Serena and Venus, and Andy Roddick remain successful American professionals. As with other professional sports, the commercial aspects of tennis have expanded significantly. More tournaments have commercial sponsors. Prize money for men and women has increased dramatically. More than 600,000 spectators attended the U.S. Open Tennis Championship in New York in 2005, and prize money amounted to more than $18 million, split evenly between men and women players (U.S. Tennis Association). Television, again, elevates the popularity and commercial benefits for players.

In the past 15 years, perhaps no individual sport has seen a more significant increase in participation and interest than golf. Once largely the preserve of members of private clubs, the number of municipal and public golf courses open to general use has expanded. In 1990, the National Golf Foundation indicated that 23 million Americans played golf. By 2005, that number climbed to 27 million. There are 16,052 golf courses in the United States, 4,372 private, 2,418 municipal (owned and operated by townships), and 9,262 public courses, an increase of 4,000 since 1990. The professional golf tour has produced an interest in the game as well. Sponsorships, prize money, television, and exceptional players like Tiger Woods and Phil Mickleson, among others, have had a major impact on the sport.

Women's professional golf has developed along similar lines. Michelle Wie, the teenage player from Hawaii, has emerged as a new star in a field of women with exceptional abilities. Prize money differs widely. Major PGA (Professional Golf Association) tournaments award winners up to $1 million and more. Women's tour events generally offer half that much. A variety of other tour programs, for senior players and those not on the PGA tour, also attract fans and prizes.

The commercial aspect of spectator/participant sports hinges, to a great degree, on equipment. The sale of bowling, tennis, and golf equipment amounts to a multibillion dollar enterprise, with a variety of companies competing for customers. They also pay star performers large sums of money to endorse their products. When Tiger Woods signed with Nike, the sports equipment company had no major golf product line. In 2005, the golf line generated $500 million in revenue. Nike pays Woods $40 million (Cheng 2006). While other golf, tennis, and bowling professionals have endorsements lower than Woods', most substantially enhance their income through sponsoring agreements with sporting goods companies. As with the other sports topics, commercialism remains a major issue.

NASCAR AND AUTO RACING

Auto sports attract a huge audience, both at the track and on television. Television ratings in the period 2000–2005 indicate that NASCAR (The National Association of Stock Car Auto Racing) is second only to professional football in viewing numbers. NASCAR produces 1,500 events in 40 states. In 2005, 17 of the top 20 sporting events in the United States show NASCAR with the highest attendance numbers. The organization claims 75 million fans, who purchase more than $2 billion in sponsored products. Fortune 500 companies provide sponsorship for NASCAR events more than any other sport. Their marketing directors have determined clearly that fan, hence product, loyalty seems especially strong among NASCAR spectators. The origins of stock-car racing as a regional sporting event in the southeastern United States have changed broadly during the past 15 years. And the fan base includes many suburban, middle-class followers across the country. NASCAR has become a national passion for millions of Americans, some of whom follow their heroes from race to race, setting up in large trailer and recreational vehicle camps outside race tracks and enjoying a growing racing fan subculture (http://www. Nascar.com).

NO PLACE LIKE HOME: STADIUMS

The end of the twentieth century heralded a new era of stadium and arena construction. Between 1990 and 1998, 46 professional sport stadiums and arenas were built or renovated. By 1999, an additional 49 were either under construction or in the planning stages. The building of a new facility typically began once owners decried their existing facilities as inadequate—meaning that the facilities lacked the luxury boxes, club seats, and advertising opportunities that represented good sources of revenue. Owners then pressured local and state government officials into negotiating stadium or arena financing deals that devoted a great deal of publicly generated funds to the construction of a new playing facility. Cities and states utilized a variety of taxes to finance new sports facilities—sales taxes, property taxes, hotel and motel taxes, car rental taxes, personal and corporate income taxes, lotteries, and "sin taxes" on alcohol and cigarettes. The efforts of city and state governments to finance new playing facilities frequently generated criticism from local community leaders, who argued that the governments should focus on more important endeavors, such as building new schools. Those criticisms usually died amidst vocal and well-financed movements to build new playing facilities.

Owners utilized a variety of methods to defray construction costs; in addition to raising ticket prices, they instituted personal seat licenses, or fees that fans paid simply for the right to purchase season tickets. Most owners typically sold great amounts of advertising space within the facilities and even sold stadium or arena-naming rights to corporations. Daniel Snyder of the Washington Redskins snagged one of the most lucrative deals when FedEx agreed to pay $75 million for the right to have its name attached to the team's new stadium. Due to takeovers in the corporate world, the names of stadiums and arenas changed frequently. Since 1996, the home of the Philadelphia Flyers and 76ers has been called the CoreStates Center, the First Union Center, and the Wachovia Center. In Houston, the Astros' new ballpark was originally called Enron Field; after an ugly scandal swept through the corporation, the team ended its affiliation with Enron and resold the ballpark naming rights to the Minute Maid Corporation.

Several economists, most notably Andrew Zimbalist, discovered that professional sports facilities do not have a positive impact on local economic development, a key finding that directly contradicts the arguments of team owners who advocate publicly financed facilities. Those economists highlighted the fact that as part of the stadium or arena deals, individual team owners, and not the city governments, received all of the revenue generated by the playing facilities. City governments, however, continued to finance new sports facilities, because they feared losing their professional teams to other cities whose governments offered lucrative stadium or arena financing deals. Most American cities regarded having professional sports teams as a mark of "major-league" status, so they sought to raise their national profiles by building facilities and attracting sports franchises. Consequently, the boom in sports facility construction altered the geography of professional sports and ushered a brief era of "franchise free agency."

One of the most infamous examples of franchise free agency happened in 1995 when Art Modell moved the beloved Cleveland Browns NFL team to Baltimore. While the Browns played at old Cleveland Municipal Stadium, Modell watched as the city helped both the Indians and Cavaliers build new facilities and construct the Rock and Roll Hall of Fame. Modell also noticed that the Cavaliers sold 92 luxury boxes worth as much as $150,000 per year and that the Indians sold 120 private suites in their new ballpark. At the same time, the Browns failed to lease 24 of their 108 luxury boxes. Those events convinced Modell that Cleveland's business community could not and would not pay for luxury boxes at a new football stadium. Consequently, Modell eagerly accepted the deal offered by the Maryland Stadium Authority, led by Governor Parris Glendening and Baltimore Mayor Kurt Schmoke, to move his franchise to Baltimore for the 1996 season. Under the 30-year agreement with the Maryland Stadium Authority, the Browns would play at old Memorial Stadium during the 1996 and 1997 seasons and then move to a new stadium next to Oriole Park at Camden Yards (a new Major League Baseball facility). The franchise would pay stadium operating expenses, but they would have use of the stadium rent-free and would keep all ticket, concession, parking, and stadium advertising revenue. As a further inducement, the Maryland Stadium Authority agreed to pay the franchise up to $75 million for their relocation expenses.

Modell's decision to relocate the Browns sparked outrage in Cleveland, especially since the team enjoyed the fourth-highest home attendance in the NFL despite having a losing record. Cleveland Mayor Michael White, who had intended to negotiate a new stadium deal with the Browns, met with NFL commissioner Paul Tagliabue and vainly sought a restraining order to prevent the Browns from moving. Eventually, Modell's team left Cleveland, but the city won the right to retain the franchise's name, history, and colors. The NFL wisely agreed to place a new team in Cleveland by the start of the 1999 season; meanwhile, Modell's team opened the 1996 season as the Baltimore Ravens. Since their return in 1999, the new Cleveland Browns have played before sold-out crowds in a new stadium built with public funds. Unfortunately for Cleveland's football fans, the Browns have ranked among the worst teams in the NFL, and the Ravens won the Super Bowl in 2001.

Around the time of the Browns' departure, the Rams left Los Angeles for St. Louis, the Raiders left Los Angeles for Oakland, and the Oilers left Houston for Nashville. Franchise free agency impacted other professional sports leagues, particularly the National Hockey League (NHL). In the NHL, the Nordiques left Quebec to become the Colorado Avalanche, the Jets left Winnipeg to become the Phoenix Coyotes, the North Stars left Minneapolis to become the Dallas Stars, and the Whalers left Hartford to become the Carolina Hurricanes. All professional sports leagues also underwent periods of expansion as they sought to uncover new markets. The NFL added three teams, Major League Baseball added four teams, the NBA added two teams, and the NHL added nine teams. In the early twenty-first century, the periods of franchise free agency and rapid expansion ended, but disgruntled owners continued to use the threat of relocation to receive concessions from state and local authorities.

—*Courtney Smith*

PROFESSIONAL TEAM SPORTS

During the late twentieth century, money drastically altered the landscape of professional sports in the United States. Since the early 1970s, three broadcast networks televised NFL games—CBS broadcasted NFC contests, NBC aired AFC contests, and ABC carried Monday Night Football. In 1994, however, the FOX network stunned the sports world by offering over a then-record $1.58 billion for the rights to televise NFC games. The move effectively ended the 30-year partnership between CBS and the NFL. Moreover, FOX's stunning action led to more lucrative television contracts for the other professional sports leagues, but the NFL continued to enjoy the most profitable television contracts. In 1998, CBS snagged the rights to televise AFC games away from NBC with a $4 billion, eight-year contract. Collectively, the NFL's eight-year television contracts with FOX, CBS, ABC, and ESPN netted the league $17.6 billion.

An increase in the average salary of professional athletes paralleled the increasing monetary value of television contracts. Prior to the 1990s, professional baseball, basketball, and hockey players enjoyed some form of free agency; in 1993, NFL players and owners finally reached an agreement that granted players true free agency. Free agency allowed players to sell their services to the highest bidder, and multimillionaire owners seemed willing to offer higher salaries as well as higher signing bonuses. In 1993, for example, the San Francisco Giants lured Barry Bonds away from the Pittsburgh Pirates for a then-record deal of $43.75 million over six years. Seven years later, Tom Hicks, owner of the Texas Rangers, questionably raised the bar by offering Alex Rodriguez a 10-year contract worth $252 million dollars, or over $25 million per year. Free agency frequently led to labor confrontations as owners somewhat hypocritically complained about escalating salaries and as players resisted attempts to cap their salaries. A devastating strike prematurely ended the 1994 baseball season on August 12, canceled the World Series, delayed the start of the 1995 regular season, and disgusted millions of baseball fans. To compound the situation, a growing gap developed between large and small market teams, because teams in large media markets generated more revenue from local television rights, ticket sales, and merchandise sales. Consequently, teams like the New York Yankees, who won four World Series titles between 1996 and 2000, carried payrolls that dwarfed the payrolls of teams like the Pittsburgh Pirates, the Kansas City Royals, and the Milwaukee Brewers.

In contrast to Major League Baseball, stability and parity reigned in the NFL because, in return for allowing free agency, owners enjoyed a hard salary cap and a strong revenue-sharing plan. The salary cap kept salaries within manageable limits, and the revenue-sharing plan allowed all NFL owners to share equally in the profits generated by the league. Consequently, small market teams, such as the Green Bay Packers, had the same opportunity as large market teams, such as the New York Giants and Dallas Cowboys, to attract free agents and win championships. The lucrative television contracts, combined with the revenue-sharing plan and hard salary cap, made it virtually impossible for NFL owners to lose money. From 1989 until 2004, the NFL's revenue increased more than 500 percent, and fans purchased nearly 90 percent of available tickets to league games. In the 2004 season, the NFL's 32 franchises shared equally in nearly $5.5 billion in total revenue—the most income, and the largest measure of financial cooperation, in the four major American professional sports. Each team received over $85 million from television contracts; teams also shared 34 percent of their individual gate receipts, the most generous amount in professional sports, and received a portion of revenue from luxury seats and club boxes.

While the NFL owners directly benefited from the salary cap and revenue-sharing plan, NFL players also wallowed in the league's riches because they received a percentage of the league's profits. Despite the presence of a hard salary cap, the average salary of NFL players more than tripled from $484,000 in 1992 to $1.3 million in 2003; the salary cap itself climbed from $34.6 million in 1994 to $80.6 million in 2004. Moreover, because owners could prorate a signing bonus throughout the length of a contract, NFL players received tens of millions of dollars simply for signing a contract. Due to that distribution of riches, NFL players remained content with the status quo, and the league avoided a costly labor confrontation (Yost 2006).

Jerry Jones, who bought the Dallas Cowboys for $140 million in 1989, tried to upset the system by negotiating personal deals with corporations, such as Nike and PepsiCo Inc., which fell outside of the NFL's revenue-sharing plan. In 1963, the league had created NFL Properties to collectively negotiate merchandise or sponsorship rights and distribute the revenues equally among the teams. In 1995, Jones challenged the authority of NFL Properties by arguing that each team should have the right to market itself individually and to take advantage of its popularity among NFL fans. At the time, the Cowboys ranked first in merchandise sales, but under the revenue-sharing plan, the team had to divide profits generated by those sales with the other NFL teams. Jones's deals with Nike and PepsiCo allowed those companies to adorn Texas Stadium, home of the Dallas Cowboys, with their familiar logos; Pepsi became the stadium's official soft drink. The NFL promptly sued Jones for violating league guidelines; Jones countersued, and the two parties eventually reached a settlement. Unwilling to endure another ugly confrontation, the NFL gave teams more freedom to make their own sponsorship deals that fell outside of the revenue-sharing system. Consequently, more teams followed Jones's example and allowed corporations to advertise or sell products within their stadiums. In the early twenty-first century, those individual sponsorship deals began to create a widening gap between large and small market teams and threatened to undermine the NFL's stability (http://nfl.com/history).

—*Courtney Smith*

TELEVISION

The popularity and broadcasting of particular prime-time television shows remained volatile and changing throughout the last half of the twentieth century. Viewers tended to show less loyalty to television shows than they had to favorite radio programs in the prewar era. The rise and fall of countless television shows during the period 1991–2005 showed a similar pattern. In the age of hundreds of channel options, few shows lasted for more than five or six years. Television programs that defied that trend vary in genre. Half-hour sitcoms like *Friends* and *Seinfeld* were the most notable examples. *Friends*, a comedy about six adults living in New York City, aired from 1994 until 2004. This program dominated the Thursday evening airwaves along with *Seinfeld*. The brainchild of its namesake Jerry Seinfeld, this show aired from 1989 to 1998. Also set in New York City, the creators of *Seinfeld* boasted that it was a show "about nothing." Members of the cast from both of these sitcoms moved on to "spin-off" shows, but none of them boast the fan base of *Friends* and *Seinfeld*.

Hour-long shows also had success during the time period. The part science fiction, part detective drama *X-Files* developed a cult following from 1993 through 2002. This television series was so popular that it inspired a movie that was released in 1998. When it launched in 1993, *X-Files* became a major hit for the relatively new Fox Broadcasting Company.

Other hour-long programs geared largely to a young adult audience thrived during the period. *Beverly Hills 90210* obtained a large following while it aired from 1990 to 2000. The show, about a group of friends in Beverly Hills, California, followed their lives from the teenage years to adulthood and from high school to college life. *Charmed*, a show about three sisters who are also witches, aired from 1998 to 2006. Vampire-themed shows like *Angel* and *Buffy the Vampire Slayer* also enjoyed success in the late 1990s and early 2000s.

Some animated programs enjoyed success over the era. Leading the way were shows like *Futurama*, *Family Guy*, *South Park*, and the eternal favorite the *Simpsons*. The latter was an Emmy and Peabody Award–winning show that had the distinction of being the longest-running animated program and the longest-running sitcom in American history. First aired in 1989, the *Simpsons* was in its seventeenth season in 2005.

At the same time, Americans have gained increased access to the world with the spread of 24-hour news networks. By 1991, CNN and Fox News Network already existed; however, MSNBC entered the news race in 1996. The arguably more conservative Fox News Network enjoyed particular success in the Republican-dominated political environment of the era. Throughout the era viewers watched as the Columbine High School massacre, the O. J. Simpson trial, the events of 9/11/2001, and both Gulf Wars unfolded on their favorite news channels. Television programming, with the many innovations in both technology and options, has remained the single most significant form of entertainment in American daily life. Average viewing time amounts to more than eight hours a day in households in the United States, and the number of homes that own one or more televisions has topped 95 percent. From sitcoms to sports, from melodrama to cooking shows, and from 24-hour news programs to various religious options, Americans consistently turn to their televisions sets for recreation and relaxation. The electronic medium of television remains the most powerful and striking technical and innovative force in American recreation and cultural life in the past half century.

TOURISM: CRUISE SHIPS

Americans spend billions of dollars annually as tourists. The ease of air travel, the broad development of resorts worldwide, and an increase in middle-class spending options have turned tourism into a major business and a key component of recreational life in the United States. The fastest-growing area of tourism has occurred in cruise ship tourism during the past 25 years. Since 1980, an annual growth of 8 percent shows an increase of as much as twice the percentage of annual growth in other tourism options. In 1997, more than eight million people took cruises for recreational purposes. North Americans (the United States and Canada) account for more than 80 percent of the passengers on cruise ships. The revenue that cruise ships derive amounts to almost $17 billion annually.

Modern cruise ship—the new tourism. Courtesy of Jolyon Girard.

In 1998, 71 ships from 24 cruise lines carried passengers to the Caribbean (50 percent), the Mediterranean (15 percent), Alaska (8 percent), the Panama Canal (6 percent), and Mexico (5 percent). Miami, Florida, has surfaced as a major hub for cruise ships, with up to 30 departures a week. Prices range widely depending on the cruise line, the length of the cruise, and the location. Cruising tourism has become one of the most popular forms of recreational activity for many Americans seeking to enhance their vacation options (www.lighthouse-foundation.org).

WIDE WORLD OF SPORTS

In 1961, ABC television began to broadcast a show entitled *Wide World of Sports*. Roone Arledge produced the program, and Jim McKay acted as the announcer for most of the series. ABC ended the program as a regular weekly event in 2006. The show captured the many forms of sport that Americans watched and sporting activities in which they participated. From rodeos in the West to *jai lai* in Florida, viewers witnessed the broad world of sports in the United States, and worldwide, unfold weekly. The program indicated how many sports activities existed in the United States and how many people took advantage of those options. This section concludes with a nod of appreciation to the idea behind the show. The section has certainly overlooked countless recreational activities about which people are passionate and involved in their recreational life. It has devoted little time to fishing or hunting as activities and to camping and hiking as recreation. Esoteric or new forms of sport are also given short notice. The impact of ski boarding, as an example, deserves time and space. Everything from billiards and shuffleboard should also join the expansive list of available sports. If the encyclopedia omits or gives short space to one's favorites, apologies are extended. In simple fact, recreational life in the United States remains so varied, with so many options and opportunities, that it becomes implausible to pay full homage or attention to all of them. A full look at recreational life, even in a time period as concentrated as 1990–2005, would require its own encyclopedia.

FOR MORE INFORMATION

Cheng, Andria. *International Herald Tribune* (September 22, 2006).

Grinols, Earl L. *Gambling in America: Costs and Benefits*. New York: Cambridge University Press, 2004.

McDonough, Will. *The NFL Century: The Complete Story of the National Football League, 1920–2000*. New York: Smithmark Publishers, 1999.

NASCAR. Turner Sports Inc. 2006. http://www.nascar.com.

Parlett, David. *Oxford History of Board Games*. New York: Oxford University Press, 1999.

Professional Bowling Association. http://www.pba.com/.

Roberts, Randy, and James S. Olson. *Winning Is the Only Thing: Sports in America since 1945*. Baltimore, MD: Johns Hopkins University Press, 1991.

Smith, Ronald. *Sports and Freedom: The Rise of Big-Time College Athletics*. New York: Oxford University Press, 1990.

Thelin, John R. *Games Colleges Play: Scandal and Reform in Intercollegiate Athletics*. Baltimore, MD: Johns Hopkins University Press, 1996.

Thompson, William N. *Gambling in America: An Encyclopedia.* Santa Barbara, CA: ABC Clio, 2001.

U.S. Tennis Association. http://www.usta.com/home/default.sps.

Yost, Mark. *Tailgating, Sacks, and Salary Caps: How the NFL Became the Most Successful Sports League in History.* Chicago: Kaplan Business, 2006.

Zimbalist, Andrew. *The Bottom Line: Observations and Arguments on the Sports Business.* Philadelphia: Temple University Press, 2006.

Religious Life

OVERVIEW

American commitment to religious and spiritual life remains a key aspect of contemporary society. Since 1990, statistics indicate a rise in formal religious participation in every religious denomination and belief. At the same time, the number of Americans who claim no religious affiliation has also grown. The increased political and social influence of evangelical Christians has become an issue of broad debate in the society. Many American political pundits believe that the religious right's support of Republican Party candidates has enabled that party to win control of Congress and the White House between 1995 and 2005. The growing scandal regarding sexual abuse in the Roman Catholic Church in America has also prompted a major national debate. While American Muslims make up a small percentage of the U.S. population, post-September 11, 2001, issues concerning terrorism and its modern roots have drawn more attention to Islam in America as a factor in the nation's religious life. In every respect, the nation continues to view religious life as a major factor in its day-to-day affairs. From school board battles regarding science, to court decisions concerning the First Amendment, to religious worship on a weekly basis, Americans view religion, positively or negatively, in serious terms. Alexis de Tocqueville suggested in *Democracy in America,* in the 1830s, that Americans took their religious life seriously. Little appears to have changed at the beginning of the twenty-first century.

EVANGELICAL CHRISTIANS

The growth and influence of evangelical Protestanism have surfaced as a major factor in American religious life. Estimates place the number of practicing evangelical Christians at more than 30 million Americans (10 percent of the population). Those numbers suggest that evangelical Christians make up the largest percentage of Protestants across the various denominations in that religion. Over the past 20 years, they became more active in public forums, arguing for greater controls over the content of mass media, the sanctity of marriage, opposition to gay rights, opposition to abortion, and less reliance on government and more on faith-based institutions to address social problems and public education than mainline Protestants and Roman Catholics also engaged in political and social issues (Bethel 2005).

The spiritual drive of evangelical Protestanism has existed in America since the Great Awakening in the early eighteenth century. The modern expression includes members of a number of Protestant faiths but has four basic characteristics: first, a personal conversion experience, essentially a "new birth" or "born-again" commitment to the faith; second, a belief in biblical authority or *sola scriptura* as the inspired word and truth of God; third, a belief in personal missionary responsibility—"as you go preach"; and fourth, a central focus on the redeeming value of Christ's life and death as the only means of salvation. While individual points of view may differ, and it remains difficult to stereotype any large group of people, most observers see those four concepts as basic to evangelical Christianity.

In public life, many adherents challenge court decisions regarding prayer in public schools and the teaching of Darwinian science without alternative access to "creationism" theories. Efforts to win election to local school boards to effect changes in curriculum have become a strategy of the evangelical Christians. The rise of televangelism and large congregational churches has added to the impact and, to some degree, the fervor of the members. Their involvement in moral political issues such as gay lifestyles, pornography, and school prayer has encouraged politicians to solicit their votes. The Republican Party has won key victories in state elections, in Congress, and even in the presidency as a result of evangelicals' political support. In terms of religious faith, few question the sincerity and depth of belief among evangelical Christians. Critics do question their conclusions and often their methods of public discourse, but it remains difficult for even their harshest opponents to argue their conviction. The very success of evangelical Christianity, reflected in sales of books on Christian themes, in the popularity of Christian broadcasting, and in the growth of churches, especially in new suburban areas, bespeaks the still intense religious atmosphere of modern America. It also encourages other religions to adopt some of the methods of evangelism and outreach.

Tied to the emotional debate regarding the separation of church and state, the active involvement of evangelical Christians in political discourse, at both the local and the national level, continues to produce a significant response. Critics contend that their efforts to seize control of local school boards are designed to impose biblical influence on the public school curriculum. At the national level, critics accuse evangelicals of too heavily imposing their social values on a society more secular and humanist than religious conviction can understand or accept. Nonetheless, those who claim commitment to evangelical Christianity maintain that they have the right and moral necessity to bring their views and opinions to the public forum. The debate continues.

ISLAM AND JUDAISM

According to the 2000 census, American Muslims and Jews made up less than 2 percent of the population of the United States; approximately four million Jewish citizens and 1,600,000 Muslims. Recent political crises on the global stage, however, have heightened American interest in and sensitivity regarding the two faiths. Not only are Muslims and Jews concerned as they practice their religion in America, but those who live in the United States who are not members of those religions also have questions and concerns. Both Judaism and Islam, like Christianity, stem from common roots. Muslims talk about believers in the three faiths as "brothers of the book," people with a root unity and background going back to the prophet Abraham. Obviously, however, the three important Western religions have not been the most ecumenical in the past or at present. The developing tension between the three faiths has as much of its animosity in politics and global diplomacy as it does in religious disagreement. The emergence of Israel as an independent Jewish state in 1947, the growing influence of Arab-Muslim oil states in the Middle East as enemies of Israel, the Palestinian conflict, and the U.S. involvement in those issues has isolated the religions along geopolitical lines (Girard 2001, 231–54).

At the same time, orthodox Muslim clerics and believers see much to dislike in the secular Western world, with much of that concern pointed at the United States. Those complex developments led, on September 11, 2001, to a violent, devastating terrorist attack on the United States. The people responsible were Muslims. Previous terrorist attacks against the United States and its facilities overseas were also attributed to Muslim terrorists. Many expected that the "9/11" attacks would provoke a violent anti-Muslim reaction in the United States. With the exception of some rare instances, that did not occur. Yet, a 2005 Cornell University poll indicated that 44 percent of Americans believe the government should restrict some civil rights and liberties for Muslim Americans. And 27 percent of those polled believed Muslims should be required to register with the government. The same poll also revealed that 22 percent favored some form of racial profiling, and 29 percent believed government agents should infiltrate Muslim American social and religious institutions to look for potential or actual terrorists. Forty-eight percent of Americans, however, believed that the government should impose no restrictions of civil liberties or rights for the religious group. To date, the U.S. government has passed no specific legislation restricting the rights of Muslim Americans. But Arabic-looking people and Muslims have complained of profiling and restrictions in travel and employment.

KWANZAA

Kwanzaa is a Pan-African cultural celebration, often confused as a religious ceremony. It is celebrated between December 26 and January 1 each year, mostly in the United States. An estimated 13 percent of African Americans celebrate the weeklong event. Dr. Ron Karenga initiated Kwanzaa in December, 1966. It celebrates seven key principles—*umoja* (unity); *kujichagulia* (self-determination); *ujima* (collective work and responsibility); *ujamaa* (cooperative economics); *nia* (purpose); *kuumba* (creativity); and *imani* (faith).

FOR FURTHER INFORMATION

Karenga, Maulana. *Kwanzaa: A Celebration of Family, Community, and Culture*. Los Angeles: University of Sankore Press, 1997.

NUMBERS

In the first decade of the twenty-first century, 52 percent of Americans claimed affiliation with a Protestant Christian religion. Twenty-four percent claimed Roman Catholicism. Two percent were Mormons. One percent was Muslim or Jewish. Buddhism and Hinduism drew more than one million faithful to those religious beliefs. Ten percent claimed no religious affiliation, and another 10 percent belonged to religious groups as diverse as Hinduism, Baha'i, Sikhism, New Age, Scientology, Wicca, or Deism. In 2004, over 224 million Americans belonged to a variety of Christian faiths, while 38 million claimed no religious affiliation (http://www.cia.gov).

RELIGION AND THE MORAL AND SOCIAL IMPERATIVES

In broad terms, Americans have tended to accept the separation of church and state, as a number of federal and Supreme Court decisions continue to confirm. Most public opinion polls tend to agree with the concept of a "wall of separation" between the government and religion, although there remains some hesitancy about prayer in schools. The 1963 U.S. Supreme Court decision, *Abington Township School District v. Schempp*, which removed school prayer and religious devotion from public schools, remains a topic of debate among Americans. In any event, efforts on the part of evangelical Christians to change local and state laws regarding prayer and curriculum have failed in virtually every instance nationwide. Usually voters in local districts or at the state level reject the ideas. When they do not, state and federal courts generally reject local or state laws that include overt forms of religion in the classroom. There are exceptions. A number of local communities and school districts have banned Halloween celebrations or limited or ended Christmas celebrations, as examples, to deflect concern that those events overtly advance particular religious beliefs in violation of the First Amendment.

In similar fashion, the display of the Ten Commandments in public, government venues has also provoked criticism from Americans who oppose the displays. While those actions do not have the support of most Americans, government officials tend to accede to complaints in the name of diversity and to avoid lawsuits. At the same time, there is little evidence to suggest that the government has crossed the wall of separation either. At the height of fear and anger over the 9/11 tragedy and throughout the ongoing global war on terrorism, Americans and their government have taken no real reprisals against Muslims living in the United States. In the new century, religion remains an important aspect of daily life in America, with all of its complex and emotional antecedents. It seems to continue to do so with respect for the First Amendment and the private right of Americans to pursue their religious and spiritual beliefs as they choose.

ROMAN CATHOLICISM: CONTRIBUTIONS AND SCANDALS

In 2004, more than 70 million Americans practiced their faith as Roman Catholics, 24.5 percent of the population. Catholicism remains the single most populous faith in America. Its parishes, hospitals, orphanages, schools, colleges, and universities have been an important part of American public and religious life for more than a century. Catholic charities and social service organizations have joined with a number of other religions to provide health and welfare services for hundreds of thousands of Americans, and millions of people worldwide. Catholic commitment to social justice remains a major aspect of the faith.

In the recent history of the church, however, Roman Catholicism has been beset with a series of scandals involving sexual impropriety among a small number of its priests. On January 6, 2002, news reports made public the first sexual abuse scandal involving a priest and a young male. Since that time, 300 lawsuits have been filed against the church and individual priests alleging sexual abuse. A number of priests have pled guilty. Other cases are pending. The archbishop of Boston, Cardinal Bernard Law, became a focus of the emerging scandal because of the manner in which the church hierarchy was apparently dealing with the issue. The church appeared more interested in covering up the scandal, moving priests to other places, and protecting the institution against lawsuits than correcting the problem. As the scandal became more public, the church responded with a series of meetings and conferences not only to confront the issue but also to combat the bad publicity. Church policy has changed and now requires the removal of any priest convicted of sexual abuse. Lawsuits have cost the Catholic Church millions of dollars in settlements. The Roman Catholic laity appear stunned, embarrassed, and angered by the scandals. The church has suffered a political and moral "black eye" unlike any in recent memory.

It remains important to note, however, that there are 46,000 priests in the United States. To date, less than 0.7 percent are involved in abuse scandals. It is also important to examine the issue of pedophiliac behavior or any form of sexual misconduct among ministers and other religious leaders outside the Catholic Church. Little research has been done in that area. While a debate has developed regarding the question of the sexual abuse as an example of homosexual behavior or pedophilia on the part of accused priests, the issue drags on in the courts and in the public discourse.

In 2005, Americans enjoyed many religious choices in a nation where religion is voluntary, not compulsory. The significance of religion is perhaps best revealed in polls taken as recently as 2006. In the 2006 poll, a wide range of respondents reported overwhelmingly that they could never vote for an atheist to be president of the United States.

SPECIAL FAITHS AND SPIRITUALITY

A variety of sects and nontraditional religious beliefs have always existed in the American experience. The Amish in Pennsylvania and elsewhere, for instance, have practiced their beliefs in the United States since the eighteenth century. Some 145,000 Native Americans continue to adhere to the traditional spiritual beliefs of their forbears. Scientology has attracted almost 80,000 adherents, some of them movie celebrities. New Age religion attracts more than 95,000 people in the United States. Wiccan (druid or pagan belief) adherents draw close to half a million believers. While the religious or spiritual conviction involved in those faiths have a variety of antecedents, it remains clear in the American religious experience that the government does not interfere in the right of believers to pursue their spiritual lives as they choose. While examples of religious intolerance have existed throughout the history of the United States, both the laws and popular expressions supporting religious tolerance have appeared to dominate mainstream American thinking since the end of World War II.

FOR MORE INFORMATION

Bethel, Alison. "Evangelical Christian Influence Grows." *The Detroit News* (February 6, 2005).

CIA Fact Book. http://www.cia.gov.

Girard, Jolyon P. *America and the World*. Westport, CT: Greenwood Press, 2001.

Harvey, Paul, and Philip Goff. *The Columbia Documentary History of Religion in America since 1945*. New York: Columbia University Press, 2005.

Steinfels, Peter. *A People Adrift: The Crisis of the Roman Catholic Church in America*. New York: Simon and Schuster, 2003.

Taylor, Mark Lewis. *Religion, Politics, and the Christian Right: Post-9/11 Powers in American Empire*. Minneapolis, MN: Augsburg Fortress, 2005.

PRIMARY
DOCUMENTS

1. FRANKLIN D. ROOSEVELT'S ADDRESS TO THE NATION FOLLOWING THE JAPANESE ATTACK ON PEARL HARBOR (DECEMBER 8, 1941)

On December 8, 1941, the day following the surprise Japanese military attack on the United States naval and air bases at Pearl Harbor in Hawaii, President Franklin D. Roosevelt delivered the following address, asking for a declaration of war on Japan, before a joint session of Congress.

Mr. Vice President, Mr. Speaker, Members of the Senate, and of the House of Representatives:

Yesterday, December 7th, 1941—a date which will live in infamy—the United States of America was suddenly and deliberately attacked by naval and air forces of the Empire of Japan.

The United States was at peace with that nation and, at the solicitation of Japan, was still in conversation with its government and its emperor looking toward the maintenance of peace in the Pacific.

Indeed, one hour after Japanese air squadrons had commenced bombing in the American island of Oahu, the Japanese ambassador to the United States and his colleague delivered to our Secretary of State a formal reply to a recent American message. And while this reply stated that it seemed useless to continue the existing diplomatic negotiations, it contained no threat or hint of war or of armed attack.

It will be recorded that the distance of Hawaii from Japan makes it obvious that the attack was deliberately planned many days or even weeks ago. During the intervening time, the Japanese government has deliberately sought to deceive the United States by false statements and expressions of hope for continued peace.

The attack yesterday on the Hawaiian islands has caused severe damage to American naval and military forces. I regret to tell you that very many American lives have been lost. In addition, American ships have been reported torpedoed on the high seas between San Francisco and Honolulu.

Yesterday, the Japanese government also launched an attack against Malaya.

Last night, Japanese forces attacked Hong Kong.

Last night, Japanese forces attacked Guam.

Last night, Japanese forces attacked the Philippine Islands.

Last night, the Japanese attacked Wake Island.

And this morning, the Japanese attacked Midway Island.

Japan has, therefore, undertaken a surprise offensive extending throughout the Pacific area. The facts of yesterday and today speak for themselves. The people of the United States have already formed their opinions and well understand the implications to the very life and safety of our nation.

As commander in chief of the Army and Navy, I have directed that all measures be taken for our defense. But always will our whole nation remember the character of the onslaught against us....

...With confidence in our armed forces, with the unbounding determination of our people, we will gain the inevitable triumph—so help us God.

I ask that the Congress declare that since the unprovoked and dastardly attack by Japan on Sunday, December 7th, 1941, a state of war has existed between the United States and the Japanese empire.

Source: http://www.ou.edu/ushistory/infamy.shtml.

2. PRESIDENT FRANKLIN D. ROOSEVELT'S FIRESIDE CHAT CONCERNING THE COAL CRISIS (MAY 2, 1943)

Between 1933 and 1944, President Franklin Roosevelt gave 30 radio addresses, known as fireside chats, to discuss domestic and foreign policy issues with the American people. They became popular examples of Roosevelt's political ability to keep in touch with the public. The following chat from 1943 addresses the dangers to the war effort of a strike by coal miners.

MY FELLOW AMERICANS:

I am speaking tonight to the American people, and in particular to those of our citizens who are coal miners.

Tonight this country faces a serious crisis. We are engaged in a war on the successful outcome of which will depend the whole future of our country.

This war has reached a new critical phase. After the years that we have spent in preparation, we have moved into active and continuing battle with our enemies. We are pouring into the world-wide conflict everything that we have—our young men, and the vast resources of our nation.

I have just returned from a two weeks' tour of inspection on which I saw our men being trained and our war materials made. My trip took me through twenty states. I saw thousands of workers on the production line, making airplanes, and guns and ammunition. Everywhere I found great eagerness to get on with the war. Men and women are working long hours at difficult jobs and living under difficult conditions without complaint.

Along thousands of miles of track I saw countless acres of newly ploughed fields. The farmers of this country are planting the crops that are needed to feed our armed forces, our civilian population and our Allies. Those crops will be harvested. On my trip, I saw hundreds of thousands of soldiers. Young men who were green recruits last autumn have matured into self-assured and hardened fighting men. They are in splendid physical condition. They are mastering the superior weapons that we are pouring out of our factories.

The American people have accomplished a miracle. However, all of our massed effort is none too great to meet the demands of this war. We shall need everything that we have and everything that our Allies have to defeat the Nazis and the Fascists in the coming battles on the Continent of Europe, and the Japanese on the Continent of Asia and in the Islands of the Pacific.

This tremendous forward movement of the United States and the United Nations cannot be stopped by our enemies.

And equally, it must not be hampered by any one individual or by the leaders of any one group here back home.

I want to make it clear that every American coal miner who has stopped mining coal—no matter how sincere his motives, no matter how legitimate he may believe his grievances to be—every idle miner directly and individually is obstructing our war effort. We have not yet won this war. We will win this war only as we produce and deliver our total American effort on the high seas and on the battle fronts. And that requires unrelenting, uninterrupted effort here on the home front.

A stopping of the coal supply, even for a short time, would involve a gamble with the lives of American soldiers and sailors and the future security of our whole people. It would involve an unwarranted, unnecessary and terribly dangerous gamble with our chances for victory.

Therefore, I say to all miners—and to all Americans everywhere, at home and abroad—the production of coal will not be stopped.

Tonight, I am speaking to the essential patriotism of the miners, and to the patriotism of their wives and children. And I am going to state the true facts of this case as simply and as plainly as I know how.

After the attack at Pearl Harbor, the three great labor organizations—the American Federation of Labor, the Congress of Industrial Organizations, and the Railroad Brotherhoods—gave the positive assurance that there would be no strikes as long as the war lasted. And the President of the United Mine workers of America was a party to that assurance.

That pledge was applauded throughout the country. It was a forcible means of telling the world that we Americans—135,000,000 of us—are united in our determination to fight this total war with our total will and our total power. At the request of employers and of organized labor—including the United Mine Workers—the War Labor Board was set up for settling any disputes which could not be adjusted through collective bargaining. The War Labor Board is a tribunal on which workers, employers and the general public are equally represented.

In the present coal crisis, conciliation and mediation were tried unsuccessfully.

In accordance with the law, the case was then certified to the War Labor Board, the agency created for this express purpose with the approval of organized labor. The members of the Board followed the usual practice which has proved successful in other disputes. Acting promptly, they undertook to get all the facts of this (the) case from both the miners and the operators.

The national officers of the United Mine Workers, however, declined to have anything to do with the fact-finding of the War Labor Board. The only excuse that they offer is that the War Labor Board is prejudiced.

The War Labor Board has been and is ready to give this (the) case a fair and impartial hearing. And I have given my assurance that if any adjustment of wages is made by the Board, it will be made retroactive to April first. But the national officers Of the United Mine Workers refused to participate in the hearing, when asked to do so last Monday.

On Wednesday of this past week, while the Board was proceeding with the case, stoppages began to occur in some mines. On Thursday morning I telegraphed to the officers of the United Mine Workers asking that the miners continue mining coal on Saturday morning. However, a general strike throughout the industry became effective on Friday night.

The responsibility for the crisis that we now face rests squarely on these national officers of the United Mine Workers, and not on the Government of the United States. But the consequences of this arbitrary action threaten all of us everywhere.

At ten o'clock, yesterday morning—Saturday—the Government took over the mines. I called upon the miners to return to work for their Government. The Government needs their services just as surely as it needs the services of our soldiers, and sailors, and marines—and the services of the millions who are turning out the munitions of war.

You miners have sons in the Army and Navy and Marine Corps. You have sons who at this very minute—this split second—may be fighting in New Guinea, or in the Aleutian Islands, or Guadalcanal, or Tunisia, or China, or protecting troop ships and supplies against submarines on the high seas. We have already received telegrams from some of our fighting men overseas, and I only wish they could tell you what they think of the stoppage of work in the coal mines.

Some of your own sons have come back from the fighting fronts, wounded. A number of them, for example, are now here in an Army hospital in Washington. Several of them have been decorated by their Government.

I could tell you of one from Pennsylvania. He was a coal miner before his induction, and his father is a coal miner. He was seriously wounded by Nazi machine gun bullets while he was on a bombing mission over Europe in a Flying Fortress. Another boy, from Kentucky, the son of a coal miner, was wounded when our troops first landed in North Africa six months ago.

There is (still) another, from Illinois. He was a coal miner—his father and two brothers are coal miners. He was seriously wounded in Tunisia while attempting to rescue two comrades whose jeep had been blown up by a Nazi mine.

These men do not consider themselves heroes. They would probably be embarrassed if I mentioned their names over the air. They were wounded in the line of duty. They know how essential it is to the tens of thousands—hundreds of thousands—and ultimately millions of other young Americans to get the best of arms and equipment into the hands of our fighting forces—and get them there quickly.

The fathers and mothers of our fighting men, their brothers and sisters and friends—and that includes all of us—are also in the line of duty—the production line. Any failure in production may well result in costly defeat on the field of battle.

There can be no one among us—no one faction powerful enough to interrupt the forward march of our people to victory.

You miners have ample reason to know that there are certain basic rights for which this country stands, and that those rights are worth fighting for and worth dying for. That is why you have sent your sons and brothers from every mining town in the nation to join in the great struggle overseas. That is why you have contributed so generously, so willingly, to the purchase of war bonds and to the many funds for the relief of war victims in foreign lands. That is why, since this war was started in 1939, you have increased the annual production of coal by almost two hundred million tons a year.

The toughness of your sons in our armed forces is not surprising. They come of fine, rugged stock. Men who work in the mines are not unaccustomed to hardship. It has been the objective of this Government to reduce that hardship, to obtain for miners and for all who do the nation's work a better standard of living.

I know only too well that the cost of living is troubling the miners' families, and troubling the families of millions of other workers throughout the country as well. A year ago it became evident to all of us that something had to be done about living costs. Your Government determined not to let the cost of living continue to go up as it did in the first World War.

Your Government has been determined to maintain stability of both prices and wages—so that a dollar would buy, so far as possible, the same amount of the necessities of life. And by necessities I mean just that—not the luxuries, not the (and) fancy goods that we have learned to do without in wartime.

So far, we have not been able to keep the prices of some necessities as low as we should have liked to keep them. That is true not only in coal towns but in many other places.

Wherever we find that prices of essentials have risen too high, they will be brought down. Wherever we find that price ceilings are being violated, the violators will be punished.

Rents have been fixed in most parts of the country. In many cities they have been cut to below where they were before we entered the war. Clothing prices have generally remained stable.

These two items make up more than a third of the total budget of the worker's family.

As for food, which today accounts for about another (a) third of the family expenditure on the average, I want to repeat again: your Government will continue to take all necessary measures to eliminate unjustified and avoidable price increases. And we are today (now) taking measures to "roll back" the prices of meats.

The war is going to go on. Coal will be mined no matter what any individual thinks about it. The operation of our factories, our power plants, our railroads will not be stopped. Our munitions must move to our troops.

And so, under these circumstances, it is inconceivable that any patriotic miner can choose any course other than going back to work and mining coal.

The nation cannot afford violence of any kind at the coal mines or in coal towns. I have placed authority for the resumption of coal mining in the hands of a civilian, the Secretary of the Interior. If it becomes necessary to protect any miner who seeks patriotically to go back and work, then that miner must have and his family must have—and will have—complete and adequate protection. If it becomes necessary to have troops at the mine mouths or in coal towns for the protection of working miners and their families, those troops will be doing police duty for the sake of the nation as a whole, and particularly for the sake of the fighting men in the Army, the Navy and the Marines—your sons and mine—who are fighting our common enemies all over the world.

I understand the devotion of the coal miners to their union. I know of the sacrifices they have made to build it up. I believe now, as I have all my life, in the right of workers to join unions and to protect their unions. I want to make it absolutely clear that this Government is not going to do anything now to weaken those rights in the coal fields.

Every improvement in the conditions of the coal miners of this country has had my hearty support, and I do not mean to desert them now. But I also do not mean to desert my obligations and responsibilities as President of the United States and Commander in Chief of the Army and Navy.

The first necessity is the resumption of coal mining. The terms of the old contract will be followed by the Secretary of the Interior. If an adjustment in wages results from a decision of the War Labor Board, or from any new agreement between the operators and miners, which is approved by the War Labor Board, that adjustment will be made retroactive to April first.

In the message that I delivered to the Congress four months ago, I expressed my conviction that the spirit of this nation is good.

Since then, I have seen our troops in the Caribbean area, in bases on the coasts of our ally, Brazil, and in North Africa. Recently I have again seen great numbers of our fellow countrymen—soldiers and civilians—from the Atlantic Seaboard to the Mexican border and to the Rocky Mountains.

Tonight, in the fact of a crisis of serious proportions in the coal industry, I say again that the spirit or this nation is good. I know that the American people will not tolerate any threat offered to their Government by anyone. I believe the coal miners will not continue the strike against their (the) Government. I believe that the coal miners (themselves) as Americans will not fail to heed the clear call to duty. Like all other good Americans, they will march shoulder to shoulder with their armed forces to victory. Tomorrow the Stars and Stripes will fly over the coal mines, and I hope that every miner will be at work under that flag.

Source: http://www.mhric.org/fdr/chat24.html.

3. GENERAL DWIGHT D. EISENHOWER'S ORDER OF THE DAY FOR D-DAY, THE ALLIED INVASION OF NORMANDY (JUNE 6, 1944)

General Dwight Eisenhower commanded Allied forces during the Normandy landings in Europe in June 1944. The following order served as his formal announcement of the commencement of the long-awaited Allied invasion of France.

Soldiers, Sailors and Airmen of the Allied Expeditionary Forces:

…In company with our brave Allies and brothers-in-arms on other Fronts you will bring about the destruction of the German war machine, the elimination of Nazi tyranny over oppressed peoples of Europe, and security for ourselves in a free world.

Your task will not be an easy one. Your enemy is well trained, well equipped and battle-hardened. He will fight savagely.

But this is the year 1944. Much has happened since the Nazi triumphs of 1940–41. The United Nations have inflicted upon the Germans great defeats, in open battle, man-to-man. Our air offensive has seriously reduced their strength in the air and their capacity to wage war on the ground. Our Home Fronts have given us an overwhelming superiority in weapons and munitions of war, and placed at our disposal great reserves of trained fighting men. The tide has turned. The free men of the world are marching together to victory.

I have full confidence in your courage, devotion to duty, and skill in battle. We will accept nothing less than full victory.

Good Luck! And let us all beseech the blessing of Almighty God upon this great and noble undertaking.

Source: http://www.classbrain.com.

4. SECRETARY OF STATE GEORGE C. MARSHALL DESCRIBES THE MARSHALL PLAN (JUNE 5, 1947)

Secretary of State George C. Marshall provided a public announcement of the European Economic Recovery Program (the Marshall Plan) at a Harvard

University Commencement Address in June 1947. The program provided billions of dollars in U.S. aid to rebuild the economies of postwar European nations.

Mr. President, Dr. Conant, members of the Board of Overseers, Ladies and Gentlemen:

I am profoundly grateful, touched by the great distinction and honor and great compliment accorded me by the authorities of Harvard this morning....

But to speak more seriously, I need not tell you that the world situation is very serious. That must be apparent to all intelligent people. I think one difficulty is that the problem is one of such enormous complexity that the very mass of facts presented to the public by press and radio make it exceedingly difficult for the man in the street to reach a clear appraisement of the situation. Furthermore, the people of this country are distant from the troubled areas of the earth, and it is hard for them to comprehend the plight and consequent reactions of the long-suffering peoples of Europe and the effect of those reactions on their governments in connection with our efforts to promote peace in the world.

In considering the requirements for the rehabilitation of Europe, the physical loss of life, the visible destruction of cities, factories, mines, and railroads was correctly estimated, but it has become obvious during recent months that this visible destruction was probably less serious than the dislocation of the entire fabric of European economy.... The feverish preparation for war and the more feverish maintenance of the war effort engulfed all aspects of national economies. Machinery has fallen into disrepair or is entirely obsolete. Under the arbitrary and destructive Nazi rule, virtually every possible enterprise was geared into the German war machine.... Recovery has been seriously retarded by the fact that two years after the close of hostilities a peace settlement with Germany and Austria has not been agreed upon....

...The farmer has always produced the foodstuffs to exchange with the city dweller for the other necessities of life. This division of labor is the basis of modern civilization. At the present time it is threatened with breakdown. The town and city industries are not producing adequate goods to exchange with the food-producing farmer. Raw materials and fuel are in short supply. Machinery, as I have said, is lacking or worn out. The farmer or the peasant cannot find the goods for sale which he desires to purchase. So the sale of his farm produce for money which he cannot use seems to him an unprofitable transaction. He, therefore, has withdrawn many fields from crop cultivation and he's using them for grazing. He feeds more grain to stock and finds for himself and his family an ample supply of food, however short he may be on clothing and the other ordinary gadgets of civilization.

Meanwhile, people in the cities are short of food and fuel, and in some places approaching the starvation levels. So, the governments are forced to use their foreign money and credits to procure these necessities abroad. This process exhausts funds which are urgently needed for reconstruction. Thus, a very serious situation is rapidly developing which bodes no good for the world....

…Aside from the demoralizing effect on the world at large and the possibilities of disturbances arising as a result of the desperation of the people concerned, the consequences to the economy of the United States should be apparent to all. It is logical that the United States should do whatever it is able to do to assist in the return of normal economic health in the world, without which there can be no political stability and no assured peace. Our policy is directed not against any country or doctrine but against hunger, poverty, desperation, and chaos. Its purpose should be the revival of a working economy in the world so as to permit the emergence of political and social conditions in which free institutions can exist.

…Any government that is willing to assist in the task of recovery will find full cooperation, I am sure, on the part of the United States Government. Any government which maneuvers to block the recovery of other countries cannot expect help from us. Furthermore, governments, political parties, or groups which seek to perpetuate human misery in order to profit there from politically or otherwise will encounter the opposition of the United States.

It is already evident that before the United States Government can proceed much further in its efforts to alleviate the situation and help start the European world on its way to recovery, there must be some agreement among the countries of Europe as to the requirements of the situation and the part those countries themselves will take in order to give a proper effect to whatever actions might be undertaken by this Government. It would be neither fitting nor efficacious for our Government to undertake to draw up unilaterally a program designed to place Europe on its feet economically. This is the business of the Europeans. The initiative, I think, must come from Europe….

…An essential part of any successful action on the part of the United States is an understanding on the part of the people of America of the character of the problem and the remedies to be applied. Political passion and prejudice should have no part. With foresight, and a willingness on the part of our people to face up to the vast responsibility which history has clearly placed upon our country, the difficulties I have outlined can and will be overcome….

…As I said more formally a moment ago, we are remote from the scene of these troubles. It is virtually impossible at this distance merely by reading, or listening, or even seeing photographs and motion pictures, to grasp at all the real significance of the situation. And yet the whole world of the future hangs on a proper judgment….

Source: http://www.hpol.org/marshall.

5. SENATOR MARGARET CHASE SMITH'S DECLARATION OF CONSCIENCE (JUNE 1, 1950)

Senator Margaret Chase Smith (R-Maine) responded to the political censorship provoked by the influence of Senator Joseph McCarthy's (R-Wisconsin)

Red Scare tactics with the following public assault on his efforts to silence public debate and free speech regarding critical national issues.

Mr. President:

…It is a national feeling of fear and frustration that could result in national suicide and the end of everything that we Americans hold dear. It is a condition that comes from the lack of effective leadership in either the Legislative Branch or the Executive Branch of our Government.

…I speak as briefly as possible because too much harm has already been done with irresponsible words of bitterness and selfish political opportunism. I speak as briefly as possible because the issue is too great to be obscured by eloquence. I speak simply and briefly in the hope that my words will be taken to heart.

I speak as a Republican. I speak as a woman. I speak as a United States Senator. I speak as an American.

The United States Senate has long enjoyed worldwide respect as the greatest deliberative body in the world. But recently that deliberative character has too often been debased to the level of a forum of hate and character assassination sheltered by the shield of congressional immunity.

It is ironical that we Senators can in debate in the Senate directly or indirectly, by any form of words, impute to any American who is not a Senator any conduct or motive unworthy or unbecoming an American—and without that non-Senator American having any legal redress against us—yet if we say the same thing in the Senate about our colleagues we can be stopped on the grounds of being out of order.

…I think that it is high time for the United States Senate and its members to do some soul-searching—for us to weigh our consciences—on the manner in which we are performing our duty to the people of America—on the manner in which we are using or abusing our individual powers and privileges.

I think that it is high time that we remembered that we have sworn to uphold and defend the Constitution. I think that it is high time that we remembered that the Constitution, as amended, speaks not only of the freedom of speech but also of trial by jury instead of trial by accusation.

Whether it be a criminal prosecution in court or a character prosecution in the Senate, there is little practical distinction when the life of a person has been ruined.

Those of us who shout the loudest about Americanism in making character assassinations are all too frequently those who, by our own words and acts, ignore some of the basic principles of Americanism:

The right to criticize;

The right to hold unpopular beliefs;

The right to protest;

The right of independent thought.

The exercise of these rights should not cost one single American citizen his reputation or his right to a livelihood nor should he be in danger of losing his reputation or livelihood merely because he happens to know someone who holds unpopular beliefs. Who of us doesn't? Otherwise none of us could call our souls our own. Otherwise thought control would have set in.

The American people are sick and tired of being afraid to speak their minds lest they be politically smeared as "Communists" or "Fascists" by their opponents. Freedom of speech is not what it used to be in America. It has been so abused by some that it is not exercised by others.

…As a Republican, I say to my colleagues on this side of the aisle that the Republican Party faces a challenge today that is not unlike the challenge that it faced back in Lincoln's day. The Republican Party so successfully met that challenge that it emerged from the Civil War as the champion of a united nation—in addition to being a Party that unrelentingly fought loose spending and loose programs.

Today our country is being psychologically divided by the confusion and the suspicions that are bred in the United States Senate to spread like cancerous tentacles of "know nothing, suspect everything" attitudes. Today we have a Democratic Administration that has developed a mania for loose spending and loose programs. History is repeating itself—and the Republican Party again has the opportunity to emerge as the champion of unity and prudence.

The record of the present Democratic Administration has provided us with sufficient campaign issues without the necessity of resorting to political smears. America is rapidly losing its position as leader of the world simply because the Democratic Administration has pitifully failed to provide effective leadership.…

…The Democratic Administration has greatly lost the confidence of the American people by its complacency to the threat of communism here at home and the leak of vital secrets to Russia though key officials of the Democratic Administration. There are enough proved cases to make this point without diluting our criticism with unproved charges.

Surely these are sufficient reasons to make it clear to the American people that it is time for a change and that a Republican victory is necessary to the security of this country. Surely it is clear that this nation will continue to suffer as long as it is governed by the present ineffective Democratic Administration.

Yet to displace it with a Republican regime embracing a philosophy that lacks political integrity or intellectual honesty would prove equally disastrous to this nation. The nation sorely needs a Republican victory. But I don't want to see the Republican Party ride to political victory on the Four Horsemen of Calumny—Fear, Ignorance, Bigotry, and Smear.

I doubt if the Republican Party could—simply because I don't believe the American people will uphold any political party that puts political exploitation above national interest. Surely we Republicans aren't that desperate for victory.

I don't want to see the Republican Party win that way. While it might be a fleeting victory for the Republican Party, it would be a more lasting defeat for the American people. Surely it would ultimately be suicide for the Republican Party and the two-party system that has protected our American liberties from the dictatorship of a one party system.

...As a woman, I wonder how the mothers, wives, sisters, and daughters feel about the way in which members of their families have been politically mangled in the Senate debate—and I use the word "debate" advisedly.

As a United States Senator, I am not proud of the way in which the Senate has been made a publicity platform for irresponsible sensationalism. I am not proud of the reckless abandon in which unproved charges have been hurled from the side of the aisle. I am not proud of the obviously staged, undignified countercharges that have been attempted in retaliation from the other side of the aisle.

As an American, I am shocked at the way Republicans and Democrats alike are playing directly into the Communist design of "confuse, divide, and conquer." As an American, I don't want a Democratic Administration "whitewash" or "cover-up" any more than a want a Republican smear or witch hunt....

...As an American, I want to see our nation recapture the strength and unity it once had when we fought the enemy instead of ourselves.

It is with these thoughts that I have drafted what I call a "Declaration of Conscience." I am gratified that Senator Tobey, Senator Aiken, Senator Morse, Senator Ives, Senator Thye, and Senator Hendrickson have concurred in that declaration and have authorized me to announce their concurrence.

Source: http://www.americanrhetoric.com/speeches/margaretchasesmithconscience.html.

6. WILLIAM FAULKNER ACCEPTS THE NOBEL PRIZE FOR LITERATURE (SEPTEMBER 10, 1950)

William Faulkner (1897–1962), a Mississippi-born poet and novelist, was one of the greatest American writers of the twentieth century. *The Sound and the Fury* and *Absalom, Absalom* were two of his noted works, many of which dealt with themes relating to southern American culture and life. The following is the Nobel Prize acceptance speech Faulkner delivered in Stockholm, Sweden, in 1950.

I feel that this award was not made to me as a man, but to my work—a life's work in the agony and sweat of the human spirit, not for glory and least of all for profit, but to create out of the materials of the human spirit something which did not exist before. So this award is only mine in trust. It will not be difficult to find a dedication for the money part of it commensurate with the purpose and significance of its origin. But I would like to do the same with the acclaim too, by using this moment as a pinnacle from which I might be listened to by the young men and women already dedicated to the same anguish and travail, among whom is already that one who will some day stand here where I am standing.

Our tragedy today is a general and universal physical fear so long sustained by now that we can even bear it. There are no longer problems of the spirit. There is only the question: When will I be blown up? Because of this, the young man or woman writing today has forgotten the problems of the human heart in conflict with itself which alone can make good writing because only that is worth writing about, worth the agony and the sweat.

He must learn them again. He must teach himself that the basest of all things is to be afraid; and, teaching himself that, forget it forever, leaving no room in his workshop for anything but the old verities and truths of the heart, the old universal truths lacking which any story is ephemeral and doomed—love and honor and pity and pride and compassion and sacrifice. Until he does so, he labors under a curse. He writes not of love but of lust, of defeats in which nobody loses anything of value, of victories without hope and, worst of all, without pity or compassion. His griefs grieve on no universal bones, leaving no scars. He writes not of the heart but of the glands.

Until he relearns these things, he will write as though he stood among and watched the end of man. I decline to accept the end of man. It is easy enough to say that man is immortal simply because he will endure: that when the last ding-dong of doom has clanged and faded from the last worthless rock hanging tideless in the last red and dying evening, that even then there will still be one more sound: that of his puny inexhaustible voice, still talking. I refuse to accept this. I believe that man will not merely endure: he will prevail. He is immortal, not because he alone among creatures has an inexhaustible voice, but because he has a soul, a spirit capable of compassion and sacrifice and endurance.

The poet's, the writer's, duty is to write about these things. It is his privilege to help man endure by lifting his heart, by reminding him of the courage and honor and hope and pride and compassion and pity and sacrifice which have been the glory of his past. The poet's voice need not merely be the record of man, it can be one of the props, the pillars to help him endure and prevail.

Source: http://www.rjgeib.com/thoughts/faulkner.

---

7. U.S. SUPREME COURT'S LANDMARK RULING ON DESEGREGATION IN *BROWN V. BOARD OF EDUCATION* (MAY 17, 1954)

Chief Justice Earl Warren gained a 9–0 unanimous court decision striking down the legal aspects of racial segregation in public education, which had existed since the court's *Plessy v. Ferguson* ruling laid down the "separate but equal" doctrine in 1896. The momentous court decision set the legal stage for the end of de jure segregation in American life.

BROWN v. BOARD OF EDUCATION, 347 U.S. 483 (1954)
347 U.S. 483

BROWN ET AL. v. BOARD OF EDUCATION OF TOPEKA ET AL.
APPEAL FROM THE UNITED STATES DISTRICT COURT FOR THE DISTRICT
OF KANSAS. * No. 1.
Argued December 9, 1952. Reargued December 8, 1953.
Decided May 17, 1954.

Segregation of white and Negro children in the public schools of a State solely on the basis of race, pursuant to state laws permitting or requiring such segregation, denies to Negro children the equal protection of the laws guaranteed by the Fourteenth Amendment—even though the physical facilities and other "tangible" factors of white and Negro schools may be equal. Pp. 486–496. (a) The history of the Fourteenth Amendment is inconclusive as to its intended effect on public education. Pp. 489–490. (b) The question presented in these cases must be determined, not on the basis of conditions existing when the Fourteenth Amendment was adopted, but in the light of the full development of public education and its present place in American life throughout the Nation. Pp. 492–493. (c) Where a State has undertaken to provide an opportunity for an education in its public schools, such an opportunity is a right which must be made available to all on equal terms. P. 493. (d) Segregation of children in public schools solely on the basis of race deprives children of the minority group of equal educational opportunities, even though the physical facilities and other "tangible" factors may be equal. Pp. 493–494.

(e) The "separate but equal" doctrine adopted in Plessy v. Ferguson, 163 U.S. 537, has no place in the field of public education. P. 495. [347 U.S. 483, 484].

(f) The cases are restored to the docket for further argument on specified questions relating to the forms of the decrees. Pp. 495–496....

...MR. CHIEF JUSTICE WARREN delivered the opinion of the Court. These cases come to us from the States of Kansas, South Carolina, Virginia, and Delaware. They are premised on different facts and different local conditions, but a common legal question justifies their consideration together in this consolidated opinion. 1 [347 U.S. 483, 487].

In each of the cases, minors of the Negro race, through their legal representatives, seek the aid of the courts in obtaining admission to the public schools of their community on a nonsegregated basis. In each instance, [347 U.S. 483, 488] they had been denied admission to schools attended by white children under laws requiring or permitting segregation according to race. This segregation was alleged to deprive the plaintiffs of the equal protection of the laws under the Fourteenth Amendment. In each of the cases other than the Delaware case, a three-judge federal district court denied relief to the plaintiffs on the so-called "separate but equal" doctrine announced by this Court in Plessy v. Ferguson, 163 U.S. 537. Under that doctrine, equality of treatment is accorded when the races are provided substantially equal facilities, even though these facilities be separate. In the Delaware case, the Supreme Court of Delaware adhered to that doctrine, but ordered that the plaintiffs be admitted to the white schools because of their superiority to the Negro schools.

The plaintiffs contend that segregated public schools are not "equal" and cannot be made "equal," and that hence they are deprived of the equal protection of the laws.

Because of the obvious importance of the question presented, the Court took jurisdiction. 2 Argument was heard in the 1952 Term, and reargument was heard this Term on certain questions propounded by the Court. 3 [347 U.S. 483, 489] Reargument was largely devoted to the circumstances surrounding the adoption of the Fourteenth Amendment in 1868. It covered exhaustively consideration of the Amendment in Congress, ratification by the states, then existing practices in racial segregation, and the views of proponents and opponents of the Amendment. This discussion and our own investigation convince us that, although these sources cast some light, it is not enough to resolve the problem with which we are faced. At best, they are inconclusive. The most avid proponents of the post-War Amendments undoubtedly intended them to remove all legal distinctions among "all persons born or naturalized in the United States." Their opponents, just as certainly, were antagonistic to both the letter and the spirit of the Amendments and wished them to have the most limited effect. What others in Congress and the state legislatures had in mind cannot be determined with any degree of certainty. An additional reason for the inconclusive nature of the Amendment's history, with respect to segregated schools, is the status of public education at that time. 4 In the South, the movement toward free common schools, supported [347 U.S. 483, 490] by general taxation, had not yet taken hold.

Education of white children was largely in the hands of private groups. Education of Negroes was almost nonexistent, and practically all of the race were illiterate. In fact, any education of Negroes was forbidden by law in some states. Today, in contrast, many Negroes have achieved outstanding success in the arts and sciences as well as in the business and professional world. It is true that public school education at the time of the Amendment had advanced further in the North, but the effect of the Amendment on Northern States was generally ignored in the congressional debates. Even in the North, the conditions of public education did not approximate those existing today. The curriculum was usually rudimentary; ungraded schools were common in rural areas; the school term was but three months a year in many states; and compulsory school attendance was virtually unknown. As a consequence, it is not surprising that there should be so little in the history of the Fourteenth Amendment relating to its intended effect on public education....

...Today, education is perhaps the most important function of state and local governments. Compulsory school attendance laws and the great expenditures for education both demonstrate our recognition of the importance of education to our democratic society. It is required in the performance of our most basic public responsibilities, even service in the armed forces. It is the very foundation of good citizenship. Today it is a principal instrument in awakening the child to cultural values, in preparing him for later professional training, and in helping him to adjust normally to his environment. In these days, it is doubtful that any child may reasonably be expected to succeed in life if he is denied the opportunity of an education. Such an opportunity, where the state has undertaken to provide it, is a right which must be made available to all on equal terms.

We come then to the question presented: Does segregation of children in public schools solely on the basis of race, even though the physical facilities and other "tangible" factors may be equal, deprive the children of the minority group of equal educational opportunities? We believe that it does. In Sweatt v. Painter, supra, in finding that a segregated law school for Negroes could not provide them equal educational opportunities, this Court relied in large part on "those qualities which are incapable of objective measurement but which make for greatness in a law school."... To separate them from others of similar age and qualifications solely because of their race generates a feeling of inferiority as to their status in the community that may affect their hearts and minds in a way unlikely ever to be undone. The effect of this separation on their educational opportunities was well stated by a finding in the Kansas case by a court which nevertheless felt compelled to rule against the Negro plaintiffs: "Segregation of white and colored children in public schools has a detrimental effect upon the colored children. The impact is greater when it has the sanction of the law; for the policy of separating the races is usually interpreted as denoting the inferiority of the negro group. A sense of inferiority affects the motivation of a child to learn. Segregation with the sanction of law, therefore, has a tendency to [retard] the educational and mental development of negro children and to deprive them of some of the benefits they would receive in a racial[ly] integrated school system."...

... We conclude that in the field of public education the doctrine of "separate but equal" has no place. Separate educational facilities are inherently unequal. Therefore, we hold that the plaintiffs and others similarly situated for whom the actions have been brought are, by reason of the segregation complained of, deprived of the equal protection of the laws guaranteed by the Fourteenth Amendment. This disposition makes unnecessary any discussion whether such segregation also violates the Due Process Clause of the Fourteenth Amendment. 12 Because these are class actions, because of the wide applicability of this decision, and because of the great variety of local conditions, the formulation of decrees in these cases presents problems of considerable complexity. On reargument, the consideration of appropriate relief was necessarily subordinated to the primary question—the constitutionality of segregation in public education. We have now announced that such segregation is a denial of the equal protection of the laws. In order that we may have the full assistance of the parties in formulating decrees, the cases will be restored to the docket, and the parties are requested to present further argument on Questions 4 and 5 previously propounded by the Court for the reargument this Term. 13 The Attorney General [347 U.S. 483, 496] of the United States is again invited to participate. The Attorneys General of the states requiring or permitting segregation in public education will also be permitted to appear as amici curiae upon request to do so by September 15, 1954, and submission of briefs by October 1, 1954. 14

Source: http://www.sefatl.org/pdf/Brown%20v.%20Board%20of%20Education.pdf.

8. PRESIDENT JOHN F. KENNEDY'S INAUGURAL ADDRESS (JANUARY 20, 1961)

President John F. Kennedy's noted inaugural address has achieved a legendary status, thanks in large part to its principle challenge contained in the words "ask not what your country can do for you; ask what you can do for your country." Equally important was the new president's commitment to continue the role of the United States as defender of liberty throughout the world.

Vice President Johnson, Mr. Speaker, Mr. Chief Justice, President Eisenhower, Vice President Nixon, President Truman, Reverend Clergy, fellow citizens:

We observe today not a victory of party, but a celebration of freedom—symbolizing an end, as well as a beginning—signifying renewal, as well as change. For I have sworn before you and Almighty God the same solemn oath our forebears prescribed nearly a century and three-quarters ago.

The world is very different now. For man holds in his mortal hands the power to abolish all forms of human poverty and all forms of human life. And yet the same revolutionary beliefs for which our forebears fought are still at issue around the globe—the belief that the rights of man come not from the generosity of the state, but from the hand of God.

We dare not forget today that we are the heirs of that first revolution. Let the word go forth from this time and place, to friend and foe alike, that the torch has been passed to a new generation of Americans—born in this century, tempered by war, disciplined by a hard and bitter peace, proud of our ancient heritage, and unwilling to witness or permit the slow undoing of those human rights to which this nation has always been committed, and to which we are committed today at home and around the world.

Let every nation know, whether it wishes us well or ill, that we shall pay any price, bear any burden, meet any hardship, support any friend, oppose any foe, to assure the survival and the success of liberty.

To those old allies whose cultural and spiritual origins we share, we pledge the loyalty of faithful friends. United there is little we cannot do in a host of cooperative ventures. Divided there is little we can do—for we dare not meet a powerful challenge at odds and split asunder.

To those new states whom we welcome to the ranks of the free, we pledge our word that one form of colonial control shall not have passed away merely to be replaced by a far more iron tyranny. We shall not always expect to find them supporting our view. But we shall always hope to find them strongly supporting their own freedom—and to remember that, in the past, those who foolishly sought power by riding the back of the tiger ended up inside.

To those people in the huts and villages of half the globe struggling to break the bonds of mass misery, we pledge our best efforts to help them help themselves, for whatever period is required—not because the Communists may be doing it, not because we seek their votes, but because it is right. If a free society cannot help the many who are poor, it cannot save the few who are rich.

To our sister republics south of our border, we offer a special pledge: to convert our good words into good deeds, in a new alliance for progress, to assist free men and free governments in casting off the chains of poverty. But this peaceful revolution of hope cannot become the prey of hostile powers. Let all our neighbors know that we shall join with them to oppose aggression or subversion anywhere in the Americas.

And let every other power know that this hemisphere intends to remain the master of its own house.

To that world assembly of sovereign states, the United Nations, our last best hope in an age where the instruments of war have far outpaced the instruments of peace, we renew our pledge of support—to prevent it from becoming merely a forum for invective, to strengthen its shield of the new and the weak, and to enlarge the area in which its writ may run.

Finally, to those nations who would make themselves our adversary, we offer not a pledge but a request: that both sides begin anew the quest for peace, before the dark powers of destruction unleashed by science engulf all humanity in planned or accidental self-destruction....

...So let us begin anew—remembering on both sides that civility is not a sign of weakness, and sincerity is always subject to proof. Let us never negotiate out of fear, but let us never fear to negotiate.

Let both sides explore what problems unite us instead of belaboring those problems which divide us.

Let both sides, for the first time, formulate serious and precise proposals for the inspection and control of arms, and bring the absolute power to destroy other nations under the absolute control of all nations.

Let both sides seek to invoke the wonders of science instead of its terrors. Together let us explore the stars, conquer the deserts, eradicate disease, tap the ocean depths, and encourage the arts and commerce.

Let both sides unite to heed, in all corners of the earth, the command of Isaiah—to "undo the heavy burdens, and [to] let the oppressed go free."...

...In your hands, my fellow citizens, more than mine, will rest the final success or failure of our course. Since this country was founded, each generation of Americans has been summoned to give testimony to its national loyalty. The graves of young Americans who answered the call to service surround the globe.

Now the trumpet summons us again—not as a call to bear arms, though arms we need—not as a call to battle, though embattled we are—but a call to bear the burden of a long twilight struggle, year in and year out, "rejoicing in hope; patient in tribulation," a struggle against the common enemies of man: tyranny, poverty, disease, and war itself.

Can we forge against these enemies a grand and global alliance, North and South, East and West, that can assure a more fruitful life for all mankind? Will you join in that historic effort?

In the long history of the world, only a few generations have been granted the role of defending freedom in its hour of maximum danger. I do not shrink from this responsibility—I welcome it. I do not believe that any of us would exchange places with any other people or any other generation. The energy, the faith, the devotion which we bring to this endeavor will light our country and all who serve it. And the glow from that fire can truly light the world.

And so, my fellow Americans, ask not what your country can do for you; ask what you can do for your country.

My fellow citizens of the world, ask not what America will do for you, but what together we can do for the freedom of man.

Finally, whether you are citizens of America or citizens of the world, ask of us here the same high standards of strength and sacrifice which we ask of you. With a good conscience our only sure reward, with history the final judge of our deeds, let us go forth to lead the land we love, asking His blessing and His help, but knowing that here on earth God's work must truly be our own.

Source: http://www.allamericanpatriots.com/m-wfsection+article+articleid-69.html.

9. FEDERAL COMMUNICATION COMMISSION CHAIRMAN NEWTON MINNOW DECLARES TELEVISION A "VAST WASTELAND" (MAY 9, 1961)

In 1961, President John F. Kennedy appointed Newton Minnow as his new director of the Federal Communication Commission (FCC). Minnow's May 1961 address before the National Association of Broadcasters served as a warning that the FCC would take a stronger look at the content of television programs. It called for self-policing by the networks and for a time had some influence on content.

Thank you for this opportunity to meet with you today. This is my first public address since I took over my new job. It may also come as a surprise to some of you, but I want you to know that you have my admiration and respect. Yours is a most honorable profession. Anyone who is in the broadcasting business has a tough row to hoe. You earn your bread by using public property. When you work in broadcasting, you volunteer for public service, public pressure, and public regulation. You must compete with other attractions and other investments, and the only way you can do it is to prove to us every three years that you should have been in business in the first place.

I can think of easier ways to make a living.

But I cannot think of more satisfying ways.

I admire your courage—but that doesn't mean I would make life any easier for you. Your license lets you use the public's airwaves as trustees for 180 million Americans. The public is your beneficiary. If you want to stay on as trustees, you must deliver a decent return to the public—not only to your stockholders. So, as a representative of the public, your health and your product are among my chief concerns. . . .

I have confidence in your health.

But not in your product.

It is with this and much more in mind that I come before you today.

One editorialist in the trade press wrote that 'the FCC of the New Frontier is going to be one of the toughest FCCs in the history of broadcast regulation'. If he meant that we intend to enforce the law in the public interest, let me make it perfectly clear that he is right—we do.

If he meant that we intend to muzzle or censor broadcasting, he is dead wrong.

It would not surprise me if some of you had expected me to come here today and say in effect, 'Clean up your own house, or the government will do it for you'.

Well, in a limited sense, you would be right—I've just said it.

But I want to say to you earnestly that it is not in that spirit that I come before you today, nor is it in that spirit that I intend to serve the FCC.

I am in Washington to help broadcasting, not to harm it; to strengthen it, not to weaken it; to reward it, not to punish it; to encourage it, not threaten it; to stimulate it, not censor it.

Above all, I am here to uphold and protect the public interest.

What do we mean by 'the public interest'? Some say the public interest is merely what interests the public.

I disagree.

So does your distinguished president, Governor Collins. In a recent speech he said, 'Broadcasting, to serve the public interest, must have a soul and a conscience, a burning desire to excel, as well as to sell; the urge to build the character, citizenship, and intellectual stature of people, as well as to expand the gross national product.... By no means do I imply that broadcasters disregard the public interest.... But a much better job can be done and should be done.'

I could not agree more.

And I would add that in today's world, with chaos in Laos and the Congo aflame, with Communist tyranny on our Caribbean doorstep and relentless pressure on our Atlantic alliance, with social and economic problems at home of the gravest nature, yes, and with technological knowledge that makes it possible, as our president has said, not only to destroy our world but to destroy poverty around the world—in a time of peril and opportunity, the old complacent, unbalanced fare of action-adventure and situation comedies is simply not good enough.

Your industry possesses the most powerful voice in America. It has an inescapable duty to make that voice ring with intelligence and with leadership. In a few years this exciting industry has grown from a novelty to an instrument of overwhelming impact on the American people. It should be making ready for the kind of leadership that newspapers and magazines assumed years ago, to make our people aware of their world.

Ours has been called the Jet Age, the Atomic Age, the Space Age. It is also, I submit, the Television Age. And just as history will decide whether the leaders of today's world employed the atom to destroy the world or rebuild it for mankind's benefit, so will history decide whether today's broadcasters employed their powerful voice to enrich the people or debase them....

Like everybody, I wear more than one hat. I am the chairman of the FCC. I am also a television viewer and the husband and father of other television viewers. I have seen a great many television programs that seemed to me eminently worthwhile, and I am not talking about the much-bemoaned good old days of *Playhouse 90* and *Studio One*.

I am talking about this past season. Some were wonderfully entertaining, such as *The Fabulous Fifties*, the *Fred Astaire Show* and the *Bing Crosby Special*; some were dramatic and moving, such as Conrad's *Victory* and *Twilight Zone*; some were marvelously informative, such as *The Nation's Future*, *CBS Reports*, and *The Valiant Years*. I could list many more—programs that I am sure everyone here felt enriched his own life and that of his family. When television is good, nothing—not the theater, not the magazines or newspapers—nothing is better.

But when television is bad, nothing is worse. I invite you to sit down in front of your television set when your station goes on the air and stay there without a book, magazine, newspaper, profit-and-loss sheet, or rating book to distract you—and keep your eyes glued to that set until the station signs off. I can assure you that you will observe a vast wasteland.

You will see a procession of game shows, violence, audience participation shows, formula comedies about totally unbelievable families, blood and thunder, mayhem, violence, sadism, murder, western bad men, western good men, private eyes, gangsters, more violence and cartoons. And, endlessly, commercials—many screaming, cajoling, and offending. And, most of all, boredom. True, you will see a few things you will enjoy. But they will be very, very few. And if you think I exaggerate, try it.

Is there one person in this room who claims that broadcasting can't do better?

Well, a glance at next season's proposed programming can give us little heart. Of seventy-three and a half hours of prime evening time, the networks have tentatively scheduled 59 hours to categories of 'action-adventure', situation comedy, variety, quiz, and movies.

Is there one network president in this room who claims he can't do better?

Well, is there at least one network president who believes that the other networks can't do better?

Gentlemen, your trust accounting with your beneficiaries is overdue.

Never have so few owed so much to so many.

Why is so much of television so bad? I have heard many answers: demands of your advertisers; competition for ever higher ratings; the need always to attract a mass audience; the high cost of television programs; the insatiable appetite for programming material—these are some of them. Unquestionably these are tough problems not susceptible to easy answers.

But I am not convinced that you have tried hard enough to solve them. I do not accept the idea that the present overall programming is aimed accurately at the public taste. The ratings tell us only that some people have their television sets turned on, and, of that number, so many are tuned to one channel and so many to another. They don't tell us what the public might watch if they were offered half a dozen additional choices. A rating, at best, is an indication of how many people saw what you gave them. Unfortunately it does not reveal the depth of the penetration or the intensity of reaction, and it never reveals what the acceptance would have been if what you gave them had been better—if all the forces of art and creativity and daring and imagination had been unleashed. I believe in the people's good sense and good taste, and I am not convinced that the people's taste is as low as some of you assume.

My concern with the ratings services is not with their accuracy. Perhaps they are accurate. I really don't know. What, then, is wrong with the ratings? It's not been their accuracy—it's been their use.

Certainly I hope you will agree that ratings should have little influence where children are concerned. The best estimates indicate that during the hours of 5 to 6 pm, 60 per cent of your audience is composed of children under twelve. And most young children today, believe it or not, spend as much time watching television as they do in the schoolroom. I repeat—let that sink in—most young children today spend as much time watching television as they do in the schoolroom. It used to be said that there were three great influences on a child: home, school, and church. Today there is a fourth great influence, and you ladies and gentlemen control it.

If parents, teachers, and ministers conducted their responsibilities by following the ratings, children would have a steady diet of ice cream, school holidays, and no Sunday school. What about your responsibilities? Is there no room on television to teach, to inform, to uplift, to stretch, to enlarge the capacities of our children? Is there no room for programs deepening their understanding of children in other lands? Is there no room for a children's news show explaining something about the world to them at their level of understanding? Is there no room for reading the great literature of the past, teaching them the great traditions of freedom? There are some fine children's shows, but they are drowned out in the massive doses of cartoons, violence, and more violence. Must these be your trademarks? Search your consciences and see if you cannot offer more to your young beneficiaries whose future you guide so many hours each and every day.

What about adult programming and ratings? You know, newspaper publishers take popularity ratings too. The answers are pretty clear; it is almost always the comics, followed by the advice-to-the-lovelorn columns. But, ladies and gentlemen, the news is still on the front page of all newspapers, the editorials are not replaced by more comics, the newspapers have not become one long collection of advice to the lovelorn. Yet newspapers do not need a license from the government to be in business—they do not use public property. But in television—where your responsibilities as public trustees are so plain—the moment that the ratings indicate that Westerns are popular, there are new imitations of Westerns on the air faster than the old coaxial cable could take us from Hollywood to New York. Broadcasting cannot continue to live by the numbers. Ratings ought to be the slave of the broadcaster, not his master. And you and I both know that the rating services themselves would agree.

Let me make clear that what I am talking about is balance. I believe that the public interest is made up of many interests. There are many people in this great country, and you must serve all of us. You will get no argument from me if you say that, given a choice between a Western and a symphony, more people will watch the Western. I like Westerns and private eyes too—but a steady diet for the whole country is obviously not in the public interest. We all know that people would more often prefer to be entertained than stimulated or informed. But your obligations are not satisfied if you look only to popularity as a test of what to broadcast. You are not only in show business; you are free to communicate ideas as well as relaxation. You must provide a wider range of choices, more diversity, more alternatives. It is not enough to cater to the nation's whims—you must also serve the nation's needs.

And I would add this—that if some of you persist in a relentless search for the highest rating and the lowest common denominator, you may very well lose your audience. Because, to paraphrase a great American who was recently my law partner*, the people are wise, wiser than some of the broadcasters—and politicians—think.

As you may have gathered, I would like to see television improved. But how is this to be brought about? By voluntary action by the broadcasters themselves? By direct government intervention? Or how?

Let me address myself now to my role, not as a viewer but as chairman of the FCC. I could not if I would chart for you this afternoon in detail all of the actions I contemplate. Instead, I want to make clear some of the fundamental principles which guide me.

First, the people own the air. They own it as much in prime evening time as they do at 6 o'clock Sunday morning. For every hour that the people give you, you owe them something. I intend to see that your debt is paid with service.

Second, I think it would be foolish and wasteful for us to continue any worn-out wrangle over the problems of payola, rigged quiz shows, and other mistakes of the past. There are laws on the books which we will enforce. But there is no chip on my shoulder. We live together in perilous, uncertain times; we face together staggering problems; and we must not waste much time now by rehashing the clichés of past controversy. To quarrel over the past is to lose the future.

Third, I believe in the free enterprise system. I want to see broadcasting improved and I want you to do the job. I am proud to champion your cause. It is not rare for American businessmen to serve a public trust. Yours is a special trust because it is imposed by law.

Fourth, I will do all I can to help educational television. There are still not enough educational stations, and major centers of the country still lack usable educational channels. If there were a limited number of printing presses in this country, you may be sure that a fair proportion of them would be put to education use. Educational television has an enormous contribution to make to the future, and I intend to give it a hand along the way. If there is not a nationwide educational television system in this country, it will not be the fault of the FCC.

Fifth, I am unalterably opposed to governmental censorship. There will be no suppression of programming which does not meet with bureaucratic tastes. Censorship strikes at the taproot of our free society.

Sixth, I did not come to Washington to idly observe the squandering of the public's airwaves. The squandering of our airwaves is no less important than the lavish waste of any precious natural resource. I intend to take the job of chairman of the FCC very seriously. I believe in the gravity of my own particular sector of the New

Frontier. There will be times perhaps when you will consider that I take myself or my job too seriously. Frankly, I don't care if you do. For I am convinced that either one takes this job seriously—or one can be seriously taken.

Now, how will these principles be applied? Clearly, at the heart of the FCC's authority lies its power to license, to renew or fail to renew, or to revoke a license. As you know, when your license comes up for renewal, your performance is compared with your promises. I understand that many people feel that in the past licenses were often renewed pro forma. I say to you now, renewal will not be pro forma in the future. There is nothing permanent or sacred about a broadcast license.

But simply matching promises and performance is not enough. I intend to do more. I intend to find out whether the people care. I intend to find out whether the community which each broadcaster serves believes he has been serving the public interest. When a renewal is set down for hearing, I intend—wherever possible—to hold a well-advertised public hearing, right in the community you have promised to serve. I want the people who own the air and the homes that television enters to tell you and the FCC what's been going on. I want the people—if they are truly interested in the service you give them—to make notes, document cases, tell us the facts. For those few of you who really believe that the public interest is merely what interests the public—I hope that these hearings will arouse no little interest.

The FCC has a fine reserve of monitors—almost 180m Americans gathered around 56m sets. If you want these monitors to be your friends at court—it's up to you.

Some of you may say, "Yes, but I still do not know where the line is between a grant of a renewal and the hearing you just spoke of." My answer is, Why should you want to know how close you can come to the edge of the cliff? What the commission asks of you is to make a conscientious good-faith effort to serve the public interest. Every one of you serves a community in which the people would benefit by educational religious instructive or other public service programming. Every one of you serves an area which has local needs—as to local elections, controversial issues, local news, local talent. Make a serious, genuine effort to put on that programming. When you do, you will not be playing brinkmanship with the public interest. . . .

Another, and perhaps the most important, frontier: television will rapidly join the parade into space. International television will be with us soon. No one knows how long it will be until a broadcast from a studio in New York will be viewed in India as well as in Indiana, will be seen in the Congo as it is seen in Chicago. But as surely as we are meeting here today, that day will come—and once again our world will shrink.

What will the people of other countries think of us when they see our western bad men and good men punching each other in the jaw in between the shooting? What will the Latin American or African child learn of America from our great communications industry? We cannot permit television in its present form to be our voice overseas.

There is your challenge to leadership. You must reexamine some fundamentals of your industry. You must open your minds and open your hearts to the limitless horizons of tomorrow.

I can suggest some words that should serve to guide you:

Television and all who participate in it are jointly accountable to the American public for respect for the special needs of children, for community responsibility, for the advancement of education and culture, for the acceptability of the program materials chosen, for decency and decorum in production, and for propriety in advertising. This responsibility cannot be discharged by any given group of programs, but can be discharged only through the highest standards of respect for the American home, applied to every moment of every program presented by television.

Program materials should enlarge the horizons of the viewer, provide him with wholesome entertainment, afford helpful stimulation, and remind him of the responsibilities which the citizen has toward his society.

These words are not mine. They are yours. They are taken literally from your own Television Code. They reflect the leadership and aspirations of your own great industry. I urge you to respect them as I do. And I urge you to respect the intelligent and farsighted leadership of Governor LeRoy Collins and to make this meeting a creative act. I urge you at this meeting and, after you leave, back home, at your stations and your networks, to strive ceaselessly to improve your product and to better serve your viewers, the American people.

I hope that we at the FCC will not allow ourselves to become so bogged down in the mountain of papers, hearings, memoranda, orders, and the daily routine that we close our eyes to the wider view of the public interest. And I hope that you broadcasters will not permit yourselves to become so absorbed in the case for ratings, sales, and profits that you lose this wider view. Now more than ever before in broadcasting's history, the times demand the best of all of us.

We need imagination in programming, not sterility; creativity, not imitation; experimentation, not conformity; excellence, not mediocrity. Television is filled with creative, imaginative people. You must strive to set them free.

Television in its young life has had many hours of greatness—its *Victory at Sea*, its Army-McCarthy hearings, its *Peter Pan*, its *Kraft Theater*, its *See It Now*, its *Project 20*, the World Series, its political conventions and campaigns, the Great Debates—and it has had its endless hours of mediocrity and its moments of public disgrace. There are estimates that today the average viewer spends about two hundred minutes daily with television, while the average reader spends thirty-eight minutes with magazines and forty minutes with newspapers. Television has grown faster than a teenager, and now it is time to grow up.

What you gentlemen broadcast through the people's air affects the people's taste, their knowledge, their opinions, their understanding of themselves and of their world. And their future.

The power of instantaneous sight and sound is without precedent in mankind's history. This is an awesome power. It has limitless capabilities for good—and for evil. And it carries with it awesome responsibilities—responsibilities which you and I cannot escape.

In his stirring inaugural address, our president said, 'And so, my fellow Americans: ask not what your country can do for you—ask what you can do for your country.'

Ladies and gentlemen: ask not what broadcasting can do for you—ask what you can do for broadcasting.

I urge you to put the people's airwaves to the service of the people and the cause of freedom. You must help prepare a generation for great decisions. You must help a great nation fulfill its future.

Do this, and I pledge you our help.

Source: http://www.terramedia.co.uk/documents/vast_wasteland.htm.

10. ROBERT MOSES'S "LETTER FROM A MISSISSIPPI JAIL CELL" (JULY 15, 1961)

Robert Moses, a Harlem-born, Harvard-educated civil rights activist, was arrested, beaten, and jailed in Magnolia, Mississippi, during the 1961 Freedom Marches to protest racial segregation in the American South. The following letter was written during his incarceration. Moses became one of the leading civil rights spokesmen of the 1960s.

We are smuggling this note from the drunk tank of the country jail in Magnolia, Mississippi. Twelve of us are here, sprawled out along the concrete bunker; Curtis Hayes, Hollis Watkins, Ike Lewis and Robert Talbert, four veterans of the bunker, are sitting up talking—mostly about girls; Charles McDew ("Tell the story") is curled into the concrete and the wall; Harold Robinson, Stephen Ashley, James Wells, Lee Chester, Vick, Leotus Eubanks, and Ivory Diggs lay cramped on the cold bunker; I'm sitting with smuggled pen and paper, thinking a little, writing a little; Myrtis Bennett and Janie Campbell are across the way wedded to a different icy cubicle.

Later on Hollis will lead out with a clear tenor into a freedom song; Talbert and Lewis will supply jokes; and McDew will discourse on the history of the black man and the Jew. McDew—a black by birth, a Jew by choice and a revolutionary by necessity—has taken on the deep hates and deep loves which America, and the world, reserve for those who dare to stand in a strong sun and cast a sharp shadow.

In the words of Judge Brumfield, who sentenced us, we are "cold calculators" who design to disrupt the racial harmony (harmonious since 1619) of McComb into racial strife and rioting; we, he said, are the leaders who are causing young children to be led like sheep to the pen to be slaughtered (in a legal manner). "Robert," he was addressing me, "haven't some of the people from your school been able to go down and register without violence here in Pike county?" I thought to myself that Southerners are most exposed when they boast.

It's mealtime now: we have rice and gravy in a flat pan, dry bread and a "big town cake"; we lack eating and drinking utensils. Water comes from a faucet and goes into a hole.

This is Mississippi, the middle of the iceberg. Hollis is leading off with his tenor, "Michael, row the boat ashore, Alleluia; Christian brothers don't be slow, Alleluia; Mississippi's next to go, Alleluia." This is a tremor in the middle of the iceberg—from a stone that the builders rejected.

Source: Peter B. Levy, ed., *Let Freedom Ring: A Documentary History of the Modern Civil Rights Movement.* Westport, CT: Praeger, 1992, pp. 94–95.

11. GEORGE C. WALLACE'S INAUGURAL ADDRESS AS GOVERNOR OF ALABAMA (JANUARY 14, 1963)

As governor of Alabama, George Wallace became one of the South's leading political opponents of integration during the 1960s and an example of the region's white opposition to racial integration. He ran for the presidency four times. In 1972, while campaigning as an Independent, he was shot in an assassination attempt and was paralyzed as a result of the assault. Below is the address delivered by Wallace in 1963 upon first assuming the governorship of Alabama.

Governor Patterson, Governor Barnett...fellow Alabamians:

...General Robert E. Lee said that "duty" is the sublimest word in the English language and I have come, increasingly, to realize what he meant. I SHALL do my duty to you, God helping...to every man, to every woman...yes, and to every child in this State....Today I have stood, where once Jefferson Davis stood, and took an oath to my people. It is very appropriate then that from this Cradle of the Confederacy, this very Heart of the Great Anglo-Saxon Southland, that today we sound the drum for freedom as have our generations of forbearers before us done, time and again down through history. Let us rise to the call of freedom-loving blood that is in us and send our answer to the tyranny that clanks its chains upon the South. In the name of the greatest people that ever trod the earth, I draw the line in the dust and toss the gauntlet before the feet of tyranny...and I say...segregation now...segregation tomorrow...segregation forever.

The Washington, D.C. school riot report is disgusting and revealing. We will not sacrifice our children to any such type of school system—and you can write that down. The federal troops in Mississippi could better be used guarding the safety of the citizens of Washington, D.C., where it is even unsafe to walk or go to a ball game—and that is the nation's capitol. I was safer in a B-29 bomber over Japan during the war in an air raid, than the people of Washington are walking in the White House neighborhood. A closer example is Atlanta. The city officials fawn for political reasons over school integration and THEN build barricades to stop residential integration—what hypocrisy!

Let us send this message back to Washington...that from this day we are standing up, and the heel of tyranny does not fit the neck of an upright man...that we intend to take the offensive and carry our fight for freedom across the nation, wielding the balance of power we know we possess in the Southland.... that WE, not the insipid bloc voters of some sections will determine in the next election who shall sit in the white House...that from this day, from this minute, we give the word of a race of honor that we will not tolerate their boot in our face no longer....

...To realize our ambitions and to bring to fruition our dreams, we as Alabamians must take cognizance of the world about us. We must re-define our heritage, re-school our thoughts in the lessons our forefathers knew so well, first hand, in order to function and to grow and to prosper. We can no longer hide our head in the sand and tell ourselves that the ideology of our free fathers is not being attacked and is not being threatened by another idea, for it is. We are faced with an idea that if centralized government assumes enough authority, enough power over its people that it can provide a utopian life, that if given the power to dictate, to forbid, to require, to demand, to distribute, to edict and to judge what is best and enforce that will of judgment upon its citizens from unimpeachable authority, then it will produce only "good" and it shall be our father and our God. It is an idea of government that encourages our fears and destroys our faith, for where there is faith, there is no fear, and where there is fear, there is no faith....

Not so long ago men stood in marvel and awe at the cities, the buildings, the schools, the autobahns that the government of Hitler's Germany had built...but it could not stand, for the system that built it had rotted the souls of the builders and in turn rotted the foundation of what God meant that God should be. Today that same system on an international scale is sweeping the world. It is the "changing world" of which we are told. It is now called "new" and "liberal." It is as old as the oldest dictator. It is degenerate and decadent. As the national racism of Hitler's Germany persecuted a national minority to the whim of a national majority so the international racism of liberals seeks to persecute the international white minority to the whim of the international colored majority, so that we are footballed about according to the favor of the Afro-Asian bloc. But the Belgian survivors of the Congo cannot present their case to the war crimes commission...nor the survivors of Castro, nor the citizens of Oxford, Mississippi....

...In united effort we were meant to live under this government, whether Baptist, Methodist...or whatever one's denomination or religious belief, each respecting the others right to a separate denomination. And so it was meant in our political lives...each...respecting the rights of others to be separate and work from within the political framework....

...The true brotherhood of America, of respecting separateness of others and uniting in effort, has been so twisted and distorted from its original concept that there is small wonder that communism is winning the world.

We invite the Negro citizen of Alabama to work with us from his separate racial station, as we will work with him, to develop, to grow....But we warn those, of any group, who would follow the false doctrine of communistic amalgamation that we will not surrender our system of government, our freedom of race and religion, that freedom was won at a hard price and if it requires a hard price to retain it, we are able and quite willing to pay it....

We remind all within hearing of the Southland that...Southerners played a most magnificent part in erecting this great divinely inspired system of freedom, and as God is our witness, Southerners will save it.

Let us, as Alabamians, grasp the hand of destiny and walk out of the shadow of fear and fill our divine destiny. Let us not simply defend but let us assume the leadership of the fight and carry our leadership across the nation. God has placed us here in this crisis. Let us not fail in this our most historical moment.

Source: Alabama Department of Archives and History, Montgomery, Alabama; "George C. Wallace, 'Inaugural Address,' 1963," *Daily Life Online.* Greenwood Publishing Group. http://dailylife. greenwood.com/dle.jsp?k=1&x=7&p=pd-3903.

12. MADALYN MURRAY O'HAIR'S ESSAY "THE BATTLE IS JOINED" (JUNE 10, 1963)

Madalyn Murray O'Hair founded the American Atheists in 1963 and initiated the *Murray v. Curlett* (1963) Supreme Court case challenging prayer in public schools. She became a noted—or notorious—spokeswoman in the battle to challenge religious influence in public life.

During the last quarter century there have been more Supreme Court and federal legal cases, more state lawsuits, and more legislation passed on both the federal and the state level—all regarding religion and state/church separation—than there had been in the first 175 years of the nation. The litigation beginning in the early 1960s has picked up in both volume and viciousness until during the last five years the major decisions issued by the Supreme Court have involved primarily religious or state/church separation issues. There is a certain anomaly here, for consistently government has stood side by side with religion against an array of individuals, who have been bravely storming the courts, attempting to coerce the government to come into compliance with or to enforce the provisions of the First Amendment to the Constitution of the United States.

Think of that: citizens suing the government to force it into conformity with the Constitution.

The battle has been inherently uneven. Government, in defense of religion, has necessarily had unlimited money, the best legal services which could be bought, the media, and its subservient courts. As many personnel as needed, in whatever layer of government, could be brought to the task. Telephone service has been free. All printing has been free. Filing fees and court costs have been waived. Politicians and government officials have endorsed the religious positions, attempting to sway the populace to an acceptance of the constitutional breach. Tax money has paid for it all. The most sophisticated theoretics have been brought to bear to rationalize fallacious arguments.

Actually, in these twenty-five years a finely tuned war has proceeded, with government doing whatever was necessary and more to delay, obfuscate, and pile up as many costs for the challenging litigants as possible. Every stumbling block has been laid in their paths. A first line of defense, apparently, has been to weary the citizen challengers with delays and money costs so that they abandon their efforts. Indeed, that has often happened: a lawsuit has stopped in a state court of appeals or at the federal appellate level for lack of funds, after spending years in court. Or it has failed from frustration in the attempt to have the issue joined.

Additionally, the courts—particularly the federal courts—have promulgated rules which immediately knock out the would-be litigants: One cannot sue the sovereign. Mere taxpayer status does not give the right to sue. One must show personal injury. One must first exhaust all administrative and other remedies before coming to court.

In order to pursue the cases, lawyers with a particular specialty (constitutional law, particularly with emphasis on the religious clauses of the First Amendment) must be found, and there are few if any such attorneys. If in 175 years there were one hundred cases, and in the last twenty-five years even 250 such cases, that is a minuscule percentage of the legal (albeit significantly important) cases of the nation. There simply are really no "specialists" in this are of law.

For several generations Leo Pfeffer, a lawyer for the American Jewish Congress, was held out to be an expert on this genre of litigation. He took an old state/church separation study, Church and State in the United States, three volumes, by Anson Phelps Stokes,[1] put out by Harper & Brothers Publishing, and edited it to one volume issued by Harper in 1950 and later by Greenwood Press, Inc. in 1964 under the authorship of Anson Stokes and Leo Pfeffer. Later editions carried only Pfeffer's name. He reedited, updated, reissued, and rewrote the book again, using only his own name, this time under the title God, Caesar and the Constitution: The Court as Referee of Church-State Confrontation, published by Beacon Press. But he was a religious man of a particular minority sect (Judaism), attempting to gain respectability and acceptance for Judaism in the United States. The American Jewish Congress is a powerful arm of Judaism in our nation, and Pfeffer came to be accepted as the authority on state/church separation. He was, in fact, often one of the lawyers making an appearance on certain of the Supreme Court cases. The Supreme Court for decades depended on the work originally written by Stokes and cited the book in its cases. In later years, the Court also quoted Pfeffer's revisions. All of this makes for difficulties in such litigation. Imagine if there was only one book ever written on criminal law or on real estate law. Additionally no law schools have any courses on state/ church separation alone—it is usually handled in a cursory way in a three-hour course on "Constitutional Law." Any lawyer approaching the subject is really on his own. Additionally, these cases are time-consuming as well as time intensive during certain periods of litigation, and victory has not historically brought a money award either to the challenger or the attorney who litigates for him. On the other hand, who among the legal profession really wants to fight for a principle instead of monetary damages? Who indeed? Every attorney must minimally pay rent, utilities, telephone, and secretarial help for his office. Often he may still be paying for his college/university tuition. He cannot devote hours of time free when he needs rather to sell his services to paying clients in order to maintain himself and his family....

Source: http://www.skepticfiles.org/american/memohbio.htm.

13. PRESIDENT JOHN F. KENNEDY'S ADDRESS ON CIVIL RIGHTS (JUNE 11, 1963)

President John F. Kennedy had shown an ambivalent attitude toward the civil rights movement in the first years of his presidency. Concerned about losing powerful white, southern Democratic votes, he privately supported civil rights issues but publicly avoided a direct commitment to the struggle. This speech suggested a shift in the president's position.

Good evening my fellow citizens. This afternoon, following a series of threats and defiant statements, the presence of Alabama National Guardsmen was required on the campus of the University of Alabama to carry out the final and unequivocal order of the United States District Court of the Northern District of Alabama.

The order called for the admission of two clearly qualified young Alabama residents who happened to have been born Negro.

That they were admitted peacefully on the campus is due in good measure to the conduct of the students of the University of Alabama who met their responsibilities in a constructive way.

I hope that every American, regardless of where he lives, will stop and examine his conscience about this and other related incidents.

This nation was founded by men of many nations and backgrounds. It was founded on the principle that all men are created equal, and that the rights of every man are diminished when the rights of one man are threatened....

... It ought to be possible, therefore, for American students of any color to attend any public institution they select without having to be backed up by troops. It ought to be possible for American consumers of any color to receive equal service in places of public accommodation, such as hotels and restaurants, and theaters and retail stores without being forced to resort to demonstrations in the street.

And it ought to be possible for American citizens of any color to register and to vote in a free election without interference or fear of reprisal.

It ought to be possible, in short, for every American to enjoy the privileges of being American without regard to his race or his color.

In short, every American ought to have the right to be treated as he would wish to be treated, as one would wish his children to be treated. But this is not the case.

The Negro baby born in America today, regardless of the section or the state in which he is born, has about one-half as much chance of completing high school as a white baby, born in the same place, on the same day... twice as much chance of becoming unemployed... a life expectancy which is seven years shorter....

This is not a sectional issue. Difficulties over segregation and discrimination exist in almost every city...producing...a rising tide of discontent that threatens the public safety.

Nor is this a partisan issue. In a time of domestic crisis, men of goodwill and generosity should be able to unite regardless of party or politics.

This is not even a legal or legislative issue alone. It is better to settle these matters in the courts than on the streets, and new laws are needed at every level. But law alone cannot make men see right.

We are confronted primarily with a moral issue. It is as old as the Scriptures and is as clear as the American Constitution. The heart of the question is whether all Americans are to be afforded equal rights and equal opportunities; whether we are going to treat our fellow Americans as we want to be treated.

If an American, because his skin is dark, cannot eat lunch in a restaurant open to the public; if he cannot send his children to the best public school available; if he cannot vote for the public officials who represent him; if, in short, he cannot enjoy the full and free life which all of us want, then who among us would be content to have the color of his skin changed and stand in his place?

Who among us would then be content with the counsels of patience and delay. One hundred years of delay have passed since President Lincoln freed the slaves, yet their heirs, their grandsons, are not fully free....

And this nation, for all its hopes and all its boasts, will not be fully free until all its citizens are free.

We preach freedom around the world, and we mean it. And we cherish our freedom here at home. But are we to say to the world—and more importantly to each other—that this is the land of the free, except for the Negroes....

...Now the time has come for this nation to fulfill its promise. The events in Birmingham and elsewhere have so increased the cries for equality that no city or state or legislative body can prudently choose to ignore them.

The fires of frustration and discord are burning in every city, North and South. Where legal remedies are not at hand, redress is sought in the streets in demonstrations, parades and protests, which create tensions and threaten violence—and threaten lives.

We face, therefore, a moral crisis as a country and a people. It cannot be met by repressive police action. It cannot be left to increased demonstrations in the streets. It cannot be quieted by token moves or talk. It is time to act in the Congress, in your state and local legislative body, in all of our daily lives.

It is not enough to pin the blame on others, to say this is a problem of one section of the country or another, or deplore the facts that we face. A great change is at hand, and our task, our obligation is to make that revolution, that change peaceful and constructive for all.

Those who do nothing are inviting shame as well as violence. Those who act boldly are recognizing right as well as reality.

Next week I shall ask the Congress of the United States to act, to make a commitment it has not fully made in this century to the proposition that race has no place in American life or law....

But legislation, I repeat, cannot solve this problem alone. It must be solved in the homes of every American in every community across our country.

In this respect, I want to pay tribute to those citizens, North and South, who've been working in their communities to make life better for all. They are acting not out of a sense of legal duty but out of a sense of human decency. Like our soldiers and sailors in all parts of the world, they are meeting freedom's challenge on the firing line and I salute them for their honor—their courage....

We have a right to expect that the Negro community will be responsible, will uphold the law. But they have a right to expect that the law will be fair, that the Constitution will be color blind, as Justice Harlan said at the turn of the century.

Source: Public Papers of the Presidents of the United States, John F. Kennedy, 1963. Washington, DC: United States Government Printing Office, 1964.

14.   CIVIL RIGHTS ACT (JULY 2, 1964)

President Lyndon Johnson used all his considerable political skills to push the 1964 Civil Rights Act through Congress. The House of Representatives passed the legislation by a vote of 290–130, and the Senate by a vote of 73–27. The most important civil rights legislation since the Reconstruction Era following the American Civil War, the 1964 measure formed the basis for all future such legislation.

To enforce the constitutional right to vote, to confer jurisdiction upon the district courts of the United States to provide injunctive relief against discrimination in public accommodations, to authorize the Attorney General to institute suits to protect constitutional rights in public facilities and public education, to extend the Commission on Civil Rights, to prevent discrimination in federally assisted programs, to establish a Commission on Equal Employment Opportunity, and for other purposes.

Be it enacted by the Senate and House of Representatives of the United States of America in Congress assembled, That this Act may be cited as the "Civil Rights Act of 1964."

Title I—Voting Rights

..."(2) No person acting under color of law shall—

"(A) in determining whether any individual is qualified under State law or laws to vote in any Federal election, apply any standard, practice, or procedure different from the standards, practices, or procedures applied under such law or laws to other individuals within the same county, parish, or similar political subdivision who have been found by State officials to be qualified to vote.

"(B) deny the right of any individual to vote in any Federal election because of an error or omission on any record or paper relating to any application, registration, or other act requisite to voting, if such error or omission is not material in determining whether such individual is qualified under State law to vote in such election; or

"(C) employ any literacy test as a qualification for voting in any Federal election unless (i) such test is administered to each individual and is conducted wholly in writing, and (ii) a certified copy of the test and of the answers given by the individual is furnished to him within twenty-five days of the submission of his request made within the period of time during which records and papers are required to be retained and preserved pursuant to title III of the Civil Rights Act of 1960 (42 U.S.C. 1974—74e; 74 Stat. 88)....

...Title II—Injunctive Relief against Discrimination in Places of Public Accommodation

SEC. 201. (a) All persons shall be entitled to the full and equal enjoyment of the goods, services, facilities, and privileges, advantages, and accommodations of any place of public accommodation, as defined in this section, without discrimination or segregation on the ground of race, color, religion, or national origin.

(b) Each of the following establishments which serves the public is a place of public accommodation within the meaning of this title if its operations affect commerce, or if discrimination or segregation by it is supported by State action....

...Title III—Desegregation of Public Facilities

SEC. 301. (a) Whenever the Attorney General receives a complaint in writing signed by an individual to the effect that he is being deprived of or threatened with the loss of his right to the equal protection of the laws, on account of his race, color, religion, or national origin, by being denied equal utilization of any public facility which is owned, operated, or managed by or on behalf of any State or subdivision thereof, other than a public school or public college as defined in section 401 of title IV hereof....

....Title VI—Nondiscrimination in Federally Assisted Programs

SEC. 601. No person in the United States shall, on the ground of race, color, or national origin, be excluded from participation in, be denied the benefits of, or be subjected to discrimination under any program or activity receiving Federal financial assistance....

Source: httm://www.historical documents.com/Civil Rights Act1964.htm.

15. PRESIDENT LYNDON B. JOHNSON'S "SPECIAL MESSAGE TO THE CONGRESS: THE AMERICAN PROMISE" (MARCH 15, 1965)

In this important speech to Congress, President Lyndon Johnson confirmed his commitment to the civil rights movement.

I speak tonight for the dignity of man and the destiny of democracy. I urge every member of both parties, Americans of all religions and of all colors, from every section of this country, to join me in that cause.

At times history and fate meet at a single time in a single place to shape a turning point in man's unending search for freedom. So it was at Lexington and Concord.... So it was last week in Selma, Alabama. There, long-suffering men and women peacefully protested the denial of their rights as Americans. Many were brutally assaulted. One good man, a man of God, was killed. There is no cause for pride in what happened in Selma. There is no cause for self-satisfaction in the long denial of equal rights of millions of Americans. But there is cause for hope and for faith in our democracy in what is happening here tonight. For the cries of pain and the hymns and protests of oppressed people have summoned into convocation all the majesty of this great government of the greatest nation on earth.

Our mission is at once the oldest and the most basic of this country: to right wrong, to do justice, to serve man.... Rarely in any time does an issue lay bare the secret heart of America itself. Rarely are we met with a challenge, not to our growth or abundance, or our welfare or our security, but rather to the values and the purposes and the meaning of our beloved nation.

The issue of equal rights for American Negroes is such an issue. And should we defeat every enemy and should we double our wealth and conquer the stars and still be unequal to this issue, then we will have failed as a people and as a nation. For with a country as with a person, "What is a man profited, if he shall gain the whole world, and lose his own soul?"

There is no Negro problem. There is no Southern problem. There is no Northern problem. There is only an American problem. And we are met here tonight as Americans, not as Democrats or Republicans, we are met here as Americans to solve the problem.

This was the first nation in the history of the world to be founded with a purpose. The great phrases of that purpose still sound in every American heart, North and South: "All men are created equal"—"government by consent of the governed"— "give me liberty or give me death." Those are not just clever words. These are not just empty theories. In their name Americans have fought and died for two centuries, and tonight around the world they stand there as guardians of our liberty, risking their lives.

These words are a promise to every citizen that he shall share in the dignity of man.... It says that he shall share in freedom, he shall choose his leaders, educate his children, provide for his family according to his ability and his merits as a human being. To apply any other test—to deny a man his hopes because of his color or race, or his religion, or the place of his birth—is not only to do injustice, it is to deny America and to dishonor the dead who gave their lives for American freedom....

...The Constitution says that no person shall be kept from voting because of his race or his color. We have all sworn an oath before God to support and to defend that Constitution. We must now act in obedience to that oath.

Wednesday, I will send to Congress a law designed to eliminate illegal barriers to the right to vote.... Open your polling places to all your people. Allow men and women to register and vote whatever the color of their skin. Extend the rights of citizenship to every citizen of this land. There is no constitutional issue here. The command of the Constitution is plain. There is no moral issue here. It is wrong to deny any of your fellow Americans the right to vote in this country. There is no issue of states rights or national rights. There is only the struggle for human rights....

We cannot, we must not refuse to protect the right of every American to vote in every election that he may desire to participate in. And we ought not, we must not wait another eight months before we get a bill. We have already waited a hundred years and more and the time for waiting is gone....

Even if we pass this bill, the battle will not be over. What happened in Selma is part of a far larger movement which reaches into every section and state of America. It is the effort of American Negroes to secure for themselves the full blessings of American life. Their cause is our cause too. Because it is not just Negroes, but really it is all of us, who must overcome the crippling legacy of bigotry and injustice. And, we shall overcome.

...The time of justice has now come. I tell you that I believe sincerely that no force can hold it back. It is right in the eyes of man and God that it should come. And when it does, I think that the day will brighten the lives of every American. For Negroes are not the only victims. How many white children have gone uneducated, how many white families have lived in stark poverty, how many white lives have been scarred by fear because we wasted our energy and substance to maintain the barriers of hatred and terror?

So I say to all of you here and to all in the nation tonight, that those who appeal to you to hold on to the past do so at the cost of denying you your future. This great, rich, restless country can offer opportunity and education and hope to all—all black and white, all North and South, sharecropper, and city dweller. These are the enemies—poverty, ignorance, disease. They are enemies, not our fellow man, not our neighbor, and these enemies too...we shall overcome....

The real hero of this struggle is the American Negro. His actions and protests, his courage to risk safety and even to risk his life, have awakened the conscience of this nation...He has called upon us to make good the promise of America. And who among us can say that we would have made the same progress if not for his persistent bravery, and his faith in democracy.

Source: Public Papers of the Presidents of the United States, Lyndon B. Johnson, 1965. Washington, DC: GPO, 1966; "Lyndon B. Johnson, 'Special Message to the Congress: The American Promise,' March 15, 1965" *Daily Life Online.* Greenwood Publishing Group. http://dailylife.greenwood.com/ dle.jsp?k=1&x=7&p=pd-3997.

16. VOTING RIGHTS ACT OF 1965 (AUGUST 6, 1965)

The Voting Rights Act served as a follow-up to the Civil Rights Act of 1964, securing specific voting rights for minorities under the Fifteenth Amendment. The House supported the bill by a vote of 333–85, and the Senate by a vote of 77–19.

SEC. 1.... Be it enacted by the Senate and House of Representatives of the United States of America in Congress [p*338] assembled, That this Act shall be known as the "Voting Rights Act of 1965."

SEC. 2. No voting qualification or prerequisite to voting, or standard, practice, or procedure shall be imposed or applied by any State or political subdivision to deny or abridge the right of any citizen of the United States to vote on account of race or color. SEC. 3.

(a) Whenever the Attorney General institutes a proceeding under any statute to enforce the guarantees of the fifteenth amendment in any State or political subdivision the court shall authorize the appointment of Federal examiners by the United States Civil Service Commission in accordance with section 6 to serve for such period of time and for such political subdivisions as the court shall determine is appropriate to enforce the guarantees of the fifteenth amendment (1) as part of any interlocutory order if the court determines that the appointment of such examiners is necessary to enforce such guarantees or (2) as part of any final judgment if the court finds that violations of the fifteenth amendment justifying equitable relief have occurred in such State or subdivision: Provided, That the court need not authorize the appointment of examiners if any incidents of denial or abridgement of the right to vote on account of race or color (1) have been few in number and have been promptly and effectively corrected by State or local action, (2) the continuing effect of such incidents has been eliminated, and (3) there is no reasonable probability of their recurrence in the future. (b) If in a proceeding instituted by the Attorney General under any statute to enforce the guarantees of the fifteenth amendment in any State or political subdivision the court finds that a test or device has been used for the purpose or with the effect of denying or abridging the right of any citizen of the United States to vote on account of race or color, it shall suspend the use of [p*339] tests and devices in such State or political subdivisions as the court shall determine is appropriate and for such period as it deems necessary. (c) If in any proceeding instituted by the Attorney General under any statute to enforce the guarantees of the fifteenth amendment in any State or political subdivision the court finds that violations of the fifteenth amendment justifying equitable relief have occurred within the territory of such State or political subdivision, the court, in addition to such relief as it may grant, shall retain jurisdiction for such period as it may deem appropriate and during such period no voting qualification or prerequisite to voting, or standard, practice, or procedure with respect to voting different from that in force or effect at the time the proceeding was commenced shall be enforced unless and until the court finds that such qualification, prerequisite, standard, practice, or procedure does not have the purpose and will not have the effect of denying or abridging the right to vote on account of race or color: Provided, That such qualification, prerequisite, standard, practice, or procedure may be enforced if the qualification, prerequisite, standard, practice, or procedure has been submitted by the chief legal officer or other appropriate official of such State or subdivision to the Attorney General and the Attorney General has not interposed an objection within sixty days after such submission, except that neither the court's finding nor the Attorney General's failure to object shall bar a subsequent action to enjoin enforcement of such qualification, prerequisite, standard, practice, or procedure.

SEC. 4.

(a) To assure that the right of citizens of the United States to vote is not denied or abridged on account of race or color, no citizen shall be denied the right to vote in any Federal, State, or local election because of his failure to comply with any test or device in any State with respect to which the determinations have been [p*340] made under subsection (b) or in any political subdivision with respect to which such determinations have been made as a separate unit, unless the United States District Court for the District of Columbia in an action for a declaratory judgment brought by such State or subdivision against the United States has determined that no such test or device has been used during the five years preceding the filing of the action for the purpose or with the effect of denying or abridging the right to vote on account of race or color: Provided, That no such declaratory judgment shall issue with respect to any plaintiff for a period of five years after the entry of a final judgment of any court of the United States, other than the denial of a declaratory judgment under this section, whether entered prior to or after the enactment of this Act, determining that denials or abridgments of the right to vote on account of race or color through the use of such tests or devices have occurred anywhere in the territory of such plaintiff. An action pursuant to this subsection shall be heard and determined by a court of three judges in accordance with the provisions of section 2284 of title 28 of the United States Code and any appeal shall lie to the Supreme Court. The court shall retain jurisdiction of any action pursuant to this subsection for five years after judgment and shall reopen the action upon motion of the Attorney General alleging that a test or device has been used for the purpose or with the effect of denying or abridging the right to vote on account of race or color. If the Attorney General determines that he has no reason to believe that any such test or device has been used during the five years preceding the filing of the action for the purpose or with the effect of denying or abridging the right to vote on account of race or color, he shall consent to the entry of such judgment (b) The provisions of subsection (a) shall apply in any State or in any political subdivision of a state which (1) the Attorney General determines maintained on November 1, 1964, any test or device, and with respect to which (2) the Director of the Census determines that less than 50 percentum of the persons of voting age residing therein were registered on November 1, 1964, or that less than 50 percentum of such persons voted in the presidential election of November 1964. A determination or certification of the Attorney General or of the Director of the Census under this section or under section 6 or section 13 shall not be reviewable in any court and shall be effective upon publication in the Federal Register....

SEC. 5.... Whenever a State or political subdivision with respect to which the prohibitions set forth in section 4(a) are in effect shall enact or seek to administer any voting qualification or prerequisite to voting, or standard, practice, or procedure with respect to voting different from that in force or effect on November 1, 1964, such State or subdivision may institute an action in the United States District Court for the District of Columbia for a declaratory judgment that such qualification, prerequisite, standard, practice, or procedure does not have the purpose and will not have the effect of denying or abridging the right to vote on account of race or color, and unless and until the court enters such judgment no person shall be denied the right to vote for failure to comply with such qualification, prerequisite, standard, practice, [p*343] or procedure: Provided, That such qualification, prerequisite, standard, practice, or procedure may be enforced without such proceeding if the qualification, prerequisite, standard, practice, or procedure has been submitted by the chief legal officer or other appropriate official of such State or subdivision to the Attorney General and the Attorney General has not interposed an objection within sixty days after such submission, except that neither the Attorney General's failure to object nor a declaratory judgment entered under this section shall bar a subsequent action to enjoin enforcement of such qualification, prerequisite, standard, practice, or procedure. Any action under this section shall be heard and determined by a court of three judges in accordance with the provisions of section 2284 of title 28 of the United States Code and any appeal shall lie to the Supreme Court.

SEC. 6. Whenever (a) a court has authorized the appointment of examiners pursuant to the provisions of section 3(a), or (b) unless a declaratory judgment has been rendered under section 4(a), the Attorney General certifies with respect to any political subdivision named in, or included within the scope of, determinations made under section 4(b) that (1) he has received complaints in writing from twenty or more residents of such political subdivision alleging that they have been denied the right to vote under color of law on account of race or color, and that he believes such complaints to be meritorious, or (2) that, in his judgment (considering, among other factors, whether the ratio of nonwhite persons to white persons registered to vote within such subdivision appears to him to be reasonably attributable to violations of the fifteenth amendment or whether substantial evidence exists that bona fide efforts are being made within such subdivision to comply with the fifteenth amendment), the appointment of examiners is otherwise necessary to [p*344] enforce the guarantees of the fifteenth amendment, the Civil Service Commission shall appoint as many examiners for such subdivision as it may deem appropriate to prepare and maintain lists of persons eligible to vote in Federal, State, and local elections. Such examiners, hearing officers provided for in section 9(a), and other persons deemed necessary by the Commission to carry out the provisions and purposes of this Act shall be appointed, compensated, and separated without regard to the provisions of any statute administered by the Civil Service Commission, and service under this Act shall not be considered employment for the purposes of any statute administered by the Civil Service Commission, except the provisions of section 9 of the Act of August 2, 1939, as amended (5 U.S.C. 118i), prohibiting partisan political activity: Provided, That the Commission is authorized, after consulting the head of the appropriate department or agency, to designate suitable persons in the official service of the United States, with their consent, to serve in these positions. Examiners and hearing officers shall have the power to administer oaths. . . .

Sec. 8. Whenever an examiner is serving under this Act in any political subdivision, the Civil Service Commission may assign, at the request of the Attorney General, one or more persons, who may be officers of the United States, (1) to enter and attend at any place for holding an election in such subdivision for the purpose [p*346] of observing whether persons who are entitled to vote are being permitted to vote, and (2) to enter and attend at any place for tabulating the votes cast at any election held in such subdivision for the purpose of observing whether votes cast by persons entitled to vote are being properly tabulated. Such persons so assigned shall report to an examiner appointed for such political subdivision, to the Attorney General, and if the appointment of examiners has been authorized pursuant to section 3(a), to the court. . . .

SEC. 10.

(a) The Congress finds that the requirement of the payment of a poll tax as a precondition to voting (i) precludes persons of limited means from voting or imposes unreasonable financial hardship upon such persons [p*348] as a precondition to their exercise of the franchise, (ii) does not bear a reasonable relationship to any legitimate State interest in the conduct of elections, and (iii) in some areas has the purpose or effect of denying persons the right to vote because of race or color. Upon the basis of these findings, Congress declares that the constitutional right of citizens to vote is denied or abridged in some areas by the requirement of the payment of a poll tax as a precondition to voting. (b) In the exercise of the powers of Congress under section 5 of the fourteenth amendment and section 2 of the fifteenth amendment, the Attorney General is authorized and directed to institute forthwith in the name of the United States such actions, including actions against States or political subdivisions, for declaratory judgment or injunctive relief against the enforcement of any requirement of the payment of a poll tax as a precondition to voting, or substitute therefor enacted after November 1, 1964, as will be necessary to implement the declaration of subsection (a) and the purposes of this section. (c) The district courts of the United States shall have jurisdiction of such actions which shall be heard and determined by a court of three judges in accordance with the provisions of section 2284 of title 28 of the United States Code and any appeal shall lie to the Supreme Court. It shall be the duty of the judges designated to hear the case to assign the case for hearing at the earliest practicable date, to participate in the hearing and determination thereof, and to cause the case to be in every way expedited. (d) During the pendency of such actions, and thereafter if the courts, notwithstanding this action by the Congress, should declare the requirement of the payment of a poll tax to be constitutional, no citizen of the United States who is a resident of a State or political [p*349] subdivision with respect to which determinations have been made under subsection 4(b) and a declaratory judgment has not been entered under subsection 4(a), during the first year he becomes otherwise entitled to vote by reason of registration by State or local officials or listing by an examiner, shall be denied the right to vote for failure to pay a poll tax if he tenders payment of such tax for the current year to an examiner or to the appropriate State or local official at least forty-five days prior to election, whether or not such tender would be timely or adequate under State law. An examiner shall have authority to accept such payment from any person authorized by this Act to make an application for listing, and shall issue a receipt for such payment. The examiner shall transmit promptly any such poll tax payment to the office of the State or local official authorized to receive such payment under State law, together with the name and address of the applicant.

SEC. 11.

(a) No person acting under color of law shall fail or refuse to permit any person to vote who is entitled to vote under any provision of this Act or is otherwise qualified to vote, or willfully fail or refuse to tabulate, count, and report such person's vote. (b) No person, whether acting under color of law or otherwise, shall intimidate, threaten, or coerce, or attempt to intimidate, threaten, or coerce any person for voting or attempting to vote, or intimidate, threaten, or coerce, or attempt to intimidate, threaten, or coerce any person for urging or aiding any person to vote or attempt to vote, or intimidate, threaten, or coerce any person for exercising any powers or duties under section 3(a), 6, 8, 9, 10, or 12(e). (c) Whoever knowingly or willfully gives false information as to his name, address, or period of residence in the voting district for the purpose of establishing his eligibility to register or vote, or conspires with another [p*350] individual for the purpose of encouraging his false registration to vote or illegal voting, or pays or offers to pay or accepts payment either for registration to vote or for voting shall be fined not more than $10,000 or imprisoned not more than five years, or both: Provided, however, That this provision shall be applicable only to general, special, or primary elections held solely or in part for the purpose of selecting or electing any candidate for the office of President, Vice President, presidential elector, Member of the United States Senate, Member of the United States House of Representatives, or Delegates or Commissioners from the territories or possessions, or Resident Commissioner of the Commonwealth of Puerto Rico. (d) Whoever, in any matter within the jurisdiction of an examiner or hearing officer knowingly and willfully falsifies or conceals a material fact, or makes any false, fictitious, or fraudulent statements or representations, or makes or uses any false writing or document knowing the same to contain any false, fictitious, or fraudulent statement or entry, shall be fined not more than $10,000 or imprisoned not more than five years, or both....

...SEC. 13. Listing procedures shall be terminated in any political subdivision of any State (a) with respect to examiners appointed pursuant to clause (b) of section 6 whenever the Attorney General notifies the Civil Service Commission, or whenever the District Court for the District of Columbia determines in an action for declaratory judgment brought by any political subdivision with respect to which the Director of the Census has determined that more than 50 percentum of the nonwhite persons of voting age residing therein are registered to vote, (1) that all persons listed by an examiner for such subdivision have been placed on the appropriate voting registration roll, and (2) that there is no longer reasonable cause to believe that persons will be deprived of or denied the right to vote on account of race or color in such subdivision, and (b), with respect to examiners appointed pursuant to section 3(a), upon order of the authorizing court. A political subdivision may petition the Attorney General for the termination of listing procedures under clause (a) of this section, and may petition the Attorney General to request the Director of the Census to take such survey or census as may be appropriate for the making of the determination provided for in this section. The District Court for the District of Columbia shall have jurisdiction to require such survey or census to be made by the Director of the Census and it shall require him to do so if it deems the Attorney [p*353] General's refusal to request such survey or census to be arbitrary or unreasonable....

SEC. 16. The Attorney General and the Secretary of Defense, jointly, shall make a full and complete study to determine whether, under the laws or practices of any State or States, there are preconditions to voting, which might tend to result in discrimination against citizens serving in the Armed Forces of the United States seeking to vote. Such officials shall, jointly, make a report to the Congress not later than June 30, 1966, containing the results of such study, together with a list of any States in which such preconditions exist, and shall include in such report such recommendations for legislation as they deem advisable to prevent discrimination in voting against citizens serving in the Armed Forces of the United States. SEC. 17. Nothing in this Act shall be construed to deny, impair, or otherwise adversely affect the right to vote of any person registered to vote under the law of any State or political subdivision. SEC. 18. There are hereby authorized to be appropriated such sums as are necessary to carry out the provisions of this Act. [p*355] SEC 19. If any provision of this Act or the application thereof to any person or circumstances is held invalid, the remainder of the Act and the application of the provision to other persons not similarly situated or to other circumstances shall not be affected thereby. Approved August 6, 1965.

Source: http://www.yale.edu/lawweb/avalon/statutes/voting_rights_1965.htm.

17. EXCERPT FROM TITLE IX OF THE EDUCATION AMENDMENTS OF 1972 (JUNE 23, 1972)

Congresswoman Patsy Mink (D-Hawaii) authored the Equal Opportunity in Education Act, commonly known as Title IX, to ban discrimination in education based on gender. The most obvious impact of the legislation was the opening of athletic opportunities for women in high school and college athletics.

Section 1681. Sex

(a) Prohibition against discrimination; exceptions. No person in the United States shall, on the basis of sex, be excluded from participation in, be denied the benefits of, or be subjected to discrimination under any education program or activity receiving Federal financial assistance, except that:

(1) Classes of educational institutions subject to prohibition in regard to admissions to educational institutions, this section shall apply only to institutions of vocational education, professional education, and graduate higher education, and to public institutions of undergraduate higher education;

(2) Educational institutions commencing planned change in admissions in regard to admissions to educational institutions, this section shall not apply (A) for one year from June 23, 1972, nor for six years after June 23, 1972, in the case of an educational institution which has begun the process of changing from being an institution which admits only students of one sex to being an institution which admits students of both sexes, but only if it is carrying out a plan for such a change which is approved by the Secretary of Education or (B) for seven years from the date an educational institution begins the process of changing from being an institution which admits only students of one sex to being an institution which admits students of both sexes, but only if it is carrying out a plan for such a change which is approved by the Secretary of Education, whichever is the later;

(3) Educational institutions of religious organizations with contrary religious tenets this section shall not apply to any educational institution which is controlled by

a religious organization if the application of this subsection would not be consistent with the religious tenets of such organization;

(4) Educational institutions training individuals for military services or merchant marine this section shall not apply to an educational institution whose primary purpose is the training of individuals for the military services of the United States, or the merchant marine;

(5) Public educational institutions with traditional and continuing admissions policy in regard to admissions this section shall not apply to any public institution of undergraduate higher education which is an institution that traditionally and continually from its establishment has had a policy of admitting only students of one sex;

(6) Social fraternities or sororities; voluntary youth service organizations this section shall not apply to membership practices—

   (A) of a social fraternity or social sorority which is exempt from taxation under section 501(a) of Title 26, the active membership of which consists primarily of students in attendance at an institution of higher education, or

   (B) of the Young Men's Christian Association, Young Women's Christian Association; Girl Scouts, Boy Scouts, Camp Fire Girls, and voluntary youth service organizations which are so exempt, the membership of which has traditionally been limited to persons of one sex and principally to persons of less than nineteen years of age;

(7) Boy or Girl conferences this section shall not apply to—

   (A) any program or activity of the American Legion undertaken in connection with the organization or operation of any Boys State conference, Boys Nation conference, Girls State conference, or Girls Nation conference; or

   (B) any program or activity of any secondary school or educational institution specifically for—

      (i) the promotion of any Boys State conference, Boys Nation conference, Girls State conference, or Girls Nation conference; or

      (ii) the selection of students to attend any such conference;

(8) Father-son or mother-daughter activities at educational institutions this section shall not preclude father-son or mother-daughter activities at an educational institution, but if such activities are provided for students of one sex, opportunities for reasonably comparable activities shall be provided for students of the other sex; and

(9) Institutions of higher education scholarship awards in "beauty" pageants this section shall not apply with respect to any scholarship or other financial assistance awarded by an institution of higher education to any individual because such individual has received such award in any pageant in which the attainment of such award is based upon a combination of factors related to the personal appearance, poise, and talent of such individual and in which participation is limited to individuals of one sex only, so long as such pageant is in compliance with other nondiscrimination provisions of Federal law.

Source: "Excerpt from Title IX of the Education Amendments of 1972" *Daily Life Online.* Greenwood Publishing Group. http://dailylife.greenwood.com/dle.jsp?k=1&x=6&p=GR2547–3985.

18.   EXCERPT FROM THE SUPREME COURT'S DECISION ON ABORTION RIGHTS IN *Roe v. Wade* (JANUARY 22, 1973)

On January 22, 1973, the U.S. Supreme Court rendered its decision in the case of *Roe v. Wade*, thereby liberalizing access to abortion for American women and overturning the criminal abortion statute, and all similar state statutes, for violating the constitutional right to privacy, especially as it pertained to a woman's decision, in consultation with her doctor, to terminate a pregnancy. However, the majority opinion, written by Justice Harry Blackmun, also noted that the right to privacy was not absolute and recognized the ability of the state to regulate or even prohibit abortions for pregnancies that had developed past the first trimester.

In view of all this, we do not agree that, by adopting one theory of life, Texas may override the rights of the pregnant woman that are at stake. We repeat, however, that the State does have an important and legitimate interest in preserving and protecting the health of the pregnant woman, whether she be a resident of the State or a nonresident who seeks medical consultation and treatment there, and that it has still *another* important and legitimate interest in protecting the potentiality of human life. These interests are separate and distinct. Each grows in substantiality as the woman approaches term and, at a point during pregnancy, each becomes "compelling."

With respect to the State's important and legitimate interest in the health of the mother, the "compelling" point, in the light of present medical knowledge, is at approximately the end of the first trimester. This is so because of the now-established medical fact, referred to above at 149, that until the end of the first trimester mortality in abortion may be less than mortality in normal childbirth. It follows that, from and after this point, a State may regulate the abortion procedure to the extent that the regulation reasonably relates to the preservation and protection of maternal health. Examples of permissible state regulation in this area are requirements as to the qualifications of the person who is to perform the abortion; as to the licensure of that person; as to the facility in which the procedure is to be performed, that is, whether it must be a hospital or may be a clinic or some other place of less-than-hospital status; as to the licensing of the facility; and the like.

This means, on the other hand, that, for the period of pregnancy prior to this "compelling" point, the attending physician, in consultation with his patient, is free to determine, without regulation by the State, that, in his medical judgment, the patient's pregnancy should be terminated. If that decision is reached, the judgment may be effectuated by an abortion free of interference by the State.

With respect to the State's important and legitimate interest in potential life, the "compelling" point is at viability. This is so because the fetus then presumably has the capability of meaningful life outside the mother's womb. State regulation protective of fetal life after viability thus has both logical and biological justifications. If the State is interested in protecting fetal life after viability, it may go so far as to proscribe abortion during that period, except when it is necessary to preserve the life or health of the mother.

Measured against these standards, Art. 1196 of the Texas Penal Code, in restricting legal abortions to those "procured or attempted by medical advice for the purpose of saving the life of the mother," sweeps too broadly. The statute makes no distinction between abortions performed early in pregnancy and those performed later, and it limits to a single reason, "saving" the mother's life, the legal justification for the procedure. The statute, therefore, cannot survive the constitutional attack made upon it here.

Source: "Excerpt from the Supreme Court's Decision on Abortion Rights in *Roe v. Wade,* 1973," *Daily Life Online.* Greenwood Publishing Group. http://dailylife.greenwood.com/dle.jsp?k=1&x=6&p=GR2547–3946.

19. PRESIDENT RONALD REAGAN'S REMARKS AT BERLIN'S BRANDENBURG GATE (JUNE 12, 1987)

President Ronald Reagan traveled to Berlin in 1987 to deliver his famous "tear down this wall" speech. It became an iconic symbol of the collapse of the Soviet Union's hold on eastern Europe and signaled the coming end of communist influence in the region. It also served as the beginning of German unification, a nation divided by the Cold War since the end of World War II.

Thank you. Thank you, very much.

Chancellor Kohl, Governing Mayor Diepgen, ladies and gentlemen: Twenty four years ago, President John F. Kennedy visited Berlin, and speaking to the people of this city and the world at the city hall. Well since then two other presidents have come, each in his turn to Berlin. And today, I, myself, make my second visit to your city.

We come to Berlin, we American Presidents, because it's our duty to speak in this place of freedom. But I must confess, we're drawn here by other things as well; by the feeling of history in this city—more than 500 years older than our own nation; by the beauty of the Grunewald and the Tiergarten; most of all, by your courage and determination. Perhaps the composer, Paul Linke, understood something about American Presidents. . . .

Our gathering today is being broadcast throughout Western Europe and North America. I understand that it is being seen and heard as well in the East. . . . For I join you, as I join your fellow countrymen in the West, in this firm, this unalterable belief: Es gibt nur ein Berlin. [There is only one Berlin.]

Behind me stands a wall that encircles the free sectors of this city, part of a vast system of barriers that divides the entire continent of Europe. From the Baltic South, those barriers cut across Germany in a gash of barbed wire, concrete, dog runs, and guard towers. Farther south, there may be no visible, no obvious wall. But there remain armed guards and checkpoints all the same—still a restriction on the right to travel, still an instrument to impose upon ordinary men and women the will of a totalitarian state.

… Standing before the Brandenburg Gate, every man is a German separated from his fellow men.

Every man is a Berliner, forced to look upon a scar.

President Von Weizsäcker has said, "The German question is open as long as the Brandenburg Gate is closed." Well today—today I say: As long as this gate is closed, as long as this scar of a wall is permitted to stand, it is not the German question alone that remains open, but the question of freedom for all mankind.

Yet, I do not come here to lament. For I find in Berlin a message of hope, even in the shadow of this wall, a message of triumph.

In this season of spring in 1945, the people of Berlin emerged from their air-raid shelters to find devastation. Thousands of miles away, the people of the United States reached out to help. And in 1947 Secretary of State—as you've been told—George Marshall announced the creation of what would become known as the Marshall Plan. Speaking precisely 40 years ago this month, he said: "Our policy is directed not against any country or doctrine, but against hunger, poverty, desperation, and chaos."

In the Reichstag a few moments ago, I saw a display commemorating this 40th anniversary of the Marshall Plan. I was struck by a sign—the sign on a burnt-out, gutted structure that was being rebuilt. I understand that Berliners of my own generation can remember seeing signs like it dotted throughout the western sectors of the city. The sign read simply: "The Marshall Plan is helping here to strengthen the free world." A strong, free world in the West—that dream became real. Japan rose from ruin to become an economic giant. Italy, France, Belgium—virtually every nation in Western Europe saw political and economic rebirth; the European Community was founded.

In West Germany and here in Berlin, there took place an economic miracle, the Wirtschaftswunder. Adenauer, Erhard, Reuter, and other leaders understood the practical importance of liberty—that just as truth can flourish only when the journalist is given freedom of speech, so prosperity can come about only when the farmer and businessman enjoy economic freedom. The German leaders—the German leaders reduced tariffs, expanded free trade, lowered taxes. From 1950 to 1960 alone, the standard of living in West Germany and Berlin doubled.

Where four decades ago there was rubble, today in West Berlin there is the greatest industrial output of any city in Germany: busy office blocks, fine homes and apartments, proud avenues, and the spreading lawns of parkland. Where a city's culture seemed to have been destroyed, today there are two great universities, orchestras and an opera, countless theaters, and museums. Where there was want, today there's abundance—food, clothing, automobiles—the wonderful goods of the

Kudamm.[1] From devastation, from utter ruin, you Berliners have, in freedom, rebuilt a city that once again ranks as one of the greatest on earth. Now the Soviets may have had other plans. But my friends, there were a few things the Soviets didn't count on: Berliner Herz, Berliner Humor, ja, und Berliner Schnauze. [Berliner heart, Berliner humor, yes, and a Berliner Schnauze.]

In the 1950s—In the 1950s Khrushchev predicted: "We will bury you."

But in the West today, we see a free world that has achieved a level of prosperity and well-being unprecedented in all human history. In the Communist world, we see failure, technological backwardness, declining standards of health; even want of the most basic kind—too little food. Even today, the Soviet Union still cannot feed itself. After these four decades, then, there stands before the entire world one great and inescapable conclusion: Freedom leads to prosperity. Freedom replaces the ancient hatreds among the nations with comity and peace. Freedom is the victor.

And now—now the Soviets themselves may, in a limited way, be coming to understand the importance of freedom. We hear much from Moscow about a new policy of reform and openness. Some political prisoners have been released. Certain foreign news broadcasts are no longer being jammed. Some economic enterprises have been permitted to operate with greater freedom from state control.

. . . We welcome change and openness; for we believe that freedom and security go together, that the advance of human liberty—the advance of human liberty can only strengthen the cause of world peace.

. . . General Secretary Gorbachev, if you seek peace, if you seek prosperity for the Soviet Union and Eastern Europe, if you seek liberalization: Come here to this gate.

Mr. Gorbachev, open this gate.

Mr. Gorbachev—Mr. Gorbachev, tear down this wall!

. . . Beginning 10 years ago, the Soviets challenged the Western alliance with a grave new threat, hundreds of new and more deadly SS-20 nuclear missiles capable of striking every capital in Europe. The Western alliance responded by committing itself to a counter-deployment (unless the Soviets agreed to negotiate a better solution)—namely, the elimination of such weapons on both sides. For many months, the Soviets refused to bargain in earnestness. As the alliance, in turn, prepared to go forward with its counter-deployment, there were difficult days, days of protests like those during my 1982 visit to this city; and the Soviets later walked away from the table.

But through it all, the alliance held firm. And I invite those who protested then—I invite those who protest today—to mark this fact: Because we remained strong, the Soviets came back to the table. Because we remained strong, today we have within reach the possibility, not merely of limiting the growth of arms, but of eliminating, for the first time, an entire class of nuclear weapons from the face of the earth.

As I speak, NATO ministers are meeting in Iceland to review the progress of our proposals for eliminating these weapons. At the talks in Geneva, we have also proposed deep cuts in strategic offensive weapons. And the Western allies have likewise made far-reaching proposals to reduce the danger of conventional war and to place a total ban on chemical weapons.

While we pursue these arms reductions, I pledge to you that we will maintain the capacity to deter Soviet aggression at any level at which it might occur. And in cooperation with many of our allies, the United States is pursuing the Strategic Defense Initiative—research to base deterrence not on the threat of offensive retaliation, but on defenses that truly defend; on systems, in short, that will not target populations, but shield them. By these means we seek to increase the safety of Europe and all the world. But we must remember a crucial fact: East and West do not mistrust each other because we are armed; we are armed because we mistrust each other. And our differences are not about weapons but about liberty. When President Kennedy spoke at the City Hall those 24 years ago, freedom was encircled; Berlin was under siege. And today, despite all the pressures upon this city, Berlin stands secure in its liberty. And freedom itself is transforming the globe. . . .

. . . Free people of Berlin: Today, as in the past, the United States stands for the strict observance and full implementation of all parts of the Four Power Agreement of 1971. Let us use this occasion, the 750th anniversary of this city, to usher in a new era, to seek a still fuller, richer life for the Berlin of the future. Together, let us maintain and develop the ties between the Federal Republic and the Western sectors of Berlin, which is permitted by the 1971 agreement.

And I invite Mr. Gorbachev: Let us work to bring the Eastern and Western parts of the city closer together, so that all the inhabitants of all Berlin can enjoy the benefits that come with life in one of the great cities of the world.

. . . With—With our French—With our French and British partners, the United States is prepared to help bring international meetings to Berlin. It would be only fitting for Berlin to serve as the site of United Nations meetings, or world conferences on human rights and arms control, or other issues that call for international cooperation. . . .

. . . One final proposal, one close to my heart: Sport represents a source of enjoyment and ennoblement, and you may have noted that the Republic of Korea—South Korea—has offered to permit certain events of the 1988 Olympics to take place in the North. International sports competitions of all kinds could take place in both parts of this city. And what better way to demonstrate to the world the openness of this city than to offer in some future year to hold the Olympic games here in Berlin, East and West.

In these four decades, as I have said, you Berliners have built a great city. You've done so in spite of threats—the Soviet attempts to impose the East-mark, the blockade. Today the city thrives in spite of the challenges implicit in the very presence of this wall. What keeps you here? Certainly there's a great deal to be said for your fortitude, for your defiant courage. But I believe there's something deeper, something that involves Berlin's whole look and feel and way of life—not mere sentiment. No one could live long in Berlin without being completely disabused of illusions. Something, instead, that has seen the difficulties of life in Berlin but chose to accept them, that continues to build this good and proud city in contrast to a surrounding totalitarian presence, that refuses to release human energies or aspirations, something that speaks with a powerful voice of affirmation, that says "yes" to this city, yes to the future, yes to freedom. In a word, I would submit that what keeps you in Berlin—is "love...."

...Perhaps this gets to the root of the matter, to the most fundamental distinction of all between East and West. The totalitarian world produces backwardness because it does such violence to the spirit, thwarting the human impulse to create, to enjoy, to worship. The totalitarian world finds even symbols of love and of worship an affront.

Years ago, before the East Germans began rebuilding their churches, they erected a secular structure: the television tower at Alexander Platz. Virtually ever since, the authorities have been working to correct what they view as the tower's one major flaw: treating the glass sphere at the top with paints and chemicals of every kind. Yet even today when the sun strikes that sphere, that sphere that towers over all Berlin, the light makes the sign of the cross. There in Berlin, like the city itself, symbols of love, symbols of worship, cannot be suppressed.

As I looked out a moment ago from the Reichstag, that embodiment of German unity, I noticed words crudely spray-painted upon the wall, perhaps by a young Berliner (quote):

"This wall will fall. Beliefs become reality."

Yes, across Europe, this wall will fall, for it cannot withstand faith; it cannot withstand truth. The wall cannot withstand freedom.

And I would like, before I close, to say one word. I have read, and I have been questioned since I've been here about certain demonstrations against my coming. And I would like to say just one thing, and to those who demonstrate so. I wonder if they have ever asked themselves that if they should have the kind of government they apparently seek, no one would ever be able to do what they're doing again.

Thank you and God bless you all. Thank you.

Source: http://www. reaganfoundation.org/reagan/speeches/wall.asp.

20. NORTH AMERICAN FREE TRADE AGREEMENT (NAFTA) TREATY (JANUARY 1, 1994)

The North American Free Trade Agreement (NAFTA) included the United States, Canada, and Mexico in a commercial trading bloc that gradually removed tariffs and other national trade barriers between the three states. Opponents of the agreement, particularly organized labor unions in the United States, saw NAFTA as a means to provide cheap labor from Mexico that would threaten their members. Advocates argued that the agreement would create a hemispheric commercial economy that would advance the economic interests of all three nations.

Article 101: Establishment of the Free Trade Area

The Parties to this Agreement, consistent with Article XXIV of the *General Agreement on Tariffs and Trade,* hereby establish a free trade area.

Article 102: Objectives

The objectives of this Agreement, as elaborated more specifically through its principles and rules, including national treatment, most-favored-nation treatment and transparency, are to:

eliminate barriers to trade in, and facilitate the cross-border movement of, goods and services between the territories of the Parties;

promote conditions of fair competition in the free trade area;

increase substantially investment opportunities in the territories of the Parties;

provide adequate and effective protection and enforcement of intellectual property rights in each Party's territory;

create effective procedures for the implementation and application of this Agreement, for its joint administration and for the resolution of disputes; and

establish a framework for further trilateral, regional and multilateral cooperation to expand and enhance the benefits of this Agreement.

The Parties shall interpret and apply the provisions of this Agreement in the light of its objectives set out in paragraph 1 and in accordance with applicable rules of international law.

Article 103: Relation to Other Agreements

The Parties affirm their existing rights and obligations with respect to each other under the *General Agreement on Tariffs and Trade* and other agreements to which such Parties are party.

In the event of any inconsistency between this Agreement and such other agreements, this Agreement shall prevail to the extent of the inconsistency, except as otherwise provided in this Agreement.

Article 104: Relation to Environmental and Conservation Agreements

In the event of any inconsistency between this Agreement and the specific trade obligations set out in:

the *Convention on International Trade in Endangered Species of Wild Fauna and Flora*, done at Washington, March 3, 1973, as amended June 22, 1979,

the *Montreal Protocol on Substances that Deplete the Ozone Layer*, done at Montreal, September 16, 1987, as amended June 29, 1990,

the *Basel Convention on the Control of Transboundary Movements of Hazardous Wastes and Their Disposal*, done at Basel, March 22, 1989, on its entry into force for Canada, Mexico and the United States, or the agreements set out in Annex 104.1, such obligations shall prevail to the extent of the inconsistency, provided that where a Party has a choice among equally effective and reasonably available means of complying with such obligations, the Party chooses the alternative that is the least inconsistent with the other provisions of this Agreement.

The Parties may agree in writing to modify Annex 104.1 to include any amendment to an agreement referred to in paragraph 1, and any other environmental or conservation agreement.

Article 105: Extent of Obligations

The Parties shall ensure that all necessary measures are taken in order to give effect to the provisions of this Agreement, including their observance, except as otherwise provided in this Agreement, by state and provincial governments.

Annex 104.1

Bilateral and Other Environmental and Conservation Agreements

The *Agreement Between the Government of Canada and the Government of the United States of America Concerning the Transboundary Movement of Hazardous Waste*, signed at Ottawa, October 28, 1986.

The *Agreement Between the United States of America and the United Mexican States on Cooperation for the Protection and Improvement of the Environment in the Border Area*, signed at La Paz, Baja California Sur, August 14, 1983.

Source: http://www.duke.edu/lib/researchguides/nafta.html.

21. PRESIDENT GEORGE W. BUSH'S 9/11 ADDRESS TO THE NATION (SEPTEMBER 11, 2001)

On September 11, 2001, terrorist attacks on the World Trade Center, the Pentagon, and an airline crash in Shanksville, Pennsylvania, resulted in the deaths of over 3,000 Americans. President George W. Bush's speech to the nation that evening initiated a response to those incidents and a new American foreign policy regarding Islamic terrorism.

Good evening.

Today, our fellow citizens, our way of life, our very freedom came under attack in a series of deliberate and deadly terrorist acts. The victims were in airplanes or in their offices: secretaries, business men and women, military and federal workers, moms and dads, friends and neighbors. Thousands of lives were suddenly ended by evil, despicable acts of terror. The pictures of airplanes flying into buildings, fires burning, huge structures collapsing have filled us with disbelief, terrible sadness, and a quiet, unyielding anger. These acts of mass murder were intended to frighten our nation into chaos and retreat. But they have failed. Our country is strong.

A great people has been moved to defend a great nation. Terrorist attacks can shake the foundations of our biggest buildings, but they cannot touch the foundation of America. These acts shatter steel, but they cannot dent the steel of American resolve. America was targeted for attack because we're the brightest beacon for freedom and opportunity in the world. And no one will keep that light from shining. Today, our nation saw evil—the very worst of human nature—and we responded with the best of America. With the daring of our rescue workers, with the caring for strangers and neighbors who came to give blood and help in any way they could.

Immediately following the first attack, I implemented our government's emergency response plans. Our military is powerful, and it's prepared. Our emergency teams are working in New York City and Washington D.C. to help with local rescue efforts. Our first priority is to get help to those who have been injured, and to take every precaution to protect our citizens at home and around the world from further attacks. The functions of our government continue without interruption. Federal agencies in Washington which had to be evacuated today are reopening for essential personnel tonight and will be open for business tomorrow. Our financial institutions remain strong, and the American economy will be open for business as well.

The search is underway for those who were behind these evil acts. I have directed the full resources of our intelligence and law enforcement communities to find those responsible and to bring them to justice. We will make no distinction between the terrorists who committed these acts and those who harbor them.

I appreciate so very much the members of Congress who have joined me in strongly condemning these attacks. And on behalf of the American people, I thank the many world leaders who have called to offer their condolences and assistance. America and our friends and allies join with all those who want peace and security in the world, and we stand together to win the war against terrorism.

Tonight, I ask for your prayers for all those who grieve, for the children whose worlds have been shattered, for all whose sense of safety and security has been threatened. And I pray they will be comforted by a Power greater than any of us, spoken through the ages in Psalm 23:

Even though I walk through the valley of the shadow of death, I fear no evil for you are with me.

This is a day when all Americans from every walk of life unite in our resolve for justice and peace. America has stood down enemies before, and we will do so this time. None of us will ever forget this day, yet we go forward to defend freedom and all that is good and just in our world.

Thank you. Good night. And God bless America.

Source: http://www.whitehouse.gov/news/release/2001/09/20010911–16.html.

22. POPE JOHN PAUL II'S SPEECH TO 12 U.S. CARDINALS ON THE SEX ABUSE SCANDAL IN THE AMERICAN CATHOLIC CHURCH (APRIL 23, 2002)

Responding to a growing public and legal sex-abuse scandal involving priests in the United States, Pope John Paul II addressed the issue in this speech to

American cardinals. The cases of pedophilia had become a national concern and were severely damaging the reputation of the Roman Catholic Church.

Dear Brothers:

I have been deeply grieved by the fact that priests and religious workers, whose vocation it is to help people live holy lives in the sight of God, have themselves caused such suffering and scandal to the young.

Let me assure you first of all that I greatly appreciate the effort you are making to keep the Holy See, and me personally, informed regarding the complex and difficult situation which has arisen in your country in recent months. I am confident that your discussions here will bear much fruit for the good of the Catholic people of the United States....

...Like you, I too have been deeply grieved by the fact that priests and religious workers, whose vocation it is to help people live holy lives in the sight of God, have themselves caused such suffering and scandal to the young. Because of the great harm done by some priests and religious, the Church herself is viewed with distrust, and many are offended at the way in which the Church's leaders are perceived to have acted in this matter. The abuse which has caused this crisis is by every standard wrong and rightly considered a crime by society; it is also an appalling sin in the eyes of God.

To the victims and their families, wherever they may be, I express my profound sense of solidarity and concern. It is true that a generalized lack of knowledge of the nature of the problem and also at times the advice of clinical experts led bishops to make decisions which subsequent events showed to be wrong. You are now working to establish more reliable criteria to ensure that such mistakes are not repeated.

At the same time, even while recognizing how indispensable these criteria are, we cannot forget the power of Christian conversion, that radical decision to turn away from sin and back to God, which reaches to the depths of a person's soul and can work extraordinary change. Neither should we forget the immense spiritual, human and social good that the vast majority of priests and religious workers in the United States have done and are still doing. The Catholic Church in your country has always promoted human and Christian values with great vigor and generosity, in a way that has helped to consolidate all that is noble in the American people....

...To the Catholic communities in the United States, to their pastors and members, to the men and women religious, to teachers in Catholic universities and schools, to American missionaries in all parts of the world, go the wholehearted thanks of the entire Catholic Church and the personal thanks of the bishop of Rome. The abuse of the young is a grave symptom of a crisis affecting not only the Church but society as a whole.

It is a deep-seated crisis of sexual morality, even of human relationships, and its prime victims are the family and the young. In addressing the problem of abuse with clarity and determination, the Church will help society to understand and deal with the crisis in its midst.

It must be absolutely clear to the Catholic faithful, and to the wider community, that bishops and superiors are concerned, above all else, with the spiritual good of souls. People need to know that there is no place in the priesthood and religious life for those who would harm the young. They must know that bishops and priests are totally committed to the fullness of Catholic truth on matters of sexual morality, a truth as essential to the renewal of the priesthood and the episcopate as it is to the renewal of marriage and family life.

We must be confident that this time of trial will bring a purification of the entire Catholic community, a purification that is urgently needed if the Church is to preach more effectively the Gospel of Jesus Christ in all its liberating force.... So much pain, so much sorrow must lead to a holier priesthood, a holier episcopate, and a holier Church.

God alone is the source of holiness, and it is to Him above all that we must turn for forgiveness, for healing and for the grace to meet this challenge with uncompromising courage and harmony of purpose. Like the good shepherd of last Sunday's Gospel, pastors must go among their priests and people as men who inspire deep trust and lead them to restful waters (Psalms 22:2).

I beg the Lord to give the bishops of the United States the strength to build their response to the present crisis upon the solid foundations of faith and upon genuine pastoral charity for the victims, as well as for the priests and the entire Catholic community in your country. And I ask Catholics to stay close to their priests and bishops, and to support them with their prayers at this difficult time. The peace of the risen Christ be with you!

Source: http://www.americanrhetoric.com/speeches/popeuscardinaladdress.htm.

23. BILL COSBY'S "POUND CAKE SPEECH," AN ADDRESS TO THE NAACP'S GALA TO COMMEMORATE THE FIFTIETH ANNIVERSARY OF *BROWN V. BOARD OF EDUCATION* (MAY 17, 2004)

In May 2004, Bill Cosby, the popular American comic, gave a speech before the NAACP criticizing contemporary flaws in the popular culture's response to the problems facing the African American community. His irreverent and challenging rhetoric angered many black Americans. Cosby called for a renewal of the kind of commitment that had existed during the height of the civil rights movement in the 1960s.

Ladies and gentlemen, I really have to ask you to seriously consider what you've heard, and now this is the end of the evening so to speak. I heard a prize fight manager say to his fellow who was losing badly, "David, listen to me. It's not what's he's doing to you. It's what you're not doing."

Ladies and gentlemen, these people set—they opened the doors, they gave us the right, and today, ladies and gentlemen, in our cities and public schools we have 50% drop out. In our own neighborhood, we have men in prison. No longer is a person embarrassed because they're pregnant without a husband. No longer is a boy considered an embarrassment if he tries to run away from being the father of the unmarried child.

Ladies and gentlemen, the lower economic and lower middle economic people are not holding their end in this deal. In the neighborhood that most of us grew up in, parenting is not going on....

The church is only open on Sunday. And you can't keep asking Jesus to ask doing things for you. You can't keep asking that God will find a way. God is tired of you. God was there when they won all those cases. 50 in a row. That's where God was because these people were doing something. And God said, "I'm going to find a way." I wasn't there when God said it—I'm making this up. But it sounds like what God would do.

We cannot blame white people. White people—white people don't live over there. They close up the shop early. The Korean ones still don't know us as well—they stay open 24 hours....

...50 percent drop out rate, I'm telling you, and people in jail, and women having children by five, six different men. Under what excuse? I want somebody to love me. And as soon as you have it, you forget to parent. Grandmother, mother, and great grandmother in the same room, raising children, and the child knows nothing about love or respect of any one of the three of them. All this child knows is "gimme, gimme, gimme." These people want to buy the friendship of a child, and the child couldn't care less. Those of us sitting out here who have gone on to some college or whatever we've done, we still fear our parents. And these people are not parenting. They're buying things for the kid—$500 sneakers—for what? They won't buy or spend $250 on Hooked on Phonics.

Kenneth Clark, somewhere in his home in upstate New York—just looking ahead. Thank God he doesn't know what's going on. Thank God. But these people—the ones up here in the balcony fought so hard. Looking at the incarcerated, these are not political criminals. These are people going around stealing Coca Cola. People getting shot in the back of the head over a piece of pound cake! Then we all run out and are outraged: "The cops shouldn't have shot him. What the hell was he doing with the pound cake in his hand? I wanted a piece of pound cake just as bad as anybody else. And I looked at it and I had no money. And something called parenting said if you get caught with it you're going to embarrass your mother." Not, "You're going to get your butt kicked." No. "You're going to embarrass your mother."...We are not parenting.

Ladies and gentlemen, listen to these people. They are showing you what's wrong. People putting their clothes on backwards. Isn't that a sign of something going on wrong? Are you not paying attention? People with their hat on backwards, pants down around the crack. Isn't that a sign of something or are you waiting for Jesus to pull his pants up? Isn't it a sign of something when she's got her dress all the way up to the crack—and got all kinds of needles and things going through her body. What part of Africa did this come from?...With names like Shaniqua, Shaligua, Mohammed and all that crap and all of them are in jail. (When we give these kinds names to our children, we give them the strength and inspiration in the meaning of those names. What's the point of giving them strong names if there is not parenting and values backing it up.)

Brown versus the Board of Education is no longer the white person's problem. We've got to take the neighborhood back. We've got to go in there....

Now, look, I'm telling you. It's not what they're doing to us. It's what we're not doing. 50 percent drop out. Look, we're raising our own ingrown immigrants. These people are fighting hard to be ignorant. There's no English being spoken, and they're walking and they're angry. Oh God, they're angry and they have pistols and they shoot and they do stupid things. And after they kill somebody, they don't have a plan. Just murder somebody. Boom. Over what? A pizza? And then run to the poor cousin's house.

...I'm saying *Brown versus the Board of Education*. We've got to hit the streets, ladies and gentlemen. I'm winding up, now—no more applause. I'm saying, look at the Black Muslims. There are Black Muslims standing on the street corners and they say so forth and so on, and we're laughing at them because they have bean pies and all that, but you don't read, "Black Muslim gunned down while chastising drug dealer." You don't read that. They don't shoot down Black Muslims. You understand me. Muslims tell you to get out of the neighborhood. When you want to clear your neighborhood out, first thing you do is go get the Black Muslims, bean pies and all. And your neighborhood is then clear. The police can't do it.

I'm telling you Christians, what's wrong with you? Why can't you hit the streets? Why can't you clean it out yourselves? It's our time now, ladies and gentlemen. It is our time. And I've got good news for you. It's not about money. It's about you doing something ordinarily that we do—get in somebody else's business. It's time for you to not accept the language that these people are speaking, which will take them nowhere. What the hell good is *Brown v. Board of Education* if nobody wants it? What is it with young girls getting after some girl who wants to still remain a virgin. Who are these sick black people and where did they come from and why haven't they been parented to shut up? To go up to girls and try to get a club where "you are nobody...." " This is a sickness, ladies and gentlemen, and we are not paying attention to these children. These are children. They don't know anything. They don't have anything. They're homeless people. All they know how to do is beg. And you give it to them, trying to win their friendship. And what are they good for? And then they stand there in an orange suit and you drop to your knees: "He didn't do anything. He didn't do anything." Yes, he did do it. And you need to have an orange suit on, too.

So, ladies and gentlemen, I want to thank you for the award—and giving me an opportunity to speak because, I mean, this is the future, and all of these people who lined up and done—they've got to be wondering what the hell happened. *Brown v. Board of Education*—these people who marched and were hit in the face with rocks and punched in the face to get an education and we got these knuckleheads walking around who don't want to learn English. I know that you all know it. I just want to get you as angry that you ought to be. When you walk around the neighborhood and you see this stuff, that stuff's not funny. These people are not funny anymore. And that's not my brother. And that's not my sister. They're faking and they're dragging me way down because the state, the city, and all these people have to pick up the tab on them because they don't want to accept that they have to study to get an education.

We have to begin to build in the neighborhood, have restaurants, have cleaners, have pharmacies, have real estate, have medical buildings instead of trying to rob them all. And so, ladies and gentlemen, please, Dorothy Height, where ever she's sitting, she didn't do all that stuff so that she could hear somebody say "I can't stand algebra, I can't stand . . ." and "what you is." It's horrible.

. . . Therefore, you have the pile up of these sweet beautiful things born by nature—raised by no one. Give them presents. You're raising pimps. That's what a pimp is. A pimp will act nasty to you so you have to go out and get them something. And then you bring it back and maybe he or she hugs you. And that's why pimp is so famous. They've got a drink called the "Pimp-something." You all wonder what that's about, don't you? Well, you're probably going to let Jesus figure it out for you. Well, I've got something to tell you about Jesus. When you go to the church, look at the stained glass things of Jesus. Look at them. Is Jesus smiling? Not in one picture. So, tell your friends. Let's try to do something. Let's try to make Jesus smile. Let's start parenting. Thank you, thank you.

Source: http://www.americanrhetoric.com/speeches/billcosby/poundcakespeech.htm.

24. KARL ROVE'S ADDRESS TO THE FEDERALIST SOCIETY (NOVEMBER 10, 2005)

In November 2005, Karl Rove, a key political advisor to President George W. Bush, gave the following speech before the conservative Federalist Society questioning the influence of judicial activism in the U.S. federal court system. Rove called for the appointment of more judges who would interpret the Constitution and the law from a literalist position.

You know, for some it's the Bavarian Illuminati. For others, it's the Knights Templar. In recent years it's been the Trilateralists, the Bilderbergers, or the neocons. But for Senators Kennedy, Durbin, Schumer and Lahey, the most successful conspiracy in the history of the mankind is one of the most visible and open, as shown by your willingness to put yourselves on display here tonight. Who would've thought that powerful members of the world's most exclusive club would be so threatened by a movement of confident, principle-driven, egghead lawyers? So, I say good evening, fellow Federalists. . . .

. . . As I was looking around the crowd here tonight I see that we—virtually everybody in this audience is—falls into one of three classifications of people. First of all, honored to have members of the federal judiciary here, and the state judiciary. So we have a bunch of judges. I saw a couple of our nominees to the bench. Fred Cavanaugh and I crossed paths here recently. (Fred, where are you?) Any of you nominees just remember you wanted the job.

And, of course, the final group of people who are here tonight are aspiring judges, so my advice to you is save your money, buy a little Kelvar [Kevlar] jacket and hope you get in the chance to get in the process 'cause it's not going to get any better soon.

You've also got here a friend of mine that I'd like to just say a word about because I've known her for 15 years. Back in Texas when the Supreme Court of Texas was a disaster—I'll have a little bit more to say about that later—she was one of the few people in the legal community who stood up and said we need to do something to change it, and I worked with her awfully, you know, for an awfully long time to see us get the changes we wanted in the judiciary, and she was a warrior. And I've worked with her the last five years and have really gotten to know her well.

In the last three years, we've served together on the judicial selection committee at the White House, and for me, the non-lawyer, it's been a fantastic experience—been like attending a graduate seminar in legal theory. If you like every one of the 200 judges that we've sent to forward to the U.S. Congress to be approved, in the last three years there hasn't been one of them who hasn't been researched, vetted, studied, analyzed, and recommended by my friend, Harriet Meyers—legal council to the President.

The Federalist Society is one of America's most important intellectual movements. Since your founding more than 20 years ago, you have made extraordinary efforts to return our country to constitutionalism....

...Consider where America stands today versus where it stood when the great William Rehnquist was named to the High Court in 1972. That was right about the time that judicial activism was most dominant. And yet, today, the wind and tide are running in our favor—due in large measure to the efforts your organization....

You've also thoroughly infiltrated the ranks of the White House. In fact, there are so many Federalists in the Administration that Andy Card, Chief of Staff, has asked me to say that there will be a special staff meeting in the back of the room, near the back doors, at the end of the dinner. We'll be discussing an important legal question, namely, the application of the principle of equidistance in the determination of seaward lateral boundaries. I, incidentally, while not a lawyer am the leading White House expert on this issue. I be—will be leading the meeting....

...I've seen this phenomenon myself for several decades. In the 1980s, in my home state of Texas, our Supreme Court was dominated by justices determined to legislate from the bench, bending the law to fit a personal agenda. Millions of dollars from a handful of wealthy personal injury trial lawyers were poured into Supreme Court races to shift the philosophical direction of the Court. It earned the reputation, as the *Dallas Morning News* said, as quote, "the best court that money could buy." Even *60 Minutes* was troubled, and it takes a lot to trouble CBS. In 1987 it did a story on the Texas Supreme Court titled "Justice for Sale."

Ordinary Texans had had enough, and they took it upon themselves to change the Court. In a bipartisan reform effort, they recruited and then elected to the Texas Supreme Court distinguished individuals like Tom Phillips, Alberto Gonzales, John Cornyn, Priscilla Owen, Nathan Hecht, and Greg Abbott. And for those of you— And for those of you [who] know something about Texas politics, this is pretty significant because all of them were Republicans. After all, Texas had gone for a mere 120 years without electing a single Republican to our Supreme Court, and then all of a sudden we were blessed with these extraordinarily able people.

I saw this public reaction to judicial activism again in Alabama. The state legislature passed tort-reform legislation in 1987. However, activist judges on the—on the Supreme Court, the trial lawyer-friendly Supreme Court, struck it down, prompting a period of "jackpot justice" at Alabama through the mid-1990s, where the median punitive-damage award in Alabama reached 250,000 dollars—three times the national average. *Time Magazine* labeled Alabama "tort hell."

Like in Texas, this led to a popular revolt against judicial activism. It began in 1994, when Republican Perry Hooper challenged sitting Chief Justice and trial lawyer favorite Sonny Hornsby. Hooper pulled off a stunning upset—outspent, outworked—he won by 262 votes out of over 1.2 million votes cast. And then, the day after the election, several thousand absentee ballots mysteriously surfaced, none of them witnessed nor notarized as required by Alabama law, and Sonny Hornsby tried to have them counted. It took a year of court battles before Hooper was finally seated. His groundbreaking victory would not have been possible without the work of many Alabamians—including a young dynamic lawyer I got to know by the name of Bill Pryor—and isn't he doing a terrific job....

...Earlier this year a federal district court judge dismissed a 10-count indictment against hard-core pornographers, alleging that federal obscenity laws violated the pornographers' right to privacy—despite the fact that popularly elected representatives in Congress had passed the obscenity laws and that the pornographers distributed materials with simulations where women were raped and killed.

Just a few months ago, five Justices on the U.S. Supreme Court decided that a "national consensus" prohibited the use of the death penalty for murderers—for murders committed under the age of 18. In its decision, the majority ignored the fact that, at the time, the people's representatives in 20 states had passed laws permitting the death penalty for killers under 18, while just 18 states—or less than 50% of the states allowing capital punishment—had laws prohibiting the execution of killers who committed their crimes as juveniles.

These attempts, and many, many more over the past decades, have led to widespread concern about our courts. While ordinary people may not be able to give you the case number or explain in fine detail the legal principles they feel are being bent and broken, they are clearly concerned about too many judges too ready and eager to legislate from too many benches....

...Scholars of American government have pointed out the Founders were determined to build a system of government that would succeed because of our imperfections, not in spite of them. They envision—envisioned judges as impartial umpires, charged with guarding the sanctity of the Constitution, not as legislators dressed conveniently in robes.

…At the end of the day, though, the views of the Founders will prevail because the core defects of judicial imperialism—including the mistaken assumption that our charter of government is like hot wax: pliable, inconstant, and easily shaped and changed.

America's 43rd President believes, as you do, that judges should base their opinions on strictly and faithfully interpreting the text of our Constitution, a document that is remarkable and reliable. William Gladstone called it (quote) "the greatest work ever struck off at a given time by the brain and purpose of man." Not bad for an Englishman.

Critics of constitutionalism say it is resistant to social change—our Constitution. But if the people want to enact or repeal certain laws, they can do so by persuading their fellow citizens on the merits through legislation or constitutional amendment. This makes eminent good sense, and it allows for enormous adaptability.

Another defect of judicial imperialism is it undermines self-government. The will of the people is replaced by the personal predilections and political biases of a handful of judges. The result is that judicial imperialism has split American society, politicized the courts in a way the Founders never intended. And it has created a sense of disenfranchisement among a great many—a very large segment of American society—people who believe issues not addressed by the Constitution should be decided through elections rather than by nine lawyers in robes.…

…The willingness of these brilliant legal minds to put aside lucrative careers in private practice to serve a greater public good should make us all optimistic and hopeful. Our arguments will carry the day because the force and logic and wisdom of the Founders—all of them are on our side. We welcome a vigorous, open and fair-minded. and high-minded debate about the purpose and meaning of the courts in our lives, and we will win that debate.

In America, conservatives are winning the battle of ideas on almost every front, and few are more important than the battle over our judiciary. The outcome of that debate will shape the course of human events, and the reason we will prevail rests in large measure on the good work of the Federalist Society and those of you in this room tonight.

The President is grateful for your support, for your tireless efforts on behalf of constitutionalism and, above all, for your dedication to the founding principles of our great country.…

Source: http://www.americanrhetoric.com/speeches/karlrovefederalist.htmlww.americanrhetoric.com/speeches/karlrovefederalist.html.

APPENDICES

With the admission of Alaska as a state on January 3, 1959, and of Hawaii as a state on August 21, 1959, the American union comprised 50 states, as shown in the following map.

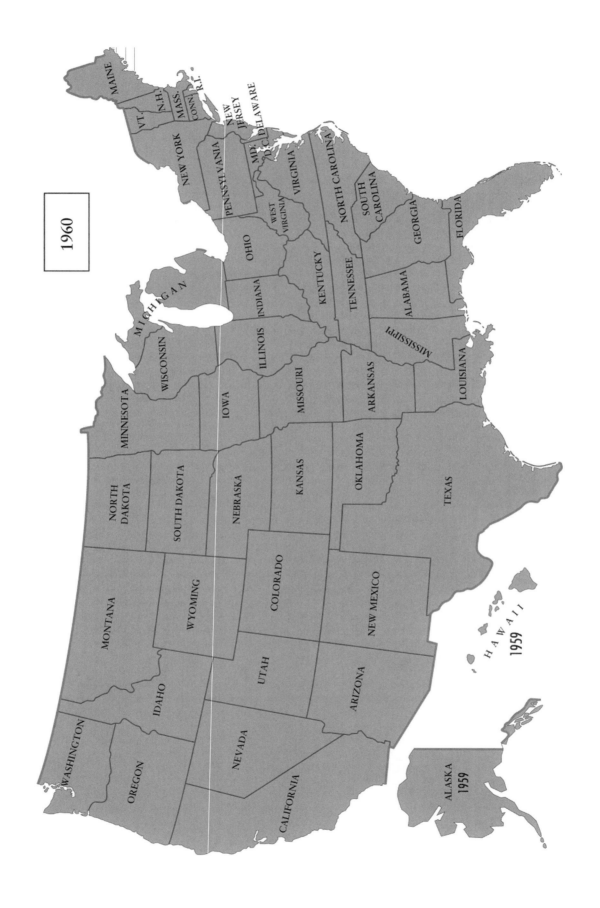

APPENDIX 2: LEGAL PUBLIC HOLIDAYS IN THE UNITED STATES AT THE START OF THE TWENTY-FIRST CENTURY

Legal public holidays, or federal holidays, are those holidays recognized by the U.S. government. Although the U.S. government has power to create holidays only for federal offices and agencies and their employees, most other national institutions and businesses, such as private banks and stock exchanges, are closed in celebration of these holidays. Many of these holidays are designated to fall each year on a Monday so as to create a longer weekend break for federal and all other workers who observe the day.

Inauguration Day, which occurs on January 20 in every fourth year following a U.S. presidential election, witnesses the inauguration of the recently elected president. It is celebrated as a federal holiday in Washington, D.C., and in certain counties of surrounding states that are likely to be affected by the inauguration festivities.

January

New Year's Day	Celebrates the start of the new year.	January 1
Martin Luther King Jr. Day	Honors civil rights leader Martin Luther King Jr., whose birthday was January 15; combined with various other holidays in several states.	Third Monday of the month

February

President's Day	Honors President George Washington, whose birthday was February 22, and thus is known officially as "Washington's Birthday"; however, it is popularly observed as a day of recognition for all American presidents (especially Abraham Lincoln, whose birthday was February 12) and thus best known as "President's Day."	Third Monday of the month

May

Memorial Day	Also known as Decoration Day and traditionally observed on May 30, Memorial Day began in the nineteenth century as a day to honor the dead of the Civil War by decorating their graves with flowers; it is now observed to honor those who served in all American wars.	Fourth Monday of the month

July

| Independence Day | Celebrates the signing of the American Declaration of Independence on July 4, 1776, and is popularly observed as the birthday of the United States. | July 4 |

September

| Labor Day | Honors the achievements of American workers and the American Labor Movement. | First Monday of the month |

October

| Columbus Day | Commemorates the landing of Christopher Columbus in the Americas on October 12, 1492, and was traditionally celebrated on October 12; in some places, it is also a celebration of Italian culture and history. | Second Monday of the month |

November

| Veteran's Day | Also known as Armistice Day or Remembrance Day, Veteran's Day is the American name for an internationally recognized holiday commemorating the signing of the armistice that ended World War I on November 11, 1918. | November 11 |
| Thanksgiving | Observed annually in the United States since 1863 when President Lincoln proclaimed a national day of thanksgiving for the last Thursday of November; it is traditionally observed as a day for giving thanks to God for the autumn harvest. | Fourth Thursday of the month |

December

| Christmas | Simultaneously celebrated as a religious holiday for Christians, who commemorate the birth of Christ, and a secular holiday emphasizing family, charity, and goodwill. | December 25 |

APPENDIX 3: POPULATION OF THE UNITED STATES BY DECADE, 1940–2000

As the following Census figures show, the population of the United States more than doubled in the 60 years between 1940 and 2000, with particular spurts in growth during the post–World War II Baby Boom period of the 1950s and the period of economic stability in the 1990s.

1940	132,164,569
1950	151,325,798
1960	179,323,175
1970	203,211,926
1980	226,545,805
1990	248,709,873
2000	281,421,906

Source: United States Census Bureau.

APPENDIX 4: PRESIDENTS OF THE UNITED STATES, 1940–2005

Listed below are the presidents of the United States who held office between 1940 and 2005, with their party affiliations and their terms of service.

Franklin D. Roosevelt[1]	Democrat	1933–1945
Harry S Truman	Democrat	1945–1953
Dwight D. Eisenhower	Republican	1953–1961
John F. Kennedy[2]	Democrat	1961–1963
Lyndon B. Johnson	Democrat	1963–1969
Richard M. Nixon[3]	Republican	1969–1974
Gerald R. Ford	Republican	1974–1977
Jimmy Carter	Democrat	1977–1981
Ronald Reagan	Republican	1981–1989
George H. W. Bush	Republican	1989–1993
William J. Clinton	Democrat	1993–2001
George W. Bush	Republican	2001–2008

[1] Died in office on April 12, 1945.

[2] Assassinated in office on November 22, 1963.

[3] Resigned from office on August 8, 1974.

Source: www.whitehouse.gov/history/presidents.

APPENDIX 5: VICE PRESIDENTS OF THE UNITED STATES, 1940–2005

Listed below are the vice presidents of the United States who held office between 1940 and 2005, with the president under whom they served, their party affiliation, and their terms of service.

John Nance Garner	Roosevelt	Democrat	1933–1941
Henry A. Wallace	Roosevelt	Democrat	1941–1945
Harry S Truman[1]	Roosevelt	Democrat	1945
Office Vacant	Truman		1945–1949
Alben W. Barkley	Truman	Democrat	1949–1953
Richard M. Nixon	Eisenhower	Republican	1953–1961
Lyndon B. Johnson[2]	Kennedy	Democrat	1961–1963
Office Vacant	Johnson		1963–1965
Hubert H. Humphrey	Johnson	Democrat	1965–1969
Spiro T. Agnew[3]	Nixon	Republican	1969–1973
Office Vacant	Nixon	October–December 1973	
Gerald R. Ford[4]	Nixon	Republican	1973–1974
Office Vacant	Ford	August–December 1974	
Nelson A. Rockefeller	Ford	Republican	1974–1977
Walter F. Mondale	Carter	Democrat	1977–1981
George H. W. Bush	Reagan	Republican	1981–1989
J. Danforth Quayle	Bush, George H. W.	Republican	1989–1993
Albert Gore Jr.	Clinton	Democrat	1993–2001
Richard Cheney	Bush, George W.	Republican	2001–2008

[1] Succeeded to the presidency upon the death of Franklin D. Roosevelt on April 12, 1945.

[2] Succeeded to the presidency upon the assassination of John F. Kennedy on November 22, 1963.

[3] Resigned from office on October 10, 1973.

[4] Succeeded to presidency upon resignation of Richard M. Nixon on August 8, 1974.

Source: http://americanhistory.about.com/library/charts/blchartpresidents.htm.

APPENDIX 6: SECRETARIES OF STATE OF THE UNITED STATES, 1940–2005

Listed below are the secretaries of state of the United States who held office between 1940 and 2005, with the president who appointed them, their party affiliation, and their terms of service.

Cordell Hull	Roosevelt	Democrat	1933–1944
Edward R. Stettinis Jr.	Roosevelt/Truman	Democrat	1944–1945
James F. Byrnes	Truman	Democrat	1945–1947
George C. Marshall	Truman	Democrat	1947–1949
Dean Acheson	Truman	Democrat	1949–1953
John Foster Dulles	Eisenhower	Republican	1953–1959
Christian Herter	Eisenhower	Republican	1959–1961
Dean Rusk	Kennedy/Johnson	Democrat	1961–1969
William P. Rogers	Nixon	Republican	1969–1973
Henry Kissinger	Nixon/Ford	Republican	1973–1977
Cyrus Vance	Carter	Democrat	1977–1980
Edmund S. Muskie	Carter	Democrat	1980–1981
Alexander M. Haig Jr.	Reagan	Republican	1981–1982
George P. Schultz	Reagan	Republican	1982–1989
James Baker III	Bush, George H. W.	Republican	1989–1992
Lawrence S. Eagleburger	Bush, George H. W.	Republican	1992–1993
Warren Christopher	Clinton	Democrat	1993–1997
Madeleine Albright	Clinton	Democrat	1997–2001
Colon Powell	Bush, George W.	Republican	2001–2005
Condoleezza Rice	Bush, George W.	Republican	2005–2008

Source: http://www.state.gov/r/pa/ho/po/1682.htm.

APPENDIX 7: CHIEF JUSTICES OF THE U.S. SUPREME COURT, 1940–2005

Listed below are the chief justices of the U.S. Supreme Court who served between 1940 and 2005, with the president who appointed them and their terms of service.

Charles Evans Hughes	Hoover	1930–1941
Harlan Fiske Stone	Roosevelt	1941–1946
Fred M. Vinson	Truman	1946–1953
Earl Warren	Eisenhower	1953–1969
Warren E. Burger	Nixon	1969–1986
William H. Rehnquist	Reagan	1986–2005
John G. Roberts Jr.	Bush, George W.	2005–

BIBLIOGRAPHY

BOOKS, 1940–1959

Adler, Selig. *The Uncertain Giant, 1921–1941: American Foreign Policy between the Wars*. New York: MacMillan, 1965.

Bailey, Thomas A. *A Diplomatic History of the American People*. Englewood Cliffs, NJ: Prentice Hall, 1980.

Barnouw, Erik. *The Golden Web: A History of Broadcasting in the United States from 1933–1953*. New York: Oxford University Press, 1968.

———. *The Image Empire: A History of Broadcasting in the United States from 1953*. New York: Oxford University Press, 1970.

———. *Tube of Plenty: The Evolution of American Television*. 2nd ed. New York: Oxford University Press, 1990.

Barton, B. *The Man Nobody Knows*. Indianapolis, IN: Bobbs-Merrill, 1925.

Benson, Robert Louis. *The Venona Story*. Washington, DC: National Security Agency, 1996.

Caute, D. *The Great Fear: The Anti-Communist Purge under Truman and Eisenhower*. New York: Simon and Schuster, 1978.

Cayleff, Susan E. *Babe: The Life and Legend of Babe Didrikson Zaharias*. Urbana: University of Illinois Press, 1995.

Chafe, W. H. *The Paradox of Change: American Women in the 20th Century*. New York: Oxford University Press, 1991.

Chase, R. "Our Country and Our Culture (Part 3)." *Partisan Review* (Sept./Oct. 1952): 567–69.

Cole, Wayne S. *Roosevelt and the Isolationists*. Lincoln: University of Nebraska Press, 1983.

Coover, R. *The Public Burning*. New York: Viking Press, 1977.

Cremin, L. *American Education, 1876–1980: The Metropolitan Experience*. New York: Harper and Row, 1988.

Davies, Richard O. *America's Obsession: Sports and Society since 1945*. Belmont, CA: Wadsworth Publishing, 2007.

DeCurtis, A., and J. Henke, eds. *The Rolling Stone Illustrated History of Rock & Roll: The Definitive History of the Most Important Artists and Their Music*. New York: Random House, 1992.

Doctorow, E. L. *The Book of Daniel*. New York: Random House, 1971.

Evans, S. *Born for Liberty: A History of Women in America*. New York: Free Press, 1989.

Faragher, John Mack, Susan Armitage, Mari Jo Buhle, and Daniel Czitrom. *Out of Many: A History of the American People*. Upper Saddle River, NJ: Prentice Hall, 2000.

Fehrenbach, T. R. *This Kind of War*. Washington, DC: Brassey's, 2000.

Friedan, Betty. *The Feminine Mystique*. New York: Norton, 1963.

Galbraith, John Kenneth. *The Affluent Society*. Boston: Little, Brown, 1958.

Goldman, Eric. *The Crucial Decade and After—America, 1945–1960*. New York: Random House, 1960.

Goodwin, Doris Kearns. *No Ordinary Time: Franklin and Eleanor Roosevelt: The Home Front in World War II*. New York: Touchstone, 1994.

Halberstam, David. *The Fifties*. New York: Random House, 1993.

Harrington, Michael. *The Other America: Poverty in the United States*. New York: Macmillan, 1962; New York: Penguin, 1981.

Harrison, C. *On Account of Sex: The Politics of Women's Issues, 1945–1968*. Berkeley: University of California Press, 1988.

Hart, J. D. *The Oxford Companion to American Literature*. 6th ed. New York: Oxford University Press, 1995.

Hayes, C. D., J. L. Palmer, and M. J. Zaslow, eds. *Families That Work: Children in a Changing World*. Washington, DC: National Academy Press, 1982.

Herberg, W. *Protestant-Catholic-Jew: An Essay in American Religious Sociology*. Garden City, NY: Doubleday, 1955.

Hine, T. *Populuxe*. New York: Knopf, 1986.

Jowett, G., and J. M. Linton. *Movies as Mass Communications*. Beverly Hills, CA: Sage, 1980.

Kaledin, E. *Daily Life in the United States, 1940–1959: Shifting Worlds*. Westport, CT: Greenwood Press, 2000; also online at http://dailylife.greenwood.com.

Kennedy, David M. *Freedom from Fear: The American People in Depression and War, 1929–1945*. New York: Oxford University Press, 1999.

Kenney, W. H. *Recorded Music in American Life: The Phonograph and Popular Memory, 1890–1945*. New York: Oxford University Press, 1999.

Kushner, T. *Angels in America: A Gay Fantasia on National Themes*. New York: Theatre Communications Group, 1993.

Lundberg, Ferdinand, and Marynia F. Farnham. *Modern Woman: The Lost Sex*. New York: Harper and Brothers, 1947.

Marcus, Greil. *Mystery Train: Images of America in Rock 'n' Roll Music*. New York: E. P. Dutton, 1982.

Marling, K. A. *As Seen on TV: The Visual Culture of Everyday Life in the 1950s*. Cambridge, MA: Harvard University Press, 1994.

Marty, M. E. *Pilgrims in Their Own Land: 500 Years of Religion in America*. Boston: Little, Brown, 1984.

May, E. T. *Homeward Bound: American Families in the Cold War Era*. New York: Basic Books, 1989.

McCarthy, Martha M., and Nelda H. Cambron-McCabe. *Public School Law: Teachers' and Students' Rights*. Newton, MA: Allyn and Bacon, 1987.

Mills, C. Wright. *White Collar: The American Middle Classes*. New York. Oxford University Press, 1951.

Mintz, S., and S. Kellogg. *Domestic Revolutions: A Social History of American Family Life*. New York: Free Press, 1988.

Olson, James, and Randy Roberts. *Winning Is the Only Thing: Sports in America since 1945*. Baltimore, MD: Johns Hopkins University Press, 1989.

Patterson, J. T. *Grand Expectations: The United States, 1945–1974*. New York: Oxford University Press, 1996.

Rader, Benjamin G. *American Sports: From the Age of Folk Games to the Age of Televised Sports*. Upper Saddle River, NJ: Prentice Hall, 1998.

Ravitch, D. *The Troubled Crusade: American Education, 1945–1980*. New York: Basic Books, 1983.

Rybczynski, W. *Waiting for the Weekend*. New York: Viking, 1991.

Shorter, E. *The Health Century*. New York: Doubleday, 1987.

Sklar, Robert. *Movie-Made America: A Cultural History of American Movies*. New York. Vintage Books, 1975; Rev. ed., 1994.

Spring, J. *The American School, 1642–1993*. 3rd ed. New York: McGraw Hill, 1994.

Steinberg, Cobbett S. *TV Facts*. New York: Facts on File, 1980.

Tennyson, Jeffrey. *Behind the Arches*. New York. Bantam Books, 1986.

Terkel, Studs. *The Good War: An Oral History of World War Two*. New York: Pantheon Books, 1984.

Tuttle, Frank W., and Joseph M. Perry. *An Economic History of the United States*. Chicago: South-Western Publishing, 1970.

Tuttle, W. M. Jr. *Daddy's Gone to War: The Second World War in the Lives of America's Children*. New York: Oxford University Press, 1993.

Tygiel, Jules. *Baseball's Great Experiment: Jackie Robinson and His Legacy*. New York: Oxford University Press, 1997.

Whitfield, S. J. *The Culture of the Cold War*. Baltimore, MD: Johns Hopkins University Press, 1991.

Whyte, William. *The Organization Man*. New York. Doubleday, 1956.

Winkler, A. *Home Front U.S.A.: America during World War II*. 2nd ed. Wheeling, IL: Harlan Davidson, 2000.

Wright, G. *Building the Dream: A Social History of Housing in America*. New York: Pantheon, 1981.

ONLINE SOURCES, 1940–1959

"Domestic Life: Children, United States, 1940–59." *Daily Life Online*. Greenwood Publishing Group. http://dailylife.greenwood.com/dle.jsp?k=1&x=6&p=GR2547–671.

"Domestic Life: Women, United States, 1940–59." *Daily Life Online*. Greenwood Publishing Group. http://dailylife.greenwood.com/dle.jsp?k=1&x=6&p=GR2547–482.

"Economic Life: Work, United States, 1940–59." *Daily Life Online*. Greenwood Publishing Group. http://dailylife.greenwood.com/dle.jsp?k=1&x=6&p=GR2547–839.

"Material Life: Housing, United States, 1940–59." *Daily Life Online*. Greenwood Publishing Group. http://dailylife.greenwood.com/dle.jsp?k=1&x=6&p=GR2547–2231.

"Recreational Life: Music, United States, 1940–59." *Daily Life Online*. Greenwood Publishing Group. http://dailylife.greenwood.com/dle.jsp?k=1&x=6&p=GR2547–3474.

"Religious Life: Religion, United States, 1940–59." *Daily Life Online*. Greenwood Publishing Group. http://dailylife.greenwood.com/dle.jsp?k=1&x=6&p=GR2547–3702.

BOOKS AND ARTICLES, 1960–1990

Banner, Stuart. *Death Penalty: An American Story*. Cambridge, MA: Harvard University Press, 2001.

Barnouw, E. *Tube of Plenty: The Evolution of American Television*. 2nd ed. New York: Oxford University Press, 1990.

Boyer, P. S. *By the Bomb's Early Light: American Thought and Culture at the Dawn of the Atomic Age*. Chapel Hill: University of North Carolina Press, 1994.

Brandon, Craig. *Electric Chair: An Unnatural American History*. Jefferson, NC: McFarland and Company, 1999.

Brumberg, J. J. *The Body Project: An Intimate History of American Girls*. New York: Random House, 1997.

Carr, Edward Hallet. *What Is History?* New York: Alfred A. Knopf, 1963.

Chafe, William H. *The Unfinished Journey: America since World War II*. 3rd ed. New York: Oxford University Press, 1995.

Chalmers, David. *And the Crooked Places Made Straight: The Struggle for Social Change in the 1960s*. Baltimore, MD: Johns Hopkins University Press, 1991.

Clark, W. B., and M. E. Hilton, eds. *Alcohol in America: Drinking Practices and Problems*. Albany: State University of New York Press, 1991.

Comstock, George S. *Television in America*. Beverly Hills, CA: Sage Publications, 1980.

Consumer's Union. *I'll Buy That! 50 Small Wonders and Big Deals That Revolutionized the Lives of Consumers: A 50-Year Retrospective*. Mount Vernon, NY: Consumer's Union, 1986.

Cremin, L. *American Education, 1876–1980: The Metropolitan Experience*. New York: Harper and Row, 1988.

Cremin, Lawrence A. "Grading America's Public Schools." *The 1984 World Book Year Book*. Chicago: World Book, 1984.

Deardorff, D. L. *Sports: A Reference Guide and Critical Commentary, 1980–1999*. Westport, CT: Greenwood Press, 2000.

DeCurtis, A., and J. Henke, eds. *The Rolling Stone Illustrated History of Rock & Roll: The Definitive History of the Most Important Artists and Their Music*. New York: Random House, 1992.

Ehrenreich, B. *The Worst Years of Our Lives: Irreverent Notes from a Decade of Greed*. New York: Pantheon Books, 1990.

Ehrman, John. *The Eighties: America in the Age of Reagan*. New Haven, CT: Yale University Press, 2006.

Farb, P., and G. Armelagos. *Consuming Passions: The Anthropology of Eating*. Boston: Houghton-Mifflin, 1980.

Flink, J. J. *The Car Culture*. Cambridge, MA: MIT Press, 1975.

Girard, Jolyon. *America and the World*. Westport, CT: Greenwood Press, 2001.

Greenfield, J. "They Changed Rock, Which Changed the Culture, Which Changed the US" in *Rock Music in America*, ed. J. Podell, 105–112. New York: H. W. Wilson, 1987.

Grmek, M. D. *History of AIDS: Emergence and Origin of a Modern Pandemic*. Princeton, NJ: Princeton University Press, 1990.

Halberstam, D. *The Fifties*. New York: Ballantine Books, 1994.

Hallowell, E. M., and J. J. Ratey. *Driven to Distraction*. New York: Pantheon Books, 1994.

Harrington, Michael. *The Other America: Poverty in the United States*. New York: Penguin, 1962; New York: Penguin, 1981.

Harris, Neil. "American Space: Spaced-Out at the Shopping Center." *The New Republic* (December 13, 1975): 23–25.

Hart, J. D. *The Oxford Companion to American Literature*. 6th ed. New York: Oxford University Press, 1995.

Haskins, J., and K. Benson. *The 60s Reader*. New York: Viking Kestrel, 1988.

Herberg, W. *Protestant-Catholic-Jew: An Essay in American Religious Sociology*. Garden City, NY: Anchor Books, 1960.

Hering, G. C. *America's Longest War: The United States and Vietnam, 1950–1975*. New York: Wiley, 1979.

Hughes, H. Stuart. *History as Art and as Science: Twin Vistas on the Past*. New York: Harper & Row, 1964.

Jackson, Kenneth T. *Crabgrass Frontier: The Suburbanization of the United States*. New York: Oxford University Press, 1985.

Jowett, G., and J. M. Linton. *Movies as Mass Communications*. Beverly Hills, CA: Sage Publications, 1980.

Kaledin, E. *Daily Life in the United States, 1940–1959: Shifting Worlds*. Westport, CT: Greenwood Press, 2000.

Karnow, S. *Vietnam: A History*. New York: Viking, 1983.

Kennan, E. *Mission to the Moon: A Critical Examination of NASA and the Space Program*. New York: Morrow, 1969.

Kenney, W. H. *Recorded Music in American Life: The Phonograph and Popular Memory, 1890–1945*. New York: Oxford University Press, 1999.

Kowinski, William Severini. "The Malling of America." *New York Times* (May 1, 1978): 35.

Lemann, N. *The Promised Land: The Great Black Migration and How It Changed America*. New York: Vintage Books/Knopf, 1991.

Levenstein, H. *Revolution at the Table: The Transformation of the American Diet*. New York: Oxford University Press, 1988.

London, H. *Closing the Circle: A Cultural History of the Rock Revolution*. Chicago: Nelson-Hall, 1984.

Marcus, G. *Mystery Train: Images of America in Rock 'n' Roll Music*. New York: E. P. Dutton, 1982.

Martin, J. K. *Drinking in America: A History*. New York: Free Press, 1982.

Marty, Myron A. *Daily Life in the United States, 1960–1990: Decades of Discord*. Westport, CT: Greenwood Press, 1997; also available online at http://dailyfile.greenwood.com/dle.jsp?k=2&bc=DBDL1331&x=24&p=P-1.

Marty, M. E. *Pilgrims in Their Own Land: 500 Years of Religion in America*. Boston: Little, Brown, 1984.

Marty, M. E., and R. Scott Appleby. *The Glory and the Power: The Fundamentalist Challenge to the Modern World*. Boston: Beacon Press, 1992.

Matusow, A. J. *The Unraveling of America: A History of American Liberalism in the 1960s*. New York: Harper and Row, 1984.

Miller, Z. L. *The Urbanization of Modern America: A Brief History*. New York: Harcourt Brace, 1973.

Millett, Allen R., and Peter Maslowski. *For the Common Defense: A Military History of the United States of America*. New York: The Free Press, 1994.

Morgan, E. P. *The 60s Experience: Hard Lessons about Modern America*. Philadelphia: Temple University Press, 1991.

National Commission on Excellence in Education, USA Research, ed. *A Nation at Risk: The Full Account*. Cambridge, MA: USA Research, 1984.

Newman, K. *Falling from Grace: The Experience of Downward Mobility in the American Middle Class*. New York: Free Press, 1988.

O'Neill, William L. *Coming Apart: An Informal History of America in the 1960's*. New York: Quadrangle-New York Times Books, 1974.

Patterson, J. T. *Grand Expectations: The United States, 1945–1974*. New York: Oxford University Press, 1996.

Rader, B. C. *American Sports: From the Age of Folk Games to the Age of Spectators*. Englewood Cliff, NJ: Prentice-Hall, 1983.

Ravitch, D. *The Troubled Crusade: American Education, 1945–1980*. New York: Basic Books, 1983.

Rybczynski, W. *Waiting for the Weekend*. New York: Viking, 1991.

Sanders, L. "Facing the Music." *Civilization* (May/June 1996): 38–39.

Schlosser, E. *Fast Food Nation: The Dark Side of the All-American Meal*. New York: Houghton-Mifflin, 2001.

Schulman, Bruce J. *The Seventies: The Great Shift in American Culture*. New York: The Free Press, 2001.

Shorter, E. *The Health Century*. New York: Doubleday, 1987.

Sitkoff, H. *The Struggle for Black Equality, 1954–1992*. New York: Hill and Wang, 1993.

Sklar, R. *Movie-Made America*. Rev. ed. New York: Vintage, 1994.

Spring, J. *The American School, 1642–1993*. 3rd ed. New York: McGraw Hill, 1994.

Steelwater, Eliza. *Hangman's Knot: Lynching, Legal Execution, and America's Struggle with the Death Penalty*. New York: Basic Books, 2003.

Szatmary, D. P. *Rockin' in Time: A Social History of Rock and Roll*. 2nd ed. Englewood Cliffs, NJ: Prentice Hall, 1991.

Tichi, Cecelia. *Electronic Hearth: Creating an American Television Culture*. New York: Oxford University Press, 1991.

Waverly, L. R. *Eating in America: A History*. New York: Morrow, 1976.

Whitehead, Barbara. *The Divorce Culture*. New York. Alfred Knopf, 1997.

Whitfield, S. J. *The Culture of the Cold War*. Baltimore, MD: Johns Hopkins University Press, 1991.

Williams, T. I., ed. *Science: A History of Discovery in the Twentieth Century*. New York: Oxford University Press, 1990.

Williamson, J. *The Crucible of Race: Black-White Relations in the American South since Emancipation*. New York: Oxford University Press, 1984.

Winn, M. *The Plug-In Drug*. New York: Viking Press, 1977.

Wright, G. *Building the Dream: A Social History of Housing in America*. New York: Pantheon, 1981.

Yankelovich, Daniel. *The New Morality: A Profile of American Youth in the 70's*. New York: McGraw-Hill, 1974.

Zaroulis, N. L. *Who Spoke Up? Americans Protest the War in Vietnam, 1963–1975*. Garden City, NY: Doubleday, 1984.

ONLINE SOURCES, 1960–1990

Center for Automotive Research. http://www.mergentonline.com.

CIA Fact book. http://www.cia.gov.

Marty, M. A. *Daily Life in the United States, 1960–1990: Decades of Discord.* http://dailyfile.greenwood.com/dle.jsp?k=2&bc=DBDL1331&x=24&p=P-1.

North American Free Trade Agreement. http://www.dfait-maeci.gc.ca/nafta-alena/menu en.asp.

Sawhill, Isabel V. "Poverty in the United States." *The Concise Encyclopedia of Economics.* http://www.econlib.org.

U.S. Census. 1990. http://www.census.gov/population/www/censusdata/hiscendata.html.

U.S. Department of Defense. http://www.defenselink.mil/.

U.S. Department of Justice. http://www.ojp.usdoj.gov.

U.S. Department of Labor. http://www.dol.gov.

U.S. Internal Revenue Service. http://www.irs.gov.

U.S. Office of Management and Budget. http://www.whitehouse.gov/omb/.

The Wall Street Journal. http://www.wsj.com/.

BOOKS AND ARTICLES, 1991–2005

Altbach, Philip G., Robert O. Berdahl, and Patricia J. Gumport. *American Higher Education in the Twenty-First Century: Social Political and Economic Challenges.* Baltimore, MD: Johns Hopkins University Press, 1999.

Bailey, Maria, and Bonnie Ulman. *Trillion Dollar Moms: Marketing to a New Generation.* Chicago: Kaplan, 2005.

Basile, Carlo, et al. "The U.S. HDTV Standard: The Grand Alliance." *IEEE Spectrum* 4 (1995): 36–45.

Beik, Millie Allen. *Labor Relations.* Westport, CT: Greenwood Press, 2005.

Bethel, Alison. "Evangelical Christian Influence Grows." *The Detroit News* (February 6, 2005): 17.

Billingsley, A. *Climbing Jacob's Ladder: The Enduring Legacy of African-American Families.* New York: Simon & Schuster, 1992.

Cheng, Andria. "Rising Top Athletes Fail to Lift Nike Stock." *International Herald Tribune* (September 22, 2006): 23.

Coker, Cheo Hodari. "Unbelievable: The Life, Death, and Afterlife of the Notorious B.I.G." *Vibe* (June 15, 2005).

Copeland, C., and J. M. De La Croix. *Encyclopedia of Contemporary American Art.* New York: Elite Associates International, 1987.

Davis, Rocio G. "Oral Narrative as Short Story Cycle: Forging Community in Edwidge Danticat's 'Krik! Krak!'" *MELUS* 26, no. 2: 65–81.

Derrida, Jacques. *The Post Card: From Socrates to Freud and Beyond.* Translated by Alan Bass. Chicago and London: University of Chicago Press, 1987.

Doss, Erika. *Twentieth-Century American Art.* New York: Oxford University Press, 2002.

Edge, John. *Hamburgers and Fries: An American Story.* New York. Putnam, 2005.

Faragher, John Mack, Susan Armitage, Mari Jo Buhle, and Daniel Czitrom. *Out of Many: A History of the American People.* Upper Saddle River, NJ: Prentice Hall, 2006.

"Fiction Is the Poor Man's Cinema: An Interview with Junot Díaz Diógenes Céspedes; Silvio Torres-Saillant; Junot Díaz." *Callaloo* 23, no. 3: 892–907.

Finler, Joel W. *The Hollywood Story*. New York: Wallflower Press, 2003.

Fixico, Donald. *Daily Life of Native Americans in the Twentieth Century*. Westport, CT: Greenwood Press, 2006.

Foucault, Michel. *The History of Sexuality*. Vols. 1–3. Paris: Gallimard, 1976, 1984.

Freidman, Thomas. *The World Is Flat*. New York: Farrar, Straus and Giroux, 2005.

Fukuyama, Francis. *The End of the World and the Last Man*. New York: Avon Books, 1992.

Girard, Jolyon P. *America and the World*. Westport, CT: Greenwood Press, 2001.

Gitlin, Todd. *Media Unlimited*. New York: Henry Holt, 2002.

Goldfield, David, et al. *The American Journey*. Upper Saddle River, NJ: Prentice Hall, 2007.

Gore, Al. *An Inconvenient Truth*. New York: Rodale, 2006.

Grier, Katherine C. *Pets in America: A History*. Durham: University of North Carolina Press, 2006.

Grinols, Earl L. *Gambling in America: Costs and Benefits*. New York: Cambridge University Press, 2004.

Harris, Robert L., Jr. "The Rise of the Black Middle Class." *The World and I Online* 14:2 (February 1999): 40. http://www.worldandi.com.

Harvey, Paul, and Philip Goff. *The Columbia Documentary History of Religion in America since 1945*. New York: Columbia University Press, 2005.

"High-Definition (HD) TV: What It Is, Why You'd Want It." *Consumer Reports* (February 2006).

"Ja Rule Calls Beef with 50 Cent 'Studio Bangin.'" *Vibe* 1, no. 10 (2005).

Korman, Amy Donohue. "The Death of the Chore." *Philadelphia* 97, no. 10 (2006): 68–69.

Magoc, Chris J. *Environmental Issues in American History: A Reference Guide with Primary Documents*. Westport, CT: Greenwood Press, 2006.

Mardorossian, Carine M. "From Literature of Exile to Migrant Literature." *Modern Language Studies* 32, no. 2 (1996): 15–33.

McCrisken, Trevor B., and Andrew Pepper. *American History and Contemporary Hollywood*. New Brunswick, NJ: Rutgers University Press, 2005.

McDonough, Will. *The NFL Century: The Complete Story of the National Football League, 1920–2000*. New York: Smithmark Publishers, 1999.

Mooney, Chris. *The Republican War on Science*. Cambridge, MA: Perseus Book Group, 2005.

Morning Edition, National Public Radio (October 23, 2006).

Parlett, David. *Oxford History of Board Games*. New York: Oxford University Press, 1999.

Pautz, Michelle. "The Decline in Average Weekly Cinema Attendance: 1930–2000." *Issues in Political Economy* 2: 2002.

Petersen, Melody. "2 Big-Selling Arthritis Drugs Are Questioned." *New York Times* (June 4, 2002).

Roberts, Randy, and James S. Olson. *Winning Is the Only Thing: Sports in America since 1945*. Baltimore, MD: Johns Hopkins University Press, 1991.

Saltzman, Arthur. "Avid Monsters: The Look of Agony in Contemporary Literature." *Twentieth Century Literature* 45, no. 2: 236.

Smith, Ronald. *Sports and Freedom: The Rise of Big-Time College Athletics*. New York: Oxford University Press, 1990.

Spring, Joel H. *American Education*. New York: McGraw-Hill, 2004.

Steinfels, Peter. *A People Adrift: The Crisis of the Roman Catholic Church in America*. New York: Simon and Schuster, 2003.

Stossel, John. "Stupid in America." ABC News (January 13, 2006).

Taylor, Mark Lewis. *Religion, Politics, and the Christian Right: Post-9/11 Powers in American Empire*. Minneapolis, MN: Augsburg Fortress, 2005.

Thelin, John R. *Games Colleges Play: Scandal and Reform in Intercollegiate Athletics*. Baltimore, MD: Johns Hopkins University Press, 1996.

Thompson, William N. *Gambling in America: An Encyclopedia*. Santa Barbara, CA: ABC Clio, 2001.

U.S. Department of Labor. *100 Years of United States Consumer Spending*. Washington, DC: United States Government Printing Office, 2006.

Williams, Juan. *Enough: The Phony Leaders, Dead-End Movements, and Culture of Failure That Are Undermining Black America—And What We Can Do about It*. New York: Crown Publishers, 2006.

———. "Where Are Today's Civil Rights Leaders?" *The Philadelphia Inquirer* (September 26, 2006): A15.

Woodin, Karen E., and John C. Schneider. *The CRA's Guide to Monitoring Clinical Trials*. Boston: Thompson, 2003.

Yost, Mark. *Tailgating, Sacks, and Salary Caps: How the NFL Became the Most Successful Sports League in History*. Chicago: Kaplan Business, 2006.

Zimbalist, Andrew. *The Bottom Line: Observations and Arguments on the Sports Business*. Philadelphia: Temple University Press. 2006.

ONLINE SOURCES, 1991–2005

About.com: "Business and Finance." http://www.inventors.about.com.

About.com: "Globalization." http://globalization.about.com/.

About.com: "Retail and Industry." http://www.retailindustry.about.com.

Center for Automotive Research. http://www.mergentonline.com.

CIA Fact book. http://www.cia.gov.

ComScore Networks—A Global Internet Provider. http://www.comscore.com.

Consumer Confidence Board. http://www.conference-board.org.

The Endocrine Society Weighs In: A Handbook on Obesity in America. http://www.obesityinamerica.org/endoedge/archive/2005_apr_endoedge.html.

Federal Trade Commission. http://www.ftc.gov/credit/.

Flaherty, Joseph. "A Perspective on Digital TV and HDTV." *HDTV Magazine*. http://hdtvmagazine.com/history/2005/06/a_perspective_o.php.

NASCAR. Turner Sports Inc. 2006. http://www.Nascar.com.

NFL History. NFL Enterprises LLC 2006. http://nfl.com/history.

The 9/11 Commission Report. http://www.9–11commission.gov/report/911Report.pdf.

North American Free Trade Agreement. http://www.dfait-maeci.gc.ca/nafta-alena/menu en.asp.

Office of National Drug Control Policy. http://www.whitehousedrugpolicy.gov/.

Professional Bowling Association. http://www.pba.com/.

Sawhill, Isabel V. "Poverty in the United States." *The Concise Encyclopedia of Economics*. http://www.econlib.org.

Securities and Exchange Commission. http://www.sec.gov/.

Shop PBS. http://www.shoppbs.org.

"Taxation in the EU from 1995 to 2002 Tax Rates." *Income and Corporate Tax Rates 2004.* http://www.finfacts.com/Private/tax/taxationeuropeanunion25.htm.

"Taxes by States." http://www.retirementliving.com/RL taxes.

U.S. Census. 1990. http://www.census.gov/population/www/censusdata/hiscendata.html.

U.S. Department of Defense. http://www.defenselink.mil/.

U.S. Department of Justice. http://www.ojp.usdoj.gov.

U.S. Department of Labor. http://www.dol.gov.

U.S. Internal Revenue Service. http://www.irs.gov.

U.S. Office of Management and Budget. http://www.whitehouse.gov/omb/.

U.S. Tennis Association. http://www.usta.com/.

The Wall Street Journal. http://www.wsj.com/.

Worldwatch Institute. http://www.worldwatch.org.

CUMULATIVE INDEX

Boldface numbers refer to volume numbers. A key appears on all verso pages.

First Great Awakening in, **1:**559; Unification Church, **4:**255; World Council of Churches, **4:**124; worship in, **1:**307–8. *See also* Baptist Church; Church of the Brethren; Episcopal Church; Reformed Church; Religions; Roman Catholic Church

Church of England, **1:**305

Church of Scientology, **4:**27

Church of the Brethren, **1:**296, 299

Church, William C., **2:**300

CIA. *See* Central Intelligence Agency

Cigarettes, **3:**58; manufacturing, **3:**247; in World War I, **3:**247–48. *See also* Smoking; Tobacco

CIO. *See* Committee of Industrial Organizations; Congress of Industrial Organizations

Circular Letter, **1:**14

Circus, **2:**309–10. *See also* Barnum, P. T.

Cities, **4:**17–18, 212; in American changes/conflict (1821–1861), **1:**394; bosses, **3:**3; in Colonial America (1763–1789), **1:**6–8, 86; craftspeople in, **1:**86–87; domestic life and, **4:**142–44; elite in, **1:**7; free blacks in, **1:**324; government in, **2:**572; leisure activities in, **1:**269; mass transit in, **2:**279–80; police in, **2:**573–74; population growth in, **2:**474; poverty in, **1:**7; shopping in, **2:**515–16; slaves in, **1:**564; stray dogs in, **2:**348; street life, **2:**515; transportation in, **1:**529–30; working-class in, **1:**251. *See also specific cities*

Citizen Cane, **4:**105

Citizenship, **2:**416–19

Citizen Soldier, **1:**428, 557

City bosses, **3:**3

Civil Aeronautics Authority, **3:**85

Civil rights, **4:**11, 38, 128; of African American, **4:**2, 103; group identity and, **4:**206–10; Kennedy, John F. address, **4:**381–83; marches, **4:**15; movement, **4:**127; reform, **4:**215–21

Civil Rights Act (1964), **4:**128, 203, 208, 209, 216; Title II-Discrimination Relief, **4:**383–84; Title III-Desegregation of Public Facilities, **4:**384–85; Title I-Voting Rights, **4:**383–84; Title VI-Nondiscrimination in Federal Programs, **4:**385

Civil Rights Act (1968), **4:**129

Clark, Ann Nolan, **4:**72

Clark, Barney, **4:**131

Clark, Dick, **4:**38, 110

Clarke, Charity, **1:**158

Clarke, Kenny, **3:**144

Clarke Matthew St. Clair, **1:**461

Clarke, William, **2:**387

Clark, Herbert L., **2:**597

Clark, Kenneth, **4:**102

Clark, Mary, **2:**239, 339

Clark, Maurice B., **2:**511

Clark, Meriwether Lewis, **2:**317

Clark, Norman, **3:**391

Clark's School Visitor, **2:**535

Clark, William, **1:**202, 350; **2:**327

Clark, William Andrews, **3:**464

Class, **3:**59–60

Clay, Cassius, **2:**177; **4:**127, 240. *See also* Ali, Muhammad

Clay, Henry, **1:**376, 383, 385–86, 575; American System of, **1:**207–8, 374, 378

Clemens, Samuel. *See* Twain, Mark

Clermont, **1:**260, 519; **2:**145. *See also North River*

Cleveland, Grover, **2:**570, 584–85; **3:**151

Cleveland Plain Dealer, **3:**314

Clifford, Anna Rawle, **1:**142

Clinton, Bill, **4:**319; election of, **4:**320; impeachment of, **4:**325; Kosovo and, **4:**325–26; Lewinsky scandal and, **4:**263, 324–25; as New Democrat, **4:**320–21; in political life, **4:**319–26; re-election of, **4:**322; as too liberal, **4:**324

Clinton, Catherine, **1:**407, 413

Clinton, DeWitt, **1:**375, 409, 521–22

Clinton, Henry, **1:**25–26

Clinton, Hillary, **4:**320, 324

"Clinton's Ditch." *See* Erie Canal

Clio, **1:**143

Clio's Nursery, **1:**424

Clipper ships, **2:**521–23, 567

The Closing of the American Mind (Bloom), **4:**237

Clotel (Brown, W. W.), **2:**104

Clothing/style, **1:**497; accessories, **1:**487–88; "American Look," **3:**245–46; aprons, **1:**491, 499; **2:**134, 137; athletic, **2:**562, 564; bicycles and, **3:**78; bishop sleeves, **1:**484; bloomers, **2:**409–10; blue jeans, **4:**200; bonnets, **2:**133–34; buckskin, **2:**412; business suits, **2:**563; bustles, **1:**488–89; **2:**275–76, 561; calico, **2:**410; capes, **2:**133; casual, **4:**305; children, **1:**152, 221, 498–501, 501; **2:**136–38, 276–77, 411–12, 564–65; collars, **1:**485; colors, **1:**486; corsets, **2:**561–62; cosmetics, **3:**79; of cowboys, **2:**411; cravats, **1:**495; **2:**135; crinolines, **1:**489; denim trousers, **2:**276, 411; Deseret Costume, **2:**410; detachable shirt collars, **2:**563; dress elevator, **2:**409; fabrics, **1:**383, 484, 486, 495, 498; fans, **1:**492; films and, **3:**80; frock coats, **1:**495; gloves, **1:**491–92, 497; hair, **1:**153–54, 494, 498, 500; **2:**136, 137–38, 276; **3:**79–80; hats, **1:**490–91, 497; **2:**135–36, 276; haversacks, **1:**117; hemlines, **3:**172, 445; hoopskirts, **2:**275, 410; of immigrants, **2:**412; imported, **4:**306; jewelry, **1:**493–94, 497, 499; Knickerbocker suit, **2:**137; laundering, **1:**486; leg-of-mutton sleeves, **1:**483; **2:**561; lounging, **1:**498; *Macaroni,* **1:**152; mail order, **2:**411; mass-produced clothing, **3:**78; in material life, **1:**481–501; **2:**129–40, 275–77, 409–12, 560–65; **3:**78–80, 172–73, 245–46, 445–47; **4:**199–200, 305–6; men, **1:**494–98; **2:**134–36, 276, 411, 563–64; in military life, American Revolution homefront, **1:**152; in military life, Continental Army makeup, **1:**116–17; Mother Hubbard dress, **2:**409, 411; mourning, **2:**139–40; "O" bodice, **1:**484; outerwear, **1:**489–90, 500; overskirt, **2:**561; pagoda sleeves, **1:**485; pantalettes, **1:**499; parasols, **1:**492; of patriots, **1:**57; philosophy of, **3:**79; pockets, **1:**484; postwar consumerism/materialism, 1945–1959, **4:**80–82; purses, **1:**493; ready-made, **2:**564–65; **3:**246; sailor suits, **1:**500; **2:**276–77, 565; shawls, **2:**133; shirts, **1:**495; shoes, **1:**492, 497, 500; **2:**276, 412; skeleton suit, **1:**221; slaves, **1:**566; **2:**138–39; sportswear, **3:**447; "street sweeper fashions," **2:**561; suspenders, **1:**497; tailcoats, **1:**495; tunics, **2:**276; undergarments, **1:**488–89, 497, 500; **3:**78, 172–73; V-bodice, **1:**484; waistcoats, **1:**495; wedding dresses, **1:**488; wigs, **1:**152–53; women, **1:**482–94; **2:**129–34, 275–76, 409–11, 560–63; for work, **3:**172; Y-bodice, **1:**483, 485

Coal: for heating, **2:**517; mining, **1:**553–54; **2:**352–53; **3:**251–53

Coale, George B., **2:**248

Coates, Henry M., **2:**257

Coca Cola, **3:**242–43; **4:**191–92

Cochise, making peace with, **2:**646–48

Cock fighting, **1:**147, 271–72

Cockrell, Francis, **2:**584

Cody, William ("Buffalo Bill"), **2:**261, 300–301, 385, 606–7

Coercive Acts (1774), **1:**17

Coffee, **1:**134, 280; **2:**121, 126–27, 270, 403

Cohan, George M., **3:**98–99, 189

Cohen, Mickey, **4:**123

Cohn, Roy, **4:**97

Coit, Stanton, **2:**530

Cold War, **4:**11, 29, 30; aggression during, **4:**96; alignments, **4:**219; "culture" of, **4:**49; defense needs, **4:**50; defined, **4:**221; education concerns during, **4:**61; Europe and, **4:**316–17; focus of, **4:**221; influence of, **4:**41, 99; intellectuals, **4:**101; victimization, **4:**39; women and, **4:**39

Coleman, T., **3:**181

Cole, Nat King, **3:**190; **4:**110

Cole, Thomas, **1:**450

Colisimo, Jim, **3:**331

Collier, George, **2:**155

Collier, John, **3:**372, 377, 397

Collier's, **2:**537; **3:**98

Collies, Charles, **2:**170

Collins, Billy, **4:**296

Collins, Eddie, **3:**340

Collins, Judy, **4:**232

Collinson, Frank, **2:**243

Collins, Phil, **4:**232

Colonial America (1763–1789): African Americans in, **1:**81–82; agriculture in, **1:**68; Anglicization of upper class, **1:**88; barn raisings, **1:**139; children in, **1:**39–42; cities, **1:**6–8, 86; craftspeople in, **1:**84; domestic life during, **1:**29–43; economic life during, **1:**68–90; education in, **1:**60–65; elite of, **1:**87–88; Enlightenment in, **1:**60; family in, **1:**29–31; farming in, **1:**68–75; glimpses of, **1:**591–92; government creation in, **1:**27–29; growing crisis in, **1:**10–14; harvesting, **1:**139; homes in, **1:**44–46; independence in, **1:**19–21, 169–72; industry in, **1:**83–84; intellectual life during, **1:**59–64; literature in, **1:**141–42; logging, **1:**139; logging bees, **1:**139; marriage in, **1:**31–34; material life during, **1:**43–65; middling order in, **1:**88–89; military life, American Revolution homefront, **1:**128–54; military life, Continental Army makeup, **1:**99–128; newspapers, **1:**95; planter aristocracy in, **1:**74–75; political life during, **1:**90–98; political structure in, **1:**90–91; population growth in, **1:**5–6; poverty in, **1:**88–89; regional food in, **1:**55–57; religious life during, **1:**65–66; representation/voting in, **1:**91–92; slavery in, **1:**75–80; spinning bees, **1:**139, 155; taxes in, **1:**8; uniting, **1:**16; women in, **1:**154–69

Colored Man's Journal, **1:**580

Colored Protective Association, **3:**138

Colt, Miriam Davis, **2:**228, 240, 340

Colt, Samuel, **1:**538–40

Colt, Stanton, **2:**470

Columbia Broadcasting System (CBS)

4:106; kinetoscopes, 3:99; large-screen projection, 3:99; ratings, 4:167; in recreational life, 4:244–45; religious, 4:123; during roaring twenties, 3:22; ticket sales, 4:62; westerns, 3:467; wide-screen epics, 4:107; during World War II, 4:63–64. *See also* Entertainment; Films; Theater; *specific movies*

Moyer, Charles, 3:393

Moynihan, Daniel Patrick, 4:138

MPAA. *See* Motion Picture Association of America

Mravlag, Victor, 3:91

Mr. Isaac's (Crawford, F. M.), 2:254

Muck, Karl, 3:13

Muhammad, Elijah, 4:217

Muir, John, 3:434–35

Mulholland, William, 3:448

Mulock, Dinah, 2:22

Mulvagh, Jane, 3:445

Mumford, Lewis, 4:66–67

Mummers Parade, 2:612; 3:199–200

Munn vs. Illinois, 2:419, 434

Munro, George, 2:386–87

Munro, Norman, 2:386–87

Munsey's Magazine, 2:537; 3:70

Murgas, Joseph, 3:176

Murphy, Charles W., 3:339

Murray, John Courtney, 4:258

Murray's Rush, 2:308

Murray, Thomas E., 2:477

Murray, W. H. H., 2:308

Murrow, Edward R., 4:54

Music: African American, 4:107–8; in American Republic (1789–1820), 1:286–87; big band, 4:110; Black spirituals, 2:303–4, 599; blues, 2:599; 3:262–63, 343; boogie woogie, 3:344; brass-band, 2:169–70, 302–3, 597; bully songs, 2:595; classical, 2:168–69; classical, on radio, 3:71; of Confederacy, 2:170–71; contemporary, 4:236; coon songs, 2:595–96; cowboys, 2:441–42; Decca Record Company, 3:94–95; disco, 4:236; drinking songs, 1:287; folk, 4:110; *Grand Ole Opry*, 3:263–64; grunge movement, 4:298; in intellectual life, 4:298–99; jazz, 2:599; 3:95, 262–63; jukeboxes, 3:95; lamentations, 2:172; making of, 2:438–42; messages in, 4:299; military, 2:169–70; in military life, American Revolution homefront, 1:151; mining, 2:441; minstrelsy, 2:169, 304–5, 592; musicals, 3:98–99; Napster, 4:299; opera, 3:464; philharmonic orchestra, 3:464; player pianos, 2:591; ragtime, 2:596–97; rap, 4:238, 298–99; in recreational life, 2:167–74, 302–6, 438–42, 447–48, 591–99; 3:94–95, 262–64, 343–44, 464; 4:107–10, 230–39; religious melodies, 1:286; rock, 4:230–36; rock and roll, 4:26, 108–10; Second New England School, 2:598; sheet music, 2:592; of slaves, 1:320–21; 2:173–74; song, 2:167–68, 593–94; swing, 3:95, 411; symphonic orchestra, 2:598; Thomas Orchestra, 2:303; Tin Pan Alley, 2:593–94; Western, 2:447–48; of Western emigrants, 2:438; white gospel, 2:305–6. *See also specific musicians*

Muskets, 1:97, 117–18; 2:84–85

Mussolini, Benito, 3:36–37

My Ántonia (Cather), 2:227, 540

Myers, Myer, 1:86–87

Mystery Train (Marcus), 4:109

NAACP. *See* National Association for the Advancement of Colored People

Nabokov, Vladimir, 4:34, 70

NACW. *See* National Association of Colored Women

Nader, Ralph, 4:14, 149

NAFTA. *See* North American Free Trade Agreement

Naked Lunch (Burroughs), 4:72

The Naked and the Dead (Mailer), 4:69

The Name of the Rose (Eco), 4:185

Napoleon III, 2:157, 292

Narrative of the Life of Frederick Douglass (Douglass), 1:565, 602–4; 2:103

Narrative of William Wells Brown, Fugitive Slave Written by Himself (Brown, W. W.), 2:104

NASA. *See* National Aeronautics and Space Administration

NASCAR. *See* National Association of Stock Car Auto Racing

Nash, Tom, 3:342

The Nashville Banner, 1:464

Nason, Tama, 4:101

Nast, Thomas, 2:185, 283, 535

The Natchez Courier, 1:464

National Academy of Sciences, 2:106

National Aeronautics and Space Administration (NASA), 4:28, 186–87

National Association for the Advancement of Colored People (NAACP), 4:102; anti-lynching protests, 3:222; founding of, 3:24; support for, 3:430

National Association of Amateur Oarsmen, 2:298

National Association of Colored Women (NACW), 3:3, 431

National Association of Stock Car Auto Racing (NASCAR), 4:336–38

National Association of Women's Lawyers, 4:145

National Association of Working Women, 4:151

National Black Political Assembly, 4:208

National Board for the Promotion of Rifle Practice (NBPRP), 2:300

National Broadcasting Corporation (NBC), 4:110, 111

National Collegiate Athletic Association (NCAA), 2:167, 299, 300; 4:113, 118–19, 332–35

National Commission of Life Adjustment for Youth, 4:58

National Committee for a Sane Nuclear Policy (SANE), 4:100

National Consumers League, 2:491

National Defense Education Act (1958), 4:61

National Education Association, 2:507

National Football League (NFL), 4:113, 240, 242

National Grange, 2:17

National Housing Act (1949), 4:51

National Housing Agency, 4:86

National Industry Recovery Act (NIRA), 3:33

National Institute of Alcohol Abuse and Alcoholism (NIAAA), 4:191

National Institutes of Health (NIH), 4:68

Nationalism, 2:2, 150; in American Republic (1789–1820), 1:206–7; new, 3:6; of Southern U.S., 1:581–84

National Labor Relations Act (1935), 3:34, 424; 4:47

National Livestock Association, 2:423

National Organization for Women (NOW), 4:40, 275

National Park System, 3:6, 151, 434–35

National Party, 2:288

National Peace Jubilee (1869), 2:302

National Police Gazette, 2:22–23, 422

National Progressive Union of Miners and Mine Laborers, 2:508

National Recorder, 1:463, 481

National Rifle Association (NRA), 2:300; 4:323

National Road, 1:260, 518

The National Journal, 1:461

National Urban League, 3:430

A Nation at Risk, 4:210–11, 293

The Nation, 2:256

Native Americans, 1:88, 387, 558; 2:96, 361, 386, 395, 539, 607, 646–48; 3:223–25, 397; 4:273; animal husbandry/hunting/fishing of, 1:314–15; British alliances, 1:127–28, 196; clans, 1:315–16; confinement of, 2:330; customs of, 3:370; depiction of, 2:384; discrimination and, 3:303; education, 3:381; family life, 3:403; farming, 1:314–15; food, 1:128; 3:318–19; games, 1:315; during Great Depression of 1929, 3:306–7, 372; Indian Wars, 2:223; during Jacksonian Age, 1:377–78; literacy, 2:21; Long Walk, 2:431; as minority, 3:370; Native American Party, 1:382; in new hunting grounds, 1:6; orphans, 2:220; Plains Indian Wars, 2:433; poverty among, 3:432; religious beliefs, 3:395; reservations, 2:430–33, 471; 3:432; rituals/ceremonies, 1:316–17; in social life, 1:313–18; suppression, 1:317; towns, 1:316–17; "Trail of Tears," 1:378; U.S. Supreme Court and, 1:377; voting and, 1:373. *See also* Creek War; French and Indian War (1754–1763); *specific Native American peoples; specific Native Americans*

Nativism, 1:382; 2:1, 148, 152–53; discrimination, 2:157–60; evangelical movement and, 2:160

Nativist Party, 2:152–53

NATO. *See* North Atlantic Treaty Organization

Natural gas, 3:358–59

Naturalization Act, 1:200

Natural law, 1:9

Navajos, 3:354, 371, 372

Navigation, 3:82–83, 450–51; Navigation Acts, 2:566. *See also* Transportation

Nazism, 4:9, 63

NBC. *See* National Broadcasting Corporation

NBPRP. *See* National Board for the Promotion of Rifle Practice

NCAA. *See* National Collegiate Athletic Association

NCAS. *See* North Carolina Academy of Science

The Nebraska Farmer, 2:400

Necessary Rules For the Proper Behavior of Children (Dock), 1:62

Negro Leagues, 4:114–15

The Negro American Family (Moynihan), 4:138

Nelson, Baby Face, 3:333

Nelson, Ozzie, 3:95

Nelson, Ricky, 4:27

Nevin, J. W., 2:456

New Almanack & Ephemeris (Rivington), 1:146

Newbold, Charles, 1:232; 2:517

New Deal, 2:586; 3:43, 128, 283–84; 4:11, 15, 88; agencies of, 3:32–33; as "creeping socialism,"

EDITORS AND CONTRIBUTORS

General Editor

Randall M. Miller
St. Joseph's University
Philadelphia, Pennsylvania

Volume Editor

Jolyon P. Girard
Cabrini College
Radnor, Pennsylvania

Section Contributors

Darryl Mace
Cabrini College
Radnor, Pennsylvania

Courtney Smith
Lehigh University
Bethlehem, Pennsylvania

Student Editorial Assistants

Stephen Beierschmidt
Michael Bergamo

Matthew Burge
Dustin Carpenter
Gregory Cavacini
Genevieve Cupaiuolo
Jamie Curenden
Brittany DeCicco
Andrea Domacinovic
Marcy Fonseca
Charles Jaxel
Ryan Kelliher
Megan Keye
John Kolesnik
Christine MaGargee
Cari MaGoffin
Kevin Mairs
Deborah Maloney
Megan McCourry
Melina Moore
Matthew Paris
Angie Peso
Kevin Quinn
Tyler Sandford
Kristine Schmid
Miriam Thompson